"DISCARD"

A FOREST

OF

KINGS

ALSO BY LINDA SCHELE

Maya Glyphs: The Verbs (1982)

The Blood of Kings:
Dynasty and Ritual in Maya Art (1986)
with Mary Ellen Miller

A FOREST OF KINGS

The Untold Story of the Ancient Maya

Linda Schele
and
David Freidel

Color photographs
by Justin Kerr

WILLIAM MORROW
AND COMPANY, INC.
New York

Copyright © 1990 by Linda Schele and David Freidel

It is the policy of William Morrow and Company, Inc., and its imprints and affiliates, recognizing the importance of preserving what has been written, to print the books we publish on acid-free paper, and we exert our best efforts to that end.

Library of Congress Cataloging-in-Publication Data
Schele, Linda.
A forest of kings : the untold story of the ancient Maya / Linda Schele and David Freidel.
p.   cm.
Includes bibliograpical references (p.).
ISBN 0-688-07456-1
1. Mayas—Kings and rulers. 2. Mayas—History. I. Freidel.
David A. II. Title
F1435.3.K55S34   1990   90-5809
972.01—dc20   CIP

Printed in the United States of America

First Edition

4 5 6 7 8 9 10

BOOK DESIGN BY RICHARD ORIOLO

THIS BOOK IS DEDICATED TO
Floyd Lounsbury
and
Gordon Willey

ACKNOWLEDGMENTS

We wish to acknowledge the many people who helped us with the ideas presented in *A Forest of Kings* and contributed to its writing and production. First and foremost is Maria Guarnaschelli, senior editor and vice-president of William Morrow and Company. When she called Linda Schele in the spring of 1986 about writing a book on the Maya for Morrow, she opened a world to us we never imagined we would or could know. She saw potential in our ideas and believed we could learn how to write for a larger audience. Throughout the process of writing, she has always been sensitive to our fears and trepidations, enthusiastic about how the work was going, merciless in breaking through the limits in our imagination, and encouraging in all things. In short, she saw something in us we did not know was there, and without her exuberant encouragement and support, we might not have tried a book of this scope or ambition. We wish to thank her also for finding Joy Parker, the third and unseen hand in this book. Much of its eloquence and readability comes from her subtle touch.

The manuscript was written using *Nota Bene* by Dragonfly Software as the primary word processor. For those interested in how collaborative writing and research worked between us, it varied from chapter to chapter, but it always required goodwill and respect from all the participants. A few of the chapters, in their first draft versions, were written sitting together in front of the computer; but most of the time, one of us structured the first draft alone and then mailed it on disk to the other, who rewrote, adapted, added, or deleted material at will in a process we called "massaging the text." The text went back and forth between both authors until each chapter became a true fusion of our different viewpoints and specialities.

Joy Parker, a professional writer who knew nothing about the Maya before she began, was commissioned to help us make the thick academese of the first version readable to a nonacademic audience. To begin her task, she flew to Austin to meet us and to tape three days of questions, answers, and just talking about the Maya world. Using these tapes, she tore into our text, learning *Note Bene* and how to use a computer as she went. She reworked each chapter in turn, clarifying the prose, cutting redundancy, and to our surprise, often asking for more detail to the text.

The idea of including vignettes in the book was inspired by Gordon Willey. At a School of American Research seminar on Terminal Classic and Postclassic Maya civilization held in Santa Fe in 1982, Professor Willey entertained the group with a wonderful fictional account of the last days of the royal court at Seibal. The vignette was taken by Jeremy A. Sabloff and David Freidel and prepared as a little in-house publication for distribution at Professor Willey's retirement celebration. Neither Professor Willey's career nor the idea of vignettes stopped there. Jeremy Sabloff has pursued the vignette concept in subsequent publications and so have we. The original draft of *A Forest of Kings* had one vignette in it—and Joy asked for more . . . and more . . . and more. To our astonishment, they worked and we became as enthusiastic about them as she.

When she was done with her version of the text, she sent it to Freidel, who answered her questions, made his corrections, and then passed it on to Schele. Having a nonspecialist as a writing partner is a wonderful barometer of clarity: When the text came back to us scrambled, we knew we hadn't explained things right in the first place. When necessary, a chapter was passed through the loop several times. *Nota Bene's* redlining feature proved an invaluable tool in this process.

A special thanks to Joan Amico for her meticulous and informed copy editing. Were it not for Richard Oriolo's skill and imagination, we would not have been able to incorporate such complex visual material in the book. Additional thanks to Bruce Hattendorf, Maria's capable and hardworking assistant, for his intelligent help; to Debbie Weiss for her professional care; to Harvey Hoffman for his patience and expertise; to Tom Nau for his commitment and skill; and to Nick Mazzella for his able guidance.

Many of the ideas in this book come from years of interchange with friends, colleagues, collaborators, and our students. We wish to acknowledge in particular the contributions to this process made by Floyd Lounsbury, Peter Mathews, Merle Robertson, William Fash, David Stuart, Nikolai Grube, Elizabeth Benson, Robert Rands, David Kelley, Christopher Jones, Juan Pedro LaPorte, Juan Antonio Valdés, Gordon Willey,

Evon Vogt, Brian Stross, Barbara MacLeod, and the many participants in the Texas Meetings on Maya Hieroglyphic Writing. In addition, we have sent chapters to various colleagues who have offered suggestions and criticisms that have been invaluable. These people include Patrick Culbert, Robert Sharer, William and Barbara Fash, Ruth Krochock, Kent Reilly, Marisela Ayala, Anthony Andrews, Peter Harrison, Linea Wren, and E. Wyllys Andrews IV. We particularly wish to thank Peter Harrison, who provided photographs of Tikal we could obtain from no other source, and McDuff Everton, who offered us his extraordinary wraparound photographs of Palenque. Finally, Justin and Barbara Kerr gave us access to their photographic archives, including roll-outs of pottery as well as photographs of the art and architecture of the major Maya sites that they have taken during their long love affair with the Maya. As valuable to us was the haven—complete with bed and breakfast—they provided each time we went to New York.

Research by Linda Schele, as it is presented in various chapters, was supported over the years by the Research Committee of the University of South Alabama, the University Research Institute of the University of Texas at Austin, and Dumbarton Oaks of Washington, D.C. Linda's research on the inscriptions of Copán has been conducted under the Copán Mosaics Project, which is under the direction of Dr. William Fash and the Instituto Hondureño de Antropología e Historia. Part of this research was completed as a Fullbright Research Scholar in Honduras from June to December 1987. Support for the CMP came from National Science Foundation (1986–1988), the National Geographic Society (1986–1989), the National Endowment for the Humanities (1986–1987), the Center for Field Research (EARTHWATCH, 1985–1988), the Wenner-Gren Foundation for Anthropological Research (1987; 1989), the H. J. Heinz Charitable Fund (1986), and Council for International Exchange of Scholars (1987).

Research on Cerros presented in Chapter 3 was carried out under the auspices of the office of the Archaeological Commissioner of Belize. Joseph Palacio, Jaime Awe, Elizabeth Graham Pendergast, and Harriot Topsey served in that office and greatly facilitated our research. The Cerros work was supported by the National Science Foundation (BNS-77-07959; BNS-78-2470; BNS-78-15905; BNS-82-17620) and by private donations by citizens of Dallas to the Cerros Maya Foundation. T. Tim Cullum and Richard Sandow served as officers of this foundation and effectively launched the research despite numerous difficulties. Their friendship, enthusiasm, and patience are greatly appreciated. Stanley Marcus, and through Mr. Marcus many other individuals, supported the work throughout its duration. Mr. Marcus has been a special mentor and friend to David Freidel throughout his career in Dallas. The research at Cerros was originally directed by Dr. Ira Abrams; without his energy and initiative, Chapter 3 would never have been written.

Research at Yaxuná presented in Chapter 10 is being carried out under the auspices of the Instituto Nacional de Antropología e Historia, México. The Directors of the INAH in Mérida, Ruben Maldonado and Alfredo Barrera, have greatly facilitated our work at Yaxuná. Dr. Fernando Robles, senior investigator of the INAH, and Dr. Anthony Andrews first took David Freidel to Yaxuná and have strongly encouraged the work at the site. The Yaxuná research is supported by the National Endowment for the Humanities (RO-21699-88), the National Geographic Society, the Provost's Office of Southern Methodist University, and private benefactors in Dallas through Mr. Stanley Marcus.

Contents

PROLOGUE: PERSONAL NOTES

I remember vividly the first time I walked down the gravel path that led into the ruins of Palenque. Surrounded by vine-shrouded bushes filled with the sounds of playing children, barking dogs, and the chest-deep thumps of tom turkeys, I walked down that path past broken buildings shaded under vine-draped trees until I came to the grass-filled plaza in front of the Temple of the Inscriptions. Inspired by the curiosity of my architect husband, this was the first time I had ever visited México. I had never before seen the rich web of life in a tropical forest nor heard the cicadas sing in twelve-tone harmony. As I walked through the lichen-painted ruins of that magic place, I felt my imagination stirred by the pathos of a lost world. The enchantment of the forest with its emerald green light and towering trees shrouded in a rich world of orchids, bromeliads, and liana vines produced a kind of exotic beauty I had never imagined. The mystery of calcium-heavy water, tumbling down the rocky streams to the plain below Palenque's escarpment, to encase rock, leaf, branch, and broken temple alike, spoke to my mind in metaphors of creation and destruction.

We were there quite by accident, for we had planned in that December of 1970 to follow the standard tourist pilgrimage to Yucatán to see the famous ruins of Uxmal, Chichén Itzá, and Kabah. Going to Palenque was a last-minute side trip. It looked close to the main highway on the map and the Sanborns Travelguide said it was worth at least a couple of hours of our time. When we left twelve days later, the direction and passion of my life was changed forever.

At the time I was a professional painter teaching art at a small university in Mobile, Alabama. Like most of my contemporaries, I lived in frustration because I knew what I did in my art was irrelevant to the society around me. No matter the rhetoric I threw at the world, I recognized in my deepest heart that the irrelevancy was real and unchangeable. Yet while teaching our "Introduction to Art" course to nonmajors (the token fine-arts class that is supposed to make modern university graduates cultured), I had built an image in my head of what art could be like if it were critical to the society that produced it. When I walked among the tumbled rocks and broken plaster of Palenque's wonderland, I knew I had found the dream made real. I had to understand how, why, when, and who had made these things.

It took three years to answer the last question: who? and, strangely enough, finding this answer was an accident also. On the last afternoon of the *Primera Mesa Redonda de Palenque,*[1] held in December 1973, Peter Mathews and I pored over the texts in the ruins of Palenque, looking for the names and dates of kings. After three hours' work, we had managed to identify five rulers, as well as the dates of major events in their lives.[2] That magic of discovery has not diminished during the intervening fifteen years. I have been an enraptured passenger on a wondrous voyage into the past and a participant in the rediscovery of something very special: the history of a people whose story had been lost in the obscurity of the past.

This time of excitement and discovery comes at the end of 150 years of inspired work by hundreds of people who built the foundation that make this time possible. Yet, even acknowledging the debt all of us owe to the scholars who went before us, this is a special time that will never come again. Only once will someone read Pacal's name for the first time or realize who built the Temple of the Cross at Palenque or Temple 22 at Copán.[3]

And know that this time of discovery is not yet over, for the decipherment of the Maya writing system, the study of their religion and politics, the excavations and analyses of the remains of their lives are not yet finished. In truth, they are barely begun. What we share in this book is but one stage in the journey, and the product of many different people and approaches. No one person is, or ever can be, responsible for the sum of discovery.

The way I have always studied the ancient Maya is to try to understand the patterns intrinsic to their art, writing, architecture, and other cultural remains. The interpretations of events the two of us offer in this book represent the way we understand those patterns now. As more decipherments are made and new data comes out of the ground, as fresh minds bring their insights to bear upon the patterns we have inherited from our predecessors and expanded in our own work, the connections that we see between these patterns will change. Interpretation in our work is an ephemeral thing that continually adapts to the changing nature of these underlying patterns. It is like the reassessment and reinterpretation of history we experience in our own lives, as we look back on events great and small that have shaped the way we see the world. Those of us in our middle years know this kind of reevaluation in how we see and understand the Vietnam War and all that surrounded it. To me, the truly magical thing is that the ancient Maya now have a history that can enter into this process of reevaluation.

—LINDA SCHELE
Austin, Texas
May 1989

I passed through Palenque for the first time just after Linda, in the summer of 1971 on my way to begin an exploration of Cozumel Island for the Harvard-Arizona Cozumel project.[4] Although I was just starting graduate school, I had been a working "dirt" archaeologist for eight years, gaining experience at projects in North America, Europe, and the Middle East. I looked forward to seeing the ruins on Cozumel, even though they were humble compared to Palenque, because I enjoy the craft of fieldwork; but I dreamed of another kind of study among the Maya.

I wanted to find a way to reveal the nature of Maya shamanism archaeologically. I wanted to know what the relationship was between political power and religious belief among the ancient Maya. My aspirations were fueled by a thorough and intensive training in social anthropology and in Maya ethnography by my mentors in college. I knew that the Maya institutions of power recorded and observed since the coming of the Europeans were imbued with the sacred and enveloped in the cosmic. The challenge was to discover a way to use archaeology to help penetrate the Christian veil and contribute to a discovery of the Precolumbian institutions of central authority.

Because Cozumel island had been a sacred pilgrimage center just before the Conquest, I did get to investigate Maya politics and religion within the context of ruins and artifacts. I found I could bridge across from the relatively rich eyewitness descriptions of Maya buildings and their functions left by the sixteenth-century explorers to the archaeological remains without great problem. Still, even though I had passed through the veil, the penetration was only beyond the historical era of Spanish chronicles. The great span of the Precolumbian past remained beyond my focus.

My next project, at Cerros in Belize, took me from the demise of Maya civilization to its Preclassic beginnings, deep into the archaeological record and far from the historical observations of the Europeans. When I first laid eyes on the great Sun mask of Structure 5C in the summer of 1977, I knew that I was going to have to train myself in Maya iconography and attempt to interpret this building in terms of its political and religious functions. I had basic training in symbolic analysis from college, but I was pretty ignorant of Maya art and knew virtually nothing of text translation.

Linda was among the several specialists in Maya art who kindly responded to my request for feedback on my first substantive article on the Cerros materials. She called me up from Austin and said, "David, you're right for all the wrong reasons. We have to talk."

That was in the fall of 1979; we have been talking ever since. Collaboration comes easily to us. The nature of archaeological research requires teamwork; general interpretation is always the product of many people pooling their insight. It is the nature of epigraphic and iconographic research among the Maya as well. Linda and I have different perceptions of the ancient Maya that draw upon different experience and training. We think together in ways that we find occasionally opaque, regularly surprising, usually stimulating, and always worthwhile. I am now an iconographer with a rudimentary command of epigraphy. She is now an advocate of structural analysis and an evolutionist. Most important, we are both something we could not have been in 1971: we are historians of the ancient Maya.

This book is a unique product of our collaboration. It draws heavily upon our personal scholarly experience with the Maya field. Of the six regions and communities anchoring our histories, we have extensively worked at, and published technical studies on, four of them (Cerros, Palenque, Copán, Yaxuná). We wrote the manuscript on personal computers, rewriting over each other's prose several times so that the initial expertise of each one of us was repeatedly leavened by the ongoing dialogue between us. Ultimately, our partner in this writing effort, Joy Parker, joined in the process. Joy's clear prose, fresh perspective, and respect for our subject smoothed the flow of our narrative and enhanced the accessibility of our often intricate concepts.

I am changed by this book. I cannot look at a Maya ruin now and think of the people who built it and lived with it as abstractions, an aggregate social force shaping the material world and coping with the process of living. Now I see Maya faces, recall Maya names, look for clues to their intentional acts, their decisions, and the events of their daily existence. History has its many limitations to be sure. Ancient Maya history was the privilege of the elite and powerful; at best it gives an accurate reflection of their views on what happened. It is mute about the lives of the ordinary people. We must look to the archaeological record for knowledge of the humble and numerous commoners whose experiences also shaped the Maya destiny. But I now feel better prepared to continue the collaborative enterprise conjoining the insight of the "dirt" archaeological record with the story left by the kings and their nobles. It will yield, I hope, something of the dialogue between the populace, the source of power, and the elite who wielded that power. The long-term history and evolution of this kind of dialogue is, for me, an important source of insight into the current human condition.

—DAVID FREIDEL
Dallas, Texas
May 1989

FOREWORD

Early in this century the word *pharaoh* burst
upon the imagination of the West and transported the modern mind into the ancient and alien
world of Egypt's living gods. Today, in the tropical
lowlands of Central America, another anthropological
revolution is uncovering a new intellectual and spiritual
legacy for the civilized world: an ancient American
civilization ruled by living gods who called themselves
ahau. [1]

Flourishing for over a thousand years (200 B.C. to
A.D. 900), the Classic Maya world was organized at its
apogee into fifty or more independent states encompassing more than 100,000 square miles of forest and plain.
The divine ahauob ruled millions of farmers, craftsmen,
merchants, warriors, and nobility and presided over
capitals studded with pyramids, temples, palaces, and
vast open plazas serviced by urban populations numbering in the tens of thousands. Outside of their realm,
the Maya engaged in war, trade, and diplomacy with
other great states in the mountains of Central México.
Theirs was a civilized world: a world of big government,
big business, big problems, and big decisions by the
people in power. The problems they faced sound familiar to us today: war, drought, famine, trade, food production, the legitimate transition of political power. It

was a world which mirrors our own as we wrestle with the present in search of a future.

Like ourselves, the Maya wrote on paper, keeping thousands of books in which they recorded their history, genealogy, religion, and ritual; but their libraries and archives perished into dust or in the flames of their Spanish conquerors. Nevertheless, hieroglyphic texts and scenes carved on buildings, stone monuments, jade, bone, and other materials impervious to decay in the tropics remain as records of their innovative political solutions to the social crises that dominated life in ancient America. These political chronicles speak in the language of a great philosophical, scientific, and religious vision—a charter for power as eternal and as flexible as the American Constitution.

The Maya conception of time, however, was very different from our own. Our old adage "He who does not know history is doomed to repeat it" might have been expressed by the Maya as "He who does not know history cannot predict his own destiny." The Maya believed in a past which always returned, in historical symmetries—endless cycles repeating patterns already set into the fabric of time and space. By understanding and manipulating this eternal, cyclic framework of possibility, divine rulers hoped to create a favorable destiny for their people. But while the Maya ahauob could know only the immediate results of the events they put into motion, we are gradually reclaiming the full scope of their historical accomplishments from the obscurity of the past.

Our challenge then is to interpret this history, recorded in their words, images, and ruins, in a manner comprehensible to the modern mind yet true to the Maya's perceptions of themselves. What we can offer here is not quite biography, for the Maya ahauob did not intend their history to be a record of personal glory so much as a cosmic affirmation of their actions. Nor can we offer a comprehensive social history, for the vagaries of time have left us with only the story of the great and victorious. Nevertheless, we can offer a history unique in the Precolumbian Americas, populated with real people, replete with the drama of battle, palace intrigue, heroic tragedy, and magnificent personal artistic and intellectual expression. History unlocks the humanity of the Maya in a way not possible by any other means, for it reveals not only what they did, but how they thought and felt about the nature of reality.

It is important that we acknowledge this history, because only then will a true picture of the Americas emerge. The American chronicle does not begin with the landing of Columbus or the arrival of the Pilgrims, but with the lives of Maya kings in the second century B.C. We who live in this part of the world inherit a written history two millennia old and as important to us as the history of the ancient Egyptians or the Chinese, a history equal in longevity to that of Europe or Asia.

Understanding the complexity of the ancient American civilizations does not come easily to us. From childhood on we have been taught in our schools that the Mediterranean is the only "cradle of civilization"; but, in fact, human beings developed the civilized state also in Northern India, China, Middle America, and Peru. The Maya are one of those societies that transformed themselves from villagers and agriculturists into a great civilization. To accomplish this transformation, they developed a high religion and extraordinary statecraft that produced a stable society for over a thousand years. More than a collection of quaint mythology and exotic rituals, their religion was an effective definition of the nature of the world, answering questions about the origin of humanity, the purpose of human life on earth, and the relationship of the individual to his family, his society, and his gods. It is a religion which speaks to central and enduring problems of the civilized human condition: power, justice, equality, individual purpose, and social destiny.

The world of that vision was informed by the power of the supernatural. Our concepts of animate and inanimate matter would not have made sense to the Maya, for to them everything was alive. The Maya cosmos was peopled with exotic creatures of all sorts and the objects and places in their physical world acquired dangerous power as they interacted with the supernatural Otherworld. Order in the cosmos was not accidental or distant from human affairs. Like the great metaphor of Maya life—the life cycle of maize—the continued well-being of the universe required the active participation of the human community through ritual. As maize cannot seed itself without the intervention of human beings, so the cosmos required sacrificial blood to maintain life. Maya life was filled with endless rituals which seem to us bizarre and shocking, but which to them embodied the highest concepts of their spiritual devotion.

With the decipherment of their writing system, the Maya joined the world's great pristine civilizations—Egypt, Mesopotamia, the Indus Valley, and China—on the stage of world history. A picture has emerged, not only of a civilization, but of a world view and the individuals who cherished that view. All of the great events in the lives of rulers—their births, accessions, marriages, conquests and defeats, their deaths, and the births of their children—were recorded on public monuments. Not only kings, but their wives and courtiers, sought a place in history through commissioning monuments of their own. Kings and their nobles marked objects of all types with their names, and artists and sculptors signed their works so that future generations could honor them. The architecture and stone monuments, the pottery, jewelry, and ritual implements found buried in the earth, speak to us of the personal histories of the people who made them. This new American history resounds with the names of heroes, kings, princes, warriors, queens, priests, artists, and scribes and the deeds and accomplishments of their lives. Ancient America created its own vision of the world, its own form of civilization, its own high religion: But it also had its Alexanders, its Myrons, its Sargons, its Ramseses.

The story we construct here is one of drama, pathos, humor, and heroics. We approach this story not as if we were examining a long-dead religion and a history of little contemporary relevance but as scholars unearthing the dynamic actions of real people. If human beings find immortality after death by the memories they leave the generations who follow them, then the Maya have been reborn through our growing awareness of the history they memorialized throughout their cities.

Come, then, and join us on a journey into the American past and meet some of the great and victorious people of Maya history.

How to Pronounce Mayan Words

Many of the words in this book will look strange to English-speaking readers because of the way Mayan words are written. Soon after the conquest, the Spanish began to convert Mayan languages from their own written forms into the Roman alphabet. To do so, they used the spelling conventions of the sixteenth century. Since the characters of the alphabet are pronounced differently in Spanish from the way they are in English, and since the Spanish system of pronunciation itself has changed over the intervening centuries, the conventions used for Maya place names and their hieroglyphic writing should be explained. The alphabet we use here, with a few moderations, is identical to that of the colonial Yucatec sources.

Mayan languages use five vowels, or, as in the case of modern Chol, six. Using the Spanish convention, these vowels are pronounced as follows:

a is like the *a* in "far" or "father."

e is like the *e* in "obey" or "prey."

i is like the double *e* in "see" or "bee."

o is like the *o* in "hello" or "open."

u is like the double *o* in "zoo" or "boo."

ä is like the final *e* in "title" or "handle."

The letter *u* becomes a special case when it falls at the end of a word or is combined with another vowel. Then it functions like the consonant *w*. The word *ahau* is pronounced *"a-haw"* and *Uolantun* is *"wo-lan-toon."* Normally, each individual vowel in a word is pronounced separately as an independent syllable, so that the place name El Baul is pronounced *"el ba-ool."*

Since the Mayan languages have several consonants not found in Spanish, the friars who first tried to write the languages had to improvise. They used *x* to record the consonant that sounds like the English *sh*. The color term *yax* is pronounced *"yash"* and the place name *Uaxactún* is pronounced *"wa-shak-tun."* When the *x* is at the front of a word, it is still *sh,* even when it precedes other consonants, as in *Xphuhil ("sh-poo-hil")* and *Xcalumkin ("sh-kal-loom-kin").* In Mayan words, *c* is always pronounced like *k,* regardless of what vowel it precedes. The month *Ceh* is *"keh"* and the day *Cimi* is *"kee-mee."*

In Mayan languages, there is also a contrast between the glottalized and nonglottalized forms of many consonants. Since this contrast is not used in European languages, English speakers find it hard to pronounce or even to hear the difference. Glottalized consonants are pronounced like the regular consonant, but with the glottis or "voice box" closed. You can hear the unvoiced glottal stop in the way New Yorkers and Englishmen pronounce words with a double *t,* such as "bottle." Glottalized consonants sound like very hard and explosive forms of the regular consonants. In this book, the unglottalized *k* sound is written with *c* while the glottalized *k* is represented by the letter *k.* For example, the word for "earth" is written *cab,* while the word for "hand" is *kab.* While these words would be pronounced the same way in English, they sound as different to the Maya as *volt* and *bolt* sound to us.

There are other pairs of glottalized and plain consonants also, but in all these cases, the glottalized member of the pair is written with an apostrophe after the regular letter, as in *b', ch', p',* and *t'.* A glottal stop is written with a simple apostophe, as in *ca'an.*

Mayan languages do not have some of the consonants that are native to English, such as the *d* sound. Conversely, Mayan has a pair of consonants unknown in English. Written as *tz* in its plain form and *tz'* in its glottalized form, the consonant is pronounced somewhat like the English *z,* but with the blade of the tongue against the ridge behind the teeth and with a sharp expulsion of breath.

The Spanish letter *j* also causes problems for English-speaking people. In Spanish, *j* is pronounced like the hard *h* in English, while their letter *h* is essentially silent. Since the Mayan consonant is more like the English *h* than the silent Spanish *h,* the letter *j* is frequently used to represent it. English speakers often make the mistake of pronouncing it like the English *j* in "jet." Our consonant *j* does not exist in the Mayan languages and thus the English pronunciation is never used. The place name *Abaj Takalik* is *"a-bah tak-a-leek"* and *Kaminaljuyu* is *"ka-mee-nal-hoo-yoo."*

In Mayan words, the accent usually falls on the last syllable, as in the following names used in this book.

Tikal	"tee-kál"
Yaxchilán	"yash-chee-lán"
Pacal	"pa-kál"
Chan-Bahlum	"chan bah-lóom"
Yax-Pac	"yash pák"
Yahau-Chan-Ah-Bac	"ya-háw chan ah bák"
Uaxactún	"wa-shak-tóon"
Kakupacal	"ka-ku-pa-kál"

In this book we will use the word *Mayan* to refer only to the languages spoken. The name of the people, used either as a noun or an adjective, will be *Maya.* We will pluralize Mayan words such as *ahau* with the pluralizing suffix *-ob* taken from the Yucatec and Chol. More than one *ahau,* therefore, is *ahauob,* which is pronounced *a-ha-wob.*

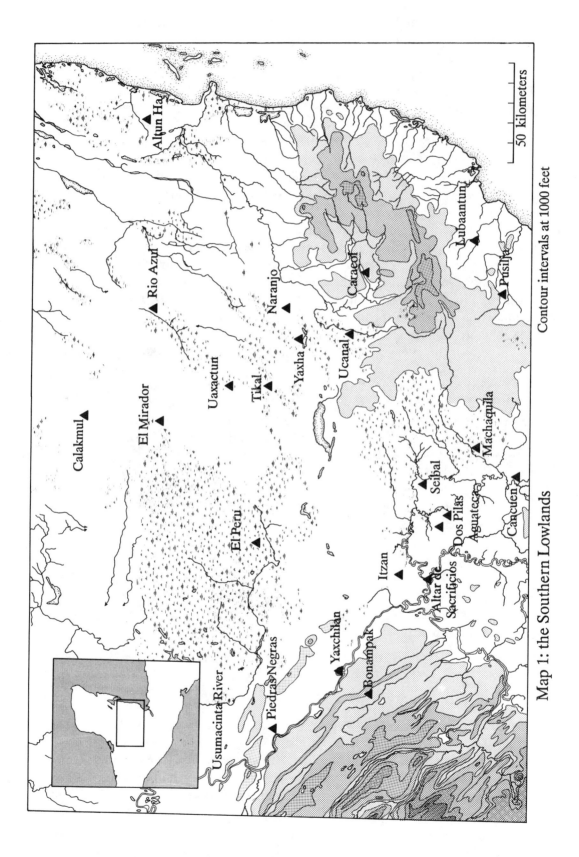

Map 1: the Southern Lowlands

Contour intervals at 1000 feet

50 kilometers

Altun Ha
Rio Azul
Naranjo
Lubaantun
Pusilha
Caracol
Yaxha
Ucanal
Uaxactun
Tikal
Machaquila
El Mirador
Calakmul
Seibal
Dos Pilas
Aguateca
Cancuen
El Peru
Itzan
Altar de
Sacrificios
Usumacinta River
Yaxchilan
Piedras Negras
Bonampak

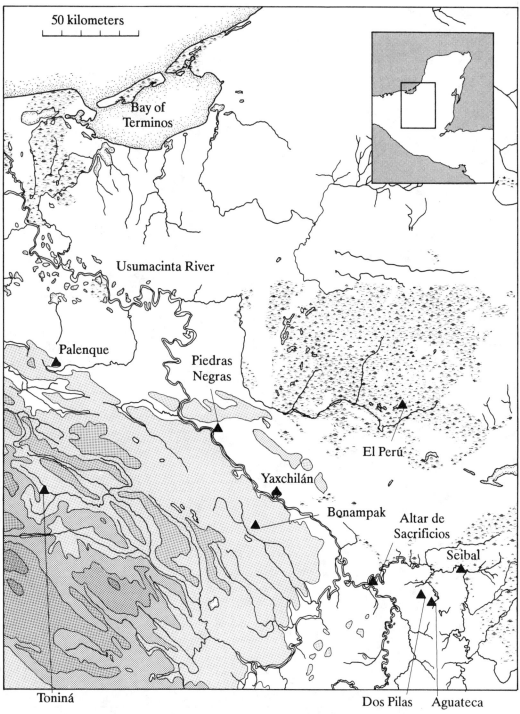

Map of the Western Region of the Southern Lowlands
Contour intervals at 1,000, 3,000, 5,000 feet
drawings of these three maps by Karim Sadr

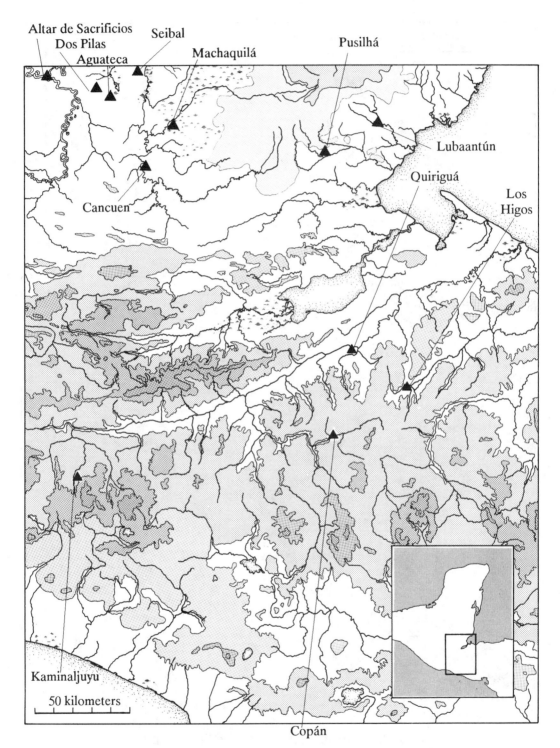

Altar de Sacrificios Seibal
Dos Pilas
Aguateca   Machaquilá   Pusilhá

Cancuen

Lubaantún

Quiriguá

Los
Higos

Kaminaljuyu

50 kilometers

Copán

Map of the Eastern Region of the Maya Region
Contour intervals 2,000, 5,000, 7,000

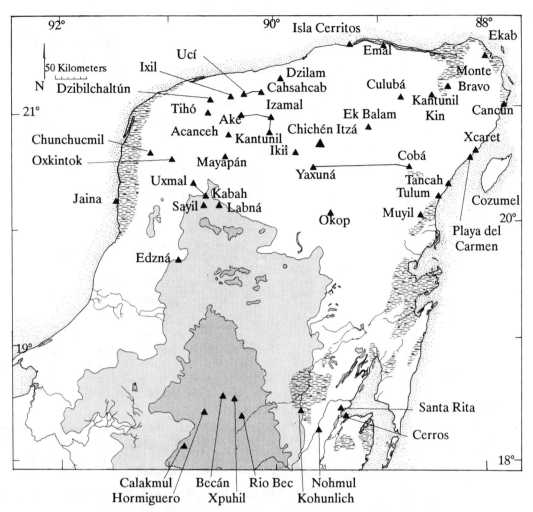

The Yucatán Peninsula and the Northern Lowlands
Contour intervals: 250, 500 feet

1100 B.C.		First settlers in the Copán Valley
1000 B.C.		Florescence of Gulf Coast Olmec; early villagers and beginnings of hierarchical social organization in the Pacific zone; the Copán Valley has permanent settlements

MIDDLE PRECLASSIC

900 B.C.		Rich tombs in the Copán Valley
600 B.C.		Tikal settled by early villagers
500 B.C.		Large towns and long-distance trading

LATE PRECLASSIC

300 B.C.		Late Preclassic period begins
200 B.C.		Early Izapa monuments with Popol Vuh mythology in the south; activity in the Copán Valley diminishes
100 B.C.		Sculpted temples begin to appear throughout the northern lowlands; carved and dated monuments and large towns in the southern zone; appearance of writing in the Maya zone; formulation of the institution of kingship
50 B.C.		Structure 5C-2nd at Cerros; North Acropolis and stelae at Tikal; Group H at Uaxactún; El Mirador the dominant lowland center; green obsidian from Teotihuacán region at Nohmul
50 A.D.		El Mirador, Cerros, and other centers abandoned

EARLY CLASSIC

120	8.4.0.0.0	First object with deciphered date (DO celt)
150	8.6.0.0.0	The kingdom of Copán established
199	8.8.0.4.0	First dated stela (Hauberg)
219	8.9.0.0.0	Reign of Yax-Moch-Xoc and founding of the Tikal dynasty
292	8.12.14.8.15	Stela 29, earliest monument at Tikal
320	8.14.2.17.6	Yat-Balam of Yaxchilán accedes and founds the lineage
328	8.14.10.13.15	Stela 9, earliest monument at Uaxactún
376	8.17.0.0.0	Great-Jaguar-Paw ends the katun at Tikal
378	8.17.1.4.12	Tikal conquers Uaxactún; first appearance of Tlaloc-war complex in Maya imagery

379	8.17.2.16.17	Curl-Snout accedes at Tikal under Smoking-Frog
396	8.18.0.0.0	Smoking-Frog ends katun at Uaxactún; Curl-Snout ends it at Tikal
411	8.18.15.11.0	Astronomically timed "accession" event at Tikal
426	8.19.10.0.0	Probable accession of Stormy-Sky of Tikal
426	8.19.10.11.17	Yax-Kuk-Mo' of Copán enacts a God K-scepter rite and establishes the dynasty
431	8.19.15.3.4	Bahlum-Kuk accedes and founds the dynasty of Palenque
439	9.0.3.9.18	Last event on Stela 31 at Tikal: Stormy-Sky's bloodletting
445	9.0.10.0.0	Tikal Stela 31 dedicated
475	9.2.0.0.0	Kan-Boar rules at Tikal
488	9.2.13.0.0	Jaguar-Paw Skull, the 14th king, rules at Tikal
504	9.3.16.18.4	New ruler (name unknown) accedes at Tikal
514	9.4.0.0.0	Summit of North Acropolis reworked at Tikal
527	9.4.13.0.0	The 19th king of Tikal rules
537	9.5.3.19.15	Double-Bird, the 21st king, accedes(?)
553	9.5.19.1.2	Lord Water of Caracol accedes
556	9.6.2.1.11	Caracol conducts "ax-war" action against Tikal
557	9.6.3.9.15	Last date at Tikal before the conquest
562	9.6.8.4.2	Caracol conducts "star war" against Tikal

LATE CLASSIC

599	9.8.5.16.12	Oldest son of Lord Water becomes the king of Caracol
603	9.8.9.13.0	Pacal the Great is born at Palenque during the reign of Ac-Kan
612	9.8.19.7.18	Lady Zac-Kuk, Pacal's mother, accedes at Palenque
615	9.9.2.4.8	Pacal of Palenque accedes
618	9.9.4.16.2	Lord Kan II, younger son of Lord Water, becomes the king of Caracol
619	9.9.5.13.8	Lord Kan II of Caracol interacts with Calakmul's king (Site Q?)
626	9.9.13.4.4	Caracol's first attack against Naranjo
627	9.9.14.3.5	Caracol's second attack against Naranjo
628	9.9.14.17.5	Smoke-Imix-God K of Copán accedes
630	9.9.17.11.14	A lord of Naranjo dies
631	9.9.18.16.3	Star war against Naranjo by Caracol
635	9.10.2.6.6	Chan-Bahlum, son of Pacal of Palenque, is born
636	9.10.3.2.12	Second star war against Naranjo by Caracol

640	9.10.7.13.5	Lady Zac-Kuk, Pacal's mother, dies at Palenque
641	9.10.8.9.3	Chan-Bahlum of Palenque is designated heir to the throne
642	9.10.10.0.0	Caracol victory stair dedicated at Naranjo
643	9.10.10.1.6	Kan-Bahlum-Mo', Pacal's father, dies at Palenque
644	9.10.11.17.0	Kan-Xul, brother of Chan-Bahlum, is born at Palenque
645	9.10.12.11.2	Flint-Sky-God K accedes at Dos Pilas
647	9.10.14.5 10	Pacal dedicates his first temple at Palenque
647	9.10.15.0.0	Shield-Jaguar, son of 6-Tun-Bird-Jaguar of Yaxchilán, is born
649	9.10.16.16.19	Jaguar-Paw of Calakmul (Site Q) born
652	9.11.0.0.0	Smoke-Imix-God K of Copán celebrates the period ending with a monument at Quiriguá and with the pattern of outlying stelae in the Copán Valley; Pacal celebrates the period ending at Palenque.
664	9.11.11.9.17	Flint-Sky-God K captures Tah-Mo' during his long military campaign in the Petexbatun
675	9.12.3.6.6	Pacal begins construction of the Temple of Inscriptions at Palenque
681	9.12.9.8.1	Shield-Jaguar of Yaxchilán accedes
682	9.12.9.17.16	Ah-Cacaw of Tikal accedes as king
682	9.12.10.5.12	Lady Wac-Chanil-Ahau, daughter of the Flint-Sky-God K of Dos Pilas, arrives at Naranjo and reestablishes its royal house
683	9.12.11.5.18	Pacal of Palenque dies
684	9.12.11.12.10	Chan-Bahlum of Palenque accedes in a ten-day-long ceremony
686	9.12.13.17.7	Jaguar-Paw of Calakmul (Site Q) accedes with Flint-Sky-God K of Dos Pilas witnessing the ritual
688	9.12.15.13.7	Smoking-Squirrel of Naranjo born
690	9.12.18.5.16+	Chan-Bahlum of Palenque dedicates the Group of the Cross in a three-day-long ceremony
692	9.12.19.14.12	Chan-Bahlum of Palenque activates the *pib na* in the temples of the Group of the Cross
692	9.13.0.0.0	Ah-Cacaw plants the first stela and builds the first twin-pyramid group after the defeat by Caracol
693	9.13.1.3.19	Smoking-Squirrel of Naranjo, grandson of Flint-Sky-God K of Dos Pilas, accedes at age five
	9.13.1.4.19	Naranjo's first attack on Ucanal: Kinichil-Cab captured under the authority of Lady Wac-Chanil-Ahau
695	9.13.2.16.0	Naranjo's second attack on Ucanal

695	9.13.3.6.8	18-Rabbit of Copán accedes
695	9.13.3.7.18	Ah-Cacaw of Tikal captures Jaguar-Paw of Calakmul (Site Q)
695	9.13.3.9.18	Ah-Cacaw dedicates Temple 33-1st with bloodletting rites 260 tuns (13 katuns) after the last date on Stela 31, the stela celebrating Tikal's conquest of Uaxactún
695	9.13 3.13.15	Tikal captures a noble of Calakmul (Site Q)
698	9.13.6.2.0	Shield-God K, son of Flint-Sky-God K, becomes king of Dos Pilas
698	9.13.6.4.17	Kinichil-Cab of Ucanal in a sacrificial ritual at Naranjo
698	9.13.6.10.4	Sacrificial ritual at Naranjo with Shield-Jaguar of Ucanal
699	9.13.7.3.8	Lady Wac-Chanil-Ahau of Naranjo stands atop her captive, Kinich-Cab of Ucanal
702	9.13.10.0.0	Stela dedication and period-ending rites at Naranjo in which Shield-Jaguar of Ucanal is bled
702	9.13.10.1.5	Chan-Bahlum of Palenque dies
702	9.13.10.6.8	Kan-Xul, the younger brother of Chan-Bahlum, accedes to the throne of Palenque
709	9.13.17.12.10	Bird-Jaguar, the son of Shield-Jaguar of Yaxchilán, is born
709	9.13.17.15.12	Lady Xoc, wife of Shield-Jaguar, lets blood from her tongue
709	9.13.17.15.13	Lady Eveningstar, mother of Bird-Jaguar of Yaxchilán, does a bundle rite with Shield-Jaguar
710	9.13.18.4.18	Smoking-Squirrel of Naranjo attacks Yaxha
711	9.13.19.6.3	Smoking-Squirrel of Naranjo attacks Sacnab
711	9.14.0.0.0	Smoking-Squirrel erects stela at Naranjo; Ah-Cacaw erects a stela and his second twin-pyramid group at Tikal
712	9.14.0.10.0	Shield-Jaguar of Ucanal undergoes a sacrificial rite at Naranjo
713	9.14.1.3.19	Smoking-Squirrel of Naranjo celebrates his first katun as king by erecting Stelae 2 and 3
715	9.14.3.6.8	18-Rabbit of Copán dedicates Temple 22 to celebrate his first katun as king
723	9.14.11.15.1	Lady Xoc, wife of Shield-Jaguar of Yaxchilán, dedicates the sculpture of Temple 23
726	9.14.14.8.1	Lady Xoc and Shield-Jaguar of Yaxchilán participate in the dedication rites of Temple 23
734	9.15.3.6.8	Ah-Cacaw's son become the king of Tikal
736	9.15.4.16.11	Shield-Jaguar of Yaxchilán enacts a flapstaff event
738	9.15.6.14.6	18-Rabbit of Copán taken captive and sacrificed by Cauac-Sky of Quiriguá

738	9.15.6.16.5	Smoke-Monkey of Copán accedes
741	9.15.9.17.16	Shield-Jaguar of Yaxchilán enacts a flapstaff event with his son, Bird-Jaguar
741	9.15.10.0.1	Bird-Jaguar (the son of Shield-Jaguar), Lady Eveningstar (the mother of Bird-Jaguar), Lady Great-Skull-Zero (the wife of Bird-Jaguar), and Great-Skull-Zero (her patriarch) let blood
742	9.15.10.17.14	Shield-Jaguar of Yaxchilán dies
744	9.15.13.6.9	Bird-Jaguar of Yaxchilán participates in a ballgame
746	9.15.15.0.0	Bird-Jaguar of Yaxchilán celebrates the period ending in his father's name
747	9.15.16.1.6	Bird-Jaguar of Yaxchilán enacts his own flapstaff ritual
749	9.15.17.12.16	Smoke-Monkey of Copán dies
749	9.15.17.12.10	Smoke-Shell, the son of Smoke-Monkey of Copán, accedes
749	9.15.17.15.14	Lady Xoc, the wife of Shield-Jaguar, dies
749	9.15.18.3.13	Bird-Jaguar of Yaxchilán goes to Piedras Negras to celebrate the first katun anniversary of Ruler 4's accession
750	9.15.19.1.1	Bird-Jaguar of Yaxchilán sacrifices captives as Chac-Xib-Chac
751	9.15.19.15.3	Lady Eveningstar, the mother of Bird-Jaguar, dies
752	9.16.0.13.17	Bird-Jaguar of Yaxchilán takes Yax-Cib-Tok captive
752	9.16.0.14.5	Chel-Te, the son of Lady Great-Skull-Zero and Bird-Jaguar of Yaxchilán, is born
752	9.16.1.0.0	Bird-Jaguar of Yaxchilán accedes in a nine-day-long ritual that ends with the dedication of Temple 22
752	9.16.1.2.0	Bird-Jaguar of Yaxchilán enacts the tree-scepter rite with Lady 6-Sky-Ahau and a God K-scepter rite with his cahal, Kan-Toc
752	9.16.1.8.6	Bird-Jaguar enacts a God K-staff event with Kan-Toc and blood-letting rite with Lady Balam-Ix
752	9.16.1.8.8	Bird-Jaguar of Yaxchilán captures Jeweled-Skull
756	9.16.5.0.0	Bird-Jaguar of Yaxchilán celebrates his first period ending in three different ceremonies: one with a cahal in attendance; a second with his wife; and a third with her patriarch and his own son, Chel-Te
757	9.16.6.0.0	Bird-Jaguar of Yaxchilán celebrates his five-year anniversary with his son, Chel-Te
757	9.16.6.9.16	Bird-Jaguar of Yaxchilán goes to Piedras Negras to confirm his support of Ruler 4's heir
757	9.16.6.11.14	Ruler 4 of Piedras Negras dies

757	9.16.6.17.17	Ruler 5 of Piedras Negras accedes
763	9.16.12.5.17	Yax-Pac of Copán, son of the woman of Palenque, accedes
766	9.16.15.0.0	Bird-Jaguar of Yaxchilán celebrates the period ending with his wife, his son, and his cahals, Great-Skull-Zero and Tilot
766	9.16.15.0.0	Yax-Pac of Copán sets up Altar G3 in the Great Plaza
768	9.16.17.6.12	Bird-Jaguar of Yaxchilán celebrates a flapstaff event with his brother-in-law Great-Skull-Zero
769	9.16.18.0.0	Yax-Pac of Copán begins remodeling Temple 11
771	9.17.0.0.0	Yax-Pac dedicates Temple 21a to celebrate the period ending
773	9.17.2.12.16	Yax-Pac dedicates the upper temple of Structure 11
775	9.17.5.0.0	Yax-Pac dedicates Altar Q
780	9.17.9.2.12	Yax-Pac's younger brother become "First Servitor" of the kingdom
780	9.17.10.0.0	Yax-Pac's scattering rite recorded in Group 9M-18
781	9.17.10.11.0	Yax-Pac dedicates the bench in Group 9N-8
783	9.17.12.5.17	Yax-Pac celebrates his first katun as king by dedicating Temple 22a; by erecting Stela 8 in the area under the modern village; and by erecting Altar T with his younger brother in the same region
790	9.18.0.0.0	Last date at Pomoná, Tabasco; last date at Aguateca
793	9.18.2.5.17	Yax-Pac celebrates his 30-tun anniversary of accession on the same day his younger brother celebrates his 13th haab as the "First Servitor"
793	9.18.3.0.0	Last date at Yaxhá
795	9.18.5.0.0	Last date at Bonampak; Yax-Pac places an altar in the Temple 22a council house
799	9.18.9.4.4	Accession of 6-Cimi-Pacal at Palenque; the last date at Palenque
800	9.18.10.0.0	Yax-Pac and his brother erect Altar G1 in the Great Plaza
801	9.18.10.17.18	Yax-Pac dedicates Temple 18
802	9.18.12.5.17	Yax-Pac celebrates his two-katun anniversary
807	9.18.17.1.13	Ballgame event on La Amelia Stela 1; last date associated with the Petexbatún state
808	9.18.17.13.4	Last date at Yaxchilán

810	9.19.0.0.0	Yax-Pac goes to Quiriguá to celebrate the katun ending; last date at Piedras Negras; last monument erected at Chinkultic; last date at Calakmul; last date at Naranjo; last date at Quiriguá
820	9.19.10.0.0	Yax-Pac's apotheosis as an ancestor is celebrated on Stela 11 at Copán
822	9.19.11.14.5	U-Cit-Tok of Copán accedes and within five years the central government collapses
830	10.0.0.0.0	The baktun-ending celebrated at Oxpemul and Uaxactún
841	10.0.10.17.15	Last date at Machaquilá
842	10.0.12.8.0	Capture on a column on the High Priest's Grave
849	10.1.0.0.0	Bolon-Tun, a Putun-type lord, dominates Seibal and builds a katun-ending complex with five stelae; last date at Altar de Sacrificios; last date at Xunantunich; last date at Ucanal
859	10.1.10.0.0	Last date at Caracol
862	10.1.13.0.0	Dedication date of the Palace at Labná
867	10.1.17.15.13	The earliest date at Chichén Itzá (the Watering Trough)
879	10.2.0.0.0	The last ruler of Tikal scattered; last date at Tikal
869	10.2.0.1.9	Fire ceremony by Yax-Uk-Kauil and another lord of Chichén Itzá; bloodletting by Kakupacal recorded in the Casa Colorada at Chichén Itzá
870	10.2.0.15.3	Dedication of Casa Colorada at Chichén Itzá
874	10.2.5.0.0	Monument erected at Comitán
879	10.2.10.0.0	Last date at Ixlú; monument erected at Quen Santo
881	10.2.12.1.8	Dedication of the Temple of the Four Lintels at Chichén Itzá by Yax-T'ul and other lords
889	10.3.0.0.0	Last date at La Muñeca; last date at Xultún; last date at Uaxactún; last date at Jimbal; last date at Seibal
898	10.3.8.14.4	Last date recorded at Chichén Itzá
901	10.3.11.15.14	Date on the Ballcourt Marker at Uxmal
907	10.3.17.12.1	Date on a capstone in the Monjas at Uxmal
909	10.4.0.0.0	Late monument with a Long Count date (Tonina)

POSTCLASSIC

1200	10.19.0.0.0	Chichén Itzá abandoned
1250	11.1.10.0.0	Founding of Mayapán

1451	11.11.10.0.0	Fall of Mayapán
1502	11.14.2.0.0	A Maya trading canoe contacted in the bay of Honduras during the fourth voyage of Columbus
1511	11.14.11.0.0	Aguilar and Guerrero shipwrecked on the coast of Yucatán
1519	11.14.18.17.16	Cortés lands on Cozumel Island and meets Naum-Pat
1521	11.15.1.8.13	Tenochtitlan, the Aztec capital, falls
1524	11.15.4.8.9	Alvarado founds Guatemala City
1525	11.15.5.2.1	Cortés meets King Can-Ek at the Itzá capital of Tayasal during his trip across Maya country to Honduras
1542	11.16.2.3.4	The city of Mérida founded by the Spanish
1618	11.19.19.9.1	Fuensalida and Orbita visit King Can-Ek of the Itzá in Katun 3 Ahau
1695	12.3.17.10 0	Avendaño's first visit to King Can-Ek of the Itzá
1696	12.3.18.8.1	King Can-Ek of the Itzá accepts Avendaño's invitation to become a Christian
1697	12.3.19.11.14	The Itzá are conquered by the Spanish and the last independent Maya kingdom falls

A
FOREST
OF
KINGS

1

TIME
TRAVEL
IN THE
JUNGLE

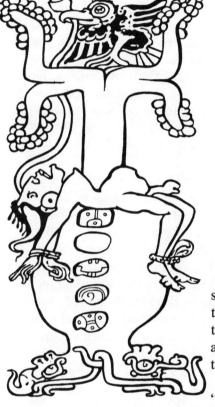

Once, many years ago, when we were just beginning our adventure with the Maya, a friend observed that to cross the Texas border into México was to enter a different world where time and reality dance to a different rhythm. After twenty years of moving in and out of that world, both of us have confirmed the truth of that observation for ourselves.

While the experiences of our first journey to that "otherworld" were distinctly our own, they have much in common with the thousands of other pilgrims who go to Yucatán out of curiosity and admiration. For Linda Schele that first journey came in 1970 when she followed the great arching curve of the Gulf Coast from Mobile, Alabama, around to the tip of the Yucatán peninsula. With three students and a husband in tow, she followed the narrow, potholed highway south from Matamoros through the vast, cactus-filled deserts of northern México, skirting the majestic Sierra Madre mountains. At the Gulf port of Tampico, she rode a dilapidated ferry across the Río Pánuco and with the gawking wonder of a first-time tourist entered a world that has known civilization for 5,000 years. The Huastecs, long-lost cousins of the Maya,[1] dwell in the mountains and the dry northern edge of this enormous region. Now we call this world Mesoamerica, a term which refers not only to geography, but to a Precolumbian cultural tradition that shared a 260-day calendar, religious beliefs including definitions of gods and bloodletting as the central act of piety, the cultivation of maize, the use of cacao as a drink and as money, a ballgame played with a rubber ball, screen-fold books, pyramids and plazas, and a sense of common cultural identity.[2] The world view that was forged by the ancient peoples of that land is still a living and vibrant heritage for the millions of their descendants.

The first time you cross the boundary into that world, you may not have an intellectual definition for what is happening to you, but you will sense a change. If nothing else, this region is greener than the desert, and evidence of people and their communities thickens around you. As you drive south, the narrow band of land next to the sea gets squeezed against the waters of the Gulf of México by the huge Sierra Madre mountains and you see for the first time the dramatic contrast between the cool, dry highlands towering above and the hot, humid, forest-covered lowlands. This central opposition is the force that molded life in ancient Mesoamerica into a dynamic interaction between the peoples who lived in these two very different environments.

Moving through the green, hilly land of the Totonacs, another great people of this ancient world, you pass around the modern port city of Veracruz where Cortés's motley band of adventurers first established a foothold during the time of the Conquest. There you enter the flat, swampy homeland of the primordial Olmec, whose dominions lined the southernmost arc of the Gulf of México. Here amid the twisted courses of sluggish, tide-driven rivers (while carefully dodging the speeding juggernauts of modern tanker trucks that frequent this stretch of road), you see where the first civilization in North America was built. The road rises out of the swamp into a small cluster of black and mottled green volcanic mountains, the Tuxtlas, the natural pyramidal heart of this land, and you can see the flat waterworld of levees and bayous stretching to the horizon in all directions. This was the land of the Olmec, who began building cities at places like San Lorenzo and La Venta by 1200 B.C. They were the people who forged the template of world view and governance that the Maya would inherit a thousand years later when they began to build their own cities.

Southern Veracruz and Tabasco finally give way to the land of the Maya as the coast bends eastward to swing north into the Yucatán Peninsula. The narrow strip of land between the mountains and the sea, which had widened out briefly into the flat expanse of the ancient Olmec kingdoms in the Isthmus of Tehuantepec, narrows again as you approach the westernmost Maya city, Palenque. It has always seemed to us that this swampy place could not make up its mind whether it wanted to be land or sea. Patches of dry land peek forlornly up through the flowering hyacinths that have replaced waterlilies to form the floating surface of the dark, still waters the Maya saw as the source of creation. Here is the gateway to the lowlands of the Maya, who developed one of the most fascinating civilizations in the annals of the ancient world.

While our first visits to the hauntingly beautiful ruins that dot the landscape of the Yucatán peninsula were different, we both learned that the Maya are not just a people of the past. Today, they live in their millions in México, Guatemala, Belize, and western Honduras, still speaking one of the thirty-five Mayan languages as their native tongue. They continue to cultivate their fields and commune with their living world in spite of the fact that they are encapsulated within a larger modern civilization whose vision of reality is often alien to their own.

Encounters between the modern Maya and those who visit their lands can also be startling. Linda Schele remembers vividly the first Maya who truly made a lasting impression on her. As an incredibly naïve gringa tourist, she was walking through the market in Mérida, when she found herself followed around by a Yucatec woman whose aged, wrinkle-creased face barely came to her shoulder. The old woman's black eyes gazed upon that foreigner—*Ix-tz'ul* in Yucatec Mayan—with disbelief, and who could blame her? At five feet eleven and dressed in heavy boots and jeans, Linda was truly an apparition from another world. That tall gringa and the tiny Yucatec shared a moment of contact, but they were from different realities indeed.

That old woman, like millions of other modern Maya, is the inheritor of a cultural tradition that began with the hunter-gatherers who settled the Yucatán Peninsula and adjacent highlands to the south eleven thousand years ago. The land her ancestors found was vast and environmentally diverse, covering nearly half a million square kilometers and ranging from high volcanic mountain ranges with narrow cool valleys to dense rain forest interspersed with swamps and rivers to the dry forest plains of the north (Fig. 1:1). This diversity meant that when the Maya became farmers around three thousand years ago,[3] they had to devise many different agricultural techniques, including the terracing of slopes, the raising of fields in swamps and rivers, and the slashing and burning of forest cover. This last technique, swidden agriculture—burning and then planting in the fertile ashes left behind—is both the most ancient and the most common farming method used in the region today.

The archaeological record from those ancient villagers, as well as the description of the Maya by their Spanish conquerors, biased though it was, speaks to us of a cultural heritage which still lives on in Maya farming communities today. Granted that much has changed in the intervening centuries, there is still a basic connection between the ancient Maya and their descendants, just as there is between the ancient Saxons and the modern British. By examining modern village life, we can recover at least a partial picture of what life in those ancient villages was like.

Just as they did in ancient times, modern Maya villagers live in household compounds occupied by extended families. Each family is made up of a group of related adults, including one or more mature couples with growing children; several unmarried adolescents; and, more often than not, a senior couple or grandparents. Such extended families provide the large number of people needed in farming, a labor-intensive way of life. Maya farmers and their families work hard. The yearly cycle

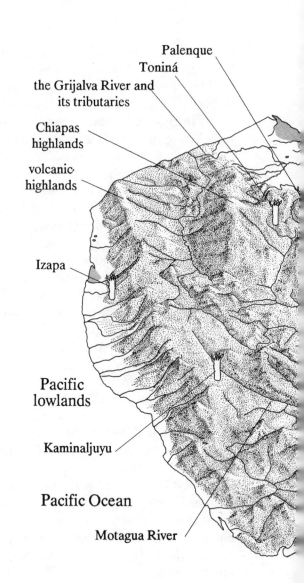

Palenque
Toniná
the Grijalva River and
its tributaries
Chiapas
highlands
volcanic
highlands
Izapa
Pacific
lowlands
Kaminaljuyu
Pacific Ocean
Motagua River

FIG. 1:1
Topographical map of the
Yucatán Peninsula and
the Maya Region
drawing by Karim Sadr

of preparing the fields, planting, cultivating, harvesting, and processing the fruits of their labor leaves only intermittent periods of unoccupied time.

Extended family organization not only provides a means of ensuring that several farmers are available during the peak periods of work, it also ensures that there are extra hands available to carry out the other necessary activities of the household. Such activities include routine tasks, such as the building and refurbishment of houses, kitchens, and storerooms, the collection of firewood, the preparation of food, and the repair and maintenance of tools. They also include more specialized craftwork, such as the weaving and decorating of cloth, the manufacture of clothing, and the making of pottery. These crafts can be either used by their makers or exchanged for other goods and services needed by the household.

Households live in compounds made up of several single-roomed dwellings. The walls of these dwellings are constructed with wooden posts

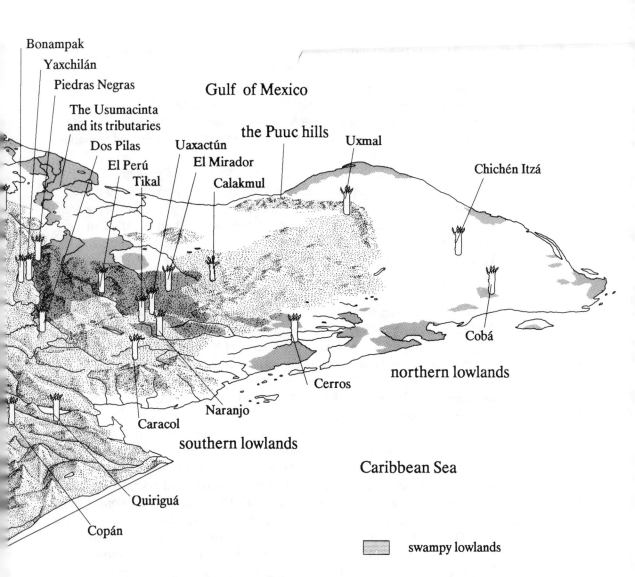

Bonampak
Yaxchilán
Piedras Negras
The Usumacinta and its tributaries
Dos Pilas
El Perú
Tikal
Uaxactún
El Mirador
Calakmul
Gulf of Mexico
the Puuc hills
Uxmal
Chichén Itzá
Cerros
Naranjo
Caracol
southern lowlands
Cobá
northern lowlands
Caribbean Sea
Quiriguá
Copán

swampy lowlands

and lime marl (more recently with cement blocks), and roofed with palm thatch or other readily available materials. These buildings are built around an open patio space, usually in the form of a quadrangle, to provide privacy from the prying eyes of neighbors. In many Maya villages, the kitchen is a separate building made of lighter materials, to allow free circulation around the smoky fire. Tools and foodstuffs are often kept in separate storerooms.

Despite the diversity in the ways that contemporary Maya communities organize their living space, they cling stubbornly and proudly to local traditions. David Freidel remembers visiting the home of a young Tzotzil Maya farmer in Chiapas. He was very pleased to regard himself as a modern man, and to prove the point he showed David a fine pocket watch that he had acquired. His house had been built by the government as part of a project to improve the living conditions of his people. It was a particularly sturdy structure, but it didn't fit with the ideals of Tzotzil

Maya houses. It had windows, which he had boarded up to avoid drafts. It had a fireplace and chimney, which his wife was using as a store cupboard. His fire was directly on the cement floor with the proper three stones and its smoke was properly blackening the rafters above. No longer a house, now it was a home. Such conservatism in daily practice is vital to the bridges we build between the living Maya and the ruined remains left by their ancestors.

There is a clear division of labor in a Maya family: men farm and women prepare the food in the home. Among the people of Yucatán these role definitions are bestowed upon children in infancy, on the day when they are first carried on their mother's hip rather than bundled in her shawl. In this ceremony children attain both gender identity and person-hood: boys are given little toy field tools, while girls are given toy house-hold utensils.

Participation in this ceremony by adults who are not kinsmen of the child is one of many small ritual ways of forging social ties among different families and even with people from outside the Maya world. As an archae-ologist working with Maya from the village of Yaxuná in Yucatán, David Freidel was asked to put a little boy on his hip in just such a ceremony. As it happened the child wasn't wearing any diapers and, much to the amusement of David's staff and Maya friends, he reciprocated the honor by making water on his sponsor.

The roles bestowed in this ceremony extend throughout the lifetime of the child. In modern Maya communities, men predominate in the public affairs of the village, while women carry substantial authority within the household and make many economic and social decisions concerning the family in conjunction with the senior men. Women are expert in crafts, especially the making of cloth and clothes.

The public authorities in Maya villages derive from three sources: offices surviving from Precolumbian institutions, those introduced by the Spanish, and those needed for working with the modern national govern-ments presiding over Maya country. In the Maya highlands, the primary hierarchy is made up of cargo officials, adult men who take on the cargo, or burden, of responsibility for organizing the festivals of the saints through the cycle of the year. In many highland communities, there are dual cargo hierarchies. One is responsible for public festivals, and the other for civil matters such as arbitrating disputes which cannot be han-dled by family patriarchs and matriarchs. Such disputes include unpaid loans, damaged property, sexual improprieties, and other infractions which the national authorities consider too minor to bother with. The cargo officials who try these cases possess an admirable philosophy of justice, one aimed at reconciliation rather than a forcibly imposed verdict from the bench. The civil hierarchy presides over these matters at the *cabildo,* a municipal building usually found on the square facing the church in the center of the community. Cargo positions are sought after years in advance, and men go to the major festivals to have their names inscribed on waiting lists up to fifteen years long.

To hold a cargo in the public life of a village is very expensive, often requiring most of the disposable income of a family and its relatives for many years. These officials have to pay for the festivals, and for the many ritual meals, flowers, incense, rockets, and other paraphernalia they use during the performance of their office. They must also live in the population center, away from their households and their fields. In this way, the accumulated wealth of families is put at the disposal of the entire community, and the men buy prestige and authority through their devotion.

The way modern Maya think about cargo officials offers us insight into the ancient attitude toward kings and nobility. Robert Laughlin, a friend of ours and a famous expert on the Tzotzil Maya of highland Chiapas, commented at a national meeting where we were presenting our views on Maya divine kingship that modern Maya cargo holders may be saints for a year, but they are still men subject to the same pleasures and needs as the rest of the community. David Freidel remembers spending the night in the home of such a cargo official, Saint John, in the ceremonial center of Zinacantan, a Tzotzil Maya community. After a rough night on the dirt floor, covered not only with warm blankets but with an abundance of fleas, David was awakened before dawn by calls from without: "Saint John, are you dead? Wake up!" To which his host replied: "No, I'm not dead, I'm a little bit alive, wait a minute, come in, come in." While the wife of Saint John busied herself with the fire, Saint Lawrence and Saint Sabastian strolled in, decked out in wide, flat beribboned sombreros and black ponchos, and everyone huddled on little stools around the growing fire. Someone produced a bottle of homemade cane liquor, a spicy and formidable potion accompanying most ritual business in the town, and a single shot glass. Drinks were poured in proper order, each shot downed in a single gulp after polite bowing to all Saints present; each gulp was followed by spitting on the earth in libation to the unseen but ever-present spiritual beings. With David's second shot, the memories of fleas faded, replaced by the delicious aroma of coffee laced with cinnamon, fresh thick corn tortillas, and meat jerky broiling on the fire. The Saints proceeded to discuss the preparation of flower arrangements in the church for the upcoming festival of Saint Lawrence: business breakfast, Maya style. Divine kings, like their saintly descendants, no doubt wove their sacred work around the daily pleasures of human life. The beautifully painted crockery from their own official meals, buried in tombs and offerings, is tangible testimony to this tradition.

Unlike its uses in our culture, hierarchy for the modern Maya is an institutional means of maintaining an egalitarian way of life in which everyone has similar material means and no one stands out as wealthy. Wealth is something intrinsically to be feared, as seen in the stories about pacts with the spirits in which people trade integrity for money. People who accumulate wealth or display it in private space are likely to be accused of witchcraft and killed or driven from the village. Unlike us, the Maya are uncomfortable with nonconformity, and such behavior only causes tension within the community.

Shamans also fulfill an important role in the public domain. They cure disease and carry out a wide range of rituals in the fields and homes of a village, and they too have their responsibilities in the public festivals. In contrast with the cargo hierarchies and modern officials, shamans are fundamentally self-selecting and egalitarian in organization. Through their prayers to the age-old divinities of their people, the shamans maintain the link with the past and help modern villagers preserve their language and their most cherished understandings of the world in the face of pressing alternatives from the national cultures.

Although in the ancient world the pressures were different, the shamanistic function has always been to conserve tradition within the community. The shamans were and are public explainers, repositories of the stories and morals of thousands of years of village experience. Their power is intimate and personal, and in the ecstasy of prayer their charisma is unquestionable. They are the keepers of a very complicated world view encoded in special poetic language. We call such knowledge oral history, but in fact it is much more than history. It is an ongoing interpretation of daily life. An example of this way of thinking can be seen in the shaman's attitude toward disease. Instead of seeing illness as an isolated, purely physical phenomenon, the shaman treats it within the context of the tensions and anxieties of interfamilial and social relationships. The curing of an individual is more than a healing of the physical being. It is a healing of the emotional being, the social being, and the social web holding the community together.

The public rituals of the shamans are occasions for the affirmation of the overarching experience of existence, the cycles of life and death and of the agricultural year, and of the community as the true center of everything important. The poetic form of the shaman's expression allows him not only to learn and remember encyclopedias of communal knowledge but to express himself effectively in ecstatic states, when he is within the true reality which all of his people know exists behind their common, daily understanding of the world.[4]

The moral and emotional burdens of being a shaman are great, but there are rewards as well. The terrible drought of 1989 finally broke in Yaxuná, Yucatán, only a few days after the village shaman, Don Pablo, had conducted a three-day-long ritual called a Cha-Chac ceremony to summon the storm gods who would bring rain to the parched lands. Having participated in the earlier ceremony, an astounded David Friedel stood in his archaeological field camp watching the rains Don Pablo had called sweep in from the northeast over the pyramids of the ancient city next to the village. With his triumph written across his face in a huge grin, Don Pablo came running over the crest of a nearby hill, clutching his hat in the gusting winds as he fled inches ahead of a gray wall of rain. A great rainbow arched over him in the brilliant orange light of the setting sun in a magnificent display that affirmed the success of his performance as shaman.

Although contemporary villages interact through modern national institutions such as the market economy, the land-tenure system, the school system, and the legal authorities, they also participate in networks of pilgrimage that come from a far older experience. Villagers attend festivals at other villages and brotherhoods of shamans gather periodically to discuss their craft. These festivals reinforce the local culture and provide opportunities for the arrangement of marriages and the choosing of godparents, acts which link families in real or fictive kinship relationships.

The Spanish overlay of Christianity and the adaptation of village life to the growing impact of modern technological life have produced changes in the Maya village. Nevertheless, there is a remarkable continuity to be seen between modern villagers and their predecessors as described by the Spanish chroniclers. Although the Maya festivals are now arranged according to the Christian calendar, the modern Maya have only switched the timing from the regularities of the katun and the Calendar Round, the ancient way of tracking time. Furthermore, household compounds both of the exalted and the humble, from Preclassic times on, have the same basic identity: small houses arranged around a plaza space. Whether the houses were made of stone and decorated with ornate sculpture, or were the simple wood and thatch constructions of the lowly farmer, the spaces inside them were the same. And both the powerful and the humble buried their dead under the stones of their courtyards so that their ancestors could remain with them and hear the sounds of their descendants' children playing over their heads.

A vivid reminder of just how strong the continuity is between the ancient and modern ways of life made itself forcefully known to us as we were in the final stages of preparing this book. From the first moment we had turned on the computer to start writing, we knew that shamanism was a fundamental part of Maya life, both ancient and modern. Yet we had only been able to *deduce* its importance to the older Maya civilization by comparing ancient imagery and the archaeological remains of ritual to the practices of modern Maya shamanism. We had no direct written evidence from the ancient Maya themselves. At the 1989 Dumbarton Oaks conference, David Stuart whispered a miracle into David Freidel's ear. He and Stephen Houston had deciphered a glyph composed of an ahau face half covered with jaguar pelt as *way,* the word for "to sleep," "to dream," "to metamorphize or transform," "sorcerer," and "animal (or spirit) companion." Here in their writing was the glyph for "shaman," identifying for all who wanted to see Maya shamans engaged in their Otherworld journeys or manifesting as their spirit companions. Perhaps the most startling coincidence of all was that less than two weeks later, we got a letter from Nikolai Grube of Germany. He had independently found the *way* reading and recognized what it meant.[5]

This continuity and many others tell us that the villagers of today are the inheritors of more than exotic ruins hidden among vine-draped forests. Moreover, their heritage is not just a collection of myths and half-remembered stories, because their ancestors carved words and images on slabs of stone, on temple walls, and on the objects they used in their ritual lives. These silent monuments hold the names and deeds of kings and nobles, and accounts of how they and their people strove for prosperity and a place in history. That history was obscured until recently, but those ancient kings now speak again through our new understanding of the words they wrote. It is the decipherment of this writing system that has given us a window into the Maya world. This book is about history as they wrote it and the world as they saw it.

How we came to know about this history is one of the great stories of archaeology. The adventure began with an eccentric nineteenth-century naturalist of dubious renown named Constantine Rafinesque. A man who seemed to just miss fame throughout his lifetime (he almost went on the Lewis and Clark expedition), Rafinesque became interested in the strange writing from México that had been published in the reports of Humboldt's and António del Río's[6] journeys through the region now known as Chiapas. After deciding this odd writing was Maya and deducing how to read the numbers, he published the first modern decipherments in the *Saturday Evening Post* of January 13, 1827, and June 21, 1828. In a wonderful historical irony, Rafinesque sent letters describing his discoveries about Maya writing to Champolion, who was already famous for his decipherment of Egyptian hieroglyphic writing.[7]

Ancient Maya writing became an abiding part of the public imagination with the publication in 1841 of *Incidents of Travels in Central America, Chiapas and Yucatán* by John Lloyd Stephens and Frederick Catherwood. With carefully detailed illustrations of the ruined cities and vine-covered stone monuments accompanying the authors' lucid and exciting accounts of their adventures, the *Travels* became a much-reprinted best seller throughout the United States and Europe. Since then, Europeans and Americans have never lost their fascination with this lost American civilization.

During the ensuing century and a half, many inspired scholars and aficionados contributed to the growing body of knowledge about the Maya and their writing system. The great German scholars Eduard Seler and Ernst Förstemann, along with the American J. T. Goodman, worked out the fundamentals of the calendar and basic questions of reading order by the turn of the century. Just as important as their discoveries was the amazing set of drawings and photographs published by the Englishman Alfred Maudslay in *Archaeology: Biologia Centrali-Americana* and by Teobert Maler in the *Memoirs of the Peabody Museum* of Harvard University .

We have often marveled at the hardships these two men and other early explorers endured to complete their work in the hot, forest-covered ruins. Their huge, bulky cameras and the glass-plate technology available to them required gargantuan strength, superhuman patience, and obsessive dedication, but these men left us a priceless heritage[8] that has been basic to the decipherment process. Those glass plates they so laboriously exposed and developed still provide the most detailed records of monuments that have either eroded into near illegibility or been destroyed by looters during the intervening century.

As the early efforts at decipherment progressed, a few people played with the idea that the texts recorded history. One of the most famous near misses was in Herbert Spinden's[9] 1913 description of the Yaxchilán Lintel 12.

> Upon the bodies of these captives are glyphs which may record
> their names and the dates of their capture. At the upper part of
> the stone are two bands of glyphs . . . which possibly contain the
> narrative of the victory or other information of historical interest.
>
> (Spinden 1913:23)

Two years later in his *Introduction to the Study of Maya Hieroglyphic Writing*, Sylvanus Morley also assumed that history was to be found in the inscriptions. He suggested it was recorded in what he called the "textual residue" left when all the calendric information was accounted for. "It is here, if anywhere, that fragments of Maya history will be found recorded, and precisely here is the richest field for future research, since the successful interpretation of the 'textual residue' will alone disclose the true meaning of the Maya writings."[10]

Ironically, these early suggestions were overwhelmed by the proposition that Maya writing concerned only the stately passage of time. J. Eric Thompson, one of the greatest Maya scholars of this century, was the leading proponent of this viewpoint. It was unfortunate for the field that he was so elegant in expressing his ideas, for the few who argued with him never matched the persuasiveness of his rhetoric. This is the way he put it:

> It has been held by some that Maya dates recorded on stelae may
> refer to historical events or even recount the deeds of individu-
> als; to me such a possibility is well-nigh inconceivable. The dates
> on stelae surely narrate the stages of the journey of time with a
> reverence befitting such a solemn theme. I conceive the endless
> progress of time as the supreme mystery of Maya religion, a
> subject which pervaded Maya thought to an extent without
> parallel in the history of mankind. In such a setting there was
> no place for personal records, for, in relation to the vastness of
> time, man and his doings shrink to insignificance. To add details
> of war or peace, of marriage or giving in marriage, to the solemn
> roll call of the periods of time is as though a tourist were to carve
> his initials on Donatello's David.
>
> (J. Eric Thompson 1950:155)

To his everlasting credit, Thompson admitted before he died that he had been utterly wrong. We'll let him speak the retraction in his own words.

> Touching on the inscriptions of the Classic period, the most
> significant achievement has been the demonstration by Tatiana
> Proskouriakoff that texts on stone monuments treat of individ-
> ual rulers with dates which probably mark birth, accession to
> power, conquests, and so on. Name glyphs of rulers or dynasties
> are given, and hints at political events such as alliances.
>
> (J. Eric Thompson 1971:v)

Proskouriakoff's accomplishment was truly monumental. Her carefully constructed logic convinced the field instantly and irrevocably that the contents of the inscriptions concerned the deeds of rulers and nobles. Retrospectively, we can't help but wonder why it took so long to recognize something that is so self-evident today. The answer seems to be that in a barrage of papers published between 1960 and 1964, Proskouriakoff, affectionately known as Tania to her friends, changed the filters before our eyes and altered forever the way we think about the Maya and who they were. Before her work the conclusion was not self-evident.

David Freidel's first encounter with Tania Proskouriakoff reveals a lot about the character of this great scholar. In the fall of 1971, sensing David's interest in Maya art, his mentor, Gordon Willey, invited him and Tania to lunch at Young Lee's Chinese Restaurant, just behind the Harvard Co-op in Cambridge. A brash first-year graduate student, and a long-haired hippie to boot, David arrived sporting a flowing Indian-silk headband. His extravagance raised no eyebrows—great teachers speak to the mind and not to outward appearances—and the conversation ranged over everything from shamanism to Darwinian evolution.

David took what he thought would be a reading course from Tania the following spring, but found that what she taught was actually a "looking" course. He sat in her laboratory in the cluttered, dreary basement of the Peabody Museum for hours on end staring at Maler's exquisite photographs of stelae, while under a small bright lamp set on a nearby desk, Tania worked away on the beautiful jades that had been dredged from the Cenote of Sacrifice at Chichén Itzá. She decided that he should work on realistic animal figures in the art on the principle that these are easiest to discern. Like all of the great Mayanists, she was a master typologist who believed that useful insight could come only through painstaking and systematic inventory of empirical patterns revealed as categories in data. She hoped David would follow this sensible approach and she shared her voluminous card catalogs with him to show her own inventory of every motif and element to be found on the known carved monuments, each accurately sketched on a separate card. This inventory undergirds her famous chronological seriation of Maya stelae. Having directed David to the proper methodological path, she did not tell him what to look for. She wanted him to come to his own conclusions about what was conveyed in the art. Periodically she and David would sit by her desk and talk, her clear, intelligent eyes, her quiet, concise words, and her warm wit contrasting sharply with her small, frail appearance and nervous chain-smoking.

Despite her patience, David perplexed and frustrated her. He wanted to interpret whole stela scenes as compositional structures and to establish the patterns of substitution that existed in the objects held or worn as helmets, girdles, and other apparel. Most of all, he wanted to go beyond the first obvious set of patterns to generate more inclusive categories that would let him understand the historical development from natural to grotesque forms. At the end of the course, she said, "David, you have some good ideas, but you need to learn discipline before you can usefully pursue them." She regarded his deductive leaps as incautious and impossible to prove. She told David that it had taken her many years of careful compilation and study before she was prepared to publicly present her "historical hypothesis." She believed that one should not publish an argument concerning Maya art, even in article form, until it was incontrovertibly proven.

While no single researcher has ever equaled Proskouriakoff's central and revolutionary contribution, there were other players[11] in the new historical approach she so elegantly propounded. In 1962, David Kelley published the first history of Quiriguá's dynasty and in 1958 and 1959, Heinrich Berlin identified the name glyphs of historical portraits at Palenque as well as glyphs referring to various Maya cities.

Yet knowing that the contents of the inscriptions concerned history did not help the historical epigraphers figure out how the Maya spelled their words. That discovery belongs to a young Russian named Yuri Knorozov, who in 1952 proposed that the Maya system was not unlike Egyptian hieroglyphics and cuneiform in that it was a mixed system composed of full word signs combined with signs representing the sounds of syllables. None of the big three, Thompson, Proskouriakoff, or Berlin, was ever able to accept Knorozov's ideas. Partly it was because the Russian bureaucracy couched his discovery in the political rhetoric of the day, but just as important was the fact that they never saw the promise of "phoneticism" fulfilled. In one of his many damning criticisms of phoneticism, Thompson[12] said it this way: "A point of some importance, I feel, is that with a phonetic system, as with breaking a code, the rate of decipherment accelerates with each newly established reading . . . . The first flow of alleged decipherments has not swollen to a river; it has long since dried up."

In retrospect, the reason the river of decipherment dried up was because only a few hearty souls were ready to ride the current of phoneticism. David Kelley, Michael Coe, and Floyd Lounsbury were the only Western scholars to give Knorozov a fair hearing until the dam broke open at the *First Mesa Redonda of Palenque*, a tiny little conference held in the village near the ruins in December 1973. At that conference, a new generation of epigraphers, including Linda Schele and Peter Mathews, were initiated into the mysteries of glyphic decipherment. They joined Kelley and Lounsbury in blending Knorozov's phoneticism with Proskouriakoff's "historical approach." During the next five years, in a series of mini-conferences sponsored by Dumbarton Oaks,[13] this group of epigraphers developed a highly successful collaborative approach and forged the last key—the axiom that the writing reflected spoken language and thus had word order that could be used to determine the function of glyphs, even when we could not read them. Thus, while we might not know what a particular glyph meant, we could figure out whether it was a verb or noun by where it fell in a sentence. That simple assumption let us begin paraphrasing inscriptions and dealing with them as whole texts. It was a breakthrough as important as phoneticism and the historical hypothesis because it gave us a larger framework in which to test readings and reconstruct history.

The conjunction of these three approaches—phoneticism, the historical approach, and syntactical analysis—began the acceleration that Thompson evoked as proof that the right system had been found. Now each new discovery ripples outward to trigger other discoveries, which in turn trigger still others. The number of glyphs deciphered and the interpretative fallout is growing exponentially. As the results of epigraphic research have been published, more and more archaeologists have realized that the Maya inscriptions and imagery offer a primary source of data about how the Maya thought about themselves. They are merging epigraphic and iconographic studies with archaeological projects designed to find out how this "history" epigraphers recover looks in the ground. This is a time of marvelous adventure and unprecedented discovery. The process is ongoing and unbelievably exhilarating to those of us privileged to participate in it.

The Maya writing system used to record this ancient history was a rich and expressive script, capable of faithfully recording every nuance of sound, meaning, and grammatical structure in the writers' language. Calligraphically, it has an unsurpassed elegance, deriving its form from the beauty of freely flowing painted line. Maya scribes, whether carving limestone, engraving jade, inscribing shell, or incising bone, never lost the eloquence of their writing's original painterly grace. And throughout their history the Maya continued to use the original medium in which writing developed—accordion-folded books made from beaten bark paper that was surfaced with a thin layer of plaster. Four of their books[14] survived the ravages of time and Spanish intervention, but they are but a pitiful remnant of the thousands of books that once formed the basis of Maya knowledge. The four we have are calendar almanacs for the timing of ritual, but we may deduce from other Mesoamerican texts we have in our possession[15] that the Maya also recorded all the details of their lives in their books: genealogy, history, learning, prescriptions for ritual, tribute, trade, mythology, views of the world and history, and perhaps poetry and personal thoughts, ambitions, and dreams. Much information has been lost in the dampness of jungle tombs, but we retain a precious and revealing fragment of this heritage in the public and personal texts they wrote on things of stone and clay.

Millions of Maya today speak languages that descend from the two languages we know were written in the ancient texts—Yucatecan, which was spoken by people living in the northern third and on the eastern edge of the peninsula, and Cholan,[16] which was spoken along the base of the southern lowlands from Palenque in the west to Copán in the east (Fig. 1:2).[17] The area between these two regions was probably occupied by both groups, with Yucatecans concentrated toward the east and Cholans to the west. Like the modern Swiss or Belgians, many of these people were and are culturally bilingual.

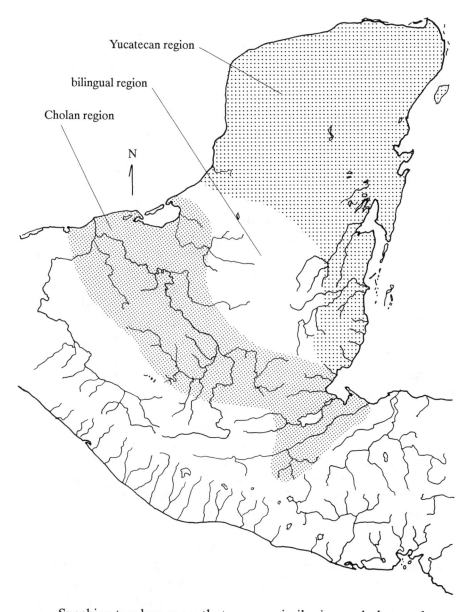

Yucatecan region

bilingual region

Cholan region

N

FIG. 1:2
Distribution for
Yucatecan and
Cholan during
the Classic
period

Speaking two languages that were as similar in vocabulary and grammar as Spanish and Italian gave the people occupying the lowlands an enormous advantage in creating a regional civilization. People living in kingdoms at opposite sides of the Maya region—Palenque on the western edge and Copán on the eastern frontier—spoke the same Cholan language, while people at Dzibilchaltún in the north spoke the same Yucatecan language as people living near Nah Tunich, a cave in the central Petén near the Belizean border. This uniformity of language was one of the factors that facilitated trade and cultural exchange between the kingdoms and gave the people of this region a sense of common identity as Maya. Although fiercely competitive, the Maya, like the ancient Greek city-states, presented a unified ethnic identity to outsiders—especially those who spoke other languages.

balam

ba - balam

balam - ma

ba - balam - ma

ba - la - m(a)

FIG. 1:3A

Even when speakers could not understand one another, the writing system acted as intermediary, much as the Chinese writing system has functioned for millennia. The wordplays that were so important in the Maya writing system and in the symbolism of their imagery usually worked equally in both Yucatecan and Cholan. Language as the source of visual metaphor provided a common base for the innovation of the symbolic expression of the Classic Maya world view and the institution of kingship. For example, in Cholan and Yucatecan, the words for "snake," "sky," and the number "four" are all pronounced in a nearly identical fashion (*can* in Yucatecan and *chan* in Cholan).[18] It made good sense to Maya artisans reaching for images to convey the sky arching overhead to portray it as a great snake. They also freely exchanged the glyphs for "sky" and "snake" in titles and names. Since both glyphs were read in the same way, it did not matter which form they used. The fact that only two languages were spoken in such a large geographic area, as much as anything, may account for the remarkable coherency of Classic Maya cultural production during the thousand years of its existence.

The writing system itself worked much like the other great hiero-glyphic systems in the world, Egyptian and cuneiform—although it came from an entirely indigenous development. Scribes could spell words with signs representing individual sounds as well as signs representing whole words. We call these "word signs" *logographs.*[19] For example, the word for "jaguar" (*balam* in Mayan) could be written simply as a picture of the head of the big cat (Fig. 1:3a). Yet in the Maya world there was more than one spotted cat—for example, there were ocelots and margays. Since confusion could arise concerning this pictorial sign, as with many others, the Maya added syllabary signs to either the front or rear of logographs in order to specify how to pronounce the initial or final consonant. For example, they could attach the syllable sign for *ba* to the front of the jaguar head or *ma* to its rear, giving the spelling *ba-balam* or *balam-ma.* Since no other word for a cat began with *ba* or ended in *ma,* readers knew that here they should pronounce *balam,* instead of any of the other possible words for "cat." This type of sign is called a *phonetic complement,* because it helps to specify the phonetic or sound value of the main glyph it accompanies.

Since these phonetic complements represented the sounds of sylla-bles, the Maya could spell the word using only these phonetic signs, thus eliminating the logograph altogether. The system they devised used two syllable signs to spell a word composed of a consonant-vowel-consonant.[20] For example, *cab,* "earth," was spelled with the sign for *ca* combined with *ba* to form *ca-b(a)* (Fig. 1:3b). The final vowel in this kind of spelling was not pronounced. In this phonetic system, the word for "jaguar" used three signs, *ba, la,* and *ma* to spell *balam(a),* again without pronouncing the final *a.*

The scribes also used other types of signs, called *semantic determina-tives,* which specified that a word should be read with a particular mean-ing. The most widely distributed sign of this sort was the cartouche that was put around the names of the days in the 260-day calendar. Composed

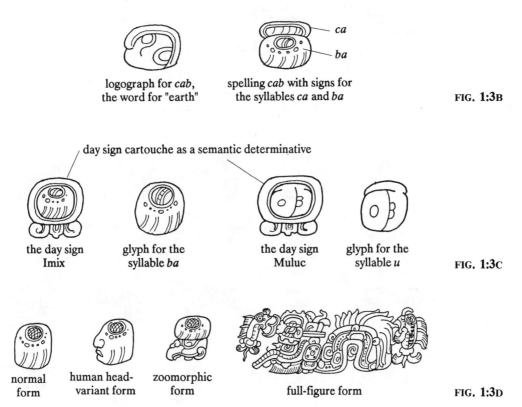

logograph for *cab*,
the word for "earth"

spelling *cab* with signs for
the syllables *ca* and *ba*

day sign cartouche as a semantic determinative

the day sign
Imix

glyph for the
syllable *ba*

the day sign
Muluc

glyph for the
syllable *u*

normal
form

human head-
variant form

zoomorphic
form

full-figure form

of a hollow circle standing on three scrolled feet, the cartouche told the reader he was looking at the name of a day. When that same sign appeared outside the cartouche, its values were entirely different. For example, the sign that recorded the day Imix became *ba* outside this cartouche and the day sign Muluc became the syllable *u* in its naked form (Fig. 1:3c).

To the despair and sometimes the bemusement of the modern epigrapher, glyphs also had many different graphic forms as well as different phonetic and semantic values. For example, the Imix graph has its regular form, a human form, a zoomorphic form, and a full-bodied form (Fig. 1:3d). The scribe chose the form that fit the space or the elaborateness of his text in the best possible way, and artistry was judged on how elegantly these various forms were combined and used, much like the ornate capital letters used in medieval manuscripts.

Syllables or words (such as *u,* the third person pronoun, "he/his, she/hers, it/its") that were frequently used soon developed many different forms, almost as if the scribes got bored writing the same word too many times in the same way. Since each of these alternative signs had its own set of plain, head, and full-bodied forms, the end product was an enormously complex system of writing in which the same word could be written in many different ways. An example of this is the word *ahau,* which could function both as a day sign and as the rank of the king (Fig. 1:4). The more important parts of a text were often rendered in the more elaborate forms and were larger in scale.

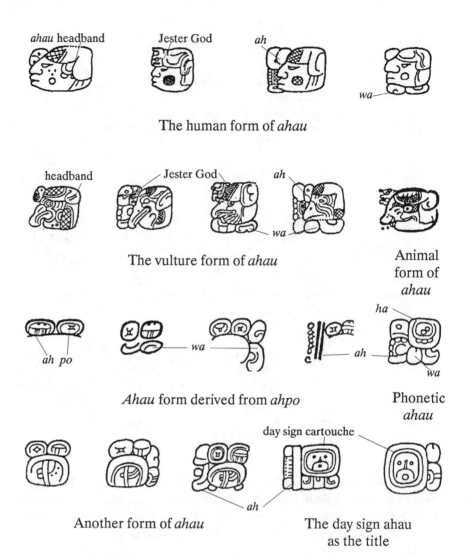

The human form of *ahau*

The vulture form of *ahau*

Animal form of *ahau*

Ahau form derived from *ahpo*

Phonetic *ahau*

Another form of *ahau*

The day sign ahau as the title

The glyphs in all their various forms were combined into phrases, sentences, and finally the larger texts that have survived into modern times. In the Maya inscriptions, the standard sentence normally began with the time of the action, followed by the action itself, the thing acted upon, and finally the actor. These sentences join with other sentences to become texts, relating sequences of times, actions, and actors, and finally to create a literature with its own style and judgments of what was good and bad writing. Today many of these conventions still survive in the oral traditions of living Maya.[21]

We have found that the surviving Maya literature falls into several genres: the ritual almanacs of the codices; texts marking the ownership of objects from earflares to houses; texts recording the formal dedication of objects, their patronage, and their artists and scribes; and finally, narrative texts. This last category has at least two subdivisions: narratives embedded into pictorial scenes which illustrate the action, and narratives which stand on their own without pictorial illustration. By combining the information recorded in these various kinds of texts, we can reconstruct the history, beliefs, and institutions of the ancient Maya.

The hieroglyphic texts are more than just a history. They constitute a literature, the only written one surviving from the Precolumbian world. The art of writing for the ancient Maya was not only the sequence and structure of words, but included making the image of the word itself. Their writing was one of the most elegant scripts of the ancient world, partially because more than any other writing system, it stayed close to its pictorial and artistic origin. Yet the art of the scribe turned not only on the beauty of the calligraphy but also on how creatively and innovatively he exploited the potential of the writing system and the conventions of text presentation themselves. To the Maya, it was not only what the text said that counted, but also how the scribe chose to say it: and not only how it was said, but also where and on what it was said.

The complexity of the system is often bewildering to the modern reader, just as it must have been to the ancient Maya who was not an expert in its use. But we must recognize that the goal of the writing system was not mass communication, in the modern sense. Few of the ancient Maya population were literate and there were no paperbacks and weekly news journals. Writing was a sacred proposition that had the capacity to capture the order of the cosmos, to inform history, to give form to ritual, and to transform the profane material of everyday life into the supernatural.

History is as much a construction of those writing it as the events it proposes to record, and this is as true of the Maya as of any other civilization. Surviving Maya texts give us, almost exclusively, only the side of the winners—those who were victorious in war, who had the power to commission the great public monuments and buildings, those wealthy enough to fill their tombs with inscribed objects, and those who could afford to buy or commission precious objects as offerings to the gods. In the best of worlds, we would also have more examples of the losers' stories, as well as the daily records of transactions, taxes, and trade, and the personal thoughts of the humans who lived that history. Time almost never gives us such a complete record. What we have lost of the Maya are the things they wrote in their books and on other perishable material. What we have is history as the kings and nobles wanted their constituents to understand it, the things of faith people wanted to take with them into death, and the words of worth they put on offerings and on the objects they used in ritual and daily life.

Given that the public histories the Maya left behind them are not necessarily the truth, we must use archaeology to provide complementary information of all sorts—some confirming the written record, some qualifying it. It is upon the pattern of conjunction and disjunction between these two records that we base our interpretations of history.

Combining the two streams of information also gives the archaeologist the chronological framework into which we put Maya history. That archaeological history begins with evidence of the first people moving into the Yucatán Peninsula about eleven thousand years ago. For thousands of years, these hunter-gatherers lived quiet lives, leaving behind the chipped stone tools they used as knives, scrapers, and projectile points for hunting game as mute witness of their existence, but by 1000 B.C., they had learned agriculture and begun to build villages.[22] This first phase of settled life is called the Preclassic period (1500 B.C.–A.D. 200). By its end, the Maya had developed a civilized way of life: the social and political institutions, centering on the institution of divine kingship, that would guide the Maya for the next thousand years.

The first subdivision of this long period, the Early Preclassic (1500–900 B.C.), was the time when the first great civilization arose in Mesoamerica. Called the Olmec by modern researchers, this remarkable people built the first kingdoms and established the template of world view and political symbolism the Maya would inherit. Occupying the swampy lowlands of southern Veracruz and parts of highland Guerrero, the Olmec were the first people to create an artistic style and symbolic expression that united different ethnic groups throughout Mesoamerica into a single cultural system.

By the Middle Preclassic (900–300 B.C.), Olmec imagery was used from Costa Rica to the Valley of México and different groups throughout the region were building large population centers and buying into the ideas of kingship and hierarchical society. The reaction of the southernmost Maya peoples to the rise of the Olmec can be seen in their rapid adoption of Olmec innovation in symbolic imagery and social institutions. The Maya in the mountain valleys of western Honduras,[23] Guatemala, and El Salvador began, like the Olmec, to organize their society along more hierarchical lines, a fact which can be extrapolated from the contents of graves from several sites. Some members of society were buried humbly in the floors of their houses, while others were sent to the afterlife accompanied by precious objects such as jade. Throughout the Middle Preclassic period the southern Maya also began raising public buildings—mounds with plazas of earth and stone. On the mountain slopes and foothills above the hot and swampy Pacific coast, other groups[24] began carving stone monuments in styles emulating the Olmec and displaying symbols that presaged the royal iconography of the Maya kings who emerged by the time of Christ. Early rulers were carved in stone along with imagery depicting the symbols of gods and the cosmos of the Middle Preclassic vision. These power images would eventually become the stelae of the lowland tradition, showing the lord frozen at the moment of communication with the Otherworld.

Although surrounded to the west and south by peoples who had elected to unite under the authority of high chieftains and kings, most of the Middle Preclassic villagers of the lowlands chose a different path of social development: tribal confederacies that could convene in the thousands to repel an enemy, but whose members recognized no power above their village patriarchs.[25] Segmentary tribal organization of this type could sustain essentially egalitarian societies of very large size, in spite of the proximity of neighboring hierarchical states. From this type of organization came the template of a kingship replicated in numerous small states, an institution that arose with great rapidity throughout the lowland country in the first century B.C. Early kings were exalted patriarchs, heads of lineages who viewed themselves as brothers because they had all descended from the same mythical ancestors.[26] Segmentary tribal organization was gradually amplified into segmentary state organization.[27]

The Late Preclassic period (300 B.C.–A.D. 100) witnessed the emergence of the rank called *ahau* and the rise of kingdoms throughout the Maya country. From this exalted rank of lords came the person who was the high king, the *ahau* of the *ahauob*. From the Pacific slopes of the southern highlands[28] to the northern plains of Yucatán,[29] these lords displayed themselves and their royal regalia on monuments carved with narrative pictures recording their ritual actions. For the first time texts accompanied these scenes, describing who acted, where, and when. It was the beginning of history for the Maya. It was also the beginning of the great political strategies utilized by kings in their creation of public art; for, to the Maya, the cornerstone of historical reality was what could be seen on the temples and public buildings of the city. More powerfully than we can imagine, their art created their reality. It is in this period that the lowland Maya first created decorated temples and the highland peoples[30] raised stone stelae inscribed with texts, and the principles of kingship were firmly established for the next thousand years.

Our story begins in this last phase of the Preclassic period and continues into the florescence of Maya civilization during the Classic period, a phase which traditionally begins with the earliest deciphered date on a stela—now A.D. 199.[31] This time of extraordinary accomplishment falls into two subdivisions: the Early Classic (A.D. 200–600) and the Late Classic (A.D. 600–900).[32] The Classic period ended with a general collapse in most of the Maya region, although in some areas, such as northern Belize and Yucatán, the Classic way of life continued unbroken into the final phase of Precolumbian history, the Postclassic. The Postclassic period lasted from A.D. 900 until the conquest of Yucatán by the Spaniards in 1541, although Maya resistance to Spanish domination continued until the Itzá, Maya Indians who lived around Lake Petén Itzá, were overwhelmed in 1697.

The inscriptions and archaeology also give us information on the world that the Maya inhabited during the Classic period, for it was very different from what we find as tourists. At the height of Classic civilization in the eighth century, the Maya landscape in all its variety supported millions of people. Although the inscriptions from that period tell us the largest domain was Tikal, a kingdom of around 500,000 souls,[33] the average dominion was much smaller, holding jurisdiction over only 30,000 to 50,000 subjects. Maya kings had to cope with a political geography of enormous complexity (Fig. 1:5), resembling the bewildering variety of kingdoms, dukedoms, baronies, and other titled lands of the European Middle Ages. A closer parallel might be the city-states of Classical Greece: little countries that were politically autonomous, yet culturally, socially, and economically interdependent.[34]

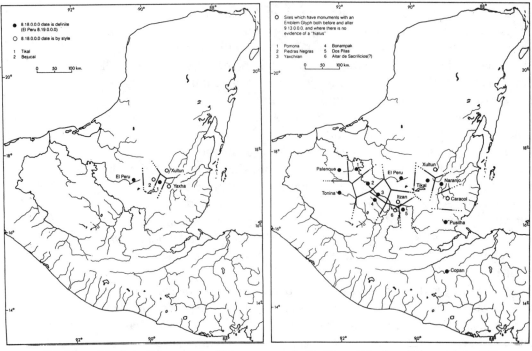

a. Emblem Glyph polities at A.D. 396   b. Emblem Glyph polities at A.D. 692

FIG. 1:5
Distribution of
Emblem Glyph
Polities in the
Classic Period as
suggested by
Peter Mathews

The first clues about the way the Classic Maya organized themselves came with Heinrich Berlin's discovery of Emblem Glyphs.[35] Today we know that these glyphs are titles signifying that people who have them in their names are either a *ch'ul ahau* ("holy lord"), *ahau* ("lord"), or *na ahau* ("noble lady") of a particular kingdom. We also know that these kingdoms were hierarchically organized and included people of many different ranks among their populations. Most of them had a main center or capital, but they also included subsidiary sites ranging from sizable towns up to very large palace compounds and eventually down to hamlets and individual farms.[36]

The glyphic inscriptions give us other kinds of information about the governing hierarchies in these kingdoms, although there was apparently some variation in organization from region to region. The main king was often referred to as the ch'ul ahau. He was always of the rank ahau, but there were also lesser ahauob within the same kingdom who had different responsibilities. Ahauob ruled subordinate population centers within the larger polity and they held important offices, such as war chief, within the main center. The subordinate town of Tortuguero, for example, was ruled by a man named Ahpo-Balam, who was a member of the royal family and an ahau of Palenque. At Copán, the half brother of the last great king ruled a portion of that city. An ahau who was also the son of a king of Naranjo achieved fame as a scribe—not a political office, yet a highly valued specialist rank. In brief, the title of ahau indicated nobility of the highest degree. It was the rank to which the king must belong, but there were many more ahauob than there were kings. This is the typical pattern

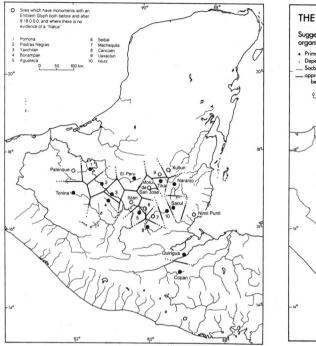

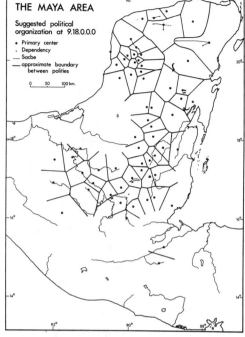

c. Emblem Glyph polities at A.D. 790   d. Suggested polities at A.D. 790

for a rank that is inherited by several offspring at each generation, as ahau certainly was during the Late Classic period. Obviously, it was in the interests of the kings to find useful work in the government of the realm for their siblings and other ahauob.

Within the kingdoms along the Usumacinta and in the forest to the west of that region,[37] secondary centers might be ruled by a *cahal,* a noble with less prestige than the ahauob, yet still intimately associated with their kings. The rank of cahal carried many of the ritual prerogatives of the ahauob and produced both provincial governors and officials at the capitals.[38] Both cahalob and ahauob were, therefore, part of the courts that administered the polities, and kings could marry women of either rank to secure political alliances.

Nobles of both ranks were sent to other capitals as emissaries of their high kings,[39] and people of both ahau and cahal rank were important witnesses to the designations of heirs and the accessions of high kings. The powerful and dangerous ritual requirements of accession, along with the preference that the king be ideally the eldest male offspring of his royal sire, suggest that kingship was not elective. Nevertheless, the many exceptions to the ideal of inheritance, including descent of the throne from older to younger brothers,[40] also show how critical the support of the nobility was to the succession.

The number of kingdoms ruled by kings grew from perhaps a dozen in the first century B.C. to as many as sixty at the height of the lowland civilization in the eighth century (Fig. 1:5d).[41] Not all polities survived this span of history, even when they were well established. There were many hazards to challenge kings—wars, intrigues, and natural catastrophes. A king was literally at risk all his life; and more than one king ended his rule, not by dying of peaceful old age but by being taken captive in a war he was too old to fight.[42] It was also true that prosperous and probably autonomous towns always existed within the political geography without ever erecting a royal stela or establishing themselves as an Emblem Glyph polity. Polities both with and without an Emblem Glyph appeared, matured, and disappeared throughout Maya history.

Political coherence and integration characterized life within the dominion of a king, but in the borderlands between these kingdoms, the opportunity must have existed for adventuresome people to maintain independent chiefdoms, or even for whole villages of unallied farmers to exist. Many civilizations tolerate such marginal folk because they service the civilized in a variety of ways, not the least of which is as a human buffer against organized enemies. In the Maya world of the forest, these in-between people likely gathered many wild plant and tree products—from which they made medicines, poisons, dyes, and incense—and trapped and hunted game for meat and hides. They then sold all these valued commodities to their brethren within the kingdoms. Keeping the border towns under control and assessing tribute were the responsibility of court nobles, and disputed jurisdiction over borderlands was likely one of the causes of wars.

The political geography of the Maya consisted of island cities of royal power in a sea of townspeople and village folk. Kings worked hard to establish firm control over the countryside and to expand their authority as far as possible in the direction of other polities. From the beginning of the institution of kingship, military confrontation was not only a fact of life but a necessary and inevitable royal responsibility. With the proliferation of polities, the civilized territories expanded at the expense of the freeholders. By the Late Classic period, kings looked out at a landscape peopled with brother lords, both enemies and allies, and at escalating conditions of war and strife.

There are certain things about the Maya landscape, about life in the tropics, and about the kind of "technology" available to the ancient Maya that help people of the twentieth century to understand a little better what their lives were really like. They were, first of all, a stone age people, without metal of any kind until several centuries before the Conquest. All they accomplished was done by means of stone tools, utilizing human beings as their beasts of burden: No animals large enough to carry cargo lived in Mesoamerica before the coming of the Spanish. Although the Maya built wide roads to link parts of their kingdoms together, they did not build highway systems. Within the jungle and the rugged mountain landscape, where the wheel was not used, highways did not make a lot of sense. The ancient Maya traveled along paths winding through the deep forests and cultivated areas, but the major arteries of their transportation were the many rivers and swamps that crisscrossed the landscape. Until very recently,[43] the canoe was the most important form of travel into the interior of the Maya region.

Carved as a single piece from a huge hardwood tree, dugout canoes plied the slow-moving lowland rivers. These rivers drained huge swamps fed by rains that could, and still do, average 150 inches a year in the southern lowlands. Some of this water flows north into the mighty Usumacinta River and its tributaries to empty into the Gulf of México. The rest of it flows east down a network of streams and rivers, large and small, emptying eventually into the Caribbean Sea. Spreading like the veins of a forest leaf, these waterways provided the natural avenues of travel and trade from the southern to the northern lowlands. When we think of lords visiting one another or items being traded between areas, we must remember that these people and trade goods were carried on the backs of bearers in litters or in tumplines[44] or in canoes paddled across the network of waterways that was the superhighway system of the ancient Maya.

These rivers were are not always gentle pathways. At the height of the rainy season, especially when the great thunderstorms and the hurricanes of summer and fall sweep in from the Gulf, these slow-moving rivers can turn into raging torrents of destruction. Conversely, in the dry season they can become too shallow to navigate. Although water, overall, is abundant in the tropics, there is usually too little of it during the dry times, and too much during the torrential rains of summer and fall. Because of these conditions, much of Maya social innovation was centered around two great problems: how to store excess water for the times it would be needed, and how to free wet, fertile swampland for farming. The building of reservoirs and massive, complicated canal systems took the labor of thousands and helped develop the concepts of community and central authority. For instance, the Maya of Tikal excavated reservoirs as they quarried stone to build the great houses of the central acropolis. In areas now in the state of Campeche, the lack of permanent water sources forced the Maya to build great rainwater cisterns under their buildings, and at Edzna, to dig kilometers of shallow canals to hold water throughout the dry season.

Further to the north, rainwater collects seasonally in low sinks, but most surface water seeps quickly into the soil and runs underground to the sea. The Maya could reach this underground water only through caves which riddled the limestone. When water dissolved the ceilings of these limestone caves, deep natural wells called *cenotes* were formed. In the northwestern corner of Yucatán, the water in these wells is close to the surface, but in other regions, for example, at Chichén Itzá, the water table is twenty meters below the surface. Such water is accessible only by long and dangerous climbing down wooden ladders or stone steps carved in the wall of the well itself. The cenotes are a major geographic feature of the northern lowlands, and for a people focused on entrances into the "Otherworld" beneath the earth, these caves and water holes became centers of social gathering and the enactment of ritual.

The other great fact of Maya life was the magnificent rain forest, full of towering, liana-draped hardwoods, such as the mahogany, chico zapote, and the most sacred tree of all, the great ceiba. The forest supports a rich web of life, but because the soil under it is thin, nutrients that seep below the surface are captured by the subsoil, which locks them away from the roots of plants. The forest has adapted to this by developing a spectacular factory of insects and fungi which live on its dank and shady floor and digest the fall of leaves, limbs, and trees, returning these precious nutrients to the great spreading roots of the trees. This cycle of life is in full view of humanity, a litany of green blossoming out of death and decay.

The rhythms of the tropical world are not the same as those of the temperate zone in which we live. For us, the central metaphor of death and rebirth derives from the change of winter to spring, but in the Maya tropics spring is the time of drought and the burning of the forest to open the fields for planting. There, the heat of the spring is unending and inescapable as the skies darken with the gritty pall of burning trees, filling lungs with soot and dimming the light of the sun.[45] The forest turns completely white as the trees dry out and many of them lose their leaves. The world becomes the color of bone and the forest smells of death.

The dry season was also the time for wars, for the muddy land dried out then and people could move to and from the battlefield with greater ease. Since planting could not be done until the rains came, there was time for war without endangering the work of farmers. Almost all the battles discussed in this book were fought between late January and early May.

When the rains finally come in late May or early June, the world awakens, literally changing overnight. Thirsty leaves and stems swell with the water of life, and the forest is transformed within hours from the colorlessness of death into a vibrant, unbelievably deep green—the color the Maya called *yax*. These rains do not bring the riotous color of northern spring, but a sudden change that even more surely emphasizes the transformation of death into life.

In the summer, the rains come in torrential tropical thunderstorms that break across the land with awesome power. In good times, they release their heavy loads of life-giving water with predictable regularity in the late afternoon or early evening, but they can inundate the land as surely as they can bring it life. Eventually, the storms of summer give way in late July and August to a short dry season called the *canícula,* letting the muddy, saturated earth dry out a little before the fall rains come in their gentle, all-day drizzle. The cold winter storms, today called *nortes,* can go on for days, chilling the normally warm climate to a bone-deep, shivering, wet cold.

There is a rhythm to tropical life that flows through the experience of all beings living there. In the rich abundance of life that thrives in the forest, in the coming of the rains, and in the terrible consequences of drought, there is a contrast of life and death, of abundance and deprivation, that teaches the lessons of life and cyclic time in metaphors of undeniable power and elegance. Their metaphor is not ours—a spring rebirth timed by the equinox. It is instead the coming of the life-giving rains timed by the summer solstice. This metaphor, however, is just as powerful and penetrating as the temperate cycle upon which the great myths of the Western world are built, and just as effective.

The institution of kingship, and the understanding of the world that fueled Maya civilization welled up out of the experience of the ancient villager. The plants and animals of the forest, the alternation of dry season with the time of rains, the rhythms of planting and burning, were the stuff from which the kings molded the symbols of their power. We are just beginning to understand the patterns of the Maya world and how they used them in the material expression of their culture.

The connections the Maya put into their public history between things spiritual and things human, between things ancestral and things current, between things of the king and things of the community, were not a matter of accident or personal taste. The Maya put them in the public forum of life because they were the things they saw as important. The inscriptions and imagery we have are the propaganda the kings thought their people would believe. They represent the strategies everyone thought gave them a chance to live beyond dying.

These texts and images are a map of the ancient Maya mind and history, of the world as they understood it. Through the words and images they inscribed upon the objects of their lives, they live again in our time. We can remember their deeds, contemplate the power and beauty of their world, and recognize that they accomplished things we honor as civilized, and in the context of human events, as great. The writing of the Maya preserves not only the history of their kings but also their sense of power and sacredness. It lets us utter their names once again—and for a moment see the world as they saw it.

2

SACRED SPACE, HOLY TIME, *AND THE* MAYA WORLD

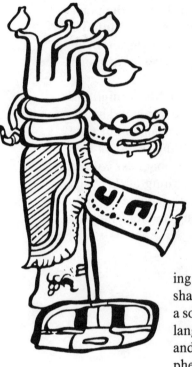

As we grow to adulthood, every human being acquires a special way of seeing and understanding the world and the human community. This is a shared conception of reality, created by the members of a society living together over generations, through their language, their institutions and arts, their experiences, and their common work and play. We call this human phenomenon "culture," and it enables people to understand how and why the world around them works.

The idea that there are as many "realities" as there are societies may be novel to many of us. Yet whether or not we are aware that we see our world through a filter, our own version of reality guides our actions just as surely as other, different versions have guided other societies around the world in both the present and the past. We in the West live as we do in part because our cultural reality constrains our ability to imagine different ways of doing things. In our world, for example, we could not imagine letting blood from our bodies, as the Maya did, in order to communicate with our ancestors. Such violence seems crazy and "uncivilized" to us. On the other hand, the ancient Maya would find our wartime custom of drafting young men to go and fight in the place of the leaders of our nation both barbaric and cowardly. Maya lords fought their own battles and a king often paid for defeat in the coin of his own capture and sacrifice.

The principal language of our reality here in the West is economics. Important issues in our lives, such as progress and social justice, war and peace, and the hope for prosperity and security, are expressed in material metaphors. Struggles, both moral and military, between the haves and have-nots of our world pervade our public media and our thoughts of the future. The Maya codified their shared model of reality through religion and ritual rather than economics. The language of Maya religion explained the place of human beings in nature, the workings of the sacred world, and the mysteries of life and death, just as our religion still does for us in special circumstances like marriages and funerals. But their religious system also encompassed practical matters of political and economic power, such as how the ordered world of the community worked.

While we live in a model of the world that vests our definitions of physical reality in science and spiritual reality in religious principles, the Maya lived in a world that defined the physical world as the material manifestation of the spiritual and the spiritual as the essence of the material. For them the world of experience manifested itself in two complementary dimensions. One dimension was the world in which they lived out their lives and the other was the abode of the gods, ancestors, and other supernatural beings. This manner of understanding reality is still true for many of the contemporary descendants of the ancient Maya.

These two planes of existence were inextricably locked together. The actions and interactions of Otherworld beings influenced the fate of this world, bringing disease or health, disaster or victory, life or death, prosperity or misfortune into the lives of human beings. But the denizens of the Otherworld were also dependent upon the deeds of the living for their continued well-being. Only the living could provide the nourishment required by both the inhabitants of the Otherworld and the souls who would be reborn there as the ancestors.[1] To the Maya, the idea of dividing the responsibility for human welfare between politicians and priests would have been incomprehensible. The kings were, above all, divine shamans who operated in both dimensions and through the power of their ritual performance kept both in balance, thus bringing prosperity to their domains.

Because the king lived in the same community as the villager, his explanations of political institutions and rituals had to be voiced in the common language of this shared reality, for the villagers were as much his constituents as were the nobles.[2] For us to understand the actions of Maya kings and their people as rational and necessary for their successful functioning in their world, we must understand how the shared reality of the ancient Maya defined the world for them.

The high art that has so fascinated the modern visitor is the public and private expression of that world view through writing and narrative imagery. This narrative representation of the actions of kings and nobles served a twofold purpose. On the most fundamental level it placed them within the framework of history. Most important, however, it underlined the cyclicality of the cosmic time in which that history unfolded. The

SACRED
SPACE,
HOLY TIME,
AND THE
MAYA
WORLD
——
65

Maya were preoccupied with demonstrating historical action as the inevitable result of cosmic and ancestral necessities. It was within this great matrix of belief that the Maya enacted the triumphs, defeats, drama, humor, and pathos of their history and strove to create the greatest and most lasting memorials to their lives.

The World They Conceived

The Maya world was made up of three layered domains: the starry arch of heaven, the stony Middleworld of earth made to flower and bear fruit by the blood of kings, and the dark waters of the Underworld below.[3] To say that the Maya considered these to be three distinct regions, however, is to give a false impression, for they believed all dimensions of existence were interrelated. Furthermore, all three domains were thought to be alive and imbued with sacred power, including the sky, which was represented by a great crocodilian monster. This Cosmic Monster made the rains when it shed its blood in supernatural counterpoint to the royal sacrifices on the earth below.

The Underworld was sometimes called Xibalba,[4] but it is perhaps closer to the original Maya understanding to think of Xibalba as the parallel unseen Otherworld into which the Maya kings and other shamans could pass in ecstatic trance. Like the world of human beings, Xibalba[5] had animals, plants, inhabitants of various kinds, and a landscape with both natural and constructed features. At sundown Xibalba rotated above the earth to become the night sky.

The human plane of existence, like the Otherworld, was a sacred place. The Maya conceived of the human world as a region floating in the primordial sea. Sometimes they represented the earth as the back of a caiman and sometimes as the back of a turtle.[6] The four cardinal directions provided the fundamental grid for the Maya community and for the surface of the world. But for the Maya, the principal axis of the Middleworld was the path of the sun as it moved from east to west on its daily journey. Each direction of the compass had a special tree, a bird, a color, gods associated with its domain, and rituals associated with those gods. East was red and the most important direction since it was where the sun was born. North, sometimes called the "side of heaven," was white and the direction from which the cooling rains of winter came. It was also the direction of the north star around which the sky pivots. West, the leaving or dying place of the sun, was black. South was yellow and was considered to be the right-hand or great side of the sun.[7] In the Maya conception east, not north, should always be at the top of maps.

This model of the world, however, was concentric as well as quadrangular. The four cardinal directions were also seen in relationship to the center, which also had its color (blue-green), its gods, its bird, and its tree (Fig. 2:1). Running through this center, the Maya envisioned an axis called *Wacah Chan* ("six sky" or "raised up sky").[8] The tree which symbolized this axis coexisted in all three vertical domains. Its trunk went

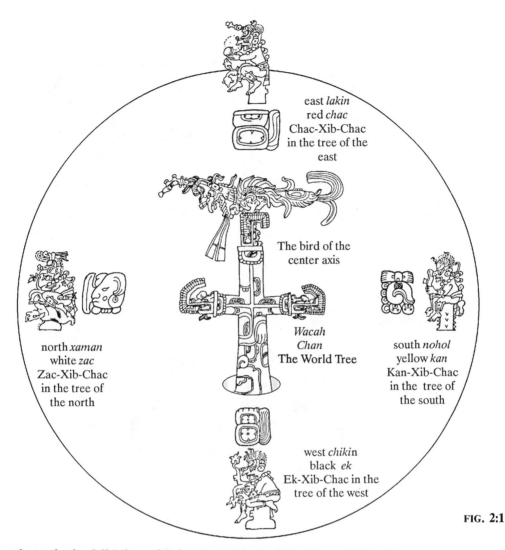

east *lakin*
red *chac*
Chac-Xib-Chac
in the tree of the
east

The bird of the
center axis

north *xaman*
white *zac*
Zac-Xib-Chac
in the tree of
the north

*Wacah
Chan*
The World Tree

south *nohol*
yellow *kan*
Kan-Xib-Chac
in the tree of
the south

west *chikin*
black *ek*
Ek-Xib-Chac in the
tree of the west

FIG. 2:1

through the Middleworld; its roots plunged to the nadir in the watery Underworld region of the Otherworld, and its branches soared to the zenith in the highest layer of the heavenly region of the Otherworld.

The geography of the human world included plains, mountains, caves, cenotes, rivers, lakes, and swamps, and the places and buildings made by people—cities and towns with their houses, palaces, temples, and ballcourts (Fig. 2:2). To the Maya, this world was alive and imbued with a sacredness that was especially concentrated at special points, like caves and mountains. The principal pattern of power points had been established by the gods when the cosmos was created. Within this matrix of sacred landscape, human beings built communities that both merged with the god-generated patterns and created a second human-made matrix of power points. These two systems were perceived to be complementary, not separate.

As we mentioned above, the world of human beings was connected to the Otherworld along the *wacah chan* axis which ran through the center of existence. This axis was not located in any one earthly place, but could be materialized though ritual at any point in the natural and human-made landscape. Most important, it was materialized in the person of the king,

SACRED
SPACE,
HOLY TIME,
AND THE
MAYA
WORLD

—

67

cauac signs   eyelids   maize god

cave as the
mouth of
the Witz
Monster

muzzle   stepped forehead

Witz ("mountain") Monster

the surface of water

otot
house

pitzil
ballcourt

nab
swamp or
shallow lake

cenote or
water hole

te-tun,
tree-stone,
the glyph for stela

sky, *chan*

earthband, *cab*

cave in earth

FIG. 2:2

who brought it into existence as he stood enthralled in ecstatic visions atop his pyramid-mountain.

There were two great symbolic representations of this center axis: the king himself, who brought it into being, and his natural analog, the World Tree. The act of communication between the human world and the Otherworld was represented by the most profound symbols of Maya kingship: the Vision Serpent and the Double-headed Serpent Bar[9] (Fig. 2:3). In the rapture of bloodletting rituals, the king brought the great World Tree into existence through the middle of the temple and opened the awesome

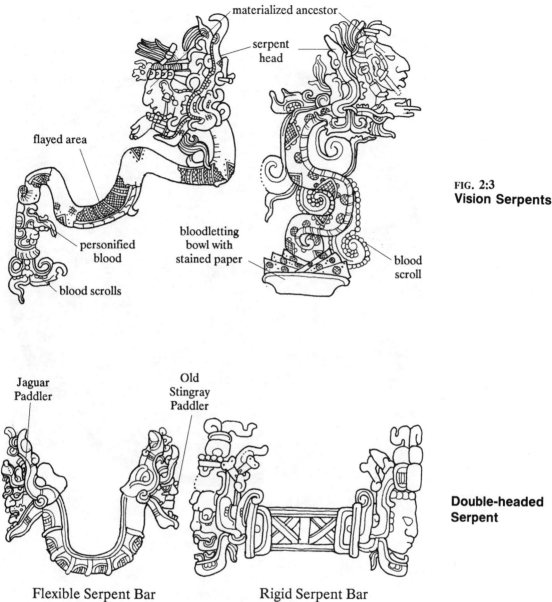

materialized ancestor

serpent head

flayed area

personified blood

blood scrolls

bloodletting bowl with stained paper

blood scroll

FIG. 2:3
Vision Serpents

Jaguar Paddler

Old Stingray Paddler

Double-headed Serpent

Flexible Serpent Bar

Rigid Serpent Bar

doorway into the Otherworld.[10] During both public and private bloodletting rituals, the Vision Serpent, which symbolized the path of communication between the two worlds, was seen rising in the clouds of incense and smoke above the temples housing the sculptured sanctums. The earthly sides of the portals were within these sanctums.

Fortunately for us, one of the greatest of Maya painters[11] left us an eloquent representation of the cosmos as his people understood it to exist. This image was painted on a tripod plate which was intended to hold the blood that helped open a portal to the Otherworld (Fig. 2:4). The opened portal itself is depicted as the Maw of the Underworld, a great bearded and skeletal-jawed serpent. Out of the jaws of this serpent come the pure, life-bearing waters of the earth and below them flow the dark, fecund

SACRED
SPACE,
HOLY TIME,
AND THE
MAYA
WORLD
——
69

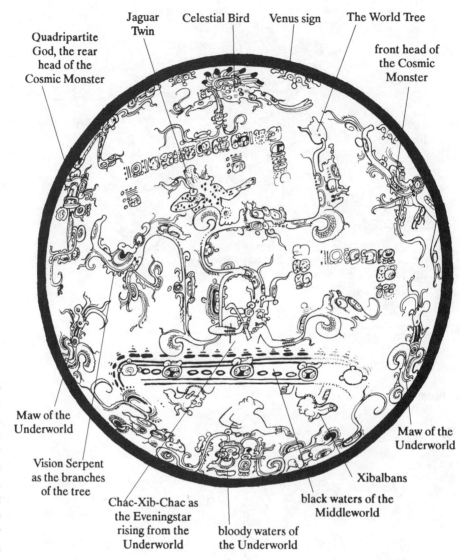

Jaguar
Twin

Celestial Bird

Venus sign

The World Tree

Quadripartite
God, the rear
head of the
Cosmic Monster

front head of
the Cosmic
Monster

FIG. 2:4
**The Maya
Cosmos**
Venus as
Eveningstar
rising from the
Underworld
in its first
appearance
after superior
conjunction

Maw of the
Underworld

Vision Serpent
as the branches
of the tree

Chac-Xib-Chac as
the Eveningstar
rising from the
Underworld

bloody waters of
the Underworld

black waters of the
Middleworld

Xibalbans

Maw of the
Underworld

waters of the Underworld. Along the upper edge of the image arches the
living sky, the Cosmic Monster, which contains within its body the great
ancestral Sun and Venus. The rains, its holy blood, flow in great scrolls
from the mouth of its crocodilian head and from the stingray spine on the
Quadripartite Monster at the opposite end. The World Tree, *Wacah
Chan*, emerges from the head of the god Chac-Xib-Chac (the Eveningstar)
as he rises from the black waters of the portal. The trunk of the World
Tree splits to become the Vision Serpent, whose gullet is the path taken
by the ancestral dead and the gods of the Otherworld when they commune
with the king as the forces of nature and destiny.

Once brought into the world of humanity, these Otherworld beings
could be materialized in ritual objects, in features of the landscape, or in
the actual body of a human performer.[12] Bloodletting, the focus ritual of
Maya life, was the instrument of this materialization.[13] The ritual of
communication was performed on the pyramids and in the plazas of the

Maya cities, which replicated in symbolic form the sacred landscape generated by the gods at creation.

The names for various parts of the Maya cityscape reinforced this symbolism. The slab-shaped monuments they carved with the images of kings were called *te-tun*, "tree-stone." Plazas filled with these tree-stones then represented the earth covered by a tropical forest (Fig. 2:5). The Maya word for temple was *yotot* ("his house"[14]) or *ch'ul na*, "holy edifice." The doors of such buildings were formed to represent the mouth of a monster (Fig. 2:6) in echo of the Maya phrase for door—"mouth of the house" (*ti yotot*).

Pyramids and temples were often decorated with images of Witz Monsters[15] (Fig. 2:7) to define them as sacred mountains (*witz*[16] is the Mayan word for "mountain" or "hill"). In this metaphor, the door of the

SACRED
SPACE,
HOLY TIME,
AND THE
MAYA
WORLD
—
71

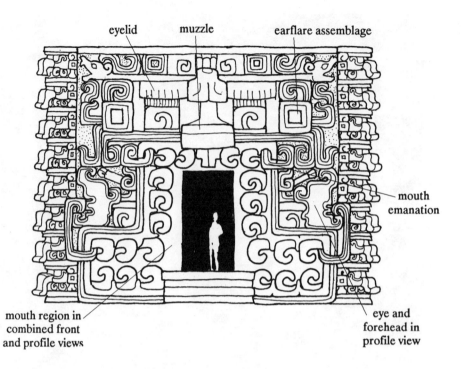

eyelid   muzzle   earflare assemblage

mouth
emanation

FIG. 2:6
Doorway
Sculpture from
Temple 1 at
Tabasqueña,
Campeche

mouth region in
combined front
and profile views

eye and
forehead in
profile view

temple is also the cave leading into the heart of the mountain. Inside the sanctum of the cave sat the portal, depicted as the skeletal Maw of the Otherworld. The royal mountain thus contained the cave that formed part of the path that led to the supernatural world. Within this cave grew the Tree of the World marking the center, the place of the portal,[17] in replication of the great ceiba trees that often grow from the entrances of caves in the natural world. A group of temples set together on a platform represented a mountain range towering over the forest of tree-stones in the plazas below. The architecture of ritual space thus replicated the features of sacred geography—the forest, the mountain, and the cave.

These same metaphors were also used by patriarchs and shamans in the humble settings of the village. Today, Yucatecan village shamans make their models of the natural world out of green saplings and corn stalks and set them up in the middle of fields, at the mouths of caves, or at the bases of natural hills.[18] Maya peasants throughout the region similarly decorate their altars and images with flowers, leaves, pine boughs, and other living links to surrounding nature. The remarkable correspondences between modern peasant shamanistic practices and ancient royal practices suggest that the ancestral shamans of the peasants, presumably also villagers, carried out modest versions of the noble ceremonies. Nevertheless, these humble rituals activated the sacred energies just as effectively as their counterparts in the great urban centers.[19]

So powerful were the effects of these rituals that the objects, people, buildings, and places in the landscape in which the supernatural materialized accumulated energy and became more sacred with repeated use.[20] Thus, as kings built and rebuilt temples on the same spot over centuries, the sanctums within them became ever more sacred. The devotion and

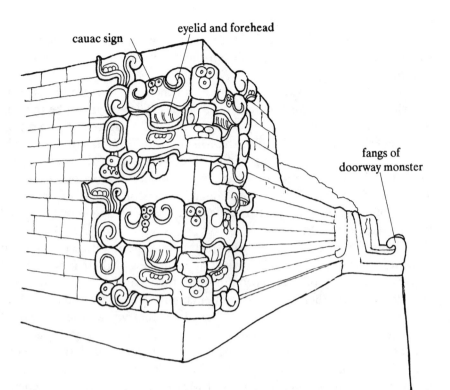

cauac sign

eyelid and forehead

fangs of
doorway monster

FIG. 2:7
Witz Monster
Masks on the
Southwest Corner
of Temple 22
at Copán

ecstasy of successive divine ahauob sacrificing within those sanctums rendered the membrane between this world and the Otherworld ever more thin and pliable. The ancestors and the gods passed through such portals into the living monarch with increasing facility. To enhance this effect, generations of kings replicated the iconography and sculptural programs of early buildings through successive temples built over the same nexus.[21]

The result was a layered pattern of power points particular to each Maya royal capital, a dynamic pattern that was both conserved and elaborated upon by successive rulers. On the larger scale, dynastic histories affected the sacred geography that had been created by the gods. As kings and nobles built temples to consolidate their power, and as king and commoner buried their dead in the houses they built, human action both added to and shifted the great magnetic centers of supernatural power that dotted the landscape. Sacred geography was affected as much by the unfolding of human history as by the intrinsic structure of the cosmos. But of course, for the Maya these were connected aspects of the same basic forces of nature.

The strategies of political competition were conceived and executed within this matrix of sacred power. Ritual, war, trade, marriage, accession, and other social activities were more likely to succeed if they were conducted at the proper place and time. Specialists in the complex patterns of time and in the movements of the heavens, like Western astrologers, kept track of the movements of the stars and planets to discover when it was favorable to proceed. As the Maya exploited the patterns of power in time and space, they used ritual to control the dangerous and powerful energies they released. There were also rituals which contained the accumulated power of objects, people, and places when they were no

SACRED
SPACE,
HOLY TIME,
AND THE
MAYA
WORLD

———

73

longer in active use.[22] And conversely, when the community became convinced that the power was gone from their city and ruling dynasts, they just walked away.

The Maya described the inhabitants of their world, both human and superhuman, in elaborate and powerful stories. These myths, like those in the Bible, not only described but also explained the nature of those beings and their relationships. Because the Maya wrote primarily upon perishable paper, our understanding of their literature and of the many forms such stories must have taken is severely limited. There is one example, however, of a Maya Bible,[23] a compilation of stories that explains the essence of living experience. It is called the Book of Council or the Popol Vuh of the Quiche Maya[24] people.

Fragmentary versions of these stories and others were written down by Maya literate both in their own script and that of their new masters, the Spanish. Many of these accounts were requested by the Spanish and incorporated into their official documents, but some made their way into carefully guarded caches of books saved by the Maya from the great burning. Other versions were transferred orally from generation to generation of living Maya, making it possible for modern scholars to record them. In fact, one version or another of the creation stories related in the Popol Vuh are found in all periods of Maya history: on the monuments of Preclassic cities like Izapa and Cerros,[25] on Classic period pottery and public art, in documents from the Colonial period, and in the modern oral tradition. There can be no doubt that the creation mythology of the ancient Maya later inspired the genesis stories of the Popol Vuh and that the Precolumbian versions of these stories described the shared world view which linked farmer and king together into a unified society.

The Heroes of Maya myth were twins. In the seventeenth-century Popol Vuh myth, they were called Hunahpu and Xbalanque. The names most securely associated with them in the Classic period are Hun-Ahau and Yax-Balam. In the version of the myth preserved in the Popol Vuh, these twins were the offspring of an older set of twins who had been called to Xibalba for making too much noise playing the ballgame. Named Hun-Hunahpu and Vucub-Hunahpu,[26] these older twins were tricked by the Lords of Death, defeated, and sacrificed. The Lords of Death buried one twin under the ballcourt in Xibalba and hung the skull of the other in a gourd tree as a warning to others so ill advised as to offend the powerful Xibalbans. Found by the daughter of a Lord of Death, the skull impregnated her by spitting in her hand. Frightened by her enraged father, the girl fled Xibalba to the Middleworld, where she wandered until she found the grandmother of the dead twins. The grandmother sheltered her and eventually she gave birth to a new set of twins, named Hunahpu and Xbalanque.

After many adventures, these twins found the ballgame gear their grandmother had hidden after the death of their forebears. The two became great ballplayers and in their turn disturbed the Xibalbans who lived in the Underworld just under the ballcourt. They too were called to Xibalba to account from their unseemly behavior, but unlike the first set of twins, they outwitted the Lords of Death and survived a series of trials designed to defeat them. On the first night they were put in the Dark House and given a torch and two cigars and told to keep them lit all night. They tricked the Lords of Death by putting fireflies at the tips of their cigars and passing a macaw's tail off as the glow of the torch.

The following day the twins played ball with the lords and allowed themselves to lose. They had till morning to come up with the four bowls of flowers that were bet on the outcome. Thinking to distract Hunahpu and Xbalanque from finding a solution to this problem, the lords had put the twins in Razor House, a place full of stone blades which were constantly looking for something to cut. The twins got the blades to stop moving by promising them the flesh of animals. This accomplished, they sent leaf-cutting ants to the gardens of the Lords of Death to bring back the bowls of flowers. In the morning the lords were enraged to find that they had been paid with their own blossoms.

The twins continued to play ball with the Lords of Death by day and allow themselves to be tested by night. They survived the Cold House, which was full of freezing wind and hail; Jaguar House, a place filled with hungry jaguars; Fire House, a place filled with raging flames; and a house filled with shrieking bats which they escaped by spending the night curled up inside their blowguns.

They did not escape the Bat House completely unscathed, however. As morning approached and the bats grew quiet, Hunahpu peeked out of the muzzle of his blowgun for a look around. Just at that moment a large bat swooped down and knocked off his head, which rolled onto the Xibalban ballcourt. Xbalanque, however, managed to replace the head with a squash, which he carved to resemble his brother's face.

In the ballgame the next day, the Xibalbans used the brother's severed head as the ball, but Xbalanque was ready for their tricks. He kicked his brother's head into the high grass at the side of the court. Out of the grass jumped a rabbit who bounced away like a ball, taking the Xibalbans with him. Xbalanque retrieved his brother's head, replaced it on his body, and put the squash in its place. He yelled at the Xibalbans that he had found the lost ball and, when play resumed, the squash splattered into bits on the court. The Lords of Death were furious when they realized they had been outsmarted once again.

As a last resort the Lords of Death decided to burn Hunahpu and Xbalanque. Learning of this, the twins instructed two seers, Xulu and Pacam, telling them what they should say when the lords asked for advice in disposing of their remains. The twins cheerfully accepted an invitation to see the great stone fire pit where the Xibalbans were brewing an alcoholic beverage. When challenged to a game of jumping over the pit, they simply jumped in.

Thinking they had won, the lords followed the advice of the two seers and ground the twins' bones, casting the powder into the river. After five days Hunahpu and Xbalanque were resurrected with the faces of catfish. On the following day they took on human form again, put on the guise of vagabond actors, and began to perform miraculous dances. Hearing of these remarkable new performers, the Lords of Death invited them to demonstrate their skills at court.

The lords were most anxious to see the remarkable dance of sacrifice in which one twin decapitated and dismembered the other. Commanded to perform, Xbalanque dismembered his brother and then brought him back to life. The Lords of Death were overwhelmed and begged to have it done to themselves. The Hero Twins gladly acquiesced, but then they did not bring the lords back to life. Thus was death outwitted and hope brought to humankind. A soul called to Xibalba in death goes with the hope that it too will outwit the Lords of Death, to emerge, like the Hero Twins, in triumph and become venerated as an ancestor.

Xibalba, like the world of humanity, contained many kinds of beings, some of which were found in both worlds and some of which were unique to one or the other.[27] The myth of the Heroes suggests, however, that while people could enter Xibalba, the Lords of Death could not visit the Middleworld except in their nonphysical manifestations—rot, disease, and death. They could not rule as sentient beings here. It was thus the human form of godhood that spanned the worlds, rather than the supernatural form, and that human form was ultimately the king. He was the earthly manifestation of the Hero Twins and he reenacted their triumph over death through ritual.

Maya artists often represented Xibalba as being underground,[28] but they also pictured it underwater with its denizens upside down relative to the human world. In at least one version (Fig. 2:4), Xibalbans lived foot to foot with humans, exactly as if they were mirror people. Xibalba was, furthermore, not always underfoot, for at night it circulated to take its place above in the night sky. The Maya saw stars and constellations, the planets and the moon, as living beings who interacted with the cycles, natural and social, of the Middleworld. To the ancient Maya the world of the stars was as alive as the world of humankind. Astronomical observation was not a matter of simple scientific curiosity, but a source of vital knowledge about Xibalba and its powers. Sky patterns reflected the actions and interactions of those gods, spirits, and ancestors with the living beings of the Middleworld. Both king and commoner adjusted their living to those patterns or suffered the consequences.

From the myth of the Hero Twins came three great axioms that appear repeatedly in the imagery of Classic Maya religion and politics. First, the Hero of the Maya vision did not overpower his enemies: He outwitted them. In the myth, the Twins tricked the Lords of Death into submitting to sacrifice. Secondly, resurrection and rebirth came through sacrifice—especially death by decapitation. The Hero Twins were conceived when the severed head of their father spit into the hand of their mother. They defeated death by submitting to decapitation and sacrifice. Finally, the place of confrontation and communication was the ballcourt. The ballgame, as we shall see in later chapters, was the arena in which life and death, victory and defeat, rebirth and triumph played out their consequences.

The rules and scoring of the ballgame remain elusive to us, but we have images of Classic people in play.[29] The ball was made of solid latex rubber shaped into a sphere slightly larger than a modern basketball. Players wore heavy padding called yokes around their waist to protect them from the bruising hardness of the ball. They also wore heavy padding on one knee and forearm to protect themselves from injury as they hit the ball or threw themselves under the flight of the ball. In ballgame scenes, players are often shown on one knee as they prepare to return the ball, and there are several examples where they have thrown themselves to the ground to prevent it from hitting the floor.

The floor of the ballcourt was usually I-shaped, but the side walls could vary considerably, although the Classic Maya generally preferred slanted walls. Markers of various sorts—stone circles at Chichén Itzá, macaw heads at Copán—were mounted high on the side walls, although we do not know if they were used in scoring the play. The center ally of the I-shape usually had three round markers about a meter in diameter distributed down its center line. These markers depict one of three kinds of scenes: bound captives, play between historical people, or play between the Hero Twins and the Lords of Death. While we do not know the rules, the iconography and archaeology associated with ballcourts clearly associate them with captive sacrifice and political pomp and circumstance.

The Shape of Time

As this page is written, our world approaches what we conceive of as two great benchmarks in time—great chronological nodes when we contemplate the symmetries of history and evaluate the progress of our species as a social organism. The year 1992 will mark the five-hundredth year since Columbus "discovered" the Americas and began the process of making us into a global community aware of who and what we are. The second great anniversary will be celebrated in the Christian world, where most of us alive now will see the end of the second millennium since the birth of Christ, known among non-Christian peoples as the "common era." The first millennium brought expectations of Christ's return—the second sees us as a species standing on the edge of what could be a great adventure into the cosmos or the extinction of all people everywhere.

On both of these days, we will pause to consider where we have been, what we have done, and what the future may have in store for us. Yet neither of these days has any intrinsic magic of its own. The millennium, for example, will turn on the first day of the month January, which happens to fall on a Sunday. The moon will be in its last quarter, Venus will be sixty days after its maximum distance from the sun as Morningstar, and we will be eleven days past the winter solstice. It will also be seven days after Christmas and twenty-five days after the 58th anniversary of Pearl Harbor. That year will see the 224th anniversary of the Declaration of Independence.

SACRED
SPACE,
HOLY TIME,
AND THE
MAYA
WORLD

—

77

We give meaning to days like this because they are the benchmarks we use to perceive that linear time has passed. By observing them we give form to the flow of time and shape to the conceptions of origins and happenings that we call history.

Time for the Maya was no different. They too devised ways of recording the passage of time. Like us, they named days in many different ways and acknowledged linkages between days and events. In this way they attempted to understand the order underlying human affairs and the cycles of the living cosmos. We count with our fingers and base our numbers on units of ten. The Maya counted with the full person, both fingers and toes, and based their system on units of twenty. The symmetries generated by these two number systems are different, but their purposes are the same. We mark the passage of decades, centuries, and millennia; they marked the passage of 20-year cycles, which they called katuns, and 400-year cycles (20×20 years), called baktuns.

In our reckoning of the solar year, we use fractions, calculating that a full year is 365.25 days. Yet how is it possible to make a quarter day? It can't be done—so instead we accumulate these quarters until we have a full day and add that day every four years to make a leap year. The Maya did not make life so complicated. Their fundamental unit was the whole day with its two halves—night and day.[30] They never altered the endless replacement of one day by the next and any fractions of years left over were simply ignored.

This endless succession of time was given order by grouping days into ever-repeating cycles ranging from the small to the inconceivably huge. Some of these cycles came from the observation of the natural world, for example, the cyclic movements of the moon, the planets, and the constellations. Others derived from the symmetries intrinsic to the numbers themselves, for example, the practice of counting in twenties. Other numbers and their repetitions were sacred and had magical properties.

This succession of days, like locations in space, were conceived as falling within a structure divided into quadrants, each with its appropriate direction and color. When the Spanish arrived, the Maya used this directional structure in their New Year's ceremonies. Their ancient forebears used this four-part structure differently: They divided the progression of time into quadrants of 819 days each. In the inscriptions recording this cycle, they said that God K,[31] a small manikin-like god who was called Kawil (see the Glossary of Gods), ruled the appropriate direction during that quadrant of time. There were four such gods, each characterized by a long-nosed face, a mirror in the forehead, a smoking celt piercing the mirror, and often a serpent foot. In this context, each of the four was distinguished by his color: the red Kawil of the east, the white Kawil of the north, the black Kawil of the west, and the yellow Kawil of the south. The exact reason for choosing 819 days as the base of this cycle is not known, but the sum is the result of $7 \times 9 \times 13$, all numbers sacred to the Maya.[32]

These quadrants provided one kind of structure to time—one that directly reflected their directional and color organization of space. Yet

The Tzolkin
day signs from
the 260-day
calendar

Imix Ik Akbal Kan Chicchan

Cimi Manik Lamat Muluc Oc

Chuen Eb Ben Ix Men

Cib Caban Etz'nab Cauac Ahau

FIG. 2:8

The Haab
month signs from
the 365-day
calendar

Pop Uo Zip Zotz' Zec

Xul Yaxkin Mol Ch'en Yax

Zac Ceh Mac Kankin Muan

Pax Kayab Cumku Uayeb

SACRED
SPACE,
HOLY TIME,
AND THE
MAYA
WORLD

——

79

each whole day also fell into many other cycles, both smaller and larger. The name and character of a day were derived from the combination of positions it occupied in these many different calendric cycles. The most important of these was the 260-day cycle, called a sacred round or tzolkin by modern scholars (Fig. 2:8). Composed of thirteen numbers consecutively combining with twenty day names, this cycle was shared by all the

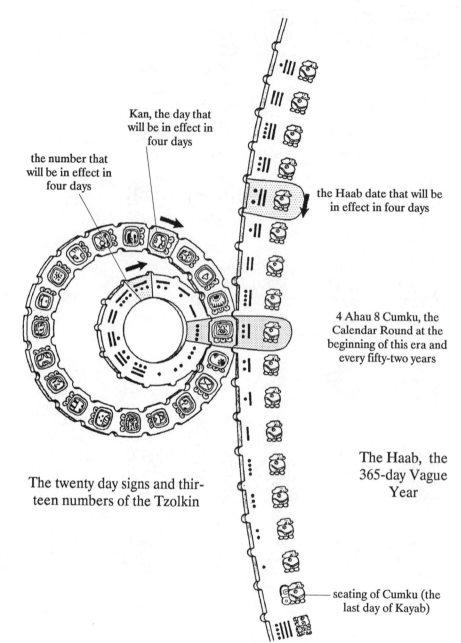

Kan, the day that will be in effect in four days

the number that will be in effect in four days

the Haab date that will be in effect in four days

4 Ahau 8 Cumku, the Calendar Round at the beginning of this era and every fifty-two years

The twenty day signs and thirteen numbers of the Tzolkin

The Haab, the 365-day Vague Year

seating of Cumku (the last day of Kayab)

FIG. 2:9
The Calendar Round and How It Worked
(after *National Geographic,* December 1975)

peoples of Mesoamerica. The tzolkin begins with the number 1 combined with the day name Imix, and proceeds to 2 Ik, 3 Akbal, and 4 Kan. After thirteen days the number cycle returns back to one. At this point, because there are more names than numbers, 13 Ben is followed by 1 Ix and so on. When we pass the 260th permutation of number and day name, 13 Ahau, we have once again arrived at the first day, 1 Imix. One easy way to visualize how the tzolkin works is to use letters for the day names so that the first twenty-five days fall in the following pattern: 1A, 2B, 3C, 4D, 5E, 6F, 7G, 8H, 9I, 10J, 11K, 12L, 13M, 1N, 2O, 3P, 4Q, 5R, 6S, 7T, 8A, 9B, 10C, 11D, 12E. It takes 260 days for the combination 1A to recur.

The tzolkin continues to repeat throughout eternity—one day following the other just as for us Monday follows Sunday every seven days forever.

A second cycle used by the ancient Maya consists of 365 days divided into eighteen months of twenty days, with five days left over at the end of the year. This short five-day month is called Uayeb, "the resting or sleep"[33] of the year (Fig. 2:9). Called both a haab and a vague year by modern scholars, this cycle mimics the solar year, but like the 260-day cycle, it is a count of whole days, one following the other in endless progression without any adjustment to the fractional remainder of the true solar year.

Each of these months had a name as do our own. Any day was named by a combination of its numerical position within the month and the name of the month itself; so, for example, the fifth day of the first month was called 5 Pop. The Maya conceived, however, that the last day of any month could also be thought of as the time that the following month was set in place. They could record this last day as the "end of" the current month, but the ancient Maya preferred to call it the "seating" (*chum*) of the upcoming month. In this haab cycle, the last day of the year would fall on "the seating of Pop" (0 Pop) and New Year's would be on 1 Pop. Conventionally, modern scholars transcribe this seating day into Arabic notation as 0, giving the impression to many beginners that the days of a Maya month were numbered 0 to 19. This impression is incorrect: they were numbered 1 to 19 or (during five-day months) 1 to 4, making the final day the seating of the following month.

The famous 52-year cycle of the Mesoamerican calendric system reflects the combination of the name of a day in the 260-day tzolkin with its name in the 365-day haab—for example, 4 Ahau 8 Cumku. The combination of these two names recurs every 18,980 (52×365) days. In the Maya system, this 52-year cycle is called a Calendar Round.

In addition to the three cycles discussed above, each day was also ruled by one of the Nine Lords of the Night, who succeeded each other in endless progression like our days of the week. The Maya also kept track of the age of the moon on each particular day and of where each day fell in the cycles of Venus and the other planets. All of these factors provided the detailed combination of cyclic information that gave each day its personality in time.

The Maya also reckoned each day in an era-based calendar that counted whole days accumulated since day zero, which they apparently conceived of as the beginning of the current manifestation of the cosmos, the fourth version of creation to exist.[34] Modern scholars call this era-based calendar the Long Count. Its basic unit was a 360-day year, which the Maya called a *tun* or "stone" because they marked the end of each of these years by setting a stone in the ground.[35] Each of these tuns consisted of eighteen months of twenty days. The months were called *uinic* (after the Maya word for "human being," since humans had twenty fingers and toes)[36] and the days *kin*. Twenty tuns composed a *katun,* 400 made a *baktun,* 8,000 made a *pictun,* and 160,000 made a *calabtun*—and so on, in multiples of twenty, toward infinity. Since we have no equivalent cycles

SACRED
SPACE,
HOLY TIME,
AND THE
MAYA
WORLD
——
81

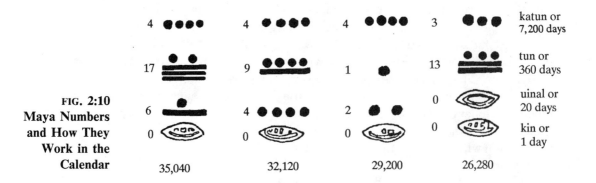

in our own calendar, we use the Maya words as the English names for the various periods in this calendar.[37]

To write the number of years that had accumulated since the base date, the Maya used a place-notation system much like ours. Instead of placing their highest numbers on the left and their lowest numbers on the right, however, they placed their highest numbers at the top of a column and their lowest at the bottom, and read them in that order. While we need ten signs to write our numbers, the Maya needed only three: a dot for one, a bar for five, and one of a number of signs for zero (Fig. 2:10). A single day was written with a dot, four days with four dots, six with a dot and bar, nineteen with three bars and four dots, and so on. To write the number twenty, they put a zero sign in the lowest position and a dot in the next one above it. Since there are only 360 days in this kind of year, there could never be a number larger than seventeen in the month position. Eighteen months was written as one year, no months, no days.

In the Maya conception, the zero day of this era-based calendar fell on 13.0.0.0.0[38] of the Long Count, 4 Ahau 8 Cumku of the Calendar Round, and on a day when the ninth Lord of the Night was ruling (Fig. 2:11). Once these day names had been juxtaposed in this way, the calendar was set for all eternity. All the simultaneous cycles that constituted time would now simply click forward one day at a time. The next day was 13.0.0.0.1 5 Imix 9 Cumku, with the first Lord of the Night ruling; followed by 13.0.0.0.2 6 Ik 10 Cumku, second Lord of the Night; and 13.0.0.0.3 7 Akbal 11 Cumku, third Lord of the Night. In our calendar, their zero day corresponds to August 11, 3114 B.C.[39]

Above we talked of the turning of the millennium as one of our own milestones in time. In the near future Maya time also approaches one of its great benchmarks. December 23, 2012, will be 13.0.0.0.0 4 Ahau 3 Kankin, the day when the 13 baktuns will end and the Long Count cycles return to the symmetry of the beginning. The Maya, however, did not conceive this to be the end of this creation, as many have suggested. Pacal, the great king of Palenque, predicted in his inscriptions that the eightieth Calendar Round anniversary of his accession will be celebrated eight days after the first eight-thousand-year cycle in the Maya calendar ends. In our time system, this cycle will end on October 15, 4772.

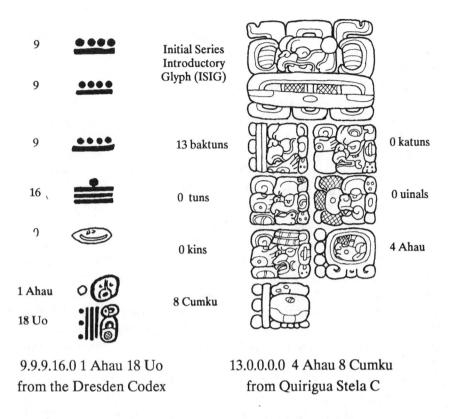

9	●●●●	Initial Series Introductory Glyph (ISIG)			
9	●●●●				
9	●●●●	13 baktuns		0 katuns	
16	▬	0 tuns		0 uinals	
꧇	⬭	0 kins		4 Ahau	
1 Ahau		8 Cumku			
18 Uo					

9.9.9.16.0 1 Ahau 18 Uo
from the Dresden Codex

13.0.0.0.0 4 Ahau 8 Cumku
from Quirigua Stela C

FIG. 2:11

Just as we can transcribe the great milestones of their time into our system, so can we express the day on which our second millennium falls in their calendar system. January 1, 2000, will fall on 9 Ahau in the 260-day Sacred Round and on the eighth day of Kankin in the 365-day haab. The Calendar Round designation is 9 Ahau 8 Kankin, which will be ruled by the third Lord of the Night. On that day, the moon will be 25 days old. Venus will be 133 days after inferior conjunction; and Jupiter will be 69 days, and Saturn 51 days, after opposition to the sun. It will be 2 years, 50 days after the beginning of the 2,282nd quadrant of the 819-day count in which the white God K will rule the north sky. And finally, that day will fall on the 1,867,260th day since the Maya zero date, expressed in the Maya Long Count as 12.19.6.15.0.

Our millennium day, of course, had no particular importance to the ancient Maya: Yet they had many such central and transitional days in their own cycles of time and they celebrated them with no less enthusiasm than we celebrate Christmas, Easter, New Year's, or the Fourth of July. For the Maya, however, what happened on such days was not merely a remembrance of days past. It was an actual reiteration of the essential events that had happened, continued to happen, and would always happen on those days. Just as we will contemplate both our past and our hopes for the future on January 1, A.D. 2000, so the Maya regularly contemplated their own history and future potential on the important days of their calendar. For the Maya, history affected the structure of time just as ritual affected the nature of matter.

SACRED
SPACE,
HOLY TIME,
AND THE
MAYA
WORLD
—
83

Political strategies and social events had to be calculated within a complex geography of sacred time, just as they were in sacred space. It was vitally important to know not just the character of a day in the major cycles of the tzolkin and haab, but its position in all of the permutations of cyclical time they measured. Certain days were important because of their relationship to Xibalba and the cosmos. The Maya reckoned this kind of importance with their own form of numerology.[40] The four surviving Maya books[41] describe which gods do what actions on different days in the many permutations of the Maya calendar. These patterns of divine action are far more complex than the relatively simple patterns we ascribe to the planets in Western astrology. For the Maya, on any given day hundreds of gods were acting and the pattern of their actions and interactions affected and were effected by the shape of sacred time and space.[42]

Yet the relationship of the kings to this timescape was not passive. While it was true that some social events, like planting and harvesting, were regular and cyclic, the actions of important humans, their births and deaths, triumphs and defeats, their records as builders and leaders, did leave their individual marks on time. Days in the history of each kingdom took on sacredness derived from the dynasts who ruled. Kings legitimized their current actions by asserting that they reiterated ancestral history. Kingly actions were likened to godly actions and exceptions to the norms of legitimate descent were explained as the reenactment of mythological or legendary history. The Maya linked their actions to gods before, during, and after the present creation and to the history of the legendary first civilization of their world—the Olmec.[43] As history accumulated for each kingdom, particular dates were remembered and celebrated for their local importance, much as different independence days are celebrated by different countries in North America. Thus, the patterns of time, like those of the physical world, had form both on the cosmic and the human scale.

The Community of Human Beings

The Maya community was embedded in the matrix of this sacred space and time. Socially, the Maya people organized themselves into families that reckoned blood membership through males and marriage membership through females. This method of organizing kinship relationships is known as patrilineal descent. The principle of selecting a single inheritor of supreme authority in the family from each successive generation usually focused on the eldest male child. This is called primogeniture[44] and it is a principle underlying hierarchical family organization from ancient China to medieval Europe. As mentioned in the previous chapter, Maya families were large, and included several generations of people under one roof or within one household compound.

The principle of reckoning through the male line made it possible for extended families to combine into larger groups, called lineages, which acknowledged a common ancestor. The Maya further combined lineages sharing an even more distant common ancestor into clans. These clans could function as very big families as circumstances warranted, often crosscutting differences in wealth, prestige, and occupation.[45] Maya families still have such clan structure in some communities today.

Some patrilineal systems regarded families within clans to be equal in status, but the structure also lent itself to hierarchical organization. One particular family could successfully claim a higher status if it could prove that it was on the direct line of descent from the founding ancestor. This was done by demonstrating that direct descent had passed through only one member of each generation. Once primogeniture designated a single inheritor of the line in each generation, it was possible to claim that there was a single line of males stretching back to the beginning of the clan, and that all other member families were descendants of a second rank. Internal ranking could be quite complicated, depending as it did on the reckoning of relative distance or closeness to the central lines of males. The principle was essentially open-ended in this respect, and the logical extreme was the ranking of each individual in each family in a pyramid of people stretching back to the beginning. While most societies, including the Maya, quit far short of this extreme, our point is that family ties were a flexible and powerful means of establishing social hierarchy.

The Maya institution of kingship was also based on the principle of inheritance of the line by a single male individual within any one generation leading back to a founding ancestor.[46] Furthermore, families and clans were ranked by their distance or nearness to the central descent line manifested in the king. Political power based on family allegiance may appear to be relatively simple compared to our own social-classes system, but it effectively integrated states composed of tens of thousands of people.[47]

Not surprisingly, the Maya applied the principle of primogeniture and the reckoning of the central line to other important social statuses in addition to the kingship. At Copán, for example, a lineage house was excavated whose patriarchs specialized in the arts of writing.[48] Their status as scribes gave the family sufficient prestige to warrant their special acknowledgment by the royal house of Copán. In the west along the Usumacinta river, members of another noble rank, cahalob,[49] provided administrators for the king and shared many of the prerogatives of the ahauob. The cahal rank was also inherited through family lines. Archaeology, text translation, and art historical interpretation give us glimmerings of many other types of kinship-based statuses. This principle of inherited status permeated the entire society and affirmed the legitimacy and prerogatives of the most exalted, as well as the most humble, of society's members.

Recent archaeology at Copán gives us a good example of the way in which the humble and the well-off maintained their integrity, even when living side by side. The residential compounds of kin groups have been classified by size and complexity into four ranks, ranging from Type 1, the lowest, to Type 4, the highest. Group 9N-8, also known as the Scribe's Compound, is a Type 4 site—a great sprawling compound with multiple courtyards and many residential buildings. Next to it sits a Type 1, the

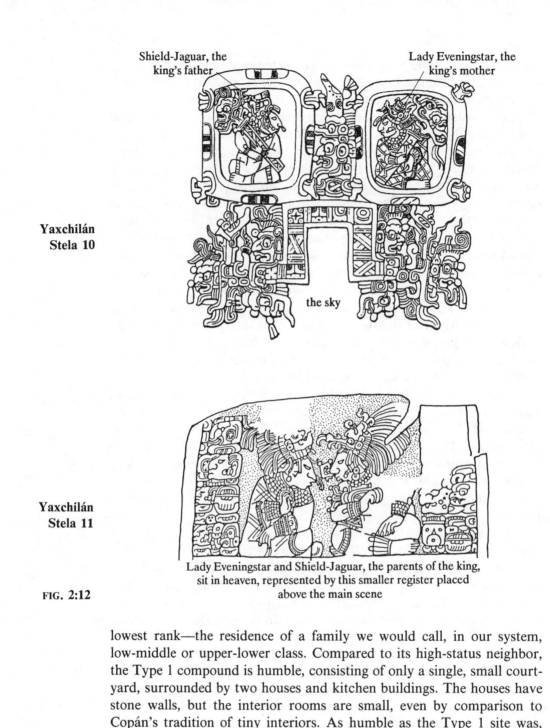

Yaxchilán Stela 10

Shield-Jaguar, the king's father

Lady Eveningstar, the king's mother

the sky

Yaxchilán Stela 11

Lady Eveningstar and Shield-Jaguar, the parents of the king, sit in heaven, represented by this smaller register placed above the main scene

FIG. 2:12

lowest rank—the residence of a family we would call, in our system, low-middle or upper-lower class. Compared to its high-status neighbor, the Type 1 compound is humble, consisting of only a single, small court-yard, surrounded by two houses and kitchen buildings. The houses have stone walls, but the interior rooms are small, even by comparison to Copán's tradition of tiny interiors. As humble as the Type 1 site was, excavations show that the lineage living there held its own against the neighboring lineage, even as the higher-ranked group expanded into more and more plaza compounds built as the family grew in size. Throughout its history, the lower-ranked compound remained spatially and, we deduce, socially independent. Within the social system of the Maya, the rights and independence of the lower-ranked lineages were protected as vigorously as those of the exalted.[50]

Public monuments erected by the Maya king during the Classic period emphasize not only his role as shaman, but also his role as family patriarch. A large percentage of the texts on stelae focus on his genealogy as the source of his legitimacy. Not only were statements of his parentage regularly included in his name phrase, but pictorial records of all sorts show the parents of the king observing the actions of their offspring, even after these parents had died (Fig. 2:12).

The titles of kings also included their numerical position in a line of succession reckoned from the founders of their lineages. These founders were usually real historical persons, but they could also be supernaturals.[51] In the realm of Copán, however, we see another type of situation. There the small population center of Rió Amarillo was governed by a group of lords belonging to a lineage who claimed descent not from the founding ancestor of the high king but from a local founder.[52] The existence of this state of affairs confirms that many subordinate lineages did not bear a real kinship status to the royal line and hence constituted allied vassals rather than relatives of inferior status. Nevertheless, the overriding metaphor of kingly authority was kinship. Kings at Copán and elsewhere used the regalia and ritual of their office to claim identity with the mythical ancestral gods of the Maya. In this way they asserted ultimate kinship authority over all of their subjects, including such subordinates as the Río Amarillo lords.

Problems with legitimate descent, such as the lack of a male heir or the death of one in war, were solved in extraordinarily creative ways. Some of the most innovative programs in the sculpture and architecture at Yaxchilán and Palenque were erected to rationalize such divergences from the prescribed pattern of descent, problems that are discussed in detail in Chapters 6 and 7. So critical was the undisputed passage of authority at the death of a king that the designation of the heir became an important public festival cycle, with magical rituals spreading over a period of a year or more. At the royal capital of Bonampak on the great Usumacinta River, exquisite polychrome murals show that these rites included both the public display of the heir and his transformation into a special person through the sacrifice of captives taken for that purpose.[53]

The sculptural record also shows the shamanistic nature of Maya kingship, central to the Classic conception of the cosmos, by depicting the divine ahau as a conductor of ritual. From the very beginning, royal monuments, such as the miniature Hauberg Stela and the San Diego cliff carving looming high above some forgotten kingdom, have depicted kings as manipulators of the supernatural domain (Fig. 2:13). Both these sculptures show a king with the supernaturals he has materialized by the ritual of shedding his blood. In the case of the Hauberg depiction, we know that this bloodletting preceded the protagonist's accession to kingly office by fifty-two days.[54] This ritual was most likely a public affirmation of his ability to open a portal to the supernatural realm. Although the verb in both these monuments is "he let blood," the Maya of these earlier times preferred to depict the materialization of the ancestor or god rather than the actual act of taking blood. There was a logical reason for this preference. By featuring the vision, rather than the sacrifice, the successful performance of the king as shaman could be documented publicly.

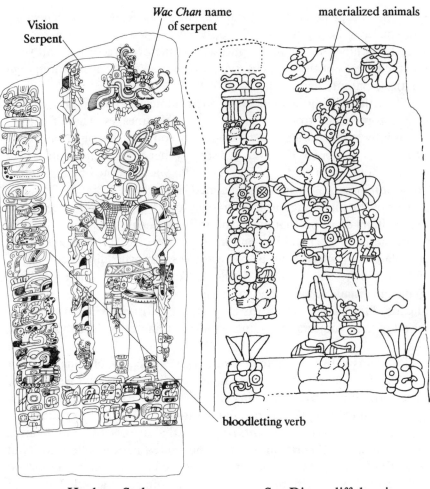

Vision Serpent

Wac Chan name of serpent

materialized animals

bloodletting verb

Hauberg Stela   San Diego cliff drawing

Throughout the Classic period, Maya public art remained focused on the ritual performances of the king, whether these rituals were part of the regular festivals that punctuated Maya life, such as the calendrically timed ritual of period endings, or special celebrations triggered by dynastic events, such as marriages, births, or deaths.

While the ritual lives of villagers and farmers were not portrayed on the public art of the ancient Maya, high-ranking nobles did have the privilege of erecting monuments. Some of these nobles erected monuments at the subsidiary sites they ruled on behalf of high kings, while others placed monuments within the courts or buildings of their own lineage compounds. These depictions take two forms: the noble acting with his king, and the noble acting alone as the protagonist. In the first type of composition, the noble can be easily distinguished from the king by his smaller size, his characteristic clothing, and his name phrases. In the second type, however, we would never know the actor was a noble, instead of a king, without being able to read the text (Fig. 2:14).

Double-headed Serpent Bar with God K emerging form the open mouths

drawing by Ian Graham

Bird-Jaguar, the king of Yaxchilán, engaged in a "fish-in-hand" ritual

FIG. 2:14
Yaxchilán
Lintel 39

Double-headed Bar with God K

Lacanjá
Lintel 1

drawing by David Stuart

Ah Zacol, the cahal who governed Lacanjá for
Knot-eye-Jaguar, the king of Bonampak

During the Classic period, the heart of Maya life was the ritual of bloodletting.[55] Giving the gift of blood from the body was an act of piety used in all of their rituals, from the births of children to the burial of the dead. This act could be as simple as an offering of a few drops of one's blood, or as extreme as the mutilation of the different parts of the body to generate large flows of this precious fluid. Blood could be drawn from any part of the body, but the most sacred sources were the tongue for males and females, and the penis for males. Representations of the act carved on stelae depict participants drawing finger-thick ropes through the wounds to guide the flow of blood down onto paper. Men with perforated genitals would whirl in a kind of dervish dance that drew the blood out onto long paper and cloth streamers tied to their wounded members. The aim of these great cathartic rituals was the vision quest, the opening of a portal into the Otherworld through which gods and the ancestors could be enticed so that the beings of this world could commune with them. The Maya thought of this process as giving "birth" to the god or ancestor, enabling it to take physical form in this plane of existence. The vision quest was the central act of the Maya world.

The practice of personal bloodletting took place not only in the temples of the mighty but at altars in the humble village as well. This fact

SACRED
SPACE,
HOLY TIME,
AND THE
MAYA
WORLD
—
89

is witnessed to by the presence of obsidian, one of the main implements of the ritual, at many ancient village sites. Obsidian is volcanic glass spewed forth from the towering fire mountains in highland regions of the Maya country. Skilled craftsmen made long thin, razor-sharp blades of the black glass, and such blades are found in virtually every lowland community context of the Maya—albeit in small quantities outside of great cities or the manufacturing towns near the natural sources of the stone. Obsidian was prized for many reasons—not only for its rarity, but for its unsurpassed ability to make clean, quick wounds. No doubt obsidian blades were used for a wide variety of cutting tasks once their main function as bloodletters was at an end, but for this primary ritual use, obsidian was to Maya propitiation of the divine what wine and wafers are to the Christian communion. What the great kings did with obsidian on behalf of all, the farmer did on behalf of his family. To be sure, the gift of obsidian from a king to his subject in return for labor, tribute, and devotion was a kind of subtle coercion. We can say this in light of the fact that the king held a virtual monopoly over the supply of obsidian and chose who was to receive it and who not. But this gift was also an affirmation of a common covenant with the divine and a common means of sustaining this covenant.[56]

The king upheld his part in this divine covenant through his enactment of many rituals of power performed for his people. Indeed he *was* power, power made material, its primary instrument. On public monuments, the oldest and most frequent manner in which the king was displayed was in the guise of the World Tree. Its trunk and branches were depicted on the apron covering his loins, and the Doubled-headed Serpent Bar that entwined in its branches was held in his arms. The Principal Bird Deity (see the Glossary of Gods) at its summit was rendered as his headdress (Fig. 2:15). This Tree was the conduit of communication between the supernatural world and the human world: The souls of the dead fell into Xibalba along its path; the daily journeys of the sun, moon, planets, and stars followed its trunk. The Vision Serpent symbolizing communion with the world of the ancestors and the gods emerged into our world along it. The king was this axis and pivot made flesh. He was the Tree of Life.

For the Maya, trees constituted the ambient living environment, the material from which they fashioned homes and tools, the source of many foods, medicines, dyes, and vital commodities such as paper. They provided the fuel for cooking fires and the soil-enriching ash that came from the cutting and burning of the forest. Trees were the source of shade in the courtyards and public places of villages and cities, and the home of the teeming life of the forest. It was natural that the Maya would choose this central metaphor for human power. Like other trees, the king was at once the ambient source of life and the material from which humans constructed it. Together, the kings of the Maya realms comprised a forest of sustaining human World Trees within the natural forested landscape of the Maya world.

The king sustained his people, but he also required much from them in the way of service. The regularities of the Maya calendar and the

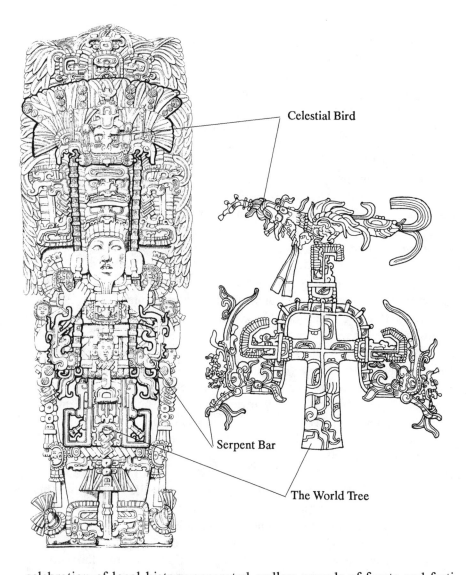

Celestial Bird

Serpent Bar

The World Tree

FIG. 2:15
The Maya King
dressed as the
World Tree

celebration of local history generated endless rounds of feasts and festivals.[57] The rich ceremonial life of the great public centers, reflected in the smaller towns and villages surrounding them, drew deeply upon the natural and human resources of the Maya. The king and his court commanded the skilled and unskilled labor of many craftsmen and commoners, whose basic needs had to be met by an even larger population of farmers, hunters, and fishermen. It is hard for us to imagine just how much patience, skill, and effort went into the creation of the elaborately decorated objects and buildings used by the king in his performance of ritual. A single small jade carving must have taken a craftsman months to complete, and we can document the fact[58] that great temples took many years of skilled work by construction specialists, carvers, plasterers, and painters as well as common laborers.

The tribute which the community gave to the royal court to finance such work was no doubt a real burden, but not necessarily a severe hardship. In times of general prosperity, which existed for most of Classical Maya history, the common folk enjoyed ready access to the basic

SACRED
SPACE,
HOLY TIME,
AND THE
MAYA
WORLD

—

91

necessities of life, both practical and spiritual. In times of hardship and privation, the commoners and nobles all suffered alike. The ancient Maya view of the world mandated serious and contractual obligations binding the king and his nobility to the common people. Incompetence or exploitation of villagers by the king invited catastrophic shifts in allegiance to neighboring kings, or simple migration into friendlier territory.[59] Such severe exploitation was a ruler's last desperate resort, not a routine policy. The king and his elite lived well. They enjoyed the most favored foods, the most pleasant home sites, the finer quality of clothing.[60] But the great public displays of the Maya were not designed just to exhibit the personal wealth of the king. They also exhibited the community's property entrusted to the king, fashioned by the hard work and inspiration of many people, and ignited into luminous power by their most prized possession, the king himself.

The practical arrangements of economic matters were never documented in the public record of ancient Maya communities. However, we can surmise that the major economic institution was the public fair[61] that accompanied every major festival in centers great and small. These public fairs were, along with daily markets in the major towns and cities, the context in which the Maya carried out their business transactions. Even as late as this century, the yearly festival of the *Señor de Escupulas,* Christ in the Sepulcher, turns a sleepy little town near the ancient center of Copán into a teeming bazaar of tens of thousands of Maya from all over that part of their country. In a single week at that festival, British merchants from neighboring Belize carried out the better part of their annual indigo trade with the Maya.

These festivals were a major part of Maya public life throughout their history. They had the practical advantage of being held on days in the calendar cycles known to everyone in the region, and were advertised far and wide by royal invitation. Many of them were occasions for visits by nobles and royalty of one kingdom to the other.[62] In the fairs which accompanied the festivals, and in the market towns in border areas between kingdoms, the Maya merchants and craftsmen transacted business under the watchful eyes of local magistrates and lords who judged contractual disputes and kept the peace of the market.[63] Family patriarchs also kept watch over merchants within their kin group and had to report directly to the king if something was amiss. Merchants calculated exchange contracts in the dirt, using pebbles and sticks to write out their numbers,[64] and honored such agreements verbally—without legal documents.[65]

The ancient Maya used various precious commodities for money— carved and polished greenstone beads, beads of red spiny oyster shell, cacao beans, lengths of cotton cloth, and measures of sea salt.[66] Such currencies were in wide demand throughout the Mesoamerican world.[67] Although currencies were probably fixed in value by the king and court within particular realms, merchants working in the uncontrolled lands between kingdoms could speculate on marginal differences in value and scarcities.[68] Even the Maya had their arbitragers.

Everyone used such money, and everyone participated in the markets and fairs. Farmers had the option of bartering for goods or turning part of their maize crop into currency for important social transactions,[69] such as marriages, christenings, funerals, and house-building parties. All such activities were expensive and required feasts and gifts. Maya men and women wore the hard currencies, jade and shell, as jewelry to display the hard work and enterprise of their families. Farmers might use money to pay tribute to their rulers, but usually they preferred to provide labor on building projects in the urban centers or service on the farms of their kings and lords. These activities enabled them to participate directly in sustaining the lives of those who sustained the prosperity of the community at large. The economy of every kingdom was administered strategically by the king and court, through both the control of the prices of Maya currencies and commodities and the management of contractual disputes and fraud in the fairs and markets.

Merchants operating beyond the borders of the kingdom were thought of euphemistically as state ambassadors bearing "gifts" to royal neighbors who acknowledged these with reciprocal "gifts."[70] Such royal business was so economically vital that the merchants involved in it were high nobles and even members of the royal household. Using the metaphor of pilgrimage, high merchants traveled to the great festivals of neighbors and distant states that controlled especially strategic goods.

The currencies used by the Maya—jade, obsidian, red spiny oyster shell, cloth, salt, and especially chocolate beans (cacao)—were prized beyond their territories and traded to all of the civilized peoples of the Mesoamerican world. In turn, different peoples produced and controlled different commodities, and traded regularly over long distances to obtain those that were outside their political domains. International relations thus were of central importance to the economic well-being of every state. The Maya king carried the burden of gathering the goods within his realm, exchanging them over long distances, and distributing the cherished goods received in return to his lords and allies. These in turn distributed the goods to their constituents in the form of gifts or exchanges. In this way, a portion of these commodities eventually filtered down into the general everyday transactions of the common folk.

In addition to managing the distribution of goods produced by his people, a Maya king also implemented agricultural work programs in the low-lying swamplands and river margins found in many parts of Maya country. In these regions, the land was not easily worked by individuals and families in a village farming community. Excavating the muck at the bottom of the swamps to create a system of raised fields and canals took organization of time and labor. The result was worth the effort: Fields were adjacent to steady supplies of water, and the canals became home to teeming schools of fish sustained by waterlilies and other evaporation-retarding plants.[71] The bottom mud became loaded with nutrients from fish excretions, thus providing rich fertilizer for the fields. It was a delicate and difficult system to maintain, but one with the prospect of enormous productivity, resulting in two or three crops a year.

SACRED
SPACE,
HOLY TIME,
AND THE
MAYA
WORLD
—
93

So important was such swamp and river-edge agriculture to the Maya state that the kings adopted waterlilies as a primary metaphor of royal power. Nobles were, literally, *Ah Nab* "Waterlily People." The heartland of Maya country is swampland, and it is more than likely that the kingdoms of the high forest, as well as the wetlands of the Petén, of the Lacandón Forest, and of northern Belize, were the greatest producers of the strategic agricultural commodities, cacao and cotton, in all of the Mesoamerican world. In these regions, the vast swamps surrounding Maya centers supported large systems of raised fields. Most of these were owned and maintained by patrilineages, but a proportion (perhaps significant in size) were maintained as royal farms through tribute labor. Both these farmers and their communities benefited in turn from the resulting prosperity of the realms. Maya kings were not only central to the economic well-being of their own constituencies. They were essential to the economic well-being of their trade partners in other parts of Mesoamerica, who depended upon them for the reliable supply of their currencies.

The understanding of currency in Mesoamerica did not parallel ours in every sense. Currency had value as a unit of economic exchange, it is true; but it also symbolized other values, far removed from the world of economics. A piece of red spondylus shell could buy something, but the same shell bead worn over the loins of a girl child represented her childhood and, when cut off in her baptism, displayed her newfound social maturity. Whole, the shell carried hematite in a dedication offering that brought the gods and sacred energy to reside in a newly built temple. A jade bead could be exchanged for some other commodity, but when placed in the mouth of a beloved grandparent who had passed on into death, it gave sustenance for the journey to Xibalba. Smeared with blue bitumen and human blood, it was cast by a shaman to divine the patterns of the sacred world and time. Carved with imagery, both the spondylus shell and the jade could be worn by a king to convey his wealth or to focus supernatural power in ritual. For the Maya things did not have an intrinsic meaning in themselves. Rather, meaning was acquired through the context of use and the way people shaped materials to function in their everyday lives and in the public life of the community.

For the Maya all things were alive and had meaning, but not everyone in Maya society was fully literate in all the levels of meaning. The farmer offering a gourd bowl of water and white corn gruel to the spirits of his field was less knowledgeable about the intricacies of royal symbolism and religion than the king who, standing in one of the great plazas of his city, offered his blood in a painted clay plate to the ancestors of all Maya. Yet the farmer knew that what he did was essentially the same. When he attended the great ceremonies in the king's plaza, the farmer could not have read the hieroglyphic inscriptions on the tree stones around him, any more than he could have expounded on the subtleties of meaning in the state religion and mythology. But then, neither can most of us expound on the principles of nuclear physics. The point is that we do not have to in order to live in our world and know it is affected by such knowledge.

The king and the farmer inhabited the same world. Even though they understood the symbology of that world on different levels, their lives in it were dynamically interconnected. The successful performance of the king as the state shaman enriched the farmer's life in spiritual and ceremonial ways. His performance in economic affairs brought wealth to his kingdom and gave his constituents access to goods from far places. Royal celebrations and rituals generated festivals that touched all parts of the community emotionally and materially. The great public works commissioned by the kings created the spaces in which these festivals and rituals took on meaning. The histories written and pictured by the kings on the tree stones standing before human-made mountains gave form to time and space in both the material and spiritual worlds.

SACRED
SPACE,
HOLY TIME,
AND THE
MAYA
WORLD

——

95

3

CERROS:
THE COMING
OF
KINGS

In an age when the word *invention* has become
synonymous with technological progress, it is
difficult for us to imagine any other kind of invention.
One of the great myths of our culture, the Myth of the
Industrial Age, teaches us that the capture of fire and
the invention of the wheel led inevitably to the combus-
tion engine, flight, and atomic energy. In this myth of
progress, only the energy harnessed by technology
drives cultural advancement. In turn, we believe that
civilized people have the responsibility to perpetuate
technological progress and to invent a viable future
through such means. We in the West see ourselves as
the inheritors of a great hope—the tradition that technology and scientific discovery will be the salvation of
humankind. However, another and more fundamental
form of invention exists.

If we judge the Maya only by our own definition
of progress, they had few technological wonders.[1] By
our standards, they were a Stone Age people lacking
even such rudimentary developments as the uses of
metal[2] and the domestication of beasts of burden.[3] Yet
few people today would deny that they possessed a high
civilization and a complex social order. If the Maya did
not invent an advanced scientific technology that harnessed natural energy, what then did they invent? The

answer to this question is simple: They invented ideas that harnessed social energy. The genius of the Maya was expressed through the creation of new visions of power. They invented political symbols that transformed and coordinated such age-old institutions as the extended family, the village, the shaman, and the patriarch into the stuff of civilized life.

It would be untrue to say that there were no technologies associated with these transformations. The writing and pictorial imagery used to interpret and record these social institutions comprised a particular type of technology—similar in nature to what in our time we call the media. Furthermore, it is no coincidence that Maya kingship and Maya writing emerged simultaneously in the century before the Common Era, for the technology of writing served the hierarchical institutions of Maya life.

Our own social institutions seem so basic and intrinsic to daily activity that we do not often realize that, like the technological side of our lives, they too are inventions. The same is true for the Maya. Their hierarchical institutions, which we recognize as the hallmarks of civilization, were *invented* as problem-solving tools during times of cultural strife.

Many of the great inventions of antiquity were social inventions. Just as the Athenian Greeks, whom we revere as spiritual forebears, invented democracy, so the Maya invented the ideas which cemented their survival as a civilization. The most powerful of these social innovations, and the cultural adaptation which instituted their great Classical florescence, was the invention of the institution of kingship. In the brief space of a century, the Maya translated the politics of village life into the politics of governance by the great ahauob, the high kings.[4]

It would be misleading for us to say that they invented this new institution whole-cloth from their own experience, because kings had been around in Meosamerica for a long time—at least a thousand years. As technological invention in our world is born of old knowledge and known technology, so the Maya transformed ancient ideas into something new and uniquely their own. Our own form of government is no different—we see it as an invention and a great experiment in human experience. Yet it is a transformation of ideas from Greece, Rome, and twenty-five hundred years of social experience inherited from our forebears.

At the time when the institution of kingship was invented, the Maya were faced with cultural tensions so great they threatened to tear their society apart. Outside forces were upsetting the heretofore carefully maintained system of social egalitarianism. Trade, both between Maya communities and between the Maya and their Mesoamerican neighbors, such as Mije-speaking peoples of the Pacific Coast, the post-Olmec people of the Gulf Coast, the Zapotecs of the Valley of Oaxaca, and the Teotihuacanos of the central Valley of México, was generating a flow of wealth that was unequally distributed among the people. In a culture which regarded the accumulation of wealth as an aberration, this turn of events created unease and social strife. At the same time, the development of raised-field agriculture and extensive water-management systems created prosperity in regions which had the means to organize the labor pool necessary to maintain these systems. As contacts with trading partners already organized into kingdoms intensified, ideas of rank and privilege further exacerbated the differences in wealth and status that had grown with the success of these commercial and agricultural enterprises. A new leadership appeared within many Maya communities—one that was hierarchical in its nature.

We know that the problem the Maya were trying to resolve was one of social inequality because that is precisely the state of affairs that the institution of ahau defines as legitimate, necessary, and intrinsic to the order of the cosmos.[5] The development of a high civilization always creates problems of social inequality, but such differences between people need not be manifested negatively. For the Maya, kingship became the primary symbol of and rationale for the noble class, the ahauob. Kingship addressed the problem of inequality, not by destroying or denying it, but by embedding the contradictory nature of privilege into the very fabric of life itself. The rituals of the ahauob declared that the magical person of the king was the pivot and pinnacle of a pyramid of people, the summit of a ranking of families that extended out to incorporate everyone in the kingdom—from highest to lowest. His person was the conduit of the sacred, the path of communication to the Otherworld, the means of contacting the dead, and indeed of surviving death itself. He was the clarifier of the mysteries of everyday life, of planting and harvesting, of illness and health. He wielded his knowledge and influence to create advantageous trade agreements for his people. He could read in the heavens the signs which told him when to war and when to maintain the peace. The farmer, the stonemason, and the craftsperson might have to pay tribute to the king, but the king compensated them for their service by giving them a richer, more enjoyable, more cohesive existence. The people reaped the spiritual benefits of the king's intercession with the supernatural world and shared in the material wealth his successful performance brought to the community.

The Late Preclassic town of Cerros (Fig. 3:1) was one of the Maya communities to experience the advent of kingship during the period of its invention.[6] This village of fisherfolk, farmers, and traders was strategically situated to command the mouth of the New River where it emptied into Chetumal Bay on the eastern coast of the Yucatán Peninsula. The people of Cerros built the early community of clustered households, and the later public center which buried it, directly on the water's edge. Edges for the Maya, whether between the surface of the earth and the underground as in a cave, between night and day, or between the sea and the shore, were intrinsically powerful and ambiguous. Cerros was at such an edge, not only physically but also culturally, for the people of this village were seafarers[7] and traders familiar with distant peoples.[8]

•

Let us imagine a day in the lives of the Cerros people at the time they had decided to adopt the institution of kingship. It is late afternoon and the heat of the day has begun to yield its brilliance to the shadows cast by the tall thatched roofs of the white one-roomed houses. Each dwelling

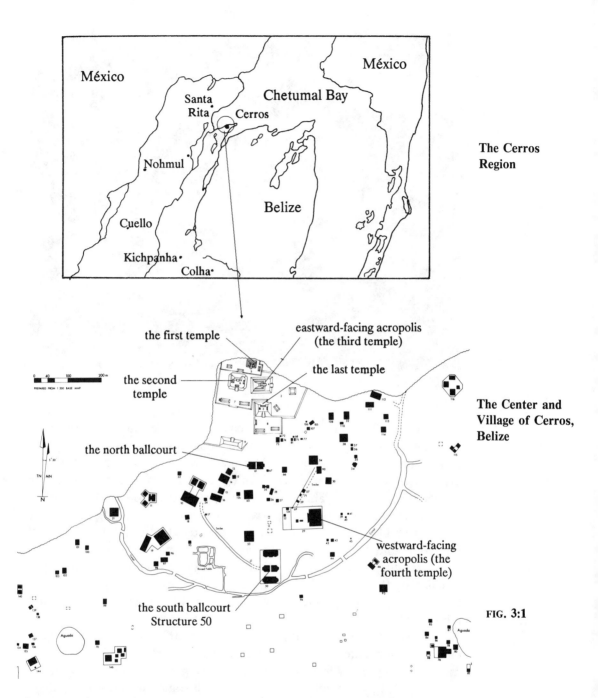

The Cerros Region

The Center and Village of Cerros, Belize

México

Chetumal Bay

México

Santa Rita

Cerros

Nohmul

Belize

Cuello

Kichpanha

Colha

the first temple

eastward-facing acropolis (the third temple)

the second temple

the last temple

the north ballcourt

westward-facing acropolis (the fourth temple)

the south ballcourt Structure 50

FIG. 3:1

is grouped around an open paved patio space filled with the cacophony of playing children. Dogs nap in the shadows and villagers busy themselves with a hundred different tasks. The women toil over large red and brown coarsely made bowls, full of maize soaking in lime, which they will grind into dough on the pink granite stones sitting before them on the plaza floor. Engrossed in quiet conversation, people are working in the shade of the house walls, weaving cotton cloth on backstrap looms, repairing nets for the fishermen, and fashioning tools of hardwood, using chipped-stone adzes made from the honey-brown chert which is abundant a few miles to the south.

stairway

terraces

FIG. 3:2
Structure
2A-Sub
4-1st

Suddenly, from farther up the coast, comes the sound of the conch-shell trumpets and wooden drums of the lookouts announcing the arrival of a trading party. Some of the elder men, who have been expecting this event by their day counts, move with dignity to the white stone and lime plaster docking area. This dock, which fronts the community's public square, creates a sharp, human-made shore for the mottled green water of the bay. The elders in their painted and dyed cotton cloaks, colorful hip cloths and turbans, jade earrings, and strings of bright orange shell beads, are unspoken testimony to the wealth and power of the community. The dignity they project is dampened somewhat by the noisy gathering of excited villagers and farmers coming in from the fields and orchards and filling the plaza behind them.

The vanguard canoes of the visitors round the point of the turbulent outer bay and enter the calmer waters close to shore. These seagoing canoes are over forty feet long, hewn from single trunks of massive trees, and propelled by multiple paddlers who both stand and sit. The paddlers attack the water in unison and with special energy as they come within sight of the community, where bonfires and billowing incense rise in greeting. From the bay, the village is a slash of white against the uniform green of fallow fields within the young forest which stretches indefinitely in both directions. While some of the boats separate from the main group to land next to the homes of trading partners, the principal voyagers disembark directly onto the dock. They are followed by a crew heavily laden with gifts for their partners and friends and for the patriarchs of the village. The leaders of each party greet each other as equals, formally and briefly, saving the speeches and conversations for the evening banquet.

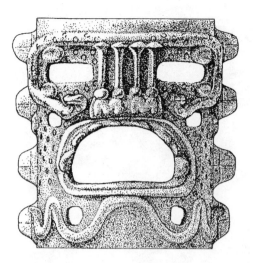

Reconstructed drum censer from
the village occupation of Cerros

FIG. 3:3
Reconstructed
by Robin Robertson

The visiting traders are themselves patriarchs, wise in the ways of the
neighboring Maya cities and the foreign peoples beyond. They are knowledgeable in magical power and its instruments, which they have brought
to trade or to give as gifts, and they are warriors capable of defending
themselves both at home and abroad. Amid loud music, noise, excitement,
and confusion, the group moves slowly across the plaza to a low red
platform which has been built to look like a stone model of a house (Fig.
3:2).[9] Sloping panels above the platform resemble thatched roofing and
lower inset panels resemble the walls of the house. Instead of a doorway
leading inside, however, there is a stairway leading up to an unobstructed
summit. In solemn dignity, the leaders ascend the platform and spatter
strips of paper with blood drawn from their ears and arms. They then burn
these papers with pellets of tree-gum incense in open bowls resting upon
clay, drum-shaped stands bearing the masks of the Ancestral Twins (Fig.
3:3).[10] This ritual is an act of thanksgiving to the gods and the ancestral
dead for a safe and successful trip. Several curers and sorcerers of the
village pray over the patriarchs and bless them on behalf of the spirits of
this place.

At the moment when the sun plunges into the sea to begin its daily
journey through the Underworld, the elders sit down to a lavish feast
consisting of red-fleshed deep-water fish, young sea turtle, pit-roasted
deer, endless varieties of steamed maize and vegetable dishes, and fresh
fruits from nearby orchards.[11] The last toasts of honey mead, quaffed from
ritual red-clay cups,[12] won't be sworn until the sun and his brother Venus,
the Morningstar, end their journey through the Underworld and rise from
the eastern sea.

Through the night the firelight flickers on the angular, bright-eyed
faces of the leaders, who have painted images over their features to encourage the illusion of their resemblance to the gods. The conversation drifts
from accounts of past glories in shared battles, to raids against enemies,
to gossip on the planned alliances of neighbors. There are practical reports
to be made on how the cotton and cacao crops are faring at home and
abroad.[13] There is also speculation about the current reliability of the kings

jewel worn on the
chest as a pectoral

FIG. 3:4
The Jewels of
Kingship Found in
an Offering at the
Summit of the
Second Temple

the small jewels worn on the king's headband

of the southern highlands who jealously trade from their sources of the black volcanic glass, obsidian, and the precious greenstones needed in the rituals that materialize the gods and insure that the earth and sea yield up their harvest.

Finally, deep into the night, the gray-haired leader of the visitors broaches the subject everyone has been waiting for. He pulls a small, soft deerskin bundle from within the folds of his cloak and opens it carefully onto his palm, revealing five stones of glowing green jade carved in the images of gods. Four of these stones are sewn onto a band of the finest cotton, ready to be tied around the head of an ahau. The fifth, a larger image that looks like the head of a frowning child, will ride on the king's chest suspended from a leather band around his neck. The trader has brought the jewels of an ahau to the patriarchs of Cerros (Fig. 3:4).[14]

The dark eyes of the principal patriarch glitter in the light of the fire. He sees before him the tools he needs to sanctify his rank among his own people. These kingly jewels assert the inherent superiority of their wearer within the community of human beings, transforming a person of merely noble rank into a being who can test and control the divine forces of the world. To have ahauob and an ahau of the ahauob will establish the Cerros community as a presence among the kingdoms of the mighty and the wealthy who rule the wetlands of the interior. Now that the people of Cerros have the means to declare themselves a place of kings, they will be able to deal with the new and changing world of kingdoms and divine power.

Slowly and deliberately, the principal patriarch takes the bundle from the visitor and puts it into a small jar, with four nubbin feet, covered with red wavy scrolls. Placing the jar at his side in the momentary quiet, he stares into the fire as if to seek his destiny. His companions silently raise their right arms across their chests and clasp their left shoulders in a reverent salute. The Cerros patriarch is in his prime. He has already proven himself in battle and he knows the rituals which call forth the gods and the ancestors from Xibalba. His family is ancient and respected in the community, and wealthy in land and water-going vessels. His gesture of acceptance is the culmination of careful discussion among the families of the village; and it carries with it the blessings of the sorcerers and curers who have prayed, sacrificed, and cast their divination stones. Some unhappy rivals and their followers will leave as enemies, but many new families will join the village as the word spreads of the new king. Cerros is too wealthy a prize to exist for long without a king, and too important a link in the trade network to pretend obscurity. The people of the community also need the resolution that kingship will bring to their own ambiguous feelings toward the wealthy and powerful among them.

•

While it is true that we have told a tale, we have tried to be faithful to the thoughts and motivations of the individuals involved. The people of Cerros did decide consciously to embrace kingship as an institution and the consequences of that decision were profound for all. In the space of two generations, this small fishing village transformed itself into a mighty acropolis. Every living soul in Cerros participated in that transformation, from the lowliest fishermen and farmers who provided food for the laborers, to the most gifted stonemasons who carved the building facades, to the shamans who gave the temples their blessing. It is difficult for us to imagine such complete and rapid social metamorphosis, but what happened at Cerros constituted nothing less than a paradigm shift.

We will never know the names of the individuals who participated in the decision to embrace kingship or of those who bore the rank and responsibilities of ahau. Because the kings of Cerros did not write the details of their lives on stone or clay, they must remain forever anonymous, but their deeds and those of their devout followers clearly declare their commitment to the vision of ahau. In the temples and buildings which remain, we have proof of the awesome energy with which they executed that vision.

Around 50 B.C., the community of Cerros began the revolutionary program of "urban renewal" which buried their village completely under broad plastered plazas and massive temples. Families conducted sacrifices over the foundations of their old homes, acknowledging for one last time the ancestors who lay buried below the floors and patios. They then smashed the vessels of their leavetaking feast, broke jade jewelry with great rocks, and scattered the bits and pieces over the homes they would never see again. Finished with one way of life, they walked outward and began building new homes in a halo some 160 acres in breadth around the

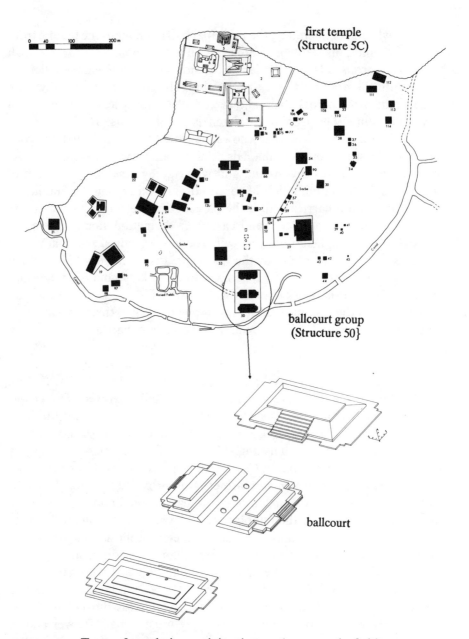

first temple
(Structure 5C)

ballcourt group
(Structure 50)

ballcourt

FIG. 3:5
The Sacred
Precinct and
the Ballcourt
Group

new center. To confirm their participation and approval of this new way
of life, some patriarchs built their front doorways facing the site of the new
temple rather than the sun path. Cerros had begun the transformation that
would turn it from village to kingdom.

These elders also participated in the rituals that prepared the site of
the new temple. Various ceremonies, the breaking of dishes from ritual
meals and the burying of water lilies and flowers in the white earth of the
temple's foundation, all helped to thin the membrane between the human
world and the Otherworld at this spot and establish it as a place of power.
This temple, called Structure 5C by archaeologists, was built directly at
the water's edge, the source of the community's livelihood. Facing south
(Fig. 3:5), it constituted the northern apex of an axis that ran southward
through the new urban center. This axis would end eventually in a great

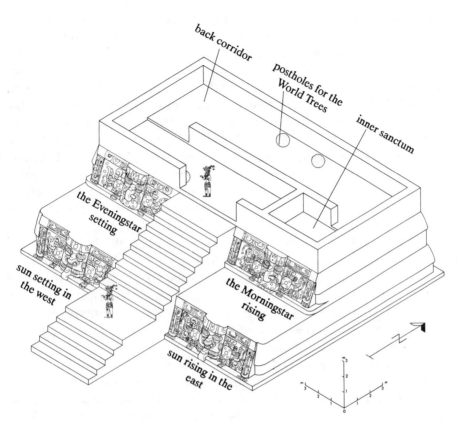

back corridor

postholes for the
World Trees

inner sanctum

the Eveningstar
setting

sun setting in
the west

the Morningstar
rising

sun rising in the
east

FIG. 3:6
The First Temple
at Cerros
(reconstructed
projection)

ballcourt built just within the reservoir canal the inhabitants had dug to define the limits of their royal capital (Fig. 3:5). Thus, while the king mandated the burial of the old village, he planned the new town that would replace it. The first temple was also in the center of the vertical axis that penetrated the earth and pierced the sky, linking the supernatural and natural worlds into a whole. This plan set the temple between the land and the sea on the horizontal axis and between the heavens and the Underworld on the vertical axis. It materialized the paths of power the king traveled through during ecstatic performance.

Since this first temple functioned as the instrument that would convey the king as shaman on his sacred journeys, the builders designed it as a public stage. The rituals that enabled the king's journey into the sacred world would be enacted in public space so that the full community could witness and affirm their successful performance. That first temple at Cerros was a masterly expression of the Maya vision, one whose effectiveness is equally impressive today. It represented not an experimental beginning, but a complete and resolved statement of a new social and cosmic order (Fig. 3:6).

How did a people who had heretofore built only houses and small buildings obtain the know-how to build temples on such a grand and architecturally complex scale? No one can be certain of the answer, but it is likely that this knowledge came from many sources. The Maya were not the first people in Mesoamerica to build pyramids. The Olmec had raised artificial "mountains" a thousand years earlier and passed the architectural form on to their successors. The pyramidal form developed primarily from the way Mesoamericans built tall buildings by piling up dirt and rock to create a mound on which they could construct a summit temple. The resulting shape emulated the shape of a mountain and created a symbolic landscape in which religious activity took place. Like the cathedrals in Europe, the pyramid temples in Maya country emerged from a long cultural tradition shared by all the peoples of the region. The lowland Maya, however, invented a new way of using the pyramid-temple: They made it a carrier of political messages by adding elaborately modeled and painted plaster facades to both the pyramid below and the temple above. These great sculptural programs became a primary expression of the political and religious doctrines underlying their form of kingship.[15]

The people of Cerros very probably also had the help of master builders,[16] stonemasons, and artisans from already established royal capitals to help them in their first building projects. It is also possible that local artists and builders had sojourned in other communities to learn necessary skills. One thing is certain: The people of Cerros did not invent the royal pyramid, but rather were part of a large number of Maya people who developed and refined its construction.

To begin their task, the builders at Cerros laid the foundation of the new temple and its plaza in layer upon layer of white earth, the soft lime marl underlying the hard capstone of this area. It was the common stuff the people used to build the platforms and patios of their houses. Then they and the elders of the community shattered precious pottery vessels, both the local work of their own craftspeople and pots obtained from trade with the south, and mixed the sherds into the white earth. To the earth and pottery, they added the flowers of fruit trees from their orchards which surrounded the new town.[17] From the foundation upward, the people made this building not only for, but with, devout and sacred action.

The ritual of beginning ended, the builders then laid down a pavement of flat hard stones upon the layers of white earth. They raised a broad platform that would hold both the temple and its plaza. Within this platform masons built a lattice of internal walls that would buttress the internal fill to keep it from spreading as the upper structures were built upon it. The spaces between these walls were filled in with vast quantities of coarse, broken limestone which laborers hauled up from nearby pits that had been driven down to excavate the white earth. When they finally finished this platform, the laborers capped the top of it with soft white lime earth into which they mixed more pottery broken in rituals of devotion and dedication. Upon this surface, the master builders then drew the outline of the temple,[18] a great T shape. The stem of this T represented a long stairway beginning at the bottom of the pyramid and extending southward onto the raised plaza, which constituted the arms of the T (Fig. 3:7). Following this outline, the builders would raise the temple and its stairway simultaneously, an effort of master builders, masons, and laborers drawn from the community, coordinated by the ruler and his counselors.

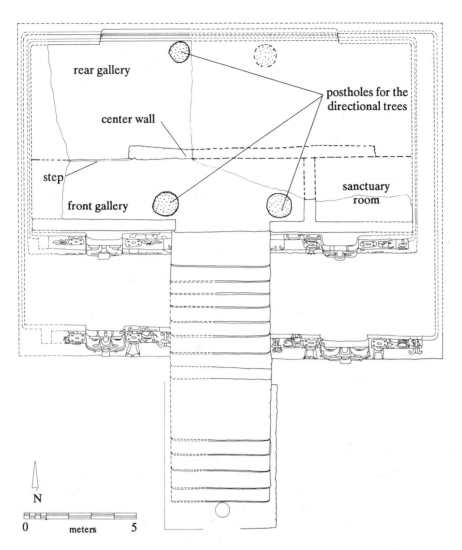

rear gallery

center wall

step

front gallery

postholes for the
directional trees

sanctuary
room

N

0   meters   5

The temple platform rose in the form of a steep pyramid with smooth outer walls made of small loaf-shaped blocks. The master builders carefully calculated the proportions of the pyramid in advance in order to accommodate the long stairway and the dimensions of the four elaborately decorated panels which would be mounted on the main, southern side of the building, facing the new plaza. While laborers built up the rubble core of the pyramid, masons fashioned four deep well-like holes which were placed symmetrically to the left and the right of the north-south axis (Fig. 3:7). These holes would contain the great trees of the four directions that would soar above the thatched roof of the temple.[19]

When the front face of the pyramid approached its full height, master masons were called in to cut and lay the special stones that would function as the armatures of the great masks and ear ornaments which would be modeled on the two upper panels (Fig. 3:8). While some masons worked on these upper panels, others supervised the construction of the stairway which linked the temple at the summit to the plaza below. Much more

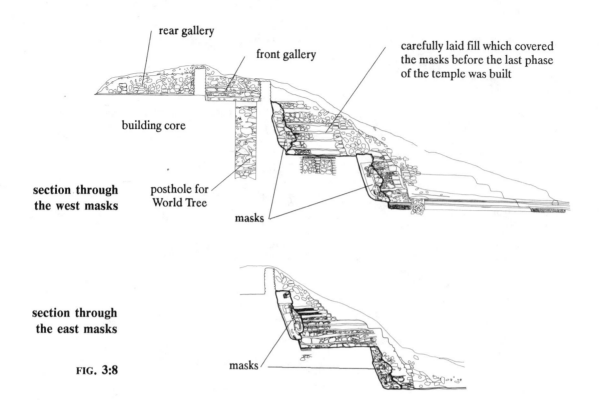

rear gallery

front gallery

carefully laid fill which covered
the masks before the last phase
of the temple was built

building core

**section through
the west masks**

posthole for
World Tree

masks

**section through
the east masks**

FIG. 3:8

masks

than a simple means of access, this stairway was the central focus of the
whole design, the place where the king would perform his public rituals.
This stairway had to be much longer than simple practicality required, for
it contained two broad landings, one in the middle of the stairway and one
at the threshold of the summit temple. During ritual, the king would pause
on the middle and the top landings to perform his ecstatic dance and carry
out sacrifice in view of his followers gathered on the plaza below (Fig. 3:9).
Four stairs led to the first landing, and nine stairs to the summit threshold.
These sacred numbers dictated the length of the whole.

At this point in the construction, it was necessary for the master
builder to pause and consult with the king, the patriarchs, and the shamans. The king had a particular decorative program in mind for this
building and it was important to follow this program in every respect. The
tricky part of the design was about to commence: the building of the front
walls of the lower terraces. These walls, like the panels already established
on the pyramid face above, would carry great masks. The builders had to
establish where to construct the retaining walls of the lower terraces so
that the king, when standing on the middle landing, would appear to be
in the center of these four great masks. Obviously, this presented a knotty
problem in optics. To create this visual impression, they had to set the
lower terrace far out in front of the pyramid core, an architecturally
awkward solution. The builders had no real choice in this matter, for the
ritual function of the facade was more important than its architectural
perfection.

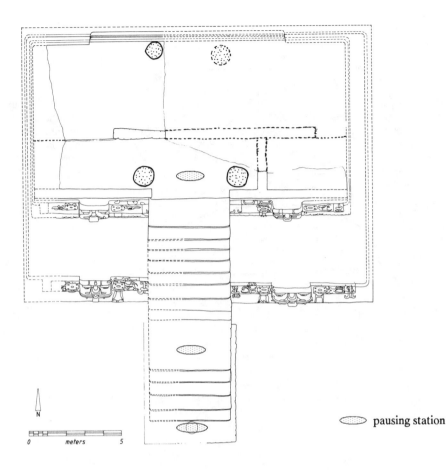

FIG. 3:9
Stations designed
for the king to
perform ritual in
his processional
ascent and descent
of the temple

⬭ pausing station

Once they had agreed upon the position of the lower terrace walls, the masons began laying a second set of armatures into the retaining wall to support the lower pair of masks. These masks had to be of the same scale and proportion as the upper ones. The Maya used strings, plumb lines, and water levels to measure the new mask armatures, but in the end the highly skilled masons adjusted the final proportions by sight. While the building designers worked out the details of each panel, masons built a lattice of walls between the outer retaining wall and the inner pyramid core. The spaces within this lattice would later be filled with loose rock and earth, and the entire terrace capped with smooth plaster.

During the construction of the pyramid and its terrace, woodcutters prepared the massive tree trunks that would be set in the four sockets in the floor of the summit temple. These would represent the trees of the four directions. After floating them as close to the construction site as possible, the people hauled and rolled these gigantic logs up into the temple where they were shaped and dropped into the floor sockets. Once anchored securely, these trees were ready for the woodcarvers and painters who would transform them into the supernatural trees at the four corners of the cosmos. The king presided over the raising of the world trees, a ceremony commemorating events that occurred at the beginning of creation.[20] Once the building was partially sanctified and activated, it had to

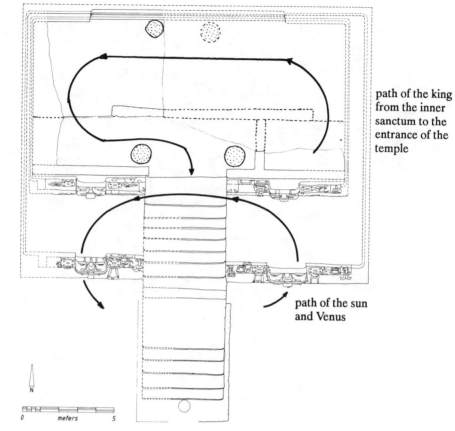

path of the king
from the inner
sanctum to the
entrance of the
temple

path of the sun
and Venus

FIG. 3:10
The Parallelism
Between the Path
of the Sun and
the Path of
the King

N

0   meters   5

be completed rapidly, for the raw power within it was potent and needed the containment that only ritual use by the king could provide. Within this sacred space the king, as shaman, could commune with the supernatural forces of the cosmos.

The masons working at the summit of the pyramid constructed the floor of the temple proper in two levels by raising the rear half of the floor a step above the front half. These two halves were separated by a wall. This design followed that of the fancy homes of prominent people within the community, who preferred a "public" space at the front of the house and a raised, more "private" back area. Unlike the homes of patriarchs at Cerros, however, the temple had walls of stone rather than walls of wood and white earth.

It was ritual need more than prosaic convenience that ultimately dictated the plan of the rooms within the pyramid. The front door of the temple was as wide as the stairway to enhance the dramatic effect of the king entering and leaving the space. The doorway leading into the back of the temple was not set directly behind the front door; rather, it was in the western end of the center wall. This design was intentional. It created a processional path through the temple interior that led the king along the east-west axis of the sun path to the principal north-south axis of the outer stairway.

FIG. 3:11
The Jaguar Sun
mask from the
east side of
Temple 5C-2nd

The journey of the king inside the temple culminated (or began, depending on the ritual) in a small room built in the eastern corner of the front gallery of the temple (Fig. 3:10). To enter this room, the king had to walk through the front door of the temple, circle to the west (his left), pass through the center-wall door into the rear gallery, and then circle back to the east to enter the room from the back gallery. In other words, he spiraled into the inner sanctum in a clockwise direction. When he left the room he reversed the spiral, moving in a counterclockwise direction—thus emulating the movement of the sun from east to west.

This little room, then, was the heart of the temple, the place where the king carried out in solitude and darkness the most intimate phases of his personal bloodletting and the most terrifying phases of his communion with the Otherworld.[21] Here he would prepare himself to meet the ancestors and the gods, fasting and practicing other kinds of trance-inducing physical mortifications. It was here also that the ritual perforation of his genitals took place and that he experienced the first shock of blood loss and the first flood of religious ecstasy. From this little room, he would travel like the sun rising from the earth to appear on the stairway before his people (Fig. 3:6). Dressed in bleached white cotton cloth that clearly showed the stains of his bloodletting, the king would speak to the ancestors on behalf of all.

With the completion of the stone construction of the pyramid, the plasterers set to work covering the walls and the stones of the stairway with the fine creamy white plaster that produced the softly modeled contours of early Maya architecture. While the plaster was still damp, they painted these surfaces bright red to provide a dramatic contrast to the dominant green of the surrounding forest.

The final work on this temple can only be described as a magnificent performance of consummate skill and cooperative effort. The panels of stone on the terraces of the pyramid base stood ready to be adorned with

Eveningstar

horizon   sky frame

Setting Sun

divine images. The artisans who applied the wet plaster and modeled the elaborate details of these four masks and their complex earflare[22] assemblages and sky frames had to work rapidly and surely (Fig. 3:11). These artisans used a few previously prepared appliqué elements that could be stuck on with plaster glue, but for the most part they had to know what the final images would look like even before they started. It was vital to shape the plaster before it cured. Even with retardants added to the plaster, the sculptors had about thirty minutes in which to apply and work the material before it hardened under their hands.

The artisans inherited some unexpected challenges from the master builders and masons: For example, the panels on the western side of the pyramid were more narrow than those on the eastern side.[23] The sculptors compensated by compressing the composition to fit the western panels. They accomplished this primarily by reducing the size of the earflares and then directing the painters to put in any details lost in the places where the plaster could not be modeled.

While the plaster was still damp, the painters began their work, adding red, pink, black, and yellow line to highlight the natural cream color of the raw plaster and to render even finer details in the images. As we saw above, the painters often put in necessary design elements that the plaster modelers left out in their haste. To finish their work before the plaster dried, the artists had to work frantically, dripping and throwing paint with the force of their strokes. Yet even these drip patterns were incorporated as part of the imagery.

Morningstar   sky frame

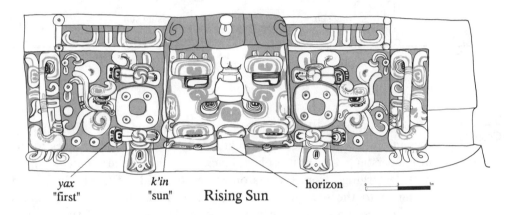

yax   *k'in*   horizon
"first"   "sun"   Rising Sun

The mastery of their craft is evident in the sureness of their drawing and the confidence of their swirling lines. The painters and sculptors knew exactly what the finished panels should look like because, just as with the written word, the panels were designed to be read as symbolic statements about the nature of the kingship and its relationship to the cosmos. And if the artisans were literate in the images of this new, revolutionary religion, then how much more so must their patron the king and his principal followers have been.

We know that the images on this temple were designed to be read because we can read them ourselves. As for actual written text, however, there is very little. While the lowland Maya of those times were literate and wrote brief, rudimentary texts on small objects,[24] they did not write full texts on any of the Late Preclassic buildings discovered so far. Instead, they used isolated glyphs as labeling devices, "tagging" objects and images to clarify and amplify their meaning.[25] Our interpretation of the art on the temple at Cerros is enhanced by such strategic glyphic clues.

The huge masks in the center of each of the four panels of the temple at Cerros derive their meaning from both the glyphic tags and the complex imagery that surrounds them. The lower masks are snarling jaguars emerging totem-pole fashion from the heads of long-snouted creatures whose lower faces merge with the pyramid. These jaguars are marked with the four-petaled glyphs denoting the sun, *kin*, identifying these beings as the Jaguar Sun God (Fig. 3:12).[26]

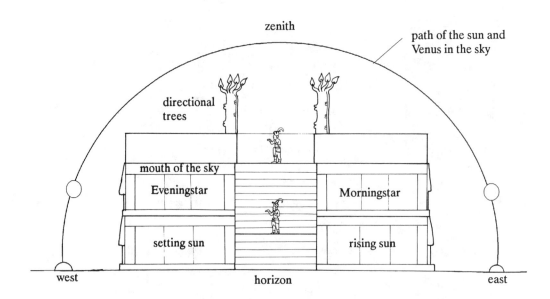

zenith

path of the sun and
Venus in the sky

directional
trees

mouth of the sky

Eveningstar

Morningstar

setting sun

rising sun

west

horizon

east

FIG. 3:13
Structure
5C-2nd and
the Cosmos

Like a puzzle with one key piece, the whole message of the temple comes into focus with these Sun Jaguars. Since this building faces to the south, a person gazing at its colorful facade would see the sun in its jaguar aspect "emerging" from the sea on the eastern side of the building and "setting" into the sea on the western side. Thus, these terrace panels symbolize the sun at the two most spectacular moments of the tropical day: dawn and dusk. Together, these sun masks display both linear time in the duration of time through the day and year and cyclical time in the return of the cycle to its beginning point over and over again; and it is significant that this path encircles the stairway along which the king must travel on his ritual journeys (Fig. 3:10). Indeed, as we shall see in the passage that follows, these masks made a special statement about kingship.

We know that, for the Maya, the Sun Jaguar represented more than a celestial body. In Classical theology, Yax-Balam, the younger of the Ancestral Hero Twins, is symbolized by the sun.[27] The older brother, Hun-Ahau, in turn, was similarly linked to the planet Venus, that bright celestial body that dances with the sun as Morningstar and Eveningstar. The logic of reading the masks that hover above the Sun Jaguars on the temple as Morningstar and Eveningstar is compelling: (1) if the lower masks denote a celestial body, so then should the upper masks in order to complete the pattern; (2) the upper image should then correspond to some celestial phenomenon hovering above the sun at dawn and dusk; (3) in astronomical terms, the heavenly body associated with the sun in exactly this relationship is the Morningstar which rises in the hours before sunrise and the Eveningstar which follows the path of the sun into the earth in the hours after sunset (Fig. 3:13).

There is other evidence to support a reading of the upper masks of the temple as Venus. Both upper masks have the long snouts that became characteristic of the Cosmic Monster, a being that was especially as-

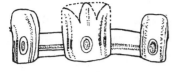

Cerros headband

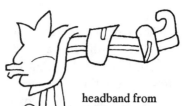

headband from
the Dumbarton
Oaks celt

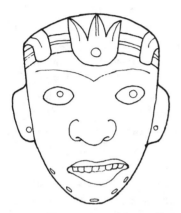

greenstone pectoral from Tikal

headband from the Oval
Palace Tablet at Palenque

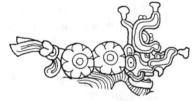

headband from Lintel
24 at Yaxchilán

Jester God
headband on the
vulture *ahau*

Jester God
headband on the
animal *ahau*

FIG. **3:14**
The Jester God

sociated with Venus and the sun as they moved through the heavens.[28] The crowns worn by these masks consisted of three jewels mounted on a headband in the same distinctive pattern as that found on the diadems of early Maya kings (Fig. 3:11). The central symbol of the kingly crown during the Classic period was the three-pointed shape in the center of this band. In its personified form, known as the Jester God,[29] it has a long-nosed head below the three-pointed shape and was worn mounted on a cloth headband by both gods and humans (see the Glossary of Gods). Since it occurs in the writing system as a glyph for *ahau,* "lord" (Fig. 3:14),[30] we can be reasonably sure that it has the same meaning as a costume element. We believe that the upper masks of this temple wore these Jester God headbands to mark them as ahau, and therefore, symbolic representations of the first king of Cerros. The Ancestral Twins, of course, are the prototypes of kingship; and in Classic imagery the Jester God headband is a diagnostic feature of the elder twin, named, not surprisingly, Hun-Ahau.[31] This headband marks the upper masks as Hun-Ahau, while the *kin* sign marks the lower as Yax-Balam, his brother.

The temple decoration was, therefore, more than just a model of the sun's daily path. It was a depiction of the Ancestral Twins, and was designed to be read in that manner by the king's constituents. When the king stood upon the stairway landing between the four great masks (Fig. 3:6), he represented the cosmic cycle of the day,[32] but he was simultaneously at the center of a four-part pattern[33] representing the lineage cycle of the Hero Twins as his founding ancestors—the first ahauob (Fig. 3:15). The lowland Maya established kingship by first crowning their gods[34] and then by proclaiming their living counterparts, the kings, as the direct descendants and spiritual manifestations of these gods.[35] The Maya manipulated their reality through art, and they did so on many levels. The images on this temple were meant to be read not only as eternal, transcendent messages, but also as political statements to be affirmed by congregations who saw them and witnessed the human performances within them. The king of Cerros as the primary ahau could exist, ultimately, because the gods of his community were also ahauob.[36]

As mentioned above, not all of the king's constituents were equally literate in the new imagery. A farmer, a noble, or a shaman reading the temple would all differ in the depth of their understanding. The point we wish to make, however, is that, on some level, the imagery *was* recognized and understood by everyone in the community and was an intrinsic part of their reality. We have examples in our own culture of symbols that are universally recognized. One would be hard pressed to find an individual who has not heard of Einstein's famous equation $E = mc^2$. The levels of understanding of that formula, however, would differ from person to person. One individual might simply recognize it as Einstein's equation. Others, because they had taken a physics course, might even know what the letters stood for and what, on a rudimentary level, the Theory of Relativity means. The highest level of understanding, corresponding to that of a Maya ahau or shaman, would be that of a practicing physicist. Regardless of how well we can talk about $E = mc^2$, it affects our reality. In a very real sense we live in Einstein's universe, just as the Maya of the Classic period lived in a reality defined by the presence of divine kings.

When the Maya of Cerros built their first royal temple, they gathered the strength of the entire community, the simple hard work of fisherfolk and farmers, the food prepared and served by their women, the leadership of their patriarchs, elders, and shamans. These individuals joined forces with the master builders, masons, and artisans (some local, some probably from other realms) to perform as an act of community the building of a sacred mountain, a portal to the Otherworld. This partnership of effort laid down in rock and white earth shows the people of Cerros as a whole acknowledging and accepting the arrival of kingship in their midst. Throughout the history of the Maya, this phenomenal cooperation was evident anytime a community embraced the institution of kingship.

However unsettling the advent of kingship might have been to the rivals of Cerros, or even to some of its inhabitants, a new social paradigm had taken root in the community. This little royal temple was only the beginning of an enormous release of social enthusiasm and energy. Within

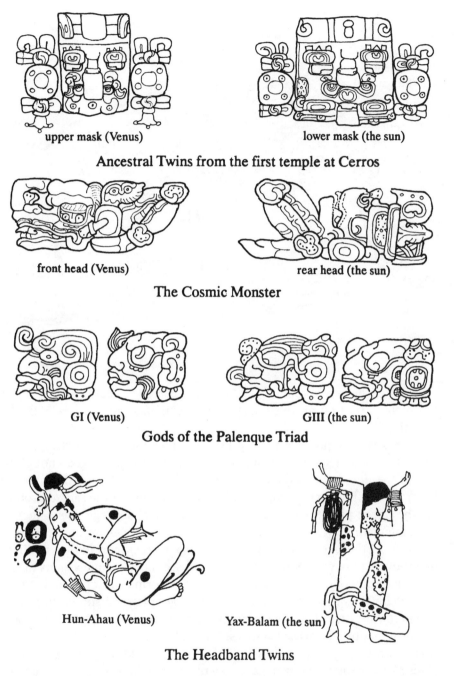

upper mask (Venus) lower mask (the sun)

Ancestral Twins from the first temple at Cerros

front head (Venus) rear head (the sun)

The Cosmic Monster

GI (Venus) GIII (the sun)

Gods of the Palenque Triad

Hun-Ahau (Venus) Yax-Balam (the sun)

The Headband Twins

a few years, a generation at most,[37] a new and very much more ambitious construction effort eclipsed the original temple and greatly amplified the royal focus of the community. This new building, called Structure 6 by the archaeologists, can truly be called an acropolis (Fig. 3:16). Measuring sixty meters long by sixty meters wide, its basal dimensions were more than three times those of the first temple. Its raised plaza stood sixteen meters above the level of the surrounding surface and was well out of view of the populace below. The function of this plaza was clearly different from that of the original temple, which was low enough to allow events upon it to be visible to anyone standing at ground level. Here, at the

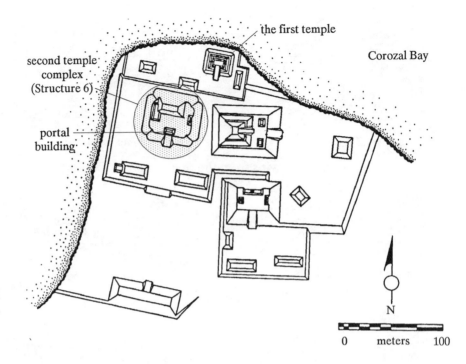

the first temple

Corozal Bay

second temple complex (Structure 6)

portal building

0   meters   100

N

summit of the new acropolis, the king could carry out actions of the most intimate nature on an open surface rather than inside the walls of the temple (Fig. 3:17).

It was now possible for the king to enter the Otherworld through bloodletting and sacrifice in full view of those few privileged enough to climb the grand stairway at the front of the pyramid, pass through the doorways of the portal temple, and stand with him on the sacred ground of the upper plaza. This change of architectural strategy was a logical development, for it took the guesswork out of the witnessing and legitimizing roles of the emergent nobility as they played their part in the establishment of royal power. Now they too could see the awesome visions of the supernatural conjured up by the magical performances of their king.[38]

Below this upper plaza was an even larger platform similar in principle to the one underlying the original temple to the north. Not so exclusive as the upper plaza, this space was still not physically or visually accessible to all, for it was partially closed off along its front edge by long buildings. This platform plaza, in turn, gave way by means of a broad grand stairway to a final lower plaza that extended 120 by 125 meters, a huge and fully accessible plaster-covered expanse capable of accommodating festival crowds numbering in the hundreds with room to spare. The new temple precinct thus had a much more complex arrangement of ritual space: three different kinds of space, all interconnected by broad stairways upon which the king could perform. Such complexity of space reflects the growing complexity of ritual activity surrounding the king and the social status attached to participation in such activity. When the king came dancing down the stairs in an ecstatic trance following a bloodletting ritual, supported on either side by his elite nobles, the first people to see him were

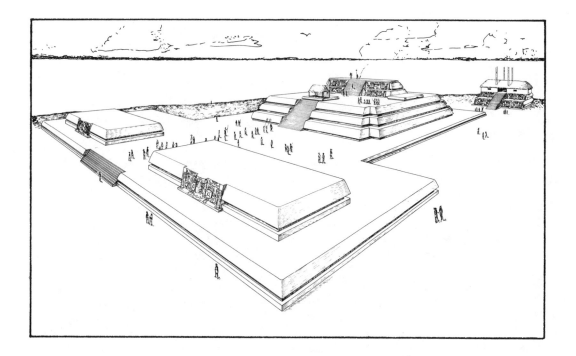

FIG. 3:17
Reconstruction
of the Second
Temple Complex
Built at Cerros.
Structure 5C-2nd
and Chetumal
Bay are in the
background
drawing by
Karim Sadr

those standing on the middle platform. These people could then join his procession and follow him down into the immense lower plaza where the general populace awaited.

The very existence of this pyramid with its carefully differentiated viewing spaces indicates the high degree of social stratification that was present at Cerros. For as long as the kingship at Cerros lasted, these social differences worked to the advantage of the government. The organization necessary to coordinate the construction of the new royal precinct required many times the effort put into the first temple. A large labor pool was required, as well as the civil machinery to guide and control it. As mentioned above, however, the coercion of local labor was alien to the Maya. This new project, like the one before it, was done by and for every member of the community, regardless of their social status.

For the people of Cerros, becoming a kingdom created liabilities as well as benefits. The new building program buried much of the original village under its immense plastered plaza. Albeit willingly, the people living in the old village proper were forced to relocate to the lands surrounding the emerging urban center. That land, however, was also being extensively quarried for the thousands of tons of rock and white earth required by the construction workers. In the course of building the temples at Cerros, its inhabitants effectively lowered the surrounding land so significantly it became necessary to build a complicated system of drainage ditches, reservoirs, and canals to keep their homes and patios from becoming flooded during the rainy season (Fig. 3:18).[39]

Another problem people faced, as they moved out from the old village, was the shortage of building materials. The amount of wealth and rank a family possessed suddenly became strikingly apparent in the type

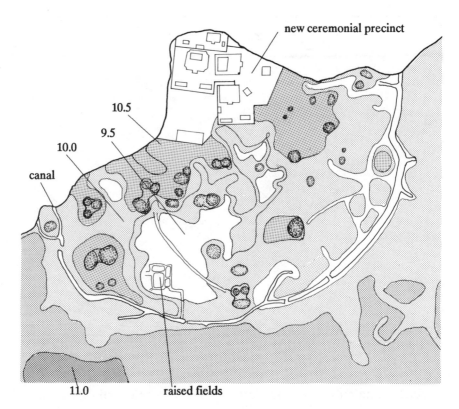

new ceremonial precinct

10.5

9.5

10.0

canal

11.0   raised fields

of new home they could afford to construct. Some individuals were able to build their new houses on raised platforms of considerable size, while other families lived on small platforms, and still others had homes at ground level. Control of all available construction materials reinforced the power of the king, for he could then dispense them as rewards for loyalty and support.

The political message of the second temple is harder to read than that of the first. The decorations on the uppermost facade, the only one excavated so far,[40] were badly damaged by natural erosion and the fires banked against them in the termination rituals conducted by the Maya when kingship at Cerros failed and the temple was abandoned. Even though only fragments of the imagery survived, we can still tell it was the same as that of the first temple: four great masks, probably of the Ancestral Heroes, flanking a stairway. The fine quality of the modeled stucco elements that were preserved, and their rich, more elaborate painted detail, demonstrate the high level of artistry involved in the decoration of this pyramid. The beauty and complexity of this building is concrete testimony to the charismatic power of the Cerros king, a ruler strong enough to attract and retain the services of skilled artisans literate in the complex theology and imagery of the new religion.

By this time in the history of Cerros, the first king had died and been replaced by a successor. We know this because of a special political message placed in the second temple. Below the summit where the new king stood for public rituals, he buried a set of royal jewels, including the

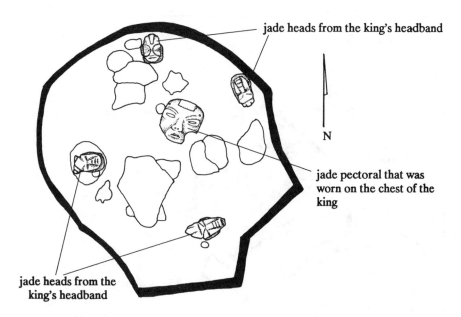

jade heads from the king's headband

jade pectoral that was worn on the chest of the king

jade heads from the king's headband

N

FIG. 3:19
The Arrangement of the King's Jewels in the Offering Bucket of Structure 6B

jades of a royal headband and the chest pectoral of a king.[41] Laid carefully face downward in the bottom of a large clay bucket, the four headband jewels were deliberately arranged in the same fourfold pattern we saw in the great masks of the first temple (Fig. 3:19). In the middle of this pattern, the king set the larger greenstone pectoral, face upward. This particular positioning was both deliberate and symbolic. This ahau pectoral rested within a fourfold pattern, just as the first king had stood within the fourfold pattern of the masks on the first temple. These powerful and magical objects were then covered (Fig. 3:20) with layers of mosaic mirrors made of bright blue hematite crystals glued to mother-of-pearl cutouts,[42] and with red-orange spiny oyster shells of the kind worn by later Maya nobles on their robes. A large red pottery plate served as the lid for the bucket, and surrounding it were four of the small pottery cups used for drinking and a jug for pouring beverages.[43]

This cache was more than a simple offering of precious materials to the gods. We believe these jewels were valued because they were the very ones owned and used by the first king of Cerros (the kingly jewels of our story). The pattern in which the precious materials were arranged echoed the pattern of power we have already seen in the first temple and established it within the summit of the second one. The second king buried them in his own temple to invoke this power and to link himself with the former king, who was presumably his ancestor. These jewels would aid him in his communication with the sacred world of the supernatural.

Later Maya kings, like the great Pacal of Palenque, would define their temples as sacred mountains and have themselves buried therein. At the beginnings of the institution of ahau, however, power lay not in the physical remains of the first king, but in the performance and settings of ritual, and in the objects of power themselves. Instead of focusing on the burial of the first king, his successor manipulated the power objects left

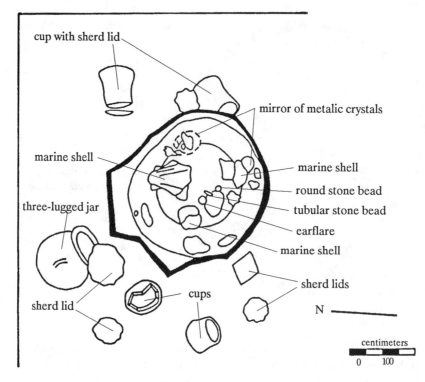

cup with sherd lid

mirror of metalic crystals

marine shell

marine shell

round stone bead

tubular stone bead

earflare

marine shell

three-lugged jar

sherd lids

sherd lid

cups

N

centimeters

0   100

by him in order to ensure the act of linkage between their reigns. All of those who worked on the new acropolis, thereby affirming the legitimacy of the succession, understood that symbolism. Just as the people of the community gave their most precious possessions in the form of labor to raise the new building, so the new king sacrificed his most precious heirlooms to its construction.[44]

Following the triumphant completion of the new royal temple, the community of Cerros began its most ambitious construction project to date: the establishment of an east-west axis to complement the north-south axis laid down by the first king. The rapidity with which the new construction project followed that of the second temple suggests that they were both part of the program of the second king of Cerros. If this is the case, then the ruler of this early kingdom truly enjoyed extraordinary power.

Directly east of the second temple (Fig 3.1), the king erected the largest of the temples at Cerros, an eastward acropolis called Structure 4. We know that the king rebuilt this structure at least once because the foundation of an earlier temple lies almost directly beneath the present structure. This practice of building one structure on top of the razed foundation of another was not uncommon with the Maya, for they believed that a location accumulated power with time. Once the portal to the Otherworld was opened, once the points of power were set in place, the membrane between the worlds was made thinner with subsequent use.

Whereas the old temple had faced the village, the new temple faced the rising sun and towered over a broad plaza of gleaming white plaster. At sixty meters along each side and twenty-two meters high, this was a

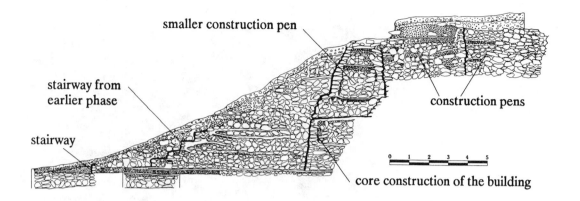

smaller construction pen

stairway from earlier phase

construction pens

stairway

core construction of the building

FIG. 3:21
Construction
Pens Inside
Structure 4A,
the Eastward-facing
Acropolis

building of respectable proportions by any Maya standards. This new acropolis, like the earlier two, buried homes and shrines that were the last vestiges of the old village and the way of life that went with it.

As with the earlier temples at Cerros, the master builders, laborers, and masons raised the new acropolis in a single enormous effort. Because of its huge size, this building required an extensive honeycomb of internal buttressing walls. Once the masons had raised these walls, laborers hurried to fill the spaces between them with alternating layers of loose boulders, gravel, and white earth. The completion of these square "construction pens" (Fig. 3:21)[45] required a good deal of work, contributed by gangs of farmers and fishermen under the watchful supervision of their patriarchs. As was always the case with the Maya, work on the temple was an act of devotion. The laborers threw their maize grinding stones, fishnet weights, and some of their personal household objects into the rubble as offerings to the ancestral gods.

Very little of the sculptural decoration of this building survived, but it was clearly meant to be the tomb of a king. Built with a steep-sided contour, it had a sepulcher at its summit. This mortuary chamber was long and rather wide as Maya tombs go, and at its northern end there was a plastered bench which would have served as the final resting place of the king (Fig. 3:22). The roof of the tomb was spanned with great stone slabs in an early example of corbel-arch construction. Strangely enough, the tomb was never occupied by its patron, a problem to which we will return.

Now that the east-west axis of the community was clearly defined, the current ruler went to work on the remaining axis. Built to the south, a westward-facing temple, Structure 29C (Fig. 3:23), complemented the eastward-facing tomb of the king and completed the north-south axis of Cerros. This last great structure was closely associated with the north and south ballcourts, which formed a triangle arrangement with the new acropolis (Fig. 3:1; 3:24).

The new pyramid was smaller than the eastward-facing acropolis discussed above, but its builders created a distinctive—and for Cerros, atypical—plan for the summit. They erected three separate temple plat-

Rubble from collapsed corbelled vault

a mixture of pottery fragments and white earth
used in the final termination rites for the building

bench in the northern end of
the tomb chamber

forms atop this pyramid, the center one facing toward the west (Fig. 3:23).
Each of these platforms had a central stairway flanked by a special iconography. On the middle pyramid, the builders mounted carved jaguar heads
with great flowing scrolls pouring out of their mouths, and small snarling
human heads emerging from the stonework above them (Fig. 3:25). These
bloody images were meant to depict the severed head of the Sun Jaguar—
the ancestral brother who died in sacrifice and was reborn as the means
of defeating the Lords of Xibalba.

The image of the severed head is a central symbol of royal power on
stelae and panels of the Classic period. Kings during this period sacrificed
highborn victims taken in war by decapitating them. The jaguar adorned
with waterlily scrolls presided over such warfare and provided it with its
central metaphor: battle as the royal hunt. Noble warriors were either prey
or predator, depending on their luck; and kings would go into battle with
ropes tied around their arms as if daring their adversaries to capture them.
This war-sacrifice complex is the central imagery we will see in the Temple
of the Sun at Palenque, the monument raised by king Chan-Bahlum to

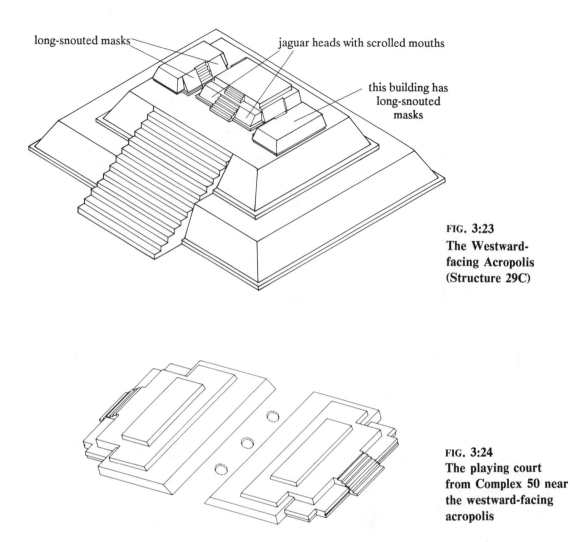

long-snouted masks

jaguar heads with scrolled mouths

this building has long-snouted masks

FIG. **3:23**
**The Westward-
facing Acropolis
(Structure 29C)**

FIG. **3:24**
**The playing court
from Complex 50 near
the westward-facing
acropolis**

celebrate his designation as heir to the throne. The westward-facing temple of Cerros, adorned with jaguar heads, was the prototype of the later Classic period complex: it was meant as a war monument.

The remaining two temple platforms faced inward toward the central temple.[46] The stairways of these flanking platforms sat between long-snouted masks, also surmounted by snarling human faces (Fig. 3:26). The jaguar images on the middle temple correspond to the lower jaguar masks of the first temple built at Cerros; and the long-snouted masks of the flanking temples echo the masks on the first temple's upper terraces. We can conclude then that the long-snouted characters on the flanking platforms represent Venus, the elder brother of the Ancestral Twins. This elder brother, as we mentioned above, sacrificed his brother, the Jaguar Sun, and then brought him back to life in order to defeat the Lords of Death in Xibalba. In the Classic Period, whenever jaguar imagery appeared, flanked on either side by Venus, the elder brother, it represented the king flanked by his kinsmen. These kinsmen were usually his father, or his mother and father, from whom he received his right to the throne.[47]

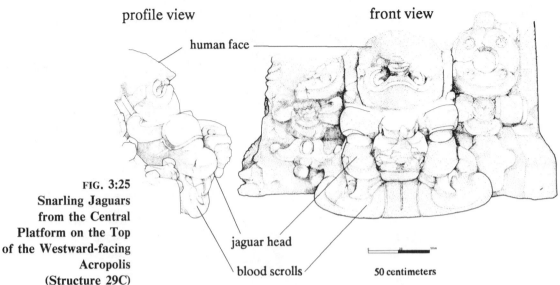

profile view   front view

human face

FIG. 3:25
Snarling Jaguars
from the Central
Platform on the Top
of the Westward-facing
Acropolis
(Structure 29C)

jaguar head

blood scrolls   50 centimeters

The ballcourts nearby were built in relationship to both the north-south and the east-west axes of the city. Within these ballcourts rituals of war and sacrifice were played out as were rituals legitimizing the descent of the new royal line. The ballgame was played for many purposes. In a more ordinary setting it could be played between friends or professionals for sport or for wager; but it more often took on a ritual or sacred aspect. Highborn captives were frequently forced to play the ballgame as members of the community looked on. As in the Popol Vuh myth, the losers were sacrificed by decapitation. Often these sacrificial victims were bound into a ball-like form and hurled down the stairs of a temple. In its most elevated form the ballgame was played as a reenactment of the Ancestral Twins' defeat of the Lords of Death in Xibalba, as related in the Popol Vuh.

These games provided the metaphorical setting for the sacrificial events by which a king or heir promoted his legitimate authority.[48] Whether the king was taking the role of supreme athlete, acting out the role of one of the Ancestral Twins, or sacrificing a captive king or noble, the ballgame had deep religious significance.

We do not know if the builder of the ballcourts and the westward-facing temple was the second or third ruler of Cerros, but that knowledge is not critical to our understanding of the development of kingship at Cerros. Expanded building programs indicate expanded ambition, if nothing else. The very existence of a war memorial and a ballcourt indicate that Cerros was looking outward, and that its new royalty was taking a growing part in the cosmopolitan and competitive world of lowland Maya kingdoms.

In the long run, however, the pressures from within and without upon this newborn kingdom were evidently more than it could withstand. The king who planned to bury himself in the summit of the eastward-facing acropolis never occupied his sepulcher—it was left open and empty. Why this happened we do not know. One possibility is that this unfortu-

profile view   front view

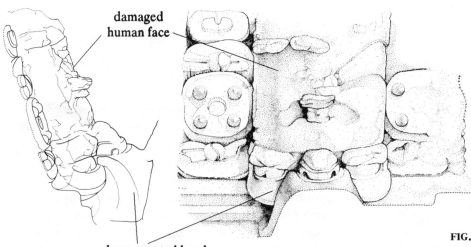

damaged
human face

long-snouted head

FIG. 3:26
Long-snouted
Monster from
the North and
South (Side)
Platforms on
the Top of the
Westward-facing
Acropolis
(Structure 29C)

nate king may have died far from home, taken captive in battle. Regardless of what the true story may have been, his successor ultimately failed to fulfill the promise inherent in the Maya vision of kingship.

The failed attempt to bury a king at the summit of the eastward-facing acropolis marked the beginning of the end of the experiment with kingship at Cerros. The heir to that ruler did manage to rally the people temporarily and to launch the construction of another temple along the designs of the first and second ones. Situated directly south of the great eastward-facing acropolis, the final temple reiterated the north-south axis of the community. It faced southward like the original two temples. This new acropolis outwardly resembled the other temple complexes, but its construction work was shoddy and no offerings were deposited in the building's summit.

Shortly after this final effort, the Maya of Cerros gave up their brief embrace of kingship and systematically released the power from the sacred mountains which they had lifted up from their own earth. The kings were gone. The nobility, once attracted by the promise of a great kingdom, abandoned the city and returned to their estates in the surrounding countryside. The remaining people banked great fires against the masks of their ancestors and lords. They sprinkled layers of white marl over the fires and then reset them. They pulled out their jade earflares (the special ear ornaments that were shaped like the end of a trumpet) and smashed them into bits, sprinkling the pieces on the piles of debris accumulating at the bases of the decorated panels. They broke the pottery from their final ritual meals as they brought the termination ritual to an end. At the last, they went down to their homes and continued to live around the ruins of their greatness as fisherfolk and farmers once more.

Many years later, after the eastward-facing temple had begun to fall into ruin, devotees returned to the summit to carry out rituals of termination to release the power of the place. Their clay offering vessels stood in solitary stacks until the stone roof of the tomb collapsed and crushed them.

We will never know exactly why the ahauob of Cerros failed, but we can hypothesize. A major difficulty might have been a problem in the transference of power between the generations within the royal line. In a system that depended less on the rules of succession than on the personal charisma and power of a leader, a weak king would not have been tolerated for very long. Another problem the people of Cerros might have experienced was the difficulty of coping with the novelty of a large scale society. While it is true that this community enthusiastically embraced kingship, intention and execution are two different things. At this point in the history of the Maya, the institution of kingship was newly invented and its practitioners were still improvising as they went along. A society based on a great experiment is a potentially unstable society.

There are reasons to suspect that these problems were common to the times in the Maya lowlands, for other early kingdoms also failed precipitously. At Cerros, however, collapse of the institution was not a matter of sudden abandonment of the place by all of its people. Just as they had once opted for kingship, now they opted against it. Maya kingdoms never maintained a standing army or a police force, so there was no one to make the people obey the king. Without the willing cooperation of the people, nobles and commoners alike, the king could do nothing.

The ahauob of Cerros re-created their world, literally transforming the place in which they and their people lived from a village into a place of kings. They could do this because their people wanted to follow their vision and celebrate its power. As mentioned above, the charisma of the king was not absolute in the Maya vision. It was subject to critical testing in performance: the abundance of crops, the prosperity of trade, the health of the people, victory in battle. We will see in later chapters that Maya kings always faced the possibility of a failure of one sort or another that could cripple a dynasty or bring it down decisively. Much of the public art erected by Maya kings was political propaganda, responding to crises resulting from these kinds of failures.

To some, this new form of Maya government might appear as a fragile sort of adaptation, subject as it was to the character and ability of a few central people and their close kin. Yet the vision of the ahau exploded into brilliant colored stucco clarity throughout the lowlands in the first century before the present era. The first Trees of Life propagated a forest of kings from the outset—in good tropical ecological adaptation, a dispersal of the species insuring that some would always survive any localized catastrophe. Individual kingdoms might fail, but the vision of the ahau as ruler endured, the most geographically extensive and long-lasting principle of governance in the history of ancient Mesoamerica.

The ahauob of Cerros—and those of Lamanai, Tikal, El Mirador, and Uaxactún, among the known early kingdoms—were masked, anonymous rulers who left little record of their personal histories among the grand royal statements of their successes and victories. This would soon change, for in the first two centuries of the present era, the written script crystallized and kings began to emerge as the chronicled figures of royal drama. In spite of their anonymity, the ancestral kings of the Preclassic period did leave a heritage to their successors in the form of their mute complexes of temple, pyramid, plaza, and plaster mask. They promoted the principle of hierarchy, focusing on architectural construction and reconstruction as the means of achieving their political objectives—principally, perpetuation of the dynasty. They created the first centers and, in the act of establishing them, also defined the notion of dominion. Like the trees of the four directions, which raise up the sky over the earth, the king was the central pillar—the Tree of Life who raised the sky that arched over his entire realm.

4

A WAR
OF
CONQUEST:
TIKAL AGAINST
UAXACTÚN

During the explosive first flush of civilized life in the Maya world, cities, like Cerros, blossomed in the towering rain forests of the lowlands. El Mirador,[1] located in the swamps and low hills of Petén, the geographic heart of the Yucatán peninsula, was the greatest of these Preclassic cities. Yet even at the height of El Mirador's glory, when its ahauob were reigning over vast temples, contenders for its greatness were growing to maturity forty miles to the south. These nascent rivals, Uaxactún and Tikal, grew steadily in power, population, and the ability to create magnificent public art throughout the Late Preclassic period, cultivating their ambition until they were ready to step into the political vacuum left by the decline of El Mirador at the outset of the Classic era.[2] Located less than twelve miles apart—not even a day's walk—Tikal and Uaxactún were perhaps too closely situated for both of them to become kingdoms of the first rank. Their competition, which is the focus of our next story, was resolved violently in A.D. 378 by means of an innovative type of warfare we call Tlaloc-Venus war, or sometimes simply "star wars."[3] The imagery and method of this new type of conflict was borrowed from the other great Mesoamerican civilization of this time, Teotihuacán, the huge city that had grown to maturity in the Valley

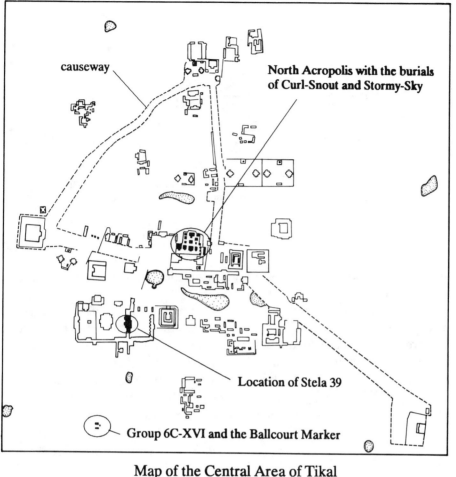

Map of the Central Area of Tikal
drawing by Kathryn Reese

of México during the third and fourth centuries. With the advent of this new kind of warfare, a new concept was incorporated into the Maya culture: the idea of empire.

Like other great Maya capitals of the interior lowland, Tikal began as a village of farmers nestled on the high ground between vast swamps. By 600 B.C., the first small groups of people had settled on the hilltop that would become the central area of the city (Fig. 4:1). These people left the debris of their lives under what would, in future years, be the North Acropolis, sanctum of Tikal's kings (Fig. 4:2), and in a *chultun*[4] located about a mile to the east of the Acropolis.[5] Even this early in their history, the villagers were using this site as a burial place. Amid the humble remains under the North Acropolis, the interred body of an adult villager was found. Lying nearby was a sacrificial offering in the form of a severed head.[6] This sacrificial practice, begun so humbly, would later be incorporated into the burial ceremonies of Tikal's kings. The household debris surrounding this burial place contained the shells of freshwater snails, which were part of the diet of these pioneers, and obsidian and quartzite

A WAR
OF
CONQUEST:
TIKAL
AGAINST
UAXACTÚN
—
131

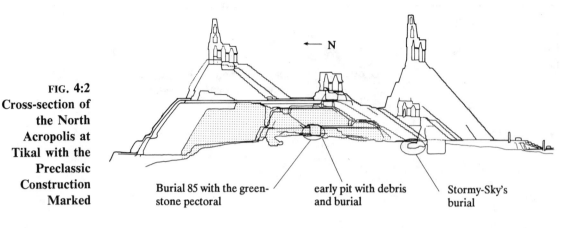

FIG. **4:2**
Cross-section of
the North
Acropolis at
Tikal with the
Preclassic
Construction
Marked

← N

Burial 85 with the green-
stone pectoral

early pit with debris
and burial

Stormy-Sky's
burial

flakes, both imported goods—obsidian from the highlands and quartzite
from northern Belize.

We do not know much about the individual lives of these early
inhabitants, but during the next four centuries they continued to multiply
and prosper. By the second century B.C. they had already expanded into
much of the "downtown" area of Tikal. At that time, they began to define
a center for the community by building stone platforms displaying the
sloping moldings and inset panels preferred by all the lowland Maya.
These platforms were the harbinger of the North Acropolis and no doubt

FIG. **4:3**
The Painting
on the Outer
Walls of
Structure 5D-
Sub-10-1st
at Tikal

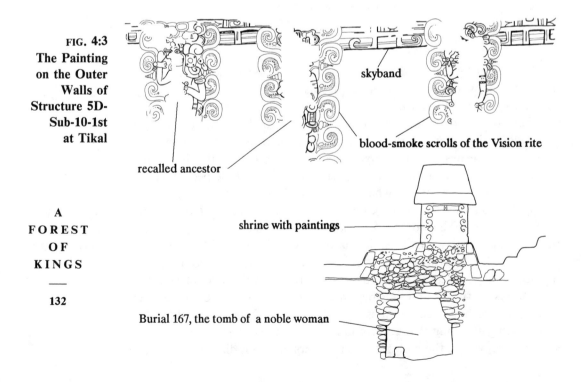

skyband

blood-smoke scrolls of the Vision rite

recalled ancestor

shrine with paintings

Burial 167, the tomb of a noble woman

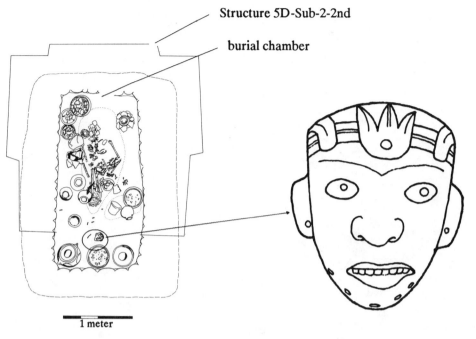

Structure 5D-Sub-2-2nd

burial chamber

1 meter

drawing of tomb by Kathryn Reese after W. R. Coe (1965a)

FIG. 4:4
Tikal Burial 85
and the Pectoral
of a King

they facilitated the rites of patriarchs and shamans defining their emergent community in relation to their neighbors and the world at large.

The first century B.C. witnessed expansion and elaboration of this Acropolis, via large public buildings and chambered burial vaults of kings and high-ranking nobles. These public buildings prefigured all the characteristics of later state architecture: large apron moldings, pyramidal platforms, steeply inclined stairs, and most important, terraces surmounted by large painted plaster masks depicting the gods fundamental to the newly emerged institution of kingship.

The North Acropolis tombs from this era reveal a unique glimpse of the newly emergent Maya ruling elite,[7] who had themselves buried in vaulted chambers set under shrinelike buildings. We find, interred in these chambers, not only the physical remains of these people and the objects they considered of value, but even some pictorial representations of them. In one of these tombs, images of Maya nobles were drawn in black line on the red-painted walls. These figures were perhaps the ancestors or kinsmen of the woman[8] buried inside the chamber. The paintings, along with the rich burial goods laid around the woman's body, mark the tomb as the "earliest interment of someone of patent consequence"[9] at Tikal. It is interesting that the deceased person in this tomb was a woman, for the Maya of Tikal, like other Maya, gave primacy to males in the reckoning of social status through the principle of patrilineal descent. This tomb, however, shows that status had transcended gender and was now ascribed to both the men and women of noble families. The foundations were laid for a hereditary elite, the clans of the ahauob.

A WAR
OF
CONQUEST:
TIKAL
AGAINST
UAXACTÚN
—
133

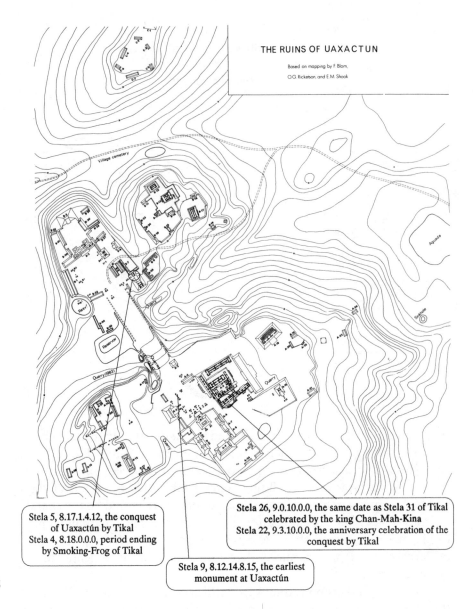

THE RUINS OF UAXACTUN

Based on mapping by F. Blom,
O.G. Rickerson, and E.M. Shook

Stela 26, 9.0.10.0.0, the same date as Stela 31 of Tikal
celebrated by the king Chan-Mah-Kina
Stela 22, 9.3.10.0.0, the anniversary celebration of the
conquest by Tikal

Stela 5, 8.17.1.4.12, the conquest
of Uaxactún by Tikal
Stela 4, 8.18.0.0.0, period ending
by Smoking-Frog of Tikal

Stela 9, 8.12.14.8.15, the earliest
monument at Uaxactún

FIG. 4:5

Other burials from the same century also featured vaulted chambers with shrines and rich offerings of pottery, food, stingray spines, and human sacrifices (if the disarticulated skeletons of an adult and an infant can be so identified). Among the buildings constructed during this time was 5D-Sub-10–1st, a small temple blackened inside by the smoke of sacrificial fires. Outside, artists decorated the shrine with elegant polychromatic paintings that were later piously defaced during the termination rituals of this phase of the Acropolis. These paintings are of people or, perhaps, of gods in the guise of people; but because the North Acropolis is the royal sanctum throughout its later history, we think these paintings depict the Tikal ruler and other nobles,[10] suspended in the red-painted blood scrolls of the Vision Rite (Fig. 4:3).

Finally, a very rich tomb, called Burial 85 by the archaeologists (Fig. 4:4), contained a headless, thighless corpse tied up in a cinnabar-impreg-

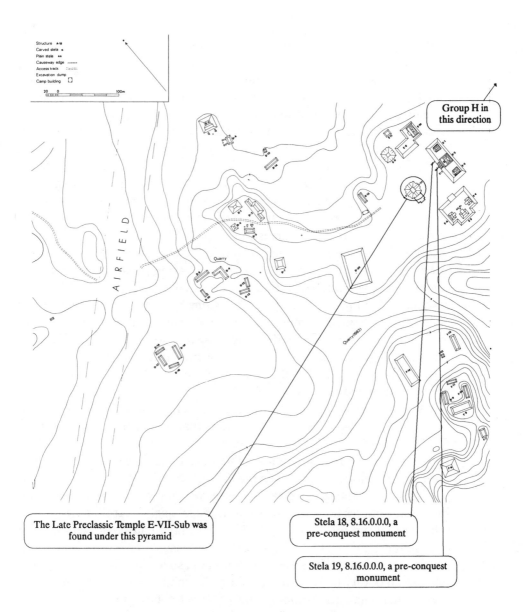

Structure A-18
Carved stela ▣
Plain stela ▣▣
Causeway edge ·······
Access track ---------
Camp building ☐

20 0   100m

Group H in this direction

The Late Preclassic Temple E-VII-Sub was found under this pyramid

Stela 18, 8.16.0.0.0, a pre-conquest monument

Stela 19, 8.16.0.0.0, a pre-conquest monument

AIRFIELD

Quarry

Quarry (1983)

nated bundle along with a spondylus shell and a stingray spine (both instruments of bloodletting rituals).[11] Sewn to the top of the bundle was a green fuchsite portrait head that once served as the chest pectoral of the ruler buried therein.[12] The human face on this pectoral wears the Jester God headdress that would be the crown of kings for the next thousand years.[13] We do not know why some of the king's bones were missing. The Maya are known to have retained bones of important relatives for relics, so that the skull and thighbones may have resided in the house of his descendants for many generations. Without further evidence the answer must remain a mystery.

The noble status of the individuals we find in these tombs is demonstrated not only by the wealth they took with them to the Otherworld, but by the physical condition of their bones. They are larger and more robust than the common people of the kingdom who were buried in other parts

A WAR
OF
CONQUEST:
TIKAL
AGAINST
UAXACTÚN

———

135

of the city.[14] They had a better diet than the people they ruled and were generally taller.

This new, ambitious elite commissioned more than just one or two buildings. During the first century B.C., the lords called upon their people to remodel the entire central area of Tikal—no doubt with an eye to the works of their rivals at El Mirador and Uaxactún. This construction proceeded in three stages. The first stage[15] involved both the renovation of the North Acropolis and the initial leveling and paving of both the Great Plaza and the West Plaza. During the second stage, the huge East Plaza was leveled and paved. The North Acropolis in the city's center was now flanked on the east and the west by two huge paved areas.[16] In the third phase, the same three areas were repaved once again, perhaps under the direction of the ruler found in Burial 85 or perhaps shortly after his interment.[17] These large plazas were the gathering places from which the common people witnessed the ritual performances of the king. The labor costs in quarrying stone, burning limestone to yield plaster, and finally building the structures, must have been enormous. If the elite of Tikal were constantly expanding this public space, we can assume that the prosperity and prestige of this kingdom were attracting a steady influx of new people whose participation in the ritual life of the kingdom had to be accommodated.[18]

During the same six centuries, Uaxactún to the north underwent a florescence as substantial and dramatic as that of its neighbor Tikal. Late Preclassic platforms in Uaxactún underlying Groups A, E, and H (Fig. 4:5) bear some of the most remarkable Late Preclassic sculpture to have survived into modern times. Temple E-VII-Sub, with its elaborately decorated platform and great plaster masks, was the first of the great Late Preclassic temples to be excavated by archaeologists.[19] At that time it was believed that, up until about A.D. 300, the Maya had possessed only the most simplistic type of farming culture. That vision of Maya history could not accommodate such an elaborate building, so for fifty years that temple stood as an oddity in Maya archaeology. Since then, excavations at Tikal, Cerros, Lamanai, El Mirador, and other sites have uncovered similar structures and shown that Temple E-VII-Sub is a typical expression of Late Preclassic kingship.

E-VII-Sub is no longer an oddity even at Uaxactún itself. Deep within and beneath the complex of the South Plaza of Group H[20] (Fig. 4:6) lies a remarkable assemblage of buildings displaying the largest program of Late Preclassic monumental masks yet discovered. This group, composed of six temples mounted on a small acropolis, was superficially buried by an Early Classic acropolis built at a later date. The largest of the masks on this buried complex can be found on the main eastern building (Sub-3) (Fig. 4:7). These massive stucco sculptures decorate the panels of the upper and lower terraces in typical Maya architectural fashion, similar to the decorative programs we have seen at Cerros. Here, however, the visual "stack" of masks does not display the celestial cycle of the sun and Venus, as found on Structure 5C-2nd at Cerros (and also on Structure E-VII-Sub at Uaxactún).[21] Instead the masks featured here are models of the sacred

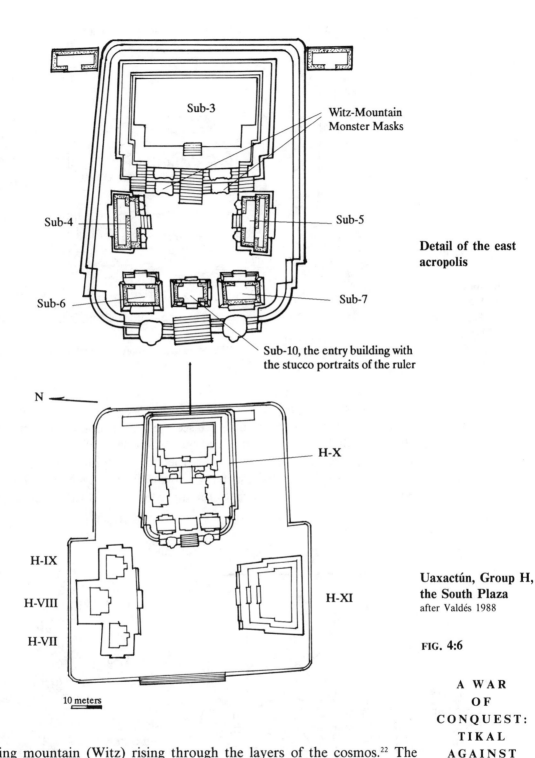

Sub-3

Witz-Mountain
Monster Masks

Detail of the east
acropolis

Sub-4

Sub-5

Sub-6

Sub-7

Sub-10, the entry building with
the stucco portraits of the ruler

N

H-X

H-IX

H-VIII

H-XI

H-VII

Uaxactún, Group H,
the South Plaza
after Valdés 1988

FIG. 4:6

10 meters

A WAR
OF
CONQUEST:
TIKAL
AGAINST
UAXACTÚN
—
137

living mountain (Witz) rising through the layers of the cosmos.[22] The lower panel displays a great Witz Monster sitting in fish-laden primordial waters with vegetation growing from the sides of its head. Above, on the upper panel, sits an identical Monster (probably the mountain peak above the waters)[23] with a Vision Serpent penetrating its head from side to side.

It is important to realize that the facade of Uaxactún Structure H-Sub-3 is simply another version of the sacred cosmos, parallel in func-

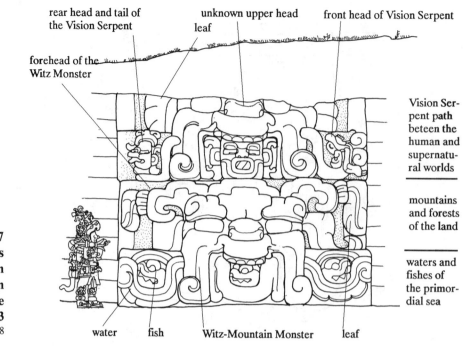

rear head and tail of
the Vision Serpent

unknown upper head
leaf

front head of Vision Serpent

forehead of the
Witz Monster

Vision Serpent path beteen the human and supernatural worlds

mountains and forests of the land

waters and fishes of the primordial sea

**FIG. 4:7
The Cosmos as
Rendered on
Uaxactún
Structure
H-X-Sub-3**
after Valdés 1988

water   fish   Witz-Mountain Monster   leaf

tion to the sun/Venus iconography of the kings at Cerros. In this particular representation of the cosmos, we see the sacred mountain rising from the primordial sea to form the land, just as the land of Petén rose above its swamps. As always, the Vision Serpent is the symbol of the path of communication between the sacred world and the human world. Here, the Vision Serpent's body penetrates the mountain just as the spiritual path

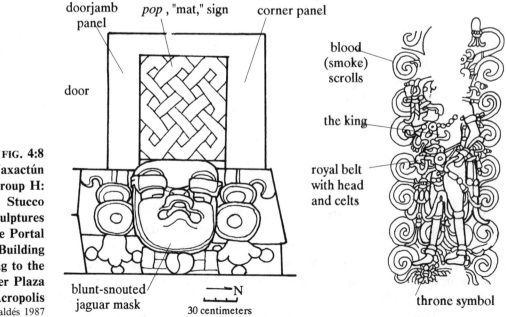

doorjamb
panel

pop, "mat," sign

corner panel

door

blood
(smoke)
scrolls

the king

royal belt
with head
and celts

**FIG. 4:8
Uaxactún
Group H:
Stucco
Sculptures
from the Portal
Building
Leading to the
Inner Plaza
of the Acropolis**
after Valdés 1987

blunt-snouted
jaguar mask

N

30 centimeters

throne symbol

the king must take penetrates down through the rock floor of the pyramid and reaches into the heart of the earth itself. Like his counterparts at Cerros and Tikal, the ahau of Uaxactún materialized that path through the rituals he conducted on the temple stairway, the physical representation of the path to the Otherworld. Behind him stood his living sacred mountains, signaling and amplifying his actions.

The ahau who commissioned this group portrayed himself on a gateway building situated in the center of the acropolis's western edge.[24] Designed to create a formal processional entrance along the east-west axis of the complex, this small Sub-10 temple has both eastern and western doors. The king and his retainers could enter through this gateway in ceremony, and at certain times of the year the light of the setting sun would shine through it as well. The stairways leading to each of the gateway doors were flanked by stucco jaguar ahau masks[25] surmounted by panels set into the walls of the temple itself. These panels carried modeled-stucco woven-mat patterns, one of the main symbols of kingship (Fig. 4:8). Stucco portraits of the king (Fig. 4:9) stood in vertical panels between these mats.

We know this is the king for several reasons. First of all, the figure represented here wears the royal costume—an elaborate ahau head and celt assemblage on a belt above a bifurcated loin apron. This apparel would become the most sacred and orthodox costume of the Classic king. This figure also stands atop a throne mat. Most important, he is encircled by the same scroll signs we saw surrounding his contemporary, the ruler of Tikal (Fig. 4:3). Here, and in the comparable shrine 5D-Sub-10–1st at Tikal, we see Late Preclassic kings memorializing themselves for the first time. They do so at the front of their principal temples, on the main axis of their sacred precincts. This practice is a prototype of what is to come,

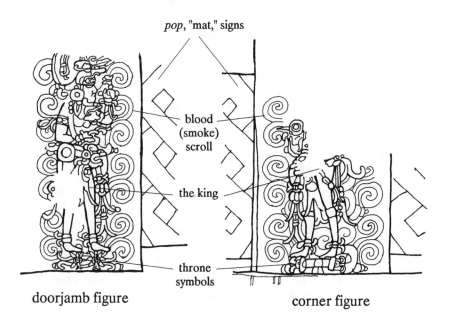

pop, "mat," signs

blood (smoke) scroll

the king

throne symbols

doorjamb figure

corner figure

FIG. 4:9
Uaxactún
Group H: Stucco
Figures of the King
Standing amid
Blood Scrolls
after Valdés 1987

A WAR
OF
CONQUEST:
TIKAL
AGAINST
UAXACTÚN

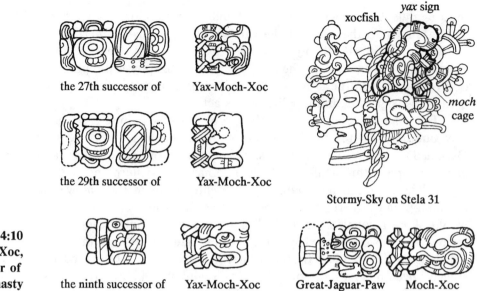

xocfish

yax sign

moch cage

Stormy-Sky on Stela 31

the 27th successor of   Yax-Moch-Xoc

the 29th successor of   Yax-Moch-Xoc

the ninth successor of   Yax-Moch-Xoc

Great-Jaguar-Paw   Moch-Xoc

FIG. 4:10
Yax-Moch-Xoc,
the Founder of
Tikal's Dynasty

for the kings of the Classic period will also raise their stelae portraits in such a place and in such a manner.

Throughout the first century A.D., neither Tikal nor Uaxactún managed to outproduce or dominate the other, but both cities continued to support the institution of kingship. We can see this by the elaborate public architecture and other, smaller ritual objects that have come into our knowledge through archaeological excavation. The imagery each city used to define its kings and to demonstrate the sacred foundations of kingly authority partook of the same fundamental understanding of the world and how it worked. Though Uaxactún may perhaps have had a slight edge, the public constructions of the two kingdoms were relatively equal in scale and elaboration.[26] Tikal and Uaxactún moved into the Classic period as full equals, both ready and able to assume the role of El Mirador when that kingdom disintegrated.[27]

Tikal's inscriptions tell us of a single dynasty which ruled the kingdom from Early Classic times until its demise in the ninth century, a dynasty that could boast of at least thirty-nine successors in its long history. The historical founder of this extraordinary dynasty was a character (Fig. 4:10) known as Yax-Moch-Xoc.[28] We have no monuments from his reign, but we can reconstruct that he ruled sometime between A.D. 219 and A.D. 238[29]—that is, at least a century and a half later than the ahau who commemorated himself on Structure 5D-Sub-10–1st in the North Acropolis. This founder, then, was not the first ruler of Tikal, but he must have performed in such an outstanding fashion that later descendants acknowledged him as the leader who established their dynasty as a power to be reckoned with. The recognition of Yax-Moch-Xoc as founder by later Tikal kings is important for another reason. It constitutes the earliest example yet recognized in ancient texts of the principle of the anchoring

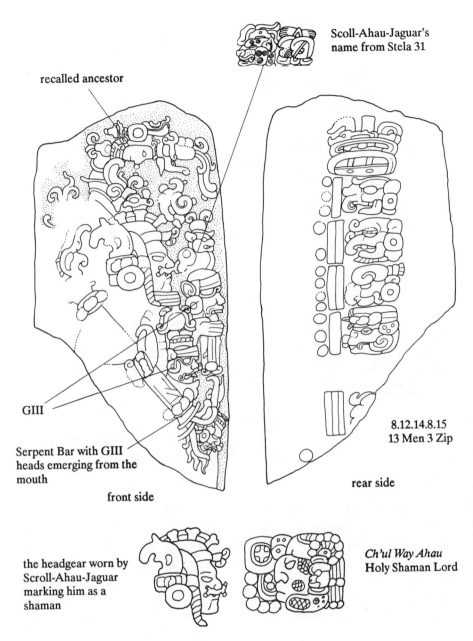

Scoll-Ahau-Jaguar's name from Stela 31

recalled ancestor

GIII

Serpent Bar with GIII heads emerging from the mouth

front side

8.12.14.8.15
13 Men 3 Zip

rear side

the headgear worn by Scroll-Ahau-Jaguar marking him as a shaman

Ch'ul Way Ahau
Holy Shaman Lord

FIG. 4:11
Stela 29,
the Earliest
Dated
Monument
at Tikal
and the King
Scroll-Ahau-
Jaguar

ancestor. From this man would descend the noble families that would comprise the inner community of the court, the royal clan of Tikal.

The earliest historical Tikal king we have in portraiture is the man depicted on Stela 29, dated at 8.12.14.8.15 13 Men 3 Zip (July 8, A.D. 292).[30] This king, Scroll-Ahau-Jaguar[31] (Fig. 4:11), appears surrounded by a complicated system of emblems which designate his rank and power. The twisted rope that hangs in front of his earflare transforms his head into the living embodiment of the glyphic name of the city. He is the kingdom made flesh.[32] Floating above him is an apparition of the dynastic ancestor from whom he received his right to rule.[33] The king's "divine" right to the throne is manifested in another kind of imagery: In his right

A WAR
OF
CONQUEST:
TIKAL
AGAINST
UAXACTÚN
—
141

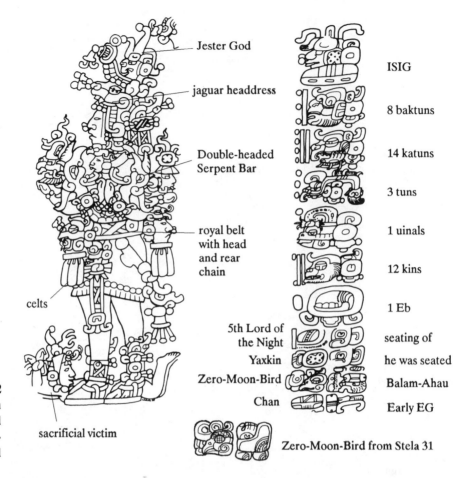

FIG. 4:12
The Leiden
Plaque and
Zero-Moon-
Bird

Jester God

jaguar headdress

Double-headed
Serpent Bar

royal belt
with head
and rear
chain

celts

5th Lord of
the Night

Yaxkin

Zero-Moon-Bird

Chan

sacrificial victim

ISIG

8 baktuns

14 katuns

3 tuns

1 uinals

12 kins

1 Eb

seating of

he was seated

Balam-Ahau

Early EG

Zero-Moon-Bird from Stela 31

arm, the king holds a Double-headed Serpent Bar from which the sun
emerges in its human-headed form. This human-headed manifestation of
the sun is none other than GIII of the Triad Gods, one of the offspring
of the first mother who existed before the present creation. GIII is also
the prototype of the second born of the Ancestral Heroes, whose Classic
name was Yax-Balam ("First Jaguar"). The Serpent Bar demonstrates the
ability of the king to materialize gods and ancestors in the world of his
people.

Another image of the Yax-Balam head adorns the chest of the king
and a third stares out from his uplifted left hand. The imagery of the
disembodied head as a symbol of kingship descends directly from Preclassic times in Mesoamerica. The Olmec, for example, were one of the first
cultures to use this symbol, portraying their shaman kings in the form of
enormous heads the height of a man. The bundle glyph that signified the
kingdom of Tikal appears, surmounting the head attached to the king's
belt and the one he materializes in the mouth of the Serpent Bar, while
the king's own name glyph, a miniature jaguar with a scroll-ahau sign,
rides upon the head in his left hand. This is the type of complex imagery
the Maya used to designate their rulers and the reason their artistic vision
was so powerful and potent.

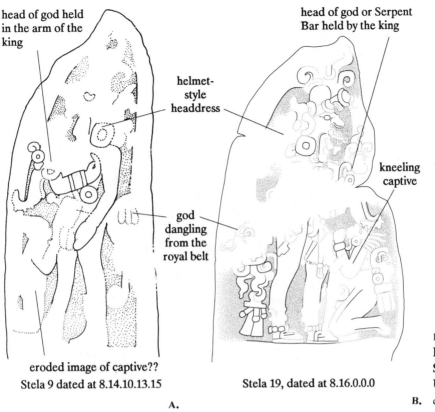

head of god held
in the arm of the
king

head of god or Serpent
Bar held by the king

helmet-
style
headdress

kneeling
captive

god
dangling
from the
royal belt

eroded image of captive??
Stela 9 dated at 8.14.10.13.15

Stela 19, dated at 8.16.0.0.0

A.

FIG. 4:13
Pre-conquest
Stelae from
Uaxactún

B. drawing by Ian Graham

The next Tikal ruler we can identify, Moon-Zero-Bird,[34] is portrayed on a royal belt ornament called the Leiden Plaque (Fig. 4:12). The inscribed text on the reverse side of this ornament records Moon-Zero-Bird's seating as king on September 17, A.D. 320. Like his predecessor, he stands holding a Serpent Bar. This time, however, we see emerging from the serpent's mouth not only the sun, but God K, the deity of lineages. This king also wears an elaborate royal belt. Hanging from this, behind his knees, is a chain with a god suspended from it. The ruler wears a massive headdress, combining the imagery of the Jester God and the jaguar, thus declaring his affiliation with both and his rank as ahau. At his feet a noble captive struggles against his impending fate as sacrificial victim.[35]

The presence of this captive documents the crucial role played by war and captive taking in early Maya kingship. The Maya fought not to kill their enemies but to capture them. Kings did not take their captives easily, but in aggressive hand-to-hand combat. A defeated ruler or lord was stripped of his finery, bound, and carried back to the victorious city to be tortured and sacrificed in public rituals. The prestige value a royal captive held for a king was high, and often a king would link the names of his important captives to his own throughout his life. Captives were symbols of the prowess and potency of a ruler and his ability to subjugate his enemies.[36]

A WAR
O F
C O N Q U E S T :
T I K A L
A G A I N S T
U A X A C T Ú N

——

· 143

Uaxactún, like Tikal, entered the Classic period with a powerful dynasty and, as with Tikal, the first public records of this royal family are fragmentary and incomplete. Uaxactún's earliest surviving monument, Stela 9, is dated at 8.14.10.13.15 (April 11, A.D. 328). The ruler depicted on it is anonymous because the glyphs containing his name are eroded beyond recall. The ritual event being recorded here is dated thirty-six years later than Scroll-Ahau-Jaguar's Stela 29 and some eight years after Moon-Zero-Bird's accession to the throne of Tikal. Although badly eroded, the scene (Fig. 4:13a) depicts essentially the same images as those found on contemporary stelae from Tikal: The elaborately dressed ruler holds a god head in the crook of his arm. We cannot identify the nature of the event taking place because that information did not survive the ravages of time and wear. But we do know, from the date, that this stela commemorated a historical occasion in the king's life and not an important juncture in the sacred cycles of time, such as a katun ending. As on the Leiden Plaque, a sacrificial victim cowers at the feet of the king,[37] emphasizing war and captive taking as an activity of crucial public interest to the ruler.

Uaxactún boasted the earliest surviving Maya monuments to record the public celebrations at the ending of a katun—Stelae 18 and 19 in Group E.[38] The image carved on Stela 18 has been lost to erosion, but Stela 19 (Fig. 4:13b) repeats the royal figure on Stela 9 and underscores the conventional nature of Uaxactún's manner of presenting rulers. The king wears the royal belt with its god image suspended on a chain behind his legs, while he holds either a god head or a Serpent Bar in his arms. A captive of noble status kneels before him with bound wrists raised as if in a gesture of supplication. We can assume from the recurrence of this captive imagery that the festivals associated with regularities in the Maya calendar required the king of Uaxactún to undertake the royal hunt for captives, just as he was required to do for accession rituals and other dynastic events. The likely source of his victims: Tikal, his nearby neighbor to the south.

The rivalry between these two cities comes into dramatic focus during the reign of an extraordinary king. Great-Jaguar-Paw, the ninth successor of Yax-Moch-Xoc, came to the throne sometime between A.D. 320 and 376. This ruler changed the destiny not only of Tikal and Uaxactún, but also the nature of Maya sacred warfare itself. Under his guidance, Tikal not only defeated Uaxactún, but emerged as the Early Classic successor to the glory and power of El Mirador as the dominant kingdom in the Central Petén region.

Despite the fact that he was such an important king, we know relatively little about Great-Jaguar-Paw's life outside of the spectacular campaign he waged against Uaxactún. His reign must have been long, but the dates we have on him come only from his last three years. On one of these historical dates, October 21, A.D. 376, we see Great-Jaguar-Paw ending the seventeenth katun in a ritual depicted on Stela 39[39] (Fig. 4:14). This fragmentary monument[40] shows him only from the waist down, but he is dressed in the same regalia as his royal ancestors, with the god Chac-Xib-

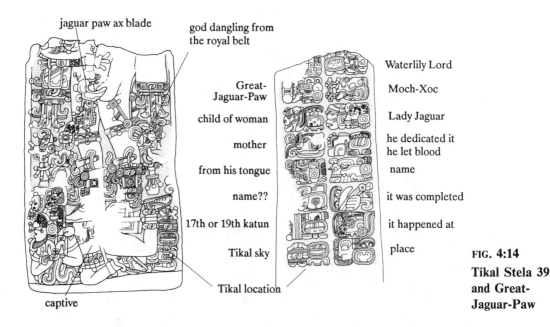

jaguar paw ax blade

god dangling from
the royal belt

Great-
Jaguar-Paw

child of woman

mother

from his tongue

name??

17th or 19th katun

Tikal sky

Tikal location

captive

Waterlily Lord

Moch-Xoc

Lady Jaguar

he dedicated it
he let blood

name

it was completed

it happened at

place

FIG. 4:14
Tikal Stela 39
and Great-
Jaguar-Paw

Chac dangling from his belt. His ankle cuffs display the sign of day on one leg and night on the other. Instead of a Serpent Bar, however, he holds an executioner's ax, its flint blade knapped into the image of a jaguar paw. In this guise of warrior and giver of sacrifices, he stands atop a captive he has taken in battle. The unfortunate victim, a bearded noble still wearing part of the regalia that marks his noble station, struggles under the victor's feet, his wrists bound together in front of his chest. He will die to sanctify the katun ending at Tikal.[41]

Warfare was not new to the Maya. Raiding for captives from one kingdom to another had been going on for centuries, for allusions to decapitation are present in even the earliest architectural decorations celebrating kingship. The hunt for sacrificial gifts to give to the gods and the testing of personal prowess in battle was part of the accepted social order, and captive sacrifice was something expected of nobles and kings in the performance of their ritual duties. Just as the gods were sustained by the bloodletting ceremonies of kings, so they were nourished as well by the blood of noble captives. Sacrificial victims like these had been buried as offerings in building terminations and dedications from Late Preclassic times on, and possibly even earlier. Furthermore, the portrayal of living captives is prominent not only at Uaxactún and Tikal, but also at Río Azul, Xultún, and other Early Classic sites.

The war waged by Great-Jaguar-Paw of Tikal against Uaxactún, however, was not the traditional hand-to-hand combat of proud nobles striving for personal glory and for captives to give to the gods. This was war on an entirely different scale, played by rules never before heard of and for stakes far higher than the reputations or lives of individuals. In this new warfare of death and conquest, the winner would gain the kingdom of the loser. Tikal won the prize on January 16, A.D. 378.

A WAR
OF
CONQUEST:
TIKAL
AGAINST
UAXACTÚN

——

145

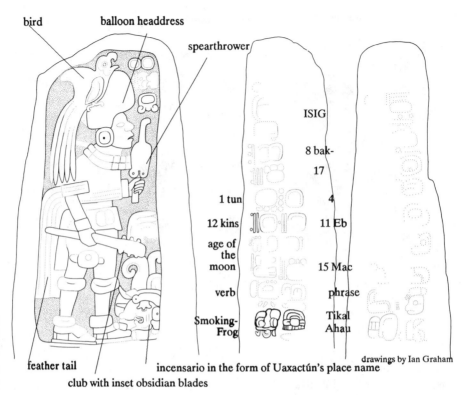

bird balloon headdress

spearthrower

ISIG

8 bak-

17

4

1 tun

12 kins 11 Eb

age of
the
moon 15 Mac

verb phrase

Smoking- Tikal
Frog Ahau

drawings by Ian Graham

feather tail incensario in the form of Uaxactún's place name

club with inset obsidian blades

FIG. 4:15
Uaxactún Stela 5
Showing Smoking-
Frog the
Conqueror

The date of the victory, 8.17.1.4.12 11 Eb 15 Mac, is recorded twice at Uaxactún (on Stela 5 and retrospectively on Stela 22) and twice at Tikal (retrospectively on Stela 31 and on a Ballcourt Marker found in Group 6C-XVI). This is one of the few non–period-ending dates ever recorded by the Maya at more than one site. As we shall see, it was a date of legendary importance for both cities. The two primary characters in this historical drama were the high king of Tikal, Great-Jaguar-Paw, and a character named Smoking-Frog.[42]

The single visual representation of this event occurs at Uaxactún on Stela 5 (Fig. 4:15), which depicts Smoking-Frog as the triumphant leader of the Tikal forces. On the rear of the monument, he proudly names himself as an ahau of Tikal, while on the front he wears the full regalia of a warrior. He grips an obsidian-bladed club, while a bird, perhaps a quetzal, flutters beside his turban. A cluster of long tails arches from the back of his belt and he stands in front of a censer much like the one that appears with Great-Jaguar-Paw on Stela 39 at Tikal (Fig. 4:16).[43]

Aside from the fact that it commemorates the war between Tikal and Uaxactún, this stela is important for another reason. On it we see depicted the first visual representation of the Tlaloc-Venus costume. This costume, with its balloon-shaped headdress and its spearthrower, is profoundly different from that which we have seen adorning Maya ahauob celebrating war and sacrifice at both Tikal and Uaxactún in earlier times. We know that this kind of regalia marks the occasion of a new type of war—conquest war. Smoking-Frog's celebration of this conquest on Stela 5 may

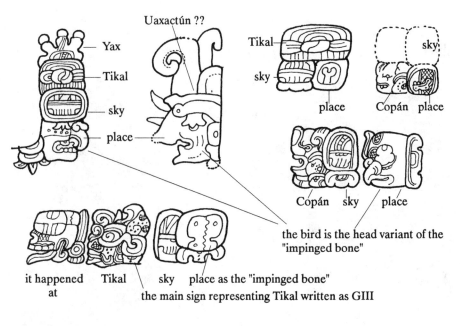

Yax

Tikal

sky

place

Tikal

sky

place

sky

Copán place

Copán sky place

the bird is the head variant of the "impinged bone"

it happened at Tikal sky place as the "impinged bone"

the main sign representing Tikal written as GIII

FIG. 4:16
The Tri-lobed
Bird and the
Place Names
of Tikal,
Uaxactún, and
Copán

mark the first known display of this complex in the imagery of public monuments, but the costume in several variations (Fig. 4:17) became one of the standard uniforms of the king as conqueror and warrior.[44]

The Maya borrowed the costume, and probably the rituals that went with it, from the great central Mexican city, Teotihuacán, whose emissaries appeared in the lowlands at about this time. Although initially adopted as a rationale for conquest, the Maya quickly made these symbols and rituals their own. This imagery held firm at the heart of Maya culture for the next thousand years. For the Maya, among many other peoples in Mesoamerica, this particular costume came to have an overwhelming association with war and sacrifice.[45] Soon after they adopted this kind of war, which we shall call Tlaloc-Venus war,[46] the Maya began timing their battles to particular points in the Venus cycle (especially the first appearance of Eveningstar) and to the stationary points of Jupiter and Saturn.[47]

We do not know why the Maya saw this association with the planets, especially Venus, as important to their concepts of war. However, the fact that later groups, such as the Aztec and Mixtec, also had such associations, which they may have inherited from either the Teotihuacanos or the Maya or both, suggests they were part of the wider Mesoamerican tradition. The date of the Uaxactún conquest, January 16, A.D. 378, has no astronomical significance that we can detect, but this event is also the earliest known appearance of the international war ritual. The astronomical associations may have come later and then spread to other societies using this type of warfare. Certainly, the association clearly had been made within forty years of the conquest because two related events in the reigns of the next two Tikal kings, Curl-Snout and Stormy-Sky, were timed by astronomical alignments (see Notes 57 and 58–5).

The subjugation of Uaxactún by Great-Jaguar-Paw and Smoking-Frog, which precipitated this new kind of war and its rituals, survives in

A WAR
OF
CONQUEST:
TIKAL
AGAINST
UAXACTÚN
—

147

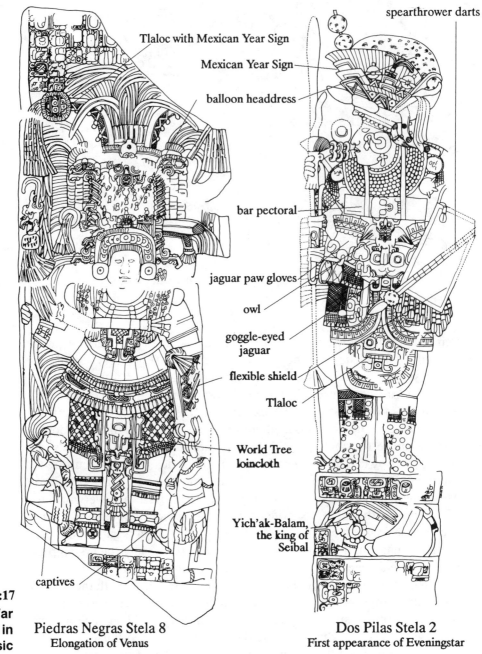

Tlaloc with Mexican Year Sign

Mexican Year Sign

balloon headdress

spearthrower darts

bar pectoral

jaguar paw gloves

owl

goggle-eyed
jaguar

flexible shield

Tlaloc

World Tree
loincloth

Yich'ak-Balam,
the king of
Seibal

captives

FIG. 4:17
**Tlaloc War
Costume in
Late Classic**

Piedras Negras Stela 8
Elongation of Venus

Dos Pilas Stela 2
First appearance of Eveningstar

the inscriptional record almost entirely in the retrospective histories carved by later rulers at Tikal. The fact that these rulers kept commemorating this event shows both its historical importance and its propaganda value for the descendants of these conquerors. Stela 31, the first of these texts, tells us that the conquest took place twelve days, four uinals, and one tun after the end of the seventeenth katun (Fig. 4:18). The passage records two actors: Smoking-Frog, who "demolished and threw down (*hom*)" the buildings of Uaxactún,[48] and Great-Jaguar-Paw, the high king

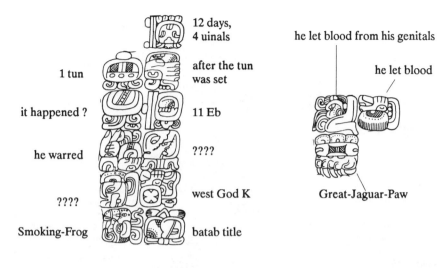

	12 days, 4 uinals		he let blood from his genitals
1 tun	after the tun was set		he let blood
it happened ?	11 Eb		
he warred	????		
????	west God K		Great-Jaguar-Paw
Smoking-Frog	batab title		

The activities of Smoking-Frog   The activities of Great-Jaguar-Paw

FIG. 4:18
**Tikal's Record
of the Conquest
of Uaxactún**
drawing by
John Montgomery

of Tikal, who let blood from his genitals[49] to sanctify the victory of his warriors.

The Ballcourt Marker, the second of these inscriptions, records the event (Fig. 4:19) using a glyph in the shape of the head of an old god. This god has a trifurcated blade over his eye and a four-petaled flower on the side of his head. This same god appears as a full-figured effigy in Burial 10 at Tikal. There he sits on a stool made of human leg bones and holds a severed human head on a plate. We do not know the precise word value intended by this glyph, but the god is clearly a deity of human sacrifice, probably by decapitation. In this conquest text, the portrait of his head is used to record one of the actions taking place on that particular day, very probably to the unfortunate captives taken at Uaxactún. These captives were very likely sacrificed by decapitation, perhaps in honor of this gruesome deity. For all of the distinctiveness of the international regalia marking this war and its political consequences, the ultimate ritual of decapitation sacrifice was the same as that which had been practiced by ahauob since time began. We shall see, however, how this international symbolism, grafted onto orthodox Maya practices, functioned as part of the propaganda that enabled Smoking-Frog to be installed as usurper king at Uaxactún.

Pictorial representations of the battle for Uaxactún have not survived, but we know enough about the way the Maya conducted warfare to reconstruct what this struggle might have been like.[50] One thing is clear: This battle would have been unlike anything the seasoned warriors on either side had ever experienced. And for the people of Uaxactún, it would be more devastating than their wildest imaginings.

A WAR
OF
CONQUEST:
TIKAL
AGAINST
UAXACTÚN

———

149

Imagine the growing sense of horror felt by the people of Uaxactún as they watched their vanquished nobility straggle into the central, daz-

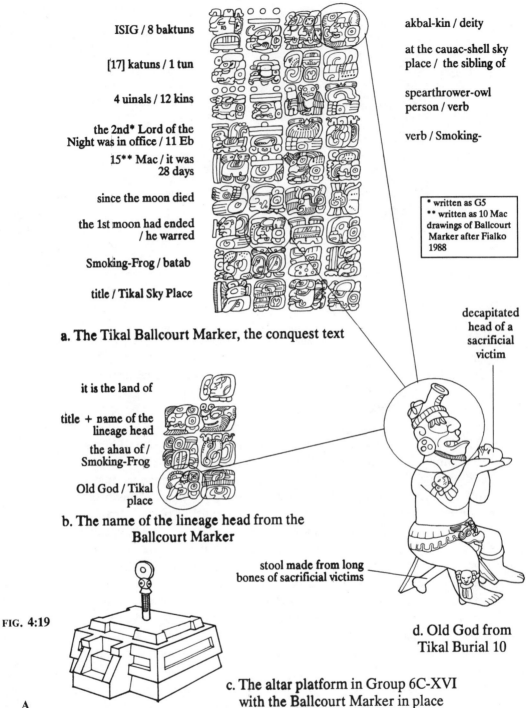

ISIG / 8 baktuns

[17] katuns / 1 tun

4 uinals / 12 kins

the 2nd* Lord of the Night was in office / 11 Eb

15** Mac / it was 28 days

since the moon died

the 1st moon had ended / he warred

Smoking-Frog / batab

title / Tikal Sky Place

akbal-kin / deity

at the cauac-shell sky place / the sibling of

spearthrower-owl person / verb

verb / Smoking-

* written as G5
** written as 10 Mac
drawings of Ballcourt Marker after Fialko 1988

a. The Tikal Ballcourt Marker, the conquest text

decapitated head of a sacrificial victim

it is the land of

title + name of the lineage head

the ahau of / Smoking-Frog

Old God / Tikal place

b. The name of the lineage head from the Ballcourt Marker

stool made from long bones of sacrificial victims

FIG. 4:19

d. Old God from Tikal Burial 10

c. The altar platform in Group 6C-XVI with the Ballcourt Marker in place

zling white plazas of their city. The clear, hard winter light of the yax-colored sky was the backdrop to a world changing before their frightened eyes. High above them on the bloodred flank of his living mountain, their king struggled to calm himself so that he might enter into the darkness of his portal with a mind clear and purposeful, to challenge his ancestors. Why this violation of all rules of the way men fight? Where was the path to escape this disaster?

It had begun well enough. He had led his warriors through the days of fasting, the rites of purification and sacrifice. Deep in the night, with his own hands he painted the strong faces of his kinsmen. In the flickering torchlight of the many-chambered men's hall, he adorned them with the black and red patterns that would terrify any who dared come against them. How proud he had been when their wives handed them the great honey-colored knives of stone and the shields which they rolled up and hung across their backs. Lastly, their wives gave them the great lances hafted with teeth of lightning, the great flint blades flaked to slice smoothly into the flesh of their enemies.

The king's principal wife, who was pregnant with their next child, had waited until the men of lesser status were prepared before she brought his battle gear.[51] His second wife stood nearby holding their infant child, and his firstborn child by his principal wife watched the proceedings with wide eyes. One day, he, like his father, would lead the men into battle in defense of the portals of the sacred mountains. Dressed in his full regalia, the king smiled at his son and led his family out into the darkness of the predawn morning.

In the still darkness his warriors awaited him, already dressed, their battle jackets tied loosely closed across their muscled chests. When he appeared in the flickering torchlight, a low-throated shout greeted him and his army began their last stages of preparation. They strapped on their helmets emblazoned with the images of their animal protectors. His ahauob donned the fearsome god masks, made in the image of the ax-wielding executioner Chac-Xib-Chac and the other denizens of the Other-world. They draped the wizened, shrunken heads of now-dead captives around their necks to let the enemy know they faced seasoned men of high reputation and proven valor.

Then there had been the rush of fear and the anticipation of glory as the warriors of Uaxactún reached the open savanna south of the city. There the battle would be fought against the age-old rivals who lived among the swamps to the south, at the right-hand side of the sun. The warming light of the rising sun had burned away the ground mist to reveal the warriors arrayed in tension-filled stillness as they waited to join in battle.

It had begun in the old ways of battle, following twenty katuns or more of honorable precedent. Standing in the waist-high grass, the old men sounded the great wooden trumpets whose piercing song cut through the bass thunder of the great war drums, the *tunkul,* filling the forest with the sound of great deeds in progress. His people stood together like a writhing vision of multicolored glory against the green of those trees, shouting insults about the ancestry of the Tikal enemy ranked in their hundreds across the sea of grass. One after another, singly or in groups, his ahauob shouted their challenges toward their counterparts across the savanna. Charging out onto the battle ground, they screamed their insults, then retreated once again to the massed safety of their own side. Their bravado and rage rippled through the ranks, transforming them into a pulsing sea of hysterical faces and trembling bodies.

A WAR
OF
CONQUEST:
TIKAL
AGAINST
UAXACTÚN
———
151

Suddenly, the tension became unbearable. The warriors' rage exploded into frenzied release as the two armies charged across the grass, trampling it into a tight mat under their thudding feet. They merged in the middle of the field in a screaming discharge of released energy, lightning blade clashing against woven shield in the glorious and dangerous hunt for captives to give as gifts to the gods.

The lines struck and intermingled in crazed chaos, screams of pain punctuating the cries of challenge. There was a brief flare of victory as Uaxactún's surging mass of men flowed across the field like a summer flood, sweeping first toward the clump of men who protected Great-Jaguar-Paw, Tikal's high king, and then back northward toward the Uaxactún lines. The entangled horde of men finally separated, and bloodied, exhausted warriors fell back toward the safety of their own side in the glaring light of midmorning. They needed to wet their dry throats with water and bind up their oozing wounds with strips of paper. Some of the warriors had taken captives who had to be stripped naked and tied down before they escaped in the heat and confusion of the battle. With such great numbers present from each city, the battle would last all day.

It was then that the treacherous enemy lord struck. Smoking-Frog, the war chief of Tikal's army, flashed an unseen signal and from the forest came hundreds of hidden warriors. In eerie silence, never once issuing challenge, they hurled a cloud of spears into the thick ranks of the Uaxactún warriors. Shocked and horrified, the king realized the enemy was using spearthrowers, the hunter's weapon, killing his people like food animals gathered for slaughter.[52]

The surprise of the attack was too great and many of his very best warriors fell to the flying lances, unable to get to safety in time. Many died and even more were crippled by a weapon that the king had seen only foreigners use in war, the foreigners who had come into their lands from Teotihuacán, the giant capital to the far west. The hidden hundreds of Tikal's militia advanced, all carrying bunches of light, obsidian-tipped darts and throwing-sticks. He heard one of his kinsmen scream as a spear drove through his cheek, turning his black-painted face red with blood.

Shouting their hatred for the enemy, the king and his captains leaped toward the Tikal general, Smoking-Frog, where he stood on the far side of the field. Jamming a wedge of bloody spears through the twisting bodies of Tikal's young men, the warriors of Uaxactún tore a pathway through enemy ranks for their vengeful king. But it was too late. Above the blare of the long wooden trumpets and the moan of the conch-shell horns, the high chants of Tikal's triumph sounded in the broken, corpse-strewn meadow. More spears rained down and the king of Uaxactún was forced to pull back to the forest with the shattered remnant of his army. The young men of the royal clan and many valiant men of the great families of Uaxactún lay dead or bound, resigned to suffer the torture that awaited them at the hands of Smoking-Frog and his ahauob.

Now in the darkness of his sanctum, the king of Uaxactún heard again that awful chant of victory. The warriors of Tikal were entering his city and he could feel the ancestral gift of his world slipping from his grasp. An unthinkable disaster had befallen him and his people. He emerged into the blinding daylight; and as his vision cleared, he saw smoke billowing from the fires of destruction, which consumed the spacious homes and public halls of his city's center. Screaming taunts of desperation, the lords of Uaxactún gathered on the sides of their living mountains, throwing their stabbing spears, rocks, and finally their bodies at the advancing and implacable Tikal forces.

In spite of all their efforts, Smoking-Frog and his company swirled around the base of the king's pyramid, killing and capturing the valiant warriors of the Uaxactún royal clan. The king and his men fought to the last. At the moment of his capture, the king of Uaxactún reached furiously for Smoking-Frog's throat. Laughing, the Tikal lord jerked him to his knees by his long bound hair. The defeated king glared up at the arrogant Smoking-Frog, costumed in the regalia of the new, barbarous warfare—the round helmet, the spearthrower, and the obsidian club. He cursed him as his captor's minions stripped him bare and tied his elbows behind his back with rough sisal rope.

They would all die. There would be no ransom. Under the code of this new, foreign battle strategy, Smoking-Frog would be able to bring his own Tikal ancestors to the portal of Uaxactún. He and his descendants would rule not only the people of the city but their venerated ancestors as well. It was an act of audacity beyond imagination: war to take not only the king but also his portal—and if possible to hold that portal captive. For as long as Smoking-Frog and his kin reigned, the people of Uaxactún would be cut off from the loving guidance of their ancestors, a people stripped of their very gods.

•

In time to come, this kind of war would require a novel alliance with the denizens of the Otherworld—an unleashing of the forces of Xibalba, particularly Venus, to conquer not only the living royal clan but also all of the apotheosized ancestors of that clan. Kings now had a policy and a strategy that would inspire dreams of conquest throughout the Maya world. Venus would prove a powerful, but treacherous ally in the realization of these dreams.

The most tantalizing mystery surrounding the conquest of Uaxactún is the identity of Smoking-Frog. Who was this warrior who appears in the inscriptions of both Uaxactún and Tikal? We know he was an ahau of Tikal because he consistently included the Tikal Emblem Glyph in his name. Second, we know he was the principal actor in the conquest of Uaxactún, despite the fact that the conquest took place under the authority of Great-Jaguar-Paw, the high king of Tikal. All of this leads us to believe that he was most likely the war chief who led Tikal's army against the rival kingdom, and as a result of his success, was installed as the ruling ahau of Uaxactún by the victorious Tikal king. We know that eighteen years after the conquest, Smoking-Frog was still at Uaxactún. On 8.18.0.0.0 (July 8, 396) he conducted a ritual to celebrate the katun ending, an event he depicted on Stela 4 (Fig. 4:20), which he planted next to his portrait

A WAR
OF
CONQUEST:
TIKAL
AGAINST
UAXACTÚN
—
153

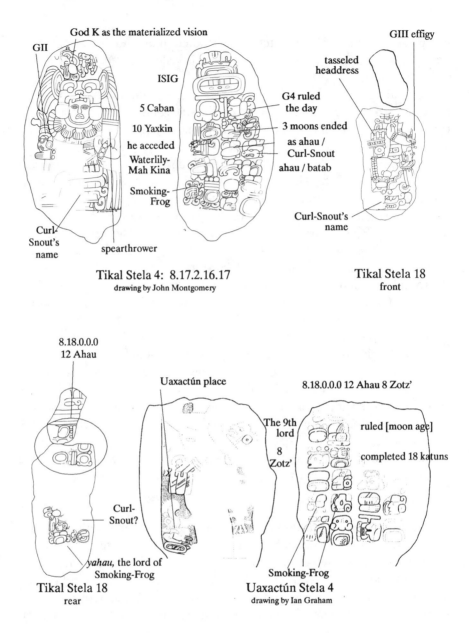

God K as the materialized vision

GII

ISIG

5 Caban

10 Yaxkin

he acceded

Waterlily-
Mah Kina

Smoking-
Frog

Curl-
Snout's
name

spearthrower

GIII effigy

tasseled
headdress

G4 ruled
the day

3 moons ended

as ahau /
Curl-Snout
ahau / batab

Curl-Snout's
name

Tikal Stela 4: 8.17.2.16.17
drawing by John Montgomery

Tikal Stela 18
front

8.18.0.0.0
12 Ahau

Uaxactún place

8.18.0.0.0 12 Ahau 8 Zotz'

The 9th
lord

8
Zotz'

ruled [moon age]

completed 18 katuns

Curl-
Snout?

yahau, the lord of
Smoking-Frog

Smoking-Frog

Tikal Stela 18
rear

Uaxactún Stela 4
drawing by Ian Graham

**FIG. 4:20
Smoking-Frog
at Tikal and
Uaxactún**

as the conqueror (Fig. 4:5). The people of Tikal didn't forget him on this occasion either. Back at his home city, Smoking-Frog was named on Stela 18 (Fig. 4:20) which recorded the celebration of the same katun ending. He was also prominently named in the retrospective histories recorded on Stela 31 and the Ballcourt Marker.

Yet even considering his prominence in the inscriptions of both Uaxactún and Tikal, we are reasonably sure that Smoking-Frog never ruled Tikal as its king. Instead, another ahau named Curl-Snout (Fig. 4:20) became high king of Tikal on September 13, 379, less than two years after the conquest. Curl-Snout apparently held his throne, however, under the sufferance of Smoking-Frog, who appears to have ruled the combined kingdom that was forged by the conquest. We would like to put forward

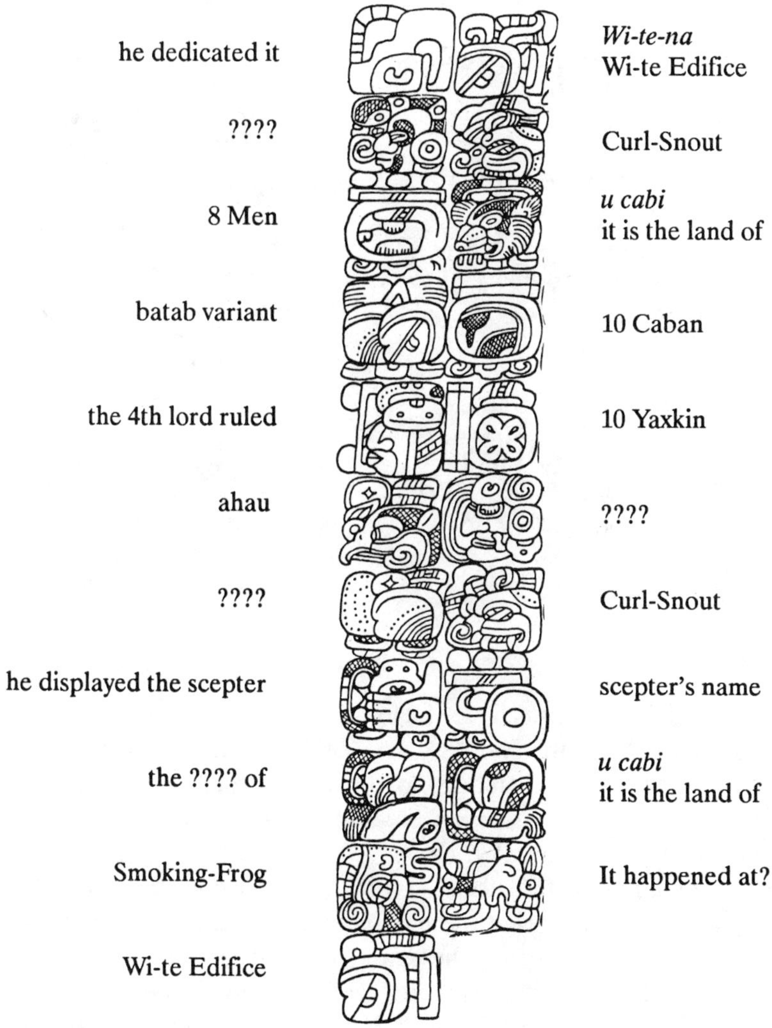

he dedicated it		*Wi-te-na* Wi-te Edifice
????		Curl-Snout
8 Men		*u cabi* it is the land of
batab variant		10 Caban
the 4th lord ruled		10 Yaxkin
ahau		????
????		Curl-Snout
he displayed the scepter		scepter's name
the ???? of		*u cabi* it is the land of
Smoking-Frog		It happened at?
Wi-te Edifice		

FIG. 4:21

Stela 31: Curl-Snout in the Land of Smoking-Frog

drawing by John Montgomery

the hypothesis that Smoking-Frog was the brother of Great-Jaguar-Paw, the high king of Tikal at the time of the battle of Uaxactún, and that Curl-Snout was his nephew.

There are several clues leading to this conclusion. One of the ways we can infer the relationship between Curl-Snout and Smoking-Frog is from the inscriptions at Tikal, which always name Curl-Snout either as the *yahau* "the noble of" (in this case, "the vassal of") Smoking-Frog (Stela 18) or as acting *u cab* "in the land of" Smoking-Frog (Stela 31). When Curl-Snout depicted himself acceding to Tikal's kingship on Stela 4 and ending Katun 18 on Stela 18, he found it advisable to record publicly his relationship to Smoking-Frog. Perhaps the most important reference to their relationship occurs on Stela 31 where an important event in Curl-Snout's life, possibly his accession, is said to have taken place "in the land of Smoking-Frog" (Fig. 4:21).[53] From these references we surmise that Curl-Snout ruled Tikal, but under the aegis of Smoking-Frog.[54]

A WAR
OF
CONQUEST:
TIKAL
AGAINST
UAXACTÚN
——
155

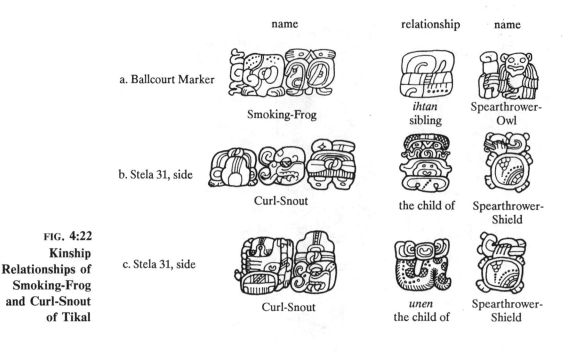

name   relationship   name

a. Ballcourt Marker

Smoking-Frog   *ihtan*
sibling   Spearthrower-
Owl

b. Stela 31, side

Curl-Snout   the child of   Spearthrower-
Shield

c. Stela 31, side

Curl-Snout   *unen*
the child of   Spearthrower-
Shield

FIG. 4:22
Kinship
Relationships of
Smoking-Frog
and Curl-Snout
of Tikal

There are additional hints as to the identity of Smoking-Frog and his relationship to Curl-Snout. The text on the Ballcourt Marker names Smoking-Frog as the *ihtan,* [55] "sibling," of a person named "Spearthrower-Owl." It is interesting that Stela 31, erected many years later by Curl-Snout's son and heir, Stormy-Sky, names Curl-Snout as the "child of" a person named by an almost identical glyph, "Spearthrower-Shield" (Fig. 4:22). We have now realized that these two seemingly different glyphs are merely different ways of writing the same thing—the shield-owl-spearthrower substitution that would become Pacal's name at Palenque and the name of the third Lord of the Night. [56] If this substitution is correctly identified, then we can assert that Smoking-Frog was the brother and Curl-Snout the son of the same man. Our remaining task is to determine the identity of the person whom these "spearthrower" glyphs name.

The solution to this mystery involves some complicated detective work. The "spearthrower" name also occurs on Stela 31 in another context. It is the title on the headdress Stormy-Sky holds aloft, prior to donning it in the public ritual depicted on the front of the monument (Fig. 4:23). A medallion attached to the front of the headdress depicts an owl with a shield on its wing and a throwing dart piercing its breast. Stormy-Sky is about to become a "spearthrower-owl-shield" person by putting on this headdress.

The last readable clause of the text on this monument tells us that Stormy-Sky performed this ritual on June 11, A.D. 439, when Venus was near its eastern elongation. [57] The glyph that records this ritual action is the same as the one recording the bloodletting event (Fig. 4:23) that Great-Jaguar-Paw performed on the day Uaxactún was conquered. The use of the same verb in both contexts is to declare a "like-in-kindness" between the two actors. If Stormy-Sky became the "spearthrower-owl"

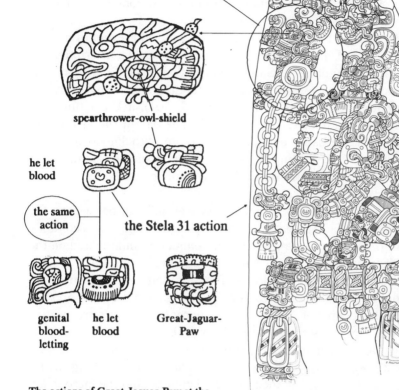

Curl-Snout recalled by Stormy-Sky's bloodletting

headdress with its spearthrower-shield medallion

spearthrower-owl-shield

he let blood

the same action

the Stela 31 action

genital blood-letting

he let blood

Great-Jaguar-Paw

The actions of Great-Jaguar-Paw at the conquest of Uaxactún

Stormy-Sky holding his headdress aloft as the holder of the spearthrower-shield title

FIG. 4:23
The Spearthrower Title and Stormy-Sky at Tikal

drawing of text and stela by John Montgomery

person by performing this rite, we may assume that Great-Jaguar-Paw had taken on this identity in the same ritual context. The "spearthrower-owl" named as the brother of Smoking-Frog and the father of Curl-Snout was none other than the first great Tikal king to call himself by that title—Great-Jaguar-Paw, the king who made war with spearthrowers his own. Furthermore, it is this very equation between grandfather and grandson that Stormy-Sky intended to portray in the first place. It is not by accident that he designated himself the "spearthrower-shield" when he reenacted his ancestor's bloodletting event. By doing so, he intended to remind his people that he was the grandson of this powerful and innovative man.

In the scenario we have reconstructed, forces from Tikal under the military leadership of Smoking-Frog, the brother of the high king, attacked and defeated the forces of their neighboring kingdom, Uaxactún, on January 16, 378. The victory placed Smoking-Frog on the throne of Uaxactún, where he oversaw the accession of his nephew, Curl-Snout, to Tikal's throne on September 13, A.D. 379. For the next eighteen years, and

A WAR
OF
CONQUEST:
TIKAL
AGAINST
UAXACTÚN
—
157

perhaps as long as twenty-six years,[58] Smoking-Frog ruled Uaxactún, possibly marrying into its ruling family as well. Even though Smoking-Frog ruled Uaxactún, however, he remained extremely important at Tikal. It's possible he was the overall ruler of the new combined kingdom that resulted from his victory in battle.

That the conquest of Uaxactún remained a glorious event of historical memory both at Uaxactún and Tikal is clear from the inscriptions at both sites. The descendants of Smoking-Frog continued to erect monuments at Uaxactún on a regular basis. One hundred and twenty-six years after the conquest, on 9.3.10.0.0 (December 9, 504), a Uaxactún ruler celebrated the conquest by erecting Stela 22. The day of the victory, 11 Eb, appears with the same conquest verb (hom, "to knock down or demolish buildings") describing the action. Even at such a late date, the borrowed glory of the battle of Uaxactún could burnish the deeds of Smoking-Frog's progeny.

Another example of this "glory by association" can be seen on the above mentioned Stela 31, erected at Tikal. This monument was commissioned by Stormy-Sky, the grandson of the conqueror, and focused on the defeat of Uaxactún.[59] Stormy-Sky's motivation in featuring this conquest was, of course, to remember the glories of his grandfather and the triumph of his kingdom against an old rival; but he also gained personal prestige by reminding his people of this event. By concentrating on retrospective historical events on this stela, Stormy-Sky was also able to emphasize the extraordinary alignment of Jupiter, Saturn, and Venus on 8.18.15.11.0 (November 27, A.D. 411, see Note 58–5) which occurred during his father's, Curl-Snout's, reign. He then used the conquest and the hierophany as a background to emphasize the importance of his own bloodletting on June 10, 439. So effective was this strategy that his own descendant, Ah-Cacaw, remembered and celebrated this same bloodletting event thirteen katuns later (9.13.3.9.18 or September 17, 695).[60]

The most extraordinary record of the conquest was inscribed on the Ballcourt Marker[61] that was recently discovered in a lineage compound south of the Lost World group. The ballgame with its decapitation and sacrificial associations had been a central component of Maya ritual since the Late Preclassic period, but the marker recording the Uaxactún conquest is not typical of the floor-mounted stone disk used in the Maya ballcourts. This Tikal marker, in the shape of a thin cylinder surmounted by a sphere and disk, is nearly identical to ballcourt markers pictured in the murals of the Tlalocán at Teotihuacán itself.[62] It rests on its own Teotihuacán-style platform and a two-paneled inscription wraps around the cylinder base (Fig. 4:19c). Its form emulates the style of Teotihuacán ballcourt markers as a reflection of the importance of the Tlaloc-Venus war in its records.[63]

The inscription is as extraordinary as the object itself. One panel records the conquest of Uaxactún by Smoking-Frog (Fig. 4:19a), while the opposite side records the accession to office of the fourth lord to rule the lineage that occupied this compound.[64] This was presumably the lineage head who went to war under the leadership of Smoking-Frog. The Ball-court Marker itself was planted in the altar on January 24, 414, some thirty-six years after the conquest of Uaxactún, but it was not commissioned by a king. It was erected by a lord who named himself "the *ahau* (in the sense of 'vassal') of Smoking-Frog of Tikal" (Fig. 4:19c).

The people who lived and worked in this ritual/residential complex were members of one of the important, nonroyal lineages of the kingdom. They were not themselves kings; but like their king and his descendants, they remembered the conquest of Uaxactún as the most glorious event in living memory. Like Stormy-Sky, they gained prestige by celebrating its memory in texts recording the history of their own lineage. This lineage presumably provided warriors, perhaps even leaders, for Smoking-Frog's army and forever gained recognition and glory by their participation.

The war and its aftermath affected more than just the two kingdoms and the people directly involved. Tikal's victory gave the lords who ruled that kingdom the advantage they needed to dominate the central Petén for the next 180 years. However, this great victory also coincided with an intensified interaction between Tikal and Teotihuacán, whose influence, as we have seen, appeared in Maya symbolism just about the time this war was fought. What did this interaction mean for the Maya culture and how far did their involvement with the civilization of Teotihuacán go? To answer this question, we must examine a little history.

During the same centuries that saw the development of lowland Maya kingdoms, the new state of Teotihuacán had simultaneously been growing to maturity in the valley of México (Fig. 4:24). We know that the lowland Maya and the Teotihuacanos had been in contact with each other from at least the first century A.D. Offerings of the distinctive green obsidian mined by the Teotihuacanos have been discovered in Late Pre-classic Maya sites at Nohmul and at Altun Ha in Belize.[65] Furthermore, the exchange of material goods was not just in one direction. Just as Teotihuacán-style objects occur at Tikal and elsewhere in the lowlands, Maya-style objects also occur at Teotihuacán. Yet even in light of this long-term exchange of exotic goods between the two regions, something very special and different, at least in scale, took place on the occasion of the war against Uaxactún. What was exchanged this time was not just goods, but a whole philosophy. The Maya borrowed the idea and the imagery of conquest war from the Teotihuacanos and made it their own.

On Stela 5 at Uaxactún (Fig. 4:15), the conqueror, Smoking-Frog, chose to depict himself in ritual war regalia of the Teotihuacán style. On Stela 4 at Tikal (Fig. 4:20), Curl-Snout, the son of Great-Jaguar-Paw, ruler of Tikal at the time of the conquest, depicted himself wearing a shell necklace, also in the style of Teotihuacán, when he acceded as king. Curl-Snout appears again on the sides of Stela 31 (Fig. 4:25), but this time in the same war regalia worn by Smoking-Frog at Uaxactún. If we recall that the Maya utilized their public art for purposes of propaganda, we can see the reasoning behind this costume. When Stormy-Sky acceded to the throne, he needed to present his father (the forebear upon whom his right

A WAR
OF
CONQUEST:
TIKAL
AGAINST
UAXACTÚN

—

159

Teotihuacán:
the Avenue of
the Dead and the
Pyramid of
the Sun

The
Talud-tablero
Style of
Architecture
Characteristic of
Teotihuacán

FIG. **4:24**

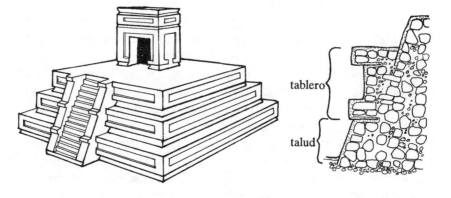

tablero

talud

to rule depended) in the most powerful light possible. What could be more prestigious than for Curl-Snout to appear in the costume worn by Smoking-Frog at the moment of his greatest triumph?

To give the impression that we are seeing Curl-Snout standing behind his son, Stormy-Sky represented him twice, on opposite sides of the stela. On one side we see the inside of his shield and the outside of his spearthrower; on the other we see the inside of the spearthrower, and the outside of the shield. Upon his shield we see the image of Tlaloc, the goggle-eyed deity that the Maya would come to associate with this particular kind of war and bloodletting ritual.[66]

Burials from this period at Tikal also give evidence of the Maya interaction with Teotihuacán. Two of our protagonists were buried in the North Acropolis at Tikal: Curl-Snout in Burial 10 and Stormy-Sky in Burial 48.[67] Both tombs include significant numbers of pots made in the

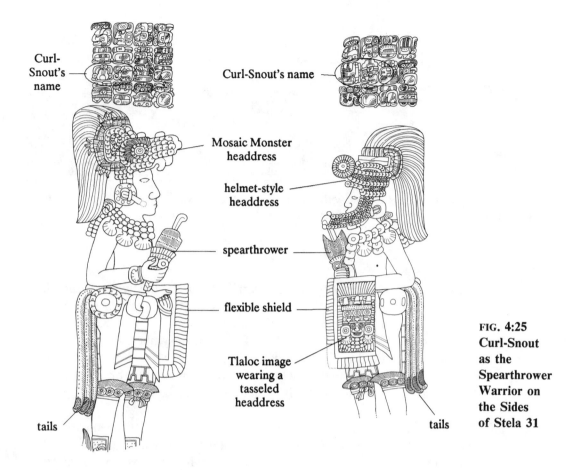

Curl-Snout's name

Curl-Snout's name

Mosaic Monster headdress

helmet-style headdress

spearthrower

flexible shield

Tlaloc image wearing a tasseled headdress

tails

tails

FIG. 4:25 Curl-Snout as the Spearthrower Warrior on the Sides of Stela 31

style of Teotihuacán, emulating imagery particularly associated with that city. Even more to the point, a special cache at Tikal called Problematic Deposit 50[68] included what may very well be the interred remains of resident Teotihuacanos of high rank. The most interesting object in this deposit is a vase that appears to depict the arrival of a group of Teotihuacanos at a Maya city (Fig. 4:26).

On this vase six Teotihuacanos, marked by their clothing, walk away from a place of talud-tablero–style architecture, the ethnic signal of Teotihuacán (Fig. 4:24), to arrive at a place that has both talud-tablero temples and stepped pyramids of Maya design. At the city of departure, they leave a child and a squatting figure, perhaps representing the family members who see them off on their long journey. Four of the Teotihuacano visitors wear the long-tailed costume we have seen at Uaxactún and Tikal. These same persons carry spearthrowers and appear to escort two other characters who carry lidded cylinders, a pottery shape particularly associated with Teotihuacán.[69] At the end of this "journey," the arriving Teotihuacanos are greeted by a person dressed like a Maya.

We do not know for sure which cities the artist intended to represent on this vessel—although it would seem logical to identify Teotihuacán as the starting point and Tikal as the point of arrival.[70] The four Teotihuaca-

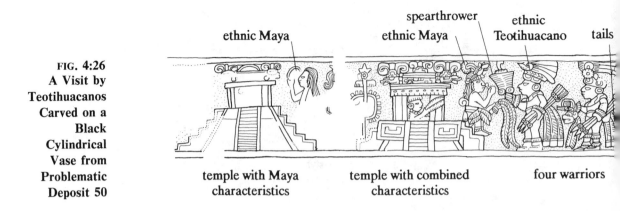

FIG. 4:26
A Visit by
Teotihuacanos
Carved on a
Black
Cylindrical
Vase from
Problematic
Deposit 50

ethnic Maya

spearthrower
ethnic Maya

ethnic
Teotihuacano

tails

temple with Maya
characteristics

temple with combined
characteristics

four warriors

nos carrying weapons constitute a warrior escort for the two vase-carrying individuals behind them. The rear figures are distinguished by tasseled headdresses of the type that also show up prominently at Kaminaljuyu and Monte Alban in contexts where Teotihuacán symbolism have merged with local traditions. The individuals who wear these headdresses are most likely special-status people who traveled as emissaries, or professional merchants representing their great city throughout western Meso-america.[71]

The appearance of this kind of imagery at Tikal has been explained in several ways, ranging from the military conquest of these sites by Teotihuacán to the usurpation of Tikal's throne by lords from Teotihua-cán or Kaminaljuyu.[72] The last alternative seems unlikely. The status of Curl-Snout as Stormy-Sky's father is certain. If we are accurate in our analysis of the "spearthrower-shield" glyph, Great-Jaguar-Paw was Curl-Snout's father and Smoking-Frog's brother. If these relationships are correctly deciphered, then we can verify an unbroken descent in the Tikal royal line during the very time Teotihuacano imagery begins appearing in such prominence.

If we dismiss conquest and usurpation, then what does the presence of this imagery imply? There is little doubt that the Teotihuacanos were physically present at Tikal, at least in small numbers, just as small numbers of lowland Maya were also present at Teotihuacán. The reason for this was not military occupation. Rather, during the fifth and sixth centuries, Teotihuacán had established a network binding the individual societies in Mesoamerica together in a great web of trade and exchange.

When the Teotihuacanos departed their city to travel among the different areas participating in that trade network, they went as tassel-headed ambassador-traders, protected by warriors. Sacred war as they defined and practiced it is registered in the murals of Atetelco and the Temple of Quetzalcoatl in their own great city.[73] The symbology in these images is clearly related, if not identical, to the Tlaloc warfare practiced by the Maya. As these Teotihuacanos spread out from their sacred city, which they believed to be the point on earth where the supernatural world

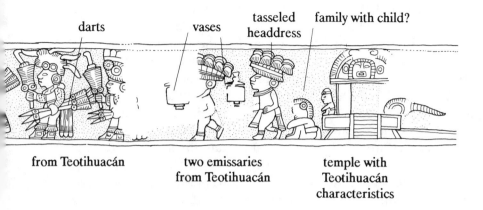

darts   vases   tasseled headdress   family with child?

from Teotihuacán   two emissaries from Teotihuacán   temple with Teotihuacán characteristics

was embodied,[74] they took their form of war and sacrificial rituals with them.

The arrival of the Teotihuacán trader-ambassadors in the central Petén may have intensified the rivalry that already existed between Uaxactún and Tikal. At the very least their presence inflated the stakes at risk—the wealth in material goods and ideas that came with controlling the trade network of the central Petén region. Certainly when Smoking-Frog depicted himself—and later on, his father—in the costume worn by the Teotihuacán warriors, it was because this costume was prestigious and important propaganda to his people. How much more impressive must the Teotihuacán symbolism have been to the people of the whole Petén region when its adoption by Tikal's rulers coincided with their conquest of Uaxactún?

Both the son and grandson of the triumphant Great-Jaguar-Paw knew the propaganda value of the Tlaloc complex. They enthusiastically adopted the imagery and its associated rituals, and then quite deliberately commemorated their ancestor's great feat whenever possible on their own public monuments. By the time Stormy-Sky erected Stela 31, this war and sacrifice ritual was firmly associated with Venus or Venus-Jupiter-Saturn hierophanies, most probably a Maya adaptation.

With the enthusiasm of the newly converted, the Maya adopted this ritual and made it their own. It survived the collapse of the Classic period civilization and is prominent at Chichén Itzá and other northern sites of the Postclassic period. It may even have traveled back to central México via Cacaxtla and Xochicalco: For it is the Maya version of the Tlaloc complex that appears at those sites at the end of the Classic period.

Why did the Maya take to this new ritual so readily and enthusiastically? Perhaps the best answer is that it helped Tikal win a staggering victory that made her kings the dominant ahauob of the central Petén. Intensified trade and political association with Teotihuacán were other likely results of this victory. As a ruler of empire, Tikal experienced an inflation of prestige perhaps unprecedented in Maya history and rarely replicated again. This conquest was the stuff of legends and the people of

A WAR
OF
CONQUEST:
TIKAL
AGAINST
UAXACTÚN
——
163

Tikal never let the story pass from memory. Thirteen katuns later another descendent memorialized this legendary conquest when he sought to rebuild the glory of Tikal after a disastrous defeat on the battlefield.

But there is more to this scenario than just the adoption of a new art of war. From early in their history, the Maya honored offerings of blood above all others as the most sacred gifts to the gods. Individuals were often sacrificed to sanctify the construction of a new building. Indeed, the people of Cuello killed and dismembered twenty-six individuals to place under the floor of a new platform they built around 400 B.C.[75] Bloodletting regalia and caches are consistently found at Late Preclassic sites. Some early communities were also fortified, suggesting that ritual war for the taking of sacrificial victims was an important part of Maya life from a very early time. The trifurcated scrolls representing blood, which flow from the mouth of the Tlaloc image, are found on the great plaster masks of Late Preclassic Maya architecture. The symbolism and ritual of the Teotihuacanos' war imagery fell on fertile ground.

The Maya did more than just borrow the imagery and ritual: They adapted it to their needs. To the Maya the Tlaloc complex with its associated jaguar, bird, spearthrower, and mosaic headdress imagery (see Note 45) meant war and sacrifice above all things. The association of this war/sacrifice complex with planetary conjunctions may have been present at Teotihuacán, but we can never test for that since the Teotihuacanos did not record dates in their art. We do not know when their rituals occurred or if the murals at Teotihuacán even represent specific historical acts. For the Maya, however, the Tlaloc complex became associated with war and sacrifice timed by the apparitions of Venus and Jupiter.[76]

The prominence of Teotihuacán-style imagery in the tombs and on the stelae of Tikal lasted only through Stormy-Sky's reign. By A.D. 475, the rulers of Tikal abandoned this way of representing themselves and concentrated on other aspects of kingship. The intensive interaction between Tikal and Teotihuacán lasted for only a hundred years, shifting thereafter to the neutral ground at Kaminaljuyu.[77] Contact between the Teotihuacanos and the lowland Maya must have continued at least until the eighth century when Teotihuacán ceased to be a major intercultural power. The first flush of intense contact is what we have observed at Tikal and it brought prestige and wealth to both parties.

From the Teotihuacanos the Maya gained a sacrificial ritual and a new kind of warfare that would remain central to their religion at least until the ninth century. We know less about what Teotihuacán gained from the interchange. The end result, however, was the establishment of an international network of trade along which moved material goods and ideas. This interaction between the peoples of Mesoamerica resulted in a florescence of civilized life, a cultural brilliance and intensity that exceeded even the accomplishments of the Olmec, the first great civilization to arise in Mesoamerica.

5

STAR WARS
IN THE
SEVENTH
CENTURY

The kingdom of Tikal throve after the conquest of Uaxactún, fulfilling the promise of its victory by becoming the largest and most prosperous Early Classic kingdom in the Maya heartland. This prosperity can be seen in the astounding proliferation of temples and public art commissioned by the ahauob of ensuing generations. The descendants of the victorious king, Great-Jaguar-Paw, launched an ambitious building program that changed the face of the city and studded the terrace in front of the North Acropolis with a forest of tree-stones. These stelae tell us something about the changing emphasis of kingship in Tikal, for the kings who reigned after Great-Jaguar-Paw's grandson, Stormy-Sky, chose a different style of representing themselves, one that emphasized their humanity by simplifying the cluster of symbolism surrounding them.[1] In place of the old-style portraits that depicted them in full royal regalia, these rulers depicted themselves (Fig. 5:1a and b) holding simple decorated staffs in rituals celebrating period endings in the Maya calendar.[2] In this manner they removed the focus of history from the arena of personal and dynastic events, like birth, accession, and conquest, and placed it instead upon the rhythms of time and the great festival cycles by which these rhythms were celebrated.

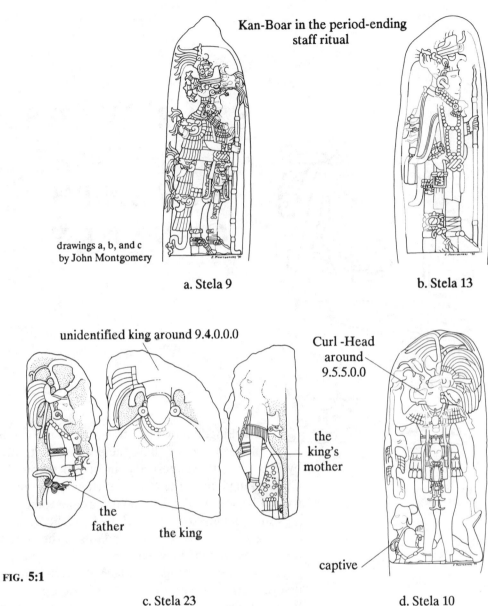

Kan-Boar in the period-ending
staff ritual

drawings a, b, and c
by John Montgomery

a. Stela 9

b. Stela 13

unidentified king around 9.4.0.0.0

Curl-Head
around
9.5.5.0.0

the
king's
mother

the
father

the king

captive

FIG. 5:1

c. Stela 23

d. Stela 10

After thirty years of depicting themselves in this style, the rulers of Tikal began experimenting again, encouraging their artisans to expand the frontiers of tradition into fresh and innovative areas. These artists created new styles by an imaginative combination of elements both old and new. Around 9.4.0.0.0 (A.D. 514), for example, the manner of depicting kings on stelae switched to a front view carved in a relief deep enough to model the king's face three-quarters in the round. Sculptors also experimented with formats that placed the king's parents on either side of the stela (Fig. 5:1c) in a modern echo of Stormy-Sky's masterpiece, Stela 31. Old themes, like the bound captive lying at the feet of the king (Fig. 5:1d), returned to stelae compositions. Eventually the styles for representing kings took their inspiration from even earlier times, creating the Maya version of the adage "Everything old is new again." In 557, the twenty-first successor, Double-Bird, commissioned a monument in a style that was popular during Tikal's first flush of conquest glory, depicting himself in shallow relief, standing profile to the viewer (Fig. 5:5). Double-Bird's monument, Stela 17, holds a unique place in the commemorative art of Tikal. It was the last monument erected before a 130-year period of silence fell upon the inscribed history of this great capital. The reason for this long silence was the conquest of the city by a new kingdom that had grown to maturity in the region to the southeast.

Piecing together the true story of Tikal's two centuries of cultural innovation is a difficult and painstaking task. Many of the existing stelae and art objects were deliberately effaced or smashed by the conquerors in the time following the erection of Stela 17. Even in such a shattered form, however, one can see the extraordinary beauty and power of Tikal's artistic accomplishments. Unfortunately, the written history that has come to us from this period is as poor and spotty as the visual one. Many of the texts that survived the destructive frenzy of Tikal's nemesis treat only of the period-ending celebrations that had become the focus of Tikal's ritual life. Although the records of the actors who entered and left the stage of history during this period are sketchy, they still provide at least a partial account of the kings who held Tikal's throne.[3] The kings we currently know from this period are as follows:

Date	Name	#	Monuments	Date
	Staff Stela			
9.2.0.0.0	Kan-Boar	12th	St. 9, 13	475
	Mah-Kina-Chan	13th	Pot, St. 8?	
9.2.13.0.0	Jaguar-Paw-Skull	14th	St. 7	488
9.3.0.0.0	"		St. 3,15,27	495
9.4.0.0.0	???	???	St. 6	514
	Frontal Style			
9.3.9.13.3	birth, Lady of Tikal	???	St. 23	504
9.3.16.18.4	accession, ??	???	St. 23	511
9.4.3.0.0	???	???	St. 25	517
9.4.13.0.0	Curl-Head	19th	St. 10, 12	527
9.5.0.0.0?	???		St. 14	534
	Profile Style			
9.5.3.9.15	Double-Bird	21st	St. 17	537

Maya date	A.D.	Tikal	Naranjo	Dos Pilas	Caracol	Calakmul
9.5.3.9.15	12/31/537	Double-Bird acts (accedes)				
9.5.12.0.4	5/7/546		Ruler I accedes			
9.5.19.1.2	4/18/553				Lord Water accedes	
9.6.2.1.11	4/11/556				ax-war against Tikal	
9.6.3.9.15	9/17/557	Double-Bird's last date				
9.6.8.4.2	5/1/562				star-war at Tikal	
9.9.4.16.2	3/9/618				Lord Kan II accedes	
9.9.5.13.8	1/9/619					lord acts at Naranjo
9.9.13.4.4	5/28/626				sacrifice of "he of Naranjo"	
9.9.14.3.5	5/4/627				ballgame and sacrifice	
9.9.17.11.14	10/4/630				death of Naranjo lord	
9.9.18.16.3	12/27/631				star war against Naranjo	
9.10.3.2.12	3/4/636				star war against Naranjo	
9.10.4.16.2	11/24/637				1 katun of rule, Lord Kan II	
9.10.10.0.0	12/6/642		victory stair dedicated by Caracol			
9.10.12.11.2	7/5/645			Flint-Sky-God K accedes		
9.10.16.16.19	10/9/649					Jaguar-Paw born
9.11.11.9.17	3/2/664			capture of Tah-Mo'		
9.12.9.17.16	5/6/682	Ah Cacaw accedes				
9.12.10.5.12	8/30/682		Lady Wak-Chanil-Ahau arrives from Dos Pilas			
9.12.13.17.7	4/6/686					Jaguar-Paw accedes
9.12.15.13.7	1/6/688		Smoking-Squirrel born			
9.13.0.0.0	3/18/692	katun ending and Stela 30 twin pyramid complex				
9.13.1.3.19	5/31/693		Smoking-Squirrel accedes			
9.13.1.4.19	6/20/693		Kinichil-Cab captured			
9.13.1.9.5	9/14/693		smoke-shell event			
9.13.1.13.14	12/12/693		smoke-shell event			
9.13.2.16.0	2/1/695		war against Ucanal			
9.13.3.7.18	8/8/695	Ah-Cacaw captures Jaguar-Paw of El Perú				Jaguar-Paw captured
9.13.3.8.11	8/21/695	sacrifice of captives				
9.13.3.9.18	9/17/695	dedication of Temple 33-1st with bloodletting rituals				
9.13.3.13.15	12/3/695	sacrificial (war?) ritual with Ox-Ha-Te of El Perú				
9.13.6.2.0	3/27/698			Shield-God K accedes		
9.13.6.4.17	5/23/698		smoke-shell event with Kinichil-Cab of Ucanal			
9.13.6.10.4	9/7/698		smoke-shell event with Shield-Jaguar of Ucanal			
9.13.7.3.8	4/19/699		sacrificial rite with Lady Wak-Chanil-Ahau			
9.13.10.0.0	1/26/702		Smoking-Squirrel dedicates stela and displays Shield-Jaguar in sacrificial rites			
9.13.18.4.16	3/23/710		Smoking-Squirrel attacks Yaxha			
9.13.18.9.15	6/28/710		sacrifice of Yaxha captive			
9.13.19.6.3	4/12/711		Smoking-Squirrel attacks Sacnab			
9.14.0.0.0	12/5/711	Stela 16 twin-pyramid complex	Venus and period-ending ceremonies			
9.14.0.10.0	6/18/711		summer solstice and Shield-Jaguar of Ucanal in sacrificial rite			

Time Sequence of the History of the Caracol-Tikal-Naranjo Wars

While we know little of the personal history of these rulers, they did leave their permanent mark upon the city in the form of the magnificent buildings raised under their patronage. Much of this construction took place in the sacred precincts of the North Acropolis. One of the most extraordinary projects commissioned there was the new version of Temple 5D-33–2nd (Fig. 5:2), a temple that covered the tomb of the great ruler Stormy-Sky.[4] During the ensuing centuries, this magnificent new temple served as the central stage front of the face of the North Acropolis, which looked out onto the Great Plaza to the south. It was an important symbol of kingship during the middle period of Tikal's history and the backdrop for all dynastic rituals conducted within the Great Plaza.

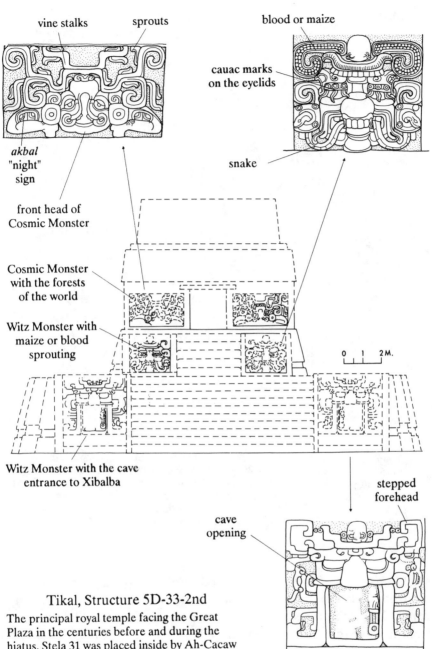

vine stalks sprouts

blood or maize

cauac marks
on the eyelids

akbal
"night"
sign

front head of
Cosmic Monster

snake

Cosmic Monster
with the forests
of the world

Witz Monster with
maize or blood
sprouting

0 1 2 M.

Witz Monster with the cave
entrance to Xibalba

stepped
forehead

cave
opening

Tikal, Structure 5D-33-2nd
The principal royal temple facing the Great
Plaza in the centuries before and during the
hiatus. Stela 31 was placed inside by Ah-Cacaw
before he built the new temple over it.

FIG. 5:2

In contrast to the novelty of the stelae of this era, Temple 5D-33–2nd
was a model of tradition. The great plaster masks that surmounted its
pyramid and its temple walls restated the symbolism of the Late Preclassic
period. This symbolic message was similar to the one we saw on Group
H at Uaxactún, a cosmology based upon the Sacred Mountains rather
than the arch of the sun and Venus.[5] The lowest masks on Temple 33–2nd
are Witz-Mountain Monsters, whose mouths have been rendered as caves
(Fig. 5:2). The middle masks represent more Witz Monsters. These have

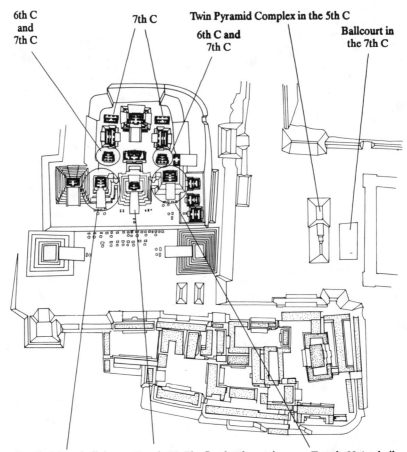

6th C
and
7th C

7th C

Twin Pyramid Complex in the 5th C

6th C and
7th C

Ballcourt in
the 7th C

FIG. 5:3
**Map of
Central Tikal**

**Temple 34-1st, built in
the 6th century to cover
Burial 10, probably
Curl-Snout's tomb**

**Temple 33. The first level contains
Burial 48, probably Stormy-Sky's
tomb. The second phase was the
principal ritual facade of the
North Acropolis during the 6th,
7th, and part of the 8th centuries**

**Temple 32-1st, built
in the 7th century to
cover Burial 195 and
the only known king
from the hiatus**

small, severed human heads and blood scrolls (or perhaps maize) emerging from their summits. The masks on the very top level of the temple
depict dragons in the shape of what is probably Venus, representing the
front head of the Cosmic Monster. Vines, representing the forests of the
world, sprout from the top of these open-mouthed heads.[6] As the king
performed his sacred rituals, this facade, like the great mask assemblages
of Preclassic Cerros, Tikal, and Uaxactún discussed in earlier chapters,
enveloped him in the ancient, orthodox, and transcendent cosmology of
the Maya people.

Temple 33–2nd was but one building in a rash of construction (Fig.
5:3) that continued into the sixth century. This renovation took place over
a period of seventy years under the direction of ten successive rulers, many
of whom sat the throne for only a short time.[7] The reason for the brief
length of their reigns is not known, but it is possible that what we see here
is the passing of the kingship from sibling to sibling at the death of a
brother.

Beginning around 9.4.0.0.0, these rulers reworked the summit of the North Acropolis into a pattern of eight buildings, a unique pattern that all future Tikal kings would honor and maintain. One of the most lasting innovations of this time, however, was the twin-pyramid complex, whose prototype was erected in the center of the East Plaza.[8] This new type of architecture, with its uncarved pillars and lack of focus on personal history, facilitated the celebration of period-ending rites, a practice that had been initiated at Tikal by Curl-Snout on Stela 18. His successors sustained that practice, developing what would henceforth be an architectural hallmark of this city and a principal focus of Tikal's festival cycle for the rest of its history.[9]

Suddenly, amid the exuberant brilliance of sixth-century life, the fortunes of Tikal's twenty-first king took a disastrous turn for the worse. He and his kingdom fell victim to a new and dangerous dynasty that had been on the rise throughout the fifth century in the forests to the southeast of Tikal. The bellicose rulers of this new kingdom, called Caracol by archaeologists, would take not only Tikal but the entire Petén region by storm, eventually controlling the politics of the Classic Maya heartland for more than a century.[10]

Caracol Goes on the Rampage

The portion of Caracol's dynastic history that survives in its inscriptions begins in A.D. 495; but the protagonist of our story, a king named Lord Water, did not accede to the throne until April 18, A.D. 553 (9.5.19.1.2). Lord Water recorded part of his personal history on Stelae 6 and 14; but until archaeologists discovered a new altar in recent excavations at Caracol, we had no idea what a deadly and pivotal role this ruler played in the drama at Tikal.

The impact of Lord Water upon the Maya world was of such proportions that even before the discovery and translation of the key texts, archaeologists and epigraphers had detected the presence of a cataclysmic pattern. The modern story of this history began in 1950 when the great Mayanist, Tatiana Proskouriakoff, published her seminal study of "style" in Maya sculpture.[11] Noting an absence of monuments between the years 9.5.0.0.0 (A.D. 534) and 9.8.0.0.0 (A.D. 593), she proposed that there must have been a hiatus[12] in Maya civilization during this time. She also noted that this hiatus corresponded to the change in ceramics styles, from the Early Classic period to the Late Classic. Another great Mayanist and a colleague of Proskouriakoff's, Gordon Willey,[13] also suggested that the Maya experienced a regional crisis at this time—a crisis so great it foreshadowed in scale and impact the great final collapse that would come in the ninth century.

Tatiana Proskouriakoff's second great contribution to Maya studies, the "historical hypothesis,"[14] contracted the time span of the hiatus somewhat. Up until the publication of this hypothesis in the 1960s, the prevailing view of the Classical Maya was that they were benign calendar priests,

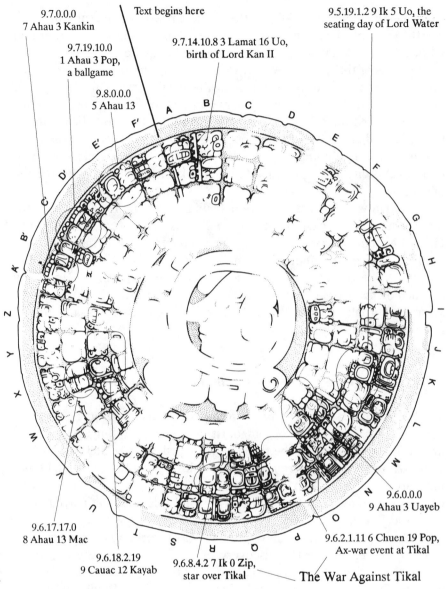

9.7.0.0.0
7 Ahau 3 Kankin

Text begins here

9.5.19.1.2 9 Ik 5 Uo, the
seating day of Lord Water

9.7.19.10.0
1 Ahau 3 Pop,
a ballgame

9.7.14.10.8 3 Lamat 16 Uo,
birth of Lord Kan II

9.8.0.0.0
5 Ahau 13

9.6.0.0.0
9 Ahau 3 Uayeb

9.6.17.17.0
8 Ahau 13 Mac

9.6.2.1.11 6 Chuen 19 Pop,
Ax-war event at Tikal

**FIG. 5:4
Caracol Altar 21**
drawing by
Stephen Houston

9.6.18.2.19
9 Cauac 12 Kayab

9.6.8.4.2 7 Ik 0 Zip,
star over Tikal

The War Against Tikal

peacefully recording endless cycles of time on stelae whose written texts would never ultimately be translated. Proskouriakoff proved beyond a shadow of a doubt that these texts not only could be read but were the history of kings and kingdoms. The retrospective histories made possible by her discovery filled in some of the gaps in time at various sites. Nevertheless, archaeologists working at Tikal still have found no stela to fill the gap between Stela 17 dated at 9.6.3.9.15 (September 17, 557) and Stela 30 dated at 9.13.0.0.0 (March 18, 692). Moreover, as we have pointed out earlier, stelae erected before this Tikal hiatus were deliberately effaced by abrading or shattering the stone.[15] Obviously, someone *intentionally* removed this history from the record. We suspect now that the culprit was

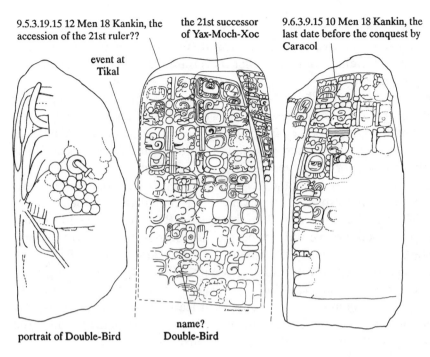

9.5.3.19.15 12 Men 18 Kankin, the accession of the 21st ruler??

the 21st successor of Yax-Moch-Xoc

9.6.3.9.15 10 Men 18 Kankin, the last date before the conquest by Caracol

event at Tikal

FIG. 5:5
Tikal Stela 17:
The Last King of Tikal
Before the Attack
by Caracol
center drawing by
John Montgomery

portrait of Double-Bird

name?
Double-Bird

none other than Lord Water, the rapacious king of Caracol, who opened a campaign of military conquest by attacking his huge neighbor Tikal.

The first clue to his role as Tikal's nemesis came in 1986 when archaeologists working at Caracol excavated a ballcourt.[16] On its central axis, they discovered a round marker (Fig. 5:4) with a long 128-glyph text circling its upper surface. The text on this "altar" begins with the birth of the king who commissioned the monument, Lord Kan II, and tells of the accession of his ancestor, Lord Water, on April 18, A.D. 553. From our point of view, however, the most important information on this marker is the text recording Lord Water's aggression against Tikal. This text tells us that on April 11, 556 (9.6.2.1.11), following the end of Katun 6, Caracol conducted an "ax-war" action "in the land of" the ahau of Tikal.[17]

We know, however, that this initial "ax war" wasn't fatal to Tikal. Shortly thereafter, on September 17, 557, the city's ruler, Double-Bird, raised his Stela 17 to commemorate a one-katun anniversary—perhaps of his own accession (Fig. 5:5). Those rituals, however, were the last re-corded in the public history of Tikal for a very long time. As the scribe of Altar 21 at Caracol exults, a "star-at-Tikal" war event, usually lethal to the loser, took place five years later, on May 1, 562 (9.6.8.4.2).[18] The tables had been turned. Caracol had mastered the same Tlaloc-Venus war that had defeated Uaxactún two centuries earlier. The long darkness at Tikal had begun.

The correspondence of Caracol's claim of victory to the all-out de-struction at Tikal shows us this claim was not a fabrication. Lord Water's war had indeed broken the back of Tikal's pride, independence, and prosperity. We are not sure, however, to what extent, or for how long, Caracol was able to maintain political dominance over its huge rival.

Present archaeology does offer us certain clues to Caracol's ubiquitous presence in the lives of Tikal's citizens. For example, Tikal's art and funerary practices exhibit influence from the region of Caracol[19] beginning with this period. We can also see, as we mentioned above, that Double-Bird and his dynasty ceased to erect stelae and other monuments, and that the building of temples and pyramids slowed down. We can speculate as to the reasons for this. Double-Bird had no doubt been captured and killed, his dynasty ended, and his remaining ahauob cut off from the vast trade routes that provided their wealth. We can vividly see the effects of this impoverishment in their burial practices. The well-stocked tombs of the Tikal nobility gave way to meager caricatures of their former glory, lacking both the quantity and quality of earlier grave goods. Tikal's oppressors permitted only one tomb of wealth—Burial 195, the resting place of the twenty-second successor of the Tikal dynasty. Never permitted to erect public monuments, this man was at least allowed the privilege of a rich burial and a dignified exit to the Otherworld, perhaps to offset the humiliation of being denied his place in history.

Lord Water enjoyed an unusually long and prosperous reign—prosperous for Caracol at least. After forty-six years as king, he died and left the throne to the eldest of two brothers, who were presumably his sons.[20] Born in 575, the older brother became king on June 26, 599, and reigned for nineteen uneventful years. The younger brother, however, was a king in the mold of his father. After acceding on March 9, 618, this young ruler took his father's name as his own and then set out to prove that the earlier victories of Lord Water had not been historical accidents. He launched a campaign that would eventually result in the defeat of Naranjo, a major kingdom located to the east of Tikal.

Lord Kan II recorded the history of his wars on Stela 3 in his own capital and on the Hieroglyphic Stairs erected in the capital of his defeated enemy, Naranjo. The earliest events of Kan II's reign still resist decipherment, but we do have allusions to a strategic alliance he formed soon after becoming king. On 9.9.5.13.8 (January 9, 619), we read that Lord Kan II performed an important but unidentified action in "the land of" an ahau of Calakmul (Fig. 5:6a), a huge kingdom lying to the north of Tikal within sight of the abandoned mountain-temples of El Mirador.[21] Whatever this action may have been, its declaration marked the beginning of an bond between Kan II and the kings of Calakmul that would prove fateful for both Tikal and Naranjo in the katuns to come. Through this alliance, and others like it, the king of Caracol would surround his intended victims with a ring of deadly enemies.

Calakmul was not new to the stage of Maya history. The city had monuments dating from the Early Classic period and was still going strong by the Late Classic. Calakmul was most probably the inheritor of El Mirador's power in the north and was a long term rival of Tikal.

The first major mention of a Calakmul king in the interkingdom politics of the times appears in the inscriptions of Yaxchilán, a city to the

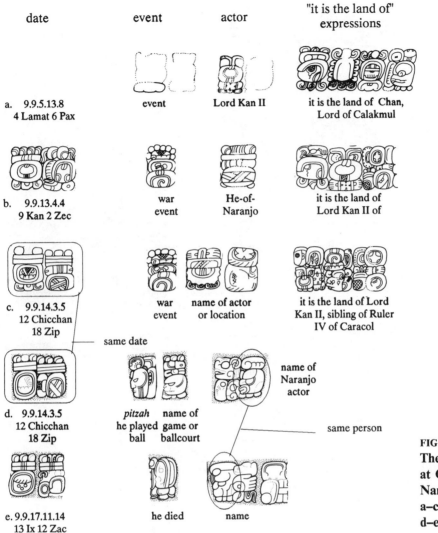

date	event	actor	"it is the land of" expressions
a. 9.9.5.13.8 4 Lamat 6 Pax	event	Lord Kan II	it is the land of Chan, Lord of Calakmul
b. 9.9.13.4.4 9 Kan 2 Zec	war event	He-of-Naranjo	it is the land of Lord Kan II of
c. 9.9.14.3.5 12 Chicchan 18 Zip	war event	name of actor or location	it is the land of Lord Kan II, sibling of Ruler IV of Caracol

same date

d. 9.9.14.3.5 12 Chicchan 18 Zip	*pitzah* he played ball	name of game or ballcourt	name of Naranjo actor

same person

e. 9.9.17.11.14 13 Ix 12 Zac	he died	name

FIG. 5:6
The War Sequence
at Caracol and
Naranjo
a–c: Caracol Stela 3;
d–e: Naranjo Stairs

west of Tikal. A passage found on Lintel 35 of the Early Classic Structure 12 records that a vassal lord of the king of Calakmul participated in a ritual at Yaxchilán on 9.5.2.10.6 (January 16, 537). The king of Calakmul is named with a Cauac-in-hand-Ix glyph, but we shall refer to him hereafter simply as "Cu-Ix."[22]

The name Cu-Ix also appears on Stela 25 at Naranjo, accompanied by the date 9.5.12.0.4 (May 7, 546). This was the most important date in the life of Naranjo's king, Ruler I, for he repeatedly celebrated anniversaries of it throughout his lifetime. We have presumed that the event was his accession, but whatever it was, the text on Stela 25 records that it took place *u cab* "in the territory" of Cu-Ix, the Ahau of Calakmul. This text suggests that the Calakmul king was important, if not instrumental, in the installation of Ruler I as the king of Naranjo. Certainly, these two references demonstrate the far-flung influence of the Calakmul king. They also suggests an envelopment strategy against Tikal involving Calakmul in the

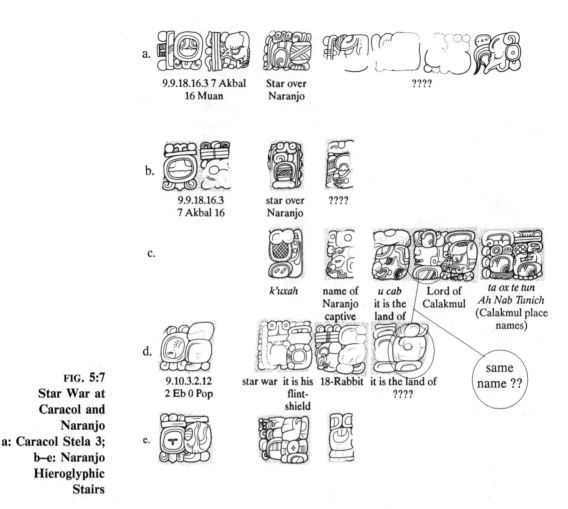

a.

9.9.18.16.3 7 Akbal
16 Muan

Star over
Naranjo

????

b.

9.9.18.16.3
7 Akbal 16

star over
Naranjo

????

c.

k'uxah

name of
Naranjo
captive

u cab
it is the
land of

Lord of
Calakmul

ta ox te tun
Ah Nab Tunich
(Calakmul place
names)

d.

9.10.3.2.12
2 Eb 0 Pop

star war
flint-
shield

it is his

18-Rabbit

it is the land of
????

same
name ??

e.

FIG. 5:7
Star War at
Caracol and
Naranjo
a: Caracol Stela 3;
b–e: Naranjo
Hieroglyphic
Stairs

north, Caracol in the south, Naranjo in the east, and, perhaps, Yaxchilán in the west.[23]

If Naranjo ever was allied with Calakmul, however, that alliance did not last long. We do not know what happened between Ruler I of Naranjo and his erstwhile ally at Calakmul; but we have evidence that in later years, the kings of Caracol felt free to skirmish with Naranjo without endangering their own alliance with Calakmul. Thus, on May 28, 626, Lord Water's second son, the rapacious Lord Kan II, launched a full-scale campaign against Naranjo. He began his military aggression by committing what we can only broadly interpret as an aggressive or sacrificial action against a lord designated in the text of Caracol Stela 3 simply as "he of Naranjo" (Fig. 5:6b). On that day, Venus was at its stationary point as Morningstar,[24] a position believed to be favorable for victory in battle.

On May 4, 627, one year after the initial battle, Lord Kan II staged his second confrontation with Naranjo. The result was again a war or sacrificial ritual, but this time events took place in his own city (Fig. 5:6c). This event was also commemorated on the stairway text at Naranjo, but here it was clearly referred to as a ballgame (Fig. 5:6d).[25] Although we do

Ruler I of Naranjo

FIG. 5:8
Painted Pot from
the Tomb in
Structure 5G-8
at Tikal

not know exactly what was meant by "ballgame" in this context, we do
know that the game was often used as a ritual for the disposition of
captives. The person recorded here as the "player" (read "captive") did
not die, however, for another three years. His name can be found next to
a glyph recording his death on October 4, 630 (Fig. 5:6e). We can't be sure,
but we think this person was Ruler I, the king who had been installed by
the Calakmul king in A.D. 546 (9.5.12.0.4). Since the inscription of
Naranjo Stela 27 describes Ruler I as "five-katun-ahau,"[26] we surmise that
he was over eighty years old when he died.

Whether Lord Kan II was recording Ruler I's death or that of some
other powerful noble in his account of these events, the end result was the
same. The death of this individual created a power imbalance at Naranjo
which invited the next stage of Caracol's war. In the following year, on
December 27, 631, when Venus as the Eveningstar first appeared in the
skies over Naranjo,[27] Lord Kan II attacked that kingdom and decisively
defeated its hapless warriors (Fig. 5:7a–b).

Why did Lord Kan II of Caracol choose Naranjo as his next target
after his victory over Tikal? Ironically, Ruler I of Naranjo may himself
have been responsible for this state of affairs. After Tikal was defeated and
its nobility stripped of their wealth and influence, the resulting power
vacuum may have tempted the king of Naranjo to betray his former allies.
He apparently reached out to Tikal in friendship and alliance, involving
himself somehow in the politics of that kingdom.

Behind all these gestures of friendship, however, might linger something even more intriguing: a love story. Sometime in the early seventh
century, nobles of Tikal mourned the death of a woman of high rank and
special status. This Tikal noblewoman was buried with extraordinary
pomp and honor. The Tikal ahauob cut her resting place into the living
rock, down under the central axis of Structure 5G-8 in the suburbs of their
benighted city. The masons then vaulted the chamber with stone in the
manner of the great ancestors of the North Acropolis, the only other
people of Tikal to have been honored with vaulted tombs. Their parting
gift to the spirit of this woman was a single beautiful polychrome bowl
with painted images of the Celestial Bird (Fig. 5:8). On its rim is a text
recording that its original owner was Ruler I of Naranjo. How it came to
Tikal we do not know, but its presence in the tomb of this woman suggests
she had some special association with Naranjo, either through marriage

STAR WARS
IN THE
SEVENTH
CENTURY

———

177

or through the exchange of gifts. The occasion symbolized by this bowl may have called down the wrath of Caracol on the aged king of Naranjo.

Neither of the accounts of this "star-war" event found at Caracol and Naranjo actually records the name of the king of Naranjo as a captive. This deletion does not prove, however, that the victim *was not* the king. We know for certain that *some* Naranjo notable was eventually sacrificed in a rather gruesome victory celebration which took place in the city of Caracol's ally, Calakmul. The Hieroglyphic Stairs the defeated Naranjanos were forced to build as a subjugation monument record that a nasty follow-up event spelled *k'uxah*[28] ("to torture" or perhaps "to eat") was perpetrated upon this individual "in the land of" the king of Calakmul (Fig. 5:7c). For the time being, Calakmul would benefit from its alliance with the top dog, Lord Kan II; but in the end, as we shall see, it would pay dearly for its role in this deadly game of war and sacrifice.

This victory seems to have temporarily sated the ambitions of Lord Kan II, for he neither attacked Naranjo nor took any more of its lords hostage for the next five years. Instead, he was content to watch and wait for Venus to once again reach an optimum battle position. On 9.10.3.2.12 (March 4, 636), such a favorable position occurred. When the Morningstar was fifteen days and .6° past its maximum elongation, he attacked Naranjo yet again. This time when he recorded his participation in the battle, he prominently featured his personal capture of a lord named 18-Rabbit (Fig. 5:7d). Ironically, 18-Rabbit gained his own kind of immortality by being the victim.

A little over a year later, on 9.10.4.16.2 (November 24, 637), Lord Kan II completed the final act in this long drama by celebrating the completion of his first katun of reign (Fig. 5:7e). Adding insult to injury, he recorded these rites not at his home city but at Naranjo on its subjugation monument, the Hieroglyphic Stairs. This ceremony must have rubbed a great deal of salt into the wound of Naranjo's defeat.

Caracol's rampage through the Petén changed the lives of noble individuals in many proud and ancient cities. Lord Kan II and his allies no doubt claimed many valuable goods from the losers as tribute. Defeated cities were forced to give up precious commodities like obsidian, shell currencies, heirlooms, craftsmen, handwoven cloth, and highly skilled artists. This tribute was the key to the domination Caracol held over this region. Because the Maya had no standing armies, conquering troops could not be garrisoned as watchdogs in a defeated city. But such policing was unnecessary. A city stripped of its wealth and its king could rarely strike back at its enemies. Loss of prestige resulted in far more than humiliation. It meant waning or destroyed political influence and the inability to recruit population and goods from the hinterlands. Without these people and goods, a city could not hope to prosper and grow.

Perhaps one of the most devastating results of defeat, however, was the stripping away of all public art. When Caracol effaced the monuments of its enemies and impoverished them to the point where they could erect no others, it was taking away their most cherished possession—history. Both Tikal and Naranjo suffered terribly in this sense. In the 130 years after the defeat of Tikal, only one king, the twenty-second, left his name in the inscribed history of the kingdom, and this not in a public space. We would not have known of him at all but for the pottery and wood texts deposited in his tomb, Burial 195, perhaps in defiance of Caracol's rule.

The lords of the allied city of Uaxactún also suffered in the wake of Caracol's victories, while no doubt appreciating the bitter irony of the situation. Tikal had been undone by the very same Tlaloc-Venus war that the brothers Great-Jaguar-Paw and Smoking-Frog had waged against Uaxactún 180 years earlier: The victors of that conflict were hoisted by the same petard of warfare they had introduced among the Maya. Yet rather than being able to celebrate the irony of the situation, the Uaxactún nobility, as part of Tikal's hegemony, found themselves deeply affected by this defeat as well. With the demise of the royal dynasty at Tikal, Uaxactún also lost the kingship, and the public ritual life of that city virtually stopped. Its leaders ceased erecting monuments in 9.6.0.0.0[29] and did not resume the practice for two hundred years.

At Naranjo, the impact of defeat was shorter-lived, but no less dramatic. On December 6, 642 (9.10.10.0.0), the victorious Caracol ruler forced the defeated people of Naranjo to dedicate the Hieroglyphic Stairs, a monument that glorified his triumph over them. This kind of stairway not only celebrated defeat and victory, but was used to dispose of captives, who were trussed into bundles and rolled down it after sacrifice in the ballgame. In their stairway, the surviving elite of Naranjo had a constant reminder of the hegemony of Caracol. That disgraceful monument was the last written record placed in public space for the next forty years.

As the katuns ground slowly by, new lords bent on revenge and on rebuilding the reputations of their cities lit sacred fires on the altars of the Petén to lighten the pall of disaster over Tikal and Naranjo. Unlike Smoking-Frog of Tikal, whose triumphs at Uaxactún inspired the admiration and imagination of an entire region, Lord Kan II and his Calakmul allies never succeeded in quelling the hatred and consolidating the submission of their enemies. In the short term, their failed experiment in empire building fired the ambitions of new challengers from the Petexbatún region to the south. These new lords from the kingdom of Dos Pilas would eventually pull Naranjo up from the ashes of defeat and jar Tikal into taking back its own. In wreaking vengeance against the former victors, however, the lords of Dos Pilas would seal the Maya doom even as they rejuvenated the dynasts of the defeated kingdoms. In the long run, the Maya struggle to forge a political unity powerful enough to match their shared vision of divine power would break on the pride of kings and their thirst for vengeance.

Dos Pilas Joins the Party

In an era of great kings who strove to stretch their power beyond traditional boundaries, the long and illustrious career of Flint-Sky-God K of Dos Pilas stands out as one of most remarkable of his times. His home

a. Dos Pilas Hieroglyphic Stair 2 East, Step 1

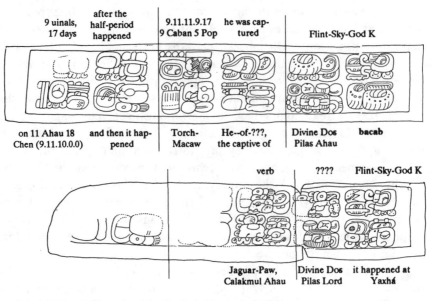

9 uinals, 17 days	after the half-period happened	9.11.11.9.17 9 Caban 5 Pop	he was captured	Flint-Sky-God K
on 11 Ahau 18 Chen (9.11.10.0.0)	and then it happened	Torch-Macaw	He--of-???, the captive of	Divine Dos Pilas Ahau	bacab

		verb	????	Flint-Sky-God K
		Jaguar-Paw, Calakmul Ahau	Divine Dos Pilas Lord	it happened at Yaxhá

b. Dos Pilas Hieroglyphic Stair 2 East, Step 3

c. Site Q, Glyphic Panel 6

9.10.16.16.19 3 Cauac 2 Ceh   he was born   Jaguar-Paw Calakmul Ahau

d. Site Q, Glyphic Panel 11

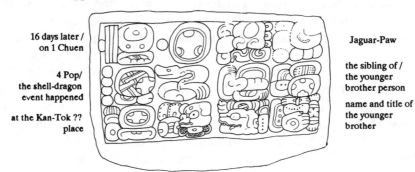

16 days later / on 1 Chuen

4 Pop/ the shell-dragon event happened

at the Kan-Tok ?? place

Jaguar-Paw

the sibling of / the younger brother person

name and title of the younger brother

FIG. 5:9 Jaguar-Paw at Dos Pilas and Site Q (Calakmul?)

was a hilltop city located near Lake Petexbatún and the Pasión River in a region that had played a significant role in Maya cultural history since the Middle Preclassic Period. Here, in the middle of the seventh century, Flint-Sky-God K declared a new kingdom, perhaps carrying with it the hopes of the house of Great-Jaguar-Paw of Tikal. This new kingdom, Dos Pilas, shared its Emblem Glyph with that ancient kingdom; and it is possible that its ruling family was an offshoot of the Tikal royal lineage—highborn individuals who left Tikal sometime after its downfall and found their way to this new region.[30]

Flint-Sky-God K was a master strategist in the game of politics and domination. He declared kingship at Dos Pilas on 9.10.12.11.2 (July 5, 645) and immediately began to consolidate his power with a series of marriage alliances with nearby kingdoms. He married a woman from the kingdom of Itzan, who bore him two sons. One son inherited both the kingship and his father's military brilliance. The other son is mentioned in the inscriptional record but never acceded to the throne.[31] Flint-Sky-God K also sent women of his own house, perhaps sisters or daughters, to marry rulers from nearby El Chorro and El Pato.[32]

At the same time, Flint-Sky-God K began a dynastic tradition of rule by conquest. He and his nobles terrified their enemies in a campaign spanning twenty years, from A.D. 664 to 684. He began his glorious saga with the capture of a lord named Tah-Mo' ("Torch-Macaw") on March 2, 664 (Fig. 5:9a). In a fashion typical of Maya warriors, Flint-Sky-God K recorded the personal names of his captives, but not the names of their kingdoms, so we do not know what city this hapless man was from. Flint-Sky-God K followed up this victory with a whole series of wars, including several of the Tlaloc-Venus variety. His ambition led him ultimately to intervene in the affairs of the central Petén kingdoms under Caracol's sway, but he did so in a cunning and circuitous way, as we shall later see.

The power he gained through his successful campaigns eventually brought Flint-Sky-God K to the attention of the powerful kingdom of Calakmul, the erstwhile ally of Caracol and the deadly enemy of Tikal and Naranjo. Part of the story of the contemporary Calakmul king, Jaguar-Paw, is told on a series of panels looted from the region of Calakmul, and part in passages from the Hieroglyphic Stairs at Dos Pilas. One of these looted panels lists Jaguar-Paw's birth date as October 9, 649 (Fig. 5:9c). Another tells us that around 9.11.10.0.0,[33] this young prince participated with Flint-Sky-God K in a ceremonial event at a place called Yaxhá (Fig. 5:9b), which was perhaps the lake region located near Naranjo. On February 25, 683, Jaguar-Paw returned to the Petexbatún region for another ritual celebration held on Lake Petexbatún near Dos Pilas[34] (Fig. 5:9d). We are not sure of the nature of these ceremonies, because that part of the text is missing, but they imply some kind of significant connection, perhaps an alliance, between Jaguar-Paw and the vigorous Dos Pilas warlord.

Whatever the relationship between the two men, it was an important one that led to the participation of Flint-Sky-God K in Jaguar-Paw's accession as king of Calakmul on April 6, 686 (Fig. 5:10a and b).[35] Jaguar-Paw's accession was also recorded at the kingdom of El Perú, to the north of Dos Pilas. We find this passage on a pair of looted stelae, recorded in association with the period-ending rites conducted by the El Perú king Mah-Kina-Balam and his wife. On one of the monuments, the El Perú lord noted that he had displayed the God K scepter in the company of Jaguar-Paw. These texts suggest that the kings of the western kingdoms traveled to Calakmul to participate in the accession ritual of Jaguar-Paw, who in turn made reciprocal visits to their kingdoms.

a. El Perú Stela 30, the accession of Jaguar-Paw

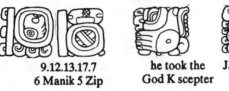

9.12.13.17.7	he took the	Jaguar-Paw	Divine
6 Manik 5 Zip	God K scepter		Calakmul
			Ahau

b. Dos Pilas Stela 13, the accession of Jaguar-Paw

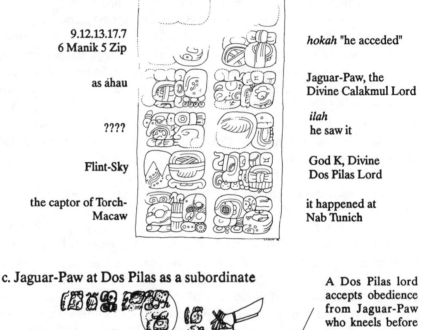

9.12.13.17.7
6 Manik 5 Zip

hokah "he acceded"

as áhau

Jaguar-Paw, the
Divine Calakmul Lord

????

ilah
he saw it

Flint-Sky

God K, Divine
Dos Pilas Lord

the captor of Torch-
Macaw

it happened at
Nab Tunich

c. Jaguar-Paw at Dos Pilas as a subordinate

A Dos Pilas lord
accepts obedience
from Jaguar-Paw
who kneels before
him

Jaguar-Paw of
Calakmul

drawing by Stephen Houston

FIG. 5:10
Jaguar-Paw
at El Perú and
Dos Pilas

At Dos Pilas, Flint-Sky-God K commemorated his participation in Jaguar-Paw's accession on his own Stela 13 (Fig. 5:10b), which he mounted on the platform supporting his great war monument, the Hieroglyphic Stairs 2. The juxtaposition of Jaguar-Paw's coronation text next to Flint-Sky-God K's war memorial associates the founding of Dos Pilas with the accession at Calakmul. By doing so, Flint-Sky-God K was paying Jaguar-Paw a powerful compliment.

This all-glyphic Stela 13 conveys first that Jaguar-Paw acceded on 9.12.13.17.7 (April 6, 686). Second, it says that this accession ritual "was seen (*yilah*)"[36] by Flint-Sky-God K, captor of Tah-Mo', at a place called Nab Tunich, the toponym designating a location somewhere within the kingdom of Calakmul.[37] Presumably, Flint-Sky-God K traveled to Nab Tunich to observe and to participate in the accession rites of Jaguar-Paw.

Regardless of the "friendliness" of this association, there is some evidence that Jaguar-Paw—perhaps before he became the king—was in a subservient position to Flint-Sky-God K, at least in some circumstances. In a scene on a looted pot,[38] Jaguar-Paw of Calakmul is painted kneeling in the position of subordination before a Dos Pilas Lord (Fig. 5:10c). We presume this Dos Pilas lord was Flint-Sky-God K or perhaps his heir.[39] The question that arises, however, is: How did a lord of Calakmul and ally of the powerful Caracol find himself in this position in the first place? Since the evidence does not exist to accurately answer that question, we can only suggest various scenarios. Perhaps Flint-Sky-God K was playing "godfather" to Jaguar-Paw, cultivating this young prince before he became the king to secure his support for the new Dos Pilas hegemony in the west. Or, in light of Flint-Sky-God K's military campaign in the Petén at this time, it is just possible that he wished to establish his own alliance with Calakmul—or at least the promise from its king that he would not interfere with the ambitions of Dos Pilas. At any rate, somehow Flint-Sky-God K made the Calakmul lords an offer they couldn't refuse.

Whatever the scenario might have been, by neutralizing the king of Calakmul, Flint-Sky-God K was able to extend his influence eastward toward the defeated city of Naranjo. It was a strategy that effectively removed Caracol as a major player in the events to come. Flint-Sky-God K's command of the primary political instruments of his time, war and marriage, forged the foundation of a new pattern of power in the Petén.

Part of Flint-Sky-God K's genius as a leader in this complex and interconnected arena of power politics was this very ability to implement different policies in different kingdoms as the situation warranted. While he was neutralizing Calakmul to the north, Flint-Sky-God K was also expanding eastward into the power vacuum left by the defeat of Tikal and Naranjo. Curiously enough, he concentrated his efforts on the lesser prize, Naranjo. This time he resorted to marriage, rather than war or political alliance, as his strategy. He sent a daughter[40] named Lady Wac-Chanil-Ahau ("Six Celestial Lord")[41] to Naranjo in order to reestablish a royal house at this ancient community after its destruction at the hands of Caracol. Although we do not know all the particulars, we can visualize her pilgrimage.

•

The journey to her new home was difficult and dangerous, for the route she had to take crossed the war-torn heart of the Petén region. In spite of the danger, the wedding party traveled in ceremonial splendor, braving the dangers hidden in the arching forest and the hot fields that lined the way to Naranjo. Lady Wac-Chanil-Ahau sat in her sedan chair

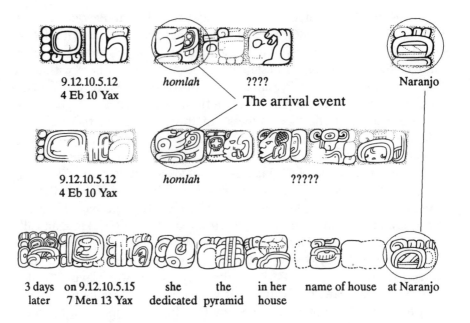

9.12.10.5.12   *homlah*   ????   Naranjo
4 Eb 10 Yax

The arrival event

9.12.10.5.12   *homlah*   ?????
4 Eb 10 Yax

3 days   on 9.12.10.5.15   she   the   in her   name of house   at Naranjo
later   7 Men 13 Yax   dedicated   pyramid   house

of dark polished wood upon royal pillows of stuffed jaguar skin, veiled from the prying eyes of village spies by a canopy of fine cotton gossamer. A company of sturdy bearers surrounded the four sweating men who carried the long poles of the sedan chair on their shoulders, ready to relieve them in the work of relaying their precious burden to its final destination. Behind came more bearers with bundles of cotton and bark cloth laden with gifts of jade, painted pottery, embroidered textiles, perfumed wooden boxes, and carved-shell diadems.

At the head of this party, the bravest and most experienced of the noble warriors of Dos Pilas strode in full battle gear, resplendent and frightening in their helmets of stuffed deer, peccary, and jaguar. The bright plumage of forest birds and the shrunken heads of defeated enemies dangled from their chests and waists. They carried throwing darts and spearthrowers, stabbing spears tipped with long leaf-shaped points of stone, and clubs studded with razor-sharp imported obsidian blades. Takers of captives and sacrificers, these men would not negotiate if confronted on the trail: They would die to the last man before letting their lady fall into the hands of the enemy. Finally, the best woodsmen of the Dos Pilas household were deployed in a wide circle around the route, moving swiftly and cautiously, alert for treachery.

•

We can imagine the courage and resolution of the Dos Pilas princess, a living declaration of war against the most powerful enemies of her family, as she traveled to her new home. The first sacred rituals she performed after her arrival lasted three days, beginning on August 30, 682 (9.12.10.5.12), in the time of the beneficent rains of late summer. One hundred and sixteen days earlier, Ah-Cacaw had resurrected the kingship at Tikal. Four years would pass before her father's journey to Calakmul

Lady   Chanil-   Divine Dos
Wac   Ahau   Pilas Ahau

a. Naranjo Stela 24, the arrival event

Lady   Chanil-   Divine Dos
Wac   Ahau   Pilas Ahau

b. Naranjo Stela 29, the arrival event

Lady   Chanil-   Divine Dos
Wac   Ahau   Pilas Ahau

c. Naranjo Stela 29, the house event

FIG. 5:11
Lady Wac-
Chanil-Ahau's
Actions upon
Her Arrival
at Naranjo

to participate in Jaguar-Paw's accession rituals. In this time of changing destinies, a young queen stood at the center of the Maya world. High on her pyramid she spilled her blood in rapture, calling forth the ancestors to witness and confirm the new destiny she brought to this place, while the gathered hosts of the city danced and sang in the broad plazas below, jeering the authors of the hated Hieroglyphic Stairs in their midst. The red towering temple mountains of Naranjo reverberated with the pulsing call of the drums and the deep moan of the shell trumpets reaching friend and foe alike across the vast green canopy of the forest: The royal ahauob of Naranjo were back. The lady from Dos Pilas and her new nobility would reckon their history from this joyous celebration for katuns to come; and under the leadership of her son, Smoking-Squirrel, they would bring back enemies to writhe and die before the monuments commemorating that fateful day.

There are four separate texts recording the events surrounding Wac-Chanil-Ahau's arrival in Naranjo, but only two of them are still legible today. In both of these texts (Fig. 5:11a–b), the glyph describing her ritual actions resembles the hand (*hom*) glyph[42] that Stormy-Sky used to record the conquest of Uaxactún on Stela 31 at Tikal. Here, however, conquest in the sense of "the destruction of buildings" couldn't possibly be the intended meaning. The action recorded on these stelae is one that led to the dedication of a pyramid three days later (Fig. 5:11c) and most likely the reestablishment of the royal house of Naranjo. As we have described in our historical reconstruction above, we believe both these events were direct results of the marriage of the daughter of the king of Dos Pilas to a noble of Naranjo. One meaning of *hom* is "borders or boundaries" and certainly these are essential qualities of a viable state. When Lady Wac-Chanil-Ahau dedicated the pyramid three days after her marriage, she was reopening the portal to the Otherworld, reestablishing the sacred connection to the ancestors, which had been broken by Naranjo's enemies so

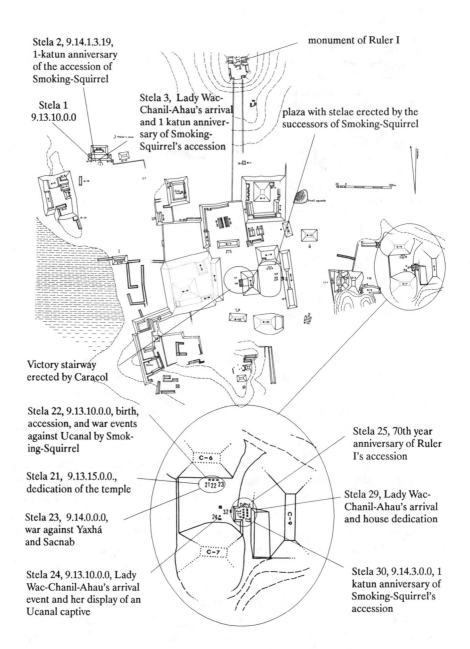

Stela 2, 9.14.1.3.19, 1-katun anniversary of the accession of Smoking-Squirrel

Stela 1 9.13.10.0.0

Stela 3, Lady Wac-Chanil-Ahau's arrival and 1 katun anniversary of Smoking-Squirrel's accession

monument of Ruler I

plaza with stelae erected by the successors of Smoking-Squirrel

Victory stairway erected by Caracol

Stela 22, 9.13.10.0.0, birth, accession, and war events against Ucanal by Smoking-Squirrel

Stela 21, 9.13.15.0.0., dedication of the temple

Stela 23, 9.14.0.0.0, war against Yaxhá and Sacnab

Stela 25, 70th year anniversary of Ruler I's accession

Stela 29, Lady Wac-Chanil-Ahau's arrival and house dedication

Stela 24, 9.13.10.0.0, Lady Wac-Chanil-Ahau's arrival event and her display of an Ucanal captive

Stela 30, 9.14.3.0.0, 1 katun anniversary of Smoking-Squirrel's accession

many years ago. This interpretation of events is further borne out by the fact that the pyramid used the Naranjo Emblem Glyph as part of its proper name, indicating that it was the Otherworld portal of this new dynasty. Naranjo had again become a place of kings, a power to be reckoned with once more.

Naranjo Strikes Back

Wac-Chanil-Ahau's efforts to found a new dynasty were not in vain. On January 6, 688, five years after the dedication of the Naranjo royal house, a male heir, named Smoking-Squirrel, was born to the royal family. This

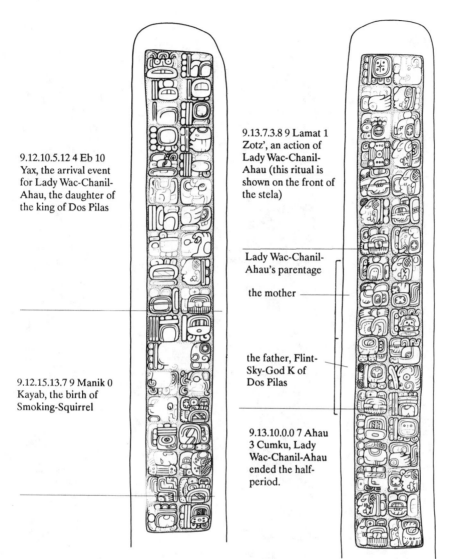

9.12.10.5.12 4 Eb 10 Yax, the arrival event for Lady Wac-Chanil-Ahau, the daughter of the king of Dos Pilas

9.13.7.3.8 9 Lamat 1 Zotz', an action of Lady Wac-Chanil-Ahau (this ritual is shown on the front of the stela)

Lady Wac-Chanil-Ahau's parentage

the mother

the father, Flint-Sky-God K of Dos Pilas

9.12.15.13.7 9 Manik 0 Kayab, the birth of Smoking-Squirrel

9.13.10.0.0 7 Ahau 3 Cumku, Lady Wac-Chanil-Ahau ended the half-period.

Naranjo, Stela 24, the text

FIG. 5:13 Lady Wac-Chanil-Ahau's Actions and Parentage

youngster was only five years old when, on May 31, 693, he became the king of Naranjo.[43] Never in all the historical texts of Naranjo do the scribes acknowledge the parentage of Smoking-Squirrel, so for many years his origins remained a mystery. It took the insight of the great Mayanist Tatiana Proskouriakoff to realize that Smoking-Squirrel was most likely the child of Lady Wac-Chanil-Ahau.

There are many clues leading to this assumption. Not only does Wac-Chanil-Ahau live long into Smoking-Squirrel's reign, but every time he erected a monument to celebrate the anniversary of his accession, he paired it with a monument dedicated to this woman. These monuments always featured the date of Lady Wac-Chanil-Ahau's arrival at Naranjo and depicted her engaging in the exact same rituals of state as her son (Fig. 5:12).[44] Smoking-Squirrel constantly portrayed himself with his mother in

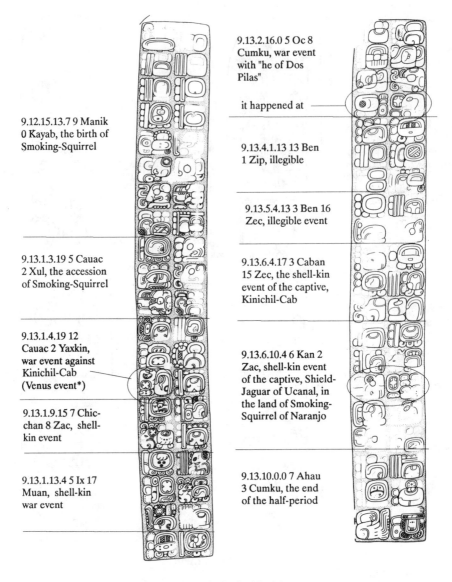

9.13.2.16.0 5 Oc 8
Cumku, war event
with "he of Dos
Pilas"

it happened at —

9.12.15.13.7 9 Manik
0 Kayab, the birth of
Smoking-Squirrel

9.13.4.1.13 13 Ben
1 Zip, illegible

9.13.5.4.13 3 Ben 16
Zec, illegible event

9.13.1.3.19 5 Cauac
2 Xul, the accession
of Smoking-Squirrel

9.13.6.4.17 3 Caban
15 Zec, the shell-kin
event of the captive,
Kinichil-Cab

9.13.1.4.19 12
Cauac 2 Yaxkin,
war event against
Kinichil-Cab
(Venus event*)

9.13.6.10.4 6 Kan 2
Zac, shell-kin event
of the captive, Shield-
Jaguar of Ucanal, in
the land of Smoking-
Squirrel of Naranjo

9.13.1.9.15 7 Chic-
chan 8 Zac, shell-
kin event

9.13.1.13.4 5 Ix 17
Muan, shell-kin
war event

9.13.10.0.0 7 Ahau
3 Cumku, the end
of the half-period

FIG. 5:14
The War Events
of Smoking-
Squirrel's Early
Years

Naranjo Stela 22, the text

this fashion for one very important reason: She was the source of his legitimacy and his link to the throne.

Smoking-Squirrel did not, however, find it to his advantage to feature his father on any of his monuments. His male parent was probably a local man whose modest achievements and social rank did not lend prestige to his son. Instead, Smoking-Squirrel capitalized on the celebrity that came from his mother's pedigree as the child of the illustrious Flint-Sky-God K of Dos Pilas (Fig. 5:13), his maternal grandfather. The texts suggest that this pedigree from Dos Pilas was considered more historically important and politically significant than even his own status as son to Lady Wac-Chanil-Ahau.

The revival of the dynasty and the ascendancy of this child to the ancestral throne of his kingdom smashed the fragile peace of the central Petén. The revived Naranjo nobility launched a campaign to reestablish the power of their royal family, challenging their enemies to meet them on the battlefield. There under a relentless tropical sun, fortune delivered many sons of noble families into their hands.

Naranjo's first victim was not its enemy Caracol, but rather a strategic border community called Ucanal which stood between Naranjo, Tikal, and the city of Lord Kan II. The kingdom of Ucanal had a hilltop capital to the south of Lake Yaxhá[45] on the west bank of the Mopán River. Probably an ally of Caracol, since it straddled the shortest route Lord Kan's marauders could take on their forays into the Petén, Ucanal was targeted perhaps as much to humiliate the kings of Caracol as to gain military victories for Naranjo.

The campaign began on June 20, 693, only twenty days after the five-year-old boy was placed on the throne. It was the day before the summer solstice, and the Eveningstar was gleaming its last before it would disappear into the glare of the sun on its journey to become the Morningstar. The warriors of Naranjo struck, taking captive a lord of Ucanal named Kinichil-Cab (Fig. 5:14). Doubtless the young king, Smoking-Squirrel, was still too tender in age to have led his army personally. Instead, it appears that Lady Wac-Chanil-Ahau took credit for the capture of the unfortunate Kinichil-Cab, for on Stela 24, she stands upon his battered body (Fig. 5:15b).

This battle and the capture of a lord of Ucanal were but the opening blows against Caracol's hold on the Petén. Naranjo continued to chip away at its enemy's strength, harassing them at every turn. One hundred days after the first attack, on September 14, 693, the warriors of Naranjo engaged Ucanal in yet another battle, this one probably on the order of a skirmish. They attacked again on December 12 of the same year. This military campaign culminated on February 1, 695, when Naranjo once again engaged the main forces of Ucanal in bloody combat, this time with a lord of Dos Pilas in attendance to participate in the victory. The major prize taken in this second full-scale battle of the war was the lord Shield-Jaguar, the unfortunate captive who is featured in the grim rites recorded on both Stela 22 (Fig. 5:15a) and Stela 2 (Fig. 5:17).[46]

Now the star of war glinted brightly for Naranjo. Smoking-Squirrel, like his earlier counterpart at Caracol, timed his battles and war-related rituals according to the position of Venus. He declared his kingship as Venus hovered on the stationary point before inferior conjunction. His first war event occurred at the helical setting of Eveningstar on the eve of the summer solstice. Finally, his second triumphant battle against Ucanal was waged when Venus rose helically as the Morningstar, exactly one cycle later.

As we have mentioned before, prestigious captives taken in battle were often kept alive for years on end. They were displayed in public rituals and often participated in these rituals in gruesome, humiliating, and painful ways. Smoking-Squirrel and Wac-Chanil-Ahau were enthusi-

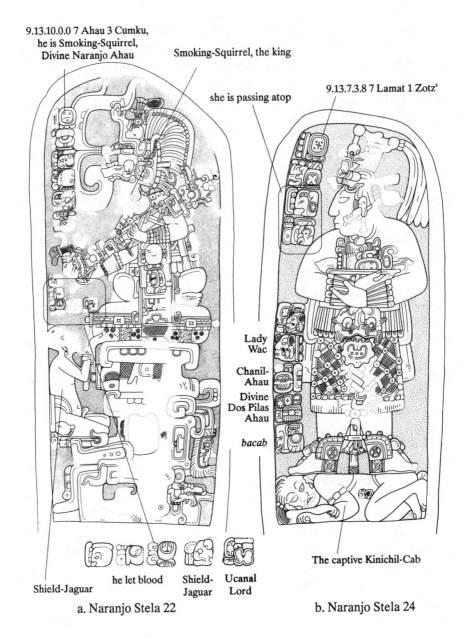

9.13.10.0.0 7 Ahau 3 Cumku,
he is Smoking-Squirrel,
Divine Naranjo Ahau

Smoking-Squirrel, the king

she is passing atop

9.13.7.3.8 7 Lamat 1 Zotz'

Lady
Wac

Chanil-
Ahau

Divine
Dos Pilas
Ahau

bacab

The captive Kinichil-Cab

Shield-Jaguar

he let blood

Shield-
Jaguar

Ucanal
Lord

a. Naranjo Stela 22

b. Naranjo Stela 24

**FIG. 5:15
Smoking-
Squirrel and
Lady Wac-
Chanil-Ahau**

astic practitioners of this sacred tradition. Kinichil-Cab of Ucanal survived his capture to reappear four years later, on May 23, 698, in an event
that was in all probability a sacrificial ritual of some sort (Fig. 5:14). Later
in the same year, on September 23, Shield-Jaguar suffered through the
same rite in "the land of Smoking-Squirrel of Naranjo." A year later, on
April 19, 699, it was Lady Wac-Chanil's turn. The hapless Kinichil-Cab
appeared again in a public ritual she conducted. On Naranjo Stela 24 (Fig.
5:15b) we see her standing on the bound, nearly naked body of this
unfortunate warrior. Finally, on 9.13.10.0.0 (January 26, 702), the day
Smoking-Squirrel dedicated both Stela 22 and Stela 24, the young king
displayed his famous captive, Shield-Jaguar of Ucanal, in a public blood-

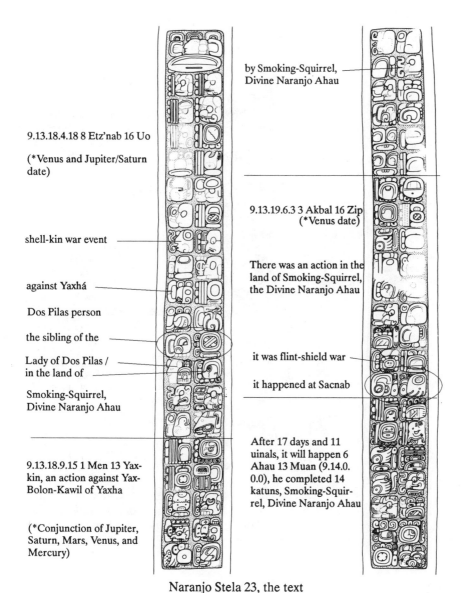

9.13.18.4.18 8 Etz'nab 16 Uo

(*Venus and Jupiter/Saturn date)

shell-kin war event

against Yaxhá

Dos Pilas person

the sibling of the

Lady of Dos Pilas / in the land of

Smoking-Squirrel, Divine Naranjo Ahau

9.13.18.9.15 1 Men 13 Yax-kin, an action against Yax-Bolon-Kawil of Yaxha

(*Conjunction of Jupiter, Saturn, Mars, Venus, and Mercury)

by Smoking-Squirrel, Divine Naranjo Ahau

9.13.19.6.3 3 Akbal 16 Zip
(*Venus date)

There was an action in the land of Smoking-Squirrel, the Divine Naranjo Ahau

it was flint-shield war

it happened at Sacnab

After 17 days and 11 uinals, it will happen 6 Ahau 13 Muan (9.14.0.0.0), he completed 14 katuns, Smoking-Squir-rel, Divine Naranjo Ahau

Naranjo Stela 23, the text

FIG. 5:16
The War Actions Against the Communities on Lake Yaxhá and Sacnab

letting ritual (Fig. 5:15a). As depicted, the ill-fated captive is nearly naked, stripped of all his marks of rank and prestige, holding his bound wrists up toward the magnificently dressed fourteen-year-old king who sits high above him on a jaguar-pillow.

In spite of his achievements, this energetic young king was still far from the fulfillment of his military ambitions. When Katun 14 was nearing its end, he began yet another series of battles, which he later recorded on Stela 23 (Fig. 5:16). This time his target was a nearer kingdom, Yaxhá, located to the south on the shores of a lake bearing the same name. It was perhaps there that his grandfather, Flint-Sky-God K, and Jaguar-Paw of Calakmul had acted together in a ritual years before. On March 23, 710, just after the spring equinox, Smoking-Squirrel attacked Yaxhá, accompa-

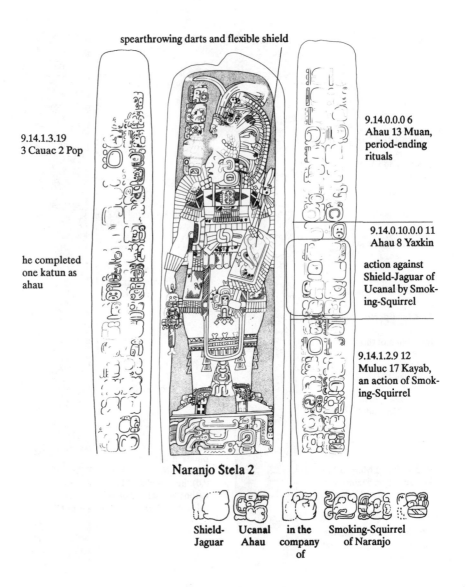

spearthrowing darts and flexible shield

9.14.1.3.19
3 Cauac 2 Pop

he completed
one katun as
ahau

9.14.0.0.0 6
Ahau 13 Muan,
period-ending
rituals

9.14.0.10.0.0 11
Ahau 8 Yaxkin

action against
Shield-Jaguar of
Ucanal by Smok-
ing-Squirrel

9.14.1.2.9 12
Muluc 17 Kayab,
an action of Smok-
ing-Squirrel

Naranjo Stela 2

Shield-
Jaguar

Ucanal
Ahau

in the
company
of

Smoking-Squirrel
of Naranjo

nied by an individual who was the sibling of either his mother or his wife.[47] On this day, Venus was making its last appearance as Morningstar and Jupiter and Saturn hung in conjunction at their second stationary points.[48] Ninety-seven days later, on June 8, shortly after the summer solstice, there was an even more spectacular alignment in the heavens, this time among Jupiter, Saturn, Mars, Venus, and Mercury.[49] On this occasion Smoking-Squirrel conducted a ritual with a prisoner from Yaxhá. We have not yet deciphered the glyphs describing this ritual, but at least part of it included the scattering of blood. A year after this rite, on April 12, 711, when Venus again appeared as Morningstar, Smoking-Squirrel went to war once more, this time on the shore of a lake adjacent to Yaxhá, a place known as *Sacnab,* or "Clear Lake."[50]

Stela 23's history ends with the battle at Sacnab, but we can pick the story up again on Stela 2 (Fig. 5:17). There Smoking-Squirrel begins his account with the celebration of the period ending on 9.14.0.0.0 at the first

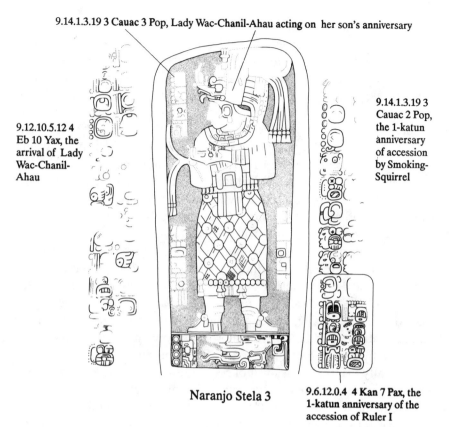

9.14.1.3.19 3 Cauac 3 Pop, Lady Wac-Chanil-Ahau acting on her son's anniversary

9.12.10.5.12 4 Eb 10 Yax, the arrival of Lady Wac-Chanil-Ahau

9.14.1.3.19 3 Cauac 2 Pop, the 1-katun anniversary of accession by Smoking-Squirrel

Naranjo Stela 3

9.6.12.0.4 4 Kan 7 Pax, the 1-katun anniversary of the accession of Ruler I

FIG. 5:18
Lady Wac-Chanil-Ahau at Her Son's First Anniversary of Rule

appearance of Venus as Eveningstar. This heavenly event was celebrated not only at Naranjo but at Copán and Tikal as well, showing how widespread these Venus rituals had become in the Maya world.[51] Two hundred days later, on the summer solstice (June 22, 712), Shield-Jaguar of Ucanal reappears in a rite which is enacted on the occasion of the maximum elongation of Eveningstar. Eighteen years of public humiliation had passed since his capture. We suspect this long-suffering prisoner did not survive this ritual, for with this date he disappears from the record.

Smoking-Squirrel's rampage through the central Petén finally ended, to the relief of neighboring kingdoms, on February 16, 713, with the first katun anniversary of his accession. As he had since the beginning of his reign, Smoking-Squirrel paired the stela commemorating this event with a stela depicting his mother, the founder of his line. Stela 2, which is essentially a war monument, stood adjacent (Fig. 5:12) to Lady Wac-Chanil-Ahau's Stela 3 (Fig. 5:18), which shows her participating in her son's anniversary celebration. In this text, Smoking-Squirrel once again memorialized her arrival. He also created some useful political propaganda by linking the date of the first katun anniversary of his own accession to the same anniversary date of Naranjo's Ruler I. Ruler I was, of course, the king who had fallen victim to Caracol's victory eighty-one years earlier. With this pair of inscriptions, Smoking-Squirrel completed the circle of defeat and triumph for Naranjo. The glory of that city had been revived by a new and vital dynasty.

Smoking-Squirrel's fame as a warrior was no doubt legend in the region of the Petén. His successful military campaigns upset the destinies of cities as dramatically as the past victories of his hated enemy, Caracol; and his postconquest strategies were cleverly designed to keep his enemies powerless. For example, by keeping his high-ranked captives, Shield-Jaguar and Kinichil-Cab of Ucanal, alive for many years, Smoking-Squirrel most likely disrupted the succession within both their families and their kingdom. This elegant strategy created chaos in a social structure where these individuals could not be replaced until after they were dead. To display these captives in public rituals over many years confirmed the military prowess and the political power of the young king among his own constituency, and sowed fear and respect among Naranjo's rivals. Smoking-Squirrel also made optimum use of the powerful allies that came to him through his mother's line. He fought his wars with the support of his formidable and aggressive grandfather, Flint-Sky-God K, and most probably Shield-God K, his mother's half brother, who became ruler of Dos Pilas on 9.13.6.2.0 (March 27, 698). These battles secured the region surrounding Lake Yaxhá, making the journey between Naranjo and the Petexbatún stronghold held by his mother's people both easier and safer.

The campaign of battles waged by Smoking-Squirrel and his people was not totally inspired by a spirit of revenge and conquest, however. This campaign was also imbued with a spiritual content, chartered by the now venerable mandates of Venus-Tlaloc warfare. Smoking-Squirrel planned his military actions according to the movements of Venus, calling upon the power of that god of conquest to sanction his aggression. The costume he wears on Stela 2, in fact (Fig. 5:17), is the Late Classic version of the same war costume we saw Smoking-Frog and Curl-Snout of Tikal wear in their first Venus war victories. Timing his attacks by Venus also gave Smoking-Squirrel the opportunity to re-create the same cosmic setting as that in which his own predecessor, Ruler I, had suffered ignominious defeat. Thus, Smoking-Squirrel's successes worked to neutralize his ancestor's defeat, proving that the god once again favored Naranjo and accepted the restoration of the dynasty.

There can be little doubt that Smoking-Squirrel's ultimate goal had always been to redeem his city from its disastrous defeat at the hands of Caracol. He accomplished this by systematically crushing Caracol's allies, and bringing a resounding finish to Caracol as a force to be reckoned with in the Petén. Once he was certain that he had reestablished the flow of history in Naranjo's favor, Smoking-Squirrel finally dismantled the hated stairs the victorious Caracol warlords had erected in his capital. Resetting it in illegible order, he created a nonsense chronicle, a fitting end for a monument erected by his enemies to rob his people of their own place in history.

One of his most telling acts of revenge was to have one of the stairs' glyph blocks transported to Ucanal. There he placed it in the center alley of the ballcourt,[52] probably in conjunction with some very unpleasant sacrificial rituals involving the defeated lords of that kingdom. The fine irony of this ceremony was surely not lost on the king of Caracol, who was forced to sit passively and watch from afar the neutralization of the monument with which his ancestor had humiliated Naranjo. What more elegant revenge could Smoking-Squirrel have conceived of than the transfer of this block to the city of Caracol's own ally?

The Giant Stirs

Almost simultaneous with Naranjo's reemergence as a power in the Petén, Tikal began to reach out and regain its position in the Maya world. The strategy used by its new king exactly paralleled Smoking-Squirrel's: a successful war waged against the alliance that had once defeated his ancestors.

It's puzzling that the two principal victims of Caracol's military rampage, Tikal and Naranjo, make little mention of each other's efforts to throw off the bonds of their mutual enemy. The reason for this rather deliberate silence is not certain. Perhaps the meddling of Flint-Sky-God K of Dos Pilas in Naranjo's affairs sowed distrust between cities that should have been logical allies. In any event, we are not yet certain if the timing of Tikal's revival was connected in any way to Naranjo's; nor do we know to what extent these cities' struggles to recoup themselves might have been mutually reinforcing.

We do know that Tikal's liberation may have begun somewhat earlier than Naranjo's. Although no stelae dated between the years A.D. 557 and 692 survived at Tikal, we know that a ruler named Shield-Skull began an ambitious remodeling project in the North Acropolis and East Plaza during the middle of the seventh century.[53] Even as the dynasty of Great-Jaguar-Paw was plotting its revenge, its kings had already begun the healing process by rebuilding the center of their city. By this act they began wiping out the evidence of Lord Water's depredations and reaffirming their own cosmic greatness. The mere fact that they got away with this new, architectural program is telling evidence of Caracol's weakening grip on the Petén in the waning decades of the seventh century.

On 9.12.9.17.16 (May 6, 682), just as Flint-Sky-God K was preparing to send his daughter Lady Wac-Chanil-Ahau to Naranjo, a new vigorous ruler, named Ah-Cacaw,[54] ascended to the throne of Tikal and began a campaign to restore the honor of its ruling family. A large man for his times, Ah-Cacaw would live into his fourth katun, and be over sixty years old when he died. At 167 cm (5 feet 5 inches), he was a veritable giant,[55] standing ten centimeters above the average height of the men of his kingdom.

No sooner had he claimed the throne than Ah-Cacaw began a tremendous new building program, rallying the pride and ingenuity of the entire metropolis with his enormous demands for both skilled and unskilled labor. He mobilized clans of masons, architects, painters, and sculptors and put them to work reshaping the most important ritual space in the city: the North Acropolis and the Great Plaza to the south of it. Embodying five hundred years of royal ritual and history, the North

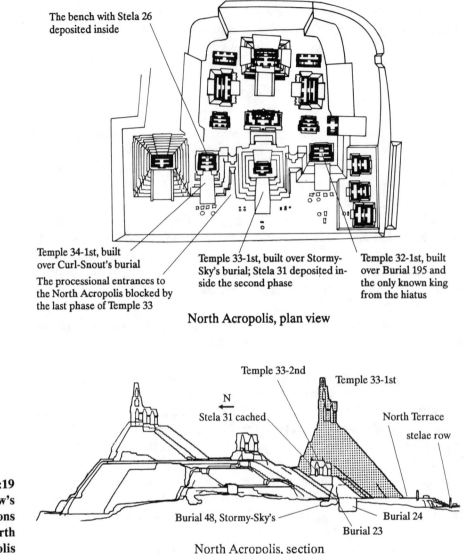

The bench with Stela 26 deposited inside

Temple 34-1st, built over Curl-Snout's burial

The processional entrances to the North Acropolis blocked by the last phase of Temple 33

Temple 33-1st, built over Stormy-Sky's burial; Stela 31 deposited inside the second phase

Temple 32-1st, built over Burial 195 and the only known king from the hiatus

North Acropolis, plan view

Temple 33-2nd

Temple 33-1st

N

Stela 31 cached

North Terrace

stelae row

FIG. 5:19 Ah-Cacaw's Renovations to the North Acropolis

Burial 48, Stormy-Sky's

Burial 24

Burial 23

North Acropolis, section

plan drawing by Kathryn Reese

Acropolis and the Great Plaza were not merely the heart of the city, they were the enduring expression of the ruling house of Tikal. Significantly, these monuments also bore the marks of the ignominious desecration placed upon them by Tikal's conquerors. Ah-Cacaw's visionary plan was not only to reclaim these monuments, but to surround them with the largest buildings ever known in the Maya world, a group of temples that would ring the Great Plaza, the ceremonial center of his revived kingdom.

The first step in Ah-Cacaw's plan was to deactivate the ritual spaces of the North Acropolis by cutting them off visually and physically from the Great Plaza. He then shifted the focus of dynastic celebration into the Great Plaza itself. To do this, he reworked the south side and ceremonial front of the North Acropolis. When he began this work, the south side of the Acropolis already held some of the finest pyramids ever built in the

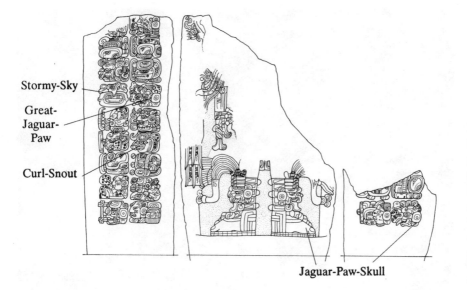

Stormy-Sky

Great-
Jaguar-
Paw

Curl-Snout

Jaguar-Paw-Skull

FIG. 5:20
Stela 26, the
pre-conquest
monument
broken by the
conquerors.
The fragments
were placed in
the bench in
Temple 34-1st.

history of the kingdom. These "sacred mountains" stood in a row behind the tree-stone forest of stelae created by Tikal's great kings (Fig. 5:19). On the right side of this magnificent temple group stood Temple 32–1st,[56] the structure built over Burial 195, the tomb of the twenty-second ruler of Tikal. Ruling around A.D. 600, this fellow was the first king to endure the darkness of a reign without history under the heel of Caracol. On the opposite end towered Temple 34–1st, built over Burial 10, the tomb of Curl-Snout, the son of the conqueror of Uaxactún and the father of Stormy-Sky.

The centerpiece of the North Acropolis's facade, however, was the magnificent Temple 33–2nd (Fig. 5:2) built before the disastrous defeat. Raised in the era of the staff kings, its exquisitely modeled and painted stucco masks displayed the original great architectural programs of the Late Preclassic period. This sacred mountain, above all others, had been the orthodox focus of royal ecstasy and the dramatic backdrop against which the stelae commemorating each king's vision stood for all to witness. Throughout much of the sixth and seventh centuries this temple remained as the indomitable image of Tikal's kingship. Under its sculptured pyramid lay Burial 48, the tomb of the great Stormy-Sky; and newly set into its base were Burial 24 and Burial 23, which was probably the tomb of Shield-Skull, Ah-Cacaw's father. It is no wonder then that this was the location Ah-Cacaw chose to raise his breathtaking Temple 33.

Ah-Cacaw's first major political act was to honorably bury two of the desecrated stelae that had been left as trash in the Great Plaza by the victorious Caracol ahauob. We can reconstruct some of what happened during these rededication rites from the archaeological record. At least two of the rituals focused upon the shattered remains of the beautiful Stela 26 (Fig. 5:20) and Stela 31, Stormy-Sky's masterpiece documenting the victory of Tikal over Uaxactún more than three hundred years earlier.

FIG. 5:21
Temples 33, 34,
and the Front
of the North
Acropolis
photograph by
Peter Harrison

Temple 34-1st. The broken fragments of
Stela 26 were placed inside the bench in
the rear chamber of the temple

Temple 33-1st. Stela 31 was placed inside the older building before the last
phase was built

Over a period of several days, Ah-Cacaw buried these stelae with great
ceremony within Temples 33 and 34 (Fig. 5:21). He would have regarded
this as a time of solemn ceremonial preparation, an initial, pivotal action
in his campaign to repair the dishonor done to his ancestral kings by the
blasphemous conquerors. In the following passage, we will visualize the
events comprising this important historical occasion.

Ah-Cacaw, a full head taller than his silent companions, halted the
procession moving across the broad plaza in the slanting orange light of
dawn. His long shadow thrust like a finger from a fist toward the forest
of tree-stones standing before the looming temple-mountains. The
crooked shadows of the stelae, in turn, fell back onto the steps which led
up to the lineage houses holding the earthly remains of his holy ancestors.
He raised his eyes to the central temple. The huge plaster faces of the gods,
mounted upon this sacred mountain, shone as brightly as they had when
first made by his ancestors long before the disastrous defeat of the twenty-
first successor of his line. It had taken the entire lifetimes of the four kings
before him to bring the kingdom back from that defeat. Now the day of
rebirth had finally arrived. As the twenty-sixth successor of Yax-Moch-
Xoc, he was determined that his brother kings would learn to respect
Tikal once more, as they had when Great-Jaguar-Paw and Smoking-Frog
had won their victory over Uaxactún.

Two of those four intervening kings were now buried in the great mountain that held the tomb of Stormy-Sky. One of them was Ah-Cacaw's father, Shield-Skull, who had begun the restoration of the city to its former glory[57] by commissioning monuments in the Central Acropolis and in the large plaza east of the ancestral mountains. Tikal's twenty-second king lay within the pyramid on the eastern shoulder of Stormy-Sky's burial temple, placing three of the kings who had suffered through the humiliation of a reign without history in the threshold zone of the ancient acropolis.[58]

The silence of his reverie was broken by the grunts of struggling men. Ah-Cacaw turned to face the stelae platform before the westernmost of the three temples at the front of the range of sacred mountains. With a unified cry of effort, six of the men straightened their backs, lifting the enormous chunk of broken stela. The stone, cradled in a net of thick ropes suspended from the thick pole they carried on their shoulders, tore at their strength as they took trembling steps toward the steep stairs that rose toward the dark inner sanctum of the western temple. Here the revered Curl-Snout, father of Stormy-Sky, lay at rest under tons of quarried stone mortared with the sweat of the laboring hundreds who had shaped his tomb into its mountain form. As the first six lords staggered up the steps, a second team of men worked to fasten ropes around the other large fragment of tree-stone that lay broken on the plaza floor. This sacred monument was Tikal history incarnate. It carried the names of the ninth successor, Great-Jaguar-Paw, Conqueror of Uaxactún; his grandson, Stormy-Sky, the eleventh successor; Kan-Boar, the twelfth successor; and the thirteenth successor, Great-Jaguar-Paw, who had been named for his illustrious forebear. Hoisting the carrying pole onto their shoulders, the second cluster of young lords staggered forward in the warming light of the rising sun.

It took the young men, all sons of the royal clan and its high-ranking allies, the entire morning to complete their task. Only five or six of them could bring their strength to bear upon the carrying pole at one time. They had to work slowly and in turns, anxious to protect the exquisitely carved text fragments from the further desecration a careless movement might cause. For three hours the king and his closest companions stood upon the steps of the sacred mountain, watching the slow and halting upward progress of the men. A crowd of witnesses gradually formed on the plaza below as patriarchs and their entourages arrived from both the city and the regions beyond. It was a quiet, tense occasion. Finally, Ah-Cacaw's lords eased the first large fragment of stone into a neat pit they had cut through the floor of the rear chamber. This pit lay just before the blank back wall of the temple, in the rear room that was the inner sanctum and the portal to the Otherworld.[59] Soon thereafter the second fragment of the broken stela was lowered into the pit.

When the young men emerged from the temple, Ah-Cacaw went to the place where the tree-stone had lain and picked up a handful of fragments left in dusty disarray on the hard plaster surface of the plaza. Cradling the broken fragments reverently against his naked chest, he carried them up the stairs and into the cool darkness of the temple. There he laid them gently into the pit with the larger pieces. Kinsmen and men of high rank followed his lead, moving single file up the stairs until all that remained of the great tree-stone lay in the pit. Ah-Cacaw had ordered that one large chunk be kept back. This fragment would be placed in another offering pit along with the altar of Stormy-Sky's tree-stone, soon to be deposited in the central temple. Burying the tree-stone fragment with the altar would link the two ritual burials so that his ancestral dead would understand his motivation. By this act, Ah-Cacaw hoped to erase the desecration visited upon their memory by the victors from the southeast and to summon their spirits to help him in the coming war.[60]

The king waited in silence until the solemn procession had ended. Then he led the shamans and the principal men of his lineage into the rear chamber where the fragments lay in their grave. In front of the pit that held the pieces of the tree-stone were three deep holes dug into the floor. These holes would hold the offerings that would both amplify the power emanating from the ancient stela and seal it into the threshold of the portal.

The mood of the crowd intensified as sounds of drumming echoed throughout the huge plaza. It seemed as if everyone in the city was present. The piercing cry of flutes and clay whistles rose from the children of Tikal. Rattles shivered on the dancing ankles of farmers, masons, and weavers, counterpointing the deep-throated rhythm of the chest-high drums arrayed along the stairs. The people—ahauob and common folk alike—sang and danced a plaintive dirge to rekindle the spirits of the desecrated tree-stones of the ancient kings.[61] At the culmination of this ritual of remembrance and burial, the gods and ancestors would turn their faces once more toward the great kingdom at the center of the world. The lineage of Tikal's kings would reign once again with honor restored.

High nobles chosen for their rank and accomplishments moved from the council houses[62] through the swirling crowd. They bore into the sanctum large offering plates called *zac lac*.[63] The waists of these men were thickly encircled by the wrappings of their hipcloths and skirts, garments made of fine cotton cloth resplendent with painted and woven patterns rendered in the bright hues of forest dyes.[64] The lordly stewards sported turbans of fine fabric, tightly bound around their long black hair with jade-studded leather headbands. Elegant tail feathers arched from the headbands to bob in time with the graceful movements of the procession. Deep-green jade beads and bloodred spondylus shell ornaments gleamed in their earlobes and against their brown chests as they moved with studied dignity, bringing their gifts to the sacred tree-stone.

Ah-Cacaw was pleased with the richness of the offerings they carried in the great plates. There were shells and coral from the distant seas to the south, east, and west,[65] purchased from coastal traders and hoarded for this day. Even more precious were the seaweed, sponges, and other living creatures the young men had conveyed inland in saltwater-filled crocks to keep them from spoiling in the tropical heat. The shamans took each offering from its plate as it was presented to them. Beside each cache pit lay a square of beaten-bark cloth. Others were spread on the floor next to the base of the broken tree. With expert grace, the shamans placed each of the offerings in its turn onto the light-brown cloth, all the while singing the story of the dark seas before the gods made the world. When the fresh sea creatures, the shells, and the coral were carefully arranged, they laid the backbones of fish and the spines of stingrays onto the prepared stacks. The royal merchants had not been able to procure enough of the stingray spines, so effigy spines carved from bone were added to the offerings. Together these tokens established the primordial sea of creation around this tree of Tikal, nourishing its spirit just as the sea had nourished the first tree, the axis of the world, at the beginning of creation.

Next, an old shaman of the royal court brought forward the divination stones—flakes of obsidian carefully incised with the images of eternal power. Eight of the flakes displayed the Jester God, that most ancient symbol of the kingship. The moon marked three others and two bore pictures of the bag of magical instruments carried by kings in rituals of state.

A warrior prince of the blood came forward next, bearing bundles of soft deer hide. The first was opened, revealing seven faceted flints, small in size but chipped by the finest knappers into irregular shapes resembling tiny amoebalike puddles of water. He unpacked other bundles and took out the blades of spears and spearthrower darts. Still more bundles contained the complex abstract shapes that decorated the wands and staves used during ecstatic ritual performance. The flints glittered in the torchlight, Tikal's famed workmanship brought to honor the tree-stone and to arm the ancestors. Their shapes focused the power of the Otherworld: Flint and obsidian were the fingernails of the Lightning Bolt, the remnants of Chac-Xib-Chac striking the rock of earth.[66]

From his own embroidered bag, the king removed a royal mosaic mirror made of jade and the silver-blue crystalline hematite forged in the southern fire mountains.[67] A precious heirloom of his dynasty, its delicate surface was mounted on a mother-of-pearl backing. He placed the mirror on top of the growing mound of offerings in the principal pit. Small balls of white stone and black obsidian were added to each offering pile. Finally, lineage patriarchs spilled precious red pigment, symbolizing their blood in enduring form, onto the carefully arranged objects. They pulled the jade and greenstone earflares and beads from their ears, smashed and ground them like maize on grinding stones, and sprinkled the fragments across the paint.[68]

The assembled lords and shamans used additional stingray spines to draw blood from their ears and tongues in the ritual that would bring the offerings to life. Then, chanting prayers, they pulled up the corners of the bark wrapping cloths, being careful to preserve the pattern of the offerings within. Folding the cloths carefully, they formed bundles[69] which were decorated with red and blue on their outside surfaces. While one man held each bundle tightly closed, another placed a band of woven fibers around it, drawing these fibers into a tight knot at the top. Cautiously and reverently, they lowered one bundle into each pit. Others were laid against the base of the broken monument.

As the sun plunged westward toward dusk, Ah-Cacaw thrust an obsidian lancet into the loose skin of his penis, drawing his own blood to both nourish and activate the resanctified tree-stone. Singing a chant to call his ancestors' attention to his offering, the king smeared his blood across the sides of the stela.[70] Satisfied that his dead had realized the honor he did them and their obligation to unleash the demons of conquest upon his enemies, the king rose, making a trail of his royal blood. Thus the divine ahau created a path for the ancestors to follow as they came out of the mountain and back to Tikal.

As the king emerged into the hot glare of late afternoon, ready to dance for his people, master builders hurried into the temple chambers. One of Ah-Cacaw's chief shamans had stayed behind to guide their work with quiet suggestions. Together, they sealed the pits with plaster so that the floor became even once again. Young men of the minor noble houses vied with one another for the honor of carrying prepared stones from the plaza up to the sanctum. Using these blocks, the master builders began to erect a wall around the broken stela, carefully and reverently placing the stones against it so that it would not be further damaged. They built up the masonry surface with mud and sand mortar until they had made a bench, a throne-altar that filled much of the rear chamber. When they were satisfied with its shape, they coated it with plaster, modeling the bench into a smooth, white surface—forever sealing the ancestral treasure deep inside. Tikal's history was safe from further depredation and empowered as a living portal awaiting the king's command. The call to war would soon come.

Festival swirled and eddied across the plazas like the floodwaters of the great rivers. There were dancing processions, pageants, and feasts of special foods and drinks served in exquisite painted vessels crafted by artists of the city and the regions beyond. Members of the royal family drew blood from their bodies and spun in ecstasy across the terraces enclosing the Great Plaza.[71] The witnessing populace responded with great devotional outpourings of their own, emblazoning the plaza in bright red. Finally, when the last light of the sun was sinking behind the horizon and the plaster on the throne-altar had cured into a hard surface, Ah-Cacaw mounted the stairs and entered the temple once again. His shamans and the principal men of his lineage accompanied him for the solemn ceremony that would end this part of the ritual.

The old shaman handed him a obsidian lancet struck free from the core only minutes earlier. Ah-Cacaw made his blood flow until the moment came when he could call forth the Vision Serpent that carried his ancestors to him. As the king sank deeply into the trance state, the shaman took the bark cloth saturated with the king's blood and laid it in a shallow pit dug in front of the newly made altar. When the blood-stained paper of Ah-Cacaw's kinsmen had swelled the pile to a respectable size, the shaman added rubber, copal, and wood to make a hot fire. Then he spun the fire drill with a bow, gradually creating enough heat to ignite the dried grass on top of the pile. The fire was slow to catch, but eventually the flames rose along the side of the altar, blackening its face with the mark of a sacrificial offering. In the smoke that swirled up into the vault high inside the roof comb, Ah-Cacaw saw the faces of his ancestors and understood that they crowned with triumph his efforts to restore their glory.

This ritual of communication with the ancestors reopened the portal that had been destroyed by their enemies in the war six katuns earlier. The burial of the tree-stone brought power back to the sacred mountains of the kingdom. In the coming days, as the celebration continued, Ah-Cacaw would also honor the desecrated tree-stone of Stormy-Sky and set it inside the great central temple-mountain. At the conclusion of these ceremonies, his people would begin work on the new mountain that would encompass and protect the repose of the ancestors. They would have to work fast, for the king intended to dedicate the new mountain on the thirteenth katun recurrence of Stormy-Sky's bloodletting. It was the kind of symmetry of time and action that the ancestors and the gods would admire.

In a state of ecstasy, Ah-Cacaw emerged from the smoking inner sanctum to the roaring shouts of his people. Pillars of fire and incense rose from lineage houses throughout the darkened city below. They knew their king would lead them back to victory and the wealth they had lost. Victory and sacrifice would keep their enemies far from the borders of the kingdom. They understood that the determination of this vigorous new king and his ambition to restore the honor of his dynasty affected all their fates. The greatness of the royal past, now recaptured, would unfold into all their futures. They prayed for the ancient strength of the great kings, knowing that the demons of war had to be driven forward to the lands of their enemies. Once unleashed, they would devour all in their path.

Shortly after entombing Stela 26, Ah-Cacaw buried Stela 31, utilizing the same sorts of dedication rituals. The most sacred memorial of Tikal's glorious military history, Stela 31 was the tree-stone upon which Stormy-Sky himself had engraved the history of the Uaxactún conquest.[72] Enemies had violently torn this magnificent stela from its place in front of Temple 33–2nd, the building next door to the temple in which Ah-Cacaw later interred Stela 26.

Lifting Stela 31 from where it lay in disgrace, the lords of Tikal carried it in honor up the stairs to the old temple. There they replanted it in the shallow pit they had dug into the floor of the rear room of the temple, laid kindling around its base, and lit a fire to disperse the power accumulated in the stone—just as they had done in the rituals described above for Stela 26. This fire also seared away the dishonor that had been done to the stela's spirit. Members of the court of Tikal, and those nobles from ancient vassal communities courageous enough to declare for the new king against Caracol, brought elaborate pottery censers in which they burned ritual offerings. After the ceremony, these censers were smashed in a termination ritual and the pieces left scattered on the floors of these soon-to-be-buried temple chambers.

Once Stela 31 was cached in its place, work crews filled the chambers of the old temple, then collapsed its vaults and roof comb, sealing in its

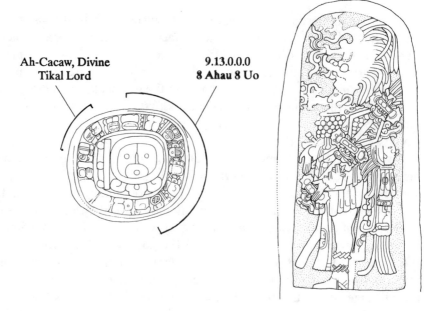

Ah-Cacaw, Divine
Tikal Lord

9.13.0.0.0
8 Ahau 8 Uo

FIG. 5:22
Tikal Stela 30
and Its Altar:
The first stela
erected by
Ah-Cacaw after
he became king

power forever. They then covered the old building with a flat-topped pyramid twelve meters tall, which would provide the construction base for a new sacred mountain which would reach 18.8 meters in height. The engineers and masons used the technique of rapid building, for no doubt Ah-Cacaw intended to strike quickly at his enemies once he had completed the reopening of his family's sacred portal to the Otherworld. Each level of the rising pyramid was divided into rectangular stone construction pens, which were then filled with mud, mortar, and rubble. When the completed temple stood atop it, this towering pyramidal base provided an impressive new backdrop for the stela row in front of the North Acropolis (Fig. 5:21). The pyramid's huge mass unified the many buildings of the North Acropolis into a range of living mountains with a single supernatural doorway on its northern horizon. Through this doorway the ancestors of Tikal would emerge once again to aid the new king as he strove to reestablish the glory they had forged before the disaster.[73]

We do not know exactly when the termination rituals for the old building, Temple 33–2nd, ended and the work on Temple 33–1st began. We can assume, however, that this building project was under way at the same time that Ah-Cacaw was raising his Twin Pyramid Complex. This complex would hold the first stela of his reign, Stela 30, and its altar (Fig. 5:22), both erected to celebrate the end of Katun 13. This Twin Pyramid Complex was the first to be built since the original complex, which had been buried under the East Plaza in Tikal's old glory days. Ah-Cacaw no doubt chose this particular style of architecture because he wanted to confirm his continuity with the earlier traditions of his dynasty. He also revived the period-ending celebrations initiated by his ancestor Stormy-Sky, especially the staff ritual that had been so prominent in the golden years after Stormy-Sky's reign. These rituals would remain central to Late Classic Tikal until its demise.

In spite of the fact that he was busily eradicating all remnants of the conqueror's influence from his city, Ah-Cacaw did not completely reject Caracol's stylistic influences in the art he created.[74] The round stone altar (Fig. 5:22) he set in front of his portrait, in fact, was carved in a style that was popular in the kingdom of Tikal's conquerors (Fig. 5:4). This style utilized Caracol's favorite device of putting the name of the katun in the center of the top surface of the altar and surrounding it with text. It is possible that Ah-Cacaw chose this style for the altar to be placed in front of his first monument precisely because he wished to neutralize the shame of Tikal's ancient defeat. This conjecture finds further support when we examine his portrait: He chose to depict himself here in a style much like that of Stela 17, the last monument of the hapless twenty-first successor, who had fallen to Caracol so many years ago.

If we had only the archaeologically excavated construction record of Temple 33 and the deposition of Stela 31, there would be little more we could say about the events surrounding its dedication. But Ah-Cacaw rightfully regarded the rekindling of the spiritual fires of his dynasty, in Temple 33–1st and the Great Plaza, to have been the most important events of his life. These were the pivotal scenes he chose to feature when he memorialized his reign on the broad hardwood lintels spanning the doorways of his great funerary house, Temple 1, high atop the huge pyramid that was built over his tomb. On the dark polished surfaces of these lintels we find Temple 33's history in wonderful detail.

The construction of Temple 33–1st must have been finished shortly after 9.13.3.0.0 (March 3, 695), for Lintel 3 tells us that the dedication events began with this period ending (Fig. 5:23). One hundred and fifty-eight days afterward, Ah-Cacaw went to war and took captive King Jaguar-Paw of Calakmul. The battle that won him this famous captive was in the same style as Caracol's war against Naranjo (Fig. 5:6) sixty-eight years earlier, and Smoking-Squirrel's recent war against Ucanal (Fig. 5:14).[75] It was Tlaloc-Venus war. There was one significant difference, however. Aside from the fact that Jaguar-Paw fell to Ah-Cacaw on August 8, 695, two days after the zenith passage of the sun, there was none of the usual astronomical significance we have come to expect in Maya warfare. Ah-Cacaw timed this victory not by the strict mandates of the heavens but by the history of his own people, marked by the thirteen katun anniversary of Stormy-Sky's war event celebrated on Stela 31.

Thirteen days after the battle in which Jaguar-Paw fell, Ah-Cacaw displayed his Calakmul captives in a ritual in which they were humiliated and probably tortured.[76] This dramatic scene, modeled in plaster, can be found on the upper facade of Structure 5D-57, one of the complex of council houses and temples called the Central Acropolis (Fig. 5:24). Here we see one of the captives, seated and with his wrists bound behind his back. He is held by a tether which stretches to the hand of the victorious king. Ah-Cacaw, standing behind the captive, is dressed in the Mosaic Monster garb of the Tlaloc complex associated with Venus war, the same costume worn by his ancestors during Tikal's conquest of Uaxactún. The

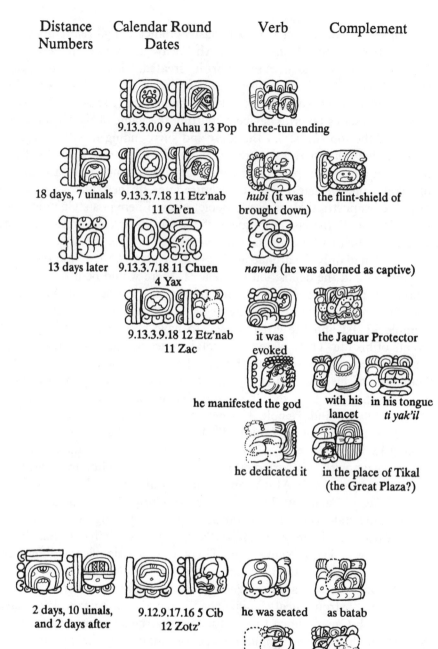

Distance Numbers	Calendar Round Dates	Verb	Complement
	9.13.3.0.0 9 Ahau 13 Pop	three-tun ending	
18 days, 7 uinals	9.13.3.7.18 11 Etz'nab 11 Ch'en	*hubi* (it was brought down)	the flint-shield of
13 days later	9.13.3.7.18 11 Chuen 4 Yax	*nawah* (he was adorned as captive)	
	9.13.3.9.18 12 Etz'nab 11 Zac	it was evoked	the Jaguar Protector
		he manifested the god	with his lancet / in his tongue *ti yak'il*
		he dedicated it	in the place of Tikal (the Great Plaza?)

FIG. 5:23 Texts recording the Dedication Rituals for Temple 33 on Lintel 3 of Temple 1 and Temple 5D-57

2 days, 10 uinals, and 2 days after	9.12.9.17.16 5 Cib 12 Zotz'	he was seated	as batab
	and then it was evoked	the Jaguar Protector	

captive pictured is not Jaguar-Paw of Calakmul himself, but someone named Ah-Bolon-Bakin, who was an ally or vassal of that captured king.

Twenty-seven days later, Ah-Cacaw sacrificed these unfortunate captives in the dedication ritual for Temple 33. He recorded this event in a triplet form, giving different types of information about the event with each repetition. This critical record was carved on Lintel 3 of Temple 1 (Fig. 5:23). First, Ah-Cacaw recorded the ritual as a dedication event in

first two clauses from the
text of Lintel 3, Temple 1

Jaguar-Paw of Calakmul   captive   of the ahau

_____

text from the plaster sculpture on Temple 5D-57

Ah-Bolon-Bakin, Ah ???

_____

remaining text from Lintel
3, Temple 1

Ah Cacaw Sky-God K Divine Tikal Ahau

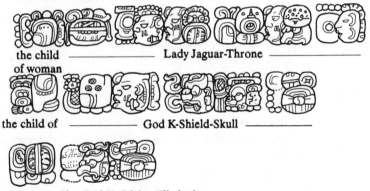

the child ——————————— Lady Jaguar-Throne ———————————
of woman

the child of ——————— God K-Shield-Skull ———————————

Ah-Cacaw Sky-God K Divine Tikal Ahau

which he himself let blood from his tongue.[77] As we shall see in the chapter on Yaxchilán, this ritual involved the piercing of the tongue to create a wound through which a cord was drawn. The blood loss and pain an individual experienced during this self-wounding process elicited a trance state in which the Vision Serpent could appear. This Vision Serpent was the conduit through which the ancestors came into the world and spoke to their descendants. We suspect that Ah-Cacaw called on Stormy-Sky, bringing him up through the sacred portal in Temple 33 to witness the dynastic renewal accomplished by his descendant.

The second passage in the triplet declares that the dedication ritual[78] took place in a location named with the main sign of the Tikal Emblem

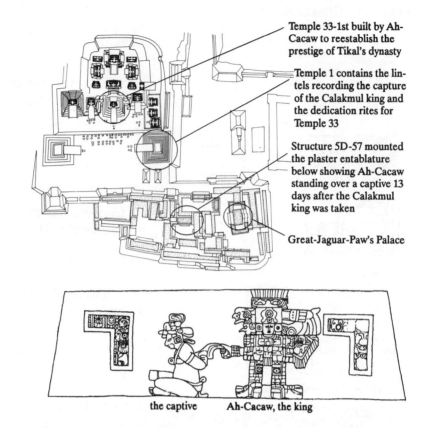

Temple 33-1st built by Ah-Cacaw to reestablish the prestige of Tikal's dynasty

Temple 1 contains the lintels recording the capture of the Calakmul king and the dedication rites for Temple 33

Structure 5D-57 mounted the plaster entablature below showing Ah-Cacaw standing over a captive 13 days after the Calakmul king was taken

Great-Jaguar-Paw's Palace

the captive   Ah-Cacaw, the king

map by Kathryn Reese and Linda Schele

FIG. 5:24 Structure 5D-57 and the Rituals of Dedication

Glyph. This location was very likely the Great Plaza, the community's spiritual center. In this passage, Ah-Cacaw asserts his legitimate right to open the portal to the Otherworld by declaring his royal pedigree as the child of Lady Jaguar-Throne and King Shield-Skull. The final description of the dedication of Temple 33 links the event to Ah-Cacaw's accession.

How do we know that the events recorded in Temple 1 refer to the dedication of Temple 33 and the refurbished Great Plaza area? The answer is that we don't, except by inference, but the evidence supporting our deduction is strong. The date of Ah-Cacaw's dedication ceremony as recorded in Temple 1 is the thirteenth katun anniversary of the last date preserved on the broken Stela 31. We know that the date on the broken stela marked a bloodletting ceremony enacted by the ancient king Stormy-Sky on the occasion of a maximum elongation of the Morningstar.[79]

The fact that Ah-Cacaw timed his own dedication rites to this thirteenth katun anniversary date was not accidental. Unlike his royal contemporaries who timed their actions in war and peace by the cycles of Venus, Ah-Cacaw chose a cycle that would connect the rebirth of his dynasty to the old Tikal of the glory days. Stormy-Sky was the pivotal hero of the old dynasty from Ah-Cacaw's point of view. We believe it was no accident that Ah-Cacaw built his magnificent Temple 33 over the tomb of this great king and there buried Stela 31, Stormy-Sky's beautifully

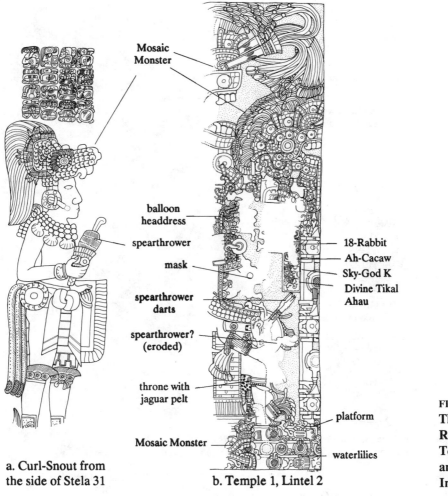

Mosaic
Monster

balloon
headdress

spearthrower

mask

spearthrower
darts

spearthrower?
(eroded)

throne with
jaguar pelt

Mosaic Monster

18-Rabbit
Ah-Cacaw
Sky-God K
Divine Tikal
Ahau

platform

waterlilies

a. Curl-Snout from
the side of Stela 31

b. Temple 1, Lintel 2

FIG. 5:25
The Dedication
Ritual for
Temple 33
and Stela 31
Imagery

carved war memorial, as part of the termination rites. As we have seen, Ah-Cacaw also timed his war against Calakmul by this thirteenth katun anniversary cycle. This 260-year anniversary was one of the most sacred cycles to the ancient Maya. It alone of the ancient cycles would survive the conquest to be preserved by the Maya in the katun wheel famous in the books of Chilam Balam in Yucatán.

More evidence for our claim can be found by comparing the imagery on Stela 31 with the scenes on the lintels of Temple 1. These scenes clearly portray the essential details of the king's performance in the Great Plaza on the occasion of the dedication of Temple 33. On Lintel 2 (Fig. 5:25b) Ah-Cacaw sits astride a throne covered with a jaguar pelt, his feet resting on a stepped base marked with bands of waterlilies representing the dark and dangerous surface of Xibalba. He wears the balloon headdress of the Tlaloc war complex and a frightful deity mask, the last earthly thing his sacrificial victims were likely to see. In his hands he holds spearthrower darts and a shield. This is the same battle gear worn by his ancestors,

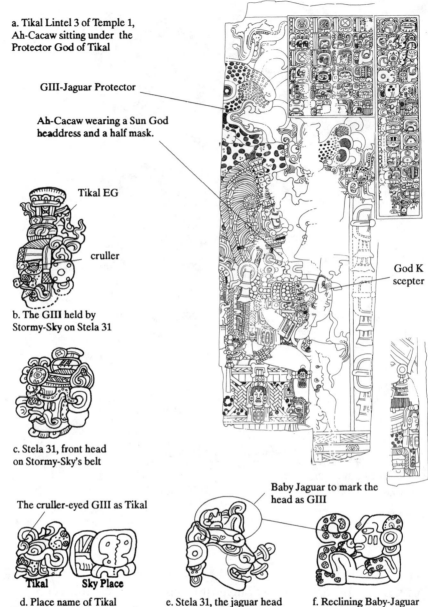

a. Tikal Lintel 3 of Temple 1, Ah-Cacaw sitting under the Protector God of Tikal

GIII-Jaguar Protector

Ah-Cacaw wearing a Sun God headdress and a half mask.

God K scepter

Tikal EG

cruller

b. The GIII held by Stormy-Sky on Stela 31

c. Stela 31, front head on Stormy-Sky's belt

Baby Jaguar to mark the head as GIII

The cruller-eyed GIII as Tikal

Tikal   Sky Place

d. Place name of Tikal from Stela 31

e. Stela 31, the jaguar head from the rear of the belt

f. Reclining Baby-Jaguar from Stela 26

FIG. 5:26
Temple 1,
Lintel 3 and
the Jaguar
Protector
drawing of lintel by
John Montgomery

Smoking-Frog on Uaxactún Stela 5 and Curl-Snout on the sides of Stela 31. The Mosaic Monster conjured up by the seated Ah-Cacaw looms above him, menacing the foes of Tikal. This monster is the same god of conquest worn by Curl-Snout as a headdress in his portrait on the left side of Stormy-Sky's Stela 31 (Fig. 5:25a). The imagery of Lintel 2 refers to much more than the individual portraits of the ancestors on Stela 31. The royal house and the city of Tikal had suffered for katuns while the star of war shone for their enemies. Now their luck had changed. Ah-Cacaw once again commanded the monsters of Tlaloc war his forebears had unleashed with the conquest of Uaxactún.[80]

The innermost lintel of Temple 1 depicts Ah-Cacaw in the other costume he wore during rituals of dedication (Fig. 5:26). Again, Stela 31 seems a likely source of inspiration for this lintel. On Stela 31, as you recall, Stormy-Sky stands holding the cruller-eyed GIII, the jaguar-featured member of the Hero Twins, in his arms. From Stormy-Sky's belt hang two more versions of the Jaguar Sun, an anthropomorphic version in front and a zoomorphic version in back. This jaguar is the great patron deity of Tikal. He is also equated with the jaguar masks modeled on Late Preclassic temples at Cerros, Uaxactún, El Mirador, and Tikal. He is found in the hand of the king in the earliest known royal portrait at Tikal, Stela 29. We suspect "jaguar" may even be one of the names of the kingdom of Tikal itself.[81]

On Lintel 3, we see the GIII-Jaguar God again, this time looming protectively over Ah-Cacaw. In this scene, the king again sits on a seat covered with jaguar pelts atop a stepped platform. In his right hand, he holds a God K scepter and in his left a round shield. He is heavily adorned with jewelry marking both his rank and his ritual role. His feathered headdress is mounted on a Roman-nosed profile of the sun god and a remnant of his huge backrack can be seen behind him. To announce his rank as ahau, a Jester God rides on his chest over a large pectoral composed of jade beads of varying sizes. Ah-Cacaw is seated on a palanquin which he has ridden into a ritual space, perhaps the Great Plaza itself, in order to conduct the public sacrifices that were part of the dedication celebrations.[82]

Out of the ruins of Tikal's broken history, Ah-Cacaw reshaped a formidable new place of power and sacrifice. Using the deeds of his ancestor Stormy-Sky as a bridge, he healed the breach in Tikal's history caused by the long years of darkness. One question remains, however: Why did Ah-Cacaw attack Calakmul?

Calakmul's alliance with Caracol in the war against Naranjo no doubt made its young king, Jaguar-Paw, a target for Tikal's wrath. Perhaps even more telling, however, was the participation of Calakmul's earlier kings in a strategy that had encircled Tikal with the enemies and allies of Calakmul. One of those erstwhile allies, the first king of Naranjo, had found himself the target of the same alliance in the waning years of his life. His descendants focused their wrathful vengeance to the south against Caracol's neighbors, while Ah-Cacaw of Tikal turned north toward Calakmul itself.

What role did Flint-Sky-God K of Dos Pilas play beyond taking advantage of the resulting power vacuum and setting his own descendants on the throne of Naranjo? We are not sure, for in his early years he had courted the young heir to Calakmul's throne and attended his accession as a powerful friend. Flint-Sky-God K won a great strategic victory at Naranjo in the power politics of the time, but he must have lost prestige when his most prized ally died at the hands of the new Tikal ruler.

Flint-Sky-God K was the founder of a vigorous new dynasty which may have been an offshoot of the Tikal royal family, but considering his alliances, he was very likely the enemy of that kingdom during its recovery.

The tangle of elite obligations and vendettas we have outlined in this chapter rivals any in recorded history. Caracol conquered Tikal and later, in alliance with Calakmul, conquered Naranjo. A branch of the defeated Tikal family may well have moved into the Petexbatún region to establish the new kingdom of Dos Pilas. Flint-Sky-God K, the founder of the Dos Pilas dynasty, then began a campaign of battles that won him the friendship of the powerful heir and soon-to-be king of Calakmul. He also sent a daughter to Naranjo to reestablish the dynasty there, after the defeat of a king who had been installed in the presence of a former ruler of Calakmul. Tikal attacked Calakmul, the ally of Dos Pilas, while Naranjo rampaged southward toward Caracol, conquering Yaxhá (which may have been subordinate to Tikal) and Ucanal. As far as we can tell, Caracol's response was to duck and hide in the deepest cover it could find, and ride out the crisis. Certainly, its fortunes declined with the reemergence of Tikal and Naranjo as major powers.

Some Thoughts and Questions

These are some of the spare facts of the matter, and with any luck more will come to light in the future. Already, however, we can sense a more subtle and treacherous diplomatic landscape behind the facts we know. Did, for example, Flint-Sky-God K deliver Jaguar-Paw into the hands of Ah-Cacaw? One can envision the young monarch of Calakmul, trapped on the battlefield and anxiously awaiting the arrival of Dos Pilas warriors who never appear, raging in frustration as Ah-Cacaw draws steadily nearer with his fierce companions. Certainly the house of Dos Pilas benefited from the outcome of this battle. The alliance of Calakmul and Caracol had spanned the entire central Petén region, holding many great families hostage. With that axis broken, with Tikal in a celebratory mood, and with relatives ruling Naranjo to the east of Tikal, the kings of Dos Pilas could enjoy a free hand in the Petexbatún , spending the next eighty years consolidating a substantial conquest state of their own.

The impact of these maneuvers on Caracol was profound. No inscriptions exist, as far as we know, from the period spanning the end of Lord Kan II's reign up until the end of Katun 17. That silence lasted for seventy years. At Calakmul, the results were different, perhaps because that kingdom was so huge and so far to the north that it managed to survive the defeat of its king without major effect. By the next period ending following the death of Jaguar-Paw, the people of Calakmul had already begun to erect stelae once more.

Whatever effects Ah-Cacaw's deeds may have had on the liberation of the Petén, his rituals of dedication and his family's program of rebuilding seem to have accomplished their primary purpose. Tikal regained its position as one of the largest and wealthiest kingdoms in the central Petén.

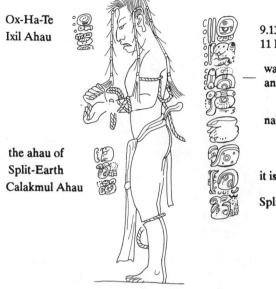

Ox-Ha-Te
Ixil Ahau

the ahau of
Split-Earth
Calakmul Ahau

9.13.3.13.15
11 Men 8 Muan

war verb (also at Naranjo
and on Lintel 3)

name of captive

it is the land of

Split-Earth

FIG. 5:27
A Captive
Ahau from
Calakmul
Carved on a
Bone from
Ah-Cacaw's
Tomb

In spite of these very substantial gains, however, the king did not rest on his laurels. The architectural remodeling of downtown Tikal and the wars of Ah-Cacaw were far from over. Less than a year after the dedication of Temple 33, Ah-Cacaw attacked Calakmul again, this time taking captive a lord named Ox-Ha-Te Ixil Ahau, who was immortalized in one of the most elegant drawings left to us by the Maya (Fig. 5:27). The artist incised the image of this man on two carved bones deposited in Ah-Cacaw's tomb. On these bones we see Ox-Ha-Te Ixil standing in public humiliation with his head bowed, stripped to his loincloth, his wrists, upper arms, and knees bound together. The battle in which he fell took place in the land of a person named Split-Earth, who was the king who apparently succeeded Jaguar-Paw at Calakmul.[83] This captive was one of his nobles. Ironically, both these Calakmul stalwarts enjoyed the privilege of history only because they accompanied a great enemy king to his grave.

At the end of the katun, 9.14.0.0.0, just when Smoking-Squirrel was attacking Yaxhá, Ah-Cacaw built his second Twin Pyramid Complex and placed Stela 14 and Altar 5 (Fig. 5:28) in the northern enclosure. On this stela, Ah-Cacaw stands front view with the staff favored by the Early Classic Tikal kings balanced on his forearms. The feathers of his backrack fan out in a torso-high circle behind him. In recognition of the first appearance of the Eveningstar, he wears the skeletal image of this celestial being as his headdress.

Ah-Cacaw may have built one more twin pyramid complex, but this one, which celebrated 9.15.0.0.0, never had any carved monuments erected within it, so we are not sure of the identity of its originator. It was not the custom at Tikal in the Late Classic period to erect stelae recording the details of the kings' lives. Instead, the kings vested public energy and historical memory into their personal twin pyramid complexes and the rites they conducted on period-endings. This new emphasis began after

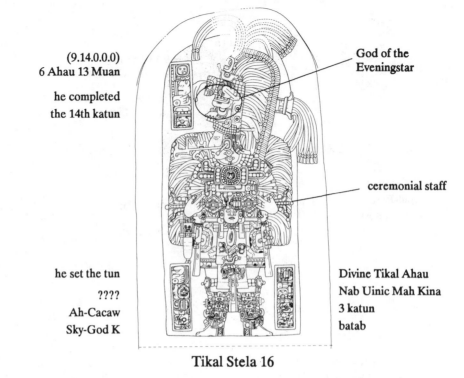

(9.14.0.0.0)
6 Ahau 13 Muan

he completed
the 14th katun

God of the
Eveningstar

ceremonial staff

he set the tun
????
Ah-Cacaw
Sky-God K

Divine Tikal Ahau
Nab Uinic Mah Kina
3 katun
batab

Tikal Stela 16

FIG. 5:28
Ah-Cacaw
Ending the
Katun as
Venus
Appeared as
Eveningstar

Stormy-Sky's death in the fifth century and it was a custom that Ah-Cacaw reinforced. For that reason we have little information about the last twenty years of Ah-Cacaw's life: A few dates with obscure events appear on the incised bones deposited in his tomb. One clear historical footnote recorded on these bones, however, is the death of Shield-God K, the son of Flint-Sky-God K of Dos Pilas.[84] Surely if Ah-Cacaw had strained good relations with the Dos Pilas family when he took Jaguar-Paw of Calakmul, he must have repaired the breach by the time of his demise.

Ah-Cacaw's son, Ruler B, succeeded him on 9.15.3.6.8 (December 12, 734). This son most likely built his famous father's funerary mountain, Temple 1, because we have evidence that the pyramid was erected after the tomb was sealed. Still, the absence of any editorial comment by this young man in the hieroglyphic texts on the masterful lintels of this temple suggests that they were completed under the watchful eye of an aging Ah-Cacaw. The devout son, no doubt, merely installed them.[85]

We are less sure about the end of Smoking-Squirrel's life at Naranjo. All we know is that his son Smoking-Batab succeeded him on November 22, 755.[86]

Many parallels can be drawn between the lives of Ah-Cacaw and Smoking-Squirrel. Both kings inherited polities that had suffered humiliating defeats at the hand of the same enemy—the kingdom of Caracol—and both kings spent their lives successfully reestablishing the prestige and central position of their kingdoms in the affairs of the Late Classic Maya world. Their strategies were essentially the same. Ah-Cacaw began his reign with the honorable deposition of desecrated monuments in the older buildings that fronted the North Acropolis, the ritual center of Tikal. Although his father, Shield Skull, had already begun the process of re-awakening the state with a preliminary rejuvenation of the North Acropolis, it fell to Ah-Cacaw to complete the program. He erected the huge Temple 33 over the stela recording the history of his kingdom's greatest conquest—the deeds of his mighty ancestors, Great-Jaguar-Paw, Curl-Snout, and Stormy-Sky. On the thirteenth katun anniversary of the last readable date on the desecrated monument, he went to war and took a captive high enough in rank and prestige to wipe away the dishonor on the spirit and history of his kingdom. With the building of Temple 33, he remade the ceremonial heart of the city into a new configuration on a scale and proportion worthy of the glory he had regained.

Smoking-Squirrel used the same tools of reclamation to reestablish his kingdom's honor. His success in war demonstrated both Naranjo's regained prowess as a military power and the renewed favor of the gods. His success as a charismatic ruler can be seen in his ability to gather the tremendous numbers of laborers and skilled craftsmen needed to remake the center of his kingdom on an even greater and more glorious scale. Smoking-Squirrel built Groups A15 and C (Fig. 5:12), both designed to reproduce the triadic arrangements of Late Preclassic buildings we have seen at Cerros and Uaxactún. His appeal was not only to size, but more important, to the ancient orthodoxy of Maya kingship. This was a pattern seized upon by Ah-Cacaw as well, for by sealing the interior courts of the old temple complex away from processional access, he turned the North Acropolis into the northern point of a new triadic group. Temple 1 formed the second point and Temple 2 the third. Thus, both kings reestablished the prestige of their defeated kingdoms by publicly and forcefully demonstrating their prowess as architects and warriors.

What we have tried to show in these histories of the Petén kingdoms is how the interrelationships of the many polities that inhabited this landscape together comprised what we call Maya civilization. In alliance, in war, and in marriage, the great families that ruled these kingdoms wove together a fabric of meaningful existence as intricate as any they wore on state occasions. The patterns of destruction and creation were shared. More important, the destiny of any kingdom hinged upon its successful performance not only within its own borders but also before the watchful eyes of its friends and foes. History was a matter of mutual interpretation and the mutual elaboration of innovative new ideas like Venus-Tlaloc warfare. In later chapters, as we shift our focus to a close-up of the inner workings of specific kingdoms, we need to bear in mind that the Maya ahauob were always performing for the wider audience of their neighboring peers. Their deeds always required the validation of that larger congregation of true and resplendent people. For the nobility, as for all the people of the community, to be Maya was to be part of the patterns of history formed by the actions of kings within the framework of sacred space and time.

6

THE CHILDREN
OF THE
FIRST MOTHER:
FAMILY
AND
DYNASTY
AT PALENQUE

Like a white, shimmering jewel, Palenque perches above the misty, deep green of the forest shrouding the waterlogged lands that stretch northward from the base of the Chiapas mountains to the swampy beaches of the Gulf of México. To the south of the city, rugged, jungle-covered hills gradually rise to climax in cold, volcanic highlands. Temples, palaces, and noble homes, all built with the distinctive sloped roofs characteristic of Palenque's architectural style, line the clear streams that bubble up from within the heart of these mountains to tumble down rocky slopes and into the rolling plain below. As if to instruct humanity in the ways of destruction and rebirth, these life-sustaining waters rise through the limestone strata to break onto the surface of the earth. Laden with calcium, the running water fashions a fantasy world of crystal lacework by encasing the decaying leaves and branches of the forest in what will become the fossil-laden strata of floriforous limestone a million years hence. The pearly deposits shroud temple and tree alike, creating a mirror to the Otherworld, like a cave turned inside out. Even today, you know you stand on sacred ground here at the western gate of the sun's journey across the world of the ancient Maya.

Palenque's magic has fascinated the Western mind

since the adventurers and explorers of the eighteenth and nineteenth centuries first published accounts of their visits. The drawings and commentaries of intrepid travelers John Stephens and Frederick Catherwood especially captured the imagination of nineteenth-century readers and created a special vision of Palenque as the lost city of an intelligent and civilized indigenous people.[1]

Yet Palenque has done more than appeal to the romantic side of the Western imagination. This city has played a crucial role in the modern study of ancient Maya history and religion, as well as in the decipherment of their writing system. The kings of Palenque left a substantial record of texts carved on the fine-grained limestone monuments of their city. Many of their most outstanding monuments are preoccupied with one issue: the relationship between the legitimate inheritance of divine status through family descent and the personal charisma of the king. As we have seen in other kingdoms, the Palenque ahauob had practical reasons for their obsession with history.

Two Palenque kings, Pacal, whose name means "shield," and his oldest son, Chan-Bahlum,[2] "snake-jaguar," stand out as primary contributors to the history of their city. They are both members of that class of remarkable people who are responsible for creating what we call a civilization's "golden age." Not only did they make their kingdom into a power among the many Maya royal houses of the seventh century; they also inspired and nurtured the exceptional beauty of Palenque's art, the innovative quality of its architecture, and the eloquence of the political and theological visions displayed in its inscriptions and imagery. The royal literature commanded by these men represents the most detailed dynastic history to survive from Classic times. Their vision wove it into the most beautiful and far-reaching expression of the religious and mythological rationale of Maya kingship left to modern contemplation.

Pacal and Chan-Bahlum recorded the essential details of their dynasty on four separate king lists. According to these family accounts, Palenque's dynastic history began on March 11, A.D. 431, when a thirty-four-year-old ahau named Bahlum-Kuk ("Jaguar-Quetzal") became the king. The descent of the royal line continued through subsequent generations of divine ahauob—with only a few minor sidesteps—into the glorious reigns of our two protagonists. Finally, the kingship failed in the hands of their progeny sometime after A.D. 799, the last date recorded in the inscriptions of Palenque. These "minor sidesteps" in the succession are the subject of our tale and the reason for the extraordinary detail of the record those ancient kings have left to us.

Pacal began his task of historical interpretation with the construction of his funerary building—the Temple of Inscriptions (Fig. 6:1). In the corridors of this magnificent temple, he mounted the first of his king lists on three huge stone slabs. These slabs comprise the second-longest[3] inscription left to posterity by the ancient Maya (Fig. 6:1d).[4] In his tomb deep under the temple, Pacal recorded the deaths of the same kings he named above. He also pictured them on the side of his coffin, as part of an ancestral orchard growing out of the cracked earth. His son, Chan-

THE
CHILDREN
OF THE
FIRST
MOTHER:
FAMILY
AND
DYNASTY
AT
PALENQUE
——
217

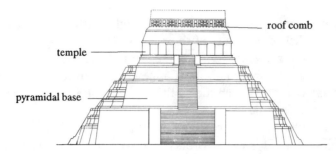

a. Temple of Inscriptions, the final phase

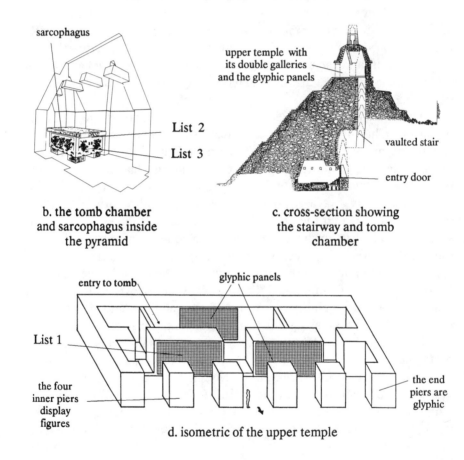

sarcophagus

List 2
List 3

b. the tomb chamber
and sarcophagus inside
the pyramid

upper temple with
its double galleries
and the glyphic panels

vaulted stair

entry door

c. cross-section showing
the stairway and tomb
chamber

entry to tomb

glyphic panels

List 1

the four
inner piers
display
figures

the end
piers are
glyphic

d. isometric of the upper temple

Bahlum, extended this ancestral list back to the founder of the dynasty—
and beyond to the divinities who established the order of the cosmos at
the beginning of this current manifestation of the universe.

Combined, these four great king lists overlap in time and recorded
history to constitute the most detailed and complete dynastic history
known from the Classic period (Fig. 6:2). When a Palenque ruler was
recorded in all four lists, we have his dates of birth, accession, and death,
as well as good information on his kinship relationships with other members of the dynasty. For those kings recorded only on Chan-Bahlum's list,

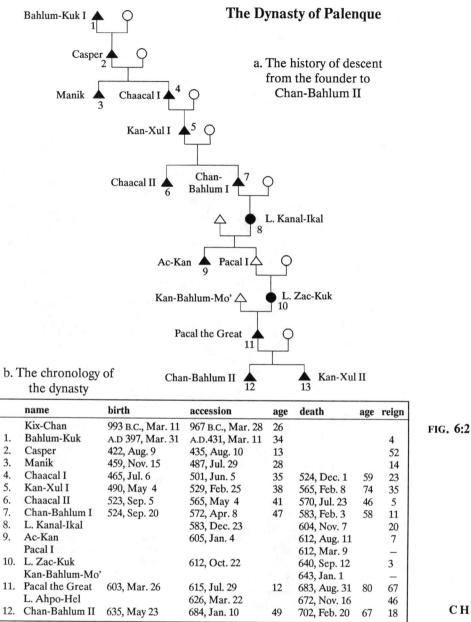

The Dynasty of Palenque

a. The history of descent
from the founder to
Chan-Bahlum II

b. The chronology of
the dynasty

	name	birth	accession	age	death	age	reign
	Kix-Chan	993 B.C., Mar. 11	967 B.C., Mar. 28	26			
1.	Bahlum-Kuk	A.D 397, Mar. 31	A.D.431, Mar. 11	34			4
2.	Casper	422, Aug. 9	435, Aug. 10	13			52
3.	Manik	459, Nov. 15	487, Jul. 29	28			14
4.	Chaacal I	465, Jul. 6	501, Jun. 5	35	524, Dec. 1	59	23
5.	Kan-Xul I	490, May 4	529, Feb. 25	38	565, Feb. 8	74	35
6.	Chaacal II	523, Sep. 5	565, May 4	41	570, Jul. 23	46	5
7.	Chan-Bahlum I	524, Sep. 20	572, Apr. 8	47	583, Feb. 3	58	11
8.	L. Kanal-Ikal		583, Dec. 23		604, Nov. 7		20
9.	Ac-Kan		605, Jan. 4		612, Aug. 11		7
	Pacal I				612, Mar. 9		—
10.	L. Zac-Kuk		612, Oct. 22		640, Sep. 12		3
	Kan-Bahlum-Mo'				643, Jan. 1		—
11.	Pacal the Great	603, Mar. 26	615, Jul. 29	12	683, Aug. 31	80	67
	L. Ahpo-Hel		626, Mar. 22		672, Nov. 16		46
12.	Chan-Bahlum II	635, May 23	684, Jan. 10	49	702, Feb. 20	67	18

FIG. 6:2

THE
CHILDREN
OF THE
FIRST
MOTHER:
FAMILY
AND
DYNASTY
AT
PALENQUE

———

219

we have their births and accessions, and a reasonable estimate of their ages at death. We can surmise the latter since we know a new king usually acceded shortly after his predecessor's death. For those kings whose names occur only on the sarcophagus and panels of the Temple of Inscriptions, we have only their dates of accession and death, and thus we cannot estimate length of life or their ages at various events. Still, these four lists taken together allow us to reconstruct the history of Palenque's dynasty for the ten generations culminating with Chan-Bahlum.[5]

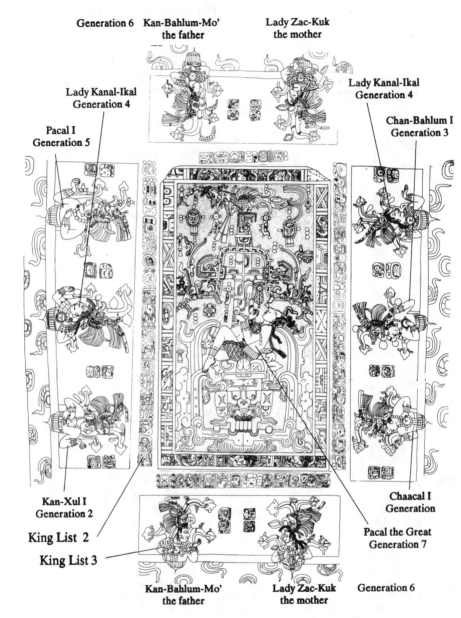

Generation 6 Kan-Bahlum-Mo'
the father

Lady Zac-Kuk
the mother

Lady Kanal-Ikal
Generation 4

Lady Kanal-Ikal
Generation 4

Pacal I
Generation 5

Chan-Bahlum I
Generation 3

FIG. 6:3
**Pacal's
Sarcophagus
and the
Portraits of
His Ancestors**
drawing by
M. G. Robertson

Kan-Xul I
Generation 2

King List 2

King List 3

Kan-Bahlum-Mo'
the father

Lady Zac-Kuk
the mother

Generation 6

Chaacal I
Generation

Pacal the Great
Generation 7

The very existence of these king lists raises questions about their context and the motivations of the men who made them. What so fascinated and troubled these men that they felt compelled to present such a comprehensive treatise on their dynasty on such important monumental spaces? Here, as in any true history, it is not so much a matter of the facts of the history as their interpretation that reveals the intentions of the chronicler. The royal preoccupation with these lists, and the parallel information that comes to us from other sources, hint of troubles in the very dynastic succession the two kings so obsessively recorded.

The essential problem, as we surmise it from their public efforts to explain it away, was to extricate dynastic succession from the same principle of lineage that originally fostered and legitimated it. As we shall see, Pacal inherited the throne of Palenque from his mother in violation of the normal patrilineal inheritance patterns that governed Maya succession. His most pressing concern, then, was to justify this departure from the normal rules. To prove his point, he and his son, who inherited the problem, made elegant and imaginative use of the Maya mythology that was the basis of social order and kingly rule.

Pacal's portrait gallery of his direct ancestors, carved on the sides of his sarcophagus, gives us his version of how each of his ancestors appeared (Fig. 6:3). Each rises with a fruit tree from a crack in the earth to create an orchard of the ancestral dead. Chaacal I in the southeast corner begins the progression through time and lineage that culminates with the mother and father of Pacal, who rise on both the north and south ends of the sarcophagus.

Within this ancestral orchard, Pacal depicted two women—his mother, Lady Zac-Kuk, and his great-grandmother, Lady Kanal-Ikal—and each is depicted twice. Why would Pacal have chosen to double the portraits of these women when he could just as easily have doubled a male ancestor or added portraits of even earlier ancestors to the portrait gallery? In the case of his mother, we might infer that he doubled her portrait precisely because she was his mother. After all, he did the same for his father, Kan-Bahlum-Mo', in spite of the fact that his father never ruled. This line of reasoning, however, cannot explain why his great-grandmother, Lady Kanal-Ikal, held an honored place on the sarcophagus. Some other factor must explain her special status.

From our vantage at least, these two women were certainly deserving of special attention. Lady Kanal-Ikal and Lady Zac-Kuk were very unusual individuals in that they are the only women we can be sure ruled as true kings. They were neither consorts nor, as in the case of Lady Wac-Chanil-Ahau of Naranjo, regents for young heirs. Yet by their very status as rulers, they created serious dilemmas for the government of their kingdom. When the throne of Palenque descended through Kanal-Ikal to her children, it became the prerogative of a different lineage, for the Maya nobility reckoned family membership through their males. Lady Kanal-Ikal and Lady Zac-Kuk were legitimate rulers because they were the children of kings and, as such, members of the current royal lineage. The offspring of their marriages, however, belonged to the father's lineage. Each time these women inherited the kingship and passed it on to their children, the throne automatically descended through another patriline. This kind of jump broke the link between lineage and dynasty in the succession.

Because the line changed twice through these women rulers, Palenque's dynasts did not belong to one patriline, but rather to three (Fig. 6:4). The first lineage to declare command of the high kingship descended from the founder Bahlum-Kuk through eight successors to Lady Kanal-Ikal. Even though they were of a different lineage, Pacal and his successors

THE
CHILDREN
OF THE
FIRST
MOTHER:
FAMILY
AND
DYNASTY
AT
PALENQUE

—

221

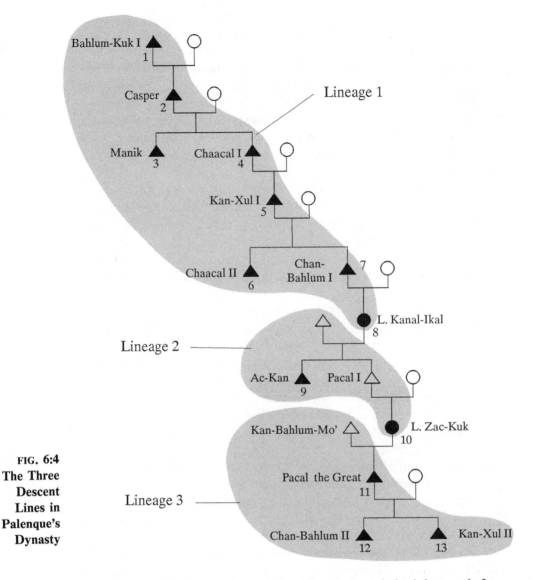

to the throne of Palenque claimed that they derived their right to rule from this man. In this respect, while they followed the traditional practice of other Maya dynasties, which also claimed descent from a founding king, they were declaring the dynastic succession to be a force transcending patrilineality.

Lady Kanal-Ikal must have been a charismatic and exceptional woman to have successfully ascended to the throne of a high kingship. What history she herself may have created lies deeply buried under later construction—if indeed she was even permitted the royal prerogative of recording personal history. In all likelihood, she would have based her legitimate claim to the kingship on her status as the child of an acknowledged ruler. Her progeny claimed the throne after her, although they belonged to the lineage of her husband—a man never mentioned by name in the Palenque chronicles. Notables in this second lineage included the king Ac-Kan and his brother Pacal, who died before he could become the high king.

Even though he himself was never a king, this first Pacal appears in the royal grove carved on the side of the sarcophagus. There is a good reason for this. In each generation, the royal line could pass through only one sibling. In this case, the first Pacal was probably the father of Lady Zac-Kuk, the next ruler and last scion of this second royal lineage.[6] The presence of the first Pacal on the side of the great sarcophagus confirms that Pacal the Great was trying to make something more than a list of kings here. He was orchestrating a careful political manipulation of an orthodox belief. By placing his direct ancestors, both kings and nonkings, into a frame of reference that both honored the rules of lineage and transcended them, he worked to establish an unshakable claim to the throne.

The third lineage began with Pacal the Great himself. As the son of a ruler, Lady Zac-Kuk, he had the same legitimate claim to the throne as Lady Kanal-Ikal's child, Ac-Kan. Difficulties arose, however, when Pacal's own children, Chan-Bahlum and Kan-Xul, followed their illustrious father to the throne. These men belonged to the lineage of their father and their paternal grandfather, Kan-Bahlum-Mo'. Hence the problems with their claim to the kingship were different from Pacal's and analogous to those of the descendant kings of the second lineage, Ac-Kan and Zac-Kuk. They were the offspring of a lineage that had no legitimate claim to produce kings.

We do not know what happened the first time one of these sidesteps in the royal dynasty occurred because we have no contemporary inscriptions from Lady Kanal-Ikal or her children.[7] The second time it happened, however, in the case of her granddaughter Zac-Kuk, the contradictory imperatives of lineage and dynasty precipitated a crisis. Lady Zac-Kuk's offspring, Pacal, and his son, Chan-Bahlum, responded to the crisis with the two extraordinarily innovative projects under discussion—the Temple of Inscriptions and the Group of the Cross. These remarkable monuments were designed to interpret the dynastic history of Palenque in such a fashion as to make their legitimate rights to the throne undeniable.

In their presentations of the dynastic sequence at Palenque, both Pacal and Chan-Bahlum recorded the descent line as if it were historically unbroken. At the same time, they substantiated their claim of legitimacy by using the current mythology, explaining the historical breaks in the descent sequence as if they were preordained by the cosmos.

Their twofold strategy was brilliant. First they declared Lady Zac-Kuk, Pacal's mother, to be like-in-kind to the first mother of gods and kings at the beginning of the present creation. This goddess was the mother of the three central gods of Maya religion—the deity complex known as the Palenque Triad. Secondly, Pacal and Chan-Bahlum asserted that Pacal was born on a day that exactly replicated the temporal symmetry of that goddess's birth. In this way they were able to imply that the human king was made of the same divine substance as the goddess. Having thereby demonstrated that the mother and son were the stuff of the gods, they declared that their own inheritance of the throne from Pacal's mother replicated the actions of the gods at the beginning of creation: the direct

THE
CHILDREN
OF THE
FIRST
MOTHER:
FAMILY
AND
DYNASTY
AT
PALENQUE

—

223

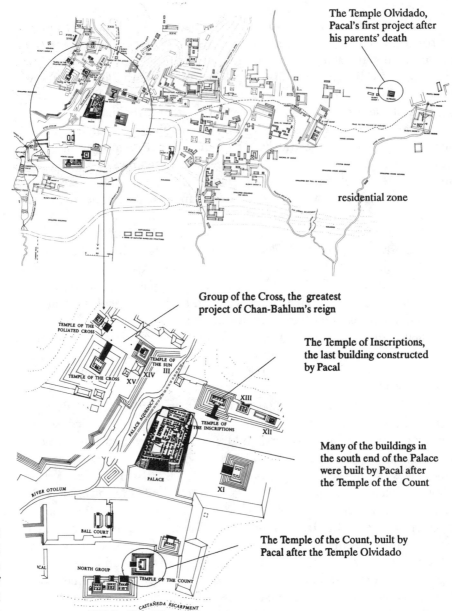

The Temple Olvidado, Pacal's first project after his parents' death

residential zone

Group of the Cross, the greatest project of Chan-Bahlum's reign

The Temple of Inscriptions, the last building constructed by Pacal

Many of the buildings in the south end of the Palace were built by Pacal after the Temple of the Count

The Temple of the Count, built by Pacal after the Temple Olvidado

FIG. 6:5 Palenque and the Public Works of Pacal and Chan-Bahlum

transmission of rule through females as well as males. Here was a radical new definition of dynastic succession that denied patrilineality as the sole fount of power. But who could possibly disagree with something that replayed creation?

Pacal's overall strategy to hold the throne was more subtle than his son's, perhaps because he acceded at age twelve while his mother was still alive and after she had been ruling for three years. Lady Zac-Kuk may have left no direct history of her reign; but like her grandmother, Kanal-Ikal, she stands out as a masterful politician, able to manipulate the rival interests of her paternal clansmen away from the succession and toward each other or outside enemies. No doubt her husband, the consort of a princess of the blood, figured prominently in her success through appeal to his own influential noble clan and his own deeds of valor. Just getting her young son on the throne was a triumph. Consolidating that victory required an acceptable historical and theological rationale for this audacious move, one that would calm the discontent of all the noble clans of the kingdom whose own high social status hinged upon lineage descent.

Lady Zac-Kuk lived another twenty-five years after Pacal's accession. While she lived, she and her husband, Kan-Bahlum-Mo', apparently sustained the alliances necessary to support her son's rule; but she very probably kept the real power in her own hands. Not until after her death in 640 did Pacal commission works that left their mark in the archaeological record of Palenque. It is also likely that during the delicate transitional period, this resplendent lady helped to craft the ingenious political resolution to the succession celebrated by her son in subsequent katuns.

In 647, seven years after his mother's death and four years after his father's, Pacal celebrated his newfound independence by dedicating the Temple Olvidado (Fig. 6:5) in the western zone of the city.[8] On the ridge side above a residential zone spanning one of two permanent water sources that coursed through the city, Pacal's architects built a new kind of temple that held the seeds of a revolution in architectural technology.[9] With its double-galleried interior, thin supporting walls, multiple doors, and trefoil vaults, this building foreshadowed the technology that would soon produce the largest interior volume and best lighting ever known in Maya architecture.

At the successful completion of his first construction project, Pacal began an extensive building campaign which included the Temple of the Count, the subterranean galleries of the Palace, House E, House B, and finally House C in the Palace which was dedicated in 659 when he was fifty-six years old.[10] With each new building, Pacal experimented with the new style and pushed the innovative technology further.

When Pacal reached his early seventies, he must have begun feeling his mortality, for he began the last great project of his lifetime: the construction of the great mortuary Temple of the Inscriptions. This building, which housed his ultimate statement on dynasty, became one of the most famous monuments in the Mesoamerican world. Built in the stylistic tradition he established with the Temple Olvidado,[11] this spectacular pyramid was a labor of imagination and complex engineering. First, the work crews cleared and leveled a section of ground next to the Palace. This site was located at the foot of the sacred natural mountain which loomed over the great central plaza opening on to the northern horizon. Against the mountain face (Fig. 6:1), a pit was dug into which the laborers set a huge block of limestone that would become Pacal's coffin when finished.

Consulting with the king, Palenque's greatest artists designed an image (Fig. 6:3) that would represent his fall down the great trunk of the World Tree into the open jaws of the Otherworld. At the same time, they incorporated a sense of resurrection into this death image. As Pacal falls,

THE
CHILDREN
OF THE
FIRST
MOTHER:
FAMILY
AND
DYNASTY
AT
PALENQUE
——
225

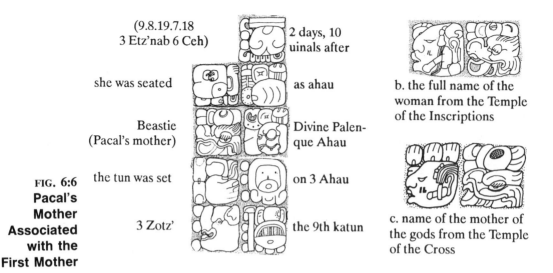

(9.8.19.7.18
3 Etz'nab 6 Ceh)

she was seated

2 days, 10
uinals after

as ahau

b. the full name of the
woman from the Temple
of the Inscriptions

Beastie
(Pacal's mother)

Divine Palen-
que Ahau

FIG. 6:6
Pacal's
Mother
Associated
with the
First Mother

the tun was set

on 3 Ahau

3 Zotz'

the 9th katun

c. name of the mother of
the gods from the Temple
of the Cross

he is accompanied by the image of a half-skeletal monster head carrying a bowl of sacrifice marked with the glyph of the sun. This particular glyph is a powerful symbol, representing the sun in transition between life and death, poised on the brink of the Otherworld. Like the sun, the king would rise again in the east after his journey through Xibalba. He was, after all, the living manifestation of the Hero Twins who had set the example of how to defeat the Lords of Death.

Around the hollowed coffin in which he would lie, the artists drew the images of his direct ancestors. These images were arranged in ascending generations, moving from south to north and from east to west, culminating with the central pivot—the king himself. When they were done with the drawings and Pacal had approved them, workmen moved in to construct a protective wall around their work. They then filled the chamber with sand and the masons and architects began to raise the pyramid. Into its center they built a vaulted stairway that would let the sculptors get to the coffin when it was no longer in danger from the construction. Down this dark stairway they would bring the body of the king when he died, setting it into the hollow at the center of the sarcophagus before they rolled the lid across the opening and sealed him in forever.

Pacal's death was still far off, however, as the great mass of rock and earth rose upward in the nine great terraces upon which the six-doored temple would rest. His masons built the foundation platform of the temple first and then raised the central and rear walls that would hold up the roof. While these walls stood unencumbered by the heavy stone vaulting of the roof, sculptors went to the special quarries where the finest sculptural stone was found. There they cut huge, thick slabs to mount within the bearing walls of the temple—two to fit into the front surfaces of the walls separating the front and back rooms, flanking the doorway into the rear sanctum; and a third to fit into the back wall of the temple in a position

Kuk

Zac- Lady

Kina Ah-Nab-Pacal

Pacal just before
he receives the
crown from his
mother

Lady Zac-
Kuk, Pacal's
mother

Double-headed
Jaguar Throne

FIG. 6:7
**The Oval
Palace
Tablet and
Pacal's
Accession**

where the light from the doorways could still shine upon it. Pacal's scribes
then drew a grid to accommodate a total of 640 glyphs which would
record Pacal's katun history and the important events of his own reign.
They reserved the last two columns of the text for his death. Then, as with
the sarcophagus, they built a protective wall around the inscriptions until
the construction of the vaults and the plastering work was completed.

The passages on these temple tablets give us our first glimpse of this
family's strategy of dynastic legitimization. Less than three years before
his own accession, Pacal recorded the accession of a woman whom he
named in a mysterious and unusual way (Fig. 6:6). This woman took the
throne on October 22, 612, 202 days before the end of the ninth katun,
when Pacal was nine years old. Her name is recorded with a glyph written
in the form of a screaming bird: Its bulging beak lies back against its
forehead, and its gaping mouth is filled with feathers. Since this strange
bird is a variant of the Palenque Emblem Glyph, we can assume that Pacal
meant to connect the woman in question with the sacred name of his
kingdom. Even more important, this same glyph was also used to name
the First Mother, affectionately dubbed Lady Beastie by scholars, who
was born before the present creation. This goddess, as we have mentioned
above, was the mother of the gods and the creatrix of Maya myth.

Is Pacal telling us, then, that the person who held the throne before
he became the king was the First Mother? In a way that is exactly what
he intended to say, for this mysterious woman was indeed a mother,
although a human one. She was his own mother, Lady Zac-Kuk,[12] who
gave him life and then the crown when he acceded to power (Fig. 6:7).
By using the name of the goddess to refer to his mother, Pacal declared
her to be analogous to the mother of the gods. By logical extension, Pacal
was then the goddess's offspring, like-in-kind to the lords who were the

THE
CHILDREN
OF THE
FIRST
MOTHER:
FAMILY
AND
DYNASTY
AT
PALENQUE

——

227

three gods of the Palenque Triad, the Late Classic version of the gods the Late Preclassic ahauob fashioned on the temples of Cerros.

The great Pacal died in his eightieth year and was buried by his sons in rituals that involved the highest and lowest people in his realm. Opened again in 1952 by the great Mexican archaeologist Alberto Ruz, his tomb contains a record of his funerary rites frozen forever in time. We can visualize the rituals that, in the final hours, sent him on his fall into the realm of Xibalba to face the Lords of Death.

•

Chan-Bahlum tasted the salty sweat that rolled into the corner of his mouth as he lowered himself to the last of the high, slippery steps that descended down through the rock of his father's sacred mountain.[13] Nearby was the vaulted tomb where his father awaited the rites that would begin his fall into the Otherworld. Dizzy from three days of fasting, the hard climb up the outer stairs, and the descent down the inner ones, Chan-Bahlum reached out to the white plastered wall to steady himself. At last, he stepped down into the dank cloud of smoke that filled the corridor at the bottom of the stairs. Masking the sweet smell of death, the blessed incense hovered around a sphere of torchlight before vanishing upward, like the Vision Serpent, following the dark path upward to the human world.[14]

His brown chest heaving like a frightened deer, Chan-Bahlum paused once more, this time to catch his breath. Sixty-seven high steps led from the world of light above, down to the gate of Xibalba. As the senior son of the dead king, and the king-elect, it had been Chan-Bahlum's obligation to descend deep into this most holy mountain to send his father on the journey only the few and the prepared survived: the journey to confront the Lords of Death and to trick them into relinquishing life once again.

The long days of fasting and grief were taking their toll. Chan-Bahlum felt all his forty-eight years weighing on him like stones upon the backs of his father's masons. Remembering his duty, he threw off his exhaustion and straightened his heavy jade pendant so that it lay squarely on his chest. His dignity restored, he turned to look into the black eyes of his younger brother. The thirty-eight-year-old Kan-Xul, by their father's decree, would be king after him. The older man looked upon the more delicate features of his brother and saw in them the image of their father as he had been in his prime. Together they continued into the tomb.

Startled from his concentrated effort, a sculptor saw the princes approaching through the swirling smoke and tore himself away from his last-minute work,[15] carving the great king's death date on the south edge of the massive sarcophagus lid. He quickly gathered his tools and the debris from his work into a net bag and slung them over his naked, sweat-damp shoulder. Pushing past the princes in the narrow confines of the hall, he mumbled apologies and began his climb out of the tomb. Kan-Xul smiled briefly to reassure his nervous brother. Even with the final rush to transform the imagery of the dead and reborn kings on the sarcophagus from painted line to carved relief, the burial rites would go without mishap. Chan-Bahlum knew it fell to him, as patriarch of Pacal's lineage, to bury his father properly and heal the wound his death had caused in the fabric of the kingdom. He was determined the ritual would go well and dispel the danger of this time.

Chan-Bahlum spoke softly to his brother and turned back toward the heavy stone door and the three steps that led up to the inner chamber. Xoc,[16] his father's adviser and a respected member of the lineage, awaited them at the door. He, along with a cadre of shamans, would assist the brothers as they sent their father into the terrifying fall to the Otherworld. First, however, they would equip the dead king with the power to rise like the dawning sun. Chan-Bahlum stepped through the triangular opening in the upper part of the tomb vault and entered the stifling hot chamber filled with the shamans who would sing the king's spirit on its way. They would contain the dangerous energies that would be left by the king's departure.

Standing on the threshold above the five stairs that led down into the tomb chamber, Chan-Bahlum paused to gaze at his father's body. Nestled in an arm-deep cavity cut into the huge limestone block that served as the sarcophagus, Pacal lay on his back with his hands at his sides. His legs were extended and his feet relaxed to the sides as if he were sleeping. The dry, wrinkled skin of the eighty-year-old man seemed transparent in the flickering light of the torches held by the shamans. The jade collar that covered his chest and the cuffs on his wrists gleamed against the red walls of the coffin. The green headband with its Jester God lay on his forehead where it would tell the Lords of Xibalba that a great king had come among them.

Chan-Bahlum and his brother advanced down the steps with slow dignity, passing between the plaster portraits of their father modeled on either side of the entrance. Their horny feet rasped on the cold limestone of the steps as they moved to the platform that had been built so that they could stand level with the body, above the floor of the chamber. Together they stepped from the platform and onto the sarcophagus itself. Chan-Bahlum walked to the right side of the hollow that held his father's body, while his brother went to the left side. Simultaneously they dropped to their knees and gazed for the last time upon their father's face. Kan-Xul reached down into the coffin to straighten the ornament in Pacal's left ear and to align the mica rectangle piece that enframed his mouth.

The two brothers locked eyes as Chan-Bahlum instructed the shamans to join them on the narrow surfaces surrounding the coffin depression and begin the final rites. Xoc stepped to his side and handed him a delicate mosaic mask of jade, shell, and obsidian formed into a likeness of his father's face. Carefully balancing his weight, Chan-Bahlum leaned forward, reaching down into the coffin to lay the mask across his father's features. The obsidian eyes of the dead Pacal stared heavenward from under the shining green brow. The visage of this great king would not be lost as his flesh decayed and left only bone.

Satisfied with the positioning of the mask, Chan-Bahlum and Kan-Xul slowly moved until they were kneeling by the dead man's waist. A

THE
CHILDREN
OF THE
FIRST
MOTHER:
FAMILY
AND
DYNASTY
AT
PALENQUE

———

229

shaman gave Chan-Bahlum a cube of jade which he laid reverently in the open palm of the right hand, already adorned with five rings of deep green jade. Another shaman gave Kan-Xul a sphere of jade to be set in the ring-laden left hand to balance the cube in the right. Leaning forward again, Chan-Bahlum set a small jade statue on the rich embroidered cloth that covered his father's genitals from whence had come the seed and the blood of the greatest of all beings in the kingdom.

Together, the brothers moved to their father's feet, each of them laying a sphere next to the sole of the foot closest to him. Lastly, Chan-Bahlum took a large hunk of jade that had been reverently and skillfully carved into the image of the patron god of the month Pax. It was an image that read *te,* the word for the tree down which the dead king was falling in the image on his sarcophagus lid and which he had embodied in his person while alive. The high-pitched, droning voices of the shamans echoed off the walls of the vaulted chamber, as they sent prayers to accompany the falling soul of the king. Satisfied that the body was prepared in the honorable manner appropriate to a high king, Chan-Bahlum and his brother stood up and stepped off the sarcophagus and back onto the platform at its south end.

Chan-Bahlum spoke softly to Xoc who disappeared through the door and called up the stairs. The sounds of the shamans' prayers counterpointed the shuffling sounds of footsteps descending the high steps from the temple above. Finally, the frightened face of a young boy appeared in the doorway. It was Chac-Zutz', scion of an important and honored cahal lineage which had served the high king for many generations. Chac-Zutz' tugged gently on the arm of the four-year-old Chaacal who lagged behind him. The youngest male issue of Pacal's line, this child might one day be the king if neither Chan-Bahlum nor his brother could produce an heir who lived long enough to inherit the throne.[17]

Chan-Bahlum stared at the two boys with dark-eyed intensity and spoke in a commanding voice, instructing them to look upon the great king who had transformed the face of the kingdom and made them all great. Chan-Bahlum and Kan-Xul stood in patient dignity while all the important men of the clan filed in behind the boys and then quickly ascended after taking this last opportunity to gaze upon the great Pacal before he was sealed forever into the Otherworld of the ancestors.

When it was done, the king-to-be gestured to the men of the royal lineage who had been chosen to help seal the coffin. After hushed consultation, two of them jumped down to the chamber floor. They handed the heavy stone lid, cut to fit inside the hollow holding the body, up to the four men standing on top of the sarcophagus. These men threaded ropes through holes drilled into each corner of the lid and then lowered it carefully onto the inset ledge around the coffin hollow. Once there, it formed a smooth stone surface across the top of the monolith. With the body now sealed in, they withdrew the ropes and dropped a stone plug into each of the drilled holes. The plug in the southwest corner had a notch cut in it so that the spirit tube, built into the stairway, could connect the chamber where the dead king lay to the world of his descendants above.

The time had finally come to pull the enormous carved lid over the top of the sarcophagus. This action would finish the sealing process and set the dead king amid the symbols that would insure success in his confrontation with the Lords of Death. Chan-Bahlum and his party stepped outside the tomb chamber to give the workers room to carry out this last difficult task. Strong young men of the ahau and cahal rank had been chosen to execute this dangerous and precise operation under the direction of the head mason who had overseen the construction of the tomb chamber. The prayers of the shamans were soon overwhelmed by the controlled pandemonium. The men whispered hoarsely to each other as they brought the equipment into the tomb. They set log rollers on top of the massive stone box that now held the king's body and arranged themselves as best they could along the sides of the carved slab. Throaty grunts underscored the straining of their muscles as they heaved at the impossibly heavy lid. From the steps above, Chan-Bahlum watched as the great lid finally began to slide slowly forward onto the rollers. Struggling and sweating, the men worked in the close space of the chamber, urging the great lid into its place. Once this was accomplished, they labored to extricate the rollers and seat the lid with the help of ropes strung from the great stone beams in the upper vaulting of the tomb.

Finally, however, it was done. The young men passed the rollers out of the chamber and up the stairs to the venting tunnels in the side of the sacred mountain. Then, more quickly than Chan-Bahlum had believed possible, they were gone, taking all the equipment and the debris of their effort with them. The urgent pandemonium diminished until suddenly only the steady chants of the shamans reverberated through the tomb. The brothers crossed the threshold and stepped down to the platform to gaze at the image of their father carved upon the lid. There they saw him poised in the first moment of his descent down the World Tree into the jaws of Xibalba—his forehead pierced by the smoking ax that marked him as the incarnation of the last born of the First Mother's sons.

Without speaking, the younger brother lowered himself onto the floor of the tomb chamber to stand at the southwest corner of the great sarcophagus. His eyes were level with the portraits of the ancestors carved on its sides. Chan-Bahlum, who had jumped to the floor at the southeast corner, reached back up to take a plaster head from Xoc, who stood on the platform above. He waited until Xoc had given another head to Kan-Xul, and then the two of them knelt down. As older brother, it was Chan-Bahlum's perogative to act first. Lying down on his belly, he crawled forward between the stone piers that supported the platform at the south end of his father's sarcophagus. It was a tight fit but he managed to wriggle between the obstacles until he could reach far under the massive stone sarcophagus, which stood on six low stone blocks.[18] With a silent call to the ancestors of his line, he stretched his arm as far inward as he could reach and gently deposited a life-sized head made of plaster. Torn from another building as an offering to help Pacal's soul in its journey, it represented his father as he had looked in his prime. Kan-Xul, in his turn, wriggled under the huge sarcophagus and placed his sculpture next to the first. The second sculpture depicted Pacal as he had looked at the age of twelve when he became king.[19]

Sweating in the heat, the two of them extricated themselves and stood to take the ritual cup and plate Xoc handed down to them. The brothers then knelt in unison, carefully balancing the containers which were filled to the brim with food and drink to succor the dead king's soul on his journey. They placed the offerings on the floor under the south side of the platform while the shamans chanted prayers asking that Pacal's journey be swift and his defeat of the Lords of Death sure. Finished with the ritual, the two brothers accepted a hand from Xoc, who helped them up onto the platform again.

Chan-Bahlum looked at the red-lidded sarcophagus once more—examining every detail of the preparations. The flickering torchlight played across the relief images of Pacal molded on the plaster walls of the chamber. In front of him, on the north end of the lid, was the carved image of his father. It almost seemed to him as if the dead king were present, sitting cross-legged on the stone platform that had supported the lid before it had been wrestled atop the sarcophagus. Chan-Bahlum stood still, lost in the memory of his father and in the anticipation of his own transformation into the high king. He was a three-katun lord in his forty-eighth year of life. To the people of his world, he was already an old man, and he wondered if the gods would give him time to leave as great a mark on the flow of history as his father had.

At his feet a plasterer worked, laying the spirit tube from the notch in the south end of the lid, across the platform, and up the five stairs to tie into the hollow pipe that ran up the vaulted stairs to the floor of the temple above. The kings of Palenque were practical men as well as people of faith. To help their ancestors ascend into the world of humankind, they created a physical path for the Vision Serpent to follow when a dead king wished to speak to his descendants.

With the spirit tube ready, only one ritual remained. Chan-Bahlum turned to his brother, who handed him the great jade belt his father had worn to mark his status as a divine ahau. The flint pendants dangling under the jade ahau heads clanked together as Chan-Bahlum grasped the leather ties and stretched the heavy belt out between his extended hands. With reverence, he stepped up onto the red surface of the sarcophagus lid and knelt upon the image of his falling father. Leaning forward, he laid the belt down on the lid, stretching it out across the god image that marked the World Tree as a holy thing. The king's belt rested above the center point of his human body, now hidden under the heavy lid. His soul could at last begin its journey, released from the case of worldly flesh, prepared for the fall to the Otherworld with food, images of his human form, and the belt that would signal his divinity and rank as he met the Lords of Death.

The shamans' song changed as Chan-Bahlum and his brother voiced their farewell, asking their father to help them when he emerged from Xibalba. Heavy with grief, they climbed the five short stairs leading out of the chamber and prepared themselves for the next stage of the ritual. Stepping down into the outer corridor, they watched as the shamans pushed the huge triangular door closed. Masons rushed down from the venting passages with baskets of wet plaster, which they threw onto the edges of the door with loud slapping noises. Using wooden spatulas and their hands, they smoothed the plaster until all evidence of the door was gone. One of them shouted an order and other men rushed down the long stairs with more plaster and stones. With the same efficient haste, they constructed a stone box at the end of the corridor setting one side of it against the now hidden door. Finishing in a rush, they cleaned up the debris, gathered their tools, and left in a silent hurry for they knew what was coming. A great king had died and it was time to sanctify his journey with a sacrifice so that he could be reborn.

In the sudden silence that fell after the workers had departed, Chan-Bahlum could hear the scuffling descent of more people, this time from the temple above. He turned and saw five captives being dragged down the stairs by the honored kinsmen of the dead king. A woman and four men would go to Xibalba this day to accompany Pacal on his journey. Some of them moaned in terror, but one young man trod forward to meet his fate with insolent pride. He was an ahau taken in battle and chosen to go with Pacal because of his arrogant courage and reckless bravado.

Chan-Bahlum grabbed the young ahau's hair and wrenched his head up so that he could see the captive's eyes. He closed his hand on the hilt of the flint knife he had brought with him for this act of sacrifice. In silence he plunged it into the captive's chest and struck up into the heart. This was the signal. His kinsmen screamed in a cacophony which echoed in the waiting ears above and fell upon the victims, slaughtering them with furious slashes of their bloodstained knives. The limp bodies of the dead were tossed in tangled abandon into the box.

With the sacrifice completed, Chan-Bahlum left the blood-splattered corridor and began to mount the stairs in slow dignity, conserving his strength for the final rite he must perform in the temple above. The muscles in his legs burned with exhaustion as he turned at the midway platform and began the climb up the second flight of stairs. His beblooded kinsmen followed him in a reverent silence broken only by their heavy breathing as they struggled with the hard climb and the residual emotions from the sacrificial ritual.

Chan-Bahlum emerged through the floor of the temple, where the spirit tube from his father's coffin ended in the head of the Vision Serpent. When he had made his careful way around the ledge beside the stairway entrance, shamans took him by the arms and stripped away his loincloth. One of them handed him a fresh blade of obsidian just struck from a core. He reached down and grasped his penis, holding it tightly as he pierced it three times with the point of the bright black razor. Handing back the blade, he pulled long strands of bark paper through the wounds and watched them turn red with the sacred blood of sacrifice. It was his first

THE
CHILDREN
OF THE
FIRST
MOTHER:
FAMILY
AND
DYNASTY
AT
PALENQUE
——
233

sacrificial act as patriarch of the royal clan, an act of symbolic birth in the midst of death.

His brother performed his own act of sacrifice, as did the men who had helped them dispatch the captives. Stained crimson with the flow from his own body and the blood of the captives below, Chan-Bahlum stepped out of the back chamber. He passed through the great katun history his father had commissioned to appear between the central piers of the outer wall. A great roar of grief rose from the gathered multitude in the plaza below as they saw him emerge, the blood on his white loincloth clearly visible in the oblique light of the setting sun. The people of the kingdom in their thousands had come to witness the beginning of the great king's journey. When Chan-Bahlum's bloodstained body appeared and cast its shadows on the whitened walls of the temple piers, they knew it was done. Like the setting sun that lit the scene, the great king was falling toward Xibalba. Hundreds began their song of grief and cut their own flesh in pious prayers for the king. Drums beat a mind-numbing rhythm accompanied by the piercing notes of clay whistles blown by people exhausted by days of dancing and fasting in preparation for this moment.

Chan-Bahlum stood above, swaying slightly, looking down on the seething mass of his people. The paper hanging down against his legs was now saturated with his blood, which dripped to stain the white plaster floor below his feet. His younger brother stood off behind his right shoulder, reddened by his own act of sacrifice. The corridor behind them was filled with the most important people of the royal clan. On the terrace just below the temple summit stood ahauob of other lineages and the cahalob who had governed the towns of the kingdoms for the king. They too had drawn blood that now stained the cloth bands tied to their wrists and hanging from their ears and loins.

Shamans stood beside hip-high braziers modeled in the image of the great Ancestral Twins, and watched Chan-Bahlum closely. He began to dance slowly in place, preparing to enter the trance of communication with the dead. When the shamans saw the trance state descend upon him, they threw handfuls of copal resin and rubber (the "blood of trees") into the fire burning in the conical bowls sitting atop the clay cylinders. Others brought shallow plates filled with blood-saturated paper from the king-to-be and his brother. As great billows of black smoke rose from the braziers, cries of wonder rose with them from the plaza below. The last light of the sinking sun lit the rising columns of smoke to tell the thousands of watchers that the ancestors had arrived. The moaning wail of conch trumpets echoed off the mountain walls and spread over the great plain below. The dead king's ancestors knew that he was coming to join them. They would go to help him in his conflict with the Lords of Death.

•

The forty-eight-year-old Chan-Bahlum waited 132 days after his father died to conduct his own rituals of accession. The responsibility of finishing his father's funerary temple fell to him, and this task provided the first step in his own campaign to prove the legitimacy of his ascent to

the forehead ax of God K

the serpent foot of God K

the child, Chan-Bahlum

a. The Temple of Inscriptions Piers

b. The Piers of the Temple

c. Chan-Bahlum's name from the end pier

Palenque lineage jaguar lord

Mah Kina Chan-Bahlum

????

Divine Palenque Ahau

THE
CHILDREN
OF THE
FIRST
MOTHER:
FAMILY
AND
DYNASTY
AT
PALENQUE

235

the throne. To do so, he asserted that he had received his power by direct transfer of authority from his dead father in an act replicating events that occurred at the time of creation. In this way, he redefined dynastic succession as a supernatural rite of ecstatic communion between the heir and the dead king, who was in the Otherworld.

The first project of Chan-Bahlum's reign demonstrates his preoccupation with this new definition of dynasty: the direct ritual transmission of power in place of the traditional system of lineage succession. While finishing his father's funerary monument, he usurped the outer piers of the temple at the summit. On these he depicted the rituals in which his father

a. Foot of the baby on
Pier C of the Temple of
Inscriptions

b. Six-fingered hand of
the figure on Pier E of
House A

c. Six-toed foot on the
North Door Panel of
the Temple of the Sun

chose him as the legitimate heir and transformed him from a human child into a living god[20] (Fig. 6:8). In this scene, modeled in brightly painted stucco, Pacal and three other adults present the six-year-old Chan-Bahlum from the edge of a pyramid. The height of this structure enabled the audience below, which consisted of the nobility and probably a large number of the commoners as well, to see and acknowledge that this child, of all Pacal's offspring, was the one who would become the next ruler.[21] Chan-Bahlum, however, mixed the portrayal of the actual ritual with images conveying the supernatural sanction of the new status this ritual bestowed upon him.

The child who is cradled in the arms of his predecessors has both divine and purely human features. His status as a divinity is emphasized by merging other parts of his anatomy with the signs of the god GII, the third-born child of the First Mother (Fig. 6:8a). One of Chan-Bahlum's legs, for example, transforms into a open-mouthed serpent in the fashion characteristic of the god. Moreover, penetrating the baby's forehead is the smoking-ax blade that is so often depicted stuck through the forehead mirror of the god. The identical symbol impales the forehead of Pacal, his father, on the sarcophagus lid in the tomb deep below to bear witness to his divine status as he falls into the Otherworld. Yet to insure that the baby on the Temple of Inscriptions piers was not taken simply to be an image of the god, he was depicted with six toes on each foot (Fig. 6:9a), a physical deformity shown repeatedly in Chan-Bahlum's adult portraits (Fig. 6:9b-d). The inclusion of this characteristic deformity affirmed the humanity of the baby figure and its personal identity as the six-toed heir Chan-Bahlum. Combining these contrasting features asserted the essential divinity of the human heir.

This ritual display of the child heir, then, constituted the public affirmation of Chan-Bahlum's new identity as a "divine human." This new identity was sanctified by the sacrifice of captives taken in battle by Pacal. Another proud father, King Chaan-Muan, depicted exactly this sequence of events explicitly and graphically in the murals of Bonampak, a contemporary Late Classic kingdom on the Usumacinta river.[22] Chan-Bahlum, like the Bonampak king, turned this ephemeral ritual of heir display into

a permanent public declaration of his legitimate status by placing it on the facade of a temple which dominated the central public plaza of his city. The fact that the temple housed his father's grave made the assertion all the more powerful.

During the time when he was finishing his father's temple, Chan-Bahlum also began work on the Group of the Cross, the buildings that would house his own version of Palenque's dynastic history—the Temple of the Cross, the Temple of the Foliated Cross, and the Temple of the Sun. In pictures and texts of unsurpassed eloquence, the new king completed the presentation of his new doctrine of dynasty as an institution transcending lineage. In order to accomplish this, it was necessary for him to reach back to the fundamental and orthodox concepts of royal authority. Chan-Bahlum approached the nebulous and paradoxical nature of political power with the vision of a great theologian and statesman. He divided his pictorial and textual treatise into three temples, thus recalling the triadic arrangement of primordial Late Preclassic royal architecture.[23] In this way, his statement evoked "origins" to the Maya—just as we "borrow" from the architecture of the Parthenon and Pantheon in our own state and religious monuments to declare the Greek and Roman origins of our cultural heritage.

The three temples of the Group of the Cross rise from the summits of pyramidal platforms. The tallest temple is in the north, the middle one in the east, and the lowest in the west (Fig. 6:10). The south side of the group is open, both to preserve the triadic form of the group and to accommodate a large audience for ritual performances. This arrangement

THE
CHILDREN
OF THE
FIRST
MOTHER:
FAMILY
AND
DYNASTY
AT
PALENQUE
——

237

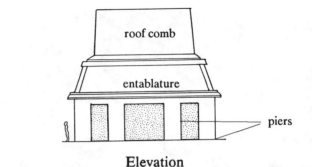

Elevation

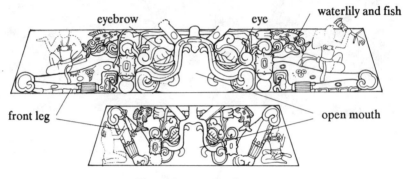

eyebrow   eye   waterlily and fish

front leg   open mouth

Entablature Sculpture

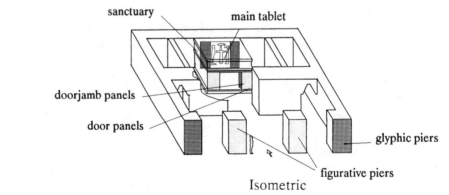

sanctuary   main tablet

doorjamb panels

door panels

glyphic piers

figurative piers

Isometric

FIG. 6:11
**The Group
of the Cross
and the Temple
Arrangement**

was all part of Chan-Bahlum's plan to assert the ancient and pristine quality of his legitimacy. Although this design violates the landscape of Palenque, which would logically dictate that the principal building face *toward* the broad plain below, not away from it, it does conform with the primarily southward orientation of the first royal temples built at Cerros and other Late Preclassic kingdoms.

Chan-Bahlum pursued the triadic theme further in the design of the buildings themselves. In each temple, three doors pierce the front wall of an interior which is divided into an antechamber and three rear sanctums (Fig. 6:11). In the central chamber of each temple his masons built the holy portals which opened into the Otherworld. These powerful foci of supernatural energy were set inside miniature houses—called by the Maya *pib na*[24] or "underground buildings"—built within the back chamber of each temple. While these little houses were only symbolically underground, they replicated in principle the real underground buildings of Palenque: the tombs of Pacal and other kings in pyramids which dotted the sacred landscape of the city.

Artists decorated the outer facades of the temples with huge plaster reliefs modeled on the roof combs, the entablatures, and on the piers between the doors (Fig. 6:11). Unfortunately, only the sculptures of the Temple of the Cross entablature remain legible. These depicted frontal views of great Witz Monsters gazing out from all four sides of the roof. The Maya thought of this temple as a living mountain. Thus, its inner sanctuary was "underground" because it was in the mountain's heart.

Into these "underground houses in the hearts of the mountains" the king would tread, alone and stripped of earthly trappings, to meet his father and his ancestors in Xibalba. He would hazard the perils of hell, as the Hero Twins had before him, to bring back life and prosperity for his people. The plaster sculptures that adorned the outer entablatures of the *pib na* declared their supernatural purpose. Great slabs of stone brought from special quarries bore the words and images that would open these portals to the Otherworld. These stone panels were set into the rear walls of the interior, and into the outer, front walls on either side of the entry doorways. Another set of inscribed doorjamb panels lined the inside of that door (Fig. 6:11).

The images used to represent the visions special to each *pib na* were all arranged in the same basic pattern. The resonances and contrasts designed into the three compositions provided a means of enriching the information they conveyed and emphasizing the unity of their spiritual source. The pictures in each temple were carved on the central axes of the main tablets set against the back wall of the *pib na* (Fig. 6:12). Each composition represented one of the three paths to Xibalba, as well as the three forms that supernatural power would take during the king's ecstatic trances. In each temple, the central image was flanked on the one side by a short figure encased in a heavy cloth costume, and on the other by Chan-Bahlum wearing simple dress. From there the action moved to the two exterior panels, following the path of the king from the Otherworld to the natural one. On the outer panels the king is shown returning in triumph from his transformational journey: He has changed from heir to the reigning monarch of Palenque.

The texts embedded in these narrative scenes tell us exactly which historical events were critical to this transformational process. The text describing the heir-designation of Chan-Bahlum was extremely important. This information appears often, always near the small figure muffled in heavy clothing. This text tells us that the rituals surrounding the presentation of the boy from atop the pyramid took place on June 17, 641,

THE
CHILDREN
OF THE
FIRST
MOTHER:
FAMILY
AND
DYNASTY
AT
PALENQUE
——
239

name of sanctuary · heir-designation text · accession text · conjunction and bloodletting

Chan-Bahlum on Jan. 20, 690

Pacal with the Quadripartite Scepter

the World Tree and the Celestial Bird

Chan-Bahlum's accession on Jan. 10, 690

the Foliated Cross

heir-designation

Jan. 10, 690, accession, image and

Witznal Mountain

Chan-Bahlum   Kan-cross Waterlily Monster   Pacal

FIG. 6:12

and ended five days later on the summer solstice when he became the living manifestation of the sun.[25] Other significant texts relate that on January 10, 684, the forty-eight-year-old Chan-Bahlum became king 132 days after his father's death. The glyphs recording this celebration are next to his portrait. They appear on the inner panels of the Temples of the Cross and the Foliated Cross, and over the shield in the center of the Tablet of the Sun.

When the scene moves to the outer panels, other important events are emphasized. In the Temple of the Foliated Cross and the Temple of the

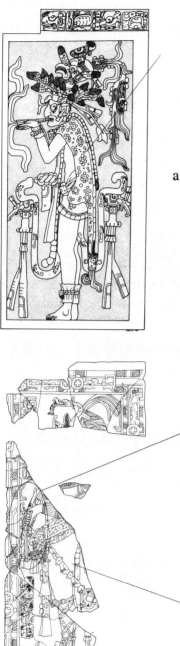

God L acting ten days after
Chan-Bahlum's accession
(Jan. 20, 690)

a. Tablets from the Temple of the Cross

Personified Perforator also
held by Chan-Bahlum on the
inner tablet

b. Tablets from the Temple of the
Foliated Cross

Chan-Bahlum in the ritual ten
days after his accession (Jan.
20, 690)

THE
CHILDREN
OF THE
FIRST
MOTHER:
FAMILY
AND
DYNASTY
AT
PALENQUE
——
241

Sun,[26] we see two different scenes from Chan-Bahlum's accession rites. In
both these temples, the left panel shows him on the first day of these rites,
and the right panel shows him at their conclusion, ten days later, when
Venus was at its greatest elongation as Eveningstar. In the Temple of the
Cross, only the culminating event of the succession rites is shown. In this
version, we see Chan-Bahlum facing God L, one of the most important
gods of Xibalba, who has evidently guided him out of the Otherworld and
back into the light of life. Finally, the text behind Chan-Bahlum on the

Tablet of the Cross puts a period to the historical proceedings by recording the three-day-long dedication rites for the completion of this monumental group on July 23, 690.

If we have accurately identified these events—the designation of Chan-Bahlum as heir, his accession as king, and his dedication of the temples—who then is the mysterious personage shown in these final narrative scenes? The answer is simple: The small muffled figure is none other than the dead Pacal, the father of the king-to-be,[27] who stands facing his child in the ritual that will make him king. Chan-Bahlum designed the inner scenes of the temples to represent places in Xibalba where he would meet his father and receive the power of the kingship from him directly. Pacal is shown transferring the kingship to his son through a ritual of transformation paralleling the one he enacted for a frightened six-year-old boy forty-two years earlier. On each of the inner panels, the son is dressed simply in the Maya equivalent of underwear, his long hair wrapped in readiness to don the heavy headdress of kingship. His father stands nearby, his chest muffled in heavy cloth wrapping bands. His neck too is bound in a thick twisted cloth which hangs down his back. This apparel most likely represents the burial clothing he wore in his own final portal deep beneath the Temple of the Inscriptions. At any rate, the costume clearly portrays him in his role as denizen of Xibalba.

On the inner panels, the dead Pacal still holds the insignia of royal power. Transformation and the passing on of authority occurred only during the ten days of the accession rites. At the end of these days and nights of fasting, sacrifice, and communion in the place of death, we finally see Chan-Bahlum coming forth from the *pib na* wielding those very power objects and wearing the age-old garb of kings. The royal belt, with Chac-Xib-Chac dangling behind his knees, girds his loins. The heavy elaborate feathered headdress adorns his brow with the responsibility of authority. On his back rests the burden of divinity symbolized by the backrack with its image of a god. This was the dress of kings when Tikal conquered Uaxactún. By donning this most ancient and powerful garb, Chan-Bahlum became the ahau of the ahauob—"the lord of lords."

The central icon at the portal of each of the three temples in the Group of the Cross specifies the nature of the cosmic power and community responsibility that defined kingship for that temple. At the portal of the Temple of the Cross, we see a variant of the World Tree (see the Glossary of Gods). This cross-shaped Tree, with the Serpent Bar of kingship entwined in its branches and the Celestial Bird standing on its crown, was the central axis of the cosmos (Fig. 6:12a).[28] Along this axis rose and descended the souls of the dead and the gods called from the Otherworld by the vision rite to talk to human beings. It was the path the Cosmic Monster took as the sun and Venus moved through its body on their daily journeys.[29] The king himself was the worldly manifestation of this axis, and this emphasized his role as the source of magical power. He was not only the primary practitioner of the rituals that contacted the Otherworld: He was the pathway itself (see Chapter 2, Fig. 2:11). In this portal the dead Pacal gives his son a scepter in the form of the monster that rests at the base of the World Tree—the same sun-marked monster that bore Pacal to Xibalba. Chan-Bahlum wields a disembodied head as an instrument of power, as had the Early Classic kings of Tikal and other kings before him.

The portal of the Temple of the Foliated Cross (Fig. 6:12b) bears a foliated variant of the World Tree formed by a maize plant rising from a band of water and Kan-cross Waterlily Monster, one of the symbols of the watery world of raised fields and swamps (see the Glossary of Gods). In the crown of this foliated tree sits a huge water bird wearing the mask of the Celestial Bird. The branches of the tree are ears of maize manifested as human heads, for, in the Maya vision, the flesh of human beings was made from maize dough. This Foliated Cross represented the cultivated world of the community through the symbol of a maize plant rising from the waters of the earth as the source of life. Maize was not only the substance of human flesh, but it was the major cultigen of the Maya farmer. As the sustainer of life, and as a plant that could not seed itself without the intervention of humans, maize was an ultimate symbol of Maya social existence in communion with nature. In this portal Pacal is shown giving his son the Personified Bloodletter. This was the instrument of the bloodletting rite and the vision quest. It drew the blood of the king and brought on the trance that opened the portal and brought forth the gods from the Otherworld.

Images of war and death sacrifice adorn the panel in the *pib na* of the Temple of the Sun. A Sun Jaguar shield and crossed spears dominate the central icon (Fig. 6:13). These images are sustained aloft by a throne with bleeding jaguar heads emerging from one axis, and bleeding dragons from the other. As at Cerros, these bleeding heads represent decapitation sacrifice. The throne and its burden of war rest on the shoulders of God L and another aged god from the Otherworld. Both are bent over like captives under the feet of victorious warrior kings.[30] This scene recalls the defeat of the Lords of Death at the beginning of time by the Hero Twins. Captive sacrifice was the source of life through the reenactment of the magical rebirth of these heroic ancestors of the Maya people. God L, who received the greetings of the new king in the Temple of the Cross, now holds up the burden of war and sacrifice. In both cases, ritual performance by the king involved Otherworld denizens in the human community.[31]

Here in the Temple of the Sun, the power object is not actually passed from the inside scene to the outside, as in the other temples; but the intent of the composition is still the same. On the inner panel, Pacal holds a full-bodied eccentric flint and a shield made of a flayed human face: symbols of war among the nobility of Palenque and other Maya kingdoms. If we move to the outer panels, on one we see Chan-Bahlum holding a bleeding jaguar on a small throne as the symbol of sacrificial death. On the opposite panel, he wears cotton battle armor with a rolled flexible shield hanging down his back. The tall staff he wields is probably a battle spear typical of the kind carried by warrior kings at other sites. The parallelism here is nicely rendered. On the one side, he is emerging from the *pib na* as a warrior prepared to capture the enemies of his kingdom; on the other, he comes forth as the giver of sacrifice, the result of victory.

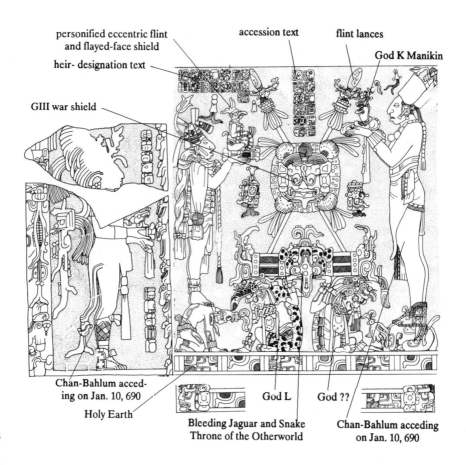

personified eccentric flint
and flayed-face shield

accession text

flint lances

God K Manikin

heir- designation text

GIII war shield

Chan-Bahlum acced-
ing on Jan. 10, 690

Holy Earth

God L

God ??

Bleeding Jaguar and Snake
Throne of the Otherworld

Chan-Bahlum acceding
on Jan. 10, 690

FIG. 6:13

Once he had memorialized the scenes of his transformation within his living mountains, Chan-Bahlum framed the imagery with the finest examples of royal literature left to the modern world by the ancient Maya. We know that, on the one hand, his actions were politically motivated and designed to gain personal glory. That knowledge, however, cannot obscure our awareness that these texts constitute a magnificent poetic vision of the universe, a remarkable expression of the high level of philosophical and spiritual development within the civilization of the Maya. These texts comprise the only full statement of creation mythology and its relationship to the institution of ahau that we have from the Maya Classic period. They define the sacred origin and charismatic obligations of kingly power.

In these texts, Chan-Bahlum resolved the relationship between lineage and dynasty by evoking the origin myths of the Maya, declaring that his own claim of descent from his grandmother replicated the practices of the gods at the time of the genesis. He pursued and elaborated the same divine symmetries his father had asserted before him, symmetries between the First Mother, First Father, and their children, and the historical realities of Palenque's dynastic succession. The First Mother was Lady Beastie, who we mentioned above as the mother of the gods and the Creatrix in the Maya vision of the cosmos. As we shall see the Palencanos

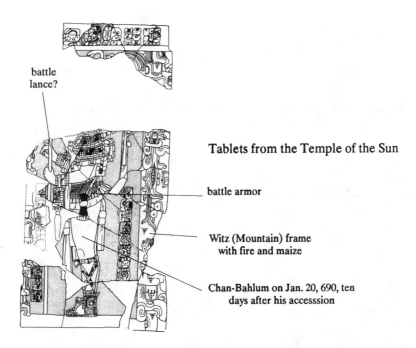

battle
lance?

Tablets from the Temple of the Sun

battle armor

Witz (Mountain) frame
with fire and maize

Chan-Bahlum on Jan. 20, 690, ten
days after his accesssion

saw her operate in their lives through her spirit counterpart, the moon. Her husband and the father of her children is called GI' (G-one-prime) by modern scholars. He established the order of time and space just after the fourth version of the cosmos was created on 4 Ahau 8 Cumku. Both the Creatrix and her husband were born during the previous manifestation of creation, but their children were born 754 years into this one.

The three children are known as the Palenque Triad because Heinrich Berlin[32] first recognized them as a unit of related gods in Palenque's inscriptions. He dubbed them GI, GII, and GIII for God I, God II, and God III. We now know that the firstborn child, GI, had the same name as his father, GI', in exactly the same pattern as the Hero Twins in the Popol Vuh where Hun-Hunahpu is the father of Hunahpu and Xbalanque. GI is a fish-barbled anthropomorphic god who wears a shell-earflare. He is associated with Venus and with decapitation sacrifice. GII, also known as God K, Bolon Tz'acab, and Kauil, is a serpent-footed god who wears a smoking-ax through his obsidian-mirrored forehead. He is the god of lineages and blood sacrifice. GIII is the cruller-eyed Jaguar God, who is also known as Ahau-Kin, "Lord Sun." See the Glossary of Gods for full descriptions and pictures.

As the most ancient and sacred of all Maya dieties, these three gods played a crucial role in the earliest symbolism of kingship we saw at Cerros, Tikal, and Uaxactún. Chan-Bahlum makes them the crucial pivot of his own claim to legitimacy. On the right half of each text, he recounted their actions in the Maya story of the beginning of the current world. On the left he recorded the connections between those sacred events and Palenque's history. Here is a chronology of the mythological events in the order they are presented. (See Fig. 6:14,15,16 for the full decipherment and drawings of these texts.)

THE
CHILDREN
OF THE
FIRST
MOTHER:
FAMILY
AND
DYNASTY
AT
PALENQUE
—
245

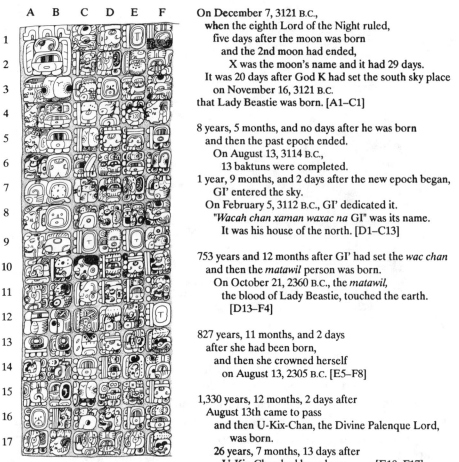

	A	B	C	D	E	F
1						
2						
3						
4						
5						
6						
7						
8						
9						
10						
11						
12						
13						
14						
15						
16						
17						

On December 7, 3121 B.C.,
  when the eighth Lord of the Night ruled,
    five days after the moon was born
    and the 2nd moon had ended,
      X was the moon's name and it had 29 days.
  It was 20 days after God K had set the south sky place
  on November 16, 3121 B.C.
that Lady Beastie was born. [A1–C1]

8 years, 5 months, and no days after he was born
  and then the past epoch ended.
    On August 13, 3114 B.C.,
      13 baktuns were completed.
  1 year, 9 months, and 2 days after the new epoch began,
    GI' entered the sky.
  On February 5, 3112 B.C., GI' dedicated it.
    "Wacah chan xaman waxac na GI" was its name.
    It was his house of the north. [D1–C13]

753 years and 12 months after GI' had set the wac chan
  and then the matawil person was born.
    On October 21, 2360 B.C., the matawil,
      the blood of Lady Beastie, touched the earth.
      [D13–F4]

827 years, 11 months, and 2 days
  after she had been born,
    and then she crowned herself
      on August 13, 2305 B.C. [E5–F8]

1,330 years, 12 months, 2 days after
  August 13th came to pass
    and then U-Kix-Chan, the Divine Palenque Lord,
      was born.
  26 years, 7 months, 13 days after
    U-Kix-Chan had been born . . . [E10–F17]

Alfardas flanking the main stairs

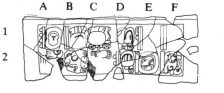

	A	B	C	D	E	F
1						
2						

On October 21, 2360 B.C.,
  GI, the matawil, touched the earth.
    3,094 years, 11 months, 10 days later
    On January 10, 692 . . .

FIG. 6:14
Tablet of the Cross: The Panels and Paraphrase Translations

The Temple of the Cross

On December 7, 3121 B.C., Lady Beastie, the First Mother, was born.
On June 16, 3122 B.C., GI', the First Father, was born.
On August 13, 3114 B.C., the 13th baktun ended and the new creation
  began.
On February 5, 3112 B.C., GI' entered into the sky and he dedicated
  the house named "wacah chan xaman waxac na GI" (the
  "World Tree house of the north").[33]

. . . and then U-Kix-Chan crowned himself
  on March 28, 967 B.C.
    He was a Divine Palenque Lord. [P1–Q3]

On March 31, 397 Kuk was born.
  It was 22 years, 5 months, 14 days after he had been born
    and then he crowned himself on March 11, 431.
      He was Divine ????? Lord. [P4–Q9]

On August 9, 422, "Casper" was born.
  13 years, 3 months, 9 days after "Casper" had been born
    and then it was August 10, 435,
      123 days after "Casper" crowned himself
        and then December 11, 435, came to pass,
          on that day 3,600 years (9 baktuns) ended. [P10–S2]

28 years, 1 month, 18 days after "Manik" had been born
  and then he crowned himself on July 29, 487. [R3-S7]

36 years, 7 months, 17 days after he had been born
  on July 6, 465,
    and then Chaacal-Ah-Nab crowned himself
      on June 5, 501. [R8–R13]

39 years, 6 months, 16 days after Kan-Xul had been born
  and then he crowned himself on February 25, 529.
    [S13–S18]

42 years, 4 months, 17 days after he had been born
  and then Chaacal-Ah-Nab crowned himself
    on May 4, 565. [T1–T6]

1 year, 1 month, 1 day after Chaacal-Ah-Nab had been
  born on September 5, 523
    and then Chan-Bahlum was born. [U6–T11]

48 years, 4 months, 7 days after Chan-Bahlum had
  been born on September 20, 524
  and 18(?) years, 8 months, 2 days. [U11–U18]

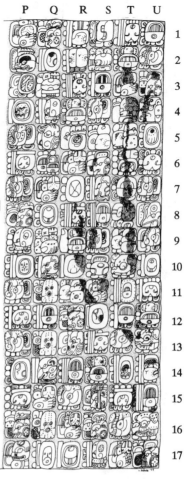

it was housed the *wacah-chan* (six-sky)
  it was the sanctuary of
    it was the holy thing of
      Lord Chan-Bahlum, the child of Lord Pacal
        and the child of Lady Ahpo-Hel.
It happened at the Waterlily Place.

THE
CHILDREN
OF THE
FIRST
MOTHER:
FAMILY
AND
DYNASTY
AT
PALENQUE
—

On October 21, 2360 B.C., GI, the child of Lady Beastie, was born.
On August 13, 2305 B.C., at age 815, Lady Beastie became the first
  being in this creation to be crowned as king.
On March 11, 993 B.C., U-Kix-Chan was born.
On March 28, 967 B.C., at age thirty-six, U-Kix-Chan, Divine Lord
  of Palenque, was crowned king of Palenque.

```
     A   B   C   D
 1
 2
 3
 4
 5
 6
 7
 8
 9
10
11
12
13
14
15
16
17
```

On November 8, 2360 B.C.
  when the eighth Lord of the Night ruled,
    it was ten days after the moon was born,
      5 moons had ended,
        X was its name and it had 30 days.
    It was 14 months and 19 days
      after God K set the west quadrant.[1] .
  It was the third birth and GII was born. [A1–D2]

  34 years, 14 months after GII, the *matawil,* had been born
    and then 2 baktuns (800 years) ended
      on February 16, 2325 B.C.
    On that day Lady Beastie, Divine Lord of *Matawil,*
      manifested a divinity through bloodletting. [C3–D11]

  It had come to pass
    on *Yax -Hal Witznal*
      in the shell place
        at the *Na-Te-Kan*[2]
          on November 8, 2360 B.C.
    2,947 years, 3 months, 16 days later[3] . . . [C12–D17]

[1] The scribe made an error here by adding rather than sub-
  tracting the Distance Number. The correct station is
  1.18.4.7.1 1 Imix 19 Pax with red and east.
[2] These three locations refer to the Mountain Monster under
  Chan-Bahlum's feet, the shell under Pacal's feet, and the
  Foliated Cross in the center of the panel (See Figure 6:12).
[3] The Distance Number should be 7.14.13.1.16.

FIG. 6:15
Tablet of the
Foliated Cross:
The Panels and
Paraphrase
Translations

Alfardas flanking the main stairs

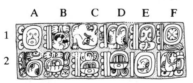

On November 8, 2360 B.C.,
  GII, the *matawil,* touched the earth.
  3,050 years, 63 days later
    on January 10, 692 . . .

A
FOREST
OF
KINGS
—

The Temple of the Foliated Cross

November 8, 2360 B.C., GII was born.
Thirty-four years later, on February 17, 2325 B.C., Lady Beastie let
her blood when two baktuns ended.

. . . on July 23, 690, GII and GIII were in conjunction.
[L1–M4]

On the next day,
   the Mah-Kina-Bahlum-Kuk Building was dedicated
   in the house of Lord Chan-Bahlum,
      Divine Palenque Lord. [L6–L9]

On the third day Lord Chan-Bahlum, Divine Palenque Lord,
   he let blood with an obsidian blade;
      he took the bundle
         after it had come to pass
         at the Waterlily Place.
      Wac-Chan-Chac Ox-Waxac-Chac acted there. [L10–L17]

49 years, 6 months, 4 days after he had been born
   and then he crowned himself,
      Lord Chan-Bahlum, Divine Palenque Lord
         on January 10, 692. [M17–P5]

6 years, 11 months, 6 days after he had been seated as *ahau*
   and then GI, GII, GIII and their companion gods
      came into conjunction.
   Lord Chan-Bahlum enacted a ritual.

In 1 year, 12 months, 4 days it will happen,
   the end of the 13th katun on March 17, 692.
And then it came to pass July 23, 690
   and then they were in conjunction
      the gods, who are the chereished-ones of,
         Lord Chan-Bahlum, Divine Palenque Lord.

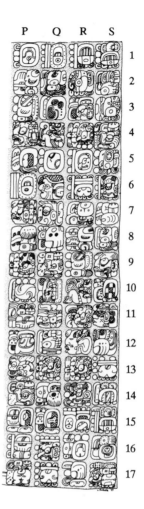

it was housed, the *Na-Te-Kan* (Foliated Cross)
   it was the *pib nail* of
      it was the divine-thing of
         Lord Chan-Bahlum, the child of Lord Pacal
         the child of Lady Ahpo-Hel.
It happened at the Waterlily Place.

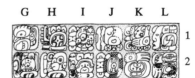

THE
CHILDREN
OF THE
FIRST
MOTHER:
FAMILY
AND
DYNASTY
AT
PALENQUE

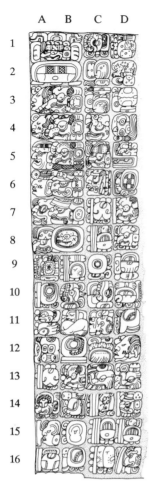

A   B   C   D

1
2
3
4
5
6
7
8
9
10
11
12
13
14
15
16

On October 25, 2360 B.C.
  the third Lord of the Night ruled,
    it was 26 days after the moon was born,
     four moons had ended,
      X was its name and it had 30 days . . . .
  It was 1 year, 46 days after
    God K set the north quadrant
    on July 24, 2587 B.C.
On that day he was born,
  Mah Kina Tah-Waybil-Ahau,
  Kin-tan "decapitated jaguar."
    Ti Nah, Zac-Bac-Na-Chan, Atin Butz', ????,
    Mah Kina Ahau-Kin.. [A1–D6]

765 years, 3 months, 6 days after the *wac-chan*
  had been set,
    and then the *matawil,* the child of Lady Beastie,
    Divine Palenque Lord, was born. [C7–D13]

3,858 years, 5 months, 16 days . . . [C1–-D16]

Alfardas flanking the main stairs

FIG. 6:16
Tablet of the
Sun: The Panels
and Paraphrase
Translations

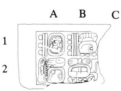

A   B   C   D   E   F

1
2

On October 25, 2360 B.C.,
  GIII, the *matawil,* touched the earth.
  [3,894 years, 11 months, 6 days later
    on January 10, 692 . . .]

The Temple of the Sun

On October 25, 2360 B.C., 754 years after the era began, GIII, the child of Lady Beastie, was born.

. . . after the present epoch began on August 13, 3114 B. C.,
   and then July 23, 690, came to pass.
      GIII came into conjunction. [D16-O6]

One day later on July 24, 690,
   the Kinich-Bahlum-Kuk Building was dedicated.
   in the house of the *Bacel-Way*
      Lord Chan-Bahlum. [N7-O12]

Three days later he materialized the divinity
   through bloodletting.
     He did it at the Waterlily Place,
      the Old God of *Kuk-Te-Witz*.[1] [N13-N16]

146 years, 12 months, 3 days after November 20, 496,
   when Kan-Xul took office as the heir-designate.
     It had come to pass at the *Toc-tan* Place.
     and then June 17, 641, came to pass.
      He (Lord Chan-Bahlum) became the heir.
      And on the fifth day after (on June 22, 641)
        Lord Chan-Bahlum became the sun
        in the company of GI. [O16-Q10]

6 years, 2 months, 17 days after he had been born
   on May 23, 635,
     and then he was designated heir. [P11-Q13]

It was 1 year, 167 days until December 6, 642,
   when 10 years ended (9.10.10.0.0),
   he warred[2] as heir. [P14-Q16]

---

[1] *Kuk-te-witz* is the ancient name for the mountain behind
   the Temple of the Foliated Cross, known today as *El
   Mirador.*
[2] This is the same war event Smoking-Squirrel of Naranjo
   enacted against Ucanal (Stela 22) and Ah-Cacaw of Tikal
   enacted against Jaguar-Paw of Calakmul.

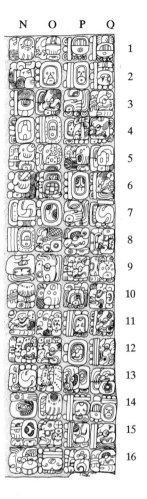

It was an action in the Mah Kina ???? Cab,
   it was the *pib nail* of
     he completed 13 katuns on March 18, 692,
Lord [Chan-Bahlum . . .]

THE
CHILDREN
OF THE
FIRST
MOTHER:
FAMILY
AND
DYNASTY
AT
PALENQUE

——

This pattern of events reveals Chan-Bahlum's strategy of dynastic legitimization. In the Temple of the Cross, the first event recorded is the birth of Lady Beastie, the First Mother. In the next passage, we are told that the First Father, GI', was born on an even earlier date.[34] Both these gods were born during the previous creation, indicating that the nature of their power comes from a time before the existence of our world. On 4 Ahau 8 Cumku, the cosmos re-formed into the new pattern of creation which manifested the present world. As the text continues, it describes how GI', the First Father, established the order of the new world on 1.9.2, 542 days after the present creation began.

Chan-Bahlum provided a lot of information about these primordial times, beyond their naked existence as dates and events. His real theological and political intentions, however, are revealed by the manner of his presentation. In the text of his accession monument, the Temple of the Cross, he recounted the birth of the First Mother as if it were the first, and not the second, chronological event in the historical sequence. Initially, when recording the birth of the First Father, he didn't even identify him. The reader had to wait until a subsequent passage to discover that this mysterious person, born eight years before creation—and 540 days *earlier* than the goddess—was in fact the First Father, GI'. Chan-Bahlum manipulated the focus of the text at the expense of the First Father specifically because the First Mother was the pivot of his strategy of legitimization.

In his accession monument, therefore, Chan-Bahlum placed the focus entirely on Lady Beastie and her relationship to the three gods of the Palenque Triad. Pacal had already set the precedent for this association by linking Lady Beastie's name to that of his own mother, Lady Zac-Kuk, implying by this reference that his mother was the human analog of the mother goddess of all Maya. Chan-Bahlum went further by contriving to make the birth date of the goddess like-in-kind to the birth date of his own father, Pacal.[35] With a little calendric manipulation, this was easily done. To the Maya, days that fell at the same point in a calender cycle shared the same characteristics in sacred time. Days that fell on the same point in many different cycles were very sacred indeed. By extension, events, such as births, which fell on days that were related cosmically, were also "like-in-kind." Because of the symmetry of their birth dates, Chan-Bahlum could declare that his father, Pacal, and the mother of the gods, were beings made of the same sacred substance.

The symmetry of sacredness between the First Mother and Pacal was vital for another reason. The mother of the gods was born in the world of the past creation; therefore, she carried into the new world the cumulative power of the previous existence.[36] The date 4 Ahau 8 Cumku represented a membrane, comprised of the horrific chaos of creation, separating the symmetry and order of the former world from that of the present one. The contrived relationship between Pacal's birth and the goddess's asserted that his birth held the same sacred destiny as hers and that this symmetry came from the time before the creation.

it was 2 days, 11 months		7 tuns
1 katun		2 baktuns
after she had been born		and then she crowned
herself		Lady Beastie
on 9 Ik		seating of Zac

The parallel Chan-Bahlum wished his people to see is both elegant and effective. He focused their attention on the old and new creation, then demonstrated that Lady Zac-Kuk and her royal clan represented the old ruling lineage at Palenque, while her son Pacal represented the new order of another patrilineal clan—a "new creation," so to speak. When his mother passed the sacred essence of the kingship on to Pacal, she successfully passed through the chaotic violation of kinship principles of succession to arrive at this new order. Chan-Bahlum's legitimate claim to the throne rested on this principle: direct transmission of the sacred essence of royal power between kings, irrespective of their gender or family.

Chan-Bahlum extended the similarity between the kings of Palenque and the gods even further by recording the births of the three gods of the Palenque Triad on the left sides of the tablets inside the *pib na*. There he emphasized their relationship to the First Mother by labeling GI (the namesake of the First Father) and GIII, who were the first and second born of her children, with the glyphic phrase "he is the child of Lady Beastie." These gods were her children, exactly as Pacal was the child of Lady Zac-Kuk. GII, the god most closely related to Maya kings, was also her child, but Chan-Bahlum chose to relate him to the First Father by setting up contrived numerology between their births, exactly as he contrived to make Pacal's birth "like-in-kind" to Lady Beastie's.[37] The equation is, of course, his own claim to legitimacy: As GII was descended from the substance of First Father so was he the descendant of the divine Pacal.

This declaration of parallelism might have been enough, but Chan-Bahlum, intent on proving his right to the throne beyond the shadow of any doubt, was not content to stop there. On the Tablet of the Cross he declared that after she brought the firstborn of the Palenque Triad into the world, Lady Beastie, at age 815, became the first living being to be crowned ruler in the new creation. The crown she wore is called glyphically *zac uinic* ("pure or resplendent person") and it is visually represented as the Jester God headband we saw first at Cerros. This glyph is the key title taken by all the subsequent kings of Palenque who were recorded on the historical side of this panel. Once again, Chan-Bahlum

THE
CHILDREN
OF THE
FIRST
MOTHER:
FAMILY
AND
DYNASTY
AT
PALENQUE

——

253

did not say that the First Father became the king: It was the goddess that he chose to emphasize. The text itself reads: "2 days, 11 uinals, 7 tuns, 1 katuns, and 2 baktuns after she had been born and then she crowned herself the *zac uinic,* Beastie, on 9 Ik seating of Zac" (Fig. 6:17).

At this point, Chan-Bahlum could certainly have rested from his labors. He had already created a simple and effective equation between the First Mother and the children of the gods on the one hand, and Lady Zac-Kuk and her descendants on the other. But instead he decided to bridge the temporal gap from the accession of the First Mother to the accession of the founder of his dynasty, Bahlum-Kuk. He accomplished this by evoking the name of a legendary king, U-Kix-Chan. We know that this man was a figure of legend because Chan-Bahlum tells us he was born on March 11, 993 B.C., and crowned himself on March 28, 967 B.C. These dates fall during the florescence of the Olmec, the first great Mesoamerican civilization. The Olmec were remembered by the Classic peoples as the great ancestral civilization in much the same way that the Romans evoked Troy from Homer's *Iliad* and *Odyssey* as their source of their legitimacy. In Mesoamerica, the Olmec, like the Greeks of the Old World, forged the template of state art and religion for their world by developing many of the symbols, the rituals, and the styles of artistic presentation that would be used by their successors for millennium.

U-Kix-Chan may not have been a real person, but Chan-Bahlum deliberately set his birth date in Olmec times. In this way he could claim that the authority of Palenque's dynasty had its roots in the beginnings of human civilization as well as in the time of the divine. The passages recording U-Kix-Chan's name began on the mythological side of the Tablet of the Cross, with his birth, and bridged to the historical side with his accession. He was immediately recognizable as human, no matter how legendary his time, because of the scale of his life. He was twenty-six years old when he became the king of Palenque; the First Mother was 815 when she took the same throne. Since their ages were read with their accessions, their status as divine versus human would have been immediately and emphatically self-evident.

From the legendary "Olmec," U-Kix-Chan, Chan-Bahlum moved to the birth and accession of the founder of his own dynasty, Bahlum-Kuk. The text then proceeded through each succeeding king, finally culminating with Chan-Bahlum I, the ancestor from whom Chan-Bahlum, the author of this text, took his name. The Palenque dynasty envisioned by him descended from the original accession of the mother of the gods.

Lady Beastie was depicted not only as the first ruler of Palenque. Chan-Bahlum also portrayed her as the first to shed her blood for the people of the community in the cathartic act which opened the path to Xibalba and allowed prosperity to flow into the human world. On the Tablet of the Foliated Cross, Chan-Bahlum recorded that thirty-four years after the birth of GII (her third-born child), Lady Beastie celebrated the end of the second baktun with a "fish-in-hand"[38] glyph (Fig. 6:18) that appears as the verb when the Vision Serpent is materialized through bloodletting. Chan-Bahlum's decision to record this vision-bringing ritual

The magic of these waterfalls at Palenque enchanted Linda Schele on her first visit to the ruins. The ancient Maya who built their city around their lifegiving pools must have seen these streams as meaningful symbols of the processes of destruction and creation. (PHOTOGRAPH © JUSTIN KERR 1972)

Tikal Temple 33 (A.D. 400–700), which was dismantled by archaeologists, was the first major building constructed by Ah-Cacaw. He placed Stela 31 inside the old temple before construction on this final version began. The enormous new temple was dedicated on September 17, A.D. 695, exactly 260 years after the last date on that early stela. (PHOTO BY PETER HARRISON)

This aerial photograph of Cerros shows Structure 5C-2nd (100 B.C.–A.D. 100), the first temple built at that center, to the right peeking out of the forest next to the shore. The eastward-facing Acropolis of a later king sits at the end of the modern dock extending into Chetumal Bay. During the first century B.C., people of Cerros experimented with kingship and then abandoned it a hundred years later to return to their lives as villagers and farmers. (PHOTO BY WILLIAM M. FERGUSON AND JOHN Q. ROYCE)

This aerial photograph of Tikal shows the North Acropolis at the top, the Great Plaza in the center, and the Central Acropolis to the lower right. Temple I is on the right of the Great Plaza and Temple II on the left. Most of the visible architecture in the North Acropolis is Early Classic (A.D. 300–600), while the Great Plaza and most of the Central Acropolis is Late Classic (A.D. 600–800). (PHOTO BY WILLIAM M. FERGUSON AND JOHN Q. ROYCE)

This aerial photograph features many of 18-Rabbit's greatest works. The Great Plaza and its forest of tree-stones (*at the top*) was built during the early eighth century. 18-Rabbit built the Ballcourt (*lower right*) six months before he was sacrificed by a rival at the nearby site of Quiriguá. The stela on the end of the Ballcourt was commissioned by his father, while the tiny altar near it was placed there by the last tragic king of Copán, the Maya kingdom that dominated western Honduras and the Motagua Valley in Guatemala. (PHOTO BY WILLIAM M. FERGUSON AND JOHN Q. ROYCE)

This wraparound photograph shows the greatest work of King Chan-Bahlum—the Group of the Cross (A.D. 692) at Palenque, México. The view is from the door of the Temple of the Foliated Cross and includes the Temple of the Sun on the left, the Palace in the center, and the Temple of the Cross on the right. (PHOTO BY MACDUFF EVERTON)

This wraparound photograph shows the south end of the Palace at Palenque. House E, the building housing Pacal's accession panel, is on the left with the Group of the Cross visible above its roof, while the Temple of Inscriptions, where Pacal is buried, nestles against the mountain on the right. (PHOTO BY MACDUFF EVERTON)

This brightly painted clay figurine (A.D. 600–800) depicts a Late Classic Maya ruler wearing the god Chac-Xib-Chac in his befeathered headdress. His ornate costume includes a royal belt around his waist, huge pendants on his chest, a decorated apron, and tasseled sandals. He wears a round shield on his left wrist and probably once had a tiny spear in his right hand. His mouth ornament is like one worn by Pacal into his grave. (PHOTOGRAPH © JUSTIN KERR 1985)

This painted vessel (A.D. 426) was found in Curl-Snout's tomb (Burial 10) inside Temple 34 of Tikal, Guatemala. The vessel shape is Maya, but the images reflect contact with Teotihuacán, the great city near modern México City. (PHOTOGRAPH © JUSTIN KERR 1964)

Lintel 41 (A.D. 755) was once mounted over a doorway into Structure 16 at the ruins of Yaxchilán in México. The carved scene depicts Bird-Jaguar standing with a wife from Motul de San José as she helps him prepare for battle. He holds a battle spear in his hand and wears a Tlaloc-war headdress. (PHOTOGRAPH © JUSTIN KERR 1985)

Lintel 24 (A.D. 700–725) was mounted over the left door of Structure 23 at Yaxchilán, México. The carved scenes depict a bloodletting rite celebrating the birth of a son to the sixty-two-year-old king, Shield-Jaguar. He holds a torch over Lady Xoc, his principal wife, as she pulls a thorn-lined rope through her tongue to sanctify the birth of a younger wife's child. This child, Bird-Jaguar, became king after ten years of competition with rivals who may have been Lady Xoc's offspring. (PHOTOGRAPH © JUSTIN KERR 1985)

Dedicated in A.D. 715, Temple 22 of Copán, Honduras, was commissioned by 18-Rabbit to celebrate the twenty-year anniversary of his accession. This extraordinary sculpted door leads to the inner sanctum where 18-Rabbit and his successors let blood and talked to their ancestors and the gods. The image represents the arch of the sky held away from the skeletal realm of the Underworld by gods called Pauahtun. (PHOTOGRAPH © JUSTIN KERR 1987)

This jade earflare (50 B.C.–A.D. 50) was once mounted on the side flanges of a headdress worn by a Late Preclassic king from Pomona, Belize. The glyphs are arranged to form a quincunx pattern with the central hole. The inscription evokes the Sun God and the Maize God and the rituals that celebrated their power. (PHOTOGRAPH © JUSTIN KERR 1985)

18-Rabbit, one of the greatest kings of Copán, as he was depicted on the east face of Stela C (A.D. 711), the first tree-stone he planted in the Great Plaza. The intense red color is the original paint. (PHOTO BY LINDA SCHELE)

These great masks (50 B.C.) were modeled from plaster on the eastern terraces of Structure 5C-2nd at Cerros, Belize. They represent the Sun God (lower mask) and Venus (the upper mask) as they rise from the horizon at dawn. (PHOTO BY JAMES F. GARBER)

The tumbled colonnade attached to the Temple of the Warriors (A.D. 850–950) at Chichén Itzá in Yucatán, México. (PHOTOGRAPH © BARBARA KERR 1975)

Stela 31 (A.D. 447), the tree-stone of the great king Stormy-Sky, as it was found inside Temple 33 at Tikal. This side represents Stormy-Sky's father, Curl-Snout, dressed as a Tlaloc warrior. (PHOTOGRAPH © JUSTIN KERR 1964)

These jade jewels (50 B.C.) were deposited in an offering in the summit of Structure 6, the second temple complex built at Cerros. The center head was worn as a pectoral, while the four smaller heads were mounted on a headband that functioned as the crown of kings. (PHOTO BY LINDA SCHELE)

Yucatec Maya conducting a *primicia* ritual at Yaxuná, Yucatán, in 1986. The boughs at the four corners of the table represent the trees at the corners of the world, while the food and drink are located on the central axis once symbolized by the *Wacah Chan* Tree. The symbolism of the altar and the ritual descend directly from Precolumbian belief and practice. (PHOTO BY DEBRA S. WALKER)

The west gallery (dedicated in A.D. 654) of the building the people of ancient Palenque called the *Zac Nuc Nah,* the "White Big House." The Oval Palace Tablet seen on the right shows Pacal receiving a headdress from his mother during his accession rites. Most of Pacal's successors were inaugurated into the office of king while seated on a throne that once sat below this tablet. (PHOTO BY MACDUFF EVERTON)

This is a photo rollout of a bowl sent by Ruler 1 of Naranjo to a noble woman of Tikal as a gift. Buried with her in Structure 5G-8, the bowl (A.D. 590–630) was decorated with images of the Celestial Bird carrying snakes in its beak as it flies across the sacred world of the Maya. (ROLLOUT PHOTOGRAPH © JUSTIN KERR 1986)

This extraordinary statue of the God of Scribes and Artists (A.D. 725–750) once decorated Structure 9N-82, the house of a noble scribe at Copán, Honduras. The net headdress, *paua,* combines with the sign on his shoulder, *tun,* to spell his name, Pauahtun, while his face is that of a howler monkey, who was an artisan in Maya myth.

Here, he holds scribal tools—a paintbrush and a shell paintpot—in his hands.

(PHOTOGRAPH © JUSTIN KERR 1985)

This photo rollout of a vase painting (A.D. 600–800) shows warfare as it was practiced in ancient times. Warriors wearing short-sleeved battle jackets, elaborate headdresses, and the shrunken heads of past victims carry stabbing spears, battleaxes, and flexible shields. They seize captives, who are disarmed but still wearing their battle finery, by their hair to bring them under control. One grabs the leg of his captor as he looks back at his companion's suffering. (ROLLOUT PHOTOGRAPH © JUSTIN KERR 1987)

A modern divination ceremony in progress before an ancient sculpture at La Demorácia in Guatemala. Copal incense hovers in front of the head, while a shaman's pouch with its rock crystals and maize seeds rests on the stone altar. Unseen in the photograph is a chocolate bar the shaman had placed in the mouth of the sculpture to bring it alive for the ritual. The same kinds of objects and rituals were used by the Precolumbian shamans two thousand years ago. (PHOTOGRAPH © JUSTIN KERR 1987)

This photo rollout of a cylindrical vessel (A.D. 600–800) shows a corpulent lord from Motul de San José leaning back against his pillow as he admires himself in a mirror held by a dwarf. Lords surround him as another dwarf, a hunchback, and a flower-bearing lord sit on the floor in front of him. The local band of three musicians plays a conch-shell trumpet and two wooden horns just offstage behind the palace wall. Three enema pots sit on the floor outside the room along with a large round pot that apparently holds the liquid sipped by the dwarf. (ROLLOUT PHOTOGRAPH © JUSTIN KERR 1981)

This is the northern vista of Palenque as seen from the Temple of the Inscriptions. The Palace, which was the main ceremonial and residential building of the king, sits in the center of the photograph, while the Group of the Cross, the accession group built by King Chan-Bahlum in the late seventh century, is seen on the right. (PHOTO BY MACDUFF EVERTON)

This photo rollout of a cylindrical vessel (A.D. 600–800) shows a scene taking place inside a palace painted with images of jaguar gods and watery quadrifoils holding the skeletal visage of a death god. A lord from Dos Pilas sits on a bench bearing a pillow for his back and a set of bundles and boxes to his left. Four lords of high rank sit on the floor in front of him, while an attendant holds an object out to him. Two of the lords face him in rapt attention, while the other two lean toward each other as they converse, perhaps about the business at hand. (ROLLOUT PHOTOGRAPH © JUSTIN KERR 1981)

This rollout of a vase painting (A.D. 600–800) shows a lord of Dos Pilas sitting on a bench in front of a large pillow. Two nobles bring him bouquets of flowers, perhaps to be used with the round-bottomed enema pot sitting on the floor between them. Other pots of various shapes sit on the bench and the floor around the principal lord. The three-glyph phrase behind his head names the artist of this vase, who may have depicted himself in the center of the scene with his paintbrush thrust into his headdress. (ROLLOUT PHOTOGRAPH © JUSTIN KERR 1989)

This Early Classic vessel (A.D. 200–450) depicts the Sun God paddling his canoe across the watery surface of the Otherworld. The nose-down peccary legs support not only the vessel but the waters of the world depicted on its sides and lid. (PHOTOGRAPH © JUSTIN KERR 1986)

A jade head (A.D. 350–500) representing the god of decapitation sacrifice that was used to record the conquest of Uaxactún on the Tikal Ballcourt Marker. (PHOTOGRAPH © JUSTIN KERR 1984)

This cylindrical vase (A.D. 600–800) was painted with a scene showing a woman from Dos Pilas dressed in a delicate, transparent lace huipil as she kneels before a lord of Motul de San José. While sitting cross-legged on a mat-covered bench inside a curtain-draped palace, he holds a small deity effigy against his chest as he extends a rattle (or perhaps an enema bag) toward her. Behind him rests a large pillow, while two large vessels sit on the floor below him. (ROLLOUT PHOTOGRAPH © JUSTIN KERR 1984)

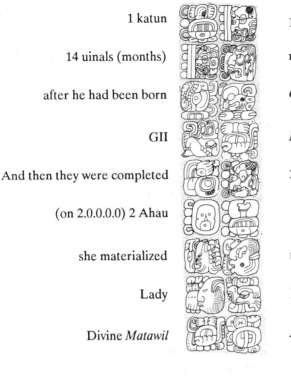

1 katun	14 tuns (years)
14 uinals (months)	no days
after he had been born	*Ch'oc* , the young one
GII	*Matawil* person
And then they were completed	2 baktuns (800 years)
(on 2.0.0.0.0) 2 Ahau	3 Uayeb
she materialized	the divinity
Lady	Beastie
Divine *Matawil*	*Ahau*

**FIG. 6:18
The First
Mother and
the First
Vision Rite
in This
Creation**

in the Temple of the Foliated Cross was not accidental. If you remember, the Personified Perforator was the instrument that Pacal, on the inner tablet, passed to Chan-Bahlum, on the outer. When Chan-Bahlum spilled his own blood in the rituals that took place within this *pib na,* he was activating his own portal and generating the energies these images represented: agricultural abundance for the human community. In Chan-Bahlum's version of the genesis story, therefore, the First Mother was not only the first being to become a ruler in this creation; she also taught the people how to offer their blood to nourish life, to maintain the social order, and to converse with their ancestors in the Otherworld. The model for human and kingly behavior was again manifested through the actions of the First Mother rather than the First Father.

Chan-Bahlum did not entirely ignore the father of the gods, however. In the Temple of the Cross, he related the story in which the First Father, GI', as a boy of ten, established cosmic order a year and a half after the creation of the present world. The text calls this action "entering or becoming the sky (*och chan*)." We can see a beautiful rendering of these actions in a scene from an ornamental pot: GI' has set up the World Tree which lifted the sky up from the primordial sea of creation. Now he crouches below it, ready to shoot his blowgun at the Celestial Bird sitting atop the Tree, imitating the glory of the sun. It was these actions, separating out the elements of the natural world and assigning them their proper roles, that brought chaotic nature into order[39] (Fig. 6:19).

In the expression of this great cosmic event at Palenque, we learn that this "entering the sky" also resulted in the dedication of a house called

THE
CHILDREN
OF THE
FIRST
MOTHER:
FAMILY
AND
DYNASTY
AT
PALENQUE

—

255

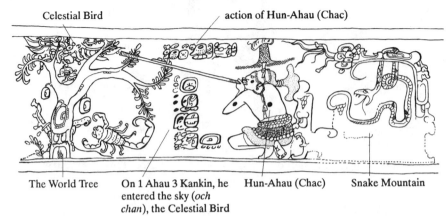

Celestial Bird   action of Hun-Ahau (Chac)

The World Tree   On 1 Ahau 3 Kankin, he   Hun-Ahau (Chac)   Snake Mountain
entered the sky (*och
chan*), the Celestial Bird

"*wacah chan xaman waxac na* GI" (see Note 33). This is the name of the structure created by GI' when he set up the World Tree. It is the dome of heaven and the movement of the constellations as they pivot around the great northern axis of the sky—the pole star. But *Wacah-Chan* was also the proper name of the *pib na* in the Temple of the Cross, which, in turn, was named for the central icon on the main tablet—the World Tree itself. When Chan-Bahlum dedicated his own temples in the Group of the Cross, he replicated the establishment of celestial order brought about by the First Father.

Chan-Bahlum made records of the rituals in which he dedicated the Group of the Cross in all three temples, but he featured them especially in the Temples of the Foliated Cross and the Sun. In both instances he created bridges between the mythological events in the left column of the tablets and the dedication rituals in the right. In this way he declared that the essential causality of these rites derived from the actions of the First Mother and Father (see Figs. 6:15 and 16 for the paraphrases and arrangements of these texts).[40]

The rituals themselves fell on three distinct days during a four-day span. On the first day (9.12.18.5.16 2 Cib 14 Mol, July 23, 690), Jupiter, Saturn, Mars, and the moon appeared in a spectacular conjunction with all four planets less than 5° apart in the constellation of Scorpio.[41] Chan-Bahlum and his people apparently envisioned this conjunction as the First Mother (the moon) rejoined by her three children (manifested as the three planets). Seen this way, this extraordinary alignment in the sky was an omen of enormous portent. On the next day (3 Caban 15 Mol), Chan-Bahlum dedicated his temples with exactly the same ritual that the First Father had enacted to establish the *Wacah-Chan* at the center of the cosmos. Chan-Bahlum's own house was named *Mah Kina Bahlum-Kuk Na,* "Lord Bahlum-Kuk House" (Fig. 6:20), therefore making it the house of the founder of his dynasty.[42] By proclaiming that his new portals to the Otherworld were also those of his founding ancestor, Chan-Bahlum joined the three patrilineages of Palenque's kingship into a coherent totality. At

| on the day | 3 Caban 15 Mol July 24, 690 | God N verb | Mah Kina Kuk building in the house | Mah Kina Chan-Bahlum, Divine Palenque Lord |

| it changed | 3 Caban 15 Mol July 24, 690 | God N verb | Kinich Kuk building in the house | Mah Kina Chan-Bahlum, Divine Palenque Lord |

| 13 Ik end of Mol Feb. 5, 3112 B.C. | God N verb | Wacah Chan Xaman Waxac Na GI | is its name | it is the house of | the north (xaman) |

FIG. 6:20
House Dedication Events from the Group of the Cross
Top, TFC, L5-M9; mid, TS, N7-O12; bottom, TC, C9-C13

their completion, the three temples of the Group of the Cross housed the divine sanction for the dynasty as a whole and gave the rationale for its descent through females as well as males.

Two days after the house dedication on 5 Cauac 17 Mol,[43] Chan-Bahlum consummated the ritual sequence with a "fish-in-hand" vision rite. The timing of this last bloodletting linked the dedication rites back to Pacal, occurring just three days short of the seventy-fifth tropical year anniversary of his accession (July 29, 615 to July 26, 690). Chan-Bahlum's final sacrifice put the finishing touch to the extraordinary document he had created. Having begun these rituals when the First Mother reassembled in the sky with her children, he ended with her action of bloodletting, completing the symmetry he had forged between the creator gods and himself.

The last event Chan-Bahlum recorded in the Group of the Cross was the activation of the *pib na* themselves on 9.12.19.14.12 5 Eb 5 Kayab, the eighth tropical year anniversary of his own accession (January 10, 684 to January 10, 692). He recorded this ritual on the jambs around the sanctuary doors, on the outer piers of the temples, and on the balustrade panels mounted on either side of the stairs rising up the pyramidal base of each temple. The most public parts of the dynastic festival were the dedication of the stairway panels and the piers. These events could be easily viewed by an audience standing in the court space in the middle of the temple group.

On each set of balustrades (see Figs. 6:15 and 16 for paraphrases), Chan-Bahlum began his text with the birth of the patron god of each temple: GI for the Temple of the Cross, GII for the Temple of the Foliated Cross, and GIII for the Temple of the Sun. On the left side of the stairs, he recorded the time elapsed between the birth of the god and the dedication of the temple. On the right he listed the actors in the dedication rituals and their actions. In this manner, he connected the birth of the god in mythological time to the dedication of the *pib na* in contemporary time.

THE
CHILDREN
OF THE
FIRST
MOTHER:
FAMILY
AND
DYNASTY
AT
PALENQUE
—
257

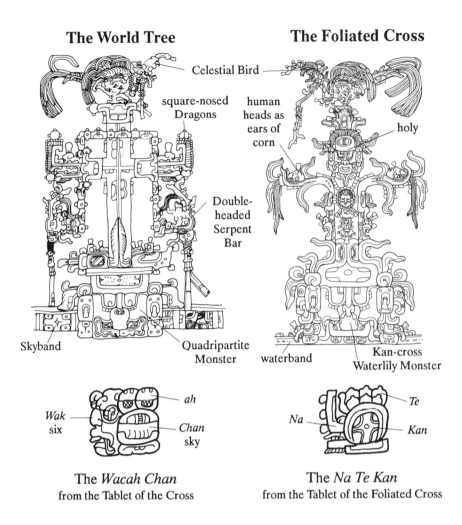

The World Tree

The Foliated Cross

Celestial Bird

square-nosed Dragons

human heads as ears of corn

holy

Double-headed Serpent Bar

Skyband

Quadripartite Monster

waterband

Kan-cross
Waterlily Monster

ah

Wak
six

Chan
sky

Te

Na

Kan

The *Wacah Chan*
from the Tablet of the Cross

The *Na Te Kan*
from the Tablet of the Foliated Cross

FIG. 6:21

Chan-Bahlum also used the four outer piers of each temple to record the dedication ceremonies. Here, once again, he depicted himself engaged in ritual. These more public displays of his political strategy were rendered in plaster relief, like the sculptures he had placed on the piers on the Temple of the Inscriptions. The inscription recording the date of the dedication festival and its events occupied the two outer piers, while the two inner ones illustrated the action. Unfortunately, only the two piers of the Temple of the Sun have survived into the twentieth century. Not surprisingly, given the temple's focus on warfare, Chan-Bahlum was portrayed in the costume of a warrior. The particular regalia he chose is that which we have already seen at Tikal, Naranjo, and Dos Pilas. The king is shown holding a square, flexible shield with a Tlaloc image on it,[44] declaring that he engaged in Tlaloc warfare. No doubt the object of his battles included those captives whose blood would sanctify the *pib na* as the gods came to reside in them.[45]

Like the balustrades, the doorjambs inside the sanctuaries are all glyphic,[46] but they record no information aside from the *pib na* dedications. All three sets of inscriptions describe the action in the same manner.

The War Stack

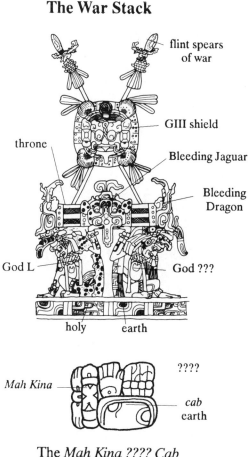

flint spears of war

GIII shield

throne

Bleeding Jaguar

Bleeding Dragon

God L

God ???

holy   earth

Mah Kina

????

cab earth

The *Mah Kina ???? Cab*
from the Tablet of the Sun

The verb "to house" is followed by the proper name of each sanctuary, followed by the glyph *u pib nail,* "his underground house." Each *pib na* was named for the central image on its inner tablet[47] (Fig. 6:21): *Wacah Chan* for the World Tree on the Tablet of the Cross, *Na Te Kan* for the maize tree on the Tablet of the Foliated Cross, and *Mah Kina ????-Cab* for the shield stack on the Tablet of the Sun.

Chan-Bahlum's final message to his people was that the performers of the "house" events were none other the gods of the Palenque Triad themselves. On the doorjambs he referred to these deities as "the cherished-ones[48] of Chan-Bahlum," while on the balustrades he called them the "divinities of Chan-Bahlum." For this event, Chan-Bahlum depicted himself in the guise of a Tlaloc warrior; but in this instance the costume symbolized more than just warfare. Dressed thus, Chan-Bahlum also became the "nurturer" of the gods[49] through his role as the provider of their sustenance—the blood of sacrifice. He offered them both the blood of captives taken in battle and his own blood.

If he himself was the principal actor, however, why did Chan-Bahlum tell us that the actors were the gods? Perhaps we are meant to

THE
CHILDREN
OF THE
FIRST
MOTHER:
FAMILY
AND
DYNASTY
AT
PALENQUE

——

259

Pacal, the father
The plaster portrait that was placed
under the sacrcophagus in his tomb

Chan-Bahlum, his firstborn son
A plaster portrait found in the rubble of
Temple XIV

understand that they acted in the divine person of the king. Although we do not have the precise phonetic reading of the verb, we suggest that each of the Triad gods came into his *pib na* on this day and brought the temples of the Group of the Cross alive with the power of the Otherworld. They were witnesses, like the nobility on the plaza below, to the awesome might of the Palenque king.

In his attempt to disengage his dynastic kingship from the prerogatives of the patrilineal clans, Chan-Bahlum brought to bear every major principle in the religion that bound the Maya states into a coherent cultural totality. As the Jaguar Sun and the Tlaloc warrior, he protected the realm from enemies. In war he captured foreign kings and nobles to offer as sacrificial instruments for the glory of Palenque. He recalled the First Father, GI', who raised the sky and established the ancestral home of creation within which his people could dwell at peace on their verdant mountainside. He also recalled the namesake of the First Father, GI, who like his father was an avatar of Venus. Just as the First Mother had shed her blood, causing maize—the raw material of humanity—to sprout from the waters of the Otherworld, so also did Chan-Bahlum shed his blood to nurture and "give birth to" the gods. The metaphor of kingship in both its human and divine dimension stretched from the contemplation of genesis to the mundane lives of farmers who plucked dried ears of maize from the bent stalks of their milpas to grind the kernels into the stuff of life.

The three gods of the Triad were known and exalted by all lowland Maya ahauob, but Chan-Bahlum and Pacal evoked them in very special ways. They gave them birth in temples which celebrated both the creation of the cosmos and the founding of the dynasty by their anchoring ancestor, Bahlum-Kuk. Called forth into this world through the unique courage and charisma of the reigning king, these three gods, like the three historical lineages leading up to Chan-Bahlum, were manifested for all to witness. All the events of the past, both human and mythological, encircled Chan-Bahlum: The dynasty existed in the person of the king.

Even the universe conspired to affirm Chan-Bahlum's assertions of divine involvement. On the day he began the rites to sanctify the buildings housing his version of history, Lady Beastie and her offspring reassembled as a group in the sky on the open south side of the Group of the Cross.

A year and a half later, on the day he celebrated his eighth solar year in office, the three gods of the Triad housed themselves. By this action they brought the sanctuaries inside the three temples, the *pib na,* alive with their power. So powerful and eloquent was Chan-Bahlum's statement of the origins of his dynasty and the preordained nature of its descent pattern, that no subsequent king ever had to restate any proofs. When later kings had problems with descent, they simply evoked Chan-Bahlum's explanation of the workings of divinity to justify their own right to the throne.[50]

Pacal's and Chan-Bahlum's vision of the Maya world has crossed the centuries to speak to us once again in the twentieth century. Their accomplishments were truly extraordinary. Pacal's tomb with its access stairway and innovative structural engineering is so far a unique achievement in the New World. The imagery of his sarcophagus lid is famous around the globe, and the life-sized plaster portrait of this king found under the sarcophagus has become an emblem of modern México (Fig. 6:22a).

Chan-Bahlum (Fig. 6:22b), in his own way, exceeded even the accomplishment of his father by creating the most detailed exposition of Maya kingship to survive into modern times. His tablets have captured the Western imagination since they were first popularized in 1841 by Stephens and Catherwood in their *Incidents of Travels in Central America, Chiapas, and Yucatán.* Chan-Bahlum's masterful performance is the clearest and most eloquent voice to speak to us of both the ancient history of kings and the religion that supported their power.

Both Pacal and Chan-Bahlum had personal agendas as they worked out the political and religious resolution to their problems of dynasty. Their success, however, was meaningful within a larger context than just their personal pride and glory. During the century of their combined lives (A.D. 603 to 702), Palenque became a major power in the west, extending its boundaries as far as Tortuguero in the west and Miraflores in the east. Under their inspired leadership, Palenque took its place in the overall political geography of the Maya world. In the end, however, Palenque's definition of dynasty as a principle transcending lineage did not provide salvation from the catastrophe of the collapse of Maya civilization. The descendants of Pacal, "he of the pyramid," followed their brethren into that final chaos when the old institution of kingship failed and the lowland Maya returned to the farming lives of their ancestors.

THE
CHILDREN
OF THE
FIRST
MOTHER:
FAMILY
AND
DYNASTY
AT
PALENQUE

——

261

BIRD-JAGUAR
AND THE
CAHALOB

In the distant past, a gleaming white city[1] once
graced the precipitous hills lining the western
shore of a huge horseshoe bend of the great river known
today as the Usumacinta (Fig. 7:1). One of the early
visitors to the ruins of that once magnificent city, Teobert Maler,[2] named it Yaxchilán. Since Tatiana Proskouriakoff's pioneering study of its inscriptions, this
kingdom has been central to the recovery of historic
information about the Maya.[3]

In Yaxchilán's heyday, visitors arriving by canoe
saw buildings clustered along the narrow curving shore
which contained and defined the natural riverside entrance into this rich and powerful community. The city
ascended in rows of broad, massive terraces built
against the face of the forest-shrouded hills that stood
as an impassive natural citadel alongside the mighty
river. From the temples (Fig. 7:2a) built upon the summits of the tallest bluffs, the lords of Yaxchilán commanded the sweeping panorama of the rich green,
low-lying forest which extended, on the far side of the
river, all the way to the hazy horizon in the northeast.
The light of sunrise on the summer solstice[4] would spill
over that horizon to shine through the dark thresholds
of the royal sanctuaries whose presence declared the
authority of the Yaxchilán ahau over all those who
lived below.

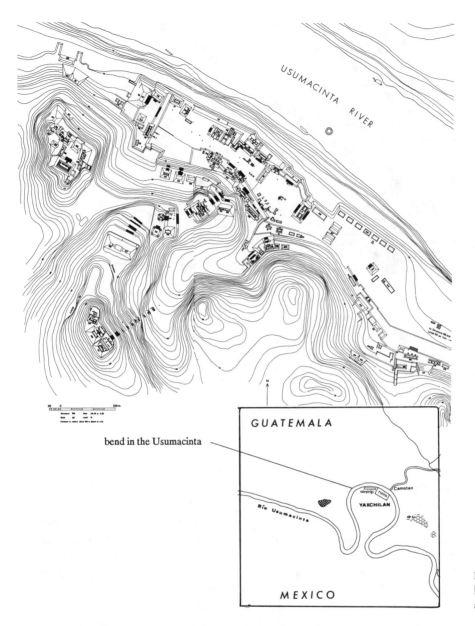

FIG. 7:1
Map of Yaxchilán
after Graham 1977

Yat-Balam, "Penis of the Jaguar,"[5] or more delicately put, "Progenitor-Jaguar," on August 2, A.D. 320, founded the dynasty that ruled this kingdom throughout its recorded history. From that day on, until Yaxchilán was abandoned five-hundred years later, the descent of the line was unbroken.[6] Of Yat-Balam's many descendants, the most famous were Shield-Jaguar and Bird-Jaguar, a father and son who collectively ruled the kingdom for over ninety years, from A.D. 681 until around A.D. 771. These two rulers stamped their vision of history upon the city with such power and eloquence that they were the first of the ancient Maya kings to have their names spoken again in our time.[7] Yet in spite of the glory of their reigns and their long-lasting effect upon history, they faced problems of descent from the father to the son. Bird-Jaguar's claim to the throne was

roof comb

entablature

bearing wall

FIG. 7:2a
**Temple 33
at Yaxchilán**

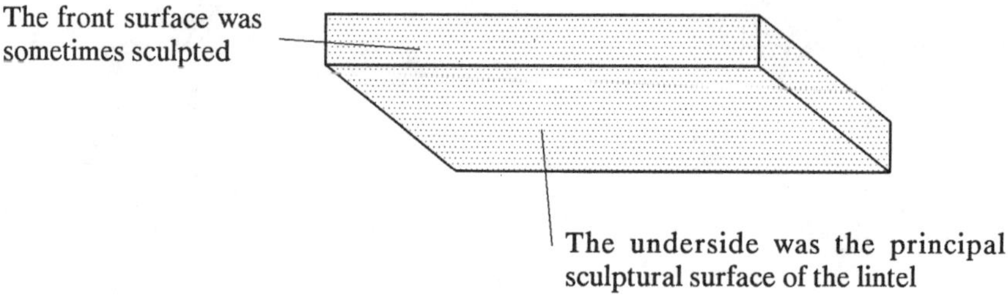

FIG. 7:2b
**Yaxchilán's
sculptors used
the stone lintels
over the doors of
the temple to
represent the
actions**

The front surface was
sometimes sculpted

The underside was the principal
sculptural surface of the lintel

vigorously disputed by powerful noble clans who were allied with other members of the royal family. Even after Bird-Jaguar overcame his adversaries and became king, many of the public buildings he commissioned were erected to retrospectively defend his own actions and prepare a secure ascent to the throne for his heir. In this chapter, we will focus on his problems and the political strategies and alliances that finally enabled him to fulfill his ambition to rule that ancient kingdom.

The history of Bird-Jaguar's ancestors in the Early Classic period does not survive in great detail. Most of the monuments from those times were either buried or destroyed as each new king shaped the city to his own purposes. However, thanks to Bird-Jaguar's strategy of reusing ancestral texts in his own buildings (Temples 12 and 22), we do have records of the first through the tenth successors of Yaxchilán. One of these venerable texts, a badly eroded hieroglyphic stairway, provides the dates of several early accessions, as well as accounts of the visits of lords from other kingdoms. These brief and sketchy early inscriptions outline the first three hundred years of Yaxchilán's history. It was a time in which its dynasty prospered and held an important place in the overall political landscape of the Maya.[8]

The foreign visitors mentioned above were ahauob sent by their high kings from as far away as Bonampak, Piedras Negras, and Tikal to participate in Yaxchilán festivals. Reciprocal visits were made as well. Knot-eye-

Jaguar, the ninth king of Yaxchilán, paid a state visit to Piedras Negras in the year 519. The relationship between these two kingdoms was apparently a long-lasting one, for another Yaxchilán ahau, presumably Bird-Jaguar, participated in the celebration of the first katun anniversary of the reign of Piedras Negras Ruler 4 in 749, 230 years later. These state visits affirm the ancient and enduring value that the kings of Yaxchilán placed upon the participation of high nobility in the rituals and festivals of their city. Public performances under the aegis of the high king, by both foreign and local lords, affirmed the power of the king and demonstrated public support for his decisions. We shall see shortly how the manipulation of such *dramatis personae* on monuments was the vital key to Bird-Jaguar's strategy of legitimization.

Our story opens around the year 647[9] with the birth of a child to the Lady Pacal, favored wife of the king, 6-Tun-Bird-Jaguar,[10] and scion of a powerful family allied to the king through marriage. The child, whom the proud parents named Shield-Jaguar, was to have a glorious career at Yaxchilán, living for at least ninety-two years and ruling as high king for over six decades. His mark on the city was long-lasting and profound, for later kings left many of his buildings untouched. Among his greatest works were the vast number of tree-stones he set among the plazas and in front of his temples on the summits of his sacred mountains. Shield-Jaguar inherited a city already built by his predecessors, but the accomplishments of his long lifetime exceeded their work by such a factor that, while much of his work is still preserved, most of theirs is forgotten, buried under his own construction and that of his son, Bird-Jaguar.

Most of Shield-Jaguar's early life is lost to us. What little biographical data we do have tells us that when he was around eleven, one of his siblings participated in a war led by Pacal, the king of Palenque we met in the last chapter.[11] This event must have lent prestige to the royal family of Yaxchilán, but their public monuments say nothing about it. We only know of this event because it was preserved on the Hieroglyphic Stairs of House C at Palenque. The fact that Pacal described his Yaxchilán cohort as the "sibling" of the eleven-year-old Shield-Jaguar tells us that, even at that early date, Shield-Jaguar had probably been named as heir. Otherwise, Pacal would have chosen to emphasize the captive's status merely as the son of a male of the royal family.[12]

Later in his life, the demonstration of the young heir's prowess as a military leader took on a special political importance—enough so that the lords of Yaxchilán required that Shield-Jaguar take a high-ranked captive before he could become king. As prelude to his accession, Shield-Jaguar went into battle and captured Ah-Ahaual, an important noble from a kingdom whose ruins we have not yet found, but which was highly important in the Maya world of that time.[13] A little over a year later, on October 23, 681, at the approximate age of thirty-four, Shield-Jaguar became high king of Yaxchilán.

Strangely enough, the only picture of Shield-Jaguar's accession rite to have survived shows not the new king but his principal wife, Lady Xoc, in rapt communion with Yat-Balam, the founding ancestor of the Yaxchilán dynasty. Lady Xoc achieved a central place in the drama of Yaxchilán's history in this and in two other bloodletting rituals she enacted with, or for, her sovereign liege.[14] Her kinship ties with two powerful lineages of the kingdom made her political support so important to Shield-Jaguar that he authorized her to commission and dedicate the magnificent Temple 23. On the lintels of that building were recorded the three rituals that comprised the apical actions of her life.

Thus, with the approval and probably at the instigation of her husband, Lady Xoc was one of the few women in Maya history to wield the prerogatives usually reserved for the high king. Unlike Lady Zac-Kuk of Palenque, however, Lady Xoc never ruled the kingdom in her own right. The hidden hand of her husband, Shield-Jaguar, underlies the political intentions of the extraordinary Temple 23. His influence can be seen in both the substance of its narrative scenes and in the texts[15] carved on the lintels that spanned the outer doorways. Constructed in the center of the city's first great terrace, and in a position to dominate the plazas that extended along the riverfront, this temple is one of the greatest artistic monuments ever created by the Maya.

The carved lintels above the doorways of Temple 23 combine to present a carefully orchestrated political message critical to Shield-Jaguar's ambition and to the future he hoped to create. Made of wide slabs mounted atop the doorjambs, these lintels displayed two carved surfaces. The first, facing outward toward the public, was composed of pure text. The second was a series of narrative scenes hidden away on the undersides of the lintels, facing downward toward the floor (Fig. 7:2b). A general viewer approaching the building could read only the text above the doorways, which recorded the dedication rituals for various parts of the temple. This text stated that the house sculpture (probably the stucco sculpture on the entablature and roof comb) had been dedicated on August 5, 723, and the temple itself on June 26, 726.[16] The all-important narrative scenes could be seen only by those privileged to stand in the low doorways and look up at the undersides of the lintels.

It is here, on the undersides of the lintels, that we see Lady Xoc enacting the three bloodletting rituals that are today the basis of her fame (Fig. 7:3). The sculptors who created these great lintels combined the sequence of events into a brilliant narrative device. If we look at the lintels from one perspective, we see that each portrays a different linear point in the ritual of bloodletting. Over the left doorway we see Lady Xoc perforating her tongue; over the center portal we see the materialization of the Vision Serpent; over the right we see her dressing her liege lord for battle. If we shift our perspective, however, we see that Shield-Jaguar intended these scenes to be interpreted on many different levels. He used the texts and the detail of the clothing the protagonists wore to tell us that this same bloodletting ritual took place on at least three different occasions:[17] during his accession to the kingship, at the birth of his son when he was sixty-one, and at the dedication of the temple itself.

Over the central door, Lady Xoc is depicted with a Vision Serpent rearing over her head as she calls forth the founder of the lineage, Yat-

Yat-Balam, the founder
recalled in the Vision Rite

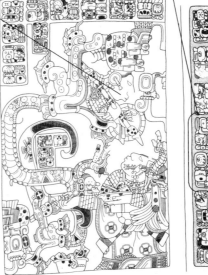

| Shield-Jaguar holding a torch for his wife | Lady Xoc pulling a rope through her tongue | Vision Serpent rising from a bowl | Lady Xoc gazing at her vision |

a. Lintel 24: the ritual on Oct. 28, 709, celebrating Bird-Jaguar's birth

b. Lintel 25: Lady Xoc's recall of the founder during Shield-Jaguar's accession rituals

| Shield-Jaguar in his battle dress | Lady Xoc holding his helmet and flexible shield | dedication of the building on June 26, 726 | Structure 23 |

c. Lady Xoc helping Shield-Jaguar prepare for battle to take captives

FIG. 7:3
Temple 23:
The Building
of Lady Xoc
all drawings by
Ian Graham

BIRD-JAGUAR
AND THE
CAHALOB

Balam, to witness the accession of his descendent Shield-Jaguar in 681[18] (Fig. 7:3a). This critical event in the lives of both the principal players was appropriately located on the center lintel, at the heart of the drama. Shield-Jaguar himself is not portrayed here, although his name does ap-

pear in the text after the "fish-in-hand" verbal phrase. The sole protagonist is the woman, who by her action as bloodletter materializes the
founder of the dynasty to sanction the transformation of his descendant
into the king. Since we know of no other pictorial representation of
Shield-Jaguar's accession,[19] we may speculate that he considered his wife's
bloodletting the most important single action in this political transformation.

Over the left door, Lady Xoc kneels before Shield-Jaguar and pulls
a thorn-laden rope through her mutilated tongue in the action that will
materialize the Vision Serpent. Shield-Jaguar stands before her holding a
torch, perhaps because the ritual takes place inside a temple or at night.
Although this lintel depicts the first stage in the type of bloodletting ritual
shown over the central door, this particular event took place almost
twenty-eight years later.[20]

The occasion for this particular act of sacrifice was an alignment
between Jupiter and Saturn. On this day those planets were frozen at their
stationary points less than 2° apart, very near the constellation of Gemini.
This was the same type of planetary alignment we saw celebrated at
Palenque when Chan-Bahlum dedicated the Group of the Cross, even
though the conjunction at Yaxchilán was perhaps less spectacular, since
it involved two planets rather than four. Significantly, this hierophany
("sacred event") took place only sixty-two days after a son was born to
Shield-Jaguar. The birth of this child on August 24, 709, and the bloodletting event that followed it on October 28, were special events in Shield-
Jaguar's reign. This bloodletting would later become the pivot of his son's
claim to Yaxchilán's throne.

Over the right door (Fig. 7:3b), the sculptors mounted the final scene.
Lady Xoc, her mouth seeping blood from the ritual she has just performed, helps her husband dress for battle. He already wears his cotton
armor and grasps his flint knife in his right hand, but she still holds his
flexible shield and the jaguar helmet he will don. Here Shield-Jaguar is
preparing to go after captives to be used in the dedication rites that took
place either on February 12, 724, or on June 26, 726.

The depiction of a woman as the principal actor in ritual is unprecedented at Yaxchilán and almost unknown in Maya monumental art[21] at
any site. Lady Xoc's importance is further emphasized by the manner in
which Bird-Jaguar centers his own strategy of legitimacy around this
building. The three events portrayed—the accession of the king, the
bloodletting on the Jupiter-Saturn hierophany, and the dedication of
the building itself, were all important events; but the bloodletting on the
hierophany was the focus of the political message Shield-Jaguar intended
to communicate. Perhaps the planetary conjunction alone would have
been enough reason for such a bloodletting to take place. We suspect,
however, that more complex motivations were involved. Later, when
Bird-Jaguar commissioned monument after monument to explain who he
was and, more importantly, who his mother was, he focused on this event
as the key to his kingdom.

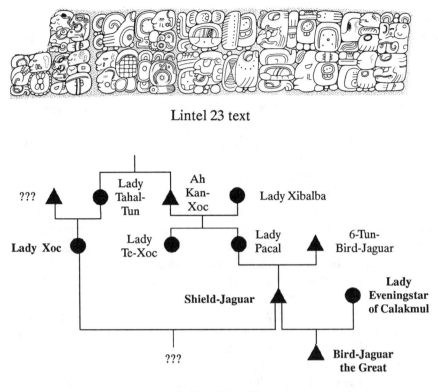

Lintel 23 text

Lady Xoc's Pedigree

Lady Eveningstar, Lady Ahau of Calakmul

FIG. 7:4
Shield-Jaguar's
Wives

There are points of interest to make about this bloodletting ritual and the birth that preceded it. Lady Xoc, patroness of this building and the giver of blood, was at least middle-aged at the time of this birth.[22] She had been shown as an adult at Shield-Jaguar's accession, twenty-eight years earlier, and she may well have been beyond her childbearing years at the time of the later bloodletting. Certainly, other inscriptions make it clear that the child in question was born to Lady Eveningstar, another of Shield-Jaguar's wives. Why, then, is Lady Xoc celebrating a celestial event linked to the royal heir born to another woman?

Some startling information about Lady Xoc's role in Shield-Jaguar's political machinations is revealed on a lintel mounted over the door in the east end of Structure 23. On its underside, this all-glyphic lintel (Lintel 23) records Shield-Jaguar's twenty-fifth year anniversary as ruler and also Lady Xoc's dedication of this extraordinary temple. On the edge of this obscure lintel, facing outward toward the viewer, we find some critical and unexpected information about Lady Xoc. The text tells us that this particular passageway[23] into the temple was dedicated by Shield-Jaguar's mother's sister—his aunt, in other words. The title sequence in this aunt's name is relevatory, for it delineates an up-to-now unknown genealogical relationship between Lady Xoc and the king (Fig. 7:4).[24] We learn here that Lady Xoc was the daughter of Shield-Jaguar's mother's father's sister. In plain English, she was the maternal first cousin of his mother, and his own maternal first cousin once removed.

What this information tells us is that Lady Xoc was distantly related to the patriline of Shield-Jaguar's mother, but he married her not because of her mother's relatives but because her father was a member of a powerful noble lineage. How do we know that her father's line was important, when it is not even mentioned in the inscriptions? We can deduce its importance from the fact that it was worthy to take a wife from the same family that provided the woman who was wife to the king 6-Tun-Bird-Jaguar and mother to the heir, Shield-Jaguar. In other words, anyone powerful enough to marry a woman from the same family that provided the queen-mother to the royal house must also be of extraordinarily high-rank. The importance of the line of Lady Xoc's father is further confirmed by the fact that it was eligible to provide a wife to the royal house in the next generation. Thus, it was a lineage important enough to take a wife from the highest levels in the kingdom and in its own right to be in a wife-giving alliance with the royal house. In fact, it is precisely this marriage alliance with Lady Xoc's father that led Shield-Jaguar to take her as his wife in the first place.

What we find amazing here is that Lady Xoc's patriline is utterly absent from the public record. On Lintel 23, Lady Xoc's relationship to that patriline is suppressed in favor of her kinship to her mother's people. As we have shown above, her mother's clan was already allied to the royal house of Yaxchilán, for Shield-Jaguar's mother was a member of that patriline. In the best of worlds, Shield-Jaguar could have safely ignored such a well-attested and secure alliance in the public record. What, then, led Shield-Jaguar to commission the extraordinary Temple 23 with its homage to Lady Xoc and her mother's clan? Why did he deliberately eliminate her father's clan from public history by redefining her importance in terms of people who were already his allies?

We suspect that the answer to this question lies in a new marriage that Shield-Jaguar contracted late in his life. His new wife, Lady Eveningstar, who bore him a son when he was sixty-one, was apparently a foreigner of high rank. On Stela 10, her son, Bird-Jaguar, recorded her name in his own parentage statement, remarking that she was a "Lady Ahau of Calakmul" (Fig. 7:4).[25] Yet Shield-Jaguar's treatment of his new wife and the powerful alliance she represented was not what we might expect. Despite the great power and prestige of Calakmul, Shield-Jaguar never once mentioned Lady Eveningstar on his own monuments. Instead, the principal concern of his late monuments was to secure support for Bird-Jaguar, the child she gave him.

To this end, he commissioned Temple 23 when his son was thirteen years old.[26] He honored Lady Xoc, who represented local alliances with two important lineages, as the major actor of the critical events in his reign. And, in the same series of lintels, he emphasized her relationship to her mother's patriline.[27] But what of her father's people, not to mention the royal house of Calakmul?

To elect a child of Lady Xoc to succeed him would have brought Shield-Jaguar strategic alliance with her father's people, a local lineage of extraordinary importance. Alternatively, to designate Lady Eveningstar's child as the heir would have sealed a blood bond with one of the largest and most aggressive kingdoms of the Petén, but it was also an alliance with a foreign power.[28] The decision for Shield-Jaguar was a difficult one: increased prospects for peace and stability within his kingdom versus an elevated position in the grand configuration of alliance and struggle embracing all of the great kingdoms of the Maya.

Temple 23 was his effort to forge a grand compromise: to honor Lady Xoc and the principle of internal alliance while building support for the child of the foreign alliance. He chose the greatest artists of his kingdom to carve what are even today recognized as great masterpieces of Maya art. In the elegant reliefs he depicted his senior wife carrying out the most sacred and intimate act of lineage fealty, the calling forth of the royal founding ancestor. When she gave her blood for his new heir, she did so in the most horrific ritual of tongue mutilation known from Maya history. No other representation of this ritual shows the use of a thorn-lined rope in the wound. Her act was one of extraordinary piety and prestige—and an act of audacity by the king, for he simultaneously consigned the mother of the heir, scion of Calakmul, to public obscurity. For Shield-Jaguar, this was a masterful three-point balancing act. By honoring Lady Xoc, he was also honoring that patriline. He used texts upon the lintels of the temple to publicly emphasize her relationship to his mother's family and thus secure that alliance. Lastly, he satisfied his foreign alliance by choosing the child of that marriage as the heir.

This strategy of compromise worked, at least while he was still alive. Perhaps Shield-Jaguar's extraordinary age was one of the contributing factors in this drama. For him to have lived long enough to marry again and to sire a child in that marriage may have surprised the lineages allied to him by previous marriages. Furthermore, any children born in his youth would have been in their middle years by the time of Bird-Jaguar's birth. By the time of Shield-Jaguar's death in his mid-nineties, many of his children may well have been dead or in advanced age themselves. Because of this factor, Bird-Jaguar's rivals would have had as legitimate a claim on the throne as he; it is likely that he faced the sons and grandsons of Lady Xoc and Shield-Jaguar. We cannot, of course, prove that these rivals existed, for they did not secure the privilege of erecting monuments to tell their own stories. This is one of those situations in which we have only the winner's version of history. Nevertheless, we know that some set of circumstances kept the throne empty for ten long years, when a legitimate heir of sufficient age and proven competence was available. We

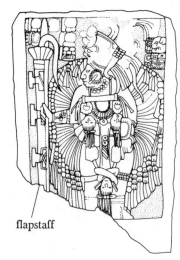

flapstaff

a. Stela 16: the first flapstaff event
by Shield-Jaguar on June 27, 736(?)

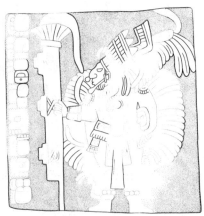

drawing by Ian Graham

b. Lintel 50: Shield-Jaguar in first
flapstaff event??

Shield-Jaguar

Bird-Jaguar

drawing by Ian Graham

c. Stela 11: Shield-Jaguar enacts
his flapstaff rite with his son
Bird-Jaguar on June 26, 741.

d. Lintel 33: Bird-Jaguar in his
flapstaff rite on June 25, 747

surmise that Bird-Jaguar needed those ten years to defeat his would-be rivals. During this long interregnum no other accessions appear in the record. There was no official king, although there may have been a de facto ruler.

There could, of course, be many reasons for such a long delay between reigns. Bird-Jaguar's own program of sculpture after he became king, however, clearly indicates what he felt were his greatest problems. The first was public recognition of his mother's status and her equality

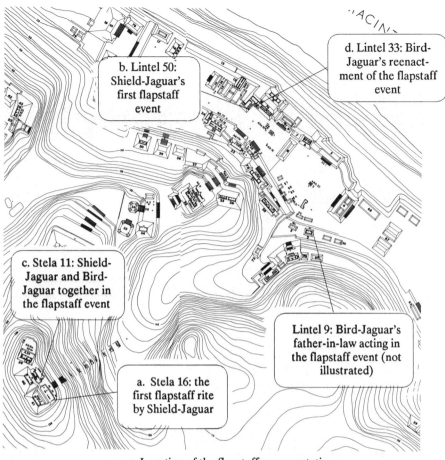

b. Lintel 50: Shield-Jaguar's first flapstaff event

d. Lintel 33: Bird-Jaguar's reenactment of the flapstaff event

c. Stela 11: Shield-Jaguar and Bird-Jaguar together in the flapstaff event

Lintel 9: Bird-Jaguar's father-in-law acting in the flapstaff event (not illustrated)

a. Stela 16: the first flapstaff rite by Shield-Jaguar

e. Location of the flapstaff representations

with Lady Xoc.[29] The second was his need to forge alliances among the noble cahal families of Yaxchilán to support his claim to the throne and force the accession ritual. He built temple after temple with lintel upon lintel both to exalt the status of his mother and to depict his public performance with those powerful cahalob. Like his father, he married a woman in the lineage of his most important allies and traded a piece of history for their loyalty.

The fathering of an heir at the age of sixty-one was not the final accomplishment of Shield-Jaguar's life. He remained a vigorous leader, both politically and in the realm of war, for many more years. Work on Temple 23 began around 723, when he was seventy-two years old. In his eighties, he still led his warriors into battle and celebrated a series of victories in Temple 44, high atop one of the mountains of Yaxchilán (Fig. 7:1). Even at eighty-four, Shield-Jaguar went to battle and took a captive, but by then he must have been feeling his mortality. He began a series of rituals soon after his last battle to demonstrate forcefully his support of Bird-Jaguar as his heir-apparent—at least according to the story Bird-Jaguar gives us. In light of the political statement that Shield-Jaguar built into Lady Xoc's Temple 23 at the height of his power, there is reason to

BIRD-JAGUAR
AND THE
CAHALOB
—
273

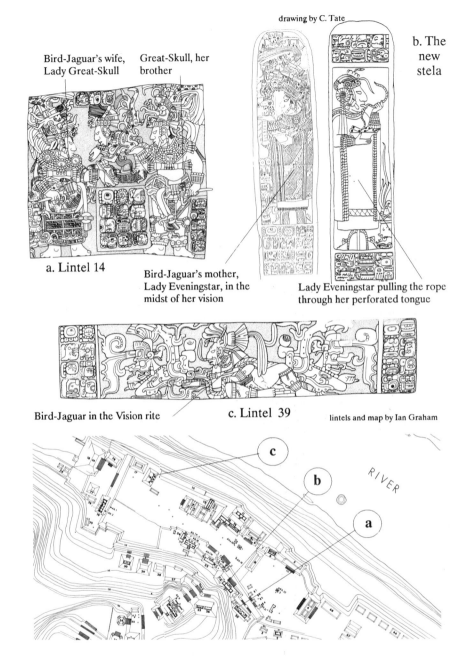

drawing by C. Tate

Bird-Jaguar's wife,
Lady Great-Skull

Great-Skull, her
brother

b. The
new
stela

a. Lintel 14

Bird-Jaguar's mother,
Lady Eveningstar, in the
midst of her vision

Lady Eveningstar pulling the rope
through her perforated tongue

Bird-Jaguar in the Vision rite

c. Lintel 39

lintels and map by Ian Graham

c

b

RIVER

a

believe that at least the essence of Bird-Jaguar's account of events leading up to his reign is true.

The series of events preceding Shield-Jaguar's death and Bird-Jaguar's ascent to the throne began on June 27, 736. On that day Shield-Jaguar, at the age of eighty-eight, conducted a flapstaff ritual (Fig. 7:5a and b), a celebration usually occurring shortly after a summer solstice. We do not know the exact nature of this ritual, but pictures of it show rulers and nobles holding a human-high, wooden staff with a four-to-six-inch-wide cloth tied down its length. This narrow cloth was decorated with elaborately woven designs and flapped openings, usually cut in the shape of a T. Shield-Jaguar recorded his first display of this staff on Stela 16, which he erected at the highest point of the city in front of Temple 41. Bird-Jaguar commissioned his own retrospective version of his father's action on Lintel 50 (Fig. 7:5b).

The next time we see this flapstaff ritual is on Stela 11, a monument erected by Bird-Jaguar soon after his accession. Designed to document events that culminated in his successful ascent to the throne, this stela includes the image of another flapstaff ritual which had occurred on June 26, 741, exactly five years after Shield-Jaguar's earlier flapstaff ceremony. In this scene (Fig. 7:5c), the shorter Shield-Jaguar,[30] who was then ninety-three years old, faces his son under a double-headed dragon representing the sky, above which sit Bird-Jaguar's ancestors.[31] Both men now hold the same flapstaff that Shield-Jaguar displayed on Stela 16. Bird-Jaguar took pains to emphasize the importance of this mutual display. He did so by depicting this scene both atop and between texts that recorded his accession to the throne, thus asserting that his father had shared this ritual with him to legitimize his status as heir. Furthermore, Bird-Jaguar set this dual depiction in front of Temple 40 (Fig. 7:5c and e), which was situated on the same hill summit as Temple 41 where Shield-Jaguar had placed his earlier depiction of the flapstaff ritual. This close juxtaposition emphasized the linkage between the two rituals and supported Bird-Jaguar's political aspirations.

This father-son flapstaff event took place only four days before the end of the tenth tun in the fifteenth katun on 9.15.10.0.0. Five days later, on 9.15.10.0.1 (July 1, 741), another ritual took place that was so important and involved so many critical people that Bird-Jaguar recorded it glyphically and pictorially three times (Fig. 7:6), in three different locations. These locations all pivoted thematically around Temple 23, the building that became the touchstone of his legitimacy.

The most distant of these depictions, Lintel 14 of Temple 20, shows two persons. One is a woman named Lady Great-Skull-Zero, and the other is a man with the same family name, Lord Great-Skull-Zero (Fig. 7:6a). This woman would become the mother of Bird-Jaguar's son and heir, and the man, who is named as her brother, was most likely the patriarch of her lineage.[32] Great-Skull-Zero belonged to a cahal lineage that was apparently an important source of political support, for Bird-Jaguar continued to depict him on public monuments, even after his own accession. In this earlier ritual, both Lady Great-Skull-Zero and her brother hold a Vision Serpent the two of them have materialized through bloodletting.[33] She also holds an offering bowl containing an obsidian blade and bloodstained paper, while he holds the head of the serpent aloft as a female ancestor materializes in its mouth. The name of this ancestor, "Lady Ahau of Yaxchilán, Lady Yaxhal," appears in the small text above the apparition's head.

It is possible that this bloodletting rite was part of the rituals of marriage between Bird-Jaguar and Lady Great-Skull-Zero, but none of the glyphs recorded on this lintel refer to marriage. Whatever the occasion, we can presume that this lady and her kinsmen were vitally important to Bird-Jaguar's successful campaign to replace his father as high king. Going against precedent, he gives them an unusually prominent place in history, depicting them as participants in this critical bloodletting ritual.

The second time we see this bloodletting is on a retrospective stela (Fig. 7:6b) found next door in Temple 21, a building in which Bird-Jaguar deliberately replayed the iconographic program of Lady Xoc's temple in celebration of the birth of his own heir.[34] This newly discovered stela[35] shows Bird-Jaguar's mother, Lady Eveningstar, engaged in the same bloodletting as his wife, Lady Great-Skull-Zero, and her brother. This stela emulates the style and iconographic detail of Lintel 25 on Temple 23, which depicts Lady Xoc materializing the founder of the dynasty at Shield-Jaguar's accession. Bird-Jaguar declares—by means of this not-so-subtle artistic manipulation—that his mother's actions were every bit as important as those of his father's principal wife.

On the front of the stela and facing the entry door, Lady Eveningstar is depicted holding a bloodletting plate in one hand and a skull-serpent device in the other, while a huge skeletal Vision Serpent rears behind her. As on Lintel 25, this Vision Serpent is double-headed and emits Tlaloc faces. The text records the date, 4 Imix 4 Mol, and states that a "fish-in-hand" vision event took place *u cab chan kina* "in the land of the sky lords." A coupleted repetition attests that "Lady Eveningstar let blood." On the rear, she is shown drawing the rope through her tongue and here the text specifies that she was "the mother of the three-katun lord, Bird-Jaguar, Holy Lord of Yaxchilán, Bacab." Bird-Jaguar very likely installed this monument to emphasize his mother's legitimate status, as well as her ritual centrality during his father's lifetime. At any rate, this stela was part of his program to assert the legitimacy of his own son and heir, whose birth was celebrated on the central lintel of this temple.[36]

Bird-Jaguar set the third depiction (Fig. 7:6c) of this critical bloodletting ritual over the central door of Structure 16, a building located at the eastern edge of the river shelf. Carved on the outer edge of Lintel 39, the scene shows Bird-Jaguar sprawled on the ground as he supports a Serpent Bar, skeletal in detail and emitting GII as the materialized vision. The date is again 4 Imix 4 Mol[37] and the action a "fish-in-hand" vision rite. Now, however, the actor is the future king himself.

Based on these three representations of this critical bloodletting, as well as depictions of similar events at other sites,[38] we can visualize this great ritual in the following vignette.

The starlit darkness broke before the first flush of light as the sun rose from Xibalba over the dark waters of the river. Venus, who had preceded his brother out of the Underworld by almost two hours, now hovered brightly near the seven lights of the Pleiades and the bright star Aldebaran.[39] Nine times had the Lords of the Night changed since the sun had taken its longest journey through the sky on the day of the summer solstice. Birds waking in the trees across the river and along the hills above the city raised a crescendo of song, counterpointing the barking of the village dogs and the squawks of brilliant red macaws flying along the edge of the water. Far in the distance, a howler monkey roared his own salutation to the new day. The celestial stage was set for an important festival and the community of people who lived along the river waited anxiously for the rituals that would soon begin.

A crowd of ahauob, cahalob, and people of lesser rank milled restlessly within the cool plaza beside the great river. The iridescent feathers of their headdresses bobbed above their animated conversations like a fantastic flock of birds. The brilliantly embroidered and dyed cloth of their garments swirled in a riot of color against the hard whiteness of the plaster floor and the distant green backdrop of the mist-shrouded forest. As dawn broke through the darkness of night, more people drifted toward the plaza from the distant hillslopes. Still more arrived in canoes, having fought the high floodwaters to cross the river so that they too could witness the great ritual announced by the king.

The king's family, arrayed in front of the gleaming white walls of the *Tz'ikinah-Nal,* the house Lady Xoc had dedicated many years ago, and the *Chan-Ah-Tz'i,*[40] the house of the seventh successor of Yat-Balam, watched the sun rise over the huge stone pier that had been built over the river on its southern side. No one could see the pier now, of course, for the great *Xocol Ha*[41] was in flood from the thunderstorms of the rainy season. The roar of the tumbling waters played a ground behind the rhythms of drums and whistles echoing through the great open spaces along the canoe-strewn shore. Merchants, visitors, pilgrims, and farmers from near and far had laid their wares along the river for the people of Yaxchilán to peruse. They too joined their voices to the cacophony of sound swelling throughout the gleaming white plazas of the city.

The royal clan stood in two groups, the hard and dangerous tension between them radiating down into the crowd below. The cahalob and ahauob of the court arranged themselves in clusters, clearly indicating their support for one or the other branch of the family. The aging but indomitable Lady Xoc[42] took up position with her kinsmen in front of the *Tz'ikinah-Nal.* In this, the place of her glory, she contemplated the irony of her fate. Here, in the most magnificent imagery to grace the city, she had commemorated her devotion to Shield-Jaguar. The finest artisans of the realm had carved the lintels in the house behind her, declaring publicly and permanently that she had materialized the founder when her lord acceded as king. And the reward for that sacrifice? She had been forced to deny her own father's kinsmen and to let her blood to sanctify the final issue of her aged husband's loins: Bird-Jaguar—son of a foreigner.

Even now the men of her father's lineage were as reluctant as she to give up their privileges as kinsmen of the king's principal wife. The gods had favored Shield-Jaguar by giving him a life span beyond that granted to other humankind. He had lived so long that most of the sons of her womb were dead, as were many of *their* sons.[43] The sharp pain of remembered grief cut through her reverie. The matriarch, soon to enter her fifth katun of life, glanced at her remaining offspring, her thwarted and angry kinsmen, and the powerful cahalob allied to her father's clan. All stood quietly, grimly, allowing the old woman her moment of bitter reflection.

Most of the witnessing emissaries from towns along the river gathered before the other royal group in anticipation of the celebration to come. Bird-Jaguar, renowned warrior, defender of the realm and future king, quietly conversed with his mother, Lady Eveningstar, and his new wife, Lady Great-Skull-Zero. They were framed by the splendor of the *Chan-Ah-Tz'i.* At thirty-one, the heir radiated a physical strength to match his valor and ambition. The bride's lineage patriarch, Great-Skull-Zero, stood beside her, accompanied by the other cahalob who, by their presence here, declared themselves allies of the king's son. Chief among them, Kan-Toc proudly and dispassionately surveyed potential friends and foes below, ready to place his prowess as warrior at the disposal of the future king.

The nobles flanking the principal players in this drama stood in small groups on the steps of the temples. Their arms folded across their chests, they spoke of the day's events, the condition of the new crop, and hundreds of other topics of concern. Some were bare-chested, but the most important lords wore blinding white capes closed at the throat with three huge red spondylus shells. This cotton garb was reserved for those privileged to serve as attendants to the king, or those who held the status of pilgrims to the royal festivals.[44] Farther away, warriors of renown in their finest battle gear stood with other notables who carried the emblazoned staff-fans of Maya war and ceremony. Other nobles sat in informal groups, engaging in lively conversation among the riot of color in the long-shadowed light of the brilliant morning. Excitement and anticipation were becoming a palpable force pulsing through the crowd of people that now included a growing number of farmers and villagers who had come in from the surrounding countryside to share in the festivities.

Shield-Jaguar, the ninety-three-year-old king, sat frail but erect upon the long bench inside the central room of the *Chan-Ah-Tz'i.* The morning light coursing through the door warmed his bony chest, bared above his white hipcloth, as he mused over the many shivering hours he had spent in such rooms in the dark time before dawn. Now with his aged cronies, the last of his most trusted lords, he sat in this venerable house that had been dedicated 286 years earlier by the seventh successor of Yat-Balam.

Shield-Jaguar's years weighed heavily upon him. This would surely be the final festival of his life—his last opportunity to seal his blessings upon Bird-Jaguar before the gods, the ancestors, and the people of his kingdom. Four days earlier, he had stood before the people with his son and heir and displayed the ceremonial cloth-lined flapstaff. It was important that all his people, noble and common folk alike, witness and accept his gift of power to Bird-Jaguar. The issue of the inheritance still tormented his spirit so powerfully he feared he was not adequately prepared for his trial with the Lords of Death. It was common scandal among all the great houses on the river that the men of Lady Xoc's lineage continued to press their claims on the king, despite all that he had done for them and for her. The kinsmen of his principal wife had become his most formidable enemies. They would surely maneuver to place one of her own offspring on the throne after his bones lay in the vaulted grave that awaited his fall into Xibalba. Bird-Jaguar would have to be a subtle and powerful leader to take and hold his rightful place as the successor of his father.

A shout from the crowd outside brought Shield-Jaguar back to the present and his immediate duty to the dynasty of Yat-Balam. The Ancestral Sun had climbed above the mouth of the eastern horizon until he hovered free of the earth. Despite the fierce glare the sun brought to the world, Venus retained his strength on this special day so that the brothers could be seen together in the morning sky, momentary companions like the aged king and his energetic son. It was one day after the halfway point of Katun 15. The bloodletting rituals about to begin would consecrate that benchmark in time and demonstrate the king's support for his youngest son.

The old man's eyes sparkled as he watched Lady Eveningstar, mother of the heir, move gracefully into the frame of light before his doorway. She would be the first to offer her blood and open the portal to the Otherworld.[45] Dressed in a brilliant white gauze huipil, high-backed sandals, and a flower headdress, she stepped forward to stand before her son. Shield-Jaguar was too frail to make the precise ceremonial cut in his wife's body and that role now fell to Bird-Jaguar. Holding a shallow plate within the circle of her folded arms, Lady Eveningstar knelt before Bird-Jaguar. The bowl was filled with strips of beaten-bark paper, a rope the thickness of her first finger, and a huge stingray spine. Her eyes glazed as she shifted her mind into the deep trance that would prepare her for what was to come. Closing her eyes, she extended her tongue as far out of her mouth as she could. Bird-Jaguar took the stingray spine and, with a practiced twist of the wrist, drove it down through the center of his mother's tongue. She did not flinch, nor did a sound pass her lips as he took the rope and threaded it through the wound.[46] She stood near the edge of the platform so that all the assembled witnesses could see her pull the rope through her tongue. Her blood saturated the paper in the bowl at her chest and dribbled redly down her chin in brilliant contrast to the deep green jade of her shoulder cape.

Bird-Jaguar removed some of the saturated paper from the plate and dropped it into the knee-high censer that stood on the floor beside his mother's left leg. After placing fresh paper in her bowl, he removed her head covering and replaced it with the skull-mounted headdress that signaled Venus war and gave honor to the brother of the Sun.[47]

Lady Eveningstar pulled the last of the rope through her tongue, dropped it into the bowl, and stood swaying as the trance state took possession of her consciousness. In that moment Bird-Jaguar saw what he had been seeking in her eyes—the great Serpent Path to the Otherworld was opening within his mother. He set the ancestral skull into her hand and stood back. That was the signal. The deep moaning voice of a conch trumpet echoed throughout the city, announcing the arrival of the Vision Serpent. Black smoke billowed and roiled upward from the god-faced censer behind Lady Eveningstar and formed a great writhing column in which Bird-Jaguar and his people saw the Double-headed Serpent and the god of Venus war she had materialized with the shedding of her blood. A song of welcome and awe rose from the crowd below as they drew blood from their own bodies and offered it to the god now born into their presence.

The crowd writhed and swayed as a tide of ecstasy coursed throughout the city. Trumpeters and drummers, caught in the tumult of their music, accelerated their rhythms to a frenzied tempo. Dancing lords whirled across the terrace below the king and his family, their glowing green feathers and hip panels suspended at right angles to their whirling bodies. People throughout the crowd drew their own blood and splattered it onto cloth bands tied to their wrists and arms. The plaza was soon brightly speckled with devotion. Smoke columns rose from censers which stood upright throughout the plaza as the ahauob and the cahalob called their own ancestors forth through the portal opened by the Lady Eveningstar.

Feeling the awesome strength of his mother's vision, Bird-Jaguar knew he had chosen the penultimate moment to publicly affirm the alliance he had forged by his marriage to Lady Great-Skull-Zero. The numbers of fierce and powerful cahalob who had allied themselves with his cause would give his rivals pause and strengthen his own claim as the rightful successor of the great Shield-Jaguar.

Motioning through the haze of smoke that drifted along the terrace from his mother's sacrifice, he signaled Lady Great-Skull-Zero and her brother to bring their own vision through the portal. His wife wore a brilliantly patterned huipil, a heavy jade-colored cape, and a bar pectoral. On her head sat the image of the Sun God at dawn to complement the symbols of Venus worn by his mother. Great-Skull-Zero, the patriarch of his wife's lineage, was richly dressed in a skull headdress, a cape, a bar pectoral, knee bands made of jade, a richly bordered hipcloth, a heavy belt, an ornate loincloth, and anklet cuffs. Both were barefoot and grasped the deified lancets of the bloodletting ritual in their hands.

Holding in readiness a shallow plate filled with paper strips, Lady Great-Skull-Zero gestured toward her brother. Like her mother-in-law, she extended her tongue far out of her mouth and permitted Great-Skull-Zero to make the cut of sacrifice. Grasping the obsidian, he pierced her tongue in one deft motion, then handed the bloody blade to Bird-Jaguar. Gazing into the eyes of his new kinsman and future king, Great-Skull-Zero remained motionless while Bird-Jaguar slashed down into his extended tongue. Bleeding heavily and deep in the vision trance, Lady Great-Skull-Zero and Great-Skull-Zero danced together, bringing forth the Serpent known as *Chanal-Chac-Bay-Chan.* [48] As the great Serpent writhed through their arms, they saw the ancestor Na-Yaxhal materialize between them. A roar rose from the plaza, coming most loudly from the throats of those lords allied with Bird-Jaguar and his wife's clan.

Finally it was time for the king's son to sanctify the day with the gift of his own blood. Bird-Jaguar was more simply dressed than Great-Skull-

Zero. His hair, worn long to tantalize his enemies in battle, was tied above his head with a panache of feathers which hung down his back. Around his neck he wore a single strand of beads, and a bar pectoral suspended on a leather strap lay against his brown chest. His wrists, ankles, and knees were bejeweled with deep blue-green strands of jade and in the septum of his nose he wore a feather-tipped ornament. His loincloth was simply decorated and brilliantly white so that his people could see the blood of sacrifice he would draw from the most sacred part of his body.

His wife, still weak from her own sacrifice, came to his side to help him with his rite,[49] but his main assistant would be an ahau who was skilled in communication with the gods. The white cape shrouding this ahau's shoulders contrasted vividly with Bird-Jaguar's sun-darkened skin. Lady Eveningstar grasped a shallow basket filled with fresh, unmarked paper in one hand, and held the stingray spine her son would use in the other. Still dazed, Great-Skull-Zero stepped in front of Bird-Jaguar, took the basket from his kinswoman's hand and placed it on the plaza floor between Bird-Jaguar's feet. Face impassive, Bird-Jaguar squatted on his heels, spreading his muscular thighs above the basket. He pulled his loincloth aside, took the huge stingray spine, and pushed it through the loose skin along the top of his penis. He pierced himself three times before reaching down into the bowl for the thin bark paper strips it contained. Threading a paper strip through each of his wounds, he slowly pulled it through until the three strips hung from his member. His blood gradually soaked into the light tan paper, turning it to deepest red. From the saturated paper, his blood dripped into the bowl between his legs. When he was done, his wife reached down for the bowl and placed the blood-stained paper of his sacrifice in the nearby censer along with offerings of maize kernels, rubber, and the tree resin called *pom*.

The rising columns of smoke revived the attention of the milling, tired crowd below. Many of the people who had drifted away to the adjacent courts and riverbank to examine the goods brought in by traders and visitors from other cities and kingdoms hurried back to the main plaza. They wanted to witness Bird-Jaguar's materialization of the god. Times were dangerous along the Xocol Ha, and they hoped for a young, vigorous ruler, skilled in battle and wily in statecraft, to lead the kingdom through the growing peril of the times.

High above the crowd, Bird-Jaguar's legs gave way beneath him as the trance state overpowered him. Sitting back onto his right hip, he stretched his legs out through the billowing smoke. In his arms, he held the Double-headed Serpent that manifested the path of communication special to kings. God K—the god called Kauil who was the last born of the three great gods of the cosmos—emerged from the mouths of the serpents. The great conch-shell trumpets sounded for the third time, warning that a god had been materialized from the Otherworld, this time by the king's son, Bird-Jaguar.

It was midmorning when the royal family's bloodletting obligations were fulfilled. Walking with a painfully careful gait, Bird-Jaguar led his mother, his wife, and Great-Skull-Zero to the bench in the *Chan-Ah-Tz'i*

**Bird-Jaguar and
the Ballgame**
the central scene from
Temple 33 stairs

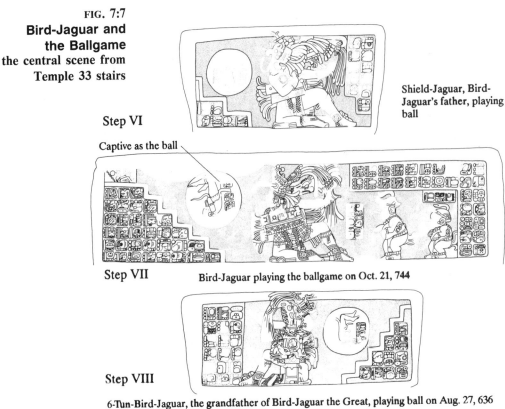

Step VI

Shield-Jaguar, Bird-
Jaguar's father, playing
ball

Captive as the ball

Step VII   Bird-Jaguar playing the ballgame on Oct. 21, 744

Step VIII

6-Tun-Bird-Jaguar, the grandfather of Bird-Jaguar the Great, playing ball on Aug. 27, 636

drawings by Ian Graham

where Shield-Jaguar had been sitting throughout the ritual. The white-caped attendants moved aside as Bird-Jaguar sat down on the right-hand side of his father.[50] His own wife, Lady Great-Skull-Zero, sat to his right. Lady Eveningstar moved to take the position on Shield-Jaguar's left, but before she could mount the bench, Lady Xoc entered and usurped that position for herself. In silent menace, the old woman forced the younger woman to take the outside position, jarring everyone present into realizing that neither she nor her kinsmen would ever yield their power without a fight. In a state of uneasy truce, the royal family watched the remainder of the rituals unfold as the ecstasy of the morning's activities ebbed into the exhaustion of afternoon.

Bird-Jaguar understood all that his father had done for him. First there had been the flapstaff ritual of four days ago and now this great blood ritual so close to the period ending celebration. His father's public acknowledgment of his favor could not be denied nor would it be forgotten. In the years ahead, this ceremonial recognition would be the most important single component of his claim to the throne. His fight would be a hard one, but now he knew that not only his father but all the ancestors of the royal clan had selected him as the inheritor of the glory of Yaxchilán. After this moment together in eternity, it was simply a matter of time and patience.

Shield-Jaguar was in his mid-nineties and not far from death when this multiple bloodletting took place. We surmise that his advanced age precluded his direct participation in this critically important rite; but, as we have seen, just about everyone else who was important to Bird-Jaguar's claim participated: his wife and her brother, who was the patriarch of her lineage, Bird-Jaguar himself, and his mother. The four-day-long sequence that began with the flapstaff event and ended in this multiple bloodletting was well-timed. Less than a year later, on June 19, 742, the old man died, and at age thirty-two Bird-Jaguar began his campaign to follow his father into office.

Bird-Jaguar's first action of public importance after his father's death was a ballgame (Fig. 7:7) he played on October 21, 744. On the front step of Structure 33, his great accession monument, his artists depicted a captive, bound into a ball, bouncing down hieroglyphic stairs toward a kneeling player.[51] The text carved on this step associated this ballgame with events in the distant mythological past, placing Bird-Jaguar's actions firmly within the sacred context of the game as it related to the larger cosmos.[52] Bird-Jaguar framed this event with the scenes he felt would most powerfully serve his political ends. Successive panels flank the central scene on the upper step[53] of the stairway leading to the temple platform. To the immediate left of his own ballgame scene, Bird-Jaguar portrayed his own father kneeling to receive a ball bouncing down a hieroglyphic stairway. On his right, his grandfather, 6-Tun-Bird-Jaguar, also kneels to receive a ball. Other panels show important cahalob engaged in the game, as well as Bird-Jaguar's wives holding Vision Serpents in rites that apparently preceded active play.

Two years later, on June 4, 746 (9.15.15.0.0), Bird-Jaguar celebrated his first big period ending. He recorded this rite in an unusual way, embedding it into the Stela 11 scene depicting him and his father engaged in the flapstaff ritual (Fig. 7:8). The text for the period ending tells us that on that day, Shield-Jaguar erected a tree-stone and that he held a staff in his hand.[54] This claim is a bit strange, since Shield-Jaguar had been in his grave for over four years (he died on June 19, 742). In reality, we know that Shield-Jaguar could not have erected a tree-stone, held a staff, nor done anything else on that date. What the reader is meant to understand is that Bird-Jaguar *acted in his place.*

Even more curious, the final phrase in this text states that these actions took place *u cab,* "in the land of" Bird-Jaguar. How had the kingdom become "the land of" Bird-Jaguar when he hadn't yet acceded to office and would not qualify for that event for another six years? The embedding of this period-ending notation into the scene of the father-son flapstaff ritual had a special intention. By this juxtaposition Bird-Jaguar implied that he and his father (even after death) acted together on both occasions, and that the kingdom had become Bird-Jaguar's by this time, if only in de facto status.[55]

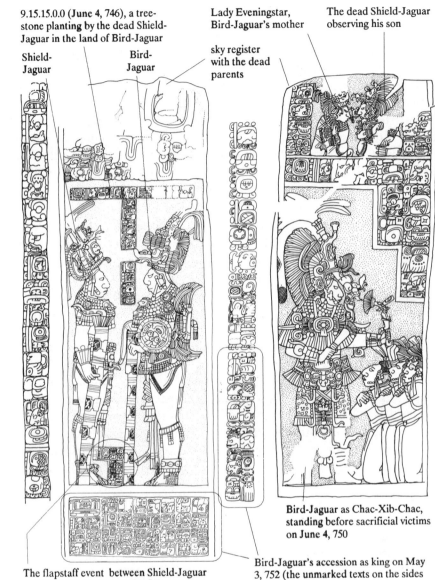

9.15.15.0.0 (June 4, 746), a tree-stone planting by the dead Shield-Jaguar in the land of Bird-Jaguar

Shield-Jaguar

Bird-Jaguar

Lady Eveningstar, Bird-Jaguar's mother

sky register with the dead parents

The dead Shield-Jaguar observing his son

FIG. 7:8
The Retrospective History on Stela 11

The flapstaff event between Shield-Jaguar and Bird-Jaguar on June 26, 741

Bird-Jaguar as Chac-Xib-Chac, standing before sacrificial victims on June 4, 750

Bird-Jaguar's accession as king on May 3, 752 (the unmarked texts on the sides record the date of accession)

The next time we see Bird-Jaguar on a monument, he is once again displaying the flapstaff (Fig. 7:5d). The date is now June 25, 747, eleven years after Shield-Jaguar's first performance of this ritual, and some six years after the father-son event. By repeating this flapstaff rite yet again, Bird-Jaguar was commemorating his growing command of Yaxchilán's ritual life.

Two years later on April 3, 749, Lady Xoc, Shield-Jaguar's principal wife, died and went to join her husband in Xibalba. She had survived him by seven years. A little over a year later—exactly four years after the 9.15.15.0.0 period ending discussed above—Bird-Jaguar conducted a ritual in which he acted as warrior and giver of sacrifices. On June 4, 750, wearing the mask of the god Chac-Xib-Chac, he presented three unnamed victims for sacrifice. He carved this scene on the temple side of Stela 11 (Fig. 7:8), opposite the depiction of the father-son flapstaff event and the unusual period ending text discussed above.[56] These three events—the flapstaff, the period ending, and the GI sacrifice—were of such central importance to his campaign for the throne that Bird-Jaguar surrounded them with texts recording his accession. One text recording that event as *hok'ah ti ahauel,* "he came out as king," was carved on the narrow sides of the tree-stone. A second text recording the event as *chumwan ti ahauel,* "he sat in reign," was carved under the scene of the flapstaff event. As a finishing touch to the program of Stela 11, Bird-Jaguar placed miniature figures of his dead mother and father in the register above the sacrificial scene. They view his performance with approval from the world of the ancestors.

Bird-Jaguar's campaign of legitimization was now close to completion, but some barriers still remained. He had yet to prove his prowess as a warrior by taking a captive of sufficient prestige to sacrifice in the accession ceremonies, and to demonstrate his potency by fathering a male child and heir. These last events were never witnessed by his mother, for she died in the following year. On March 13, 751, Lady Eveningstar went to join her rival, Lady Xoc, in the Otherworld.

With the principal female players in this historical drama dead, Bird-Jaguar embarked on the last phase of his crusade. On February 10, 752, 357 days after the end of the sixteenth katun, Bird-Jaguar went to war and took a captive named Yax-Cib-Tok, a cahal of an as-yet-unidentified king.[57] Eight days later, on February 18, Lady Great-Skull-Zero bore him a son, Chel-Te-Chan-Mah-Kina. This son would later take Shield-Jaguar's name when he himself became the king. With these events Bird-Jaguar's long struggle for the throne came to an end. Seventy-five days later he was crowned king of Yaxchilán.

Like the multiple bloodlettings that preceded Shield-Jaguar's death, this capture and the birth of Bird-Jaguar's heir loomed large in his program of propaganda. He inscribed the capture on a glyphic step (Fig. 7:9a) located in front of a door leading into Temple 41, the structure built by his father on the highest point of the city. This was the location where Shield-Jaguar himself had erected the depiction of his first flapstaff ritual and the stelae recording the most famous captures of his career. By inscribing the record of his own battle triumph on this building, Bird-Jaguar associated himself with his father's triumphs as a warrior.

Bird-Jaguar also mounted a pictorial representation of this capture (Lintel 16, Fig. 7:9b) inside Temple 21. Temple 21, if you remember, was the structure designed to parallel the glory of Lady Xoc's magnificent Temple 23. In the scene on this lintel, Bird-Jaguar, dressed in battle armor, stands before his seated captive who bites on his thumb in a gesture of submission or fear.

Bird-Jaguar also depicted the rituals celebrating the birth of his son in two separate locations, maximizing the political implications of the event in the public record. He placed the bloodletting ritual that cele-

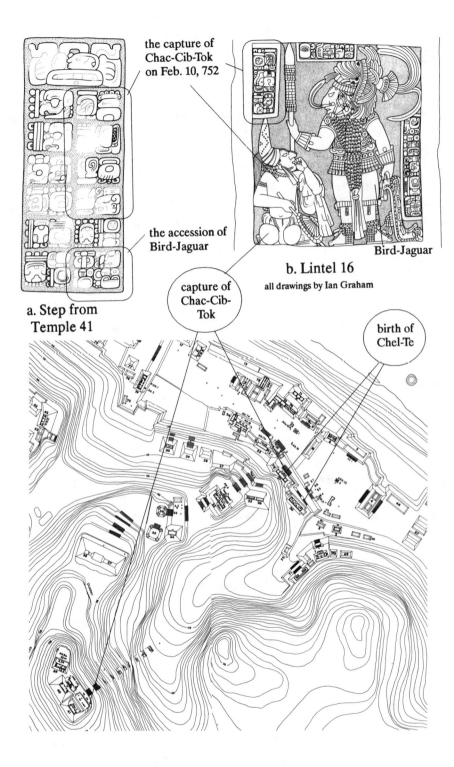

the capture of
Chac-Cib-Tok
on Feb. 10, 752

the accession of
Bird-Jaguar

a. Step from
Temple 41

capture of
Chac-Cib-
Tok

birth of
Chel-Te

Bird-Jaguar

b. Lintel 16

all drawings by Ian Graham

brated the birth over the right-hand doorway of Temple 21, next to the central capture scene described above. If we look at this scene (Fig. 7:9c), we see Bird-Jaguar preparing to draw blood from his own genitals, while one of his wives, Lady Balam, Lady Ahau of Ix Witz,[58] pulls a rope through her tongue while holding a plate filled with blood-splattered paper.

Lady Balam of Ix Witz   Bird-Jaguar

Bloodletting celebrating the birth
of Chel-Te on Feb. 18, 752

c. Lintel 17

Vision rite by Lady 6-Tun on Mar. 28, 755

d. Lintel 15

FIG. 7:9
**The Events
Leading to
Bird-Jaguar's
Accession**

This depiction corresponds to Lintel 24 in the program of Temple 23, the bloodletting celebration at the birth of Bird-Jaguar himself. Obviously, Bird-Jaguar wished the audience to draw some parallels. In the earlier bloodletting on Temple 23, Lady Xoc was shown acknowledging the birth of a son to a co-wife, Lady Eveningstar. Here Lady Balam acknowledges the birth of her husband's heir, also the child of another wife. The only logistical difference is that Lady Great-Skull-Zero is not a foreign wife, as Lady Eveningstar had been, but a woman from a prominent cahal lineage of Yaxchilán. In addition, Temple 21 houses the stela (Fig. 7:6b) that depicts Bird-Jaguar's mother in the critical 9.15.10.0.1 bloodletting, which we described in such detail in the vignette. The presence of this stela linked yet another critical bloodletting ritual to the birth of the heir.

In an adjacent temple (Temple 20), Bird-Jaguar mounted another representation of the birth rituals. In this second depiction, Lady Great-Skull-Zero, the mother of the newborn child, holds a Personified Bloodletter in one hand and a bloodletting bowl in the other (Fig. 7:10b). Against her ribs she grasps the tail of a Vision Serpent which winds its way across empty space to rest in the hand of the infant's father, Bird-Jaguar. The text recording the birth sits immediately in front of the human head emerging from the Vision Serpent's mouth. This head most likely represents either an ancestor recalled to witness the arrival of the infant heir or the infant himself, Chel-Te-Chan, being metaphorically born through the mouth of the Vision Serpent. This birth scene is mounted in the same building as Lintel 14, which shows Lady Great-Skull-Zero holding the Vision Serpent with Great-Skull-Zero in the great 9.15.10.0.1 bloodletting rite (Fig. 7:6a and 7:10c). Thus, in both Temples 20 and 21, Bird-Jaguar connected the birth of his heir and the taking of his captive to the multiple bloodletting event that was so fundamental to his political claim.

With these last two acts—the taking of a captive and the production of an heir, Bird-Jaguar became the king. It is curious that after all his long

drawings by Ian Graham

Bird-Jaguar with captives, but the date and captive names are eroded

a. Lintel 12

Bird-Jaguar

The bloodletting rite by Bird-Jaguar and Lady Great-Skull for the birth of Chel-Te on Feb. 18, 752

b. Lintel 13

Lady Great-Skull

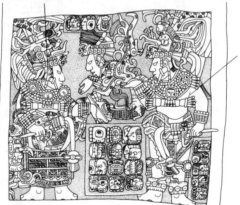

Great-Skull, the head of Lady Great-Skull's lineage

FIG. 7:10
**The Events in
Temple 20**

The 9.15.10.0.1 bloodletting at the end of Shield-Jaguar's life

c. Lintel 14

struggles for the throne, he was never particularly interested in picturing this hard-won accession rite. He did, however, inscribe *textual* records of this event on Stela 11, the steps of Stela 41, and on the lintels of Structure 10, which he built directly across the plaza from Lady Xoc's building.

The only actual surviving picture of his accession appears in Temple 33, one of the largest and most important constructions he commissioned during the first half of his reign. Built on a slope above and behind the

a. Lintel 1

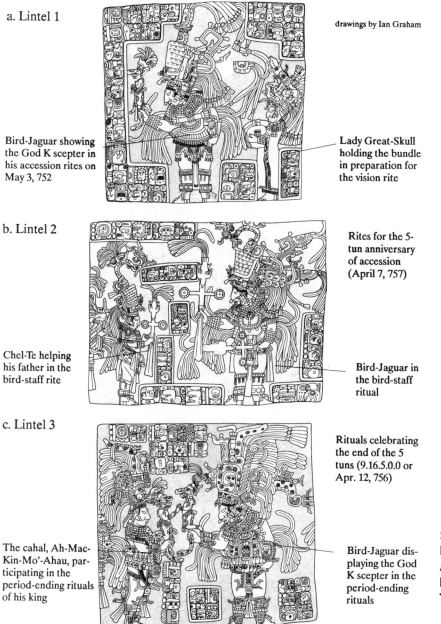

drawings by Ian Graham

Bird-Jaguar showing
the God K scepter in
his accession rites on
May 3, 752

Lady Great-Skull
holding the bundle
in preparation for
the vision rite

b. Lintel 2

Rites for the 5-
tun anniversary
of accession
(April 7, 757)

Chel-Te helping
his father in the
bird-staff rite

Bird-Jaguar in
the bird-staff
ritual

c. Lintel 3

Rituals celebrating
the end of the 5
tuns (9.16.5.0.0 or
Apr. 12, 756)

The cahal, Ah-Mac-
Kin-Mo'-Ahau, par-
ticipating in the
period-ending rituals
of his king

Bird-Jaguar dis-
playing the God
K scepter in the
period-ending
rituals

**FIG. 7:11
Historical
Actions
Recorded in
Temple 33**

string of buildings documenting his right of accession (Temples 13, 20, 21, 22, and 23), this building has a lintel over each of its three doors and a wide step portraying the ballgame events discussed earlier (Fig. 7:7) on its basal platform. The accession portrait is over the left door (Lintel 1, Fig. 7:11a). There, Bird-Jaguar depicted himself holding the manifestation of GII[59] outward toward an audience we cannot see. Behind him stands the mother of his new son, Lady Great-Skull-Zero, holding a bundle to her chest.[60] The verb in the text over her head records that she will soon let blood,[61] just as Lady Xoc did for Shield-Jaguar on the day of his accession

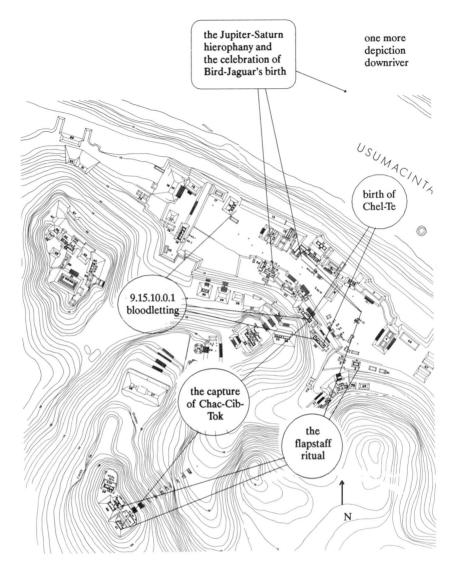

the Jupiter-Saturn
hierophany and
the celebration of
Bird-Jaguar's birth

one more
depiction
downriver

USUMACINTA

birth of
Chel-Te

9.15.10.0.1
bloodletting

the capture
of Chac-Cib-
Tok

the
flapstaff
ritual

N

FIG. 7:12
**The Events
Legitimizing
Bird-Jaguar's
Reign**

(Lintel 25, Fig. 7:3b). Presumably, as the bloodletter for the king, she, like her predecessor Lady Xoc, would be responsible for materializing the founder of the dynasty. Her name is also written in a form that identifies her as the mother of the heir—the child who would become the second Shield-Jaguar.

Bird-Jaguar's accession rites culminated nine days later with the dedication of a new building, Temple 22, located on the river terrace immediately adjacent to Temple 23, Lady Xoc's memorial (Fig. 7:12). Into this new building, he reset four very early lintels. These lintels were presumably removed from the important ancestral building now encased within the new construction. As mentioned earlier, the inclusion of lintels and inscriptions from the buildings of his ancestors was a very important part of Bird-Jaguar's political strategy.

On the brand-new lintel he placed over the central doorway of Temple 22, he commemorated the dedication of the earlier temple, which had been named *Chan-Ah-Tz'i* by King Moon-Skull, the seventh successor in the dynasty. This ancient dedication had taken place on October 16, 454. The inclusion of the earlier texts was meant to link Bird-Jaguar's dedication of the new *Chan-Ah-Tz'i* temple to the actions of the ancestral king. The official dedication of Temple 22 took place on May 12, 752, nine days after Bird-Jaguar had become the new king.

Obviously, Bird-Jaguar had to have begun construction of Temple 22 at a much earlier date for its dedication rituals to have played a part in his actual accession rites. This is but one more example of the extent of the power he wielded before he officially wore the crown. His choice of this building as his first construction project, and the one most closely associated with his accession rites, was deliberate. Not only was Temple 22 a new and impressive version of his illustrious ancestor's *Chan-Ah-Tz'i,* it stood right next door to Lady Xoc's pivotal building. Through this construction project, Bird-Jaguar asserted both his mastery of Lady Xoc's imagery and his connection to a famous and successful ancestor. The purpose of this building (and Temple 12, in which he reset another group of early lintels), was to encase and preserve earlier important monuments and to declare his status as the legitimate descendant of those earlier kings.

This construction project was just the opening shot in a grand strategy that would completely change the face of Yaxchilán over the next ten years (Fig. 7:12). Bird-Jaguar dedicated the new *Chan-Ah-Tz'i* just nine days after his accession. To the left of the adjacent Temple 23 and attached to it, he built Temple 24 (dedicated on September 2, 755). Its lintels recorded the deaths of his immediate ancestors: his grandmother's on September 12, 705; Shield-Jaguar's on June 19, 742; Lady Xoc's on April 3, 749; and his own mother's on March 13, 751.

While still working on the huge terrace that supported the group of buildings surrounding Temple 23, Bird-Jaguar began construction on yet another temple, Temple 21. This structure also replicated the magnificent lintels of Lady Xoc's building. Bird-Jaguar designed the program on this temple around the following scenes: his capture of Yax-Cib-Tok; his own bloodletting in celebration of his son's birth; and a bloodletting rite that took place on March 28, 755, probably as part of the dedication rites for the temple itself (Fig. 7:9d). The giver of blood in the final event was Lady 6-Tun, a woman from Motul de San José, another of Bird-Jaguar's wives. These images, of course, deliberately echoed the lintels of Temple 23. Bird-Jaguar intensified the association of this new building with Lady Xoc's monument by planting inside it the stela recording his mother's pivotal bloodletting rite on 9.15.10.0.1. Carved in a style emulating the Lintel 25 masterpiece from Lady Xoc's temple, this stela depicts Lady Eveningstar (Fig. 7:6b) wearing the same costume as her rival while materializing the same double-Tlaloc-headed Vision Serpent. This, and other imagery, shows us how obsessed Bird-Jaguar was with equating his mother with Lady Xoc.

Temple 13 with the flapstaff events and
Lady Eveningstar's bundle rite

Lady Xoc's temple with her celebration
of Bird-Jaguar's birth

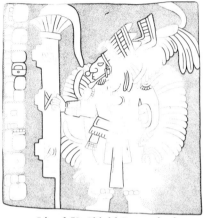

a. Lintel 50: Shield-Jaguar in the
first flapstaff ritual on June 27,
736 ???

FIG. 7:13
The
Historical
Events in
Temple 13

b. Lintel 32: Lady Eveningstar (Bird-
Jaguar's mother) in the bundle ritual with
Shield-Jaguar on Oct. 29, 709 (one day after
Lady Xoc's bloodletting on Lintel 24)

c. Lintel 33: Bird-Jaguar's flapstaff ritual
on June 25, 747

drawings by Ian Graham

A
FOREST
OF
KINGS
—
292

Next to this building, he constructed Temple 20, which had three
lintels showing many of the same events. One depicts his wife, Lady
Great-Skull-Zero, and her patriarch participating in the great 9.15.10.0.1
bloodletting. A second shows his wife letting blood along with Bird-Jaguar
in celebration of the birth of their son. The third lintel depicts the ritual
display of four captives by Bird-Jaguar and an unnamed noble. This lintel
has been tentatively dated to November 13, 757.[62]

Across the plaza from Temple 23, Bird-Jaguar constructed three more buildings: Temples 10, 12, and 13. In Temple 12, he reset another series of Early Classic lintels. These recorded the first through the tenth successors of the dynasty, and the accession of the tenth king, Ta-Skull, on February 13, 526. This building, along with Temple 22, honored the members of the long dynasty of Yaxchilán from which Bird-Jaguar descended, and preserved important public records which would have otherwise been lost when he covered over earlier structures during the course of his building program.

To the west of Structure 12, Bird-Jaguar commissioned a great L-shaped platform surmounted by two buildings housing two sets of lintels. The first set, Lintels 29, 30, and 31, are all glyphic and record his birth, accession, and the dedication of the building itself (Temple 10) on March 1, 764. The other building (Structure 13) housed pictorial lintels of extraordinary interest (Fig. 7:13). The first, Lintel 50, shows Shield-Jaguar's original flapstaff ritual, the event that began Bird-Jaguar's race for the throne.[63] Balancing Shield-Jaguar's flapstaff rite is Lintel 33. This lintel, found over the right-hand door of the temple (Fig. 7:13c), shows Bird-Jaguar conducting his own flapstaff event eleven years later on June 25, the summer solstice of the year 747.

Lintel 32 (Fig. 7:13b), found over the middle door, shows Bird-Jaguar's mother, Lady Eveningstar, in a bundle rite. According to his inscription, this rite took place the day after his father persuaded Lady Xoc to let her blood in acknowledgment of Bird-Jaguar's birth. The masterly representation of Lady Xoc's extraordinarily painful suffering is just across the plaza, so we may assume that Bird-Jaguar used Lintel 32 to show that his own mother was also directly involved in the rituals surrounding his birth. In fact, she holds a bundle that very probably contained the bowl, rope, and lancet used in the bloodletting rite. By this means, he asserted that her role on that occasion was every bit as important as Lady Xoc's. As a finishing touch, he framed his mother's participation in the bundle ritual with the flapstaff events he considered to be a key part of his legitimization. The program of this building thus links those crucial events together into a single web of causality. It is retrospective history at its best. Bird-Jaguar masterfully orchestrated events, with their many shades of meaning and connections, to fit the conclusions he wished his people to accept as fact.

With the completion of this last building, Bird-Jaguar had accomplished his campaign of political legitimization. His major problem now was to maintain the loyalty of his nobility and secure their support for his own son. His own problems with the succession appear to have marked him deeply; so much so that the efforts of his remaining years were spent in a concentrated effort to insure that his own heir did not suffer the same fate.

Bird-Jaguar began this new campaign with a set of buildings constructed on the slopes above the river shelf. Pivotal to the program was the huge Temple 33, which he flanked with Temple 1 to the west, and Temple 42 to the east (Fig. 7:14). The ten lintels on these three buildings

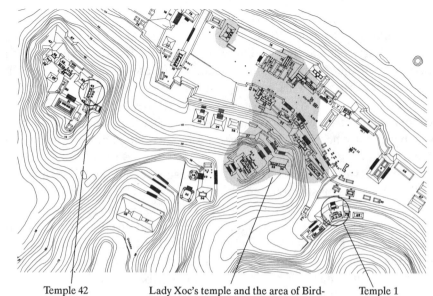

Temple 42   Lady Xoc's temple and the area of Bird-   Temple 1
Jaguar's program to prove his legitimacy

record a sequence of events beginning with Bird-Jaguar's accession and culminating with its fifth anniversary. He repeated the same narrative strategy he had used in the building sequence which centered around Temple 23: the repetition of key scenes in more than one location. In this way he was able to feature several different people, thereby allowing many of his nobles and allies the prestige of appearing with the king in the permanent public record of history (Fig. 7:14).

Forty days after his accession, Bird-Jaguar staged the first of these ceremonial events, a bundle ritual, on June 12, 752, ten days before the summer solstice (Fig. 7:15a). One pictorial representation of this event shows us Bird-Jaguar (on Lintel 5 of Temple 1) holding a tree-scepter in each hand, while Lady 6-Sky-Ahau, another foreign wife, this time from Motul de San José,[64] holds a bundle. In the second depiction of this ritual (Lintel 42 of Temple 42), Bird-Jaguar appears not with his wife but with Kan-Toc, one of his most important cahalob.[65] The king holds out a GII Manikin Scepter, an important symbol of the kingship, toward this cahal, who is shown gripping a battle ax and shield.

We do not know the occasion for this ritual event, but Bird-Jaguar found it politically advantageous to represent it on these two lintels—one displaying a foreign wife who probably brought a powerful alliance with her, and the other featuring one of his most important nobles. In the Maya tradition, subordinate nobles were rarely depicted on the same monuments as the high king. Here Bird-Jaguar is obviously flattering his cahal, perhaps cementing his allegiance by publicly acknowledging his importance. The same reasoning would apply to the monument depicting his foreign wife. She must have brought her own set of alliances with her when she came to marry the king of Yaxchilán.

Later in the same year, on October 16, 752, Bird-Jaguar staged another series of rituals, once again depicting each of them in double imagery. During the first ceremony, he displayed a strange-looking staff mounting a basket with a GII miniature sitting atop it (Fig. 7:15b). In one version of this ritual (Lintel 6, Temple 1), Kan-Toc, the same cahal we saw above, stands before the king. He is holding bloodletting paper in one hand and a jaguar-paw club in the other. In the contrasting depiction (Lintel 43 of Temple 42), another wife, Lady Balam of Ix Witz, stands with Bird-Jaguar. She holds a bloodletting bowl with a bloodstained rope hanging over one side. She is the same wife we saw letting blood on Lintel 17 to celebrate the birth of Bird-Jaguar's heir. Here Bird-Jaguar watches her let blood again in an event occurring either just before or just after his scene with the cahal. Note that the paper held by Kan-Toc in the alternate depiction now rests in Bird-Jaguar's hand. The fact that the paper is depicted in both scenes lets us know we are seeing different moments in the same ritual.

This particular ritual apparently lasted for several days, for two days later Bird-Jaguar reappears on Lintel 7 (Fig. 7:15c), this time holding the GII Manikin Scepter. Another of his wives appears with him, hugging a large bundle to her chest. While we cannot positively identify the woman depicted here (her name is badly eroded), we are reasonably certain she is another foreign wife, this time a second wife from Motul de San José.[66]

The final episode in this series of lintels records the most famous and important capture of Bird-Jaguar's lifetime—the taking of Jeweled-Skull (Fig. 7:15d). Once again, he commissioned two versions of the event. As before, one shows him acting with a cahal and the other with a wife. On Lintel 41, Lady 6-Sky-Ahau of Motul de San José stands before the king, who is dressed in full battle regalia including cotton armor and lance. She has been helping him dress for war in the same type of ritual we saw Lady Xoc perform for Shield-Jaguar thirty-one years earlier. In this scene, however, the action is a little farther along than that shown on the earlier Lintel 26 (Fig. 7:3c). Here Bird-Jaguar is already fully dressed in the Tlaloc war costume and ready to enter the battle.

The capture itself appears on Lintel 8 of Temple 1. Bird-Jaguar, dressed in the battle gear his wife had helped him don, holds the unfortunate Jeweled-Skull by the wrist. Kan-Toc, the cahal he had shown twice before, yanks on the bound hair of his own captive. The manner of Bird-Jaguar's presentation is highly important. Not only does he share his moment of victory with a subordinate, he represents the two captures[67] as equally important.[68] If it were not for the more elaborate detail of Bird-Jaguar's costume and the larger size of the text describing his actions, a casual onlooker might be hard-pressed to identify who was the king and who the lord. Both protagonists are about the same size and occupy the same compositional space.

Why would Bird-Jaguar share the stage of history with his wives and cahalob? In the age-old political traditions of the Maya, the high king's performance of public ritual affirmed the legitimacy of his power and gained public support for his decisions. Few rulers before Bird-Jaguar had

Bird-Jaguar   Lady 6-Sky-Ahau   the cahal, Kan-Toc   Bird-Jaguar

Lintel 5   a. events on June 12, 752   Lintel 42

Bird-Jaguar displays a bird-scepter while his wife holds a bundle forty days after he acceded as king

On the same day, Bird-Jaguar holds a God K scepter before his cahal, Kan-Toc, who is armed for battle

the cahal, Kan-Toc   Lady Balam   Bird-Jaguar

Bird-Jaguar

FIG. 7:15
The
Complementary
Representations
of Events
in Temples 1
(left) and 42 (right)

Lintel 6   b. events on Oct. 16, 752   Lintel 43

Bird-Jaguar displays the basket-staff with his cahal, Kan-Toc

Bird-Jaguar displays the basket-staff with his wife, Lady Balam of Ix Witz

felt compelled to document these mutual performances in monumental narrative art. By allowing his subordinates onto the stage of public history, Bird-Jaguar was actually sharing with them some of his prerogatives as king.

Shield-Jaguar had used this same strategy to deal with his wife Lady Xoc and the lineage she represented. Bird-Jaguar was merely extending this strategy further to include the cahal lineages whose alliances he needed to secure his own position and to insure that his son inherited the throne without dispute. Notice, however, that Bird-Jaguar produced his heir with a woman of this internal cahal lineage, opting for a different

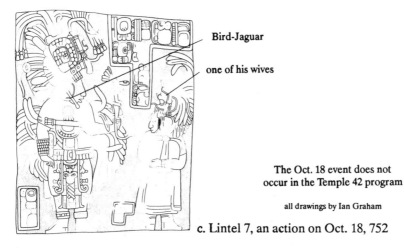

Bird-Jaguar

one of his wives

The Oct. 18 event does not
occur in the Temple 42 program

all drawings by Ian Graham

c. Lintel 7, an action on Oct. 18, 752

Bird-Jaguar displays the God K scepter
before his wife, who holds a bundle two
days after the basket-staff event

Lady 6-Sky-Ahau

Bird-Jaguar

the cahal, Kan-Toc,
and his captive

Bird-Jaguar
and his captive

Lintel 8   d. events on May 9, 755   Lintel 41

Bird-Jaguar and Kan-Toc with their battle
captives

Lady 6-Sky-Ahau with Bird-Jaguar in a
prebattle ritual (perhaps dressing or
bloodletting)

solution than his father had with his marriage to a foreigner. We suspect
he did not want his own son, Chel-Te, to face the opposition from the
internal lineages that had very probably kept him off the throne for ten
years.

Setting his son and heir into the midst of this web of alliance became
the preoccupation of the second half of Bird-Jaguar's reign, and the strategy and emphasis of his political art reflect his new goal (Fig. 7:16). The
centrally placed Temple 33 was the first sculptural program designed to
focus on the problem. In it Bird-Jaguar employed a uniquely Yaxchilán
strategy. At Palenque, in the Group of the Cross, and in the murals at

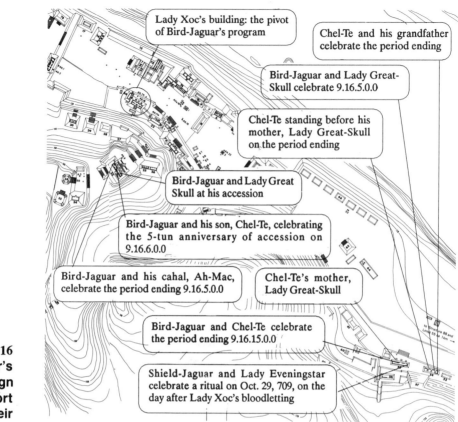

Lady Xoc's building: the pivot of Bird-Jaguar's program

Chel-Te and his grandfather celebrate the period ending

Bird-Jaguar and Lady Great-Skull celebrate 9.16.5.0.0

Chel-Te standing before his mother, Lady Great-Skull on the period ending

Bird-Jaguar and Lady Great Skull at his accession

Bird-Jaguar and his son, Chel-Te, celebrating the 5-tun anniversary of accession on 9.16.6.0.0

Bird-Jaguar and his cahal, Ah-Mac, celebrate the period ending 9.16.5.0.0

Chel-Te's mother, Lady Great-Skull

Bird-Jaguar and Chel-Te celebrate the period ending 9.16.15.0.0

Shield-Jaguar and Lady Eveningstar celebrate a ritual on Oct. 29, 709, on the day after Lady Xoc's bloodletting

FIG. 7:16
Bird-Jaguar's Campaign to Support His Heir

Bonampak, other Maya kings recorded specific rituals which were designed to publicly affirm a child's status as the chosen heir. Bird-Jaguar never recorded a similar heir-designation rite for his own son, Chel-Te. Instead, he repeatedly depicted himself and the most important of his cahalob in public performance with his heir.

This new strategy was begun with the celebration of the five-tun period ending on 9.16.5.0.0 (April 12, 756). Once again, Bird-Jaguar created multiple representations of the event. He mounted the first of these depictions over the right-hand door of Temple 33 (Fig. 7:11c). In this scene, Bird-Jaguar holds a GII Manikin Scepter out toward the smaller figure of a cahal. This noble, named Ah Mac, is someone we have not seen before. The cahal holds his own Manikin Scepter and wears the same type of clothing as the king, although his headdress is different.

The second depiction of this period-ending rite is located several hundred meters up the river in Temple 54[69] (Fig. 7:16), one of the first of a series of buildings to be erected in that new area of the city. On the central lintel (Fig. 7:17b), Bird-Jaguar is depicted with his wife, Lady Great-Skull-Zero, celebrating the period ending with a bundle rite. The bundle holds the bloodletting instruments he will use to draw his holy blood. The composition of this scene echoes both his accession portrait on Temple 33 (Fig. 7:11a) and the bundle rite celebrated by his own father and mother to commemorate his birth (on Lintel 32, Fig. 7:13b). The

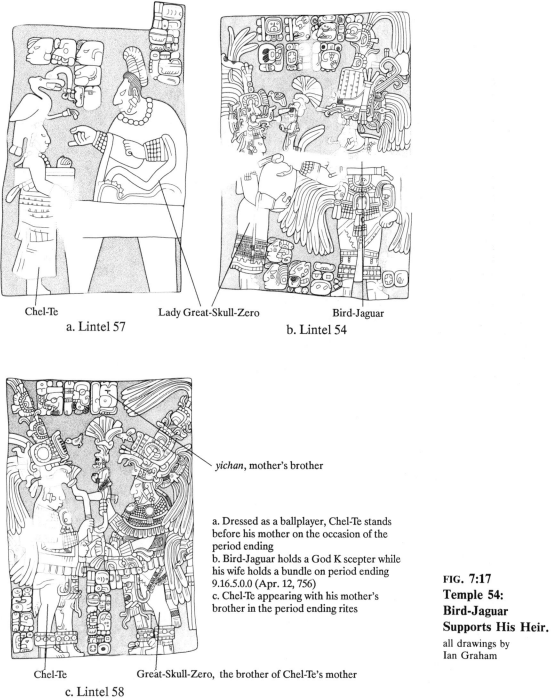

Chel-Te

a. Lintel 57

Lady Great-Skull-Zero

Bird-Jaguar

b. Lintel 54

yichan, mother's brother

a. Dressed as a ballplayer, Chel-Te stands before his mother on the occasion of the period ending

b. Bird-Jaguar holds a God K scepter while his wife holds a bundle on period ending 9.16.5.0.0 (Apr. 12, 756)

c. Chel-Te appearing with his mother's brother in the period ending rites

Chel-Te   Great-Skull-Zero, the brother of Chel-Te's mother

c. Lintel 58

FIG. 7:17
Temple 54:
Bird-Jaguar
Supports His Heir.
all drawings by
Ian Graham

replication of these earlier ritual actions was designed to deliberately link all these actions together in one great string of causality. Just as Shield-Jaguar and Lady Eveningstar had performed the bundle ritual before them, so would Bird-Jaguar and Lady Great-Skull-Zero reenact it for both his accession and this period ending. The parallel Bird-Jaguar wished to

a. Lintel 51: Lady Great-Skull (??) sitting on a zoomorphic altar while she holds a Vision Serpent

b. Bird-Jaguar performs period-ending rites with Chel-Te on 9.16.15.0.0 (Feb. 19, 766)

c. Shield-Jaguar holds a God K scepter before Lady Eveningstar, who holds a bundle, on Oct. 29, 709 (one day after Lady Xoc's bloodletting on Lintel 24)

drawings by Ian Graham

a. Lintel 51

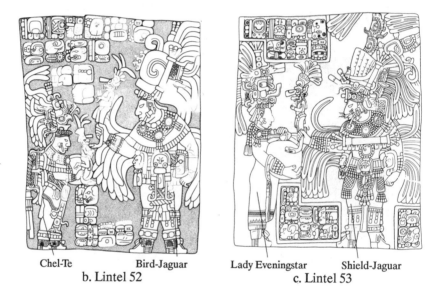

Chel-Te　　　Bird-Jaguar

b. Lintel 52

Lady Eveningstar　　Shield-Jaguar

c. Lintel 53

FIG. 7:18
The Historical Actions in Temple 55

draw is obvious: The first pair of actors were his own parents; the second were the parents of his heir, Chel-Te.

The bundle ritual conducted by Bird-Jaguar and Lady Great-Skull-Zero is linked to Chel-Te by the events depicted in the lintels over the flanking doorways. Over the right portal, Chel-Te stands before Great-Skull-Zero (Fig. 7:17c), the patriarch of his mother's lineage. Great-Skull-Zero is depicted here precisely because he is Chel-Te's mother's brother. Exactly this relationship (*yichan*[70] in Mayan) stands between his name and the heir's below.

Over the left door (Fig. 7:17a), Chel-Te stands before his mother who sits on a bench and gestures to him with her right hand. Since the flanking scenes have no date, we presume that all three lintels depict different actions that took place on the same day. First, Bird-Jaguar and his wife enacted a bundle rite; next, Chel-Te presented himself to his mother; finally, he appeared before his maternal uncle, who was the head of his mother's clan. The goal of these juxtapositions was not to glorify Bird-Jaguar, but to show his wife's lineage giving public support to his son as the heir.

One year later, Bird-Jaguar depicted himself and his son over the central door of Temple 33 (Fig. 7:11b). The date is 9.16.6.0.0 (April 7, 757), and the event, the celebration of his fifth year in office as king. Both father and son display the same bird scepters Bird-Jaguar held out to Lady 6-Sky-Ahau forty days after his accession on June 12, 752 (Lintel 5, Fig. 7:15a). Bird-Jaguar chose this location carefully. Temple 33, if you remember, is the building that housed the only picture of Bird-Jaguar's accession. It was also prominently located on the slope immediately above the temple program of legitimization. By depicting his son's participation in this important ritual at this key site, Bird-Jaguar hoped to document in public and permanent form Chel-Te's status as the heir.

Nine years later, Bird-Jaguar erected another series of lintels for his son, elaborating upon strategies he had used in earlier buildings. Going upriver again, he built a new temple next to the one that showed his son and wife celebrating the five-tun period ending. This time the event he chose to focus on was the fifteen-tun ending date, 9.16.15.0.0 (February 19, 766). Over the center door (Fig. 7:18), he depicted both himself and his son displaying GII Manikin Scepters in these period-ending rites.[71]

Bird-Jaguar took a different strategy, however, in the two flanking lintels. Over the right door, he showed a woman, presumably his wife Lady Great-Skull-Zero, holding a Vision Serpent in her arms as she materializes a vision. Over the left door (Fig. 7:18c), he repeated for the second time the scene of his mother Lady Eveningstar acting with Shield-Jaguar on the occasion of his own birth during the Jupiter-Saturn hierophany. This juxtaposition is critical. The center lintel proves that Bird-Jaguar acted with his son, and the left lintel relegitimizes his own claim to the throne by declaring once again that his mother acted with his father in the same ritual sequence his father memorialized with Lady Xoc. This is but another example of Bird-Jaguar's oft-repeated declaration that his mother was as good and as exalted as his father's principal wife. Clearly the man "doth protest too much."

Any problems Bird-Jaguar encountered, either because of his mother's status or because of rivals with better claims to the throne, would very likely be inherited by his son. Aware of the difficulties his heir might still face, Bird-Jaguar was not yet willing to rest on his laurels. He apparently used the same period-ending date, 9.16.15.0.0, to seal the allegiance of yet another cahal for his son. This fellow, Tilot, ruled the territory on the other side of the river from a subordinate town called La Pasadita. Three lintels mounted on a building at that site show Bird-Jaguar acting in public with Tilot. On the center lintel (Fig. 7:19b), Bird-Jaguar scatters blood on the period ending while Tilot stands by as his principal attendant. Flanking this critical scene is a picture of Tilot and Bird-Jaguar standing on either side of an unfortunate captive taken in battle on June

Tilot Cahal   Bird-Jaguar

a. Bird-Jaguar and the La Pasadita cahal, Tilot, stand over a captive taken in battle on June 14, 759

b. Bird-Jaguar scatters blood with Tilot on the period-ending 9.16.15.0.0 (Feb. 19, 766)

c. Tilot stands before the seated heir, Chel-Te, in acknowledgment of his allegiance

drawing by Ian Graham

a. Lintel 1

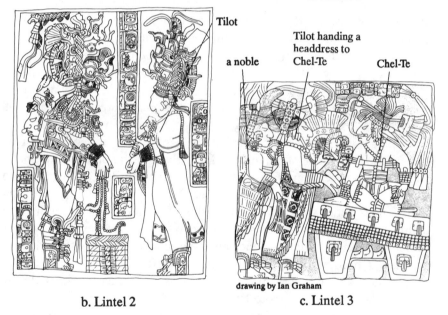

Tilot

a noble   Tilot handing a headdress to Chel-Te   Chel-Te

drawing by Ian Graham

FIG. 7:19
The La Pasadita
Cahal and
Bird-Jaguar

b. Lintel 2   c. Lintel 3

14, 759 (Fig. 7:19a). On the other side (Fig. 7:19c), Tilot stands before Chel-Te, who sits on a bench as either king or heir.

These lintels lent prestige to Tilot by depicting him in public performance with the high king. The third scene, however, was the payoff, for it shows this powerful cahal in public performance with Bird-Jaguar's son, Chel-Te. The price Bird-Jaguar paid for this allegiance was the personal elevation of Tilot into a co-performer with the king; but by sharing his prerogatives and his place in history, Bird-Jaguar reinforced the submission of this cahal to his own authority and secured Tilot's loyalty to the heir.

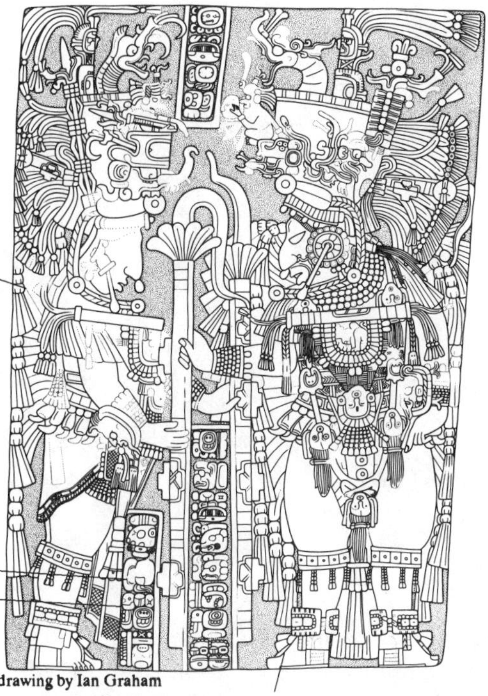

Great-Skull-Zero, the
brother of Bird-Jaguar's
wife, holds the flapstaff
with the king

yichan
ahau

drawing by Ian Graham

Bird-Jaguar in the flapstaff ritual wearing the same costume his father, Shield-Jaguar,
wore in the Stela 16 ritual. The composition recalls Shield-Jaguar and Bird-Jaguar on
Stela 11 and the first ritual by Shield-Jaguar thirty-two years earlier.

**FIG. 7:20
Bird-Jaguar
and Great-Skull
in the Last
Flapstaff Ritual**

The last monument Bird-Jaguar erected during his life continued his effort to secure the succession. It also brought his story full circle. Set on Lintel 9 (Fig. 7:20), the single lintel within Temple 2, a building situated on a terrace just below Temple 1,[72] this scene shows Great-Skull-Zero, the patriarch of the queen's lineage, conducting a flapstaff ritual with Bird-Jaguar. As we mentioned above, this was the ritual first enacted by Shield-Jaguar on June 27, 736 (Fig. 7:5a and b). It was also the ritual Bird-Jaguar enacted with his father on June 26, 741, just before Shield-Jaguar died (Fig. 7:5c). It was the ritual depicted on Lintel 33 as well (Fig. 7:5d), on June 26, 747, with Bird-Jaguar as the sole actor. This final ritual took place on June 20, 768, nearly thirty-two years after its first enactment.

The flapstaff rituals had always been critical to Bird-Jaguar's strategy to prove himself the legitimate heir to Shield-Jaguar. To show himself enacting the same event with his brother-in-law was an extraordinary elevation of that cahal's prestige. But his reason for allowing such honor to fall to Great-Skull-Zero is also patently clear from the text on Lintel 9. There Great-Skull-Zero is named *yichan ahau*, "the brother of the mother of the ahau (read 'heir')." Bird-Jaguar participated in this double display to insure that Great-Skull-Zero would support Chel-Te's assumption of the throne after Bird-Jaguar's death. The strategy apparently worked, for Chel-Te took the throne successfully and was known thereafter as the namesake of his famous grandfather, Shield-Jaguar.

Ironically, even though Bird-Jaguar had had problems demonstrating his right to the throne on his home ground, his regional prestige had been secure even before he was formally installed as king. The king of

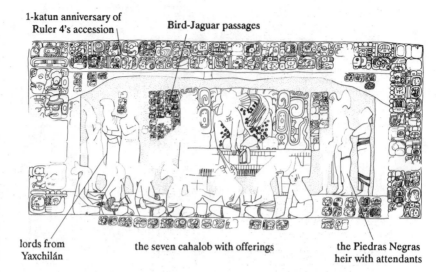

1-katun anniversary of
Ruler 4's accession

Bird-Jaguar passages

FIG. 7:21
Bird-Jaguar at
Piedras Negras for
the Heir of Ruler 4:
Piedras Negras
Lintel 3

lords from
Yaxchilán

the seven cahalob with offerings

the Piedras Negras
heir with attendants

Piedras Negras had felt his presence prestigious enough to invite him to participate in the designation of the Piedras Negras heir; and this event took place *three years* before Bird-Jaguar was even crowned. Bird-Jaguar's royal visit is recorded in an extraordinary wall panel (Fig. 7:21) commissioned retrospectively by Ruler 7 of Piedras Negras. The panel depicts a palace scene where a celebration is taking place. The occasion is the heir-designation of Ruler 5, Ruler 7's predecessor. The events recorded on the wall panel are these: On July 31, 749 (9.15.18.3.13), Ruler 4 of Piedras Negras celebrated the end of his first twenty tuns as king, in a ritual witnessed by Jaguar of Yaxchilán,[73] who had come down the river by canoe to participate in it. The date of this anniversary falls during the period when Yaxchilán was without a king. We cannot identify the Yaxchilán visitor with absolute certainty, but it was most likely Bird-Jaguar, who would have come as the de facto king of Yaxchilán.

When next Bird-Jaguar appears in a Piedras Negras text, his name and actions are clear. The cahalob portrayed in the scene on this particular wall panel are divided into four groups. The king of Piedras Negras sits on a bench and talks to the seven cahalob seated on the step below him. An ornamental pot divides them into two groups—one of three and another of four people. On the king's immediate right stands an adult and at least three smaller figures, one of which is the heir to the Piedras Negras throne.[74] At the king's far right stands a group of three lords talking among themselves. The texts around and in front of this latter group identify these people as Yaxchilán lords; and, according to the text next to the Piedras Negras king, one of them is the great Bird-Jaguar himself.

This scene took place on October 20, 757 (9.16.6.9.16), during the fifth year of Bird-Jaguar's reign. He had come down the river to conduct a bundle rite for the designation of the Piedras Negras heir. This ritual was apparently celebrated just in the nick of time, for forty-one days later, on November 30, Ruler 4 died. Ruler 5, the heir whose inheritance Bird-Jaguar publicly affirmed, took the throne on March 30, 758 (9.16.6.17.17).

Interestingly enough, Bird-Jaguar's visit to Piedras Negras was never recorded in the public forum at Yaxchilán. It would seem that the Piedras Negras heir and his descendants are the ones who gained prestige from this visit and wished to record it for their posterity. What then did Bird-Jaguar gain? Presumably, if he went to Piedras Negras at the behest of Ruler 4 to give his public support to the Piedras Negras heir, he secured reciprocal support for his own son's claim.

Bird-Jaguar's political problems and his use of monumental art to work out solutions were by no means novel either to his reign or to the political experience at Yaxchilán. Other Maya rulers, such as Pacal and Chan-Bahlum of Palenque, had their own problems with succession. Within the history of the Classic Maya, however, Bird-Jaguar's solution— sharing the public forum with powerful political allies—was new. The fact that this strategy worked so well would gradually lead to its adaptation by other kings, up and down the Usumacinta River, in the years to come.

Before Bird-Jaguar, Maya kings did not depict themselves on public monuments with cahalob, regardless of how noble or powerful these nobles might have been or how important to the king's political machinations they were. In indoor mural paintings, of course, the practice was different. Even in the very early murals of Uaxactún, the court, not just the king, was represented. On stelae and architectural lintels, however, kings normally depicted only themselves and occasionally family members—especially mothers and fathers from whom they claimed legitimate inheritance. Cahalob could and did commission monuments to celebrate important events in their lives, but they erected them in their own house compounds or in the subordinate communities they ruled for the high kings. Bird-Jaguar was the first to elevate his cahalob to stand beside him in the public eye. He did so to secure their support for his claim to the throne. That alliance must have been a fragile one, however, for he was forced to share the stage of history with them again and again in order to maintain the alliance, both for himself and his son.

Bird-Jaguar was not the first Maya king to find himself in a struggle to command the succession. Primogeniture can go wrong as often as right, especially when ambitious offspring from multiple marriages are competing for the throne. We can be sure that Bird-Jaguar was not the first son of a foreign wife to compete for a Maya throne. Others before him manipulated the system and strove to use the nobility to support their claim. Bird-Jaguar, however, was the first to exalt those cahalob by depicting them standing beside him in the public record, and we know he did not do so out of a sense of largess. Those cahalob he portrayed with him sold their loyalty for a piece of Yaxchilán's public history. The price they—and the people of the city—paid was more than sworn fealty to the king. The precedents established by Bird-Jaguar were dangerous and eventually debilitating. A king with Bird-Jaguar's personal charisma and ferocity in battle could afford to share the power of the high kingship; but the legacy of conciliar power he left to the cahal families he honored was not so well commanded by his descendants.

8

COPÁN:
THE DEATH
OF
FIRST DAWN
ON MACAW
MOUNTAIN[1]

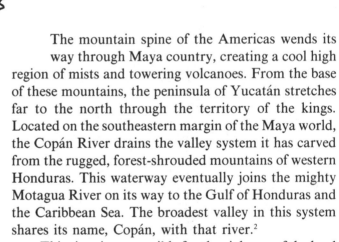

The mountain spine of the Americas wends its way through Maya country, creating a cool high region of mists and towering volcanoes. From the base of these mountains, the peninsula of Yucatán stretches far to the north through the territory of the kings. Located on the southeastern margin of the Maya world, the Copán River drains the valley system it has carved from the rugged, forest-shrouded mountains of western Honduras. This waterway eventually joins the mighty Motagua River on its way to the Gulf of Honduras and the Caribbean Sea. The broadest valley in this system shares its name, Copán, with that river.[2]

This river is responsible for the richness of the land in the Copán Valley. Each year during the rains of summer and fall, floodwaters deposit the alluvial soils from the mud-laden river waters onto the valley floor. The resulting fertile bottomlands follow the ambling path of the river through low foothills and the higher ridge lands of the rugged mountains (Fig. 8:1). On their upper reaches, these mountains are covered by pine forests, while deeper in the valley, they are covered with tropical growth—including the mighty ceiba, the sacred tree of all Mesoamericans.

From the dawn of time, the Copán Valley was an inviting place to live. Between 1100 B.C. and 900 B.C.

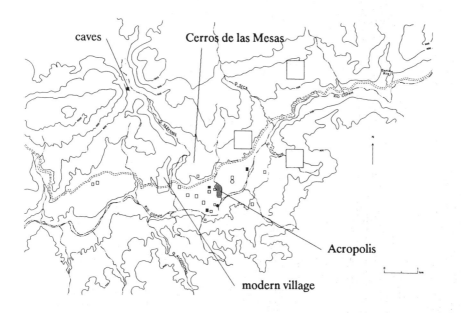

FIG. 8:1
Locations of Early Pottery in the Copán Valley

the first settlers, who were just learning to rely on agriculture to feed themselves, drifted into the valley from the Guatemalan highlands or perhaps the adjacent mountains of El Salvador. These earliest immigrants lived in temporary camps, enjoying a good life in the tall gallery forest along the water's edge. They hunted deer, turtle, rabbit, and peccary[3] among the trees and ate the maize and beans they harvested from clearings they had cut with stone axes. By 900 B.C., their farmer descendants had built permanent homes and spread out to occupy the entire valley. There, throughout the bottomlands and foothills, they left the debris of their pottery cooking vessels and the bowls, plates, and cups of their daily meals. Eventually these people established at least three villages—one in the Sepulturas Group, another in the area called the Bosque, and the last under the Great Plaza later built by Copán's kings (Fig. 8:9).

These prosperous pioneering farmers buried their loved ones under their patio floors within earshot of the children and descendants working and playing above them. In proximity to their homes and families, ancestral spirits could dwell happily in the Otherworld. When the family patriarch stood on the patio and conducted a bloodletting, he knew the ancestors were below his feet—close at hand should he want to call them forth. The departed were buried with an array of gifts and personal belongings, including quantities of highly prized jade, as well as incised and painted pottery with sacred images the Maya had borrowed from the Olmec—the creators of the first great interregional system of thought and art in Mesoamerica.[4]

These rites for the beloved dead show us that the people of the valley had already begun the process that led to the creation of social stratification, for the privileged were more able than others to take rich offerings with them into Xibalba. The differences in social standing among families in the villages, engendered by bountiful harvests or success in varying

COPÁN:
THE DEATH
OF
FIRST DAWN
ON MACAW
MOUNTAIN

—

307

commercial enterprises, would become both the foundation of kingship and its burden in the centuries to come. During the Middle Preclassic period, however, the people in the Copán Valley were blessed with an unfailing abundance of all the requirements of life. Their prosperity may well have outstripped even their contemporaries in the lowlands of the Petén, for the quantity of jade found in their tombs exceeds all other burials known from that time.[5]

By contrast, we know little of the Copanecs who lived in the valley during the Late Preclassic period (300 B.C.–A.D.150). This was the time when their Maya brethren in the lowlands, at places like Cerros, Tikal, and Uaxactún, were acknowledging their first kings. In contrast, Copán saw a major reduction of population and building activity during this 450-year span. Archaeologists have found traces of human activity from the first three centuries of this period in only two locations—one south and the other southwest of the Acropolis. And even this weak trace disappears from the record during the last 150 years of this period.

Scholars working on the history of the Copán Valley have no explanation for this curious lapse. This inexplicable disappearance of population from a thriving area becomes even more enigmatic when compared with Maya activities in both the Pacific areas to the south and the lowlands to the north. In all other parts of the Maya world, the Late Preclassic was a time of exuberant innovation and social experimentation. It was a time when the institutions of government achieved their Classic forms with the invention of kingship. To all appearances, however, the valley of Copán was seriously depopulated, and those who lived among the remnants of a more glorious past did not participate in the events sweeping the Maya society of that time. Kingship, for the Copanecs, would come to the valley only in later years when the mythology and symbolism of governance had already been developed.

By A.D. 200, however, the valley of Copán had recovered and her people had joined the mainstream of Classic Maya life. The construction of the first levels of the Acropolis stimulated a series of building projects, including floors and platforms that would serve, in future centuries, as the foundations for the Great Plaza, the Ballcourt, and the Acropolis of Copán's cultural apogee (Fig. 8:1). During this early time, farmers and craftspeople settled the rich agricultural bottomlands north of the river, building their homes as close as possible to the valley's growing center of power.

This pattern of settlement created no difficulties in the beginning when there was plenty of farmland and only a moderate number of people to support. But slowly the surrounding green sea of maize and forest gave way to a city of white and red plazas—with fine structures of stone, wood, and thatch—all jostling for position. Soon, social standing and proximity to the dynamic pulse of the city became more important to these exuberant people than their own food production. Meter by meter, over the centuries, they usurped the richest cropland, constructing their lineage compounds on acreage that used to be fields, gradually forcing the farmers up into the margins of the valley.[6] These new urban elite established particu-

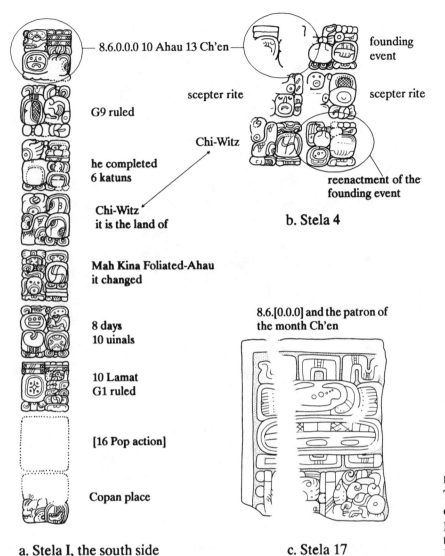

8.6.0.0.0 10 Ahau 13 Ch'en

G9 ruled

he completed
6 katuns

Chi-Witz
it is the land of

Mah Kina Foliated-Ahau
it changed

8 days
10 uinals

10 Lamat
G1 ruled

[16 Pop action]

Copan place

a. Stela I, the south side

founding
event

scepter rite

scepter rite

Chi-Witz

reenactment of the
founding event

b. Stela 4

8.6.[0.0.0] and the patron of
the month Ch'en

c. Stela 17

FIG. 8:2
The Founding
of Copán as a
Kingdom
b–c: drawing by
B.W. Fash

larly dense neighborhoods around the Acropolis, in the area now under the modern village of Copán, and on the ridge above it at a spot called El Cerro de las Mesas. Aristocrats and commoners alike vied with each other for the privilege of residing in the reflected brilliance of the Acropolis and the concentration of power it represented.

The Classic dynastic chronicles of Copán refer to this dawning era of the kingdom in ways that closely match the archaeological evidence. Later Copán kings remembered the date A.D. 160 as the year their kingdom was established as a political entity. At least three kings recorded 8.6.0.0.0 (December 18, A.D. 159) as a critical early date of the city, and Stela 1 (Fig. 8:2) records the date July 13, A.D. 160, in connection with the glyph that signifies Copán both as a physical location and a political entity. Unfortunately, the area of the text that once recorded the precise

COPÁN:
THE DEATH
OF
FIRST DAWN
ON MACAW
MOUNTAIN
—

309

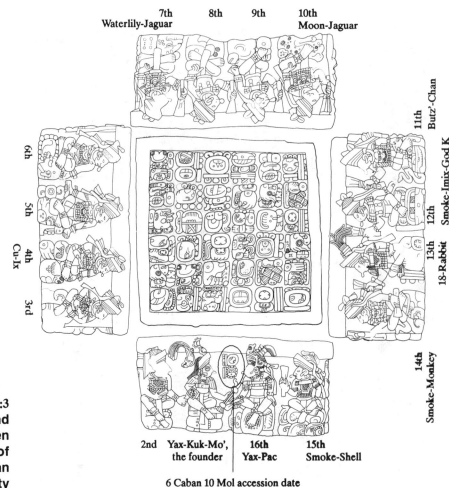

7th   8th   9th   10th
Waterlily-Jaguar   Moon-Jaguar

6th

5th

4th
Cu-Ix

3rd

11th Butz'-Chan

12th Smoke-Imix-God K

13th 18-Rabbit

14th Smoke-Monkey

2nd   Yax-Kuk-Mo',   16th   15th
      the founder   Yax-Pac   Smoke-Shell

6 Caban 10 Mol accession date

FIG. 8:3
Altar Q and the Sixteen Successors of the Copán Dynasty

event is now destroyed, but we believe that later Copanecs honored this date as the founding of their kingdom.[7]

By A.D. 426, Copán's ruling dynasty was founded and the principle of kingship was accepted by the elites reemerging in the valley society after the dormancy of the Late Preclassic period. No doubt here as elsewhere in the Maya world, the advent of this institution consolidated the kingdom, creating a politically coherent court in which the ahauob could air their differences and rivalries while at the same time presenting a unified front to their followers.

Yax-Kuk-Mo' ("Blue-Quetzal-Macaw"), who founded the ruling dynasty, appears in the historical and archaeological record[8] about 260 years after the recovery from the Late Preclassic slump. We know that he founded the dynasty of kings who led the kingdom of Copán throughout the Classic period. All the subsequent kings of Copán counted their numerical position in the succession from him, naming themselves, for example, "the twelfth successor of Yax-Kuk-Mo'."[9] In all, sixteen descendants followed Yax-Kuk-Mo' onto Copán's throne, and these kings ruled the valley for the next four hundred years.

#	Name	Accession	Death	Other dates
1	Yax-Kuk-Mo'			426–435?
2	unknown			
3	unknown			
4	Cu-Ix			465 ± 15 yrs
5	unknown			
6	unknown			
7	Waterlily-Jaguar			504–544 +
8	unknown			
9	unknown		551, Dec. 30	????
10	Moon-Jaguar	553, May 26	578, Oct. 26	
11	Butz'-Chan	578, Nov. 19	626, Jan. 23	
12	Smoke-Imix-God K	628, Feb. 8	695, Jun. 18	
13	18-Rabbit-God K	695, Jul. 9	738, May 3	
14	Smoke-Monkey	738, Jun. 11	749, Feb. 4	
15	Smoke-Shell	749, Feb. 18	????	
16	Yax-Pac	763, Jul. 2	820, May 6 –6 mos.	
17	U-Cit-Tok	????	822, Feb. 10	

In actuality, Yax-Kuk-Mo' was not the first king of Copán. It is probable, however, that he earned the designation of founder because he exemplified the charismatic qualities of the divine ahau better than any of his predecessors. It is important to remember that here, as at Palenque and the other kingdoms that acknowledged such great statesmen, the definition of a founding ancestor served a deeper social purpose. Aristocrats who descended from Yax-Kuk-Mo' constituted a distinct cluster of noble families, the clan of the kings, by birth superior to all the other elite in the valley. In principle, these people owed the reigning monarch a special measure of loyalty and support.

The earliest date associated with Yax-Kuk-Mo', 8.19.0.0.0, (February 1, 426), appears as retrospective history on Stela 15, a monument of the seventh successor, Waterlily-Jaguar. At the other end of the historical record, Yax-Pac, the sixteenth successor and the last great king of the dynasty, also recorded events in the life of Yax-Kuk-Mo'. He did so on his Altar Q (Fig. 8:3), which he called the "Altar of Yax-Kuk-Mo'." Yax-Pac used the sides of the altar to unfold the sixteen successors of his line, beginning with the founder and ending with himself. On the top, he inscribed two important deeds of Yax-Kuk'-Mo'.[10] There we can read that on 8.19.10.10.17 (September 6, 426), Yax-Kuk-Mo' displayed the God K scepter of royal authority. Three days later on 8.19.10.11.0 (September 9) Yax-Kuk-Mo' "came" or "arrived" as the founder of the lineage[11] (Fig. 8:4a and b). Yax-Pac recorded these two events as if they were the fundamental actions that spawned the dynasty and the kingdom. His commemoration of these events was critical to his campaign for political support from the many ahauob who reckoned their aristocratic pedigree from this founder. Later in the chapter we shall see why Yax-Pac was so anxious to associate himself publicly with the charismatic founder of his dynasty.

COPÁN:
THE DEATH
OF
FIRST DAWN
ON MACAW
MOUNTAIN

——

311

5 Caban 15 Yaxkin
8.19.10.10.17

he displayed
the God K
scepter

founder

Ahau Yax-Kuk-Mo'

a. Altar Q

8 Ahau 18 Yaxkin
8.19.10.11.0

tali
he arrived

founder

Kina Yax-Kuk-Mo'

b. Altar Q

9.0.0.0.0 8 Ahau 13 Ceh

c. Stela J

he displayed the
God K scepter

Mah Kina   Yax-Kuk-   Three-
            Mo'   Mountain
                        Ahau

FIG. 8:4
Yax-Kuk-Mo',
the Founder
of the Copán
Dynasty

The thirteenth successor, a particularly powerful man named 18-Rabbit, also evoked these early rituals of Yax-Kuk-Mo' as the basis of authority over his own ahauob. On Stela J, 18-Rabbit inscribed his own accession and that of his immediate predecessor, Smoke-Imix-God K, in an intricate text rendered in the form of a mat, the symbol of the kingly throne. On the first strand of the mat, he linked 9.13.10.0.0, the day this extraordinary monument was dedicated, to 9.0.0.0.0 (December 11, 435), a day when Yax-Kuk-Mo' performed another "God K-in-hand" event (Fig. 8:4c).

Recent excavations under the Acropolis have turned up a building erected either during or shortly after the reign of Yax-Kuk-Mo'. Discovered under the Temple of the Hieroglyphic Stairs (10L-26), this newly excavated temple once held in its back chamber a stela dated at 9.0.0.0.0.[12] Yax-Kuk-Mo' is recorded as the king in power when the baktun turned, while his son, the second king of the dynasty, was the owner of this tree-stone. Most important for our understanding of Copán's history, the text associates the name of Yax-Kuk-Mo' with the same date that would be evoked by his descendant, 18-Rabbit. Yax-Kuk-Mo' was not an invention of later kings who were fabricating a glorified past for political reasons. Yax-Kuk-Mo' did rule Copán, and in doing so he left a sacred legacy of tree-stones and temples to his descendants that is now coming to light in the excavations of the Acropolis.

This early temple, which is called Papagayo by the archaeologists,[13] was built only a few meters away from the first Ballcourt, which had been built during an earlier predynastic time. These two buildings became two of Copán's central metaphors of power throughout its recorded history—the temple of kings and the ballcourt portal to the Otherworld. As the centuries progressed, the successors of Yax-Kuk-Mo' commissioned temple after temple, building layer upon layer until that first temple and its companions grew into a range of sacred mountains overlooking a forest of tree-stones in the Great Plaza below.[14]

Papagayo temple held not only the 9.0.0.0.0 tree-stone, but also a step placed inside it during a remodeling project by the fourth successor, a ruler named Cu-Ix. Its text and accumulating evidence from ongoing excavations show that Papagayo was embedded in predynastic architecture and that it remained a focus of dynastic activity for centuries after the founder died.[15] This marvelous little temple emerged from obscurity when a tunnel was excavated into the southwest corner of the Temple of the Hieroglyphic Stairs.[16] Both the step and the above-mentioned stela are part of the growing body of inscriptions from the Early Classic period that have been emerging in recent excavations. Among the early kings who have been identified from this collection of inscriptions are the first ruler, Yax-Kuk-Mo'; his son, the second ruler; the fourth, Cu-Ix; the seventh, Waterlily-Jaguar, who left us two tree-stones (Stelae 15 and E) in the Great Plaza; the tenth, Moon-Jaguar, who left at least one tree-stone in the area under the modern village; and the eleventh, Butz'-Chan, who erected a tree-stone both in the village area and in the growing Acropolis. (See Fig. 8:3b for a summary of chronology that has been recovered to date.)[17]

Late Classic Copanec kings considered that their authority sprang from Yax-Kuk-Mo' and his charismatic performance as king. From his reign onward, Copán's dynastic history unfolded steadily until the system itself collapsed four hundred years later when the civilization of the Classic Maya as a whole failed. Many of the works of Copán's earliest kings still lie buried under the Acropolis and inside other structures, and are just beginning to come to light. Unfortunately, even when we uncover a buried building or find a fragmentary stela, we rarely find names associated with it. The reason for this is clear. Inscriptions are often unreadable, either because they were already old and worn when they were buried or because they were ritually "terminated" when they were placed in their final resting places. Earlier monuments were torn down to make room for the newer ones, and older buildings were either buried or broken up to be recycled as building materials. There is reason to suspect, however, that the destruction and reuse in construction of inscriptional materials was not a casual matter. The Copanecs, like other Maya, probably defused the power of places and objects they wished to cover or dispose of through special termination rituals involving defacement and careful breakage. These rituals are a source of much of the damage to early inscriptions at Copán.

Our access to recorded history really begins in earnest with the twelfth successor, Smoke-Imix-God K. This ruler stands out as a man of extraordinary accomplishment in a world that produced many great kings. One of the longest-lived kings in Copán's history, he reigned for sixty-seven years, from A.D. 628 to 695. He presided over the Late Classic explosion of Copán into a major power in the Maya world, expanding the dominion of its dynasty to the widest extent it would ever know. The

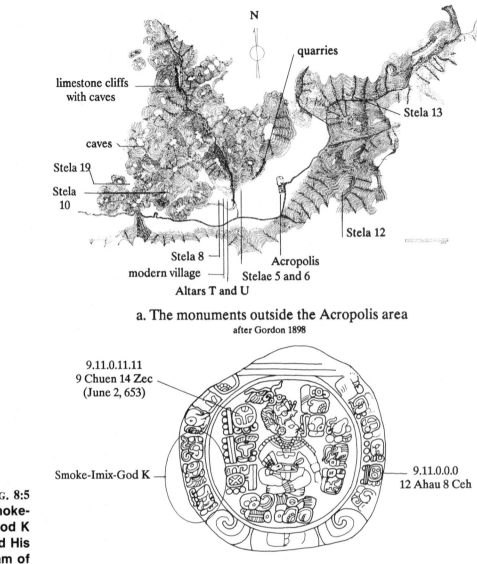

a. The monuments outside the Acropolis area
after Gordon 1898

9.11.0.11.11
9 Chuen 14 Zec
(June 2, 653)

Smoke-Imix-God K

9.11.0.0.0
12 Ahau 8 Ceh

FIG. 8:5
Smoke-
Imix-God K
and His
Program of
Monuments

b. Altar L from Quiriguá

period ending on 9.11.0.0.0 (A.D. 652) represented one of the pinnacles of his reign. On that date, he erected a series of stelae throughout the valley, making it his personal sacred space in the same manner that other kings marked out the more modest spaces of pyramid summits and plazas for their ecstatic communion.[18] At the eastern entrance to the valley, he set Stelae 23, 13, 12, and at the western entrance, Stelae 10 and 19, all pivoting off Stelae 2 and 3 set up in the huge main plaza north of the Acropolis (Fig. 8:5a). Thus Smoke-Imix-God K activated the entire city of Copán and its valley as his Otherworld portal. Even recalcitrant lords of the noble lineages might hesitate to plot intrigue within the supernatural perimeter of a king so favored by the Ancestors.

FIG. 8:6
The Great
Plaza and
a Forest of
Tree-Stones

Smoke-Imix-God K's conversion of the entire community of the Copán Valley into a magical instrument bent to his will was more than a boastful gesture. Under his aegis, the Copán nobility enjoyed prestige and wealth at the expense of their rivals in neighboring cities. They were the dominant elite of Maya civilization's southeastern region.[19] On the same 9.11.0.0.0 period ending, Smoke-Imix-God K celebrated his preeminence over his nearest neighbor, Quiriguá, by erecting Altar L there[20] (Fig. 8:5b). In years to come this nearby kingdom, which straddled the rich trade routes of the Motagua River, would throw off the yoke of Copán in a spectacular battle. As Smoke-Imix-God K pursued his dream of empire, however, that day was far in the future. While the king grasped lands to the north and west on the Motagua, Maya lords, most likely from his own city, established themselves in the Valley of La Venta on the Chamelecón River between Copán and their non-Maya neighbors to the east.[21] In the hands of the powerful and ambitious Smoke-Imix-God K, Copán may have been one of the largest Maya royal territories of its time.

In A.D. 695, 18-Rabbit succeeded Smoke-Imix-God K and began his own transformation of his ancestors' work. Where his predecessor had defined the boundaries of the sacred valley, 18-Rabbit chose the pivotal center of Copán as the stage for his own contribution to the glorious history of the dynasty. Exhorting the truly exceptional sculptors, architects, scribes, and artisans of his time to extend their arts well beyond the limits of precedence, 18-Rabbit brought about the creation of many beautiful dramas in stone. In the course of a lifetime, he transformed the center of Copán into a unique and beautiful expression of Maya royal power that has endured to the present, unfailingly touching the most dispassionate of modern visitors.

COPÁN:
THE DEATH
OF
FIRST DAWN
ON MACAW
MOUNTAIN
—
315

One of his many projects was the remodeling of the Ballcourt. 18-Rabbit capped the older markers created by his predecessors with new images emphasizing his personal role as the incarnation of the Ancestral Hero Twins in their triumph over the Lords of Death. Next to the Ballcourt and within the adjacent space of the Great Plaza, 18-Rabbit also created a symbolic forest of te-tunob (Fig. 8:6). Within this magnificent grove each tree-stone bore his portrait in the guise of a god he had manifested through ecstatic ritual. All the tree-stones found in the Great Plaza were placed there between 9.14.0.0.0 and 9.15.5.0.0 (A.D. 711–736).[22]

One of 18-Rabbit's final projects focused on the Acropolis directly south of his Ballcourt. There he rebuilt one of the ancient living mountains of his forebears, a monument referred to today as Temple 22.[23] 18-Rabbit commissioned his best artists to decorate this amazing building inside and out with deeply carved stone sculpture. Outside the temple, great Witz Monsters reared at the four corners of the cosmos, while the doorway of the inner sanctum, the king's portal to the Otherworld, was framed by an arching Celestial Monster—the sky of the apotheosized Ancestors—laced with the blood scrolls of royal sacrifice (Pl. #). This sky of the king was held aloft by Pauahtunob, the age-old burden-bearers who stand at the four points of the compass and lift the heavens above the earth. Here they allowed the king to enter the darkness where only divine ahauob could go and return alive.

The magnificence of 18-Rabbit's work lay not in the themes, which were traditional for Copán and all Maya ahauob, but rather in their execution. Unlike Pacal and Chan-Bahlum at Palenque, 18-Rabbit revealed no special political agenda in his efforts. Instead he focused solely upon the centrality of the king in the life of the state. From Smoke-Imix-God K he had inherited a court of nobles already accustomed to governing neighboring cities. To control these noble subordinates, 18-Rabbit needed to energetically and eloquently assert the prerogatives of his kingship over them. As we can see from the examples of his monumental art shown above, he accomplished his purpose with theological sophistication and poetic passion. Few kings in Maya history have ever wielded the canon of royal power with results as truly breathtaking as those of 18-Rabbit. But this balance of power was not to hold for long. From the clear vantage afforded us by hindsight, we can understand the root of the disaster that ended his reign. His beautiful expressions of the pivotal role of the divine king were aimed at a noble audience who would become increasingly convinced of their own ability to manage the affairs of the kingdom without the king.

The beginning of the end can be seen in the monumental art created by these very nobles. As the prosperity of the kingdom overflowed from the king to the valley elite, this elite began putting up monuments which, although erected in private and not public space, emulated royal practices. During 18-Rabbit's reign, for example, a lineage of scribes occupying Compound 9N-8 built an extraordinary family temple (Structure 9N-82-Sub; Pl. #) dedicated to God N, the patron god of writing, and hence, of history itself. The texts of the temple mention the high king and probably also his predecessor, Smoke-Imix-God K.[24] Not only were the nobility of 18-Rabbit's reign privileged to commission such elaborately decorated buildings, they were able to take full advantage of the extraordinary artistic talent flourishing in the community of this time. In the case of Structure 9N-82, the scribes' lineage was able to hire one of the finest masters in the valley to execute their sculpture.

During 18-Rabbit's forty-two-year reign, Copán not only flourished as an artistic center of the first rank, but also became an multi-ethnic society, drawing in non-Maya people from the central region of Honduras around Lake Yojoa and Comayagua.[25] The recruitment of these people into the city created a truly cosmopolitan state, but one in which a slight mythological adjustment had to be made. Traditionally, the high king had always been the living manifestation of the special covenant which existed between the Maya people and their supernatural ancestors. By bringing in people from a non-Maya ethnic group, however, 18-Rabbit had to expand upon this tradition. There is not the slightest hint of unorthodox ritual in his monuments. Still, his lavish amplification of the cult of the king as god and supernatural hero may register his public appeal to barbarians less knowledgeable in Maya theology, and more impressed by pageantry, than local aristocrats. He may have persuaded such new converts to Maya culture that he was indeed *their* advocate to the Otherworld, just as he was the advocate for his own people. Whether or not he enacted such a strategy, he did succeed in enhancing the power base of his kingdom and increasing the population of the valley.[26]

As had happened in other ambitious Late Classic kingdoms, the path of war and expansion taken by Copán finally turned back upon itself. The unfortunate 18-Rabbit reaped the whirlwind caused by his predecessor's actions. In mid-career and at the height of his glory, he had installed a new ruler named Cauac-Sky (Fig. 8:7) at Quiriguá, the kingdom brought under the hegemony of Copán by his father, Smoke-Imix-God K. The installation ritual, a "God K-in-hand" event, had taken place on January 2, A.D. 725, in "the land of (*u cab*)" 18-Rabbit of Copán.[27] Thirteen years after this accession, Cauac-Sky turned on his liege lord and attacked, taking 18-Rabbit captive in battle and sacrificing him at Quiriguá on May 3, 738.[28]

The subsequent fate of Copán was profoundly different from that of Tikal or Naranjo after their defeat by Caracol. In their excavations, archaeologists have found no evidence that Quiriguá dominated Copán at all. The population of Copán continued to burgeon, its lords pursued their architectural plans, and its merchants plied their trade with the rest of Honduras. In other words, everything was business as usual. A person looking at the record of the city's economic and social life would never guess that anything had changed.[29]

Although it is possible that Cauac-Sky just wasn't able to dominate so vast a neighbor from his more modest city, a more convincing explanation to this puzzle emerges. The absence of effect in the archaeological record may register a fundamental reaction of the Copán people them-

COPÁN:
THE DEATH
OF
FIRST DAWN
ON MACAW
MOUNTAIN

—

317

Quiriguá, Stela E, west

12 Caban 5 Kayab
9.14.13.4.17

he displayed the
God K scepter

Cauac-Sky

in the land of

[18-Rabbit]-God K, Copán Ahau

3 days, 13 uinals, 6 tuns

and then it
happened

4 Ahau 13 Yax
9.15.0.0.0.0

event

6 days, 14 uinals, 1 tun

and then it
happened

6 Cimi 4 Zec
9.15.6.14.6

he was
sacrificed

18-Rabbit-
God K

FIG. 8:7
**Cauac-Sky,
Divine Quiriguá
Ahau, and the
Capturer of
18-Rabbit, the
King of Copán**

A
FOREST
OF
KINGS
—
318

selves. The death of the king precipitated no faltering in the orderly world of the nobility and common folk, perhaps because they were coming to believe that they could get along without a king. Apparently, the ruling dynasty was in no position to challenge that belief for quite some time. According to the inscriptional record, it took the dynasty almost twenty years to recover the prestige it lost when 18-Rabbit succumbed to his rival. Ultimately, this failure fooled the patriarchs of the subordinate lineages into believing that their civilized world could survive quite well without a king at the center.

There was still a king at Copán, however, even if he was an unremarkable one. Thirty-nine days after the defeat of 18-Rabbit, on a day close to the maximum elongation of Venus as Morningstar,[30] a new king named Smoke-Monkey acceded to the throne. We have not been able to associate this king with any stelae or structures at Copán. In fact, the only historical episode of his reign that we know of was recorded by one of his descendants. This event, a first appearance of Eveningstar, was recorded in Temple 11 by the sixteenth successor of the dynasty, Yax-Pac.[31] After ruling for ten silent years, Smoke-Monkey died, and Smoke-Shell, his son,[32] became the king on February 18, 749.

Although Smoke-Shell reigned only fourteen years, he succeeded in reestablishing the tradition of glorious public performance, if not the glory, of his dynasty. In contrast to the long decades of humiliation that were the price of defeat paid by the ahauob of Tikal and Naranjo, Smoke-Shell brought his kingdom back from the ignominy of defeat within a katun. The strategy he used featured two main components: an ambitious building program and a judicious political marriage.

Shortly after taking the throne, Smoke-Shell began reconstruction work[33] on one of the oldest and most sacred points in the city center—the locus that had grown over that very early temple that contained the 9.0.0.0.0 temple and its adjacent Ballcourt. The magnificent result of his effort, the Temple of the Hieroglyphic Stairs (Structure 10L-26), is one of the premier monuments of the New World and a unique expression of the supernatural path of kings.[34] Inscribed upon this stairway of carved risers is the longest Precolumbian text known in the New World, comprising over twenty-two hundred glyphs.[35] This elegant text records the accessions and deaths of each of the high kings of the Yax-Kuk-Mo' dynasty. This record of Copán's divine history rises out of the mouth of an inverted Vision Serpent, pouring like a prophetic revelation of the cosmos, compelling the ancestors of Smoke-Shell to return through the sacred portal he had activated for them. Flowing upward in the midst of this chronicle sit the last five successors of the dynasty, Smoke-Monkey, 18-Rabbit, Smoke-Imix-God K, Butz'-Chan, and Moon-Jaguar, carved in life-sized portraits (Fig. 8:8). These ancestors are girded in the battle gear of Tlaloc-Venus conquest war we have seen in full bloom at Tikal, Caracol, and Dos Pilas. In his version of history, Smoke-Shell proclaimed the prowess of his predecessors as warlords despite the personal defeat of 18-Rabbit by a vassal ahau.

COPÁN:
THE DEATH
OF
FIRST DAWN
ON MACAW
MOUNTAIN

—

319

upper muzzle of Vision Serpent

rabbits to mark the identity of the figure

18-Rabbit

flexible shield from the Tlaloc war costume

the king's loincloth

lower jaw of Vision Serpent

FIG. 8:8
18-Rabbit
Emerging
from the
Gaping Mouth
of a Vision
Serpent

As the building on his portal progressed, Smoke-Shell sent to a faraway, exotic place to bring a new wife to Copán. From the opposite side of the Maya world, a royal woman from the famous kingdom of Palenque crossed the dangerous lands to marry her new husband and bear him a son who would become the next king.[36] His strategy echoes the marriage alliance between Naranjo and Dos Pilas that revived the Naranjo dynasty after its defeat by Lord Kan of Caracol. This marriage likely occurred late in Smoke-Shell's life, for his heir came to the throne when he was less than twenty years old.

Smoke-Shell's efforts to revive the dynasty and to persuade his nobility to follow him apparently succeeded only in the short term. He bequeathed his child, Yax-Pac, a variety of problems touching every stratum of society, from the highest to the most humble. In every long-lived dynasty, the pyramid of royal descendants increases every generation until an enormous body of people exists, all sharing the prerogatives of royal kinship. Not only are these people a drain on the society that must support them, but they create political problems by intriguing against one another. The general nobility was also growing in wealth and power at this time. Needless to say, Yax-Pac would have to be a very strong king to control and satisfy all these political factions. In addition to this, the valley of Copán was plagued by a variety of economic and ecological problems. The rulers of Copán, by and large, had done their job too well. The valley

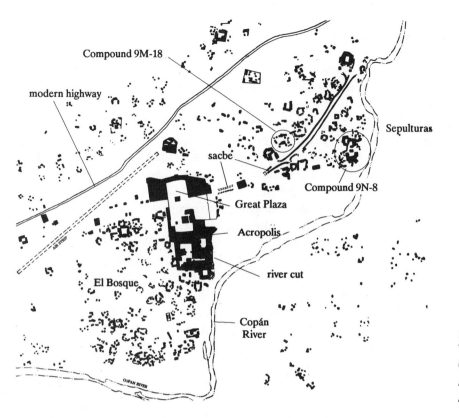

FIG. 8:9
The Urban
Concentrations
Adjacent to the
Acropolis

resources had been overdeveloped and strained to their very limits. Now it seemed that the trend toward progress was reversing itself.

Overpopulation was one of the primary problems Yax-Pac would have to deal with during his reign. The kingdom had continued to grow at a steady rate during the two reigns following 18-Rabbit's capture. Throughout the eighth century, more and more residential complexes[37] sprang up on the rich bottomlands around the Acropolis (Fig. 8:9). The region within a one-kilometer radius of the Ballcourt contained over fifteen hundred structures, with an estimated density of three thousand people per square kilometer. At least twenty thousand people were trying to eke out a living from the badly strained resources. This population simply could not be supported by local agriculture alone, especially since the best land was buried under the expanding residential complexes around the Acropolis.[38]

When Yax-Pac came to the throne, he inherited a disaster in the making. Over the generations, expanding residential zones had covered the best agricultural lands, forcing farmers into the foothills and then onto the mountain slopes. There they were forced to clear more and more forest to produce maize fields. Clearing, in turn, caused erosion. Shorter fallow periods were depleting the usable soils at an even faster rate, just when the kingdom was required to feed the largest population in its history.[39]

COPÁN:
THE DEATH
OF
FIRST DAWN
ON MACAW
MOUNTAIN

——

321

Deforestation caused other problems as well. People needed wood for their cooking fires, for the making of lime in the construction of temples,[40] for building houses, and for dozens of other domestic and ritual uses. As more and more people settled in the valley, the forest gradually retreated, exposing more and more of the poor soils on the mountain slopes and causing more erosion. The cutting down of the forest also affected climate and rainfall, making it yet more difficult for people to sustain themselves. With an insufficient food supply came malnutrition and its resultant chronic diseases, rampant conditions that affected the nobility as well as the common people.[41] The quality of life, which was never very good in the preindustrial cities of the ancient world, fast deteriorated toward the unbearable in Copán under the pained gaze of its last great king.

As his father had before him, Yax-Pac continued to place the focus of his royal performance upon dynastic history, holding up the values of his predecessors as the canon by which he would guide Copán through the dangers and crises of the present. After becoming king on July 2, 763, Yax-Pac's first action on Copán's beautiful stage[42] was the setting of a small carved altar representing the Vision Serpent into the Great Plaza amid the tree-stones of his rehabilitated predecessor, 18-Rabbit (Fig. 8:20). This small altar celebrated 9.16.15.0.0, the first important period ending after his accession.

Shortly thereafter, the young ahau turned his attention to an ancient temple standing on the northern edge of the Acropolis, overlooking the forest of tree-stones. This old temple had been built by the seventh successor of the dynasty and named on its dedication step "Holy Copán Temple, the House of Mah Kina Yax-Kuk-Mo'."[43] At the base of the temple stairs, Yax-Pac's father, Smoke-Shell, had erected Stela N, his final contribution to Copán's public history. Yax-Pac chose the locale of that old temple as the site of his greatest work. There he planned to raise Temple 11, one of the most ambitious structures ever built in the history of the city. In the tradition of his forebears, he encased the old temple in the new, shaping the imagery of the new temple into a unique and spectacular expression both of cosmic order and of the sanctions that bound the fate of the community to that of the king. Through this building and the Otherworld portal it housed at the junction of its dark corridors, Yax-Pac began his lifelong effort to ward off the impending disaster that hung over the valley.

We are not sure of the exact starting date for the construction of this temple, but work on it must have begun in the first few years of Yax-Pac's reign. Six years later, on March 27, 769, following the celebration of the equinox, Yax-Pac dedicated the Reviewing Stand on the south side of the temple. This Reviewing Stand faced the inner court and temples of his forebears which studded the West Court of the Acropolis. Built against the first terrace of the pyramid that would eventually support Temple 11, the Reviewing Stand was a metaphorical Xibalban Ballcourt, complete with three rectangular markers set into the plaza floor below in the pattern of a playing alley (Fig. 8:10). Jutting outward into the West Court, this stairway was a place of sacrifice where victims were rolled down the stairs

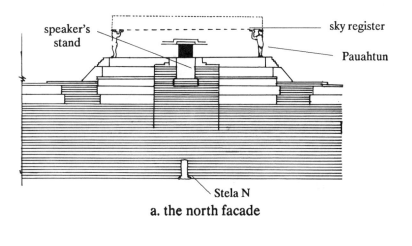

speaker's stand

sky register

Pauahtun

Stela N

a. the north facade

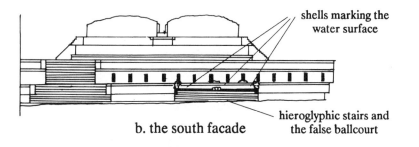

shells marking the water surface

hieroglyphic stairs and the false ballcourt

b. the south facade

FIG. 8:10
**Yax-Pac and
Temple 11**

as if they were the ball.[44] The stair itself carried an inscribed history of its dedication rituals, naming the structure as a ballcourt. Huge stone conch shells marked the terrace as the surface of the Xibalban waters through which the ax-wielding executioner god Chac-Xib-Chac (an aspect of Venus, the firstborn of the Twins) rose when he was brought forth by the king's ecstasy.

Yax-Pac further indicated that the entire West Court was under the murky waters of the Underworld by placing two floating caimans[45] atop the platform opposite the Reviewing Stand. The southern side of this pyramid was thus a representation of Xibalba. It was the "place of fright," the Otherworld where sacrificial victims were sent into the land of the Lords of Death to play ball and to deliver messages from the divine ahau.[46] With the construction of such an elaborate, theatrical ballcourt, Yax-Pac was making an important statement about his strategies for the kingship: He would require himself to excel in battle against noble enemies and bring these enemies here to die.

As the king set about preparing his new temple and the supernatural landscape surrounding it, he reached back to 18-Rabbit, the source of both his dynasty's success and its profoundest failure. In August of the same year in which he dedicated the Reviewing Stand, Yax-Pac built within the Acropolis what would be the first of many bridges to his paradoxical

COPÁN:
THE DEATH
OF
FIRST DAWN
ON MACAW
MOUNTAIN
——

323

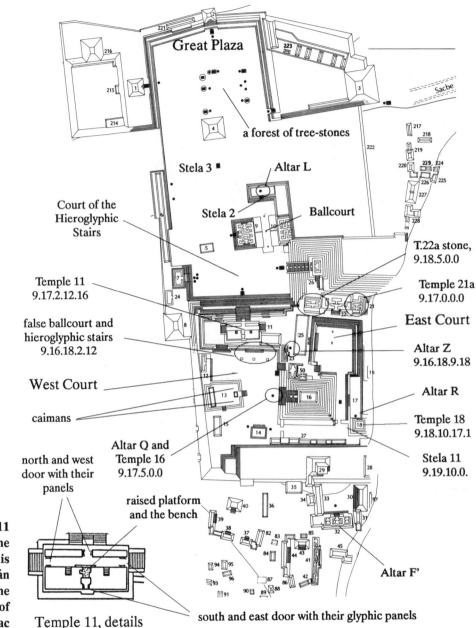

Great Plaza

216

215

214

1

221

223

Sacbe

3

a forest of tree-stones

4

Stela 3

Altar L

Court of the
Hieroglyphic
Stairs

Stela 2

Ballcourt

6

5

222

217

218

219

220

229 224

226 225

227

228

T.22a stone,
9.18.5.0.0

Temple 11
9.17.2.12.16

7

24

26

21

22

Temple 21a
9.17.0.0.0

East Court

8

11

25

false ballcourt and
hieroglyphic stairs
9.16.18.2.12

Altar Z
9.16.18.9.18

West Court

23

50

caimans

12

13

16

17

Altar R

north and west
door with their
panels

14

15

18

Temple 18
9.18.10.17.1

Altar Q and
Temple 16
9.17.5.0.0

27

Stela 11
9.19.10.0.

raised platform
and the bench

35

34

33

30

29

28

97

FIG. 8:11
The
Acropolis
of Copán
and the
Works of
Yax-Pac

40

36

39

38

37

82 83

85

32

31

45

Altar F'

84

44 43

41

94 95

93 96

91

87

90 89

42

86 88

Temple 11, details

south and east door with their glyphic panels

ancestor. The king set Altar Z on the platform between Temple 22—the
magnificent temple created by 18-Rabbit on his first katun anniversary—
and Temple 11, the structure that would become his own cosmic building
(Fig. 8:11). Yax-Pac may also have set another important precedent with
this small monument, for we think it makes mention of a younger brother
of the king.[47] This inscription is significant because it indicates the beginning of a trend in Yax-Pac's strategies in regard to the public record. In
the course of his lifetime, Yax-Pac peopled Copán's stage of history with

| the Pauahtun from the northeast corner | inscription | the raised platform surrounded by the Skeletal Maw to the Otherworld |

an ever-increasing troupe of ahauob. This is a strategy we have seen before at Yaxchilán—sharing power is always better than losing it.

The first katun ending of Yax-Pac's life was a significant one. Not only was it the first major festival of his young career, but by coincidence it fell on the day of a partial eclipse, followed sixteen days later by the first appearance of Venus as Eveningstar.[48] To celebrate the katun ending,[49] Yax-Pac sandwiched a tiny building, Temple 21a, between 18-Rabbit's great cosmic building, Temple 22, and the now-destroyed Temple 21.[50] The small scale of Temple 21a and its position between the two huge buildings suggests Yax-Pac had assigned most of the available labor to the ongoing construction of Temple 11. Yet regardless of the scale, Yax-Pac was clearly intent upon associating himself with the earlier king. Perhaps Smoke-Shell had successfully restored 18-Rabbit's reputation and he was, by that time, remembered more for the accomplishments of his reign than the ignominy of his death. Nevertheless, the repeated efforts by Yax-Pac to embrace the memory of this ancestor suggest that there was a pressing need to continue the process of rehabilitation not only of 18-Rabbit but also of his dynasty in the face of a disenchanted nobility.

On 9.17.2.12.16 1 Cib 19 Ceh (September 26, 773), two years after the katun ending, Yax-Pac dedicated Temple 11. The magnificent cosmic statement he made in this monument would become the basis of his fame. Before the passage of time had sullied its original splendor, this building was truly one of the most unusual and intriguing temples ever built in the Precolumbian Maya world. Facing the northern horizon, this two-story-high temple with wide interior vaults towered over the Ballcourt and Great Plaza. Its principal north door opened through the mouth of a huge Witz Monster,[51] which glared down at the gathered populace below. At each of the two northern corners of this microcosmic world stood a giant Pauahtun (Fig. 8:12a), its huge hands holding up images of the Cosmic Monster, arching across the roof entablatures in symbolic replication of

COPÁN:
THE DEATH
OF
FIRST DAWN
ON MACAW
MOUNTAIN
——
325

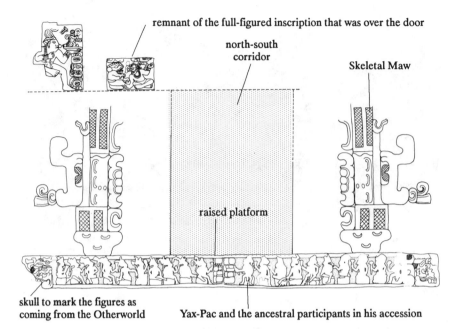

remnant of the full-figured inscription that was over the door

north-south
corridor

Skeletal Maw

raised platform

skull to mark the figures as
coming from the Otherworld

Yax-Pac and the ancestral participants in his accession

the arch of heaven and the planetary beings who moved through that path on their supernatural journeys.[52] It was as if he took the magnificent sculpture at the heart of Temple 22, 18-Rabbit's greatest building, and turned it inside out so that it became the outer facade rather than an arch over the door to the inner sanctum. Today, fragments of the scaled body of this Cosmic Monster litter the ground around the fallen temple.

Yax-Pac designed the ground floor of this temple with a wide east-west gallery crossed by a smaller north-south corridor. In this way he engineered an entrance to the building from each of the four cardinal directions—north, east, south, and west. Just inside each of these four doors, panels facing one another record historical events important to Yax-Pac's political strategy and the dedication of the temple itself.[53] What is curious about each pair of texts is that one is in normal reading order, while the other facing text reads in reverse order as if you are seeing a mirror image. It is as if you were standing between the glass entry doors of a bank—the writing on the door in front of you would read normally while the writing behind you would be reversed. If you were standing

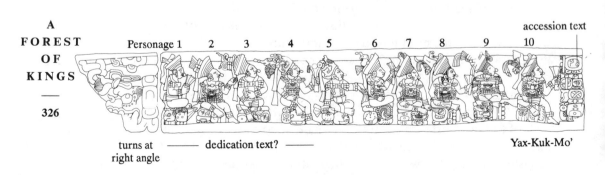

accession text

Personage 1   2   3   4   5   6   7   8   9   10

turns at ——— dedication text? ———
right angle

Yax-Kuk-Mo'

outside, however, the texts on both door would read in the proper order. In Temple 11, of course, the walls are not transparent, but this made no difference, since the audience addressed by these texts consisted of the ancestors and the gods. Apparently, they could read through solid walls. Furthermore, each pair of texts is designed to be read from a different direction starting with the north door: To read them in proper order (that is, "outside the bank doors") the reader would have to circulate through all four of the directions. This attention to the "point of view" of the gods is not unusual in Maya art.

Just to the south of the place where the two corridors cross, Yax-Pac built a small raised platform set within the skeletal, gaping jaws of the Maw of the Otherworld. The carved image of this great Maw was set at both the southern (Fig. 8:12b) and northern (Fig. 8:13) entries onto the platform. He made the northern side special by replacing the lower jaw of the Maw with a bench depicting twenty ancestral figures, ten each on either side of an inscription recording his accession as king (Fig. 8:14). These were the dynasts who had preceded him onto the throne of Copán.[54] Yax-Pac had brought them forth from the land of the ancestors to participate in his accession rite. Their sanction of this rite was forever frozen in this stone depiction, serving as a testament to those privileged elite who would enter the temple to see and affirm.

Temple 11 was the greatest work of Yax-Pac's life. To be sure, he built other buildings during his reign, but none so grand in size, ambition, and conception as this one.[55] Temple 11 was an umbilicus linking the kingdom of Yax-Pac to the nurturing, demanding cosmos: the final great expression at Copán of the Maya vision. Its lower level, especially to the south, manifested the underwater world of Xibalba.[56] The great rising Acropolis that supported it was the sacred mountain which housed other portals into the Otherworld. The temple roof was the sky held away from the mountain by the Pauahtunob at the corners of the world. The front door was the huge mouth of the mountain, the cave through which the king entered sacred space. At the heart of the temple was the raised platform defined as the portal to the Otherworld. This building sealed the covenant between Yax-Pac, his people, and their collective destiny. Its enormous size and grand scope were designed to proclaim the power of the king to rally his people in the face of their difficulties. It may not have been the finest Maya temple ever built—the sculptures weren't anywhere

FIG. **8:14**
Temple 11
bench

Waterlily-Skull to mark the location as the Otherworld

11   12   13   14   15   16   17   18   19   20

Yax-Pac

turns at
right angle

| 11 Men?? | 13?? Pax | event | names? | *utom* | 9.17.10.0.0 12 Ahau 8 Pax | he |
| [9.17.3.16.15??] | | | | it will happen | | scattered drops |

near the artistry of 18-Rabbit's. Nor was it the most architecturally sound—the vaults were so wide they had to be reinforced because the walls started to fall down as soon as the builders began to raise the second story. Nevertheless, this temple was the statement of authority the young king hoped would help keep disaster at bay.

Yax-Pac continued to refine his fundamental statement of charismatic power during the next three years in construction projects that altered the west side of the Acropolis. At the five-year point of Katun 17, three years after he had dedicated Temple 11, he set Altar Q (Fig. 8:3) in front of the newly completed Temple 16, a massive pyramid he built at the heart of the Acropolis. Replete with images of Tlaloc warfare and the skulls of slain victims, Temple 16 replicated the imagery of his father's great project—Temple 26—as Temple 11 had reproduced Temple 22 of 18-Rabbit's reign.[57]

Altar Q, a low, flat-sided monument, was more suited to the functions of a throne than those of an altar. It depicted each of the sixteen ancestors seated upon his own name glyph. The whole dynasty unfolded in a clockwise direction, starting with Yax-Kuk-Mo' and culminating with Yax-Pax himself. His ancestors sit in front of a monument celebrating war while they ride just below the surface of the symbolic sea he created in the West Court. The program of imagery is an elegant and powerful statement of power. Ironically, the charisma of the divine lord as exemplified in battle and conquest belied the reality of Yax-Pac's circumstances, for this was to be the last great exhortation of kingship to be built in the valley of Copán.

For all of its elegance and centrality, the West Court and Altar Q mark a change in strategy for Yax-Pac. Up to this time, kings had acknowledged the passage of sacred time with buildings, sculptures, and inscriptions erected only in the ceremonial heart of the community. Now, however, Yax-Pac also began to write his history outside the Acropolis by traveling to the residential compounds of his lords to conduct royal rituals within their lineage houses. This was clearly a comedown for an "ahau of the ahauob," made necessary by the need to hold the allegiance of his lords in the face of civil disaster.[58]

The next important period-ending date that Yax-Pac celebrated, 9.17.10.0.0, was commemorated not only in the royal precinct of the

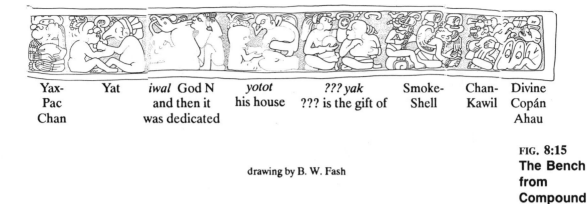

| Yax-Pac Chan | Yat | *iwal* and then it was dedicated | God N | *yotot* his house | *??? yak* ??? is the gift of | Smoke-Shell | Chan-Kawil | Divine Copán Ahau |

drawing by B. W. Fash

FIG. 8:15
The Bench from Compound 9M-27

Acropolis, but also in the household of a noble family of the city. The date and description of the scattering rite that Yax-Pax enacted is inscribed on a bench in the main building of Group 9M-18[59] (Fig. 8:9), a large noble household to the east of the Acropolis. Yax-Pac's action is recorded as an event still to come in the future at the time the patriarch dedicated his house, the place where he held court over the affairs of his family and followers (Fig. 8:15). Strangely the name of the patriarch was not included on the bench. Instead it records a dedicatory offering given in the name of Smoke-Shell, Yax-Pac's father.[60] Perhaps the lineage patriarch felt he should not place his name so close to that of his liege lord, so he remained anonymous. Nevertheless, he brought prestige to his own house and weight to the decisions he made astride this bench by focusing on the high kings as the main actors in his family drama.

Shortly after the period ending, another lineage benefited from Yax-Pac's ritual attention, and bragged about it inside the new house of their leader. The scribal lineage living in Group 9N-8 (Fig. 8:9) dismantled the magnificent structure an earlier patriarch had commissioned during the reign of 18-Rabbit and put a new, larger building in its place. The elegance of this building was unmistakable. Its upper zone was sculpted with mosaic images of the lineage's own patriarch; and on either side of the door that led into the large, central chamber of the building, a Pauahtun, one of the patron gods of their craft, rose dramatically from the Maw of Xibalba.

Almost all of the floor space of this chamber was occupied by a bench[61] on which the patriarch sat to conduct the business of the lineage. This bench (Fig. 8:16) records that on 9.17.10.11.0 11 Ahau 3 Ch'en (July 10, 781),[62] this patriarch dedicated his new house while the king participated in those rites with him. As Yax-Pac had done for the lineage head of Compound 9M-18, he honored this patriarch by participating in rituals on his home ground. The king was breaking precedent, going to his subordinate rather than the other way around. At Yaxchilán, Bird-Jaguar had also gone to his subordinate across the river at La Pasadita, but in that instance he had functioned as the principal actor while the cahal was clearly in a position of subservience. In the scribes' building, Yax-Pac's

COPÁN:
THE DEATH
OF
FIRST DAWN
ON MACAW
MOUNTAIN

———

329

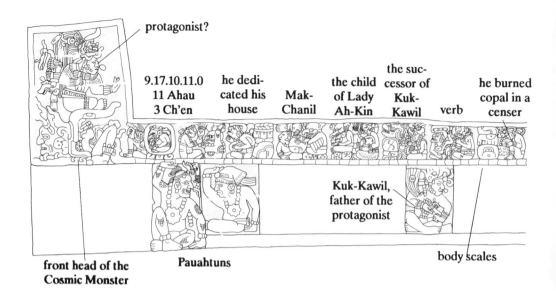

protagonist?

9.17.10.11.0
11 Ahau
3 Ch'en

he dedi-
cated his
house

Mak-
Chanil

the child
of Lady
Ah-Kin

the suc-
cessor of
Kuk-
Kawil

verb

he burned
copal in a
censer

Kuk-Kawil,
father of the
protagonist

body scales

front head of the
Cosmic Monster

Pauahtuns

name closes the text, but the noble is given equal billing. Furthermore, this text doubles as the body of a Cosmic Monster, imagery directly associated with the royal house of Copán. Four Pauahtunob hold up the bench in the same way that they hold up the sky in Temples 22, 26, and 11. The head of this scribes' lineage utilized the same symbolic imagery as his king, and he did so apparently with Yax-Pac's approval.

Yax-Pac thus gave away some of the hard-earned royal charisma of his ancestors to honor the head of this lineage. Was this the act of a desperate man? In all likelihood the king was fully aware of the potential danger in his capitulation to the nobility, but regarded it as a necessary step in his efforts to save the kingdom from impending economic disaster. He was clearly seeking solutions to immediate political problems threatening the peace and stability of the domain destiny had placed in his hands. Like Bird-Jaguar of Yaxchilán in the west, Yax-Pac tried to secure the continuing loyalty of the patriarchs of his kingdom by sharing his prerogatives with them, particularly the privilege of history.

Once Yax-Pac had embarked on this policy, he pursued it systematically and creatively during the second half of Katun 17. He raised monuments in the community at large and in the main ceremonial center and "lent" his historical actions to the monuments of significant others in the political arena of Copán. In the region now under the modern village of Copán (Fig. 8:5), the king erected two monuments to celebrate the first katun anniversary of his accession. Here, in the village area, he planted Stela 8 (Fig. 8:17), on which he recorded this anniversary and a related bloodletting which took place five days later. As we have seen so often before, the anniversary date fell on an important station of Venus: the maximum elongation of the Morningstar.[63] Yax-Pac also chose to record his parentage on this stela, reminding his people that he was the child of the woman from Palenque. This is the only monument ever to mention

it was made of clay | the house offering | Yax-Pac | Chan-Yat | Divine Copán Ahau | a katun batab

??? | name

the protagonist?

bloodletter

rear head of the Cosmic Monster

Pauahtuns

FIG. 8:16 The Bench from Structure 9N-82

Yax-Pac's relationship to his mother, and it is possible that he did so here in order to lend prestige to his half brother by the same woman.

The second monument celebrating Yax-Pac's first katun anniversary, Altar T, also graced the central plaza of the town. Here, for the first time, we are formally introduced to Yahau-Chan-Ah-Bac, the king's half brother by the woman Smoke-Shell had brought from Palenque to rejuve-

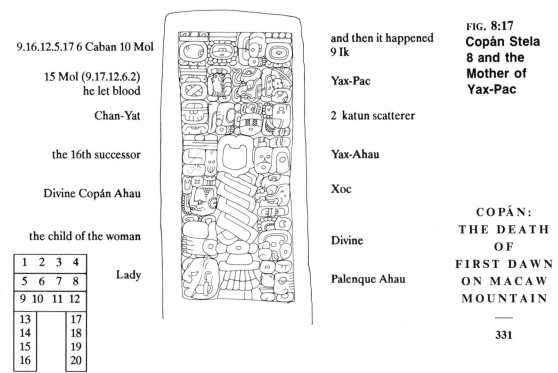

9.16.12.5.17 6 Caban 10 Mol

15 Mol (9.17.12.6.2) he let blood

Chan-Yat

the 16th successor

Divine Copán Ahau

the child of the woman

Lady

and then it happened 9 Ik

Yax-Pac

2 katun scatterer

Yax-Ahau

Xoc

Divine

Palenque Ahau

1	2	3	4
5	6	7	8
9	10	11	12
13		17
14		18
15		19
16		20

Reading Order

FIG. 8:17 Copán Stela 8 and the Mother of Yax-Pac

COPÁN:
THE DEATH
OF
FIRST DAWN
ON MACAW
MOUNTAIN

—

331

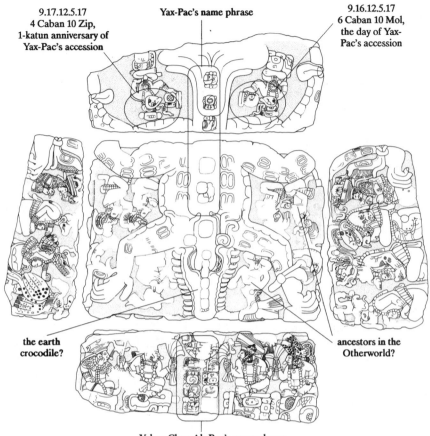

9.17.12.5.17
4 Caban 10 Zip,
1-katun anniversary of
Yax-Pac's accession

Yax-Pac's name phrase

9.16.12.5.17
6 Caban 10 Mol,
the day of Yax-
Pac's accession

the earth
crocodile?

ancestors in the
Otherworld?

FIG. 8:18
Altar T and
Yahau-Chan-
Ah-Bac

Yahau-Chan-Ah-Bac's name phrase

nate the lineage.[64] As we shall see shortly, this sibling would become an important protagonist in the saga of Copán during the twilight of its dynasty.

Altar T was decorated on three sides with twelve figures, some human and some animalistic. All of these figures faced toward a central inscription referring to the half brother (Fig. 8:18). The figures on Altar T emulate the style of Altar Q, Yax-Pac's great dynastic monument of twenty years earlier.[65] This design was chosen quite intentionally to honor the king's half brother. The top surface has a rendering of the image of ' a great crocodile sprawling in the waters of the earth. Waterlilies decorate his limbs, and his rear legs and tail drape over the corners and the back of the altar. Like fanciful scales, the king's name marches down the spine of the crocodile, and the tail of the great beast falls between two humanlike figures personifying the date of Yax-Pac's accession and its anniversary twenty years later. Sitting among the extended legs of the floating crocodile in the world under its belly are six human figures, presumably ancestors. To be sure, Altar T and its imagery celebrated the first katun anniversary of Yax-Pac's accession, but the protagonist whose name sits under the nose of the crocodile is the half brother, Yahau-Chan-Ah-Bac himself.

A
FOREST
OF
KINGS

———

332

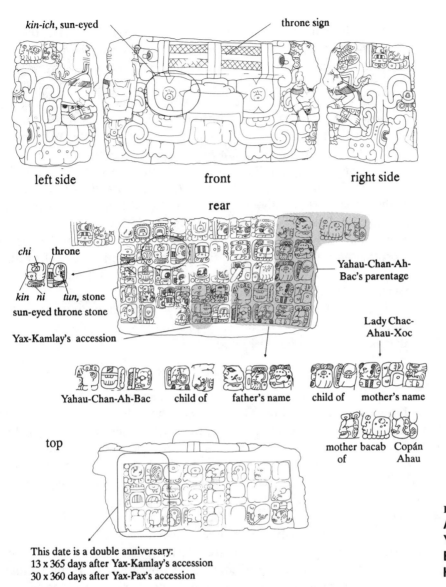

kin-ich, sun-eyed

throne sign

left side

front

right side

rear

chi throne

kin ni tun, stone
sun-eyed throne stone

Yax-Kamlay's accession

Yahau-Chan-Ah-Bac's parentage

Lady Chac-Ahau-Xoc

Yahau-Chan-Ah-Bac

child of

father's name

child of

mother's name

mother bacab of

Copán Ahau

top

This date is a double anniversary:
13 x 365 days after Yax-Kamlay's accession
30 x 360 days after Yax-Pax's accession

FIG. 8:19
Altar U and Yahau-Chan-Ah-Bac, the King's Half Brother

We know Yahau-Chan-Ah-Bac was the half brother of the king because his status as child of the king's mother was prominently inscribed on Altar U, a monument he himself raised (Fig. 8:19) in the town which once existed under the modern village. The "sun-eyed throne stone,"[66] as the Copanecs called it, depicts a sun-eyed monster flanked by two old gods who sit at the open Maw of the Otherworld. The inscriptions on the rear and top surface retrospectively document Yahau-Chan-Ah-Bac's participation in rituals on 9.18.2.5.17 3 Caban 0 Pop (January 25, 793) and the seating on January 29, 780, of yet another player on Copán's historical stage. Named Yax-Kamlay, this man, who may have been a younger full brother of the king, also played a crucial role in the last half of Yax-Pac's reign. The name Yax K'amlay means "First Steward"[67] so that this full

COPÁN:
THE DEATH
OF
FIRST DAWN
ON MACAW
MOUNTAIN
—
333

brother may have functioned in a role like "prime minister," while the half brother, Yahau-Chan-Ah-Bac, governed the district of the ancient city under the modern village area for the high king. This type of governance, rule by a council of brothers, ultimately failed in Copán, but it succeeded at Chichén Itzá, as we shall see in the next chapter.

The altar stone was dedicated on June 24, 792, a day near the summer solstice, but the text also records events later than this date. We surmise that the altar was commissioned as an object in anticipation of its function as a historical forum. The anticipated rituals occurred on the day 9.18.2.5.17 3 Caban 0 Pop (January 25, 793), a day that happily coincided with the thirtieth tun anniversary (30×360) of the king's accession and the thirteenth haab anniversary (13×365) of Yax-Kamlay's seating. Yahau-Chan-Ah-Bac, who dedicated the altar, honored both his kingly half brother and the man who was the king's first minister by celebrating this unusual co-anniversary. It was Yahau-Chan-Ah-Bac, however, who is clearly the protagonist of the inscription.

Let us stop for a moment and imagine what the king would have seen as he led a procession from the Acropolis to the village on the day these anniversaries were to be celebrated.

•

Yax-Pac paused on the causeway near the ancient tree-stone erected by his ancestor, Smoke-Imix-God K, when the valley had known happier times and lived in hope. He could see the visage of his ancestor etched by the shadows cast in the sharp morning light. The great te-tun displayed two faces—a proud human one facing the rising sun, and another masked with the image of the Sun God watching the ending of the days. Smoke-Imix was forever caught in his act of sacrifice, eternally materializing the sacred world for his people with the shedding of his blood.[68]

For a moment, Yax-Pac wondered what kind of immortality his forebear had won with the great tree-stone he had erected halfway between the Acropolis and the old community now governed by his younger half brother, the son of the royal woman from Palenque. He was grateful that the ancestors had provided him with such a capable sibling. The vigorous, optimistic Yahau-Chan-Ah-Bac strove to give him the labor and tribute necessary to keep the kingdom together in these hard times, and now he was overseeing the celebration of the thirtieth tun of reign. By coincidence, Yax-Pac's anniversary fell on the same day that ended the thirteenth haab of Yax-Kamlay's administration. They would commemorate the two anniversaries together.

Yax-Pac walked twenty paces ahead and paused again when he saw the smaller tree-stone[69] visible in the small compound to the west of the double portrait of his ancestor. This portrait of Smoke-Imix was less impressive in scale, but equally important, for it preserved the memory of the king as warrior, celebrating the half-period of Katun 12. On that day, Venus had stood still just after he had journeyed across the face of his brother, the Sun, to become Morningstar.[70] 18-Rabbit had made his debut as the heir on the occasion of that period ending. Who among the nobility remembered, or respected, such things nowadays? There was a coughing and shuffling of silent impatience in the halted entourage behind him. He ignored them.

As the low, long-shadowed light of the morning sun rose above the mountains rimming the far side of his lands and broke through the mist, Yax-Pac sighed and turned back to look across the valley. He gazed with pride on the Kan-Te-Na, Pat-Chan-Otot,[71] the house he had dedicated soon after the solar eclipse at the end of Katun 17. Silhouetted against the beams of brilliant yellow light,[72] it towered above the Acropolis, echoing the huge mountains that rose above the valley floor in the distance. The sacred mountains beyond the sacred portals built by the men of his dynasty were bare now, like bones drying in the sun. It was winter and those mountains should be green with growth from the fall rains, but all he saw was bone-white rock and the red slashes of landslides scarring the faces of the witzob. The stands of forest that had once graced the ridgetops were only memories now in the mind's eye of the very, very old. Even the occasional patches and scraggly survivors he had found in his childhood wanderings were gone—not a single sapling reared its silhouette against the blue sky.

Thirty tuns ago today he had followed his father, Smoke-Shell, onto the throne. Then he had been a young man who had not even seen the end of his first katun. He had harbored great hopes of a glorious and prosperous reign, but the gods and the ancestors seemed to be turning their backs on the people of the sacred Macaw Mountain.

Yax-Pac's eyes swept across the valley, catching an occasional glimmer of light from the distant waters of the river. Mostly he saw the white houses of his people—hundreds of them—filled with children, many of them sick and hungry. Smoke still rose from the kitchen fires, but Yax-Pac knew the young men had to walk many days now through wider and wider strips of barren land to find firewood. From time without beginning, the earth had yielded up her abundance—wood to cook the bountiful harvests of earlier generations and to make the plaster covering for the buildings and plazas commissioned by the ancestors. What was one to make of a world without trees? The earth itself was dying, and with it all must eventually die.

In the glory days of his grandfathers, his people had believed in the favor of the gods and in the endless cycles of wet and dry that gave rhythm to the passage of days and life to the earth. More and more children had been born, and more and more people had come from distant lands to live in his valley. The more there were, the more they needed fuel and lumber, and the more they cut the forest. The river ran red with the soil of the mountains, naked now, having given up their flesh to the hard storms of summer and the floods of the winter months. Always there was too much rain, or not enough. The hard rains washed away the earth and the rock below could no longer nourish the seeds of the sacred maize. Too much of the good land along the river was under the houses of the noble clans.

COPÁN:
THE DEATH
OF
FIRST DAWN
ON MACAW
MOUNTAIN

——

335

The farmers had been driven higher and higher up the stony mountainsides looking for land that could hold their crops. Some of them even had to tie ropes around their waists as they worked the nearly vertical walls of the mountainsides. Anywhere the hard rock cradled a shallow pocket of earth, they planted their seed and hoped the young sprouts of maize would find enough water and nourishment to lift their delicate leaves into the air.

Yax-Pac felt a shiver run up his back in the cold morning air. It was only thirty-five days after the winter solstice, but already it was clear that there had not been enough rain during the fall and winter. His people were facing another bad year, with too many mouths to feed with what little the earth yielded to the hard labor of his farmers. He knew in his heart that they must somehow bring back the forest, for it was the source of life. But what was he to do? His people were sick and dying already. They had to cut and burn the scraggly bush that patched his land like scabs to plant their crops or death would win its final battle with the people of the land of Yax-Kuk-Mo'. He saw no way out of this losing battle with the Lords of Death, except more prayer and sacrifices to the gods and the ancestors of the Otherworld. If they would only hear the cry of his people and touch the earth with the gift of gentle rain, perhaps the times of his fathers would return.

Yax-Pac's eyes traveled up again toward the impassive face of Smoke-Imix and he shivered once more. This was the face of his ancestor which turned toward the west and the death of the sun. Straightening his shoulders, Yax-Pac firmly dismissed all thoughts of doom from his mind and resumed his march toward the house of his brother. Today they would meet to celebrate the years of their reigns: Yax-Pac as the king would be together with his younger brothers and councillors, Yahau-Chan-Ah-Bac and Yax-Kamlay. Perhaps, in the quiet moments between their public performances in the rituals, he would have time to talk to the two men who shared the burden of rule with him. They all longed for the old days when there was plenty of everything and no end in sight for the glory of Copán. Maybe together they could get the ancestors to pay attention to the plight of the children of Yax-Kuk-Mo'. Pondering the past and his grim vision of the future, Yax-Pac resolved to harness the power and will of his people. While he lived in this world, all of his thoughts, the wisdom of his ancestors, the skill of his scribes and artisans, would be bent to the salvation of his people and his kingdom.

•

This remarkable co-anniversary and the two men who shared it with the king were also celebrated in the Acropolis at almost the same time. On 9.18.5.0.0 when Altar U was about to be completed, Yax-Pac set a small throne stone inside the back chamber of Temple 22a, the council house (*Popol Nah*) that had been erected next to 18-Rabbit's Temple 22 by his successor, Smoke-Monkey.[73] On the throne, he celebrated his own katun anniversary (which had been commemorated by Altar T and Stela 8 in the Village area), the co-anniversary he had shared with Yax-Kamlay,

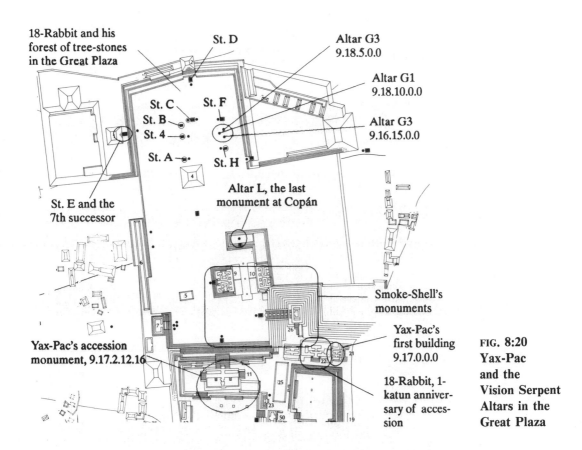

18-Rabbit and his forest of tree-stones in the Great Plaza

St. D

Altar G3
9.18.5.0.0

Altar G1
9.18.10.0.0

Altar G3
9.16.15.0.0

St. C
St. B
St. 4
St. A
St. F
St. H

Altar L, the last monument at Copán

St. E and the 7th successor

Smoke-Shell's monuments

Yax-Pac's first building
9.17.0.0.0

Yax-Pac's accession monument, 9.17.2.12.16

18-Rabbit, 1-katun anniversary of accession

FIG. 8:20
Yax-Pac and the Vision Serpent Altars in the Great Plaza

and finally the hotun ending. This final date he associated with Yahau-Chan-Ah-Bac so that all three of them appear prominently together. In the council house built by his grandfather in the dark years after 18-Rabbit's defeat, Yax-Pac celebrated his own council of siblings.[74]

The altars of Yahau-Chan-Ah-Bac and Yax-Kamlay signal Yax-Pac's radical intentions in his efforts to sustain the government, for these brothers must have stood as close to the status of co-regent as the orthodox rules of divine kingship could allow. Furthermore, the two altars Yax-Pac erected in the old village area constituted major historical and theological statements. Not only did the king and his half brother call upon Copán's best artists and scribes to execute their new vision of authority, but they communicated this vision in a style that was highly innovative, even in the expressive and daring tradition of Copán's artisans.[75] These large, dramatic, boulderlike altars were the first to combine glyphs and zoomorphic figures, and the first altar monuments to stand on their own without a stela to accompany them.

Yax-Pac shared his royal prerogatives with his brothers in response to the growing stress in the valley as social and economic conditions worsened. He also invited people of lesser status, such as the lords of Compounds 9M-18 and 9N-8 to share royal privilege by erecting monuments memorializing the king's participation in the dedications of their

COPÁN:
THE DEATH
OF
FIRST DAWN
ON MACAW
MOUNTAIN

—

337

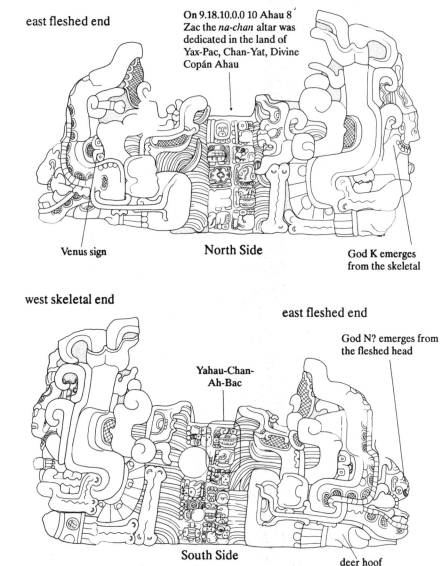

west skeletal end

east fleshed end

On 9.18.10.0.0 10 Ahau 8 Zac the *na-chan* altar was dedicated in the land of Yax-Pac, Chan-Yat, Divine Copán Ahau

Venus sign

North Side

God K emerges from the skeletal

west skeletal end

east fleshed end

God N? emerges from the fleshed head

Yahau-Chan-Ah-Bac

South Side

deer hoof

FIG. 8:21
Altar G1:
Yahau-Chan-
Ah-Bac in the
Great Plaza

houses. In this way, he broadened his power base. Perhaps the pressures were different, but Yax-Pac, like Bird-Jaguar of Yaxchilán, chose to share his power in order to conserve it. For a while, his strategy worked. In the end, however, the precedents of sharing central power with nonroyal patriarchs destroyed the divinity that had sustained the Copán kingship for more than seven hundred years.

As Copán declined, bits of her history slowly began to slip from the grasp of her people. Neither Yax-Pac nor his lords left any major monuments that celebrated the turning of the katun on 9.18.0.0.0. For reasons yet unknown, the next hotun, 9.18.5.0.0 (September 15, 795), saw a lot of activity. Yahau-Chan-Ah-Bac's Altar U, found in the town beneath the

Stela 11 was on the other side of this wall

a. View of Temple 18 from Temple 22

b. The dedication panels from the outer chamber of Temple 18

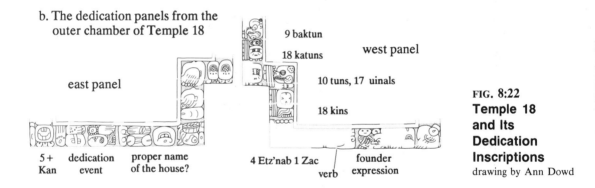

east panel

9 baktun

18 katuns

west panel

10 tuns, 17 uinals

18 kins

5 + dedication proper name
Kan event of the house?

4 Etz'nab 1 Zac founder
verb expression

FIG. 8:22
**Temple 18
and Its
Dedication
Inscriptions**
drawing by Ann Dowd

modern village, mentioned that period ending and it was celebrated in Temple 22a as we discussed above. Perhaps more important was Yax-Pac's return to the forest of tree-stones erected by 18-Rabbit in the Great Plaza. On the eastern side of this plaza, between Stelae F and H, he set another of the Vision Serpent altars (G2) next to the first monument (Altar G3) he had erected there just after he became the high king (Fig. 8:20).

Five years later on the half-period, 9.18.10.0.0, the third of these Vision Serpent monuments, Altar G1, was erected. With this monument in place, the triangular portal set in the middle of 18-Rabbit's tree-stone forest was completed. This altar, right in the ceremonial center of the city,

COPÁN:
THE DEATH
OF
FIRST DAWN
ON MACAW
MOUNTAIN
—

339

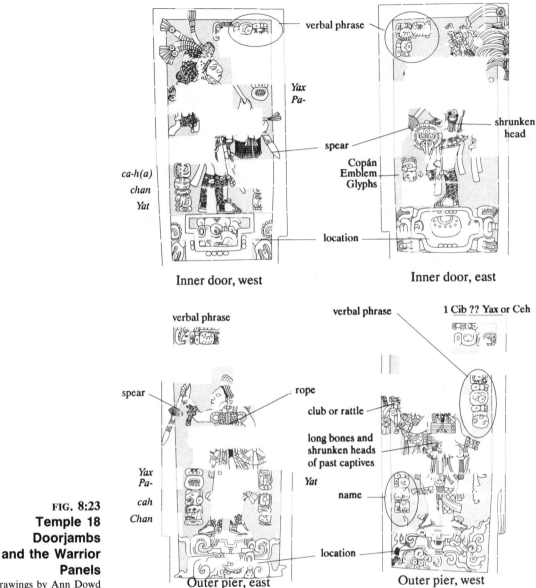

FIG. 8:23
**Temple 18
Doorjambs
and the Warrior
Panels**
drawings by Ann Dowd

also affirmed the political duality binding Yax-Pac to his half brother, Yahau-Chan-Ah-Bac. This superb sculpture, called the "*na-chan* altar" by the Copanecs, presented a double-headed image of the Cosmic Monster, skeletal at one end and fleshed at the other (Fig. 8:21). Each side of its body displayed a special text. On the north side, the dedication of the altar "in the land of Yax-Pac" was recorded; on the south, Yahau-Chan-Ah-Bac's name. The placement of this altar was highly significant. It was one thing for the half brother to get star billing in the town under the modern village, but entirely another for him to be featured in the sacred precinct in the center of the kingdom. The Acropolis and the Great Plaza had always been the sanctuary of the divine kings.

Yax-Pac's next project, Temple 18 (Fig. 8:22a), must have been under construction during the time of this same 9.18.10.0.0 period ending. This temple is the last building Yax-Pac ever built on the Acropolis, and its smaller scale is good evidence of the reduced assets available to the king less than twenty-five years after he dedicated his magnificent Otherworld portal in Temple 11. Set on the southeast corner of the Acropolis, directly across from Temple 22, this final royal sanctuary contained an elaborate vaulted tomb chamber that was looted in ancient times.[76]

Yax-Pac placed this building in one of the most potent points in the city, an area that had been the focus of his attention for thirty years. This temple completed a skewed southward triangle with Temples 21a and 22a, anchored on Temple 22, the sacred building housing the portal of his ancestor 18-Rabbit (Fig. 8:11). The inscription carved into the interior walls of the outer chamber of this temple recorded the date of its dedication as 9.18.10.17.18 4 Etz'nab 1 Zac (August 12, 801), the day of the zenith passage of the sun (Fig. 8:22b). The imagery carved on the jambs of the doors in the outer and the center walls is a radical departure from precedent at Copán and reflects the dark final days of its dynasty. Yax-Pac and a companion (most likely his half brother) wield spears and strut in the regalia of warriors (Fig. 8:23) at the place of the waterlily. They wear cotton armor, shrunken heads, ropes for binding captives, and the bones of past victims. Grasping shields and weapons, they are ready for battle with Copán's foes.

The symbolism on these two doors reflects a change in strategy in direct correspondence with the violent death throes of Copán. In this last building, Yax-Pac did not reiterate the cosmic sanction of his reign. Instead, he announced his success and prowess as a warrior. Although all Copán's kings had been warriors and sacrificial executioners, this choice of portraiture is unusual in Copán's history.

The Hieroglyphic Stairs built by Smoke-Shell emphasized the role of the ancestral kings as warriors, and this same Tlaloc-war iconography was prominently displayed on Temple 16 and Temple 21. Nevertheless, these were merely ancestral portraits or stage backdrops for rituals. Such rituals may have required wars to provide victims to send to the Otherworld in the tradition of Maya political life, but the Copanec tradition since the time of Yax-Kuk-Mo' had been to show the ruler standing in the portal of the Otherworld. It was his role as communicator with the ancestral dead and the materializer of the gods that preoccupied Copán royal portraiture.

In all of the city's long history, this is the only building on which the king is actually shown in battle, wielding the weapons of war.[77] We can only assume the role of king as active warrior became increasingly important to his public image as the crisis within his kingdom deepened. None of Yax-Pac's enemies are mentioned by name, but neighboring kingdoms may well have been making forays, or perhaps the non-Maya peoples who had always lived just beyond the borders decided to move against the failing kingdom. Copán may also have been suffering from internal political problems. The nobles who had ruled parts of the kingdom for the high

COPÁN:
THE DEATH
OF
FIRST DAWN
ON MACAW
MOUNTAIN

—

341

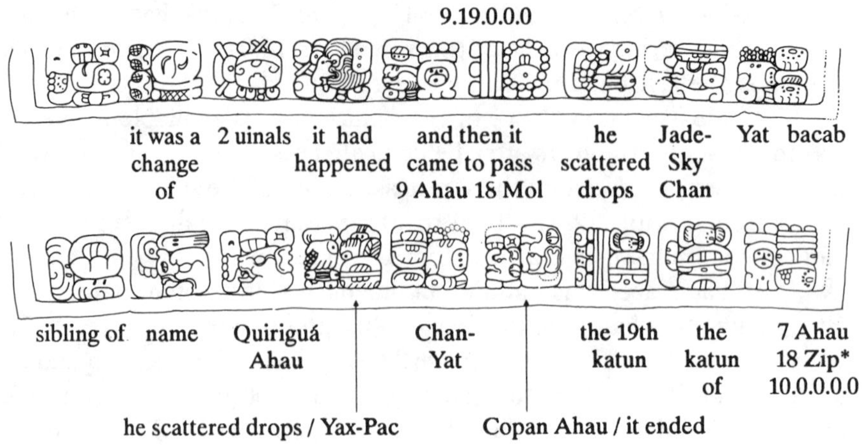

9.19.0.0.0

| it was a change of | 2 uinals | it had happened | and then it came to pass 9 Ahau 18 Mol | | he scattered drops | Jade-Sky Chan | Yat | bacab |

FIG. 8:24
Quiriguá Structure 1 and Yax-Pac's Scattering Rite
*Dots in the numbers are reconstructed

| sibling of | name | Quiriguá Ahau | | Chan-Yat | | the 19th katun | the katun of | 7 Ahau 18 Zip* 10.0.0.0.0 |

he scattered drops / Yax-Pac   Copan Ahau / it ended

king, especially in its expanded version, may have decided to strike out on their own. War apparently was the only means at Yax-Pac's disposal to fend off these challenges. Sadly, when authority fails, force is the last arbiter.

In spite of these upheavals, the machinery of the state ground on. Yax-Pac recorded the end of his second katun as king on 9.18.12.5.17 2 Caban 15 Pax (December 4, 802), on a beautifully carved stone incensario. This incensario is the only monument we have identified so far from the second half of that katun.[78] We do have one other record of Yax-Pac's activities from the end of this katun, albeit an unusual one. Yax-Pac paid a state visit to Copán's old rival, Quiriguá, in order to perform a scattering rite on 9.19.0.0.0 (June 28, 810) (Fig. 8:24). This visit was unusual on two counts. First of all, kings rarely traveled to neighboring kingdoms; they preferred to send ambassadors.[79] Second, this sort of scattering rite was usually performed at the homesite, not in another king's city. As far as we know, Yax-Pac did not perform a similar sacrificial ritual at Copán, although we know he was still ruling there, for his death was commemorated there some ten years later.

Yax-Pac died shortly before 9.19.10.0.0 (May 6, 820).[80] Although he had struggled valiantly to retain the loyalty and cooperation of the nobles in his valley, his strategy did not ultimately succeed. After seven hundred years, the central authority in the valley of Copán had less than a decade of life left.

Although we do not know the exact date of Yax-Pac's death, his survivors chose this half-period date (9.19.10.0.0) to commemorate his entry into the Otherworld. On that day they erected Stela 11 in the southwest corner of the platform supporting Temple 18 (Figs. 8:11 and 8:22), the last building he constructed. The imagery on this stela (Fig. 8:25) depicts Yax-Pac standing in the watery Otherworld holding the bar of office. In this instance, however, the bar is missing the serpent heads that symbolized the path of communication between the supernatural world and the human world.[81] Yax-Pac no longer needed them for he was already among the supernatural beings, a state marked by the smoking

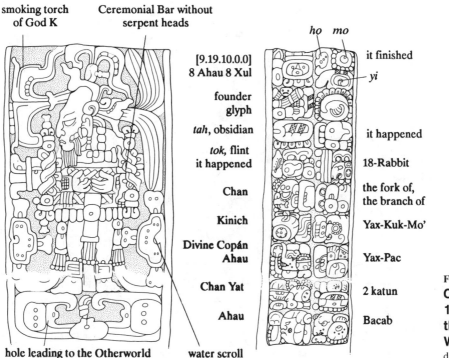

smoking torch of God K

Ceremonial Bar without serpent heads

[9.19.10.0.0]
8 Ahau 8 Xul

founder glyph

tah, obsidian

tok, flint
it happened

Chan

Kinich

Divine Copán
Ahau

Chan Yat

Ahau

hole leading to the Otherworld

water scroll

ho   mo

it finished

yi

it happened

18-Rabbit

the fork of,
the branch of

Yax-Kuk-Mo'

Yax-Pac

2 katun

Bacab

FIG. 8:25
**Copán Stela
11: Yax-Pac in
the Underwater
World of Xibalba**
drawing by B.W. Fash

torch piercing his forehead. In the Otherworld Yax-Pac was manifested as God K, the deity of kings and their lineages.[82]

The inscription on this strange rounded stela is enigmatic, but we have hints of its meaning. The verb is a phonetic spelling of *hom,* the verb we have already seen recording Tikal's war. Here, however, the word does not refer to the destruction of war, but rather to the other meaning of the verb, "to terminate" and "to end"—as, for example, "to end a katun." Following *hom* is the glyph that stands for "founder" or perhaps "lineage" or "dynasty" in other texts at Copán. Putting all this together, we understand this text to mean that the people of Copán believed the dynasty of Yax-Kuk-Mo' had ended with the death of Yax-Pac.[83]

Yax-Pac was not, however, the last king of Copán. Although his reign was a difficult one, he was fortunate in one respect. He lived long enough to gain a place in history, but died soon enough to avoid the final tragedy. The king who oversaw those last days of kingship at Copán was named U-Cit-Tok. His is perhaps the saddest story of all the Maya kings we have met, for he inherited a world that had already fallen apart. There were too many people, too much of the forest gone, too many nobles grabbing honor and power for their own benefit, too little faith in the old answers, too little rain, and too much death.

This tragic man became the new king on 9.19.11.14.5 3 Chicchan 3 Uo (February 10, 822),[84] a day that contained some of the old astronomical associations beloved by the Maya. It was the day of disappearance for the Morningstar and a time of conjunction between Mars and Jupiter, which were just visible in the hours before dawn. The accession rituals of

COPÁN:
THE DEATH
OF
FIRST DAWN
ON MACAW
MOUNTAIN

—

343

9.19.11.14.5 3 Chicchan 3 Uo, he was seated

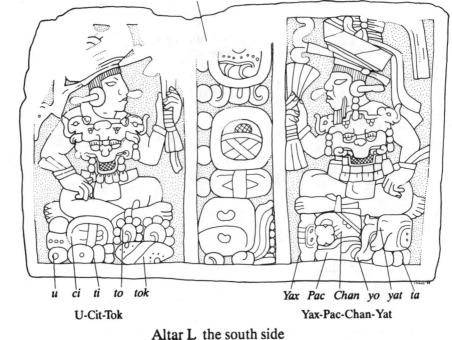

FIG. 8:26
U-Cit-Tok,
the Last King
of Copán

u   ci   ti   to   tok

U-Cit-Tok

Yax Pac Chan yo yat ta

Yax-Pac-Chan-Yat

Altar L the south side

that day were commemorated on an altar placed on the mound at the
north end of the Ballcourt (Fig. 8:11) near Stela 2, the old monument that
commemorated Smoke-Imix-God K and the earlier days of Copán's glory.

The south side of the altar (Fig. 8:26) depicts the new king seated
across from Yax-Pac in direct emulation of Altar Q, and in the tradition
pursued by Yahau-Chan-Ah-Bac on his monument. As on Altar Q, the
Calendar Round sits between the two kings, but U-Cit-Tok felt the need
to qualify its meaning even further by writing *chumwan,* "he was seated,"
after it.[85] On the left, in the same place occupied by Yax-Kuk-Mo' on
Altar Q, the new ruler sits on his own name glyph, holding out a fanlike
object toward his predecessor. On his opposite side, in the same position
he occupies on Altar Q, sits Yax-Pac. Perched on *his* name glyph, Yax-
Pac mirrors the position and clothing of his successor, passing on, by
analogy, the power and sanction of his divinity. It was not the younger
version of the king that U-Cit-Tok wished to evoke, but the divinity of the
mature and aged Yax-Pac. The pattern of Yax-Pac's beard emulates his
portrait on Stela 11, the image of his last and irreversible journey into
Xibalba.

The final hours of the kings of Copán are frozen in this amazing altar.
On the other side is a scene of two figures, seated profile to the viewer while
engaged in some sort of ritual (Fig. 8:27). We will never know what the
sculptor intended to depict here because the altar was never finished.[86] In
the middle of his cutting the imagery into the stone, the central authority
of Copán collapsed. The sculptor picked up his tools and went home,
never to return to his work on the altar. Copán's dynastic history ended

FIG. 8:27
Altar L, north side

with the echoing slap of that sculptor's sandals as he walked away from the king, the Acropolis, and a thousand years of history. The kings were no more, and with them went all that they had won.

The residential compounds beyond the Acropolis continued to function for another century or so. Some of the lineages even profited enough from the disintegration of central power to continue adding to their households. But without the central authority of the king to hold the community together, they lost it all. The lineages would not cooperate with each other without the king to reduce their competition and forge bonds of unity between them. Toward the end, one of the buildings in Compound 9N-8 collapsed onto an occupant, but his relatives never even bothered to dig him out. It was the final straw—the people simply walked away.[87] Within two centuries of the demise of the last king of Copán, 90 percent of the population in the Copán Valley system was gone.[88] They left a land so ravaged that only in this century have people returned to build the population back to the levels it knew in the time of Yax-Pac. Today, history is tragically replaying itself, as the people of Copán destroy their forests once more, revealing yet again the bones of the sacred witzob—but this time we are all threatened by the devastation.

COPÁN:
THE DEATH
OF
FIRST DAWN
ON MACAW
MOUNTAIN

—

345

9

KINGDOM
AND
EMPIRE AT
CHICHÉN ITZÁ

Maya kingdoms were dying as the tenth cycle of the baktun neared its end. The epidemic of political chaos spread a thousand miles across the base of the Yucatán Peninsula, from Palenque to Copán; and in the southern lowland country, few dynasties endured into the ninth century. Yet in the northern part of the peninsula, in the dry forest lands of the northeast, in the rugged hill country of the west, on the northwestern plain, and along the coasts, Maya states not only flourished during the Terminal Classic period, but grew in strength and numbers (Fig. 9:1).[1]

The cultures of these northern lowlands were distinctive from those in the south in several respects. The northerners, for example, developed architectural techniques using concrete wall cores surfaced with veneer block masonry.[2] They used this construction technique to render elaborate programs of political and religious imagery (Fig. 9:2) in complex stone mosaic facades and wall carvings. Further, the northern Maya developed a historical tradition of their own, distinct from the south's, collected in books called the Chilam Balam. In them, each community compiled and kept its own version of history, which, after the Spanish conquest, was transcribed from its original hieroglyphic form into an alphabetic system using Spanish letters to record

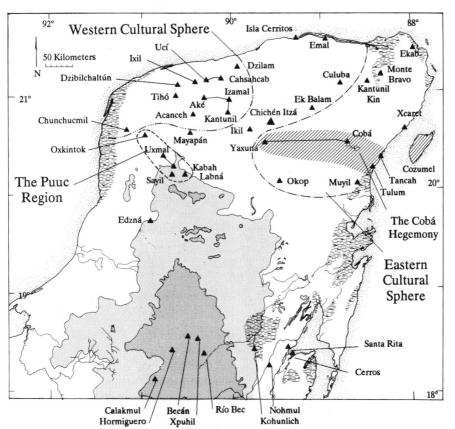

FIG. 9:1
The Yucatán
Peninsula and
the Northern
Lowlands
Contour intervals:
250, 500 feet

Mayan words.[3] The histories kept in these many books describe successive incursions of foreigners from outside Yucatán, some from as far away as central México. Because these Classic period societies of the northern lowlands had a significantly greater interaction with outsiders than the Maya in the south, they assimilated a greater amount of foreign culture. This interaction resulted in their developing a more international outlook in politics and trade.

In spite of its international tradition, the northern region merges into the southern lowlands without geographic interruption; and from the time of the earliest kingdoms, the Maya living in both regions were linked, linguistically, culturally, economically, and politically.[4] Although the destinies of southern and northern kings in the Terminal Classic period diverged, they ultimately shared a common root. Since the institution of ahau was at the heart of government in both regions, we must look at the distinctive ways the northerners modified its relationship to central leadership in order to understand how the northerners transcended the limitations that led to failure in the south.

The social catastrophe of the ninth century was the culmination of the gradual faltering of Maya kingship over a thousand years of history and many ingenious attempts to accommodate change. Yet in the end, this chain reaction of collapsing governments became the catalyst that pushed some of the peoples of the north toward a fundamental revision of the basic institution of ahau.

KINGDOM
AND
EMPIRE AT
CHICHÉN
ITZÁ
—
347

Few of the Maya kingdoms were able to make the crucial transition from one form of government to another. The southern kingdoms of the Terminal Classic period tried, but their leaders failed because they attempted to solve their burgeoning social problems using methods that were fast becoming obsolete: the time-honored politics of the divine dynasties. The aggrandized kingdoms of such men as Great-Jaguar-Paw and Lord Kan II were never able to establish stable empires because they could not transcend the pride and exclusivity of the kingship—pride that compelled conquered dynasties to resist the acknowledgment of permanent subordination; exclusivity that prevented would-be emperors from effectively sharing power. On the other hand, some ahauob in the northern lowlands did succeed in perpetuating central government in this time of turmoil. Like the conqueror kings in the southern lowlands, the Itzá lords sought to break out of the limitations imposed by many small, competing realms. The way they accomplished this was to forge a conquest state and hegemonic empire with its capital, Chichén Itzá, in the center of the north. This city witnessed the birth of a social and political order based upon a new principle of governance, *mul tepal,* "joint rule."

For a few centuries, Chichén Itzá ruled the Maya of the north without rival. The ahauob of Chichén Itzá honored many of the religious and political protocols laid down by generations of kings before them. Yet, at the same time, they were revolutionizing the ancient royal institutions, creating new policies, rituals, and symbols partly inspired by foreign traditions. At the height of their power in the lowlands, they extended the boundaries of their military and economic interests—and their religious and political vision—to the point where all of Mesoamerica knew of Chichén Itzá, as either a valuable ally or a formidable enemy.

Our last royal history will recount the transformation of Chichén Itzá, its rise and triumph through foreign invasion and alliance—through

FIG. **9:3**
**The Castillo
Seen from the
Front of the
Temple of the
Warriors**
photo by Justin Kerr

war on an unprecedented scale, diplomacy, and brilliant political innovation. It is also the story of the Itzá's opponents in this struggle: the orthodox Maya ahauob of Cobá and the innovative and international ahauob of the Puuc hills region. In their conflicts with Chichén Itzá, these powers endured and lost the closest thing to a world war the northern Maya would experience before the coming of the European conquerors.[5]

At the northern apex of the ancient city of the Itzá, the Castillo rises into the clear air above the dry forest that stretches away into the distance across the flat plain (Fig. 9:3) of central Yucatán. This structure is a mute but eloquent testimony to the engineering elegance and revolutionary vision of a city that, in its heyday, stretched for at least twenty-five square kilometers[6] beyond its wide central plazas (Fig. 9:4). Here at the heart of the community, the vision is a silent one. Unlike the kings of the south, the last divine lords of Chichén Itzá chose not to use hieroglyphic texts on their stelae and buildings to proclaim their histories and triumphs. Instead, these rulers pursued a magnificent architectural program of bas-reliefs carved on piers, walls, pillars, and lintels. The decision to tell their story in pictures unencumbered by the written word was a deliberate one, for these cosmopolitan Maya had changed the institution of ahau and the kingship derived from it.

Archaeology and the carved-stone inscriptions found in other parts of the city also give testimony to this transformation. These two sets of evidence, however, tell two quite different, though ultimately related, versions of Chichén Itzá's history.[7] During the Late Classic period, while the southern lowland kingdoms flourished, new cities came to prominence in the range of low hills called the Puuc in the northwestern part of the peninsula.[8] While divine ahauob ruled these cities,[9] the culture of their people shows strong ties to the Gulf Coast region and highland México. These ties can be seen in features of architectural decoration and ceramic

KINGDOM
AND
EMPIRE AT
CHICHÉN
ITZÁ

—

349

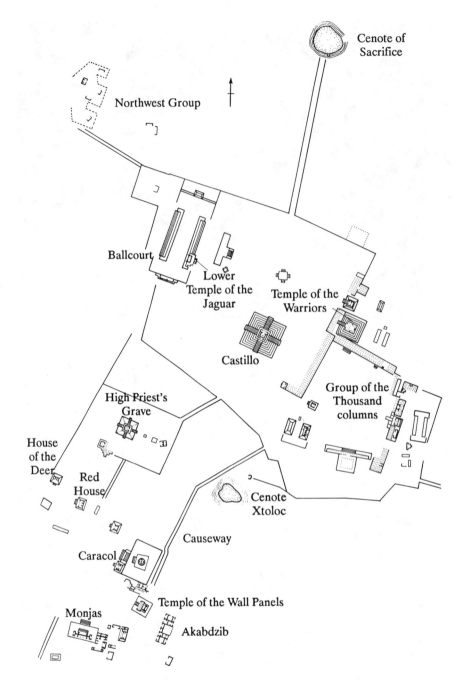

Cenote of
Sacrifice

Northwest Group

Ballcourt

Lower
Temple of the
Jaguar

Temple of the
Warriors

Castillo

High Priest's
Grave

Group of the
Thousand
columns

House
of the
Deer

Red
House

Cenote
Xtoloc

Causeway

Caracol

Temple of the Wall Panels

Monjas

Akabdzib

FIG. 9:4
Map of
Chichén Itzá
after Kilmartin
1924

styles. One group of foreigners, called by archaeologists the "Putún" or "Chontal" Maya,[10] traded with the Puuc communities during the Late Classic period, and heavily influenced their culture. Indeed, the elite of the Puuc region may well have regarded themselves not only as ethnically Putún, but also as the political inheritors of the great traditions of the southern Classic period kingdoms. Described as crude barbarians by the Yucatecan Maya in some of their later books, these Chontal speakers were probably no more barbarian than the Germanic generals who, by diplomacy and force, took over Roman provinces in the waning years of that civilization.

While the Puuc hills in the west nurtured a prosperous and cosmopolitan constellation of new cities, the eastern region witnessed the establishment of a huge Late Classic state with its capital at Cobá. With more than seventy square kilometers of homes, temples, house-lot walls, and stone causeways, Cobá was undoubtedly the largest city in the northern region of Maya country.[11] Beyond its teeming multitudes and towering pyramids, Cobá reached out for the agricultural produce and human labor of the surrounding towns. These communities were physically linked to the great city by stone roads that helped to reinforce the alliances and obligations between the noble families of vassals and the ahauob in the center.[12] In contrast to the Maya of the Puuc cities, the people of Cobá and their kings sustained strong cultural ties to the southern kingdoms. The style of their great pyramids reflected Petén traditions and their divine lords raised tree-stones with extensive, and unfortunately badly eroded, hieroglyphic texts. Like the ahauob of Palenque and Copán, the nobility of Cobá apparently regarded themselves as frontier stalwarts of a great Maya tradition with its heart in the southern lowlands.

Archaeological research documents that, soon after the consolidation of these distinctive western and eastern kingdoms in the northern lowlands by the end of the eighth century, a series of strategic coastal strongholds was established by canoe seafaring peoples. These people were called the Itzá by archaeologists, after references to them in Books of Chilam Balam.[13] These coastal Itzá used pottery styles which would become characteristic of Chichén Itzá, and they brought with them foreign goods, such as Mexican obsidian, both black and green.[14] Eventually, these merchant warriors founded a permanent port facility on an island off the northern coast, at the mouth of the Río Lagartos, where they could command a rich trade in the sea salt prized in México and elsewhere. Called Isla Cerritos,[15] this small island was literally transformed by artificial construction into a single round and massive platform with masonry docking along its entire periphery for the large dugout canoes used by these peoples.

At some juncture in their expansion along the coastal areas, the Itzá moved inland to establish a new state in the north. Although the Chilam Balam books claim the Itzá incursions came from the direction of Cozumel Island and the east coast of the peninsula, the archaeological evidence suggests they came directly inland from their outposts along the coast. It is hardly accidental that their final major capital at Chichén Itzá was established in the center of the northern plain, directly south of their port at Isla Cerritos. That central zone, however, was already a frontier between the state of Cobá to the east and the Puuc cities to the west and south. The Itzá marched provocatively into a region that was already occupied by formidable kingdoms. It is clear that they intended to stay. The first step in their plan was the conquest of Izamal, a kingdom that boasted one of the largest and most famous pyramids in the north.[16] Once they had overcome Izamal, the Itzá armies kept right on going. They

KINGDOM
AND
EMPIRE AT
CHICHÉN
ITZÁ

—

351

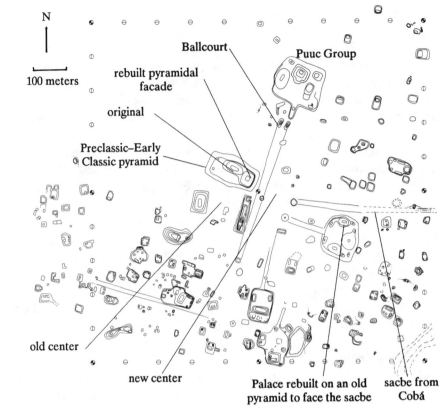

N

100 meters

Ballcourt

Puuc Group

rebuilt pyramidal
facade

original

Preclassic–Early
Classic pyramid

**FIG. 9:5
Yaxuná and
Terminal Classic
Modifications**

old center

new center

Palace rebuilt on an old
pyramid to face the sacbe

sacbe from
Cobá

aimed for a border city between Cobá and the Puuc, an ancient center
known as Yaxuná (or Cetelac, as some call it).

The massive pyramids of Yaxuná had been raised by kings in the
Preclassic and Classic periods and were the largest such structures in the
central northern lowlands. Following a decline in the Late Classic period,
Yaxuná experienced a resurgence of both population and prestige in the
Terminal Classic. At the time of the Itzá incursions, Yaxuná was probably
a sizable town, marking the boundary between Cobá's sphere of influence
and the Puuc cities to the west. In this flat land without rivers, there were
only two clear geographic markers: the deep natural wells, called *cenotes,*
and the sacred mountains raised by ancestral peoples. Both were used by
the northern Maya to stake out political centers and frontiers. Yaxuná had
large ancient pyramids and the aura of power and legitimacy such places
contain. It also had a great natural well. Both of these landmarks made
it the logical choice for a border city.

The Itzá could not take Yaxuná immediately because the king of
Cobá and the rulers of the Puuc cities claimed it as their own. By dint of
diplomacy or force of arms, these two kingdoms initially repelled the
invaders' advance, thus forcing the Itzá to chose another nearby sacred
spot for their new capital. The Itzá established their new city at a another
cenote that would come to be known as *Chichén Itzá,* "the Well of the
Itzá." This site was located twenty kilometers to the north of Yaxuná.

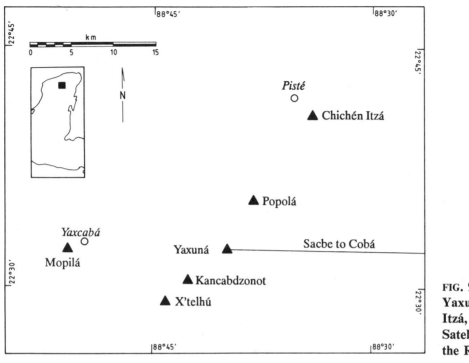

FIG. 9:6
Yaxuná, Chichén
Itzá, and the
Satellite Sites of
the Region

This first confrontation was but the opening round in a grim war for control of the northern part of the peninsula. Responding to the new intruders, the king of Cobá commissioned the construction of the most ambitious political monument ever raised by the Maya: a stone road one hundred kilometers long, linking the center of Cobá to the ancient center of Yaxuná. Townsmen and villagers living along the route of this sacred causeway quarried three quarters of a million cubic meters of rock from the earth for its construction. They filled the masonry walls and packed down tons of white marl on the road's surface, using huge stone rolling pins. This road declared Cobá to be master of a territorial domain covering at least four thousand square kilometers, nearly twice the size of the southern lowland kingdom of Tikal at its height.[17]

At Yaxuná, the arrival of the masonry road triggered a frenzy of building activity on the foundations of the ancient ruins (Fig. 9:5). Early Classic buildings were quarried to provide building blocks for the new temples and palaces that rose at the edges of the broad plaza area where the Cobá road ended. Masons removed the rubble and stone from the sides of the Preclassic Acropolis and piled it up again into a pyramid twenty-five meters high, facing eastward toward Cobá. To this conglomerate of old and new, the Yaxuná people added a ballcourt and its associated temples and platforms. We know that the Puuc cities also had their part in the rebuilding of Yaxuná because the style of the new buildings emulated the Puuc tradition, rather than that of Cobá.

Surrounding this new seat of authority, the inhabitants founded a perimeter of smaller communities, one almost exactly midway between

KINGDOM
AND
EMPIRE AT
CHICHÉN
ITZÁ

———

353

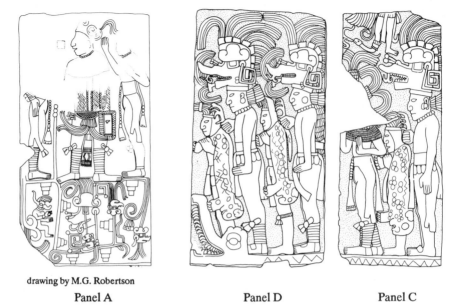

drawing by M.G. Robertson

Panel A   Panel D   Panel C

Yaxuná and Chichén Itzá (Fig. 9:6). To decorate their small palaces, artisans of these towns carved stone bas-reliefs displaying the warriors of the polity taking captives (Figs. 9:7 and 9:8). They also displayed bas-reliefs of the accession of their lords, including one who acceded to the rank of *cah,* a variant of the *cahal* status of nobles in the southern lowland kingdoms (Fig. 9:9).

Ultimately, however, the efforts of the Puuc cities and Cobá to remain in power in the center of the northern lowlands failed. After many years of bitter fighting, Chichén Itzá's armies won the battle on the fields of Yaxuná. The rebuilding of that city ended almost as soon as it had begun. Quarried blocks of stone lay strewn at the base of ancient platforms, abandoned in hasty retreat before the masons could use them. The occupants of the perimeter communities likewise fled, leaving their little decorated palaces unattended and their homes to fall into ruin.

We cannot say how long this war lasted, but its final outcome is certain. The war reliefs of Yaxuná[18] were cast down from their buildings to be rediscovered a millennium later by archaeologists (Fig. 9:10). The inhabitants of Chichén Itzá, by contrast, went on to expand their city, adding many ambitiously conceived buildings dedicated to their triumph and glory. The cities of the Puuc region and the great capital of the northwestern plain, Dzibilchaltún,[19] likewise collapsed as political capitals. As Chichén Itzá prospered, these rival kingdoms were eventually abandoned. The final occupation of Uxmal also shows the presence of the pottery styles of Chichén Itzá.[20] Cobá may not have been abandoned in the wake of this catastrophe, but it experienced a slow, steady decline in public construction.[21]

The archaeology of Chichén Itzá itself yields an enigmatic and controversial picture of these events.[22] Traditionally, archaeologists regarded the city as having had two major occupations: an earlier "Maya" commu-

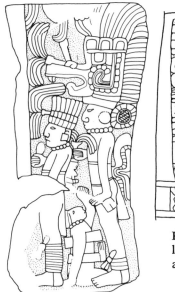

Panel from Mopilá showing a seated lord dressed as a deity and named as a cahal

Panel from Popolá showing lords and a supplicating captive

Panel from Yaxuná showing a lord dancing on a Waterlily Monster

FIG. 9:8   **FIG. 9:9**   **FIG. 9:10**

nity with Puuc-style temples and palaces, including dedicatory lintels with hieroglyphic texts; and a later "Toltec" or foreign community established by Mexican conquerors and their Maya allies. In reality, Chichén Itzá shows evidence of having always been a single city occupied by a remarkable, increasingly cosmopolitan nobility. This nobility manipulated diverse political expressions in their public art—some Maya, some Mexican—but all aimed at reinforcing and consolidating their authority.

This revised vision of Chichén Itzá as a single, unified culture is based upon a realization that the pottery style of the "Toltec" city was at least partly contemporary with the pottery style of the Puuc and "Maya" Chichén. It is also based upon recognition that the settlement organization of the city is unitary: A network of stone roads links principal groups into a whole. Finally, although the artistic style of the "Toltec" part of the city is distinctive, this style also utilizes Maya hieroglyphic texts.[23] The royal patrons of this "Toltec" complex in the northern section of Chichén Itzá may have favored murals and sculpture over texts, but they were not illiterate foreigners. They were true Maya citizens.

What the archaeology of Chichén Itzá does suggest is that several generations of rulers built public architecture and sculpture to commemorate their increasing success in war and trade. As the ahauob of Chichén Itzá worked to forge a conquest state that incorporated the territories of their enemies, the political statements they commissioned departed more and more from the prototypes they had inherited from the southern kings. These kings abandoned narrative portraits with inscribed texts in favor of assemblies of portraits carved on pillars in the great colonnades or en-

KINGDOM
AND
EMPIRE AT
CHICHÉN
ITZÁ

——

355

graved on the interior walls of their temples. Throughout this book we have shown how changes in the strategies of public art reflect improvisations in the institution of ahau. In the case of the Itzá, these changes were designed to legitimize not only conquest but also consolidation. We have seen such improvisation before in the case of Early Classic Tikal, but here the strategy is more comprehensive, reaching into the very essence of the institution of ahau itself—namely its focus upon the lineal connection between males of descending generations.

The political organization of Chichén Itzá, as conveyed in its hieroglyphic texts, was revolutionary even before the initiation of the nonglyphic public art programs. This innovativeness is particularly evident in the treatment of family relationships between ahauob,[24] as we shall see shortly. The nobles of this city shared extraordinary privileges with their rulers. The texts of Chichén Itzá are scattered throughout the city in places traditionally reserved for the use of kings: on the stone lintels spanning the doorways of public buildings; on the jambs of these doorways; on freestanding piers in doorways, an architectural fashion of the Terminal Classic period; and on friezes decorating the interiors of these buildings.

The written history of Chichén Itzá covers a remarkably short span for a city of such importance. The dates associated with these texts are all clustered within the second katun of the tenth baktun. The earliest clear date at the site, July 2, A.D. 867, is inscribed on a monument that was found lying on the ground. This monument, known as the Watering Trough Lintel, has a deep corn-grinding-metate surface cut into it. Recently, the intriguing question has arisen that an inscription on a temple called the High Priest's Grave,[25] traditionally regarded as the latest date at the site (10.8.10.11.0 2 Ahau 18 Mol, or May 13, A.D. 998) might actually have been carved much earlier. We suggest instead that this date fell on 10.0.12.8.0 (June 20, 842) and is thus the earliest date in the city. This alternative makes better sense in light of the tight clustering of the other inscribed dates found within the city. The date inscribed on the High Priest's Grave is only one of several texts, including several undeciphered historical ones, on the temple. Hence it clearly falls into the phase of public literacy in the city.

At the same time, the High Priest's Temple is architecturally a prototype of the four-sided Castillo with the famous serpent sculptures on its stairways.[26] The Castillo is the focal point of the later northern center only a few meters to the north and east of it. The imagery within the High Priest's Temple, including a bound noble on a column and a serpent-entwined individual over the inner dais, clearly anticipates the iconography of buildings in the great northern center such as the Temple of the Chac Mool and the Temple of the Warriors. This earlier placement of the High Priest's Grave would tie the "Toltec" northern center to the "Maya" southern center architecturally and spatially. If confirmed, it would also make the original implementations of the "Toltec" iconographic and architectural styles which lack inscriptions completely contemporary with the "Maya" styles found with the dedicatory monuments throughout the southern districts of the city.

The restricted distribution of dates at Chichén Itzá is commensurate with the intent of the texts, for they do not delineate a dynastic history like those we encountered in the southern kingdoms. The inscriptions of the southern cities focused on the commemoration of major events in the lives of kings and their significant others, often tying these events to major conjunctions in the cycles of time. The focus of attention in the Chichén Itzá texts is upon rituals of dedication carried out by *groups* of lords. The historical information given consists not of personal history but of dates, names, and the relationships among the actors who participated in these rituals.

The Temple of the Four Lintels is one of three Puuc-style buildings containing inscribed monuments in a group that terminates the main north-south *sacbe,* or roadway, of the city (Fig. 9:11). The assemblage of lintels from this building illustrates the general rhetoric of these inscriptions. The name of the principal protagonist is listed, along with the date of the inscription and the action being commemorated. This information is followed by a statement of his relationship to a second person. This second person may then be qualified as the agent of yet another ritual in the overall process of dedication. Finally, in a couplet structure, there is a reiteration of the dedication by the principal individual, followed by a listing of two more individuals who are said to be related to one another. The date of this particular dedication, July 13, A.D. 881, is thrice recorded on the lintels of this temple.

This focus upon dedicatory rituals and their participants leaves us with only a brief and enigmatic history of the important people of Chichén Itzá. We are not told when these people were born or when they acceded, warred, or died as we were in the southern kingdoms. We do, however, have some glimmering of the kinds of rituals being carried out. In the Four Lintels texts, there are references to the drilling action which creates new fire[27] and several of the individuals named carry a "fire" title. Furthermore, two of these lintels carry images on them which, when found in other scenes at Chichén Itzá, pertain to sacrifice. The most prominent images are the bird which claws open the chests of victims to extract the heart and the serpent which rises above the sacrifice.[28]

The Casa Colorada is a sizable temple south of the main city center and next to the sacbe leading to the southern group containing the Temple of the Four Lintels. Here, a hieroglyphic frieze records a series of events that took place on two different dates, 10.2.0.1.9 6 Muluc 12 Mac (September 15, 869),[29] and 10.2.0.15.3 7 Akbal 1 Ch'en (June 16, 870). Again, we see the names of several different lords listed along with the ritual actions they performed on these days. We find recorded, among others, a "fish-in-hand" bloodletting ritual and the ceremonial drilling activity associated with the creation of fire (Fig. 9:12). Here, as in the case of the Four Lintels texts, the emphasis is again upon a series of individuals who are named as agents of different actions.

KINGDOM
AND
EMPIRE AT
CHICHÉN
ITZÁ

—

357

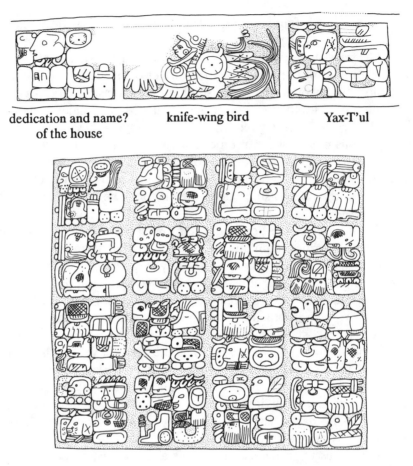

dedication and name?   knife-wing bird   Yax-T'ul
of the house

FIG. 9:11
Lintel 1 of the
Temple of
the Four Lintels
drawing by
Ruth Krochock

The bridge between the textual programs and the purely artistic programs in the city can be found on the carved doorway column in Structure 6E1[30] (Fig. 9:13). In this one instance, the artist wrote out the names of the individuals glyphically, but rendered their actions in portraits. On the doorway column of this building, we see four striding figures. One of them carries a handful of throwing-stick darts and a severed human head. The others carry axes of the kind used in decapitation sacrifice[31] and knives used in heart-extraction rituals at Chichén Itzá.[32] Here then we have a group of titled individuals[33] who are participants in, or witnesses of, a death sacrifice. Another glyphic inscription is found in the nearby Temple of the Hieroglyphic Jambs (Structure 6E3). This temple is associated with a particular kind of elite residence called a Patio Quad structure,[34] which finds its most spectacular expression in the Mercado, a colonnaded palace in the main northern center. In the past this Patio Quad type of house has been attributed to the "Toltec-Chichén Itzá," illiterate foreigners living within the city. The presence of these traditional Maya-style glyphs on a building which is clearly the household shrine of this group, however, is but one more example that the "Maya" and "Toltec" styles existed simultaneously in time, as part of one unified culture.[35]

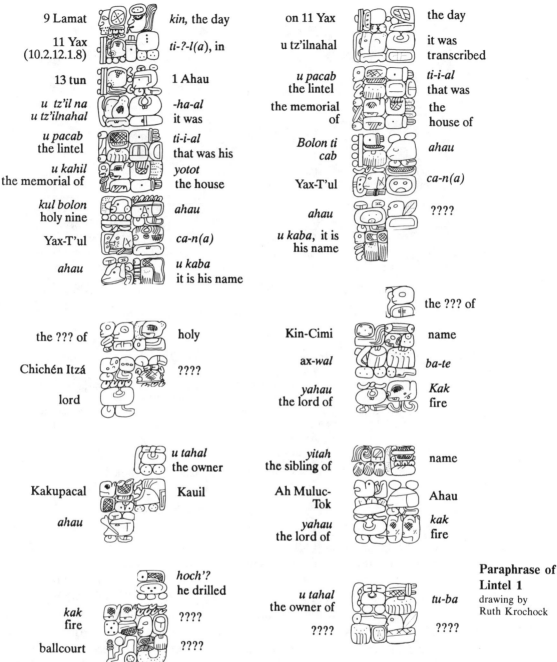

9 Lamat	*kin,* the day	on 11 Yax	the day
11 Yax (10.2.12.1.8)	*ti-?-l(a),* in	*u tz'ilnahal*	it was transcribed
13 tun	1 Ahau	*u pacab* the lintel	*ti-i-al* that was
u tz'il na u tz'ilnahal	*-ha-al* it was	the memorial of	the house of
u pacab the lintel	*ti-i-al* that was his	*Bolon ti cab*	*ahau*
u kahil the memorial of	*yotot* the house	Yax-T'ul	*ca-n(a)*
kul bolon holy nine	*ahau*	*ahau*	????
Yax-T'ul	*ca-n(a)*	*u kaba,* it is his name	
ahau	*u kaba* it is his name		

			the ??? of
the ??? of	holy	Kin-Cimi	name
Chichén Itzá	????	ax-*wal*	ba-*te*
lord		*yahau* the lord of	*Kak* fire

	u tahal the owner	*yitah* the sibling of	name
Kakupacal	Kauil	Ah Muluc-Tok	Ahau
ahau		*yahau* the lord of	*kak* fire

	hoch'? he drilled		
kak fire	????	*u tahal* the owner of	*tu-ba*
ballcourt	????	????	????

Paraphrase of Lintel 1
drawing by Ruth Krochock

Any overview of the monumental art of Chichén Itzá raises nearly as many questions as it answers. Who were these mysterious lords who did not care to celebrate their births, accessions, and triumphs as Maya rulers had done before them? This is a matter which is not easily resolved. First of all, the actual number of historical individuals recorded in the texts is still a point of controversy. Those people we *can* identify with relative certainty are listed in Figure 9:14. Second, sorting out the kin relationships at Chichén is a perplexing task. The relationships we are sure

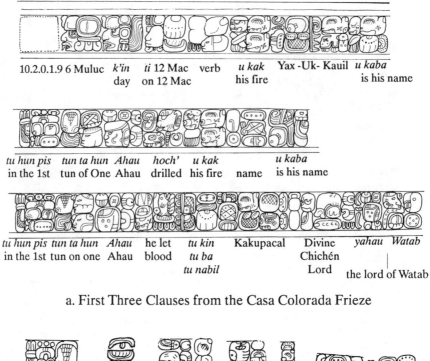

a. First Three Clauses from the Casa Colorada Frieze

| 10.2.0.1.9 6 Muluc | *k'in* day | *ti* 12 Mac on 12 Mac | verb | *u kak* his fire | Yax -Uk- Kauil | *u kaba* is his name |

| *tu hun pis* in the 1st | *tun ta hun* tun of One | *Ahau* Ahau | *hoch'* drilled | *u kak* his fire | name | *u kaba* is his name |

| *tu hun pis* in the 1st | *tun ta hun* tun on one | *Ahau* Ahau | he let blood | *tu kin tu ba tu nabil* | Kakupacal | Divine Chichén Lord | *yahau* Watab the lord of Watab |

| *tu yox pis tun* in the 3rd year | *u caban* it is the territory of | Divine Chichén Lords | *Kinich Hun-Pic- Tok* | *Kul Cocom* | *yahau* Jawbone the noble of Jawbone |

FIG. 9:12   b. The Last Clause from the Casa Colorada Frieze

of are given in Figure 9:15. The connections here are between women of ascending generation and their progeny, as expressed in the glyphic expressions "mother of" and "child of mother."

At the most, these glyphs tell us that there were two, perhaps three, generations of women who were mother, grandmother, and possibly great-grandmother to the major group of men named as "siblings" in these texts. The kinship ties among these five men can be determined in the following ways: (1) Two of them, Kakupacal and Kin-Cimi, are the children of the same mother, and (2) four of them are named in the kind of *yitah,* or "sibling," relationship we have seen recorded at Caracol and Tikal. Kin-Cimi, Ah-Muluc-Tok, Wacaw, and Double-Jawbone are all named in this "sibling" group. Since Kakupacal and Kin-Cimi share the same mother, Kakupacal can also be added to this group of brothers.

We have seen siblings before in the royal histories of the Maya, but not in sets of five. Moreover, although there are many more discoveries to be made in these texts, as of now there is no clear evidence that any one of these individuals was superior in rank to any of the others. All carry such noble titles as ahau and *yahau kak,* "lord of fire," but there is no single individual whom we can identify with certainty as king. This situa-

tion is exacerbated by the presence of at least one, and perhaps two, more such sibling sets in these texts, as shown in Figure 9:14. While there may eventually be evidence to suggest generational relationships among the groups, for the present there are no clear father-son relationships in any surviving record from Chichén Itzá. The dates of the texts in question cover a span of time which is relatively brief by Maya standards, and the texts imply contemporaneous actions by these people. The native chronicles of the Itzá declare that Chichén Itzá was ruled by brothers in its heyday[36]—and a brotherhood of princes is exactly what we see emerging from the ancient texts.

There are precedents for the sharing of power between a Maya king and his key relatives. Smoking-Frog and Curl-Snout of Tikal ruled their expanded domain together. Yax-Pac of Copán had co-regents of a sort in his brothers. Bird-Jaguar of Yaxchilán elevated his cahalob, his noble kin, and his supporters to stand beside him on the royal monuments of the realm. Of course, the king had always been an ahau, like many of the nobles around him. The dissolution of the kingship into a council of nobles, however, was still a fundamentally new and revolutionary definition of power and government for a people who had acknowledged sacred kings for a thousand years.

At the time of the Spanish Conquest, the Maya had a word for this kind of government: *multepal,* joint or confederate government.[37] It was a multepal that ruled Mayapán, the last regional capital of the northern Maya, which was established after the fall of Chichén Itzá, during the Late Postclassic period (A.D. 1200–1450) and just before the Spanish conquest.[38] Within the Mayapán government, there was a particularly powerful family, the Cocom, whose patriarch was generally regarded as the

**KINGDOM
AND
EMPIRE AT
CHICHÉN
ITZÁ**

—

361

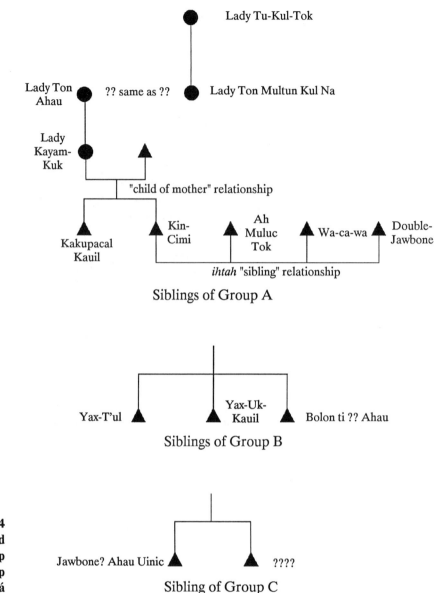

Lady Tu-Kul-Tok

Lady Ton Ahau ?? same as ?? Lady Ton Multun Kul Na

Lady Kayam-Kuk

"child of mother" relationship

Kakupacal Kauil   Kin-Cimi   Ah Muluc Tok   Wa-ca-wa   Double-Jawbone

ihtah "sibling" relationship

Siblings of Group A

Yax-T'ul   Yax-Uk-Kauil   Bolon ti ?? Ahau

Siblings of Group B

Jawbone? Ahau Uinic   ????

Sibling of Group C

"first among equals." There was also a rival political faction, the Xiu, whose family patriarch was high priest of the cult of Kukulcan and carried the title of Ah Kin Mai, Priest of the Cycle. Neither of these leaders, however, could successfully claim to rule their constituents in the manner that the Classic period southern kings did. We are convinced that the present textual evidence at Chichén Itzá points to an earlier and precedent-setting multepal as the institution of government in that city.

The Cocom family of the Conquest period claimed to be the descendants of the ancient rulers of Chichén Itzá. According to legend, the Cocom returned to the territory of the city of the sacred well after the fall of Mayapán in A.D. 1450.[39] Chichén Itzá texts from the end of the Classic period provide some support for their claim to be the former rulers of that city. In the text of the Casa Colorada frieze discussed above, Yax-Uk-

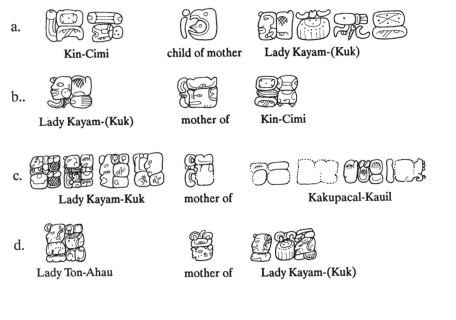

a.
Kin-Cimi   child of mother   Lady Kayam-(Kuk)

b..
Lady Kayam-(Kuk)   mother of   Kin-Cimi

c.
Lady Kayam-Kuk   mother of   Kakupacal-Kauil

d.
Lady Ton-Ahau   mother of   Lady Kayam-(Kuk)

FIG. 9:15
Kinship Phrases
from Chichén
Itzá

(a) Temple of the 3 Lintels, Lintel 3; (b) Temple of the One Lintel;
(c) Monjas, Lintel 3; (d) Monjas, Lintel 3a

Kauil, Kakupacal, and other notables are associated with Hun-Pik-Tok, who is called "Divine Cocom, the ahau (vassal) of Jawbone-Fan" (Fig. 9:12).[40] The name Hun-Pik-Tok also appears on the lintel from the Akab Tzib, where he is again named the vassal of the "Divine Cocom" overlord, Jawbone-Fan. The ancient pedigree of the Cocoms is thus confirmed by their appearance in the inscriptions of Kakupacal and his siblings in the early history of Chichén Itzá.

Since neither Hun-Pik-Tok nor Jawbone-Fan is tied to any of the sibling sets, we have no way of knowing what kin relationship they may have had with Kakupacal and his siblings. Hun-Pik-Tok, moreover, does not get the amount of historical attention we have seen on the monuments of other Maya kings. Instead, he is, at most, an antecedent presence to the sibling sets, either providing them with some form of legitimacy or acting as their ally. Nevertheless, we can assume from all of this evidence that the multepal form of government probably did not originate at Mayapán, as some have believed, but in Chichén Itzá itself.

We also know that Chichén Itzá, like the more orthodox Maya kingdoms, also used an Emblem Glyph, which can be loosely translated as "divine Chichén Itzá lord."[41] The main phrase of the Chichén Itzá Emblem Glyph is comprised of male genitalia and a *le* sign. Male genitalia are one of the most ancient and venerable of titles taken by kings, and probably connote the concept of "progenitor."

The Emblem Glyph was widely used in the names of Chichén's leaders: Several members of the sibling sets used the Emblem Glyph as a title. This "male-genitalia" glyph even occurs as part of the name of the oldest female appearing on the monuments. In the name of this woman,

KINGDOM
AND
EMPIRE AT
CHICHÉN
ITZÁ

———

363

the grandmother of the five brothers, the glyph probably simply connoted the simple idea of an ancestress. In the southern kingdoms, contemporaries of the ruler could also refer to themselves with the Emblem Glyph title. In those cases, however, there was never any ambiguity as to which of these lords was the high king and which were in positions of subordination. The ambiguous nature of the hierarchical labels at Chichén is just one more piece of evidence supporting the concept of confederate rule.

The texts we have surveyed so far give us only a glimpse of Chichén Itzá's rich and complex-history. To examine the culture and political structure further, we must turn to the richer and more extensive political statements found in the imagery on its public art. Here we find a marked thematic contrast to the art of the southern lowland Maya kingdoms, particularly those of the Late Classic period. Chichén Itzá's many carved panels, pillars, piers, lintels, sculptures, and murals do not celebrate the king, but rather groups of people, particularly in processional arrangements.

One of the most spectacular of these stone assemblies is the gallery of notables carved on the squared columns of the Northwest Colonnade and the Temple of the Warriors (Fig. 9:16). The Northwest Colonnade is a spacious, beam-and-mortar roofed building found at the base of the raised pyramid crowned by the Temple of the Warriors. The gallery of notables is, literally, a frozen procession representing 221-plus striding men. These stone figures frame the processional route which leads to the temple stairway (Fig. 9:17).[42]

For the most part, the individuals portrayed are warriors, as the name of the building complex implies. The majority are armed with spearthrowers, although some carry bunched spears and others clubs studded with ax blades. There is also a depiction of another defensive

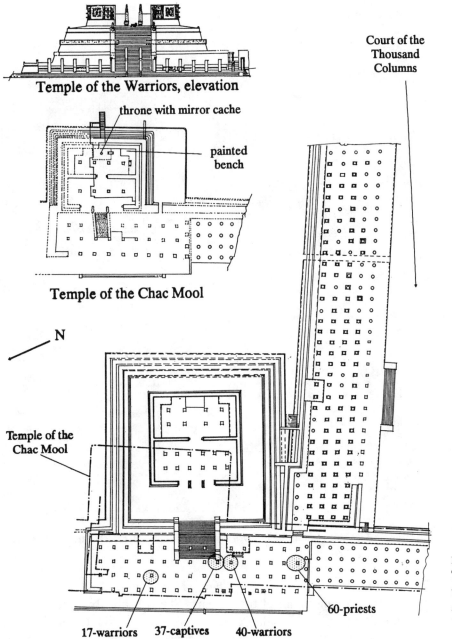

Temple of the Warriors, elevation

throne with mirror cache

painted
bench

Court of the
Thousand
Columns

Temple of the Chac Mool

N

Temple of the
Chac Mool

17-warriors   37-captives   40-warriors

60-priests

FIG. 9:17
Temple of
the Warriors
after Marquina
1950

KINGDOM
AND
EMPIRE AT
CHICHÉN
ITZÁ
———
365

weapon, a curved stick evidently used to parry spears hurled by enemies.[43] These weapons are associated with the Tlaloc-warfare complex which we saw operating among southern lowland kingdoms. In the art of Chichén Itzá, however, there are abundant and explicit depictions of the actual waging of war with such weapons. Some of the warriors in the procession are clearly veterans, proudly displaying their amputated limbs. Each is an individual portrait, differing in details from the others (Fig. 9:18). In addition to the warriors, there are other important people. Some have been identified as sorcerers or priests by the regalia they wear and the fact that

a. Column 17: Warriors

b. Column 40: Warriors

FIG. 9:18
Temple of the
Warriors: Sample
Columns from
the Colonnade
after Morris,
Charlot,
and Morris 1931

c. Column 37: Captives with bound wrists

d. Column 60: Priests carrying offerings

they are not armed (Fig. 9:18d). There is also one intimidating old matriarch striding among all of these men.[44] She is probably either the matriarch of the principal sodality or a representative of the Moon Goddess Ix-Chel, also known as Lady Rainbow, consort of the high god Itzamna and the patroness of weaving, childbirth, sorcery, and medicine. This figure echoes images from elsewhere in the city and we find her as well in the Temple of the Jaguars across the great platform from the Temple of the Warriors.

In the center of the procession, on the columns in front of the stairway leading upward to the sacrificial stone, the Chac Mool, there is an assembly of prisoners. This group of bound captives confirms the essential intent of the overall composition—to celebrate victory in war. Despite the brilliant and innovative architectural framework, the political message here is the same as the one we have seen throughout our earlier histories—

capture and sacrifice of rival lords by the powerful. There is one significant difference, however. In the monumental art of the southern kingdoms, we have seen prisoners stripped, humiliated, and often mutilated. Here, the captives are dressed in rich regalia, in most respects the same kind of attire worn by the highest ranking of the victorious warriors surrounding them (Fig. 9:18c). Obviously, the Itzá preferred to absorb their enemies rather than destroy them.

Although the elite of Chichén Itzá clearly had ties to the non-Maya kingdoms of Mesoamerica, the winners celebrating here are as clearly "Maya" in their appearance as their victims. Let us pause now to imagine what a procession like this would have been like in the days when Chichén was entering into the era of its glory.

A bewhiskered, grizzled face swam before the eyes of the adolescent boy as the old steward shook him awake in the cold dampness of the colonnaded hall. It was still dark in the plaza in front of his family compound. Inside, the red-painted walls and heavy wooden rafters glinted in the flickering torchlight, festooned with stone-edged weapons and sparkling gear. Already the boy's elder kinsmen were dressed in their sleeveless jackets of embroidered cotton armor. Their golden-feathered, greenstone-studded helmets shone in the dim light. As the men engaged in animated conversation, the small blue birds, which hung like diadems from the front of their helmets, bobbed with the movements of their heads. They reminded the boy of the pretty little birds that swooped among the swarms of insects at half-light, devouring them by the thousands, like the Itzá overwhelming their enemies on the field. The men's green-feathered backshields were emblazoned with the fearful insignia of their family and their city. Schoolboys from the villages vied with one another to supply the long strips of cotton[45] with which the men strapped each other's arms and legs for war.

Laughter and casual conversation filled the boy's ears, and his belly growled as the scent of hot corn gruel laced with chocolate and chili filled his nostrils. He moved quickly to join the others. No battle today. Instead, they would march in victory to the great council hall of the lords.

Accompanied by the ancient shamans, his father emerged from the family shrine which sat on a steep platform across the plaza. The blood of last evening's sacrifices stained their long robes and matted their flowing hair. The boy's heart swelled with pride as he remembered the lords the men of his family had taken captive in the campaign of the hill towns. His older brother had told him how the shouts of victory had mingled with the screams of terror as the women of the vanquished had fled their burning homes.

If the sacrifices were finished, the boy knew it was getting late. As he dressed hastily, he could hear the defeated nobles in their finery being assembled by his siblings on the plaza before the great hall. The drums of his clan began sounding the march. Still straightening his helmet, the boy rushed down the stairs to join the procession as it moved off led by his father, their great captain.

Drumsong and the smoke of morning temple fires rose from the arcade of tall shade trees and fruit orchards lining the road. Dawn was just turning the sky pale-blue as the boy's clan reached the main thorough-fare, joining the other groups of warriors who were pouring in greater and greater numbers from the paths among the trees. Together, they headed northward on the great white limestone road. The jogging rhythm of the warriors surrounding him propelled the boy forward, even as he strained to catch a glimpse of the prisoner-kings of the enemy whom the high lords of the council paraded among them. The company marched the battle dance of the Itzá, a frightening, sinuous rush of warriors that carried death to all who opposed it. The massive red walls of the first house of the siblings loomed to the boy's right as the swelling ranks of the army emerged onto the plaza of the old center. Their arrival was punctuated by a roar of approval from the crowds lining every side.

The great captains danced forward, reenacting the capture of their enemies. Uttering his distinctive hawklike war cry, the boy's father grabbed a valorous ahau by the hair and pushed him off balance, stabbing his spear into the air. Up ahead, the procession slowed as the vast stream of men expanded out onto the broad avenue, flanked on one side by the Observatory and on the other by the Red House. Elbowing past the intent ranks of his clan and their provincial allies, the young boy maneuvered himself to the edge of the battle group. It was his responsibility, he reminded himself as the older men gave way, to stand at the exposed edge of his family's ranks, moving them at the signals from his father and his elder siblings.

Moving forward with the impetus of the men-at-arms, the boy passed the old Castillo, its sacred cave now sealed by the graves of seven great lords.[46] It loomed high above the far side of the parade. The new Castillo, still under construction, rose proudly before them, surrounded by a sea of city folk. As the crowd fell back cheering, the army writhed onto the blinding white plaza and danced across to the Great Ballcourt. Also unfinished, this structure was vast beyond all imagining, encompassing an awesome vision of victory and sacrifice at the heart of the mighty city. The sweet stench of death filled the boy's nostrils as he passed the huge skull rack before the Ballcourt. The hollow-eyed heads of defeated enemies glared back at him, sending a shiver down his spine as he contemplated their earthly remains mounted in row upon row on the tall wooden rack. The older trophies shone in the morning light with the creamy-white brillance of naked bone, while others taken more recently still bore the flesh and hair of their unfortunate owners. All hung as grim reminders of what the wargame would bring for some of the prisoners today.

At full strength now, the army swirled around the Castillo, gyrating to the reverberation of hundreds of great wooden drums and the wail of the conch trumpets. Thousands upon thousands of warriors arranged in long sinuous lines moved with the discipline of years of combat, pushing back the crowds to the edges of the plaza and up onto the flanks of the buildings. The prisoners moved in their midst, each one the ward of a great veteran. The boy's father signaled his son to shift his battle group into formation along the eastern side of the great northern plaza, joining the others of his province. In a moment the wargames would begin in earnest.

Vibrating with tension, the men faced a wide sea of their compatriots across the plaza. When the signal whistles and cries rose from their captains, they rushed forward to engage each other as they had engaged the enemy in the battle of the hills. The crowd roared encouragement. More warriors rushed forward in the melee to dampen the danger of accident. Circles opened in the crowd as brave enemies were freed from their bonds and given weapons with which to pantomime deadly combat with the Itzá's best heroes. Dart duels cut alleyways throughout the ranks as men moved out of the line of fire.[47] The dance of death progressed, parry and thrust, the groans of surprise at a sudden wound. Some Itzá would join their ancestors today if they were not alert.

In the midst of this melee, the boy saw his father squaring off against his highest-ranked prisoner, both armed with stabbing spears. The two men closed vigorously, wrestled, and then closed again. The lord fought well, but the boy's father was in better condition and soon had his prisoner down on the plaza with a spear under his chin. There was a pause. Suddenly the father raised up his enemy and gave him back his spear. He gazed into his face and then turned his back to him as he would to a sibling and trusted battle companion. The decision he offered his enemy was to die taking his captor with him. Such a death, however, would be a humiliating act of cowardice. Better by far to live as a younger sibling, a prince of the hated Itzá and their city of the new creation. The captive grasped his spear tightly and, for a moment, the boy thought his father's time had come. But then the captive's fingers slowly relaxed, his eyes dropped, and he fell into line behind his captor as the group came back together again and moved off toward the council house.[48] The boy felt a flush of pride. Not all of the lords would have taken such a chance, but he knew his father held his position in the high council by means of his courage as well as his wisdom.

The boy's battle party moved forward to the steps of the Temple of the Warriors, the council house of the Itzá nation. The ambassadors from distant allied cities in the western mountains were arrayed along the front of the halls with their piles of sumptuous gifts. Dressed in long skirts, the dreadful shamans of the city moved among them, waving their crooked staffs and billowing censers and muttering incantations against treachery. The lords of the council gathered on the steps with their highest-born prisoners, announcing the names of those who had joined the nation and those who had chosen to go to the Otherworld today. Those who chose death were honored with ritual celebration before being led through the lower hall and up the steps to the stone of sacrifice. There, as the sun stood high in the sky at midday, one after the other they received the gentle death, so called because no one ever made a sound when his heart was cut out. The great Vision Serpent rose in the clouds of incense surrounding their lifeless bodies.

KINGDOM
AND
EMPIRE AT
CHICHÉN
ITZÁ

—

369

South Bench: six of the fourteen figures carved on the side

Fragments of the North Bench: warriors seated on jaguar seats

The sacrifices continued through the afternoon, and the warriors, engaged in their games on the plaza, clustered like angry bees around a hive until the sun sank in bloody splendor. The boy amused himself with the games and wondered if he would ever get to sacrifice in the Great Ballcourt when it was finished by the master builders and masons of the defeated hill cities. Mostly, however, his thoughts were with his father, sitting in the council house plotting the future of the city. Now that there was peace in the land, the Itzá could look outward to the world beyond and the challenges it would bring.

•

The eternal stone rendering of this procession in the Temple of the Warriors depicts figures wearing three of the basic motifs of Tlaloc warfare we have seen in the southern lowlands (Fig. 9:18a): the Tlaloc mask, the year-sign headdress, and the clawed-bird warrior. In the temple above this procession, a second gathering of portraits was carved on twenty more columns. Here there are no prisoners, but only warriors and dignitaries. These figures, ranged along the back wall of the hall before the throne dais, embody some particularly fine expressions of this particular artistic program. Although these familiar images of warriors and important dignitaries frame the ritual space which the leader occupied, as we have come to expect in the lineage houses of the earliest Maya kingdoms, they are also different. This great procession of VIPs stands in place of the traditional Classic symbol of the domain—the carved portrait of the victorious king. The throne is still upheld by the customary small warrior figures, but at Chichén Itzá, the Maya did not attempt to record the personal identity of the man who sat there.

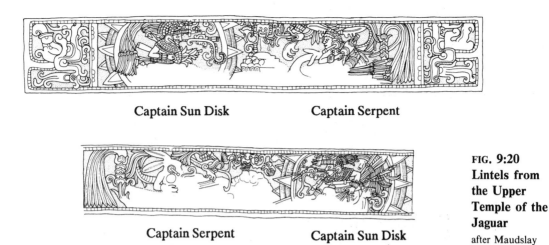

Captain Sun Disk   Captain Serpent

Captain Serpent   Captain Sun Disk

FIG. 9:20
Lintels from
the Upper
Temple of the
Jaguar
after Maudslay

The same principle holds true for the Temple of the Chac Mool, an earlier council house buried beneath the Temple of the Warriors. Above the benches that line the walls of this building's inner sanctum, brightly painted murals portray seated lords, wearing masks of the gods who ruled their cosmos. Seated upon jaguar-skin pillows, some of these lords extend offerings in flat bowls, while others sport shields and carry ax scepters with the bottom portion carved to represent the body of a snake. These scepters resemble the Manikin Scepters of royal office displayed in the southern lowlands (Fig. 9:19, south bench). Still other lords (Fig. 9:19, north bench) carry spearthrowers and throwing spears while they sit on thrones carved to represent full-bodied jaguars. This kind of jaguar throne, even more than the jaguar-skin pillow, was the furniture of rulers among the southern lowland peoples. Yet here we have not a single preeminent personage but whole assemblies of nobles seated upon this type of throne.

The message of this mural is clear. Once again, the throne is empty. What is being depicted with that empty throne is the historical *idea* of a central public persona in the city's government, not a real individual. Each of the surrounding figures is depicted in a distinctive manner. They are clearly meant to represent real people. The government of Chichén Itzá, in both its earlier manifestation in the Temple of the Chac Mool, and in its later and more splendid expression in the Temple of the Warriors, is pictured as an assembly, a multepal. What are we to make of the historical legends that claim Kukulcan ruled this city, or of the heroic captains such as Kakupacal and Hun-Pik-Tok of the Cocom, who are likewise mentioned? The answer to that question will have to wait on further archaeological evidence, for these figures certainly do not seem to be centrally focused upon in the public art.

The Great Ballcourt, directly across from the Temple of the Warriors complex, expands and complicates the political program. Here, in addition to an assembly of lords, we see other images of central importance. These figures are known as Captain Sun Disk and Captain Serpent (Fig. 9:20).[49] Captain Sun Disk carries a spearthrower and throwing spears and

KINGDOM
AND
EMPIRE AT
CHICHÉN
ITZÁ

—

371

warriors with spearthrowers

Captain
Sun Disk

Captain Serpent   warriors with spearthrowers

FIG. 9:21
Lower Temple
of the Jaguars:
The Upper
Registers
after Maudslay

sits inside a nimbus identified by its triangular protrusions as the sun. Captain Serpent also carries the weapons of war, but he sits entwined within the coils of a great feathered snake.

The importance of the individuals bearing these insignia is clear in the assembly compositions, such as the one found in the Lower Temple of the Jaguars (Fig. 9:21), where Captain Sun Disk looks down upon the upward-gazing Captain Serpent from his place on the central axis of the overall picture. But there are problems in attempting to identify these insignia as the regalia of real people. First of all, in the imagery of the Classic Maya, the nimbus means simply that the individual so portrayed is a revered ancestor.[50] Captain Sun Disk's position in the compositions of the Great Ballcourt is variable. In two of the main pictures, however—the one found in the North Temple at the apex of the playing court, and the one in the Lower Temple of the Jaguars across from the Temple of the Warriors—Sun Disk is at the top of the overall picture, the favored locality in Classic Maya art for dead predecessors. Second, the Serpent insignia is not confined to one individual, even on the Great Ballcourt scenes. In the Lower Temple of the Jaguars, for example, there are two Serpent Captains, one feathered and the other decorated with cloud scrolls.[51]

Two serpent captains within a composition could be interpreted as indications of the presence of particularly important individuals; but if we go back to the Temple of the Warriors, there are entire processions of serpent captains (Fig. 9:22). Therefore, we can only conclude that the insignia pertains not to an individual but to some important status. Even more significant is the fact that a serpent captain is also found among the prisoners arranged before the stairway of the Temple of the Warriors (Fig. 9:18). This status then is not even peculiar to Chichén's own elite.

It is a difficult task to discover individuals who stand out as unequivocal leaders in a program devoted to assembly. The sun-disk status is a real one, and perhaps it pertains to an individual ancestor, but the iconography

Detail of the four central figures flanking a tripod plate and offering. These and many of the other figures on the dais have serpents rearing behind them.

FIG. 9:22
West side of the
Dais in the
Temple of the
Warriors

of this image never shows Captain Sun Disk actively engaged in any of the scenes as a leader. The Serpent insignia is also important, but it too pertains to many people among the nobility at Chichén Itzá.

What can be derived with certainty from these public monuments is that the government of Chichén Itzá carried out successful campaigns of war against its enemies. The murals of the Upper Temple of the Jaguars (Fig. 9:23) are explicit illustrations of the kind of warfare actually fought with the spearthrower and throwing spear displayed in Tlaloc warfare throughout the Classic period in the southern lowlands. This battle scene, and others in the Temple, show that these wars were fought within the communities of the vanquished. Women are shown fleeing their homes as the battle rages around them. It was the kind of war that resulted in "the tearing down of vaults and buildings," or *hom* as it was written in the texts of Tikal and Caracol.

As always, the penalty of defeat was capture and sacrifice. Victims had their hearts torn out by warriors dressed in the guise of birds, while the great feathered serpent floated above them.[52] Others were shot with arrows or had their heads chopped off. Decapitation sacrifice was particularly associated with the ballgame, as displayed in the reliefs of the Great Ballcourt (Fig. 9:24), but it was also associated with fire ritual, as seen in mural paintings along the basal wall of the Temple of the Warriors. Like their cultural predecessors, however, the people of Chichén Itzá adhered to the ancient Maya notion of the ballgame as a metaphor for battle, and of the ballcourt (or its architectural surrogates in stairways and plazas)[53] as the primary setting for decapitation sacrifice. Indeed, the Great Ballcourt at Chichén Itzá was evidently constructed as a monument to the successful completion of the Itzá's wars of conquest.[54]

The volume of sacrifice at Chichén Itzá is grimly commemorated in the skull-rack platform[55] next to the Great Ballcourt. We have reason to suspect, however, that not all of the kings and nobles captured by Chichén Itzá ended up on the skull rack. The well-dressed prisoners paraded in the

KINGDOM
AND
EMPIRE AT
CHICHÉN
ITZÁ
—
373

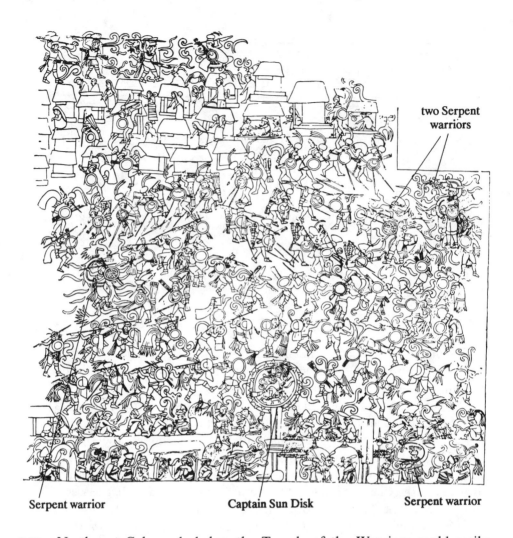

two Serpent
warriors

Serpent warrior   Captain Sun Disk   Serpent warrior

FIG. 9:23
Mural Painting
of a Battle from
the Upper
Temple of the
Jaguar
after Tozzer
1957

Northwest Colonnade below the Temple of the Warriors could easily blend in with the victors if freed from their bonds. There are also processing dignitaries in the Lower Temple of the Jaguar that bear a remarkable resemblance to lords of the Yaxuná area (Fig. 9:25). The message here is clear. In a government organized around the principle of confederation and assembly, the major political consequence of war need not be the defeat and humiliation of a rival dynasty. Instead, this dynasty might be incorporated into the expanding cosmopolitan state. In a city already housing numerous ahauob, there may well have been room for the vanquished.

  At its height, Chichén Itzá ruled supreme in the Maya lowlands. We do not know how far its elite extended their claims to dominion, but surely they prevailed over most of the northern lowlands. After the founding of their kingdom, the Puuc cities fell and Cobá slowly dwindled to insignificance. There were some hold-out polities in the southern lowlands, but these intrepid survivors of disaster provided no challenge to a city the size of Chichén Itzá and most likely attempted to negotiate an advantageous relationship with its government. How far beyond the lowlands Chichén Itzá's lords may have extended their domain is still an open question. During this period many fortified capitals of highland México—Cacaxtla,

A
FOREST
OF
KINGS

——

374

severed head   decapitated body with
snakes as spurting blood

**FIG. 9:24
Decapitation
Scene in the
Relief of the
Great Ballcourt**

Xochicalco, and Tula, to name but a few—show significant connections
to the Maya world. We suspect that in future investigations, more of
Chichén Itzá's Maya legacy will be found in the other cultures of México
that so astounded the Spaniards.

One idea that the Maya of Chichén Itzá did not pass on to their
Mesoamerican neighbors was divine kingship and its concomitant hieroglyphic literature. This does not, however, imply a paradox in our vision
of the last great burst of Maya social innovation. In order to perpetuate
the principle of kingship in this period of crisis, to expand it beyond the
limitations that caused its demise in the south, the Maya lords of Chichén
Itzá terminated the office of king and the principle of dynasty that had
generated it. We do not believe, as some have said, that the people of
Chichén Itzá were vigorous Mexican foreigners. Their leaders were Maya
ahauob as well as participants in the culture of Mesoamerica. Their enemies, at least among the Puuc cities, were similarly cosmopolitan. If
earlier Classic iconographic allusions are any guide, the Itzá were certainly not utilizing novel tactics in warfare. They were adhering to the
same four-hundred-year-old precepts of Classic Maya Tlaloc-Venus warfare we have already seen in the south.

The key to success for the Chichén Itzá lords lay in their redefinition
of the political consequences of defeat in war. They turned away from the
dynastic blood feuds of the past and moved toward effective alliance and
consolidation. This consolidation would become the guiding principle of
empire among the next great Mesoamerican civilization, the Culhua-
Mexica. At the core of this principle of alliance is the notion of *itah,*
"sibling" or "kinsman of the same generation." Two siblings perpetuated
the first Maya conquest state, that of Tikal and Uaxactún. It was this very
principle of brotherhood that Bird-Jaguar invoked in his manipulation of
his noble supporters. Even as the lords of the Puuc region desperately
fought to withstand Chichén Itzá, they began to declare *itah* relationships
among themselves.[56]

KINGDOM
AND
EMPIRE AT
CHICHÉN
ITZÁ

—

375

**FIG. 9:25
Warriors from
Chichén Itzá
and the
Yaxuná Region**

Warrior dressed as GI from the Lower
Temple of the Jaguars at Chichén Itzá

Warrior from Panel 1 at X'telhú

With Chichén Itzá, the first and last Mesoamerican capital among the Maya, we come full circle in the history of their kingship. The divine lords who emerged in the Late Preclassic period to dance upon their sculptured pyramids were first and foremost ahauob, members of a category of being that made them all essentially the same substance. They were siblings in a brotherhood that began with the Ancestral Twins and prevailed throughout all subsequent history. The reassertion of the idea of brotherhood marked the dismantling of that first principle undergirding kingship: dynasty. When the Ancestral Heroes, through the magic of sacrifice, killed one another and brought each other back to life in the Place of Ballgame Sacrifice in Xibalba, they became father and son to each other. So divine kings brought life out of death and were brought to life by the sacrifices of their fathers before them. The lords of Chichén Itzá did not celebrate dynasty, nor did they contemplate sacrifice as kings. They were brothers and ahauob together, as their ancestors were at the beginning of time.

THE END *OF A* LITERATE WORLD *AND ITS* LEGACY *TO THE* FUTURE

Naum-Pat, Halach Uinic ("true human"), felt the gentle waves of the dark, glittering sea lap against his feet as he watched the strange canoes bob against the stars. They were vast floating palaces really. Lit from within with lamps and torches, their tall masts and rigging graced the cool moonlight of Lady Ix-Chel.

"Mother of all," he whispered to himself, "where did these foul-smelling barbarians come from?"

He sighed in astonishment and worry. He had been a seaman all his life. Like his people a thousand years before him, he had plied the deep blue waters and treacherous shallows in great canoes, laden with honey, salt, slaves, chocolate—treasure of all kinds. He had fought enemies upon its rolling surface; he had ridden out the great storms that tormented its waters; he knew every port and people that graced its shores. The sea was his, world of his ancestors, great and dangerous and rich in precious, holy things. Now it had vomited up this monstrosity—a canoe that was a house. The light-skinned barbarians wielded great power, no doubt about it. A shiver ran up his spine. They would be worse and more dangerous than the Aztec *pochteca*—those dangerous merchants from the west who were extending the Mexica empire toward the ancient lands of the true people.

On the temple mountain yesterday, that old fool of a priest had addressed these new strangers as if they were gods. He had blown incense on them only a moment before they had pushed him aside and entered the sanctuary. After defiling and smashing the sacred images of the gods, they had opened the bundles and handled the holy objects of the ancestors, taking those made of sun-excrement—the yellow metal the foreigners coveted. Metal-lovers, these strange creatures wore helmets, armor, and great knives of the bright and hard substance. Wonderful stuff, he thought as he contemplated the price such objects would bring in the Mexica ports. He cursed the hairy strangers, calling upon the powers of the Otherworld to open the sea and consume them . . . and soon.

Worse than looting the temple—other pirates had done that—these men had raised up the World Tree in the form of a wooden cross. They had opened a book—small, black, and poorly painted, but still a book— and read from it in their unutterable tongue. The chilan, his city's prophet and interpreter for the gods, had watched from the crowd at the base of the temple, shaking his head in fear and wonder.

Naum-Pat shuddered with the horror of the memory of what the strangers had done. As he did so, the words of the famous prophecy of the Chilam Balam went through his mind.

"Let us exalt his sign on high, let us exalt it that we may gaze upon it today with the raised standard," the great prophet had exhorted them so many years ago. "Great is the discord that arises today. The First Tree of the World is restored; it is displayed to the world. This is the sign of Hunab-Ku on high. Worship it, Itzá. You shall worship today his sign on high. You shall worship it furthermore with true goodwill, and you shall worship the true god today, lord. You shall be converted to the word of Hunab-Ku, lord; it came from heaven."

Naum-Pat had watched in stunned disbelief as the strangers threw down the *kulche',* the images of the gods, in the Holy House, and put the wooden Tree in its place. A groan had escaped his throat as he saw the prophecy materialize before his eyes. They had put up the Yax-Cheel-Cab, the First Tree of the World. For the people it had been a very powerful sign. The local chilan had been disturbed enough to send word by courier canoe to the chilanob on the mainland.

Like the chilan, Naum-Pat had seen the raising of the Tree as a powerful portent, but somehow the strangers' black book had frightened him more. In all the world, only real human beings, only Maya, had books. Others, like the Mexica, had pictures of course, but not the written words of ancestors and heroes, not the prophecies of the star companions. Books were records of the past, they were the truth, the guide to the cycles. The strangers' metal knives were powerful weapons, but many weapons of the Maya could kill just as efficiently. It was the books that Naum-Pat feared, for with books came true knowledge, knowledge that could vanquish his people's present and capture and transform their future.

Naum-Pat could not imagine the strangers attacking his people on the neutral ground of Cozumel, Lady Ix-Chel's sacred isle. They had come ashore with smiles and gifts of clear stones that were like strangely-colored obsidian. He had planned a feast for them tomorrow in the council hall and would treat them distantly, yet with dignity. But what of the future? Was this the beginning of the time of discord and change the great chilanob had predicted? The fear in his belly whispered that it was so. As Naum-Pat turned his back to the quiet beach and headed home, his thoughts turned to his children.

·

In the Maya world, *its'at*, "one who is clever, ingenious, artistic, scientific, and knowledgeable," was used with the same respect and in the same contexts we use the word "scientist" today. That *its'at* also meant "artist" and "scribe" was no accident. For the Maya, as for ourselves, the written word held the key to their future survival. Writing was the power of knowledge made material and artifactual. It was the armature of wealth, prosperity, and the organized labor of the state. It was the wellspring from which flowed knowledge and lore, orally repeated and memorized by the common folk in their songs and prayers.[1] The arrival of the Spanish changed all that and subverted Maya literacy to the ambitions of the Europeans.

But the beginning of the end of literacy occurred centuries before the Conquest, with the Great Collapse of the southern lowland kingdoms in the ninth century A.D. As much time separates us from Columbus as separated Naum-Pat from the Classic kings. He and his proud people were still Maya, still civilized, and their elite were still able to read and write, but they lived in a dark age of petty lords and small temple mountains.[2] His age, like our own medieval period, was dimly lit by the flickering lamp of literacy and the collective memory of a great past; but his people's hope for future greatness was snuffed out by the Spanish conquerors. What brought down the awesome power crafted by the kings of our histories and made them, by the time the Spanish appeared, only a dim memory to their descendants?

The end of the Classic period witnessed a major transformation of the Maya world, one that would leave the southern lowlands a backwater for the rest of Mesoamerican history. Sometimes, as at Copán, the public record stopped dramatically, virtually in mid-sentence. Other kingdoms died in one last disastrous defeat as at Dos Pilas. For many, however, the end came when people turned their backs on the kings, as they had done at Cerros eight hundred years earlier, and returned to a less complicated way of living. Regardless of the manner in which the southern kingdoms met their doom, it is the staggering scope and range of their collapse that stymies us. This is the real mystery of the Maya and it is one that has long fascinated Mayanists and the public.[3]

We have no final answer to what happened, but as with all good mysteries, we have plenty of clues. At Copán, the last decades of the central government were those of the densest population. The voiceless remains of the dead, both commoner and noble alike, bear witness to malnutrition, sickness, infection, and a hard life indeed. In the central Petén, where raised fields played an important role in people's sustenance,

THE END
OF A
LITERATE
WORLD
AND ITS
LEGACY
TO THE
FUTURE

——

379

the agricultural system was productive only as long as the fields were maintained. Neglect of the fields during conditions of social strife, such as the growing military competition between Late Classic ruling lineages, likely led to their rapid erosion and decay.[4] Rebuilding these complex agricultural systems in the swamps was beyond the capabilities of individual farmers without the coordination provided by central governments, so they moved out as refugees into areas where they could farm—even if that meant jostling the people already there.

The collapse also came from a crisis of faith. The king held his power as the patriarch of the royal lineage and as the avatar of the gods and ancestors. Ecological and political disaster could be placed directly at his feet as proof of his failure to sustain his privileged communication with the gods. Moreover, because of the way the kings defined themselves and their power, the Maya never established enduring empires, an arrangement that would have created new possibilities of economic organization and resolved the strife that grew in ferocity and frequency during the eighth century. Kings could become conquerors, but they could never transcend the status of usurper, for they could never speak persuasively to the ancestors of the kings they had captured and slain. Each king wielded the written word and history to glorify his own ancestors and his own living people.

As time went on, the high kings were driven to unending, devastating wars of conquest and tribute extraction. In part they were urged on by the nobility. During the Early Classic period, this class comprised a relatively small proportion of the population, but even by the time of Burial 167 in the first century B.C. in Tikal, they were growing rapidly in both numbers and privilege. Averaging about ten centimeters taller than the rest of the population, they enjoyed the best food, the greatest portion of the wealth, and the best chance of having children who survived to adulthood. Since everyone born to a noble family could exercise elite prerogatives, it did not take too many centuries of prosperity for there to be an aristocracy of sufficient size to make itself a nuisance to governments and a burden to farmers. Increasing rivalry between nonroyal nobles and the central lords within the kingdoms appears to have contributed to the downfall of both.

The situation forced the gaze of the nobility outward toward neighboring kingdoms and the tribute they could win by military victory. In the short term, the strategy worked, but in the long term that kind of endemic warfare caused more problems than it solved and eventually the rivalry of the nobility helped rupture the central authority of the king.

Foreign relations were also troublesome at the end of the Classic Period. In the wake of the collapse of Teotihuacán in the late seventh century, other regional civilizations like El Tajín, Xochicalco, and Cacaxtla made a bid for power. Barbarians and marginally civilized peoples in the borderlands between the ancient great powers, like the Chontal Maya–speaking people living in the Tabasco coastlands, also asserted control of trade routes and established new states in both the highlands and lowlands. These merchant warriors, called the Putún, meddled in the affairs of Maya kingdoms and eventually established new hybrid dynasties that prospered at the expense of the traditional Maya governments.

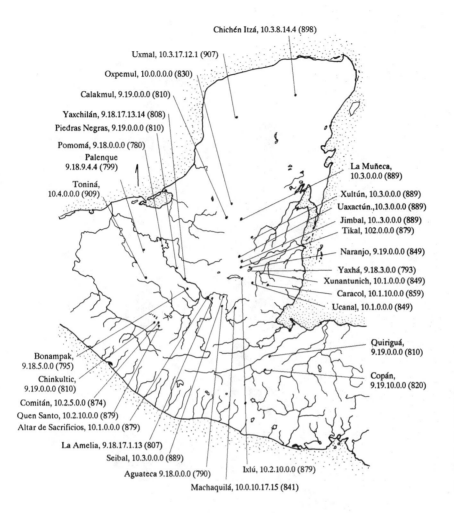

Chichén Itzá, 10.3.8.14.4 (898)

Uxmal, 10.3.17.12.1 (907)

Oxpemul, 10.0.0.0.0 (830)

Calakmul, 9.19.0.0.0 (810)

Yaxchilán, 9.18.17.13.14 (808)
Piedras Negras, 9.19.0.0.0 (810)

Pomomá, 9.18.0.0.0 (780)
Palenque
9.18.9.4.4 (799)

Toniná,
10.4.0.0.0 (909)

La Muñeca,
10.3.0.0.0 (889)

Xultún, 10.3.0.0.0 (889)
Uaxactún.,10.3.0.0.0 (889)
Jimbal, 10..3.0.0.0 (889)
Tikal, 102.0.0.0 (879)

Naranjo, 9.19.0.0.0 (849)

Yaxhá, 9.18.3.0.0 (793)
Xunantunich, 10.1.0.0.0 (849)
Caracol, 10.1.10.0.0 (859)

Ucanal, 10.1.0.0.0 (849)

Quiriguá,
9.19.0.0.0 (810)

Bonampak,
9.18.5.0.0 (795)

Chinkultic,
9.19.0.0.0 (810)

Copán,
9.19.10.0.0 (820)

Comitán, 10.2.5.0.0 (874)
Quen Santo, 10.2.10.0.0 (879)
Altar de Sacrificios, 10.1.0.0.0 (879)

La Amelia, 9.18.17.1.13 (807)
Seibal, 10.3.0.0.0 (889)
Aguateca 9.18.0.0.0 (790)

Ixlú, 10.2.10.0.0 (879)

Machaquilá, 10.0.10.17.15 (841)

**FIG. 10:1
The Last
Inscriptional
Dates Before the
Collapse of the
Classic Maya
Civilization**

The failure of the Maya way of life did not descend upon them with the dramatic suddenness of a volcanic explosion, a shattering earthquake, or a sweeping plague. The Maya had time to contemplate their disaster during the century it took for their way of life to disintegrate into a shadow of its former self. By A.D. 910, the Maya of the southern lowlands built no more temple-mountains to house their portals into the Otherworld and they erected no more tree-stones to commemorate the glory of their kings and cahalob. Throughout the lowlands, they abandoned literacy as part of the public performance of their kings (Fig. 10:1) and retreated from the society they had built under their leadership.

We have observed the sad end of the kings of Copán, but U-Cit-Tok was not alone in his suffering, nor was he the first to watch central government fall amid growing crisis. On the other side of the Maya world, at Palenque, the last words written in the historical record occur in a pitiful little inscription carved on a blackware vase. This vase was not even found in a royal context but in a slab-covered tomb under the floor of a

THE END
OF A
LITERATE
WORLD
AND ITS
LEGACY
TO THE
FUTURE

———

381

FIG. 10:2
Piedras Negras
Stela 12

modest residential compound below the escarpment where the great ceremonial precinct of the old glory days was located. The man who recorded
his accession in the text tried to enhance his renown by calling himself
6-Cimi-Ah-Nab-Pacal[5] after the great king who had brought Palenque to
glory one hundred and fifty years earlier. The vase, however, was made
in some obscure town on the swampy plain north of Palenque, and was
probably a barbarian Putún Maya gift to an otherwise silent king.[6] Within
fifty years of this date, Palenque had been abandoned and reoccupied by
wandering tribesmen who lived atop the debris in the disintegrating buildings, leaving broken fragments of ballgame yokes and *hachas* lying forlornly about. As at Copán, one of these wanderers was killed when the
north building of the Palace collapsed[7] and no one dug his body out to
give it honorable burial.

At Piedras Negras, a venerable and powerful kingdom on the Usumacinta River southeast of Palenque, the last king closed the history of his
domain on a glorious high note of artistic achievement. Stela 12 (Fig. 10:2)
is a masterpiece showing the ritual display of captives taken in a war with
the small kingdom of Pomoná[8] downriver on the Usumacinta, perhaps in

a ploy to stop people from the flourishing Putún homeland farther down-river from coming up into the territory of the ancient kingdoms. If this was the intention of the Piedras Negras lords, it did not work. The victory over those unfortunate Pomoná lords apparently did not contribute to the survival of Piedras Negras. Pomoná's last recorded date fell in the year A.D. 790, while the victor lasted only another twenty years. The last inscription at Piedras Negras celebrated the end of the nineteenth katun in A.D. 810.

This same twenty-year period saw the demise of Yaxchilán farther upriver on the Usumacinta. Like Palenque, Yaxchilán went out with a whimper rather than a bang, but as with Piedras Negras, the last inscription speaks of war. Bird-Jaguar's son Chel-Te had indeed lived to rule, testimony to his father's political success. Chel-Te, in his turn, sired a son whom he named after an illustrious ancestor—Ta-Skull, the tenth successor, who had made the alliance with Cu-Ix of Calakmul[9] in the sixth century. The last Ta-Skull, however, did not live up to the memory of his ancestor. He commissioned only a single lintel, mounted in a tiny little temple that he built next to the lineage house where Bird-Jaguar, his paternal grandfather, had given the flapstaff to Great-Skull-Zero, his grandmother's brother (Fig. 7:20). The all-glyphic lintel Ta-Skull set above the solitary door of this new temple celebrated his victory in war, but the victory must have been hollow one. Not only does the paltry scale of the building signal Yaxchilán's drastic decline, but its inscription was the work of a inept artisan. The glyphs started out large on the left and got smaller and smaller as the scribe ran out of room to the right. Like his liege, the writer had failed to plan ahead. He was not alone, for the kings of Bonampak and other smaller centers in the region fell silent at the same time.

Onward upstream at Dos Pilas in the Petexbatún region, the story was the same. During a final battle at the capital of the famous Flint-Sky-God K and his conqueror progeny, a desperate nobility threw up a huge log stockade[10] around the sacred center of their city, trying to shield themselves against the vengeance wreaked on them by their former victims. The kings who oversaw the last public history of that dying kingdom were forced to erect their tree-stones at other places than their capital. One Dos Pilas king recorded an image of himself in A.D. 790 on a stela at Aguateca at the southern end of his dynasty's conquered territories. On the northern frontier, the last-known Dos Pilas king struggled to retain control of the Pasión River. He raised two stelae at the little community of La Amelia, at the northeastern edge of his greater realm, on the Pasión River near its confluence with the Usumacinta. He also raised several tree-stones at the strategic site of Seibal. These last-known (Fig. 10:3a) images of a Dos Pilas king, elegant, dynamic, and confidently carved, show him valiantly playing ball. The recorded date is A.D. 807. Such play usually celebrated victory and sacrifice, in remembrance of what the Heroic Ancestors had won and sacrificed in the beginning. But we know in hindsight that the Lords of Death won this time. This man's kingdom probably ended in a violent cataclysm soon thereafter. Within a few years

THE END
OF A
LITERATE
WORLD
AND ITS
LEGACY
TO THE
FUTURE

—

383

a. La Amelia Stela 1   b. Chinkultic Stela 9

of the Dos Pilas ballplayer stelae, barbarian kings, probably from down-river, had taken Seibal, its prize vassal, and had effectively cut its trade routes to the Usumacinta River and the Petén.

The end of Katun 19 in A.D. 810 saw the last gasp of many kingdoms throughout the lowlands; 9.19.0.0.0 also marked the end of the royal history declared by two great dynasties in the central Petén heartland, the old rival kingdoms of Naranjo and Calakmul. Calakmul was the strongest of these realms, for its king was able to raise three stelae (15, 16, and 64) on that date. All three present him in front view, standing atop a captive and holding a shield and a God K scepter. Evidently this special show of power exhausted his fund of local support for public historical celebrations, for we don't hear from him again. For an indefinite time thereafter, kings without history (or at least, without texts discovered by archaeologists) must have ruled at Calakmul, for one holy lord of this capital did evidently witness a katun rite at Seibal thirty-nine years later. Indirectly then, we know that Calakmul still continued to exist, even after the end of its own known texts.

Naranjo's final historical ruler erected only one monument—Stela 32—but it was an extraordinary one. Unusually large, this tree-stone celebrates both the ruler's accession and the katun ending. Shown seated on a great cosmic throne, the king holds a Double-headed Serpent Bar drawn in an exaggerated style that seems to turn everything into flying scrolls.

Turning to the far southwest of the Maya world, we find what is perhaps the most interesting of these 9.19 stelae, a tree-stone erected at Chinkultic (Fig. 10:3b) in highland Chiapas. This carving bears stylistic affinities to the emerging art of the Puuc region in the northern lowlands and ultimately to Itzá monuments at Chichén Itzá.[11] Since dated monuments were not known in this part of Chiapas in earlier times, Chinkultic's appearance on the stage of history may reflect the beginning of a diaspora, a movement of literate Maya nobility from the lowlands into the highlands.[12] They might have been looking to a new political order as well as to a new land, their eyes turned to the Chontal-speaking Putún and the revolutionary state of Chichén Itzá.

Since the greatest part of Maya history took place during the four hundred years of the tenth baktun (9.0.0.0.0–10.0.0.0.0), one would think that the end of the cycle, with its promise of new beginnings, would have been celebrated with hope and enthusiasm by the Maya kings who survived to witness its completion. Ironically, the reverse is true. It was as if they all thought of it as a time of ill omen. Only the king of the resurgent Uaxactún dynasty and the ahau of Oxpemul, a little center north of Calakmul, celebrated the end of this great cycle.

Twelve years into the eleventh baktun, a captive event recorded on the High Priest's Grave establishes Itzá presence at Chichén Itzá on 10.0.12.8.0 (June 20, A.D. 842). The High Priest's Grave is a massive, four-sided pyramid with Feathered Vision Serpent balustrades. Like the Pyramid of the Sun at the great city of Teotihuacán, it was built over a cave to mark it as a place of "origin." The raising of the Temple of the High Priest's Grave with its captive iconography marked (Fig. 10:4a) the triumph of a new social and political order in the northern lowlands and a new era of barbarian, hybrid Maya states throughout the Maya world. Through the symbolism of the cave, it also declared the new state to derive from the same origin as the great states of earlier times.

Yet not all the new rulers chose revolution. Some attempted to build on the foundation of ancient Maya kingship. The earliest Chichén Itzá date is remarkably close to the last date (10.0.10.17.15; A.D. 841) at Machaquilá, a kingdom just west of the then-defunct Dos Pilas hegemony. That last Machaquilá king, One-Fish-in-Hand-Flint (Fig. 10:4b), depicted himself without the deformed forehead and step-cut hair that had been the ethnic markers of the Classic Maya elite. Either his people had abandoned the old style by then, or they were intruders who knew how to use Maya symbolism in the old orthodox ways. In light of contemporary events at neighboring Seibal, we think this lord was a Putún trying vainly to rekindle the ancient royal charisma at an old hearth of power. At Machaquilá, the ruler sided with the orthodox Petén ritualists, while at Seibal, as we shall see, the lords worked to create a new vision out of the tattered remains of the old kingship.

With the end of the first katun in the new cycle (10.1.0.0.0) came the last surge of historical kingship in the southern lowlands. On that date a lord raised a monument at Ucanal, the old border town between Naranjo and Caracol, and another lord celebrated at Xunantunich, a hilltop citadel

THE END
OF A
LITERATE
WORLD
AND ITS
LEGACY
TO THE
FUTURE

——

385

a. Chichén Itzá, High Priest's Grave
drawing by Peter Mathews

b. Machaquilá Stela 5
drawing by Ian Graham

FIG. 10:4

in Belize above the river trail leading eastward to the Caribbean coast. Ucanal's monument is particularly noteworthy because it is carved in a style that had grown to prominence in the region around Tikal late in Baktun 9. It shows the Ucanal ruler (Fig. 10:5) standing with one of his lords on top of a struggling, belly-down captive, scattering his blood in celebration of the katun ending. Above him, floating in a S-shaped scroll of blood, lies a Tlaloc warrior of the type who haunted Ucanal a hundred and fifty years earlier during the Naranjo wars. Together, the king and his colleague, who ruled other cities on the headwaters of the rivers emptying into the Caribbean, defined a new eastern frontier of the old royal territory. Beyond them to the east, in the rich river valleys of Belize, some communities survived and even flourished, but these Maya eschewed royal history.[13] To the south and west, other Putún, wise in the ways of the literate kings, raised stelae in chorus at Altar de Sacrificios on the Usumacinta and at Seibal on the Río Pasión.

The simultaneous expression of literate kingship at several surviving capitals reveals the different kinds of strategies their royalty chose in order to cope with changing times. While the Pasión was now the domain of Putún kings trying to forge new and more effective ritual formulae, the territory to the north of this river, the old heartland of Petén, belonged

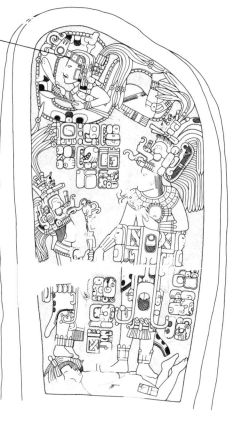

Tlaloc-warrior ancestor

FIG. 10:5
Ucanal Stela 3
drawing by Ian Graham

to conservative kings determined to stick to the old ways. These men were caught between the astute merchant warriors working their way along the rivers in the south, the rising Itzá hegemony in the north, and other barbarians who carried their commerce along the Caribbean coast and up the rivers of Belize. The world of the holy lords shrank back upon its Petén birthplace, its ancient capitals shattering into petty fiefdoms.

At Seibal, to celebrate the end of the first katun in the new baktun, a new king commissioned one of the greatest displays of creative artistry of the Late Classic period—the extraordinary Temple A3. That Seibal king, like One-Fish-in-Hand-Flint of Machaquilá, appears to have been a foreigner,[14] for he too wore his hair long and had the undeformed forehead of barbarian outsiders. Nevertheless, he knew the Classic Maya way and used it to create one of the most innovative statements of kingship in Maya history.

The new ruler, Ah-Bolon-Tun-Ta-Hun-Kin-Butz' (Ah-Bolon-Tun, for short), came to Seibal after the disappearance of its last Dos Pilas overlord. He took charge and revitalized Seibal enough to make it a major player in the politics of the time. To celebrate the end of the first katun of the new baktun, Ah-Bolon-Tun commissioned a temple with four stairways, each facing one of the cardinal directions. In this respect, he designed this temple to parallel the High Priest's Grave at Chichén Itzá.[15]

THE END
OF A
LITERATE
WORLD
AND ITS
LEGACY
TO THE
FUTURE

———

387

a. Seibal Stela 11

b. Seibal Stela 13
drawing by Ian Graham

In contrast to the one at Chichén, however, this building clearly declared the personal power of the king. Ah-Bolon-Tun decorated his temple with an elaborate polychrome and modeled stucco frieze displaying four larger-than-life portraits of himself over the doorways, each holding offerings and standing at his portals to the Otherworld. He also portrayed other people, perhaps the witnesses to his celebration, as well as monkeys, birds, and other animals—all in a great profusion of corn plants. The effect was no doubt quite spectacular, a world-renewal ceremony that all could admire and understand.

He placed one tree-stone inside the building and one at the bottom of each stairway to form the quincunx pattern so important to ancient Maya imagery. On the eastern tree-stone, he holds a staff and stretches his right hand out in the scattering gesture. On the northern tree-stone (Fig. 10:6a), he holds the Cosmic Monster as a ceremonial bar and records that three Ch'ul-Ahauob, one from Tikal, one from Calakmul, and one from Motul de San José witnessed the period-ending rites at Seibal.[16] This passage affirms that those three ancient capitals, or some local pretenders to their titles, were still active at this time and that the political landscape was stable enough to make royal visits worthwhile. The record of this gathering of holy Maya lords in the southern kingdoms shows that the conservative holdouts in Petén may have attempted to insulate themselves from change, but that they were prepared to deal with and acknowledge the barbarian kings.

The western te-tun shows Ah-Bolon-Tun holding the Vision Serpent, named Hun-Uinic-Na-Chan, as if it were a ceremonial bar. On the south te-tun, the king wears the jaguar-costume of GIII and holds up God K's head in his right hand. The central tree-stone shows him holding a round shield in his left hand and lifting up the Manikin Scepter in the other. These five images depict Ah-Bolon-Tun in some of the most important costumes of Classic Maya kings, but never had these costumes been assembled into one composition in this way, nor had the Cosmic Monster and Vision Serpent been merged with the ceremonial bar in quite this manner. In addition to his innovative treatment of these themes within the Maya canon, he also introduced new symbols—ones shared by the Itzá at Chichén Itzá.[17]

Many modern scholars have taken Ah-Bolon-Tun to be a Chontal-speaking intruder from the lower reaches of the Usumacinta.[18] While he may have been from an intruding group, it hardly matters. As we have seen, Ah-Bolon-Tun was a practiced and skillful manipulator of the Classic Maya imagery of kingship and therefore an acceptable Maya ruler. Moreover, his contemporaries in the old dynasties of other kingdoms dealt with him as a legitimate ahau. Unfortunately, whatever synthesis of the ancient kingship with barbarian beliefs he tried to put together soon began to unravel.

His successors gamely attempted to sustain the effort, but evidently lacked his command of the old orthodoxy. They erected tree-stones to celebrate the next two katun endings and by doing so they give us clear and poignant documentation of a people who were losing their roots in this ancient culture. Each image became more confused than the last, diminishing not only in the skill with which the drawings were executed but also in the very syntax of symbols that gave Classic Maya art its meaning (Fig. 10:6b). The last Seibal imagery would have seemed gibberish to the literate Maya of earlier generations.

The central Petén kingdoms managed to stave off most intruders, although some barbarians probably established an outpost on the east end of Lake Petén-Itzá at Ixlú. While the newcomers built architecture like their cousins at Seibal,[19] the images their king raised on tree-stones were perfectly standard and deliberately echoed the canon of period-ending presentations particular to Tikal. They were trying to buy into the old orthodoxy. On 10.1.10.0.0 and again on 10.2.0.0.0 (A.D. 879), this king erected tree-stones showing him materializing the Paddler Gods through bloodletting (Fig. 10:7a). The Tlaloc-marked, spearthrower-wielding warrior we saw at Ucanal floats in blood scrolls along with the Paddler Gods. More revealing, however, is a round altar that accompanied Stela 2. In his own name, this Ixlú lord claims status as a Ch'ul-Ahau of Tikal, while his reference to the gods repeats exactly the prose of an earlier stela at Dos Pilas.[20]

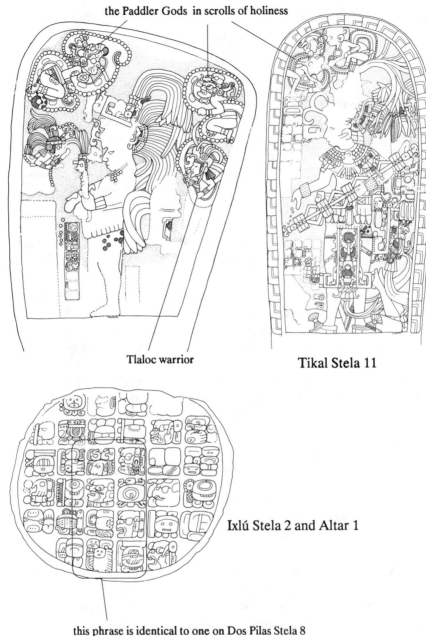

the Paddler Gods in scrolls of holiness

Tlaloc warrior

Tikal Stela 11

Ixlú Stela 2 and Altar 1

FIG. 10:7   this phrase is identical to one on Dos Pilas Stela 8

The kings of Tikal had lost more than the area at the east end of Lake Petén-Itzá. The last king of Tikal erected his only tree-stone in the middle of the forest of kings in front of the North Acropolis. The image is fairly well wrought, with the figure presented in front view holding the ribbon-decorated staff that had become prominent with the staff-kings four hundred years earlier (see Fig. 5:1a and b). In order to display the detail of the backrack in the manner of the traditional style, the artist wrapped it out to the king's side in a completely unrealistic pose. A bound captive

a. Jimbal Stela 1

b. Xultún Stela 10
drawing by Eric Von Euw

FIG. 10:8

lies belly down behind the king's ankles, echoing both the old style of composition and the kingdom's former glory. As in the case of Ixlú and Ucanal, small figures float above in the blood scrolls of the king's vision. All in all, the image is conservative and deeply concerned with remaining faithful to the old way of doing things. In contrast to the innovative king of Seibal, this Tikal ahau was a fundamentalist.

Perhaps he had reason, for his domain was a shadow of its former self. The final years of Tikal saw the kingdom fragmented into a series of petty, competing domains. All claimed legitimacy as the seat of the Ch'ul-Ahau of Tikal. While the dynasty of its old nemesis, Caracol, erected its last tree-stone in 10.1.10.0.0 (A.D. 859), Tikal's old subordinate, Uaxactún, which had reestablished its independence, erected its own tree-stones until 10.3.0.0.0 (A.D. 889). In this final irony, Uaxactún's monumental art lasted twenty years longer than its former master's.

Furthermore, on the border halfway between Uaxactún and Tikal, yet another lord had established himself as an independent king at the little site of Jimbal (Fig. 10:8a). This ahau erected a tree-stone on the same date as his Tikal rival—10.2.0.0.0, and like his Ixlú contemporary, he used the Tikal Emblem Glyph in his name. Here again the Paddler Gods float in blood scrolls above the king. This king outlasted the Tikal king by twenty years and erected another all-glyphic tree-stone on 10.3.0.0.0 (A.D. 889) on the same date as the lord of Uaxactún.

THE END
OF A
LITERATE
WORLD
AND ITS
LEGACY
TO THE
FUTURE

——

391

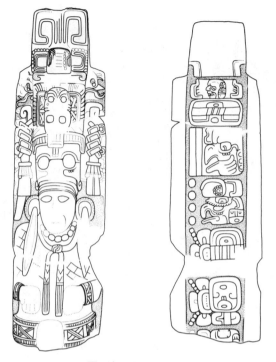

Toniná Monument 101

drawing by Peter Mathews

To the north of Tikal near Calakmul, a king of the site now called
La Muñeca erected a tree-stone on the katun-ending in A.D. 889. Xultún,
a little-studied kingdom northeast of Uaxactún, had sustained a tradition
of stela erection since Cycle 8 times, but it too ended on 10.3.0.0.0 (A.D.
889). Like Tikal, the last performances of Xultún's artists (Stelae 3 and
10) evoked the old tradition, but at Xultún, the artistic convention called
for the king to be portrayed displaying small effigy gods of the Baby Jaguar
and Chac (Fig. 10:8b). We don't yet know the reason why this date
marked the ending of monumental art at so many different sites.

The diaspora up the headwaters of the Usumacinta into the highlands
can be seen in two more stelae in Chiapas—one at Comitán dated to A.D.
874 and one at a place called Quen Santo in A.D. 879. The last historical
declaration of the Classic Maya kings was raised not too far away, also
in the Chiapas highlands, at the unlikely kingdom of Toniná. A bellicose
realm during most of its Late Classic existence, Toniná's most glorious
moment came when its king captured Kan-Hok-Xul, the aged second son
of Palenque's most famous king, Pacal. For a brief time, the same Toniná
king also had a Bonampak lord as his subordinate.[21] Perhaps the military
skill of Toniná's warriors preserved them longer than other Classic-period
kingdoms, or perhaps it was their isolated position at the western edge of
Maya territory in a valley off the major trade routes. Whatever it was,
Toniná's people retained their Classic heritage longer than any other Maya
kingdom. Their last king erected a tree-stone (Fig. 10:9) to celebrate the katun 10.4.0.0.0, which fell on January 20, A.D. 909. This was the last kingly
portrait and inscription ever mounted publicly by the Maya of the south-

a. Sun disk with corner serpents from Chichén Itzá mural (after Spinden 1913)

b. Ancestor cartouche from House A at Palenque (drawing by M.G. Robertson)

FIG. 10:10

ern lowlands, and it conformed exactly to the generations-old artistic tenets of that kingdom.

However, the collapse of the southern lowlands was not the end of Maya civilization. In the northern lowlands where rainfall rather than raised-field agriculture was the mainstay of the economy, kingdoms prospered as never before in the ninth and tenth centuries. It is in the north, rather than in the south, that the Maya finally established empires over the dominions of kings. As we have seen, the greatest of these empires had its capital at Chichén Itzá, a city with allies at Tula in highland México but with no equal in Mesoamerica during the eleventh century A.D. First cousins of Ah-Bolon-Tun's people at Seibal, the Itzá constructed a world without kings—a world that was instead ruled by councils of lords.

The Classic Maya view of a world without kings was of a world beyond the pale, a barbarian place without true order. The Chilam Balam chronicles of the northern lowland Maya suggest that the ahauob of Chichén Itzá were sufficiently barbarian to devise such a state. These confederate lords were also Maya enough to regard their solution as a perpetuation of a time-honored practice. They transformed kingship into an abstraction, vested in objects, images, and places, rather than in the individual identity and written words of a person. Their principal image of kingship was not the living king, but a dead king sitting on his sun disk, an icon that had developed from the Classic period ancestor cartouche. Captain Sun Disk may or may not have been an actual person, but his identity as an individual was not the critical message. The function of this imagery was to symbolize the idea of an ancestral king presiding as a spirit over the realm of Chichén Itzá.

For the Itzá the image of such an ancestral king was an anonymous human sitting inside the sun disk wielding the spearthrower and darts of Tlaloc war (Fig. 10:10a). His image could be replaced by a mirror, another ancient symbol of kingship from the Classic period. These two critical symbols of kingship at Chichén, the mirror and the ancestral king, were found together in a cache inside one of the earliest and most important temples at Chichén Itzá—the Temple of Chac Mool, the structure that

THE END
OF A
LITERATE
WORLD
AND ITS
LEGACY
TO THE
FUTURE
——
393

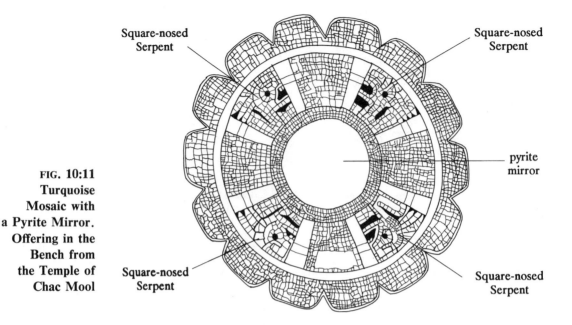

Square-nosed Serpent

Square-nosed Serpent

pyrite mirror

Square-nosed Serpent

Square-nosed Serpent

**FIG. 10:11
Turquoise
Mosaic with
a Pyrite Mirror.
Offering in the
Bench from
the Temple of
Chac Mool**

was later buried inside the Temple of the Warriors. Under the throne seat inside this earlier temple, the ruling council placed a hollowed-out stone column. Inside was a sun disk (Fig. 10:11) carefully wrapped in a sacred bundle, along with stones of divination, the bodies of a finch, representing the warriors of Chichén, and of a pygmy owl, symbolizing Tlaloc war.[22]

In the center of the disk was a golden mosaic mirror of iron pyrite. Surrounding it was a gleaming turquoise mosaic version of the sun disk divided into eight compartments. A profile serpent with a crest of feathers arcing around its head occupied every other compartment, forming a pattern like the four-serpent design that decorated the Classic period ancestor frame (Fig. 10:10b). These crested serpents are the late versions of the Vision Serpent we saw rising in the scene of Shield-Jaguar's accession, spitting out the image of the founder dressed in the garb of Tlaloc war.

At Chichén Itzá, this mosaic mirror was not passed through the generations from king to king. Instead, it was set into the throne to endow it with power and authority. The person who sat on that throne was rendered the temporary steward of ancestral power, a "two-day occupant of the mat," as the enemies of the Itzá scornfully called them.

Kukulcan, the Feathered Serpent—Quetzalcoatl of the Mexicans and the Vision Serpent of the southern Maya—became the second great abstract symbol of kingship. While images of serpents—feathered, scroll-covered, and plain—abound in the art of Chichén, nowhere in the existing texts is this being given a person's name. The role of the Feathered Serpent as it writhed between the victims of sacrifice and the hovering ancestor above was clearly derived from the Vision Serpent of Maya kingship. But for these Itzá Maya, the Vision Serpent ceased to be the instrument the king used to communicate with the ancestors and became a symbol of the

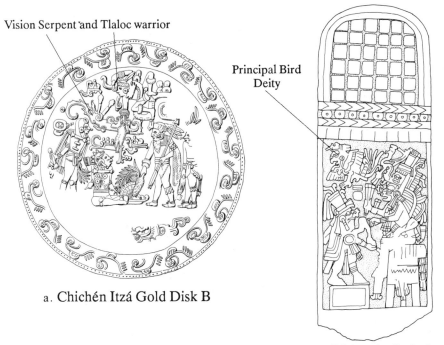

Vision Serpent and Tlaloc warrior

Principal Bird Deity

a. Chichén Itzá Gold Disk B

b. Mayapán Stela 1   FIG. 10:12

divinity of the state.[23] At the time of the Spanish Conquest, the cult of Kukulcan, the Feathered Serpent, was still the cult of the Maya nobility in Yucatán.

The revolutionaries at Chichén Itzá and the final orthodox kings of the Petén seem to have converged on a central and shared ritual theme in their pursuit of political survival: the Vision Serpent and the calling forth of the Gods and Ancestors through it. In a set of gold plates called the Battle Disks, dredged from the Cenote of Sacrifice at Chichén Itzá, acts of war (Fig. 10:12a) and sacrifice are depicted. Above many of these scenes writhe Feathered Serpents, Vision Serpents, and blood scrolls embracing Tlaloc warriors, bird warriors, and even GIII, the ancient Sun deity. The similarities to southern lowland images of the same period are striking and underscored by other correspondences in the iconography and epigraphy of these disks and the Cycle 10 monuments of the south.[24] But while the southerners tried to call forth the ancestors to reinforce the ancient definitions of kingship, the lords of Chichén called them forth to proclaim a new order of power. The economic and military success of Chichén Itzá in this contest was undeniable and may have served to seal the doom of the holdouts in Petén.

However, while the Maya of the northern lowlands did succeed in transforming the structure of their government to establish an empire, Chichén at its height was a capital without a public history, without the written declarations of kings embedded into its stone walls. It was a capital that turned its back on a thousand years of Maya royal practice and relegated literacy to the books of chilanob, men who were sorcerers and prophets, but not kings. Joining the ranks of the nonliterate peoples of Mesoamerica, this kingdom looked to the larger world of the Mexican and the Gulf Coast peoples for its prosperity and future. The result of the success of Chichén lords was the Mayanization of Mesoamerica.[25]

Chichén Itzá was a great state indeed, but once literate history had been disengaged from the central authority, Maya lords would never again harness the beliefs and aspirations of their own people as once they had. How long that state endured is still a matter of debate among scholars, but it evidently became the template for a cyclic form of government in which power became centralized at one regional capital, then dissolved to re-form elsewhere. After the fall of Chichén Itzá, another regional capital arose in the northern lowlands at Mayapán—founded by Cocom lords who claimed descent from the lords of Chichén Itzá.

The lords of Mayapán also erected their own tree-stones, but they had become something very different from those of the Classic lords. Their imagery shows gods (Fig. 10:12b) like those in the Dresden and Madrid codices, books that prescribed the timing and nature of ritual. One badly damaged image appears to show a Yax-Cheel-Cab, the First World Tree, mentioned in the prophecy of Chilam Balam. A bird flutters in the sky above the tree in an image that recalls the World Trees at Palenque. Mayapán flourished for a time and then disintegrated as the factions comprising its government struggled among themselves for power. Although the Spanish cut short the bickering among the several small states ruled by these factions, the pattern of cyclical centralization was a precedent the Maya would have likely continued.

The last king of the Maya to reign independently was a man named Can-Ek, king of the Itzá who fled after the kingdom of Mayapán failed to the region that had once been ruled by the Ch'ul-Ahauob of Tikal. The last Can-Ek (a name probably meaning Serpent-Star[26]) was at least the third ruler of that name to appear in Spanish chronicles. The first greeted Cortés and his expedition as they made their way across the Petén to Honduras in 1525.

Another Can-Ek met a second Spanish *entrada,* or "expedition," to the Itzá made in 1618 by the Padres Fuensalida and Orbita. Their goal was to convert the Itzá to Christianity. Can-Ek's reaction to their message bears witness to the power accorded the written word among the Maya. Can-Ek told the padres that, according to the prophecies of the katuns—which projected history to predict the future—their spiritual message was not correct. The padres described his reaction in these words:

"The time had not yet arrived in which their ancient priests had prophesied to them they were to relinquish the worship of the Gods; because the period in which they then were was Oxahau, which means Third Period . . . and so they asked the padres to make no further attempts in that direction, but to return to the village of Tipú and then, on another occasion, to come again to see them."[27]

Finding the Itzá unwilling to listen, the priests left, and several other attempts to convert the Itzá during the next seventy years were met by the same intransigence and sometimes even with violence. It was not until 1695 that the resistance of the Maya to Christianity eased. At that time another padre, Andrés de Avendaño y Layola, accompanied by two other Franciscans and a group of Maya from the town of Tipú in northern Belize, journeyed to the shores of Lake Petén-Itzá to a town named Chacan.[28] After a long night filled with fear and overactive imaginations fueled by memories of past massacres, the three Franciscans emerged from their hut in the morning to see a wedge of flower-adorned canoes emerging out of the glare of the rising sun. The canoes were filled with resplendent warriors playing drums and flutes. Sitting in the largest of the canoes at the apex of the wedge rode King Can-Ek, whom the Spanish chronicler described as a tall man, handsome of visage and far lighter in complexion than other Maya.[29]

Dressed with all the elegance of his station, King Can-Ek wore a large crown of gold surmounted by a crest of the same metal. His ears were covered with large gold disks decorated with long dangles that fell to his shoulders and shook when he moved his head. Gold rings adorned his fingers and gold bands his arms. His shirt was made of pure white cloth elaborately embroidered with blue designs, and he wore a wide black sash around his waist to mark his status as priest of the Itzá. His sandals were finely wrought of blue tread with golden jingles interwoven. Over everything else, he wore a cape made of blue-flecked white cloth edged with an blue-embroidered border. It bore his name spelled in glyphs.[30]

After Can-Ek stepped ashore onto a mat, his men followed him off the canoes while keeping the music going without a break. Silence fell across the plaza when he raised the feather-mounted stone baton he held in his hand. The black-dressed priests of the Chacans came forward to do the king reverence and argue for the sacrifice of the foreigners who had invaded their lands.

Protecting his guests from the Chacan priests, Can-Ek returned to his canoe, taking the Spanish and their party with him for the two-hour canoe trip to his home island. There he hosted Avendaño and his fellow padres in his own house, where they were fed and tended by two of his unmarried sons and two of his unmarried daughters, all of very attractive appearance, according to the Spanish commentator. With the help of two interpreters, Gerónimo Zinak and Ah-Balan-Chel, Avendaño tried to convince Can-Ek that the time prophesied by the Chilam Balam and the katun histories was soon to come.

Can-Ek listened politely to what Avendaño had to say and told him to return another time. That time came later in the same year when Avendaño, in yet another entrada, journeyed south from Mérida through the land of the Cehaches, past the huge ruins of Tikal,[31] and to the shore of Lake Petén-Itzá. Once again Avendaño and his party waited for Can-Ek in Chacan. When the Itzá arrived, "they came in some eighty canoes," Avendaño wrote, "full of Indians, painted and dressed for war, with very large quivers of arrows, though all were left in the canoes—all the canoes escorting and accompanying the petty King, who with about five hundred Indians came forward to receive us."

THE END
OF A
LITERATE
WORLD
AND ITS
LEGACY
TO THE
FUTURE

—

397

The time Avendaño had spent learning to speak Mayan and to know Maya prophecies as thoroughly as the Maya's own chilanob was about to bear fruit. He was to use Maya memory of history to turn their future to his own ends.

Can-Ek must have known it was a special moment too, for in the trip back to Tayasal he tested the courage of his Spanish guest. While they were in the canoe surrounded by painted and befeathered Maya warriors of fierce demeanor, Can-Ek reached down to place his hand over Avendaño's heart. "Are you frightened?" he asked. Hoping to elicit signs of fear, Can-Ek found instead a man prepared to die for what he believed. Avendaño looked up at the fearsome ahau and told him he had come in fulfillment of the very Maya prophecies that earlier Can-Ek had used against Padres Fuensalida and Orbita.

"Why should my heart be disturbed?" he retorted. "Rather it is very contented, seeing that I am the fortunate man, who is fulfilling your own prophecies, by which you are to become Christians; and this benefit will come to you by means of some bearded men from the East; who by signs of their prophets, were we ourselves, because we came many leagues from the direction of the east, ploughing the seas, with no other purpose than borne by our love of their souls, to bring them, (at the cost of much work) to bring them to that favor which the true god brings them."[32]

Avendaño had turned the tables on Can-Ek. In an act of bravado and perhaps of remarkable insight, he reached up and mimicked Can-Ek's challenge by putting his own hand on the king's chest and asking, "Are you now the one who is disturbed by the words of your own prophets?" Can-Ek replied, "No," but he was putting a good face on the matter, for his own action would soon show he had accepted that the time foretold by the prophecy had come.

When Avendaño landed at Tayasal, the capital of the Itzá, he and his men were led, for the second time that year, through the streets to Can-Ek's palace. In the center of the house sat a round stone pedestal and column which the Itzá called *Yax-Cheel-Cab,* "First Tree of the World." On the western side of the pedestal base, the ill-made (according to Avendaño) mask of a deity called *Ah-Cocah-Mut* rested. Since *mut* is the word for both "bird" and "prophecy," we take the image to be the remnant of the Celestial Bird that stood on the crown of the Wacah Chan Tree in Classic-period imagery. Here was the sad echo of the image on Pacal's sarcophagus, of the great tree-stones of the Classic period, of the tree carved on the stela of Mayapán, and of the tree Naum-Pat saw the Spaniards raise in the temple on Cozumel.

In a temple behind the Yax-Cheel-Cab, Avendaño saw a box holding a large bone. He realized later he had seen the remains of the horse Cortés had left with the first Can-Ek 172 years earlier.

Avendaño and his companions spent several days in Tayasal, surrounded wherever they went by curious and suspicious Itzá. He complained that neither the admonitions of the king nor the protest of the Spaniards forestalled the curious Maya, who touched them everywhere including "the most hidden parts of a man."[33] All the time Avendaño used the old prophecies to work on Can-Ek's mind. When he finally convinced the Itzá king to be baptized, Can-Ek remained suspicious, demanding to know what the bearded priest intended to do, "since they thought that there was some shedding of blood or circumcision or cutting of some part of their body." The king, like the suspicious Xibalbans of the Popol Vuh, volunteered a child to try it first. Satisfied that he would sustain no physical injury, he suffered himself to be baptized, and soon thereafter three hundred of his people followed his example.

In the midst of these conversion efforts, "governors, captains, and head men of the four other Peténs or islands,"[34] arrived at Tayasal splendid in the riotous color of their full war regalia. Avendaño calmed them down by inviting them to share food and drink. In his own words, he "treated them kindly, speaking to them more frequently and pleasantly, discoursing with them in their ancient idiom, as if the time had already come (just as their prophets had foretold) for our eating together from one plate and drinking from one cup, we, the Spaniards, making ourselves one with them."[35]

To argue with these new lords, who would soon prove to be formidable enemies, Avendaño spoke to them in Yucatec, read their own books to them, and used their katun prophecies to convince them it was time to accept conversion. He described these books in detail.

> It is all recorded in certain books, made of the bark of trees, folded from one side to the other like screens, each leaf of the thickness of a Mexican *Real* of eight. These are painted on both sides with a variety of figures and characters (of the same kind as the Mexican Indians also used in their own times), which show not only the count of the said days, months and years, but also the ages and prophecies which their idols and images announced to them, or, to speak more accurately, the devil by means of the worship which they pay to him in the form of some stones. These ages are thirteen in number; each age has its separate idol and its priest, with a separate prophecy of its events.
>
> (Means 1917:141)

The hostile chiefs, especially one named Covoh, did not like his words and soon drove Avendaño and his companions out of Tayasal in a dangerous, near-fatal retreat through the forest. But a year later, another expedition came back, this one armed and prepared to take on the stubborn Itzá by force, if necessary. After a few hours of token resistance, the Itzá gave up and fled their island home, leaving the houses of their gods and the site of their Yax-Cheel-Cab to be ravaged by the Spaniards. After 178 years of resistance, the Itzá gave up with barely a whimper on March 13, 1697, the day 12.3.19.11.14 1 Ix 17 Kankin in the Maya calendar.[36]

The Long Count position of the fall of Tayasal is not that important because the Maya had long since given up the Long Count as a way of keeping time, but they had retained the count of the katuns. The ends of the katuns were the ages Avendaño described. Named for the ahau day

THE END
OF A
LITERATE
WORLD
AND ITS
LEGACY
TO THE
FUTURE

———

399

on which each twenty-tun cycle ended, the katun cycled through the full thirteen numbers used in the tzolkin count. Because the 7,200 days that make up a katun are divisible by 13 with a remainder of –2, the ahau number of each successive katun drops by two. 13 Ahau is followed by 11 Ahau, 9 Ahau, 7 Ahau, 5 Ahau, 3 Ahau, 1 Ahau, 12 Ahau, and so on until the count runs through all the numbers. This unit of thirteen katuns formed the basis of the katun prophecies that Avendaño used against Can-Ek; each katun ending within the thirteen had its prophecy. The date of Avendaño's visit fell in the katun that ended on 12.4.0.0.0 10 Ahau 18 Uo (July 27, A.D. 1697).

The Chilam Balam of Chumayel records the following prophecy for Katun 10 Ahau:

> Katun 10 Ahau, the katun is established at Chablé. The ladder is set up over the rulers of the land. The hoof shall burn; the sand by the seashore shall burn. The rock shall crack [with the heat]; drought is the change of the katun. It is the word of our Lord God the Father and of the Mistress of Heaven, the portent of the katun. No one shall arrest the word of our Lord God, God the Son, the Lord of Heaven and his power, come to pass all over the world. Holy Christianity shall come bringing with it the time when the stupid ones who speak our language badly shall turn from their evil ways. No one shall prevent it; this then is the drought. Sufficient is the word for the Maya priests, the word of God.
>
> (Roys 1967:159–160)

8 Ahau, the katun that followed 10 Ahau, was even more ominous than the prophecy above, for throughout Maya history as it was recorded in the katun prophecies, 8 Ahau was a katun of political strife and religious change. These prophecies were the basis of Avendaño's success and Can-Ek's resigned acceptance of baptism and eventually his defeat.[37] The fatalism that was at the heart of Can-Ek's thinking came from the katun prophecies. This fatalism was part of the legacy of the Classic-period attitude toward history and its relationship to cyclic time and supernatural causality. Classic-period scribes emphasized the connectedness among the actions of their living kings, the actions of ancestors in the historical and legendary past, and the actions of gods in the mythological past. We do not think men like Jaguar-Paw, Smoking-Frog, Chan-Bahlum, Bird-Jaguar, and Yax-Pac believed that the past dictated the present, but that these events unfolded within the symmetries of sacred time and space. They looked for symmetries and parallelisms as part of their political strategies, and when they could not find them, they very probably manufactured them. The result of this type of thinking, transformed by the exigencies of the Collapse and then the Conquest, became predictive history and produced the fatalism of Can-Ek.

The Spaniards who met Naum-Pat on the island of Cozumel, and 178 years later convinced Can-Ek that his world had come to an end, brought with them a different vision of history and the importance of human

events. In their view, which we of the Western world have inherited, the history of the New World began with the arrival of Columbus. The eyewitness accounts of these times registered the cataclysmic clash of worlds and realities that was the Conquest and its aftermath; but, as with the story of Can-Ek, we see these events only through the eyes of the Conquerors, not of the peoples they found and changed forever.

Yet as we have shown, the peoples of Mesoamerica had a long and rich historical tradition preserved in many different forms, including myth, oral literature, ritual performance, the arts, painting, and writing. The Maya had kept their written history pristine and untainted by foreign interests for sixteen hundred years before those first Spaniards stepped ashore and surprised Naum-Pat. The conquerors knew the importance of written history to the identity of the people they subdued and used this knowledge to their own ends. They worked to destroy glyphic literacy among the Maya by burning their books and educating Maya children, when they allowed education at all, in Spanish and Latin only.[38] Their logic was clear and compelling: Native literacy perpetuated resistance to the Conquerors and their religion. Denied public history, the stubborn Maya continued to write their own books in secret, eventually in the Roman alphabet as they learned the ways of the Europeans. There are *h-men* among the Yucatecs today who still read and keep a book of prophecy in the tradition of the Books of Chilam Balam, and the Maya of highland Guatemala still observe and record the ancient count of days and use it to make sense of their lives.

Driven underground, glyphic literacy and the history that went with it was lost until the process of decipherment began to remove the veil. Because we can once again read their words, the ancient Maya are no longer a mute receptacle of our vision of what they must have been. We of the modern world no longer see the historical Maya as our immediate intellectual forebears envisioned them—as serene astronomer priests telling their charges when to plant the crops. Neither were the ancient Maya the "rational economic" people of some current theoretical schemes of social science, nor mindless automatons "behaving" without will or self-awareness as they lived their lives and left witness of their existence in the archaeological record. They were, as occasion warranted, warlike, politically acute, devout, philosophical, shortsighted, inspired, self-serving human beings. Their rulers were fully engaged in managing governments and ruling large populations through the myths and symbolisms they shared with their people. The language and images they used are ones their distant descendants can still understand today.

Recently, Linda Schele had a unique opportunity to observe firsthand the shift of the ancient Maya into the active voice and the potential this transformation holds for the Maya of the modern world. In 1987 while working on the archaeological project in Copán, Honduras, Linda was the guide to a group of American linguists and Maya Indians from the highlands of Guatemala and Chiapas, México, who came to visit those ancient ruins. During that afternoon and the following day, she shared what she knew of the ancient kings of the city. Some of the visitors were bored and

THE END
OF A
LITERATE
WORLD
AND ITS
LEGACY
TO THE
FUTURE

—

401

others distracted or doubtful, but for the most part, the Maya and Americans alike were enchanted with what those working at the site had learned. Most of all, they came to the realization that the ancient inscriptions could actually be read. A few grasped that there was powerful history locked up in those silent stones.

They finished the final tour and ate a late lunch together before piling back into their buses to begin the long trip home. While they ate, the leader of the Maya, a Cakchiquel named Martín Chacach Cutzal,[39] asked Linda if she would come to Antigua, Guatemala, that summer and give a workshop on the ancient writing system to a group of modern Maya. She thought about it (for about five minutes) and realized that a lifetime's dream was about to come true. The modern Maya had asked to learn about the writing and the history of their forebears. Linda[40] traveled to Antigua and, amid the earthquake-shattered ruins of a Spanish church, went on a marvelous four-day journey of discovery into the ancient past with forty Maya men and women.

During the last day, they all worked on reading the Tablet of the 96 Glyphs from Palenque, one of the most beautiful inscriptions ever carved by the ancient Maya. Everyone cut up a drawing of the inscription and, following Linda's lead, taped the disassembled text down onto a large sheet so that they could write a translation below each glyph. The resulting grid displayed the structure of the text, showing how its time statements, verbs, and actors worked.

The final session had to end with the text only half translated so that everyone could prepare for the traditional closing ceremony required for such events. Excited with the results, even though they were only half done, almost everyone came forward to express their feelings about the magic that had happened during those four days. Exuberant that it had worked so well, Linda was nevertheless disappointed and a little hurt when one of the most enthusiastic participants, a Kekchi named Eduardo Pacay, known as Guayo to his friends, disappeared without saying a word.

Two hours later, everyone reassembled for the closing ceremony, which was held at the headquarters of the "Francisco Marroquín" project. A polyglot of conversation in at least ten languages floated over the sounds of a marimba as everyone drank rum and cokes or soft drinks and nibbled on snacks of beef, chicken, beans, and tortillas. Finally done eating, everyone stood or sat around the courtyard of the old house as the formal ceremony began in which gifts were given to the teachers and everyone got a diploma declaring that they had participated. Toward the end, Guayo and the two other Kekchi who had been in his team appeared carrying the meter-high chart they had made during the workshop. They opened the tightly rolled paper, and while two of them held it stretched out, Guayo read their translation—in Kekchi. Before forty awestruck witnesses, a Maya read aloud one of the ancient inscriptions in his own language for the first time in four hundred and fifty years.[41] That day, 12.18.14.3.5 1 Men 3 Xul in the ancient calendar,[42] was 291 years after Can-Ek's conversion and 1,078 years after the last dated monument of the Classic period.

The magic of that moment was special to Guayo and his friends, but it was equally important to the rest of us. In the "world history" courses that punctuate our childhood education, we learn to place a special value on written history and the civilizations that possess it. In antiquity, history was a very special and rare kind of consciousness and it is a momentous event in our own time when we rediscover a lost reality encapsulated in written words. The Maya inscriptions that have been unlocked by the decipherment offer us the first great history of the Americas.

Maya history as we have presented it is, of course, a construction of our times, sensibilities, and intellectual agendas. The ancient Maya who lived that history would have seen it differently, as will their descendants. Even our own contemporaries who work with different patterns of data and different agendas will eventually change some of the details and ways of interpreting this information; but that is only the natural result of time and new discoveries. Yet for all the limitations that lie within the proposition that history cannot be separated from the historian, these very limitations are part of the nature of all history—ours as well as theirs. Each generation of humanity debates history, thus turning it into a dynamic thing that incorporates the present as well as the past. This process has been happening with American history both before and after Columbus; it is happening to the history of the last fifty years even as we watch events unfold with mind-boggling rapidity on the evening news. It will happen to the Maya history we have constructed here. But you see, that is the miracle. There is a now Maya history that can be debated and altered into a dynamic synergy with the present and the future. And with that synergy our perception of the history of humanity is changed.

THE END
OF A
LITERATE
WORLD
AND ITS
LEGACY
TO THE
FUTURE

—

EPILOGUE:
BACK
TO THE
BEGINNING

On a warm night in May of 1986, Linda and I, Mary Miller, and many friends celebrated the opening of the Blood of Kings exhibition at the Kimbell Art Museum in Fort Worth by letting a little blood from our fingers onto paper and copal incense and burning the offering. I carefully wrapped the ashes, along with the obsidian blades we had used, in a paper bundle. The following summer, I buried the bundle in the cement benchmark at the center of Yaxuná, a place where I hope to work for ten more years. So we take our thoughts and our feelings for the ancient Maya from this book and from our distant homes back to the Maya field with us, Linda to Copán, me to Yaxuná. Maybe we are a little superstitious, but I'd rather think we're empathetic, for the Otherworld still shimmers over the Maya landscape even as we of the West pass through it in oblivious innocence.

Don Emetario, captain of the Maya workmen at Yaxuná, and my friend, took me aside at the end of the summer's work in 1988 to tell me this story. A few years ago he was walking home to the village from his fields along the modern dirt road that cuts through the ruins of Yaxuná. It was dusk, and in the reddening light he saw a tiny boy standing before him, naked and bald. Thinking it might be his son, Emetario cried out to him, but the child ran off the road and disappeared into a hole in the rocky surface of the ancient community. Emetario ran home for a flashlight and peered down into the hole, but all he could see was something furry like a night animal. Was this the "lord of money (the Earthlord)"? Emetario asked me. I replied that there are always strange things to be found in ruins, but that I did not know what it was he saw.

I rather suspect that Emetario's cousin, Don Pablo, knows more than I do about such things. Don Pablo is a H-men, a "known," or shaman, of the village, who also works for the Yaxuná project. On the last day of our work in the summer of 1988, Don Pablo was working with our photographer in the southern end of the community, clearing the grass from stone foundations for pictures. In the course of the conversation, he regarded the principal acropolis of the south, a fine raised platform with three buildings upon it, erected in the Preclassic period, at the dawn of Maya history.

"Here was a great temple," he said, "but the portal is now closed."

We cannot open the Maya portals to the Otherworld with excavation alone, no matter how careful and how extensive. For the portals are places in the mind and in the heart. We, as pilgrims from another time and reality, must approach the ruined entrances to the past with humility and attention to what the Maya, ancient and modern, can teach us through their words as well as their deeds. So our book is a beginning for us on that path—I look forward to hearing what Don Pablo has to say about our progress.

DAVID FREIDEL
Dallas, Texas
September 1988

UPDATE 1991

Since *A Forest of Kings* went to press, new information relevant to our stories has been discovered. In the 1990 season, excavators in the Caracol Project under the direction of Arlen and Diane Chase discovered several new stelae. According to project epigrapher Nikolai Grube, one of these records an attack on Tikal during the war in which Lord Kan II conquered Naranjo in A.D. 637. Simultaneously, in the Dos Pilas project under the direction of Arthur Demarest, excavators cleared a hieroglyphic stairway, which Stephen Houston and David Stuart, the project epigraphers, analyzed as recording the capture of Shield-Skull, the father of Ah-Cacaw of Tikal on the date 9.12.6.16.17 11 Caban 10 Zotz' or May 3, A.D. 679. Because we knew only of Caracol's conquest of Tikal in A.D. 562 when we wrote our story of this period, we could not explain why it had taken so long for Tikal to recover from this single defeat nor why the broken stelae had been allowed to lie unattended in the Great Plaza for over a hundred years. Now it seems likely that Tikal was defeated and devastated at least two more times after the first Caracol victory and that Flint-Sky-God K and his allies disfigured the monuments in the Great Plaza only three years before Ah-Cacaw's accession in A.D. 682.

The third great discovery came from Nikolai Grube, who deciphered the glyph for "dance"*(ak'ot)* in May 1990. This new discovery is particularly important to the Bird-Jaguar story in Chapter 7 because the Flapstaff, Basket-staff, and Bird-staff rituals as well as the display of the God K scepter and the bundle can now be identified as public dances. Dance, it turns out, has been one of the focal acts of Maya ritual and political life even until today.

LINDA SCHELE
Austin, Texas
February 1991

GLOSSARY
OF GODS
AND ICONS

The **Baby Jaguar** appears frequently in paired opposition with Chac-Xib-Chac in scenes of dance and sacrifice. He most often appears with the body of a infantile human, although he may also be represented as an adult, fully zoomorphic jaguar. In both aspects, he wears a scarf and is associated with the sun. His human aspect sometimes wears a cruller, associating him with GIII of the Palenque Triad. The Baby Jaguar is particularly important at Tikal in the early inscriptions where it appears as if it were the name of the kingdom. At minimum, it was considered to be a god particularly associated with Tikal, perhaps as its patron. The Baby Jaguar also appears in early inscriptions at Caracol. See Chac-Xib-Chac.

Bicephalic Bar, see Serpent Bar.

Blood is represented by a bifurcated scroll, sometimes with plain contours and sometimes with beaded outlines representing the blood itself. To mark the scroll as blood rather than smoke or mist, the Maya attached a number of signs representing precious materials: *kan,* "yellow," *yax,* "blue-green," *chac,* "red," shells, jade jewelry like beads and earflares, obsidian, mirrors of various materials, "zero" signs, and bone. This imagery merges with that of God C, which imparts the meaning "holy" or "divine." Blood is the holy substance of human beings. See God C.

The **Bloodletting Bowl** is a flat, shallow plate with angled sides, called a *lac* in Mayan. It held offerings of all sorts and was often used in caches in a lip-to-lip configuration in which a second bowl was used as the lid. In bloodletting scenes, the bowl usually holds bloodied paper, lancets of various sorts, and rope to pull through perforations.

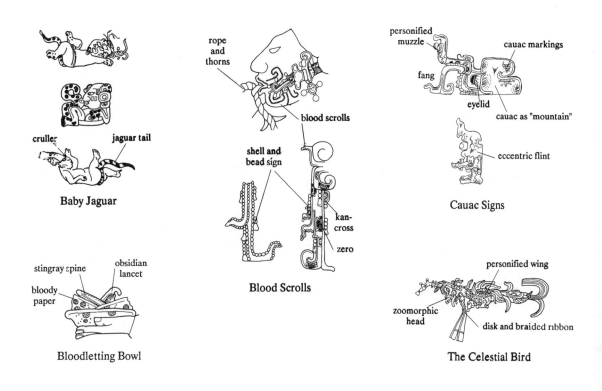

Baby Jaguar

cruller   jaguar tail

stingray spine   obsidian lancet

bloody paper

Bloodletting Bowl

rope and thorns

blood scrolls

shell and bead sign

kan-cross

zero

Blood Scrolls

personified muzzle   cauac markings

fang

eyelid   cauac as "mountain"

eccentric flint

Cauac Signs

personified wing

zoomorphic head   disk and braided ribbon

The Celestial Bird

Cab or **Caban,** see Earth.

Cauac Signs consist of a triangular arrangement of disks in groups of three, five, or more, combined with a semicircular line paralleled by a row of dots. These signs derive from the day sign Cauac, but in the iconography they mark both things made of stone and the Witz Mountain Monster. When they appear in zoomorphic form or with a wavy contour, cauac signs mark the Eccentric Flint. Combined with the God C–type head, the cauac signs refer to sacred stones, like altars. When the zoomorphic form has eyelids and a stepped forehead, it is the Witz Monster or Living Mountain. See Witz Monster.

The **Celestial Bird,** also known as the Serpent Bird and the Principal Bird Deity, has a long tail, personified wings, and the head of a zoomorphic monster. Often it appears with a round object and woven ribbon held in its mouth, with a trefoil pectoral around its neck, and a cut-shell ornament attached to a jade headband. In its most common representation it sits atop the World Tree or astride the body of the Cosmic Monster. In its earliest manifestations, it appeared prominently in the Late Preclassic art of the southern highlands. There it represented the idea of nature out of control but brought into order by the Hero Twins and their avatar on earth, the king.[1] This concept of the king as the guardian of ordered nature first came into the iconography of the lowland Maya with the image of this bird, especially in the context of the World Tree.

The **Celestial Monster,** see Cosmic Monster.

The **Ceremonial Bar,** see Serpent Bar.

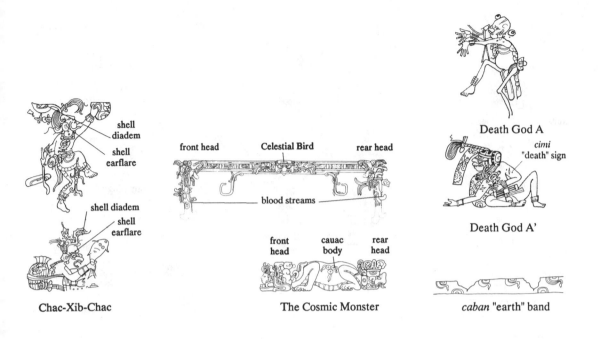

shell diadem
shell earflare

shell diadem
shell earflare

Chac-Xib-Chac

front head   Celestial Bird   rear head

blood streams

front head   cauac body   rear head

The Cosmic Monster

Death God A

cimi "death" sign

Death God A'

caban "earth" band

Chac-Xib-Chac is frequently paired with the Baby Jaguar in early inscriptions, while in Late Classic pottery painting they occur together in scenes of dance and sacrifice. Chac-Xib-Chac can appear in anthropomorphic or zoomorphic form, but he is distinguished by a shell diadem, a fish fin on the face of his human version, a shell earflare, and his frequent wielding of an ax. All but the shell diadem and the ax are features shared by GI of the Palenque Triad, and in fact the two may be aspects of the same entity. Chac-Xib-Chac was the prototype of the great god Chac of the Maya of Yucatán at the time of the Spanish Conquest. Kings frequently portray themselves in the guise of Chac-Xib-Chac or wear him behind their legs suspended on a chain. On the Cosmic Plate (Fig. 2:4), he is identified by date and actions as Venus as Eveningstar.[2] See Baby Jaguar.

The **Cosmic Monster,** also known as the Celestial Monster and the Bicephalic Monster, is a dragon-type monster with a crocodilian head marked by deer ears. The body has legs, usually terminating in deer hooves with water scrolls at the joints. Its body sometimes resembles a crocodile marked with cauac signs, but it can also appear as a sky band or as the lazy-S scrolls of blood. At Yaxchilán, the Monster appears with two crocodile heads, but usually the rear head is the Quadripartite God, which hangs upside down in relation to the front head to mark it as a burden of the Cosmic Monster. The front head is usually marked as Venus while the Quadripartite Monster is the sun. Together they represent the movement of Venus, the sun, and by extension, the planets across the star fields at night and the arc of heaven during the day. The Cosmic Monster marks the path between the natural and the supernatural worlds as it exists on the perimeter of the cosmos. See World Tree and Quadripartite Monster.

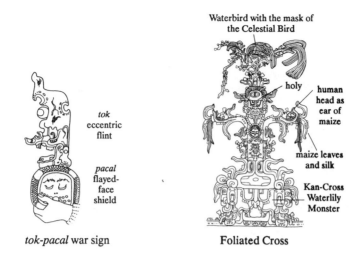

tok
eccentric
flint

pacal
flayed-
face
shield

tok-pacal war sign

Waterbird with the mask of
the Celestial Bird

holy

human
head as
ear of
maize

maize leaves
and silk

Kan-Cross
Waterlily
Monster

Foliated Cross

The **Death God** (God A) appears as an animated skeleton, sometimes with the gas-distended belly characteristic of parasitical disease or the decay of a corpse. There appear to have been many versions of this god, differentiated by slight variations in the anatomy, the objects carried, and the actions done in the scene. These variations may represent different aspects of the same god, or just as likely, different Lords of Death named for various diseases or actions.

The **Directional Gods,** see Four-Part Gods.

The **Double-headed Serpent Bar,** see Serpent Bar.

Earth is represented by bands marked with *cab* signs from the glyph meaning "earth." These bands may be split to represent a cleft from which a tree grows or ancestors emerge. In some representations, earth bands may also represent the concept of territory or domain.

Eccentric Flint and **Flayed-Face Shield** combine a flint lance blade or an eccentric flint with a shield made from a flayed human face. It is an object transferred from ancestor to king in the accession rites at Palenque. At other sites, like Tortuguero, Yaxchilán, and Tikal, this symbol combination is directly associated with war and capture.

The **Foliated Cross** is a maize tree, representing the central axis of the world in the symbolism of cultivated nature. At its base is the Kan-cross Waterlily Monster representing the canals and swamps of raised-field agriculture. Its trunk, like that of the *Wacah Chan* tree, is marked with the God C image meaning "holy" or "sacred." Its branches are ears of maize with a living human head substituting for the grains of maize as a reference to the myth of creation in which human flesh was shaped from maize dough. Perched on its summit is the great bird of the center, in this context represented as the Waterbird associated with the canals around raised fields. The Waterbird wears a mask of the Celestial Bird. See World Tree.

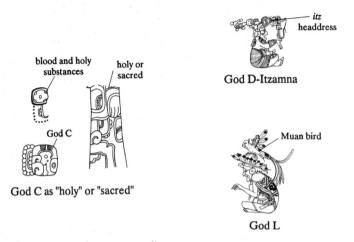

blood and holy substances

holy or sacred

God C

God C as "holy" or "sacred"

itz headdress

God D-Itzamna

Muan bird

God L

The **Four-Part Gods:** Many gods in the Maya system occur in repetitions of four associated with the directions and colors of the four-part division of the world. In the Dresden Codex, Chac (God B) is the principal god shown in a four-part set, but in the Classic period the Pauahtunob[3] or Bacabob are the most frequent deities shown in four repetitions. In the 819-day count of the Classic inscriptions, GII (God K) appears in fourfold division associated with colors, directions, and the appropriate quadrants of the sky. See Pauahtun, GII, and Chac-Xib-Chac.

GI, GII, GIII, see the Palenque Triad.

God B, see Chac-Xib-Chac.

God C is a monkey-faced image that will often have representations of blood drops and other precious materials attached to it. The phonetic reading of the glyphic version as *k'ul,* the Maya word for "divinity," "holy," or "sacred," identifies the icon as a marker for the same quality. When the image is associated with the depiction of a living being, such as a king or deity, it marks that being as a "divinity." When it is merged with the image of a thing, such as a tree, stream of blood, or a house, it marks the image as a "holy" thing. See Blood and World Tree.

God D is the most difficult of the old gods to identify iconographically. He has large square eyes, an overhanging nose, a toothless mouth, and wears a headband embossed with a hanging flower. His glyphic name in the codices and the Classic inscriptions is Itzamna. In glyphic expressions at Naranjo and Caracol, which are structurally similar to those naming the Palenque Triad, he appears paired with GIII or the Baby Jaguar.

God K, see Palenque Triad (GII).

God L is one of the aged gods who appear principally in scenes of Xibalba. He is frail and bent with age, wrinkled in feature, and has a huge nose overlapping a toothless mouth. He is a smoker, preferring huge cigars or smaller cigarettes. His most important costume element is a headdress in the form of the mythological bird named Oxlahun Chan (13 Sky). He has

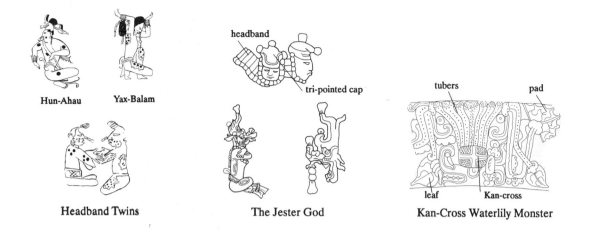

Hun-Ahau Yax-Balam Headband Twins The Jester God Kan-Cross Waterlily Monster

headband tri-pointed cap tubers pad leaf Kan-cross

a house in the Otherworld, where he is attended by the beautiful young goddesses who personify the number two. His rule of Xibalba is chronicled by a rabbit scribe.[4] He is also the god who presided over the assemblage of gods when the cosmos was ordered on 4 Ahau 8 Cumku.

God N, see Pauahtun.

The **Headband Twins,** who are characterized by ornate headbands displaying the Jester God of kings, occur most frequently in pottery scenes where they are named as Hun-Ahau and Yax-Balam. In their fully human aspect, they are the Classic period prototypes of the Hero Twins of the Popol Vuh. The Hun-Ahau Twin carries large dots on his cheek, arms, and legs and functions in the writing system as the anthropomorphic variant of the glyph for lord, *ahau.* In the Dresden Codex, this Twin appears as the god Venus in his manifestation as Morningstar. His Twin is marked by patches of jaguar pelt on his chin, arms, and legs, and by a cut shell, read as *yax,* attached to his forehead. This god functions also as the personification of the number nine and the glyph *yax,* meaning "blue-green" or "first." See Palenque Triad.

The **Hero Twins,** see Palenque Triad and Headband Twins.

The **Jester God** began as the personified version of the tri-lobed symbol that marked headband crowns of Late Preclassic kings. By the Classic period, this personified version had become the zoomorphic version of the glyph for *ahau.* Putting a headband with the Jester God, the *ahau* sign, or a mirror on any animal or human head glyph converted its meaning to *ahau.* Named for the resemblance of its pointed head to a medieval jester's cap, this god can appear in miniature form held by the king; but it is most commonly attached to the headband of the king or worn on his chest as a pectoral. The Jester God will sometimes have fishfins on its face.

The **Kan-cross Waterlily Monster** is a special version of the waterlily distinguished by the presence of a Kan-cross on its forehead. Often the root formations, blossoms, and pads of the waterlily emerge from its head.

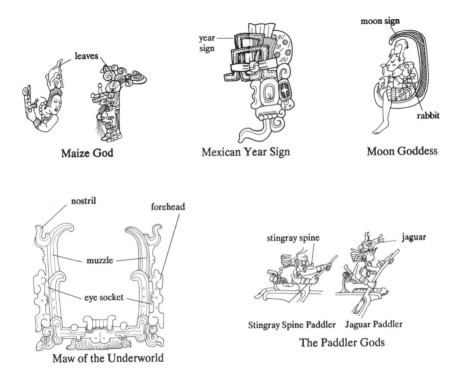

Maize God

Mexican Year Sign

moon sign

rabbit

Moon Goddess

nostril

forehead

muzzle

eye socket

Maw of the Underworld

stingray spine

jaguar

Stingray Spine Paddler   Jaguar Paddler

The Paddler Gods

It is especially associated with the water environment of agricultural canals. See Waterlily Monster.

The **Maize God** was represented by a beautiful young man with maize foliation growing from his head. He is identified with the older set of Twins who were the father and uncle of the Hero Twins[5] and his most common representation is as the Holmul Dancer.

The **Maw of Xibalba** is depicted as the great gaping head of a skeletal zoomorph. This creature has much in common with the mouth of the Witz Monster, but it is always represented with skeletal features and split-representation of two profiles merged at the lower jaw, whereas the mouth of the Witz Monster is shown either in profile or front view as the natural mouth of a fleshed creature. The Maw symbolizes death or the point of transition between the natural world and the Otherworld of Xibalba. In Temple 11 at Copán, the mouth of the Witz Monster was the outer door of the temple itself, while the central platform inside the building was the Maw to Xibalba. In that context, one reached the Maw by entering the mountain. A possible interpretation of the contrast in these images is that the Maw is the portal on the side of the Xibalbans, while the mouth of the Witz Monster is the portal in the world of humans.

The **Mexican Year Sign** is a trapezoidal configuration that is associated with the Tlaloc sacrifice complex. Its name comes from the function of a similar sign which marks year dates in the Aztec codices. See Tlaloc.

The **Moon Goddess** in her Classic period form often sits in a moon sign holding a rabbit. Her head functions both as the numeral "one" and as pho-

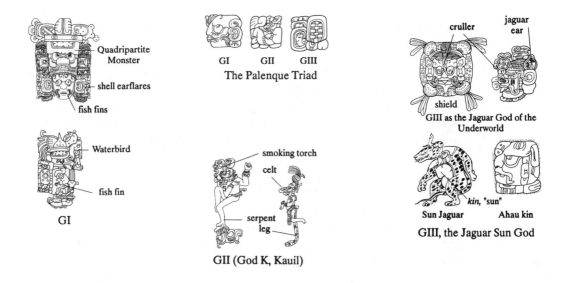

Quadripartite Monster

shell earflares

fish fins

Waterbird

fish fin

GI

GI   GII   GIII
The Palenque Triad

smoking torch

celt

serpent leg

GII (God K, Kauil)

cruller

jaguar ear

shield

GIII as the Jaguar God of the Underworld

Sun Jaguar

kin, "sun"

Ahau kin

GIII, the Jaguar Sun God

netic *na.* Since *na* was also the word for "noble woman," the head of the Moon Goddess precedes female names, distinguishing them from the names of male nobles. In the codices and the Yucatec Colonial sources, the Moon Goddess was called Ix-Chel and she may appear as an aged woman with a toothless mouth.

The **Paddler Gods** are named from their appearance on four bones from the burial chamber of Ah-Cacaw of Tikal. In the scenes incised on these offerings, they paddle the canoe of life carrying the king's soul through the membrane between the worlds and into death. The Paddlers appear with special frequency in references to period-ending rites, where they are born of the king's blood offering. Both gods have aged features. The Old Stingray God is distinguished by squint-eyes and a stingray spine piercing the septum of his Roman nose. He sometimes wears the helmet of a mythological fish called a *xoc.* His twin is also aged, but he is distinguished by a jaguar pelt on his chin, a jaguar ear, and sometimes a jaguar helmet. From glyphic substitutions, we know this pair represents the fundamental opposition of day and night. The Old Stingray God is the day and the Old Jaguar God the night.[6]

The **Palenque Triad** is composed of three gods most fully described in the inscriptions and imagery of Palenque where they are asserted to be the direct ancestors of that kingdom's dynasty. Sired by the mother and father of the gods who had survived from the previous creation, they were born only eighteen days apart. Although their kinship to human kings is detailed only in the inscriptions of Palenque, we surmise they were considered to be ancestral to all Maya kings and thus central images in Maya iconography.

GI, the first born of the Triad, is human in aspect and distinguished from his brothers by a shell earflare, a square-eye, and a fish fin on his cheek. He is particularly associated with the imagery of the incense burner in the Early Classic period and as a mask worn by kings during rituals. GI often wears the Quadripartite Monster as his headdress and is associated with the Waterbird.

GII, the last born of the Triad, is always zoomorphic in aspect. His most important feature is a smoking object—such as a cigar, torch holder, or ax head—which penetrates a mirror in his forehead. He may appear as a reclining child, as a scepter held by a ruler, or as an independent full-figured being. His face always has the zoomorphic snout traditionally called a long-nose, but his body is often shown as human with a leg transformed into a serpent. He is thus the serpent-footed god. He is also called God K,[7] the Manikin Scepter, and the Flare God and has been identified with the Maya names Tahil, Bolon Tzacab, and Kauil.[8] GII is particularly associated with the ritual of bloodletting, the institution of kingship, and the summoning of the ancestors. He is the god most frequently shown on the Double-headed Serpent Bar.

GIII, the second born, is also human in aspect, but he is marked by a jaguar ear and a twisted line called a cruller underneath his eyes. GIII is also called the Jaguar God of the Underworld and the Jaguar Night Sun. His most frequent appearance is as an isolated head worn on a belt, carried in the arm, or surmounted on shields carried by kings and nobles. Both GI and GIII have Roman-nosed, square-eyed faces, long hair looped over their foreheads, and human bodies. GI and GIII will often appear as twins.

The **Pauahtuns** (also known as God N) are aged in feature with snaggleteeth, small human eyes, and a wrinkled visage. They often wear net headbands in combination with cauac or "stone" markings on their bodies as spellings of their name, *paua* ("net") plus *tun* ("stone"). Characteristically, they wear a cut-shell pectoral or their bodies emerge from a conch shell or turtle carapace. The version that wears waterlilies in addition to the net headband might have the body of a young man.

The Classic Maya represented the Pauahtuns as beings who held up the four corners of the world. Sometimes they were the sky and sometimes the earth. The image of the Pauahtuns as world bearers is seen, for example, on Temples 11 and 22 of Copán. Pauahtuns are also depicted with scribes and artisans on painted pottery and on sculpture, as in the case of the Scribe's Palace at Copán. The number five is personified as Pauahtun.

The **Personified Perforator** is a blade of flint or obsidian, or sometimes a thorn or a stingray spine attached to the ubiquitous long-nosed head that personifies inanimate objects in the Maya symbol system. Its other critical feature is a stack of three knots, a symbol that evokes bloodletting with the perforator.

Principal Bird Deity, see Celestial Bird.

The **Quadripartite Monster** appears in three major versions: as the rear head of the Cosmic Monster, as an independent image at the base of the World Tree, and as a scepter or headdress. It never has a body and its head

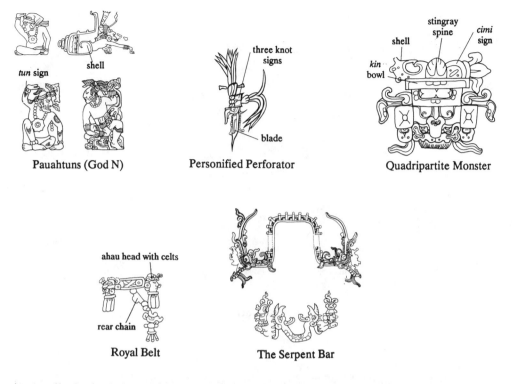

Pauahtuns (God N)

tun sign

shell

Personified Perforator

three knot
signs

blade

Quadripartite Monster

shell

stingray
spine

cimi
sign

kin
bowl

ahau head with celts

rear chain

Royal Belt

The Serpent Bar

is usually fleshed above the muzzle and skeletal beneath it. A flat bloodletting bowl marked with the sign for the sun, *kin*, forms its forehead and a stingray spine, a shell, and crossbands rest in the bowl. The stingray spine represents the blood of the Middleworld; the shell symbolizes the water of the Underworld; and the crossbands are the path of the sun crossing the Milky Way, a sign of the heavens which can be represented by a bird's wing in Early Classic examples. GI of the Palenque Triad often wears this image as its headdress. The Quadripartite Monster represents the sun as it travels on its daily journey through the cosmos. See Cosmic Monster, World Tree, and GI.

The **Royal Belt** consists of a heavy waistband to which jade heads were attached at the front and sides. Typically, these heads, which read *ahau,* surmount a mat sign (or an equivalent sign of rule) and three celts made of polished jade or flint. A chain hung from the sides of the belt to drape across the back of the wearer's legs where a god hung from the chain. Many examples of the dangling god are identified iconographically as Chac-Xib-Chac. This dangling version of Chac-Xib-Chac also occurs as the head variant of an important title reading *chan yat* or in some versions *chan ton.* The first paraphrases as "celestial is his penis" and the second as "celestial is his genitals."

The **Serpent Bar,** also known as the Bicephalic Bar, the Double-headed Serpent Bar, and the Ceremonial Bar, is a scepter carried in the arms of rulers, usually held against their chests. To hold the Bar, Maya rulers put their hands in a formal gesture with their wrists back to back and their thumbs turned outward. Its original function in the Late Preclassic period was to symbolize "sky" based on the homophony in Mayan languages

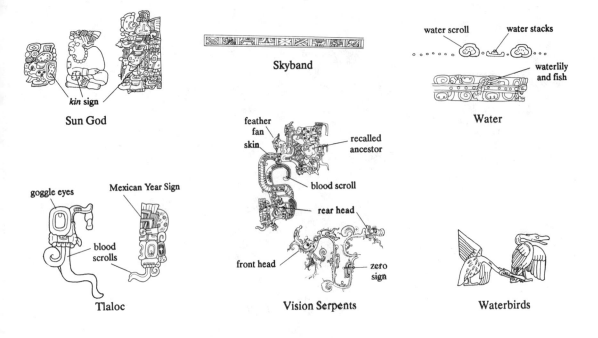

kin sign

Sun God

Skyband

water scroll   water stacks

waterlily
and fish

Water

goggle eyes   Mexican Year Sign

blood
scrolls

Tlaloc

feather
fan
skin

recalled
ancestor

blood scroll

rear head

front head

zero
sign

Vision Serpents

Waterbirds

between *chan*-"sky" and *chan*-"snake." In Early Classic times, kings began to hold the double-headed snake as a scepter. Since it had originally marked the environment through which the gods move, its structural position in Maya symbolism overlaps partly with the Vision Serpent. In its fully developed form, it signals both sky and the vision path, as well as the act of birthing the gods through the vision rite.[9] See Vision Serpent.

Serpent Bird, see Celestial Bird.

The **Skyband** consists of a narrow band divided into segments by vertical bars. Inside each segment is a glyph for a planet, the sun, the moon, or other celestial objects.

The **Sun God** is related to GIII of the Palenque Triad. This particular version features a Roman-nosed human head with square eyes and squint-like pupils in the corner. The four-petaled flower *kin* marks the head as the image of the sun.

Tlaloc is a symbol of war and bloodletting consisting of a jawless head with blood scrolls emerging from its mouth and large circles around its eyes. It is associated with spearthrowers, darts used as weapons, and a certain type of flexible, rectangular shield. Warriors dressed in the costume of this complex usually wear a full-body suit made from a jaguar pelt. Often, a horned owl will also occur with this imagery. This symbolic complex and its sacrificial meaning is shared by many contemporary Mesoamerican societies, including Teotihuacán, which may have lent this ritual complex to the Maya during the Early Classic period.

Twins and Oppositions: The principle of twinning and opposition is at the heart of Maya cosmological thought. Paired gods, like the Paddlers who represent day and night, are common in Maya religious imagery. Some twins represent oppositions and others are actual twins, born of the same parents. Any god could, however, if need be, appear alone outside its normal pairing. New oppositions could also be generated by new pairings. The most famous examples of twins are the Ancestral Heroes of the Popol Vuh, who are related mythically and historically to several of the frequently shown twins of the Classic period. Another context in which oppositions appear with regularity is in the glyphs that introduce Distance Numbers. In this context, the oppositions function as metaphors for the concept of change, the replacement of one thing by another. Some of the oppositions expressed in this context are male-female, life-death, wind-water, Venus-moon, blood-water. The principle of paired oppositions remains today a fundamental characteristic of Mayan languages and metaphor. See Headband Twins, Paddlers, Palenque Triad, Chac-Xib-Chac, and Baby Jaguar.

The **Vision Serpent** is usually depicted as a rearing snake, sometimes with feathers lining its body and sometimes with its body partially flayed. Personified (or "Holy") Blood is usually attached to its tail as a symbol of the substance which materializes it. It symbolizes the path out of Xibalba through which the ancestral dead and the gods enter the world when they are called in a bloodletting rite. Normally, Vision Serpents are depicted with a single head, but two-headed versions are known. The Maya apparently softened the distinctions between Vision Serpents and Double-headed Serpent Bars because they considered them to be related in meaning.[10] See Serpent Bar.

Wacah Chan, see World Tree.

Water is the substance in which the world floats. It is shown welling up out of the portal to the Otherworld. In at least some images, water is the atmosphere of Xibalba and actions which occur there take place as if they were underwater. Water is depicted in two ways: as Water Bands composed of alternating rows of dots, scrolls, and stacks of rectangles representing the surface of water, especially shallow water as in swamps or agricultural canals; and as bands filled with the images of waterlilies. Because *nab,* the word for "waterlily," was homophonous with words for "lake," "swamp," and "river," Waterlily Bands represented these bodies of water. Waterlily Bands often merge with the symbolism of Blood Bands. A Water Hole is a glyphic and symbolic version of water contained under the earth, in cenotes, and perhaps in rivers. It is related to the glyphic and iconic version of the Maw of the Underworld.

The **Waterbird** represents a generic class of bird the Maya associated with water, especially the waters of rivers, swamps, and the canals of raised-field agriculture. This bird usually has a long neck, but as in the case of the Palenque Emblem Glyph bird, it can also have a short neck. The head has the crest of the heron and the upturned, bulging beak of the cormorant. See the Celestial Bird.

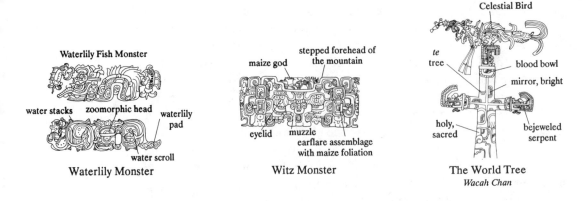

Waterlily Fish Monster

water stacks zoomorphic head waterlily pad

water scroll

Waterlily Monster

stepped forehead of the mountain

maize god

eyelid muzzle

earflare assemblage with maize foliation

Witz Monster

Celestial Bird

te tree

blood bowl

mirror, bright

holy, sacred

bejeweled serpent

The World Tree
Wacah Chan

The **Waterlily Monster** is the personification of lakes, swamps, and other bodies of still water. It is characterized by the pads and blossoms of the waterlily and in some cases it will appear with an Imix glyph (distinguished from other *imix* glyphs by cross-hatching in its center) in its forehead. This particular version is closely associated with the tun and uinal glyphs that are used in Long Count notations. A particularly important title of Classic nobility was based on the uinal substitution as a reference to the nobility as "people of the waterlily" or, perhaps, "people of the swamps and lakes."

The **Witz Monster** is the symbol of the living mountain. It is depicted as a four-legged zoomorphic creature marked with the distinctive signs of the Cauac and "stone." To differentiate the Witz Monster from the zoomorph representing "stone," the Maya portrayed the mountain with eyelids and a stepped cleft in the center of its forehead. On pottery, the mouth of the Witz Monster is often depicted agape. The Witz Monster was placed on temples to transform them into sacred, living mountains. Its open mouth then became the entry into the mountain, symbolizing both the doorway of the temple and the mouth of a cave. To specify which mountain they were picturing the Maya would attach icons to the Witz or write its name within its eyes. See Cauac Signs.

The **World Tree** is the central axis of the world. Called the *Wacah Chan* ("six sky" or "raised up sky") in the glyphs, it appears in the form of a cross marked with God C to denote it is a divine or holy thing. The bejeweled, squared-snouted serpents which usually terminate its branches represent flows of liquid offering—human blood and its analogs, rubber, copal, and the red sap of the ceiba tree. Draped in the branches of the tree is the Double-headed Serpent Bar of kings and perched on its summit is the Celestial Bird Deity, who is the bird of the center in the directional model of the world. The World Tree often emerges from behind the rear head of the Cosmic Monster. The front head of the same creature can be depicted as its roots. The Tree is the path of communication between the natural and supernatural worlds as it is defined at the center of the cosmos. The Cosmic Monster is the same path of communication configured for the periphery of the cosmos. The king personifies this World Tree in his flesh. See Foliated Cross.

NOTES

PROLOGUE

1. This conference, organized by Merle Greene Robertson at Palenque, was a pivotal meeting, bringing together thirty-five of the most active people in Maya studies. The acceleration of the glyphic decipherment and iconographic studies can be traced to this meeting and the timely publication of its results a year later.

2. Our work with the dynastic history of Palenque was built on Berlin's (1968) identification of the rulers we called Pacal, Kan-Xul, Chaacal, and Kuk, and Kubler's (1969) discussion of persons he called Sun-Shield and Snake-Jaguar. Kelley (1968) demonstrated the phonetic reading of one king's name as Pacal or "shield." Our work identified two new kings and an accession phrase that allowed us to fill in the gaps in Berlin's and Kubler's earlier work.

3. David Kelley was the first to read Pacal's name as it was originally pronounced; George Kubler identified the builder of the Group of the Cross as Snake-Jaguar (a name we later translated into Chol as Chan-Bahlum); and David Stuart read the inscription that dated Temple 22 and thus identified its builder as 18-Rabbit.

4. The Harvard-Arizona Cozumel Project was directed by Jeremy A. Sabloff and William L. Rathje and was principally funded by the National Geographic Society. See Freidel and Sabloff (1984) for a description of the ruins on the island.

FOREWORD

1. *Ahau* is glossed in the Motul dictionary, one of the earliest colonial sources on Yucatec Maya, as *"rey o emperador, monarca, principe o gran señor"* ("king or emperor, monarch, prince or great noble"). In the inscriptions of the Classic period, the high king was an *ahau*, but so were many of the high nobles in his court. The inscriptions record that the king took the office of *ahau* when he became king and that he was a *k'ul ahau*, "holy (or divine) lord" of his kingdom. We shall use the *ahau* title to refer to Maya of this highest rank, and following the custom of using pluralizing suffixes from other languages as legitimate forms in English, we will pluralize *ahau* in the Maya fashion as *ahauob*.

Chapter 1: Time Travel in the Jungle

1. Huastec is recognized by modern linguists as a Mayan language. Archaeologically and linguistically, the separation between Huastec and other Mayan languages occurred very early—probably by 2,000 B.C.

2. The term Mesoamerica was invented by Paul Kirchhoff (1943) as both a cultural and geographic term to identify a region limited by aboriginal farming, which did not extend into the deserts of northern México, to an eastward limit defined by Mayan-speakers and their cultural and economical influence.

3. There is still much controversy over the relationship between the hunter-gatherer populations who have left scattered stone-tool evidence of campsites in the Maya highlands of Guatemala and in the lowlands of Belize and the farming populations which emerge in the Middle Preclassic period (1000–400 B.C.) Some scholars believe that substantial new populations of farmers moved into the lowlands at the beginning of this period, bringing with them settled village life, the use of ceramic vessels, and the use of domesticated plants. They suggest that these are the true ancestors of the civilized Maya. However, Fred Valdez (personal communication, 1989), reports the presence of preceramic archaic occupation directly underlying the Middle Preclassic village at the site of Colha in northern Belize. With further research, the relationship between an indigenous hunter-gatherer population and the ensuing village farming populations will become clearer. Migration of peoples between the Maya highlands and the adjacent lowlands certainly did occur in antiquity, as it is continuing to occur today.

4. To say that the shaman conserves culture is only partly accurate, for his constant improvisation of interpretations must be anchored in the changes his people constantly experience from the world around them. His actions are indeed homeostatic in all senses of that word: They work to heal the contradictions in village priorities which inevitably come with the imposition of change from without. These actions conserve things of value by constantly reshaping the changes the Maya perceive in their world to fit fundamental cherished ideas which can be traced thousands of years into the past.

5. We called Stephen Houston and David Stuart asking them if they would send a letter to us documenting the new reading so that we could refer to it. Houston's and Grube's letters arrived within twenty-four hours of each other. This is typical of the growing dynamism in the field of decipherment. As more and more decipherments are made, they in turn generate new readings, so that when a critical mass is reached, many people at once come to the same conclusions. Houston and Stuart (1989) have since published their evidence for this reading.

6. Humboldt included five pages from the Dresden Codex in his 1810 narrative of his scientific travels in México with botanist Aimé Bonpland. Del Río's travels were published by Henry Berthoud of London in 1822 in a book called *Description of the Ruins of an Ancient City,* which included seventeen plates depicting stone carving from Palenque.

7. Our recounting of these interesting events is all based on George Stuart's (n.d.) detailed study of the history of publication and research in the field.

8. Ian Graham, director of the *Corpus of Maya Hieroglyphic Writing,* follows in their footsteps by publishing fine drawings and photographs of Maya inscriptions. Merle Greene Robertson is another of the great archivists. She has spent the last thirty years making rubbings, photographs, and drawings of Maya inscriptions and carvings.

9. This description was included in his *A Study of Maya Art* (1913). Completed originally in 1909 as his doctoral dissertation, Spinden's work represents the first systematic study of Classic period iconography. Many of its observations and connections still hold good today.

10. Morley (1915:26) proposed this methodology and actually applied it to become the first to suggest a war event at Quiriguá. Shortly after this time, however, he began a lifelong campaign to photograph and analyze all the Classic period inscriptions he could find. The two resulting works, *The Inscriptions of Copán* and *The Inscriptions of the Petén,* are still critically important resources, but in both, Morley paid almost exclusive attention to calendric material. He was never again interested in the "textual residue," which ironically he systematically excluded from his drawings.

11. The critical papers outlining these discoveries were all published between 1958 and 1964, including Berlin (1958 and 1959), Proskouriakoff (1960, 1961a, 1961b, 1963–1964), and Kelley (1962).

12. This statement was published in the preface to the 1971 edition to his (Thompson 1971:v) *Maya Hieroglyphs: An Introduction,* but it was but one of several devastating

criticisms he published against phoneticism as proposed not only by Knorozov but also by Whorf (Thompson 1950:311–312). His voice was powerful enough to shut down debate until the mid-seventies. Although there are still holdouts against phoneticism today, many of them strident in their opposition, the accumulated evidence, and especially the productivity of the phonetic approach, has convinced most of the working epigraphers that Knorozov was right. We are still engaged in energetic debate about details and individual readings, but there is wide consensus as to how the system works.

13. Elizabeth Benson, director of the Pre-Columbian Library and Collections of Dumbarton Oaks until 1979, called a series of mini-conference between 1974 and 1978. The participants, David Kelley, Floyd Lounsbury, Peter Mathews, Merle Robertson, and Linda Schele, worked out detailed paraphrases of the inscriptions of Palenque. This work resulted not only in many new decipherments but in the important methodology of paraphrasing based on syntactical analysis of the texts.

14. Three of the four known Maya books are named for the cities where they are now found: the Dresden Codex, the Madrid Codex, and the Paris Codex. The fourth, the Grolier Codex, resides now in the Museo Nacional de Antropología e Historia of México. Made of beaten-bark paper folded in an accordion form, each codex combines pictures and written text drawn in bright colors on plaster sizing. The Maya read their books by folding the leaves from left to right until reaching the end of one side; they then turned the codex over and began reading the other side.

15. Codices from the Mixtec recorded lineage histories as the land documents of their communities. Aztec sources record tribute lists, histories of various sorts, and calendric almanacs and were used to carry news from one part of the empire to another.

16. Yucatecan is the ancestor of modern Yucatec, Itzá, and Mopán, while Cholan diversified into Chol, Chontal, Chorti, and the extinct language, Cholti. Most linguists consider that the diversification into these daughter languages occurred after the Classic period ended (A.D. 900).

17. The descendant languages of these two proto-languages were found in approximately this distribution at the Conquest, but with the now extinct Cholti language spoken in the area between Chol and Chorti. Examples of glyphic spelling specific to one or the other language occur in roughly similar distributions, suggesting that they were in approximately the same distributions during the Classic period. Yucatec and Chol also evidence profound interaction in their vocabularies and grammars beginning during the Late Preclassic period, although they diverged from each other many centuries earlier.

18. This particular homophony has long been known to epigraphers and iconographers, although Houston (1984) was the first to fully document its use in the writing system.

19. We use the word *logograph* rather than *pictograph* because most word signs were not pictures of the things they represented. All pictographs are logographs, but most logographs are not pictographs.

20. The Russian scholar Yuri Knorozov (1952) first identified the way the phonetic spellings work, but it was many decades before his work became generally accepted by Western scholars.

21. Kathryn Josserand has explored the discourse structure of hieroglyphic texts and found a fruitful comparison of the ancient patterns to the modern. She has found that many of the features that the ancient Maya repeatedly used, such as couplets (Lounsbury 1980), oppositions, building a text toward a peak event, and disturbance in syntax around the peak, are still used today.

22. Continuities in their toolmaking techniques suggest these people gradually developed village societies between 1500 and 1000 B.C., at least in the eastern Caribbean coastlands of Belize, where there is a gradual shift toward settled village life along the shores of the rivers. R. S. MacNeish (1982) carried out a survey in Belize and discovered the sites and stone artifacts dating from the archaic, prefarming period.

Up until 1988, radiocarbon samples from the remarkable village site of Cuello in northern Belize dated the earliest Maya farmers at roughly 2000 B.C. This period of occupation fell in the Early Preclassic period of Mesoamerica. The weight of evidence (as announced by Norman Hammond, the excavator of Cuello, at the Austin Maya Hieroglyphic Workshop in 1988) now favors redating the Cuello village occupation about a millennium later, in what archaeologists call the Middle Preclassic period.

23. By 900 B.C., hierarchical society was established in the Copán Valley, resulting in a burial tradition with wide-ranging access to exotic goods, especially jade. These burials, especially Burial XVIII-27, are among the richest so far known from the early

period in the Maya region (W. Fash n.d. and Schele and M. Miller 1986: 75, Pl. 17).

24. The groups in the Pacific lowlands have long been accepted to have been Mayan-speaking. Linguists, especially Terrence Kaufman, Lyle Campbell, Nicholas Hopkins, Kathryn Josserand, and others, now propose that those peoples were speakers of the Mije-Zoquean language family with the Zoqueans living in the western region closer to the Isthmus and with Mije groups in the east toward El Salvador (Kaufman, personal communication, 1989). If this distribution is correct, then much of the early symbolism of kingship from that region derives from the Mije-Zoquean cultural tradition, rather than the Mayan.

25. This kind of social organization is called segmentary because it consists of politically autonomous groups who, for purposes of trade, ritual communion, marriage, and the management of hostilities, regard themselves as descendants of common ancestors and hence as segments of a large family. The lowland Maya developed other forms of social organization as their society became more complex—patron-client relationships, for example, between noble families and families devoted to crafts and skilled labor. Nevertheless, the segmentary lineage organization remained a fundamental building block of Maya society and politics throughout the span of the civilization. The period of civilization has been called segmentary state organization and this is a reasonable label in light of the enduring role of kinship in the hierarchical structure of royal governments.

The archaeological investigation of the origins of Maya complex society in the lowlands is proceeding at a very rapid pace in the interior of the peninsula. Richard Hansen and Donald Forsyth (personal communication, 1989) have recently discovered that the community of Nakbe near El Mirador contains pyramidal mounds of 18 to 28 meters elevation dating to the Middle Preclassic period, perhaps between 600 and 300 B.C. This discovery indicates that before the advent of the Late Preclassic period, some lowland Maya communities were already experiencing the centralization of ritual activity and the concentration of labor power characteristic of the ensuing era of kings. The people of Copán already enjoyed extensive trade contacts and access to precious materials such as carved greenstone during this Middle Preclassic period. Recently, the elaborately decorated Swazy ceramics of northern Belize were redated from the Early Preclassic period into this Middle Preclassic period. Several sites in northern Belize, including Cuello and Colha, were sizable villages with centralized ceremonial activity and extensive trade contacts during this period. The famous Olmec heartland site of La Venta in the Gulf Coast lowlands flourished during the same era and was clearly importing vast quantities of exotic materials from highland sources. Some of the La Venta sources may well be situated in the Motagua drainage in the southeastern periphery of the Maya lowlands.

Viewing this shifting landscape, we now suspect that during the Middle Preclassic period, a long-distance trade network, a "jade trail," crossed the interior of the peninsula from the Caribbean coast of Belize, through the vicinity of El Mirador, and thence across to the Gulf Coast lowlands. We suspect a pattern similar to the situation after the collapse of the southern kingdoms in the ninth century. Then, a few complex societies endured in the interior to form a demographic archipelago across the sparsely inhabited forest. These societies facilitated trade in exotic commodities and also provided local products for export. This pattern may also exist at the outset of the demographic buildup leading to the emergence of civilization in Preclassic times. Eventually, further discoveries in the interior may push the origins of the institution of ahau back into the Middle Preclassic period. Even were this to be the case, however, ethnographic analogy with other areas of the tropical world, such as Central Africa, shows that small complex societies can coexist with large tribal societies for centuries without the tribal societies developing into states. The empirical record of the Late Preclassic still suggests that the institution of kingship coalesced and dominated Maya lowland society in a rapid transformation during the last two centuries B.C.

26. We discuss the structural transformations of kinship ideology which accompanied the invention of Maya kingship in Freidel and Schele (1988b).

27. See John Fox's (1987) study of this kind of organization among the Postclassic Quiche of the Guatemala highlands.

28. Lee Parsons (personal communication, August 1987) excavated a Late Preclassic offering in a major center of the Pacific slopes area which contained a set of three carved greenstone head pendants suitable for wearing as a crown. One of these head pendants is the Jester God, the diagnostic diadem of ahau kingship status from the Late Preclassic period until the Early Postclassic period (Freidel and Schele 1988a). On Stela 5 at the site of Izapa, a major center of the Late Preclassic period in the southern highlands, the Jester

God diadem is also depicted worn by an individual in authority (Fields n.d.). Under the circumstances, there is reason to believe that the institution of kingship predicated on the status of ahau was present in the southern regions of the Maya world as well as in the lowlands to the north during the Late Preclassic period.

29. There is a massive four-sided pyramid at the northern lowland site of Acanceh in Yucatán which Joesink-Mandeville and Meluzin (1976) correctly identified as Preclassic on the basis of a partially preserved monumental stucco mask illustrated by Seler (Seler 1911). The iconography of this monumental mask is commensurate with the royal iconography of Late Preclassic buildings at Cerros (Freidel and Schele 1988b). The famous northern-lowland bas-relief in Loltún Cave depicts a Maya king. Although not firmly dated by epigraphy or archaeological context, the style of the royal regalia is Late Preclassic (Freidel and Andrews n.d.).

30. The city of El Mirador raised stelae in the Late Preclassic period (Matheny 1986), and Richard Hansen (1988) has discovered Late Preclassic-style stone stelae at the site of Nakbe, near that great city. We have yet to find any with hieroglyphic writing.

31. This early date is recorded on the Hauberg Stela (Schele 1985c and Schele and M. Miller 1986:191). The names of the phases of Maya history—Preclassic, Classic, and Postclassic—are misleading in that civilized life and with it public works of enormous size began earlier than the Classic period. Although an important temple of the Late Preclassic period was excavated at Uaxactún early on (Ricketson and Ricketson 1937), it was not until the last fifteen years that archaeologists finally began to uncover the truly amazing accomplishments of the lowland Maya during the Late Preclassic period.

32. The latest dated monument from the Classic period is found at the site of Toniná. It has the date 10.4.0.0.0 or the year 909.

33. Pat Culbert (1988 and personal communication, 1986) gives an overall population distribution of 200 people per square kilometer for the entire Maya region. He estimates a population of 500,000 at Tikal.

34. We will describe the Maya state with several words, including kingdom, domain, dominion, and polity—a word that technically connotes territoriality and political dominion without additional qualifications as to the nature of the organization or whether it can be considered a nation or a state.

35. Berlin (1958) noticed this special type of glyph in the inscriptions of many different sites. He showed that it is composed of two constants—the "water-group" affix, which we now know to read ch'ul ("holy"), and the "ben-ich" affix, which reads ahau—and a variable, which corresponded to the city in which the Emblem Glyph was found. Since he could not decide whether this new type of glyph referred to the city as a place or to its ruling lineage, he decided to call it by a neutral term—Emblem Glyph.

Peter Mathews (1985a, 1985b, 1986) has done the most recent work on Emblem Glyphs. Following Berlin's and Marcus's (1973 and 1976) work, he observed that the rulers of some neighboring communities, such as Palenque or Tortuguero, are both named as ahau of Palenque, suggesting that the territorial entity named by the Palenque Emblem Glyph is larger than the capital city. He also noted that in star-shell war events the main signs from Emblem Glyphs appeared as if they were locations. Combining these data, he proposed that Emblem Glyph are titles, naming the person who has it as a ch'ul ahau ("holy lord") of a polity. Stuart and Houston (n.d.) have additionally recognized glyphs representing geographical features and separate population centers within an area described by a single Emblem Glyph. Finally, we have evidence from Copán that noble lineages tracing their descent to different founders, and presiding over distinct communities within the realm, nevertheless used the same Emblem Glyph. The Copán Emblem Glyph appears on Altar 1 of Río Amarillo in the name of a governor who ruled that subordinate site, and at the same time traced his descent from a founder other than the founder of Copán's royal line (Schele 1987d). Emblem Glyphs thus denote a kingdom or polity as a territorial and political entity with a hierarchy of social positions and different geographical and urban locations within it.

36. Joe Ball (1989) reports that in the Buena Vista region of northern Belize the larger palace complexes are distributed at five-kilometer intervals throughout the region he surveyed. In between the larger compounds, residential clusters and single-family holdings are found distributed at regular intervals. He has found pottery at the smaller compounds that was probably made at the large Buena Vista center. More important, in debris at Buena Vista, he also has found very well-made pottery with the name of the king of Naranjo (Smoke-Squirrel, whom we shall meet in one of our histories) painted on the rim. Seiichi Nakamura (1987) and the Japanese team working in the La Venta Valley near

Copán in Honduras have found the same pattern. One of the largest sites in their survey area, Los Higos, has a stela in the style of Copán, while at least one second-level site had an ahau important enough to have received an incised alabaster vase as a gift from Yax-Pac, the high king of Copán. This gifting down of elite goods was apparently one of the ways Maya kings retained the loyalty of their subordinate lords.

37. Research to date by Mathews and Justeson (1984:212–213) and Stuart (1984b and 1986c) has documented the use of this *cahal* title only in sites of these regions. However, other Maya polities certainly had parallel constructions of political ranking and may also have used this title. Stuart and Houston (personal communication, 1987) have now expressed doubts as to the phonetic value of this title glyph, although they do not question its basic meaning. We will continue to employ it as a useful technical term for this rank that is already known in the literature.

38. Cahalob appear as attendants to kings at Yaxchilán and Bonampak, but they also ruled sites like Lacanjá and El Cayo under the authority of the high kings of larger cities. At least one, Chac-Zutz', was formerly identified as a king of Palenque, but it is now clear he was in fact a cahal probably serving as a war captain to the high king (Schele n.d.b).

39. The inscriptions from kingdoms up and down the Usumacinta record royal visits by people who are named the *yahau*, "the ahau of," the high kings of allied kingdoms (Schele and Mathews n.d.). These royal visits appear to have been one of the important methods of establishing and maintaining alliances between kingdoms and within them.

40. Lateral descents of this kind are recorded several times in the inscriptions of Palenque, Tikal, Caracol, and Calakmul, among others (Schele n.d.e). Enough examples are now documented to presume that brother-brother inheritance was an accepted pattern, which may still survive in the highlands of Guatemala. In many of the Maya groups living there, the youngest son inherits the house of his parents and is responsible for caring for them in their old age. Often the son will become owner of the house and the responsible male of the household while his parents are still alive.

41. Mathews (1986) generally requires the presence of an Emblem Glyph to define a polity, but since Emblem Glyphs usually do not occur in the northern inscriptions, he used other less certain data to suggest polity boundaries in this northern region. His resulting map of Late Classic polities shows a network of small states covering all of the lowlands, and if anything, his numbers may be overly conservative.

42. Kan-Xul of Palenque and 18-Rabbit of Copán were both captured late in their lives after long and successful reigns. They were apparently sacrificed by their captors—the rulers of the smaller towns of Toniná and Quiriguá, respectively.

43. When we went to Palenque the first time in 1970, the Chols and Tzeltals living south of Palenque had to rely on canoes to carry cargo from their homes in the Tulijá Valley to Salto de Agua and Villahermosa. At that time there were many men who knew how to make dugout canoes, but when the new road was built from Palenque to San Cristóbal de las Casas, this region opened up to truck and bus travel. The younger generation uses modern transportation and the art of canoe making is being lost. See Hopkins, Josserand, and Cruz Guzman (1985) for a description of canoe making and its role in Chol society.

44. This carrying system places the cargo in a band passed across the bearer's forehead and down his back. The weight is thus distributed into the muscles of the neck and onto the back, allowing amazingly heavy loads to be carried substantial distances. This method is still used throughout Central America, where one often sees small children walking down the highway bent under the huge load of firewood they carry back to their houses each day. Their parents will carry 100-pound sacks of grain using the same method.

45. We have all seen recent photographs of the pall of smoke from the burning forest hanging over the Amazón Basin. In the dry season, this is a fact of life across the Maya landscape as well. We might suppose that it would not have been nearly as bad during the Classic period, but archaeology and settlement-pattern studies suggest that the population of the Classic period at least equaled current levels and may well have exceeded them. At the height of the Classic period, soot from dry-season fires would have hung as oppressively over the landscape as it does today.

CHAPTER 2: SACRED SPACE, HOLY TIME, AND THE MAYA WORLD

1. The scene on the Acasaguastlan pot (Schele and M. Miller 1986:181, 193–194) suggests that in Classic Maya thought these two planes of existence were more than just

reciprocally dependent. The scene shows the Sun God in the midst of a vision represented by mirrored Vision Serpents—one manifesting day and the other night. Interspersed among the folds of these Vision Serpents are the beasts of the field and forest, elements representing the human community, the waters of both worlds, and sacrificial ritual which communicates between the two. The "waking dream" of the god is the world in which human beings live. On the other side of the equation, David Stuart (1984a, 1988c) has shown that the Maya believed that this vision rite, when performed by kings and other human beings, "gave birth" to the gods. Through this process, the beings of Xibalba, both supernaturals and ancestors, were materialized in the world of humans. If this reciprocity of the vision rite in both worlds was widely believed (and there is evidence to suggest it was), then the world of human experience came into existence as a vision of the gods, while humanity gave the gods material presence in the Middleworld of people through performance of the same rite. In a very real sense, each plane of existence is materialized through the vision rituals performed by inhabitants of the other.

2. This is more than mere speculation. One of the results of the revolution in Maya hieroglyphic translation is confirmation of the hypothesis that what Maya villagers think of the world today, what their ancestors thought of it at the time of the Spanish Conquest, and what the Classic Maya kings thought of it are all transformations of one and the same model (Vogt 1964). These connections are possible only if, in fact, the villagers of the Classic period, the direct ancestors of the post-Conquest villagers, also shared this model of reality.

3. These layers are represented in the three elements surmounting the sun-marked bowl of sacrifice in the forehead of the Quadripartite Monster. This symbol, which rests at the base of the World Tree or rides on the tail of the Celestial Monster, represents the sun as it moves through these domains. In turn, the three domains are symbolized by the signs resting in the sacrificial plate, with the crossed bands representing the heavens, the stingray-spine bloodletter representing the blood of sacrifice composing the Middleworld of earth, and the shell representing the watery world of Xibalba.

4. *Xibalba* is the Quiche Maya term used in the Popol Vuh for the Underworld. Recinos notes the following about the derivations of this word: "*Chi-Xibalba.* In ancient times, says Father Coto, this name *Xibalbay* meant the devil, or the dead, or visions which appeared to the Indians. It has the same meaning in Yucatán. Xibalba was the devil, and *xibil* to disappear like a vision or a phantom, according to the *Diccionario de Motul.* The Maya performed a dance which they called *Xibalba ocot,* or 'dance of the demon.' The Quiché believed that Xibalba was the underground region inhabited by the enemies of man."

While Xibalba is traditionally regarded as the name of the Underworld, and certainly this is the principal spatial location of Xibalba in the Quiche Popol Vuh (Tedlock 1985), we suggest that the Classic Maya regarded the Otherworld as an invisible, pervasive, ambient presence. Even in the Popol Vuh, there are celestial aspects to Xibalba as interpreted by Dennis Tedlock: "They [the Ancestral Hero Twins] choose the Black Road, which means, at the terrestrial level, that their journey through the underworld will take them from east to west. At the celestial level, it means that they were last seen in the black cleft of the Milky Way when they descended below the eastern horizon; to this day the cleft is called the Road to Xibalba." (Tedlock 1985:38; brackets ours). Tozzer's (1941:132) annotated discussion of Landa's understanding of Maya hell and heaven likewise reveals the fact that in Yucatán at the time of the Spanish Conquest, the Maya supernatural abode of gods and ancestors traversed the Underworld, Middleworld, and heavens.

Our analyses of the texts and images pertaining to the Otherworld of the Classic Maya suggest that this is a parallel world revealed in trance. The ritual public spaces of the kings, where people congregated to witness sacrifice, were explicitly designed to convey the idea that they were in the Otherworld (see the acropolis plazas of king Yax-Pac at Copán in Chapter 8). We believe that in the thrall of great public ceremonies, the combination of exhaustion, bloodletting, intoxication, and expectations of trance yielded communal experiences of the Otherworld denizens conjured forth by royalty. Such experiences confirmed the legitimate power of the kings who bore primary responsibility for the interpretation of the visions.

5. The Popol Vuh stories give the best and most humorous view of Xibalba. We recommend the translation by Dennis Tedlock (1985). Michael Coe has done more than any other scholar to associate the Popol Vuh vision with imagery from the Classic period. See Michael Coe (1973, 1978, and 1982) and Schele and M. Miller (1986) for more detailed discussion of Xibalba and Maya concepts of the afterlife.

6. Thompson (1950:10–11) was the primary proponent for the crocodile identification. Puleston's (1976) work on the iconography associated with raised fields supported Thompson's ideas. Recently, Taube (1988) has presented convincing evidence that the turtle was also used as a symbol for the land surface of the world.

7. The expressions for the directions vary greatly from language to language, and depend to some degree on whether the speaker faces east or west when naming them. East has different names in different Mayan languages: In Yucatec, it is *lakin* or "next sun"; in Cholti, it is *tzatzib kin* or "strong sun"; in Chorti, it is *wa'an kin,* "risen sun"; and in Chol, it is *pasib kin* or "arrived sun." North is *xaman* (there is no etymology for this word) in Yucatec; in Chol *chäk iklel* and in Tzeltal *kini ha'al* refer to the north as the direction of winter rains. In Chorti north is *tz'ik,* "left (side of the sun)," and in Tzotzil it is *xokon winahel,* the "side of heaven." West is *chikin,* "eaten sun," in Yucatec and *yaram kin,* "below the sun," in Lacandón. In Chol *bählib kin,* "set sun," or *mahlib kin,* "gone away sun'—as well as *malel kakal,* "gone away sun" in Tzotzil—refer to the west as the leaving or setting position of the sun. South, known as *nohol* in Yucatec and *nool* in Cholti, is the great side of the sun, because this direction is on the right-hand side as one faces the rising sun.

8. The glyph *wac ah chan* is recorded in the Temple of the Cross at Palenque as the name of the sanctuary inside the Temple and by extension the name must refer to the central image of the interior panel. That central image is the World Tree. (See Chapter 6 for a discussion of the Temple of the Cross.) Nicholas Hopkins in the 1978 Texas Workshop on Maya Hieroglyphic Writing was the first person to suggest a decipherment for the glyph naming this axis as "stood-up or raised up sky," and David Stuart's (personal communication, 1986–87) work with the proper names of buildings and stelae contributed greatly to the recognition of this *wac ah chan* as a proper name.

9. David Stuart (1988c) has made an argument that the Double-headed Serpent Bar is another manifestation of the path of communication between the Otherworld and our world.

10. As we shall see, other important people in addition to kings could participate in opening the portal to the Otherworld through elicitation of the Vision Serpent. As long as the Maya had kings, they remained the pivotal characters in such royal dramas.

11. This plate was painted by the same artist who executed the famous Altar de Sacrificios vase. See Schele and M. Miller (1986:304–307, 310–312) for a detailed analysis of this plate.

12. Symbols representing the power of objects began as a profile polymorphic image directly attached to objects such as earflares and bloodletters during the Late Preclassic period, personifying such objects as alive with power (Schele and M. Miller 1986:43–44 and Freidel and Schele 1988b). Objects and people continued to be decorated with these little power polymorphs in public art throughout the Classic period. The metaphysics of this way of regarding the material world is cogently summarized by the great Mayanist ethnographer E. Z. Vogt speaking of the modern highland Maya of Chiapas: "The phenomenon of the inner soul is by no means restricted to the domain of human beings. Virtually everything that is important and valuable to the Zinacantecos also possesses an inner soul: domesticated plants, such as maize, beans, and squash; salt; houses and the fires at the hearths; the crosses; the saints in the churches; the musical instruments played in ceremonies; and the Ancestral Gods in the mountains, as well as the Earth Lord below the surface of the earth. The ethnographer in Zinacantan soon learns that the most important interaction going on in the universe is not between persons, nor between persons and objects, as we think of these relationships, but rather between inner souls inside these persons and material objects, such as crosses." (Vogt n.d.:10–11). Crosses, we should add, are further described by Vogt: "In Chiapas they symbolize 'doorways' to the realm of the Ancestral Gods who live inside the hills and mountains and/or represent Ancestors themselves, as the Classic Maya stelae depict rulers or royal ancestors" (Vogt n.d.:25). David Stuart (personal communication, 1989) has associated these same concepts with the God C "water group" set of signs. This set reads *ch'ul,* "holy" or "sacred," in the writing system.

13. The Spanish describe the Maya drawing blood from all parts of their bodies as their principal act of piety. In Classic representations and post-Conquest descriptions, the most important rites required blood from the penis or tongue, although it could also be drawn from any part of the body (Joralemon 1974 and Thompson 1961). The ritual served two primary purposes in the understanding of the ancient Maya: as the nourishment and sustenance of the gods and as the way of achieving the visions they interpreted as commu-

nication with the other world (Furst 1976). The Maya believed this bloodletting–vision rite gave birth to the gods (Stuart 1984a, 1988c), and thus materialized them in the human world. Every important dynastic and calendric ritual in Maya life required sanctification through bloodletting (Schele and M. Miller 1986). It brought the central axis into existence and allowed communication with the ancestral dead and the gods.

14. Mayan languages have two words for "house": *otot* is a "house," but the word incorporated the idea that someone possesses it (analogous perhaps to "home" in English). *Na*, on the other hand, is a building that does not include ownership in the concept of the word. The word *otot* cannot be uttered without implying that the house is owned—it is always someone's house. *Na* was used in the proper names of temples, but *otot* is the glyph used to name the category of object to which "temple" belonged. Temples were sacred houses owned by the gods and the spirits of the ancestral dead who resided in them. Thus we know that the ancient Maya thought of the temple as an inhabited place.

15. The term "monster" has been in Maya scholarly literature since Spinden's (1913) first study of Maya iconography, but it is a loaded term to English speakers recalling the Frankensteinian tradition in literature and films. Nevertheless, "monsters" in our own tradition usually exhibit features combining animal and human or distorting the normal features of either to the level of the grotesque. The Maya generated their images of supernatural creatures in the same way, combining animal with human or exaggerating the features of both to produce an image that could never be mistaken for a being from the natural world. It is in this sense that we use the term "monster," without intending to associate it with any of the negative connotations that have become attached to the word. We use it in its original sense of "something marvelous, a divine portent or warning, something extraordinary or unnatural" and "an imaginary animal (such as a centaur, sphinx, minotaur, or heraldic griffin, wyvern, etc.) having a form either partly brute and partly human, or compounded of elements from two or more animal forms" (OED:1842–1843).

16. David Stuart (personal communication 1987) first recognized the glyph for *witz* in its many permutations at Copán and interpreted it as "mountain." Most important, he found a passage on the Hieroglyphic Stairs where *witz* is written with the zoomorphic image formerly identified as the Cauac Monster. Distinguished from the cauac zoomorph meaning "stone" by the presence of eyelids and a stepped indention in the forehead, this "mountain" image is the long-nosed god, so prevalent in Maya art and on buildings, which has in the past been called Chac. Rather than referring to the raingod, however, the image identifies the temple as a "mountain" as well as a sacred house. The doorways of temples at Copán and especially in the northern regions are often built in the form of this monster to identify them as the *ti' otot* "mouth of the house." The mouth of the mountain is, of course, the cave, and Maya mythology identifies the road to Xibalba as going through a cave. The Maya not only used natural caves as the locations of bloodletting and vision ritual (MacLeod and Puleston 1979), but the inside of their temple was understood to be the cave pathway to the Otherworld. The ritual of bloodletting materialized the World Tree as the path to the supernatural world. See "Kingship and the Maya Cosmos" in *The Blood of Kings: Ritual and Dynasty in Maya Art* (Schele and M. Miller 1986: 301–316) for a detailed examination of the imagery associated with this pathway.

17. These are elementary and pervasive metaphors of shamanistic ecstasy (see Mircea Eliade 1970:Chapter 8). It is our basic working hypothesis that Maya royal charisma was essentially shamanistic as this concept is defined by Eliade (see Freidel and Schele 1988a).

18. Ritual activities of the modern Maya generally involve the creation of altars, arbors, and corrals which, in their essential features, realize the structure of the world given in this model: four trees at the corners, or six poles holding up the altar. And the associations given by modern "knowers" of these rituals are the same as those to be found in the ancient royal performances: the fourfold arrangement of the cosmos; the use of sacrifice (now chickens, turkeys, deer, or pigs), and most significant, the principle that the created "place" is a conduit to the supernatural. The fact that the modern village Maya, and their direct village ancestors as described by the conquering Spanish, performed ritual that is resonant with that of Precolumbian Maya, albeit of elite and royal status, clearly implies that the knowledge and the performance were the province of the commoner ancients as well.

19. The pervasive quality of access to the supernatural in shamanistic cosmology is well articulated by Mircea Eliade: "Although the shamanic experience proper could be evaluated as a mystical experience by virtue of the cosmological concept of the three communicating zones [heaven, earth, underworld], this cosmological concept does not

belong exclusively to the ideology of Siberian and Central Asian shamanism, nor, in fact, of any other shamanism. It is a universally disseminated idea connected with the belief in the possibility of direct communication with the sky. On the macrocosmic plane this communication is figured by the Axis (Tree, Mountain, Pillar, etc.); on the microcosmic plane it is signified by the central pillar of the house or the upper opening of the tent— which means that *every human habitation is projected to the 'Center of the World,'* or that every altar, tent, or house makes possible a break-through in plane and hence ascent to the sky." (Eliade 1970:264–265; brackets ours, italics original.)

20. Vogt (n.d.) describes the staffs of high office among the modern peasant Maya of the highland region in terms strictly commensurate with this hypothesized attitude of the ancient Maya toward sacred objects and facilities. For example, he states, "The batons are washed and censed in communities such as Chamula in order not only to rid them of accumulations of sweat and dirt, but also to rid them symbolically of any mistakes made by a predecessor serving in the same position. Note that the first washing in Chamula rids the batons of sweat and dirt, and administrative errors, while the water and liquor used in the second and third cleanings are served to the officials who in drinking these liquids renew the sacred power that has come down to them from the Ancestral Gods via these batons. Note also that the silver-headed batons are believed to be infallible; if administrative errors have been made, they are the mistakes of human officials who hold these batons while serving in high offices" (Vogt n.d.:39–40). Similar repeated ritual results in accumulative power endowed in the silver coin necklaces of the saints housed in Zinacantan center (Vogt 1976:127–128).

21. New excavations of Temple 26 at Copán have demonstrated that the iconography of the Ballcourt at Copán remained the same in all of its manifestations from Early Classic through Late Classic times. Other buildings, such as Temple 22, retained the same sculptural program through different construction phases, suggesting that those particular foci were symbolically defined early in the city's history and remained unchanged through subsequent centuries. When new buildings were to be constructed, the Maya performed elaborate rituals both to terminate the old structure and contain its accumulated energy (Freidel and Schele n.d. and Schele 1988b). The new structure was then built atop the old and, when it was ready for use, they conducted elaborate dedication rituals to bring it alive. These dedication and termination rituals permeate the archaeological record and they represent a major component of the history recorded in the inscriptions at many sites.

22. The containment rituals were elaborate and their effects widespread in the archaeological record. The portrait images of both humans and deities were effaced, often by destroying the left eye and nose. Color was removed or whitewashed and sculpture slashed, broken, burned, or sometimes carefully sealed in. Holes were drilled in pottery vessels and other objects were broken or effaced to contain their power. In an earlier building under the summit of Temple 26 at Copán, a circle of charcoal and broken stingray spines, remaining from a ritual conducted to terminate an earlier version of the temple, was recently discovered (W. Fash 1986). At Cerros, this ritual involved the careful burial of the old facade and rituals in which hundreds of pottery vessels were broken over the building. The huge percussion holes that mar the Olmec colossal heads are also remnants of termination rituals (Grove 1981), reflecting the long-term presence of this ritual and its underlying definition of sacred energy in Mesoamerican thought.

23. The Old Testament Bible is a complex compilation of history, law, poetry, and prophecy (Drane 1983:22–23) written down over an extended period of time by several authors (Spuhler 1985:113) during the emergence of the Hebrew nation as a state. Behind the Bible is a long history of literacy and of literature both in Greater Mesopotamia and in Egypt. In these respects, the Quiche Popol Vuh is quite comparable. It too is a complex compilation of law, poetry, and history pertaining to a nation. It is also subsequent to a long history of literacy in bordering territory and related society, namely among the lowland Maya. The parallels between the histories of the Old Testament and earlier sacred literature from Mesopotamia are often striking, particularly with respect to Genesis (Spuhler 1985:114–115). In the same fashion, the parallels between the Creation story in the Popol Vuh and the allusions to Creation in the sacred literature of the Classic lowland Maya are beginning to become clear. It is important to bear in mind, however, that the Popol Vuh does not register direct transmission of the Classic Maya cosmology or theology any more than the Old Testament registers directly the beliefs of Sumerians. In both instances, we are dealing with long and complicated literary and theological traditions. Ultimately, our interpretations of the Classic Maya reality must be anchored in the contemporary Classic period texts, images, and archaeological record.

24. The surviving version of the Popol Vuh combines stories of the great protagonists of Maya myth, the Hero Twins called Hunahpu and Xbalanque, with creation stories and the dynastic history of the Quiche. Found in the town of Santo Tomás Chichicastenango by the Spanish priest Ximénez in the seventeenth century, the book records the history of Quiche kings to the year 1550. Ximénez hand-copied the original and transcribed it into Spanish. The original is now lost, but we have the copy made by Ximénez. Of the three English versions by Recinos (1950), Edmonson (1971), and Tedlock (1985), we recommend the Tedlock version as the easiest reading for those interested in knowing these stories. The Popol Vuh is one of the finest examples of Native American literature known to the modern world.

25. See Freidel and Schele (1988b) and Cortez (1986).

26. Karl Taube (1985) associated the older set of twins with the maize god and the image from pottery painting known as the Holmul Dancer.

27. Many of the underworld creatures pictured on Classic Maya pottery have Emblem Glyphs in their names. Houston and Stuart (1989) have shown these beings are the *way* or "coessences" of the ahau of those kingdoms.

28. See Michael Coe's (1973, 1978, 1982) works on Maya pottery painting for a corpus of images showing Xibalba and its denizens.

29. There are as many modern myths about the Precolumbian ballgame as there are ancient ones. The most persistent is that the winner was sacrificed, because the loser was considered unworthy. There is absolutely no evidence supporting that curious idea and the stories of the Popol Vuh, our most detailed information on the game, clearly demonstrates that the loser not the winner was the victim of sacrifice. The father and uncle of the Hero Twins were decapitated after they lost to the treacherous Lords of Death. The most interesting recent work on the Precolumbian ballgame is Ted Leyenaar's (1978) documentation of a game still played in the state of Sinaloa. His photographs of the equipment and the play resemble Classic Maya imagery to a remarkable degree.

30. All Maya calendar counts are in whole days. Since fractions were not available, the Maya used only whole-day adjustments to account for remainders in cycles of fractional lengths. For instance, a lunation is approximately 29.53 days long. To account for the accumulating error in a whole-day count, the Maya alternated a 29-day and 30-day moon to give a 29.5-day average. However, even this approximation soon accumulated discernible error between where the count said the moon should be in its cycle and what one observed in actuality. To adjust for that error, the Maya would place two 30-day months back to back, with different sites using different formulas of 29- and 30-day sequences. None of these approximations produced a particularly satisfactory result. With the true tropical year of 365.2422 days, they did not even try. Instead they kept a simple whole-day count that proceeded day by day without attempting to adjust for the .2422 day that accumulated each year. They were aware of the length of the true solar year and reckoned by it when necessary so that rituals would fall on the same point within it—for example, on a solstice. In their calendar, however, they let the count of days drift, with their New Year's day, 1 Pop, falling one day later in the solar year every fourth repetition. See Floyd Lounsbury (1978) for a detailed discussion of the Maya calendar and number system.

31. The use of letters of the alphabet to name these gods comes from Schellhas (1904), the first modern scholar to systematically study their images and glyphic names in the codices. God K, the deity of the 819-day count, appears in four versions which are distinguished by the color glyph and direction of the four quadrants through which the count moves. The first 819-day-count station began 6.15.0 before the creation day and is associated with the birth of the mother of the gods in the text of the Temple of the Cross at Palenque (Lounsbury 1976 and 1980; Schele 1981 and 1984b).

32. No apparent relationship to astronomical or seasonal periodicities has been discovered, so that we presume the cycle is based on numerology.

33. Barbara MacLeod (personal communication, 1987) has proposed that *uayeb* is an agentive noun derived from the Chol word *wäyel,* "to sleep." *Uayeb* (the five-day month at the end of a year) is, thus, the "resting or sleeping" part of the year.

34. The Maya, like other Mesoamerican people, believed the world had been created more than once and then destroyed. Each creation used one form of matter that was destroyed by its opposite, for example, a world of fire destroyed by water. Aztec myth makes the current creation the fifth to exist. The writers of the Popol Vuh described these successive creations as the attempts of the gods to create sentient beings who would recognize their greatness. The gods tried different solutions: animals, people of mud, and

then wood. Finally in the fourth attempt, they succeed in creating humanity of maize dough. If this seventeenth-century version corresponds to the ancient myth, the current existence is the fourth version in the cosmos to have been created.

35. Justeson and Mathews (1983) have proposed that the name of this 360-day year is Yucatec and derived from the practice of setting stones to mark the end of years in this count.

36. The ancient Maya called these twenty-day months *uinic* or "human being" because people have twenty fingers and toes just as a month had twenty days. Modern scholars most often use the term *uinal* because that is the term found in the Colonial sources from Yucatán. Both terms were apparently extant in the Classic period, for both spellings occur in the inscriptions; however, there is a preference for *uinic* over *uinal.* The Maya apparently thought of the month as a "person," while they thought of the year as a "stone-setting."

37. Except for *katun,* these terms are coined by modern scholars from Yucatec dictionaries of the Colonial period. Each term is a Yucatec number, *bak, pic, calab,* combined with *tun,* the word for year or stone.

38. We transcribe the Maya vertical arrangement into a left to right format using arabic numbers with periods separating the various cycles. The highest cycle, the baktun ("400-stone"), is written 13.0.0.0.0: 13 baktuns, no katuns, no tuns, no uinals, no days.

39. The thirteenth 400-year period of the Maya Calendar is soon to end. 13.0.0.0.0 will occur again on December 23, 2012, but this date falls on 4 Ahau 3 Kankin, rather than on the creation day, 4 Ahau 8 Cumku. From the ancient inscriptions, we know that the Maya did not consider it to be the beginning of a new creation as has been suggested. At Cobá, the ancient Maya recorded the creation date with twenty units above the katun as in Date 1 below.

```
13.13.13.13.13.13.13.13.13.13.13.13.13.13.13.13.13.13.13. 0. 0. 0. 0 4  Ahau      8  Cumku
               13.13.13.13.13.13.13.13. 9.15.13. 6. 9 3  Muluc    17  Mac
                               1. 0. 0. 0. 0 8 5  Lamat     1  Mol
```

These thirteens are the starting points of a huge odometer of time: each unit clicks over from thirteen to one when twenty of the next unit accumulate. The baktun clicked from thirteen to one four hundred years after the creation date. The Olmec lived during the fifth 400-year cycle; the earliest written dates in Mesoamerica fall into the seventh cycle; and Classic history took place in the last quarter of the eighth and all of the ninth 400-year cycle. The latest Long Count date known is 10.4.0.0.0 at Toniná. Since dates rarely required that numbers higher than the baktun be written, the Maya regularly excluded them from their dates.

We have one exception to this practice at Yaxchilán, where a scribe wrote a date on the stairs of Temple 33 with eight of the larger cycles above the baktun recorded (Date 2 above). The Yaxchilán scribe intended to set this important historical date in its larger cosmic scale, and by doing so told us that all of the higher cycles of the calendar were still set at thirteen during Maya history. Another inscription, this one from the Temple of Inscriptions at Palenque, projects into the future to the eightieth Calendar Round of the great king Pacal's accession. They give us a count of the precise number of days it will take to come to this date which happens to be only eight days after the end of the first 8,000-year cycle in this creation (Date 3 above). The pictun will end on October 15, 4772, in our calendar and the anniversary will occur eight days later on October 23, 4772.

Combining the information from all these dates, we have reconstructed the nature of Maya time in this creation. On the day of creation, all the cycles above the katun were set on 13, although this number should be treated arithmetically in calendric calculations as zero. Each cycle within the calendar is composed of twenty of the next lowest units, moving in the order 20, 400, 8,000, 160,000, 3,200,000, 64,000,000, and so on toward infinity. With this information, we can project how long it will take to convert the highest thirteen in the Cobá date to one—41,341,050,000,000,000,000,000,000,000 tropical years.

These huge numbers are meant, of course, to represent the infinite scale of the cosmos, but they give us other kinds of information. Although the Long Count appears to record a linear concept of time, it, like the other components of Maya calendrical science, was cyclic. Different eras came and went, and each era was itself composed of ever larger cycles, one within the other and all returning to a starting point. The metaphor used by modern scholars is that of a wheel rolling back on its starting point. It is the huge scale of the higher cycles that allowed the Maya to unite linear and cyclic time. From a human point of view, the larger cycles can be perceived only as a tangent, which has the appearance of a straight line. We use this type of scale in the same way to build a cyclic concept into our essentially linear definition of time—our cosmologists place the "Big Bang" 15,000,000,000 years ago and they contemplate the possibility that it was but one of many "Big Bangs."

40. Lounsbury (1976) has discussed "contrived numbers," as deliberately constructed time distances which link days before the creation date to days in the historical present. The function of these contrived relationships is to demonstrate that some historical date was "like-in-kind" (on the same point in many of the important cycles of Maya time) to the pre-creation date. The worlds that exist on either side of that creation date (13.0.0.0.0 4 Ahau 8 Cumku) have their special symmetries and patterns of sacredness. To demonstrate that a historical date is "like-in-kind" to a pre-creation date is to say it has the same characteristics and brings with it the symmetry and sacredness of the previous pattern of existence.

41. These four books, named for the cities in which they are found or for their first publishers, are the Dresden Codex, the Madrid Codex, the Paris Codex, and the Grolier Codex. Made of beaten-bark paper coated with a fine plaster surface and folded like accordions, the books record in pictures and writing which gods and what acts were associated with days in the calendar. Tables for anticipating the cycle of Venus and eclipses of the sun are also included as books of learning and prognostication for calendric priests specializing in the use of the calendar.

42. In trying to understand how the ancient Maya thought about time and space, modern people can think of the fabric of time and space as a matrix of energy fields. These fields affect the actions of human beings and gods, just as the actions of these beings affect the patterns within the matrix. For the Maya, it was a relationship of profound and inextricable interaction.

43. At Palenque, Tikal, and Copán, historical texts recall events that occurred during Olmec history, 1100–600 B.C., or in Late Preclassic times, 200 B.C. to A.D. 200. The texts at Palenque and Tikal imply that each of those dynasties had ruled during those early times, although archaeology has shown that neither kingdom existed during Olmec times. The symbolic relationship they meant to imply was similar in nature to the Aztecs' proclamation of themselves as the legitimate descendants of the Toltec or our own invocation of Rome or Athens as the source of our political ideology.

44. When we started writing this book, we presumed that primogeniture was the primary system of inheritance and that the examples of brother-brother successions were historical rarities. Our research, however, has shown that lateral succession was far more frequent than we had believed (Schele n.d.e.). We still believe that primogeniture was the preferred pattern, but that lateral succession from older brother to younger brother was also acceptable.

45. William Haviland (1968) provides a lucid and remarkably prescient discussion of Classic Maya kinship organization from the vantage of ethnohistorical, archaeological, and ethnological information. The epigraphic data generally support the patriclan organization he describes.

46. Although clan structure is a common social institution in the preindustrial world, in the case at hand there is a specific glyph that designates the founding ancestral king of a royal Maya clan (Schele 1986b). This characterization of Maya elite organization is documented in Classic Maya history and is not an extrapolation backward from the period of the Spanish Conquest. The function of designating a founding ancestor is to define a group of descendants as relatives and to internally rank these people.

47. Several reconstructions of the Classic period kinship system have been posited based on evidence from the inscriptions and languages, but we find the evidence for a patrilineal and patrilocal system to be by far the strongest. The major proponents of this system have been Haviland (1977) and Hopkins (n.d.).

48. This lineage compound was excavated during the second phase of the Proyeto Arqueología de Copán. Dr. William Fash first proposed the identification of this compound as the residence of a scribal lineage, an interpretation we accept (W. Fash 1986 and 1989).

49. The glyph for this rank was first identified by Mathews and Justeson (1984) as a title for a subordinate rank. David Stuart (1984b) greatly expanded their discussion by analyzing the distribution and iconographic context for the title. Although the proposed decipherment of the title as *cahal* is disputed by some epigraphers, we shall use it as a convenient way of identifying this office, accepting that the reading may change in the future.

50. The type-rank system used in the Copán Valley survey developed during Phase I of the Proyecto Arqueología de Copán (Willey and Leventhal 1979). Phase II of the PAC excavated one example of each of the four types under the direction of Dr. William Sanders. These four excavated examples have been consolidated and are now open to the public. The excavations will be published by the Instituto Hondureño de Antropología e Historia in a series of volumes entitled *Excavaciones en el area urbana de Copán*. The information related here comes from personal conversations with Dr. William Fash, who participated in the excavations (see also W. Fash 1983b).

51. Peter Mathews (1975) first identified the "numbered successor" titles as a way of recording lineage successions, an idea that was elaborated by Berthold Riese (1984). We subsequently found these counts are reckoned from a named ancestor who occurs with the notation "first successor" (Schele 1986b and Grube 1988). In the Group of the Cross at Palenque and on Altar 1 at Naranjo, a complementary succession is reckoned from mythological ancestors who lived beyond the bounds of human history—that is, before this manifestation of creation materialized on 4 Ahau 8 Cumku.

52. Recorded on Altar 1, the Río Amarillo ruler names himself as an ahau of the Copán polity, but lists his lineage as descended from its own founder (Schele 1987d).

53. Chan-Bahlum's heir-designation (Schele 1985b) began five days before the summer solstice of 641 and ended on December 6 of the following year. Muan-Chan of Bonampak began the rites for his heir on December 14, 790, and ended them on August 6, 792, with a battle in which he took captives for sacrifice. He memorialized this series of rites in the amazing murals of Temple 1 at Bonampak (M. Miller 1986b).

54. See the chapters "Kingship and the Rites of Accession," "Bloodletting and the Vision Quest," and "Kingship and the Maya Cosmos" in *The Blood of Kings: Ritual and Dynasty in Maya Art* (Schele and M. Miller 1986) and Stuart (1984a, 1988c) for a full discussion of these rituals and their representations in Maya art.

55. Peter Furst (1976) first discussed this bloodletting ritual as a quest for a vision which the Maya interpreted as communication with the supernatural world. Furst associates this bloodletting ritual with similar beliefs in many other societies, and he has been a longtime advocate of the role of shamanism in the institution of rulership from Olmec times on. David Stuart (1984a and 1988c) has added rich detail to our understanding of the complex of imagery and texts associated with bloodletting. Bloodletting has been discussed in the context of both rituals and objects manufactured for use in ritual by Schele and M. Miller (1986).

56. David Joralemon (1974) provides a clear iconographic discussion of the prismatic-blade bloodletter. Schele (1984a and n.d.d) describes the epigraphic and iconographic evidence for obsidian as a material from which prismatic-blade bloodletters were made. Freidel (1986a) reviews some of the larger economic implications of the control by governments of obsidian as a prized ritual commodity.

57. All Maya communities would have celebrated the great regularities of the Maya calendars: the hotun (five-year) endings within a katun, the katun (twenty-year) endings, New Year's, the 819-day count, the coming of the rains, important points in the solar year, such as solstices and the zenith passages, and stations in the planetary cycles. But each great city also had its own histories that generated a series of local festivals celebrating the founding of the city, the date associated with its special patron gods, the anniversaries of its great kings and their births, triumphs, and deaths. Thus the system of festivals combined those occasions celebrated by all Maya with a complementary series derived from the individual histories of each dynasty. Both kinds of celebrations appear in the glyphic record.

58. David Stuart has been instrumental in identifying a set of verbs recording rituals of dedication for temples as well as for their plaster and stone sculptures. His date for the dedication of Temple 11 at Copán (September 26, 773) is four years after the dedication of the Reviewing Stand on the south side of the building on March 27, 769. At Palenque, we have about the same time span in the Temple of Inscriptions. The last date in the ongoing history of the interior panels is October 20, 675, some eight years before the death of Pacal on August 31, 683. The 675 date appears to be the last historical date recorded before the tablets were sealed inside a containing wall to protect them during the rest of the construction. Given that the center and back walls must have been standing so the huge panels could be set in them, we deduce that the construction and decoration of the temple took about nine years.

59. At the time of the Spanish Conquest, Maya rulers in the northern lowlands were explicitly concerned with the well-being of their farming populations precisely because ill

treatment encouraged migration, which they could not easily impede (Roys [1962]; N. Farris [1984] on demographic fluidity). During the Precolumbian era, the periodic abandonment and reoccupation of some centers and the clear evidence of demographic fluctuation at others indicates similar principles in operation. See Freidel (1983).

60. Analysis of skeletal materials at Tikal by Haviland (1967) suggests that Classic elite populations enjoyed taller stature and generally somewhat greater physical robusticity than the commoners.

61. The public fair is, and was in antiquity, a temporary marketplace established in town squares near the important civic and religious buildings during religious festivals. Such fairs occurred in cycles and were also no doubt occasioned by great historical events in the lives of rulers. (See Freidel [1981c] for a discussion of this economic institution among the Maya.)

62. See Schele and Mathews (n.d.) for a discussion of visits between elites.

63. R. L. Roys (1957) summarized descriptions of marketplaces on the north coast of the peninsula.

64. Since the place-notation system of the Maya used only three marks—one, five, and zero—addition and subtraction were simple geometric operations that could be conducted with any handy material laid out on a grid drawn in the dust. To add, the two numbers were laid side by side and then collapsed into a sum. The twenties only needed to be carried up to obtain the answer. Subtraction reversed the process and was, thus, a simple geometric operation, which like addition required no memorization of tables. Multiplication was more difficult, but still possible without tables or much training. The system allowed the illiterate to do simple arithmetic needed for trade and exchange without formal education.

65. Colonial period sources describe verbal contracts, but there is no reason to suppose that contracts, tribute lists, and some form of accounting were not kept in written form, especially since we have just these sorts of documents from the Aztec of Central México. Unfortunately, the writing surface that would have been used for such purposes, bark paper sized with plaster, did not survive in the tropical forest that was home to the Classic Maya.

66. See Landa's descriptions of life in Yucatán shortly after the conquest (Tozzer 1941) and Roys's (1943) discussion of Indian life during the Colonial period of Yucatán.

67. See Freidel (1986a) for a recent discussion of Mesoamerican currencies.

68. For a discussion of Maya merchant activities and such speculation see Freidel and Scarborough (1982).

69. ". . .they traded in everything which there was in that country. They gave credit, lent and paid courteously and without usury. And the greatest number were cultivators and men who apply themselves to harvesting the maize and other grains, which they keep in fine underground places and granaries so as to be able to sell (their crops) at the proper time." (Tozzer [1941:96], parens original)

70. Such visits by high-ranked nobles who represented high kings are documented at Yaxchilán and Piedras Negras (Schele and Mathews n.d.) and at least one vessel from Burial 116 of Tikal depicts such a visit by lords from the Usumacinta region who display gifts before Tikal lords (see W. R. Coe [1967:102] for a drawing of this scene). In fact, the offering of gifts, especially cloth and plates full of various substances, is one of the most commonly represented scenes on Maya pottery.

71. Dennis Puleston (1976 and 1977) accepted the central importance of raised-field agriculture to ancient Maya civilization and proceeded with experimental reclamations of ancient canals to see how the system worked. The experiment not only yielded information on the productivity of the system, but demonstrated how the Maya used the animals and landscape associated with it—water lilies, water birds, fish, and caiman—as important components of their cosmic model and their royal symbolism.

CHAPTER 3: CERROS: THE COMING OF KINGS

1. Some modern visitors are awed by the architectural scale and design of Maya ruins. Yet the architectural techniques they used—corbeling and the post-and-lintel system—were primitive even by the standards of the ancient world. The most spectacular exploitations of the corbel systems are found at Palenque and in the use of concrete core construction in some northern lowland kingdoms. The most wonderful technology of the Maya, from our vantage, was their agricultural system. Despite evidence in some instances that the Maya over exploited and allowed the degeneration of their land, generally their

success in producing food and commercial crops was nothing short of spectacular. In an age when modern nations are allowing the rapid destruction of the tropical forest belt of the globe, we have much to learn technologically from the Maya who maintained a civilization of millions for over a thousand years in such an environment.

2. The Maya knew of metals from at least the Early Classic period onward, because their tribal and chiefly neighbors in lower Central America used them. The lowland Maya chose not to use metals, for reasons yet unknown, until very late in their history.

3. There were no eligible beasts of burden in Mesoamerica at the time of the emergence of farming village life. The largest animals—the tapir, the peccary, the deer, and the large felines—were categorically unsuited either to domestication or service as burden carriers.

4. The regional timing of the establishment of large-scale public centers in the Maya lowlands is a matter of continuing debate. Matheny (1986) and Hansen (1984) place the initial construction of the Tigre complex at El Mirador in the second century B.C., while W. R. Coe (1965a) identifies major public construction at Tikal somewhat later, in the middle of the first century B.C. The Tikal dating is commensurate with the dating at Cerros in Belize (Freidel and Scarborough 1982). Our position is that while the point dates of radiocarbon samples range over roughly a century, 25 B.C. to 125 B.C. for the earliest decorated buildings in the lowlands (perforce the earliest evidence of the kingship they celebrate), the statistical range of possibility for the radiocarbon assay representing an actual absolute date shows an overlap of all the reported contexts. For example, a date from Structure 34 at El Mirador of 125 B.C. $\pm$ 90 years and a date from Structure 2A-Sub 4 at Cerros of 50 B.C. $\pm$ 50 years, have a statistically high probability of being contemporary.

5. We have outlined the technical arguments from iconographic and archaeological evidence for this interpretation of Maya history in a series of papers, principally Freidel and Schele (1988b).

6. Cerros ("hills") is the modern name of this place; its original name was lost long ago.

7. The evidence for sea travel by the people of Cerros is principally in the form of faunal remains of reef and deep-water fish (Carr 1986b). Dugout canoes made from great tree trunks are traditional to the Maya of Belize and are made even today in some parts of the country.

8. The evidence for long-distance trade between Cerros and people to the north along the coast of Yucatán, down into the mountainous regions of the southern highlands, and into the interior of the southern lowlands is derived from analyses of exotic materials which do not normally occur in down-the-line trade between neighbors. The Cerros people had available, for example, distinctive marine shells from the northern coast of the Peninsula (Hamilton n.d.) and their craftspeople were familiar with a wide range of foreign styles, which they used freely in the pottery manufactured at the site (R. Robertson n.d). Additionally, there are numerous examples of exotic materials at the site which must have been traded in from other parts of Belize or from the southern highland region (Garber 1986).

9. A simple public platform of this description is Structure 2A-Sub 4–1st, which, like the first true royal temple at Cerros (Structure 5C-2nd) was built as part of the final phase of the nucleated village underlying the later ceremonial center (Cliff 1986). Similar platforms preceded the construction of royal temples in the North Acropolis at Tikal in Guatemala during the same time period (W. Coe 1965a).

10. Clay drums with cutout and appliqué faces were found as smashed fragments in the deposits of the nucleated village at Cerros. Elements of the iconography include the "cruller" of GIII (a Sun God and the younger of the Ancestral Heroes Twins) and shark teeth, a signal of GI, who characteristically wears a fish barbel and is associated with Xoc, the shark (see the Glossary of Gods). These drums initiate a long tradition of effigy vessels and vessel supports among the lowland Maya (Freidel, Masucci, Jaeger, and Robertson n.d.).

11. The reconstruction of vegetal environment and foodstuffs is based on research carried out by Cathy Crane (1986). The fish and game animals have been identified by Carr (1986a and 1986b).

12. The vessels, affectionately termed "beer mugs" by the Cerros crew, are very effectively designed to hold beverages: graspable, narrow at the straight rim, and weighted on the flat base to discourage tipping. They are identified by Robertson as appropriate for liquids and their context is associated with burials and high ritual (R. Robertson 1983).

13. Cathy Crane has positively identified cotton at Cerros; the presence of cacao is a more tenuous identification, but there are some macrobotanical remains that look promising.

14. These are, in fact, the jewels of an ahau that were found deposited in a dedicatory cache at the summit of Structure 6B at Cerros (Freidel 1979; Garber 1983; Freidel and Schele 1988a). Structure 6 was the second royal temple to be built at Cerros, and it was erected while the first, Structure 5C-2nd, was still open and in use. The location and design of Structure 6 shows that it was constructed by the successor of the patron of Structure 5C-2nd. It is hence likely that the jewels found buried in the summit of Structure 6B belonged to the first king of Cerros, patron of Structure 5C-2nd.

15. See Freidel (1979; 1983) and Freidel and Schele (1988b) for technical discussions of the origins and distribution of the lowland Maya sculptured pyramid.

16. We do not know how the building crafts of the ancient Maya world were divided, but we suspect they did not have architects in the sense of the modern world—that is, specialists who design buildings and are responsible for iconographic programs as well as engineering. More likely, the Maya had specialists, perhaps entire lineages, who were trained in the art of building. Their training, however, would have been less as artists responsible for what the building said, and more as master craftsmen responsible for how the message was executed. We have chosen to use the term "Master Builder" for this specialty, rather than architect, in the tradition of Frank Lloyd Wright, I. M. Pei, or Mies van der Rohe.

17. These activities have the prosaic title of "termination rituals" in our present scholarly reports (Robertson and Freidel 1986), but the practice clearly encompassed both beginnings and endings of major ritual work such as building temples, rebuilding temples, and finally abandoning them. We believe that the vessels broken on such occasions first held the foods of offering and ritual meals, as found among contemporary Maya. The identification of the fruit-tree flowers is based upon palynological analysis in progress by Cathy Crane. A complete anther of a guava flower is a likely prospect in light of the clustering of four preserved grains of this tree in the deposit.

18. Although we did not find the outline under this particular building, this is a known Maya practice in the preparation of superstructures (Smith 1950) and a logical deduction in light of the fact that the building and stairway were built in a single construction effort. We know, therefore, that their finished proportions were determined by the initial work.

19. These sockets for massive posts are more than 3.5 meters deep and 1.2 meters in diameter. If the size of the posts used in modern postholes throughout the Maya area (Wauchope 1938) can be taken as a guide, these temple posts rose 6 to 9 meters above the floor level of the summit temple or superstructure. The walls of the summit temple rose about 2 meters, hence these temple posts rose far above the roof of the temple.

20. The raising of the great posts constitutes one of the episodes in the Quiche Popol Vuh (Edmonson 1971; Tedlock 1985). These posts are called *acante*, "raised up or stood up tree," in the rituals of the Yucatec-speaking Maya at the time of the Spanish Conquest (Tozzer 1941; Roys 1965). The raising of these posts defined the sacred space within which the shaman communed with the supernatural forces. We have given the technical discussion of this interpretation of Structure 5C-2nd's posts in Freidel and Schele (1988a).

21. The plan of this temple, while unusual, is not unique. Across the bay from Cerros, there is an Early Classic temple at the community called Santa Rita (D. Chase and A. Chase 1986). The plan of this Early Classic building, constructed a few centuries after Structure 5C-2nd at Cerros, is more complex but comparable in principle to the one described here. Maya temples generally featured an inner sanctum where the most intimate features of ritual action took place, as described further in Chapter 7 in the context of Chan-Bahlum's accession monuments. The distinctive character of the Cerros example is that the path of entry into the inner sanctum corresponds to the path of the sun.

22. These assemblages consist of a fairly constant set of elements. The center ornament was usually made of jade which had been shaped into a thin-walled cylinder with one end flaring out into a flat surface, often carved to resemble a flower. This part, which is called an earflare because of its shape, was carved by drilling, sawing, and abrasion with reeds, string, sand, and water. During the Early Classic period, this main earflare often had a quincunx design with bosses arranged around the central hole at the four corners. The Maya depicted a curling leaf of maize sitting above the earflare and a large counterweight, often made of shell or pearl, hanging below it. Another popular arrangement had a finger-sized cylinder, which was drilled through its long axis, hanging diagonally from

the center of the earflare. To hold it out from the face, a thin string, possibly made from deer or cat gut, was threaded through the center drill-hole, through a bead on the end of the cylinder, back through the drill-hole, and finally through the pierced earlobe to a pearl or shell counterweight.

23. As described by Schele and M. Miller (1986) for Classic period examples, and by Landa (Tozzer 1941) with respect to the carving of sacred wooden images at the time of the Spanish Conquest, Maya artists may well have performed major public work of this kind in altered states of consciousness achieved by fasting, bloodletting, and the use of intoxicants. Once executed, the error in the proportions of the building may have been left in the design as a divine expression to be accepted and accommodated rather than corrected.

24. The earliest archaeologically documented inscribed object in the lowlands is a bone bloodletter found in a Late Preclassic period burial at the site of Kichpanhá, a few miles south of Cerros in northern Belize (Gibson, Shaw, and Finamore 1986).

25. On this building there are also special raised and modeled glyph panels attached to earflare assemblages. Such panels are also found on other Late Preclassic buildings at Cerros, Structures 6B and 29B. Similar panels are further reported or illustrated on Structure N9–56 at Lamanai (Pendergast 1981), Structure 34 at El Mirador (Hansen 1984), and on Structure H-Sub 8 at Uaxactún (Valdés 1988). The principle of glyphically "tagging" earflare assemblages, the central power objects of the entities represented as head masks on such panels, is thus a widespread convention in the Late Preclassic period. So far, only the glyphs "tagging" the earflares on Structure 5C-2nd have been read, as discussed further on in this chapter.

26. This four-petaled flower regularly appears on the cheek of the Sun God in its young human, old human, and cruller-eyed GIII aspects during the entire Classic period.

27. In the great creation myth of the highland Quiche Maya, given in their Book of Council, the Popol Vuh (Edmonson 1971; Tedlock 1985), the ancestral Hero Twins, Hunahpu and Xbalanque, apotheosize as the sun and the moon rather than the sun and Venus. Actually, the younger twin could be associated in the Classic period with the moon as well as the sun (Schele and M. Miller 1986:308–309), while the elder twin was the Sun in the first opposition and Venus in the second. It is important to grasp that such multiple natures as jaguar/sun/moon or Venus/Celestial Monster/sun are not exclusive and unchanging, but rather inclusive and dynamic. The Waterlily Jaguar, for example, the quintessential predator in royal warfare, can be associated with both the sun as it manifests the Sun God and with Venus in the Venus-timed war rituals discussed in Chapter 4. These "aspects" constitute statements of momentary affinity and resonance. The fact that some of these connections are remarkably enduring and pervasive in Maya thought does not belie the perpetual necessity of reiteration in ritual to re-create and sustain them. Ultimately, the charismatic supernature of the king is dependent upon a logic which mandates his inclusion in such cosmic categories.

28. One of the creatures especially associated with Venus, as described in the Glossary, is the Celestial Monster. Derived from a crocodilian model, this beastie was long-snouted, like the Cerros creature.

29. Schele (1974:49–50) dubbed this figure the Jester God because of the resemblance of its tri-pointed head to a medieval court jester.

30. The Maya writing system uses special signs called semantic determinatives to specify particular meanings when a value could be in doubt. One of these determinatives is the cloth headband worn by kings. In various manifestations, the headband can have the regular ahau glyph attached, as well as a mirror and, most importantly for our purpose, a Jester God. Whenever this ahau-Jester God headband is present, the glyph, whether it is a human head, a vulture, a rodent, or whatever, reads ahau. To wear this headband in the Classic period is to be an ahau.

31. The Headband Twins are the particular manifestation under discussion. Named glyphically as Hun-Ahau and Yax-Balam, this set of twins has one member marked by large body spots and the Jester God headband, while the other sports a cut-shell yax sign on his forehead and jaguar pelt on his chin, arms, and legs.

32. There are additional details in the iconographic program of Structure 5C-2nd which confirm this interpretation. The glyph panels "tagging" the earflare assemblages on the eastern side of the building contain the word *yax,* meaning "green" and "first." Here they denote that the sun and Venus of the eastern side are "first," as they should be at dawn. On the western side of the building, the Venus image on the upper panel is being disgorged from the split representation of the framing sky/snake (in Cholan languages, the

words for "sky" and "snake" are homophonous [*chan/chan*]), signaling that the movement is "down" as it should be in the setting of the sun with the Eveningstar above it.

33. The Maya shaman establishes a four-part perimeter of sacred space. Inside of this space he can pass over the threshold to the Otherworld. We detail the manner in which Late Preclassic kings harnessed shamanistic ecstasy to their emerging definitions of royal charisma in a recent professional article (Freidel and Schele 1988a).

34. There are Late Preclassic masks wearing the Jester God headdress in Group H at Uaxactún, a remarkably preserved and recently excavated temple complex in the interior of the lowlands (Valdés 1988).

35. There are other potential interpretations of these images which we are exploring, including the prospect that the "first" Venus and sun, on the eastern side, represent the ancestors, while the western Venus and sun represent the human king and his heir (Freidel n.d.).

36. Reading "between the lines" in this fashion is the key to understanding the people and politics behind the masks and ritual portraits of Maya art. Although such interpretations are subject to dispute and discussion as to their content, there is no doubt that the Maya intended their art and public texts as political propaganda as well as offerings of devotion. The documentation of this strategy is to be found in the texts of royal temples of the Classic period, as described in subsequent chapters.

37. The earliest public architecture at Cerros, Structure 2A-Sub 4–1st, the small and undecorated pyramid next to the dock, has a radiocarbon date of 58 B.C. $+$ 50 years from a single large piece of carbonized wood from a sealed plaster floor. The abandonment ritual of the latest public building, Structure 29B, provided us with a piece of burnt wood which registered 25 B.C. $+$ 50 years. What must be understood here is that any radiocarbon date is only the best statistical approximation of the age of an object: the $+$ years give a range into which the date may fall. The wider the $+$ range, the higher the probability that the date falls within that range. The beginning and ending dates of public architecture at Cerros fall within the $+$ range of each other, indicating a range of as little as fifty and as much as one hundred years for all of the public architecture of Cerros to have been built. Other archaeological evidence from the site supports this dating. For example, no change in the style or technology of ceramics occurs between the earliest and the latest building (R. Robertson n.d.). And only eight distinct construction episodes, a very low number for most Maya sites, have been detected in the stratigraphic sequence of architecture (Freidel 1986c). Together, this evidence supports the view that Cerros underwent a veritable explosion of public construction in the first century B.C.

38. Group H at Uaxactún (see Chapter 4) has this same internal court entered through a portal building atop an acropolis.

39. Vernon Scarborough has written detailed discussions of the impact of construction activity on the surrounding landscape at Cerros (Scarborough 1983; 1986).

40. The excavations in temples and pyramids at Cerros were limited in scope compared to those carried out in some Maya centers because the archaeological project had many other research objectives to address as well. Future excavation at the site will no doubt expose more examples of the elaborate stucco work of Late Preclassic royal architecture. Despite the limitations of the record at Cerros, this remains the largest analyzed and reported sample of such decoration from a Maya site. Uaxactún, El Mirador, and Lamanai promise to provide substantive new samples as excavations at those sites are reported and extended.

41. These are the jewels in our little story of the traders' landing at Cerros.

42. The grasping of a mirror is one way of signifying accession to the rulership in the texts of the Classic period (Schele and J. Miller 1983).

43. The ancient Maya believed the sacred liquids could be transmuted into other forms, resulting in a group of substances that were transformations of one another. This group included blood, fire, smoke, water (Freidel 1985), but other liquids, gases, and vapors were also related (Schele and M. Miller 1986).

44. Offerings of precious and powerful objects are common in the record of Maya royal temples. These are typically called dedicatory offerings with the connotation that the objects were given to the gods by the devout to sanctify buildings and carved stone monuments, like stelae. William Coe's detailed monograph on the offerings from one Maya center, Piedras Negras (W. Coe 1959), documents the complex symbolism of these objects. The cache from Stela 7 at Copán and newly found caches from Temple 26 incorporate ancestral heirlooms made of jade. Such objects were principally used in shamanistic rituals performed by kings to materialize sacred beings in this world (Freidel and Schele 1988a).

The burial of such objects in buildings or carved monuments enhanced their power to function as the pathways of this type of communication and as portals to the Otherworld. Just as the caching of whole objects focused sacred power, the reciprocal act was to smash and burn objects to release sacred power prior to scattering or sprinkling. In an earlier phase of Temple 26, for example, large numbers of valuable greenstone jewelry were shattered in pit fires set on the four sides of a temple to be buried by new construction. This last kind of termination ritual (R. Robertson n.d.) was often carried out in the same general cycle as dedicatory rituals (Walker n.d.).

45. The technique of using internal buttressing of this kind is common in Maya architectural construction. It was especially valuable when large-scale buildings were being raised rapidly. The Maya masons employed loose angular rubble when they could in such projects, and provided vertical stability by capping off the rubble with small rocks, gravel, and dirt which could then support another layer of large loose boulders. The internal walls provided lateral stability.

46. Although the resulting arrangement resulted in ridiculously narrow alleyways between the flanking stairways and the central platform, the plan was intended to emulate a conventional arrangement now known on the thirty-three-meter-high pyramid at Lamanai, which also dates to the Late Preclassic (Pendergast 1981). This arrangement can also be seen on a pyramid at El Mirador (Matheny 1987). The three-temple arrangement of small temples or temple-platforms is one of the more important architectural traditions of Late Preclassic architecture.

47. This pattern is best illustrated in the tri-figure panels of Palenque (Schele 1979), but it is also found at other sites. The famous Stela 31 at Tikal (Jones and Satterthwaite 1982) depicts king Stormy-Sky flanked by portraits of his father, Curl-Snout.

48. See Schele and M. Miller (1986:241–264) and M. Miller and Houston (1987) for further discussion of the Classic Maya ballgame.

CHAPTER 4: A WAR OF CONQUEST: TIKAL AGAINST UAXACTÚN

1. Some of the largest buildings ever constructed in the Precolumbian world were built at El Mirador at least two centuries before the Pyramids of the Sun and Moon at Teotihuacán. See Ray Matheny's description of El Mirador and its amazing architecture in the *National Geographic Magazine* (September 1987).

2. The political collapse of El Mirador remains one piece in the puzzle of the Protoclassic period as discussed in Chapter 1. The city was not completely abandoned after its heyday, but the modestly prosperous Classic period inhabitants never again laid claim to dominion in a landscape populated by an increasing number of rival kings.

3. We call this complex Tlaloc-Venus war because of the imagery worn by its practitioners and the regular association of its conduct with important stations of Venus, Jupiter, and conjunctions of Jupiter and Saturn (Kelley 1975, 1977a, 1977b; Closs 1979; Lounsbury 1982, Schele 1984a, n.d.c). The "star-war" nickname comes from the way the Maya recorded the event by using a Venus sign (Kelley argued that it was simply "star") over the glyph for "earth" or the main sign of the Emblem Glyph of the kingdom attacked. See Note 45 for further discussion.

4. A pit with a constricted neck dug into the bedrock by the ancient Maya.

5. W. R. Coe (1965a and 1965b) has published detailed descriptions of these very early occupations as well as the Late Preclassic and Early Classic periods of Tikal.

6. William Coe (1965b:1406) himself makes this suggestion.

7. The empty Late Preclassic period tomb at the summit of Structure 4 at Cerros also testifies to the practice of burying exalted dead in the early temple complexes, but in actuality the notion of the corpse as a worthy inclusion in the power structure of places does not appear pervasively until the Classic period. Tikal may prove precocious in this ritual activity.

8. W. R. Coe (1965b:15) identifies the main burial (two skeletons were found in the chamber) as a female.

9. See W. R. Coe (1965a:15–17 and 1965b:1410–1412) for full descriptions of this tombs and its contents. Coggins (1976:54–68) discusses the stylistic affinities of the tomb.

10. The archaeological record is rapidly changing with respect to the early public depictions of Maya kings. Richard Hansen (1989) reports the presence of carved stone stelae at Nakbe, a satellite of El Mirador, which carry the same kind of elaborate scroll

work found here. Because these early representations often depict the individual as masked, their identification as historical people is somewhat problematic.

11. See W. R. Coe (1965b:21) and Coggins (1976:79–83) for detailed descriptions of this tomb and its contents.

12. The mask is about the same size relative to a human body as other pectorals known archaeologically (Schele and M. Miller 1986:81, Pl. 19) and in Maya depictions of rulers. Most telling are the five holes drilled in the lower edge to suspend the cylinder and bead arrays normally depicted with such pectorals.

13. This three-pointed symbol of ahau, initially a geometric element, was worn as the central diadem of a characteristic headband with three jewels (viewed from the front). The three-jewel crown is seen on the foreheads of the upper masks of Structure 5C-2nd at Cerros with the geometric forms as described in Chapter 3. On the stucco masks of gods in Group H at Uaxactún (Valdés 1987), the three-jewel crown appears with snarling humanoid faces in the personified form that would become the Jester God of Classic period imagery.

14. William Haviland (1967:322–323) notes that around A.D. 1, a difference in average height could be seen between those people buried in lavish tombs and the rest of the population at Tikal. This difference continued to grow during the Early Classic period marking what Haviland sees as the development of a ruling elite who had consistent access to better nutrition.

15. Christopher Jones (n.d.) has associated the construction phases detected in the North Acropolis, Great Plaza, and East Plaza with the dynastic history of Tikal as recovered from the inscriptions.

16. Chris Jones (n.d.) also speculates that the eastern and western causeways were built at this time as "formalizations of the old entrance trails into the site center."

17. Chris Jones (n.d.) suggested an association between these massive building projects and the ruler in this burial.

18. One of the basic historical problems facing Mayanists is the relatively great size of Petén centers and communities of the Late Preclassic period compared to other parts of the lowlands. One explanation would hold that El Mirador, Tikal, and Uaxactún among other centers had early special relationships with those kingdoms of the southern mountains and Pacific slopes regions that show precocious complexity and which supplied the lowlands with strategic commodities (Sharer 1988). We agree that such special relationships are a possibility and that commerce would have attracted more farmers to the region from elsewhere in the lowlands. At the same time, the real potential of the swampy interior for ordinary farmers lies less in its proximity to the highlands than in the development of intensive agriculture based upon effective water management. The great Late Preclassic public works of El Mirador, Tikal, and Uaxactún suggest to us that these governments attracted and commanded labor for many other overtly practical projects, particularly raised-field agricultural plots. Intensive agriculture, of course, would not only guarantee the prosperity of commoners. It would also generate the surplus of commodities necessary to sustain a flourishing trade with the highlands. This "agricultural attraction" hypothesis, however, points to the great antecedent civilization in Mesoamerica's swampy lowlands: the Olmec of the Gulf Coast. We anticipate the future discovery of more direct relationships between the lowland Olmec of such centers as La Venta and the Middle Preclassic pioneers who first farmed the swamps of Petén.

19. This famous building was reported by Oliver and Edith Ricketson (1937) as part of their work for the Carnegie Institution of Washington.

20. In 1985, Juan Antonio Valdés (1988) began excavations of Group H as part of the Programa de Patrón de Asentamiento. Trenches excavated that year into the platform yielded only Mamon and Chicanel ceramics, dating all interior construction phases to the Preclassic period. In total, he found seven construction phases including the most extraordinary and complete example of Late Preclassic masked architecture now known.

21. Freidel has discussed the comparative iconography of Structures 5C-2nd and E-VII-Sub, suggesting that both display the Sun cycle surmounted by Venus (Freidel 1979; 1981a).

22. The meanings applied to particular buildings were by no means mutually exclusive. *Witz* is a general term meaning "mountain," which was applied in glyphic and symbolic form to Maya buildings to define them as the living mountain. In principle, all Maya pyramids were Witz Monsters. On some buildings, such as Structure 5C-2nd or Structure E-VII-Sub, the animus of the mountain itself is a relatively minor component of the overall decoration, specifically given in the lowermost frontal masks on those

buildings from which the larger and more important sun masks emerge. On other buildings, such as the one discussed here, the Witz aspect is central. Still other buildings, as we shall see at Palenque and Copán, emphasize the World Tree which grows from the heart of the mountain. These are not different messages, but aspects of a single unitary vision. The aesthetics of Maya ritual performance encourage such creative and diverse expression of nuance.

23. Because the specific signal of the Witz monster is his crenelated forehead, as seen on the lower Monster, we have to be cautious in identifying the upper Monster as another Witz, for the top of the mask is destroyed. Nevertheless, the rest of the mask, including the blunt snout surmounted by a human nose, "breath" scrolls flanking the gaping mouth, and the eye panels, comprise a virtual replication of the lower, complete mask. When the Late Preclassic architects intend a primary contrast in meaning between masks at different vertical points in a mask stack, as on Structures 5C-2nd and E-VII-Sub, they usually distinguished them by using different muzzle forms and other features. Hence it is likely that the upper mask here replicates the primary meaning of the lower mask.

24. All the other buildings in the group have a single room that was entered from a door on the court side of the building. Sub-10 has a door on both the inner and outer sides with flanking plaster masks on both sides of the substructural platform. One entered the group by mounting a stairway rising up the platform from the plaza to the west of Structure H-X, which was a mini-acropolis flanked by a north and south building. Once atop Structure H-X, one could walk to either side of Sub-10, but the main processional entrance was up its short western stair, through the building, and down the east stairs. The use of a building as a gateway into an acropolis is also found on Late Preclassic Structure 6 at Cerros.

25. The Late Preclassic architectural jaguar mask varies from the strikingly naturalistic animal depictions of Structure 29 at Cerros, to the blunt-snouted snarling zoomorphic image of the sun on Structure 5C-2nd at Cerros, to the anthropomorphic version found here in which the fangs are reduced to residual incurving elements within the mouth panel. What began as a broad incisor-tooth bar under the square snout on the sun jaguar of Structure 5C-2nd is here reduced to the single projecting tooth which will be characteristic of divinity and the Ancestors in the Classic period. This anthropomorphic jaguar, however, still carries the squint eyes and bifurcated eyebrows of the 5C-2nd version. On Structure 29 at Cerros, the appearance of this humanoid ahau is enhanced by its physical emergence from a naturalistic jaguar head. At Tikal, Early Classic Temple 5D-23–2nd has a comparable humanoid ahau mask emerging from a jaguar head. In this case, the jaguar carries the mat symbol in its mouth (A. Miller 1986: Fig. 9). The particular ahau masks on Temple H-Sub-10 at Uaxactún are framed below by enormous knots, signaling that they are in fact giant replicas of the girdle heads worn on the belt of the king. Schele and J. Miller (1983) have discussed these *ahau pop* and *balam pop* ("king/mat" and "jaguar/mat") images of kingship.

26. The full extent of Late Preclassic construction is not known in either case, and massive constructions at Tikal likely hide very substantial public monuments of this period (Culbert 1977).

27. Recent excavations at the site of Calakmul in southern Campeche suggest that it was a kingdom with a substantial Late Preclassic and Early Classic occupation. David Stuart (personal conversations, 1989) reminded us that the pyramids of El Mirador are visible from the summits of Calakmul's largest buildings. That great kingdom was very probably a significant player in the demise of El Mirador, and as we shall see in the next chapter, a vigorous rival of Tikal and Uaxactún for dominance of the central Maya region.

28. The name glyph in Early Classic texts (Fig. 4:10) consists of *yax* ("first" or "blue-green"), a bamboo square lashed at the corners with rope, and the head of a fish. Lounsbury and Coe (1968) suggested a reading of *moch* for the "cage" portion of the glyph, and Thompson (1944) proposed a reading of *xoc* for the mythological fish head in this name. In some examples, these two signs are preceded by *yax,* perhaps giving Yax-Moch-Xoc as the full name. It is interesting that this *moch-xoc* glyph appears in the name of Great-Jaguar-Paw on Stela 39, although that ruler is listed as the ninth successor, rather than the founder.

29. Peter Mathews (1985a:31) first proposed this calculation, which Jones (n.d.) subsequently supported by showing that the 349 tuns between the accessions of the eleventh and twenty-ninth successors divides into an average reign of 19.3 tuns. The kings who ruled between 375 and 455 were the ninth, tenth, and eleventh successors, with the eleventh successor, Stormy-Sky, acceding in 426. Giving an average reign of one katun

each to the ten rulers who preceded him places the founding date of the lineage somewhere between 8.9.0.0.0 (A.D. 219) and 8.10.0.0.0 (A.D. 238). These calculations fit well with the known archaeological history of Tikal and with the appearance of historical monuments and portable objects inscribed with historical information dated between A.D. 120 and A.D. 200 (Schele and M. Miller 1986:82–83, 199).

30. Chris Jones (n.d.) speculates that Stela 36 is even earlier than Stela 29. Found in a plaza at the end of the airfield at Tikal about 3.5 kilometers from the North Acropolis (C. Jones and Satterthwaite 1982:76), this stela may depict one of the unknown rulers between the founder and the ninth successor. The location of this very early monument away from Tikal's center is curious in any case.

31. Mathews (1985a:44) associates this scroll-jaguar image with another scroll-ahau-jaguar, a glyph at C5 on Stela 31 that he suggests is the name of a ruler. Unfortunately the date associated with this character fell in the destroyed section of Stela 31, so that we are not able to identify this personage as the same ahau portrayed on Stela 29 or as a different one because royal names could be reused in the Maya culture, as in the kingdoms of Western Europe.

32. The main sign of the Tikal Emblem Glyph is a bundle of strands bound together by a horizontal band tied in a knot. The anthropomorphic version of this bundle glyph is a Roman-nosed head with a twisted rope or jaguar tail hanging in front of the ear. The kings on Stela 29 and other later monuments wore headdresses with a twisted rope or jaguar tail in the same position as a way of marking themselves as the living embodiment of the Emblem Glyph and thus of the kingdom. This same head substitutes for an ahau glyph half-covered with a jaguar pelt, which Schele (1985a) read *balan-ahau* or "hidden lord" in an earlier study of the substitution patters of these glyphs.

In October, 1989, Stephen Houston and David Stuart informed us they had read the same glyph not as *balan-ahau* but as *way*, the word for "sorcerer" and "spirit (or animal) companion." Nikolai Grube sent a letter to us at almost exactly the same time detailing his own reading of this glyph and its head variant. All three suggested to us that the kings on Stela 29 and 31 are depicted in their their roles as "sorcerers" and one who can transform into their animal companions in the Otherworld. We accept their observations and further suggest that when this *way* head appears in the position of an Emblem Glyph on the lintels of Temple 4 that it refers to the king as the *ch'ul way,* "the holy shaman."

33. The floating figure on Stela 29 is not named, but we can reconstruct its function from other representations. At Tikal there are two kinds of floating figures: gods materialized through bloodletting, as on Stela 4 and Stela 22, and ancestors recalled by the same rite. This latter type of image is specifically named on Stela 31 as the father of the protagonist Stormy-Sky. Since the floating figure on Stela 29 is patently human, we presume he is the ancestor from whom Scroll-Ahau-Jaguar received the throne.

34. Schele and M. Miller (1986:121) called the Leiden Palenque ruler Balam-Ahau-Chaan, while Mathews (1985a:44) called this ruler "Moon-Zero-Bird," based on the occurrence of his name glyph on Stela 31 at D6-C7 and on the Leiden Plaque at A10. Fahsen (1988b) followed Mathews in the name usage and identified a new occurrence of his name on Altar 13 at Tikal.

35. See Schele and M. Miller (1986:63–73, 110, 120–121, 319) for detailed discussions of the iconography and inscription on the Leiden Plaque.

36. David Webster (1977), among other Mayanists, believes that warfare during the early phase of the lowland civilization was instrumental in the establishment of an elite warrior class. These warlords, in his view, launched wars of conquest against less organized neighbors, which yielded them land and booty for their followers. Rising population and a diminishing ratio of arable land to people spurred this kind of warfare and precipitated elitism among the lowland Maya in Webster's scenario. Webster argues his case from the instance of an impressive early fortification surrounding the center of Becán (Webster 1976). While we find Webster's work stimulating, we see no clear empirical support for a general condition of conquest warfare during the Late Preclassic period and the first centuries of the Early Classic. Ancient Maya farming settlements, beginning in the Preclassic, were characteristically open and rather dispersed across the landscape until the Terminal Classic period (A.D. 800–1000; see Ashmore 1981). Although Maya centers certainly contained acropolis constructions suitable for defense as citadels, walled forts of the kind used by populations experiencing direct attack and capable of withstanding siege are not common among these people. Where internecine warfare is aimed at ordinary settled populations in modern and historical preindustrial societies, it often generates a response of nucleated and defended communities. In this regard, a number of Terminal Classic and

Postclassic Maya are indeed fortified in this fashion (Webster 1979). Our own position is based upon substantive information from texts and images. From the Maya vantage, warfare explicitly served to prove the charisma of kings and high nobility. Ethnohistorical documents (Roys 1962) confirm that such charisma was fundamental to the attraction of population into emergent and flourishing polities (see also Demarest 1986: Chapter 7.) In particular, kingdoms of the Petén, in our view, required and utilized massive organized commoner labor—not only to create and refurbish centers, but also to create and maintain the intensive agricultural systems upon which their economies depended. While the impact of warfare on Maya commoners remains to be elucidated archaeologically, there is positive epigraphic and iconographic evidence to identify the advent of conquest warfare among these people at the close of the fourth century A.D. Preliminary results from research projects aimed at investigating the consequences of conquest warfare (Chase n.d.) indicate that victory indeed economically benefited the winners at the expense of the losers, probably through rigorous tribute extraction (see Roys [1957] for a discussion of predatory tribute at the time of the European Conquest).

37. The front of the Stela 9 is badly eroded, but the shape, size, and detail of the object in the crook of his right hand correspond to Tikal and Xultún monuments showing rulers holding heads in the guise of deities. The eroded area in front of his legs probably depicted a kneeling captive.

38. An earlier katun ending, 8.4.0.0.0, is recorded on a broken celt in the collections of Dumbarton Oaks (Schele and M. Miller 1986:84–85). Coggins (1979:44–45) suggested that the emphasis on the celebration of the katun cycles was introduced via Uaxactún from Teotihuacán and that the celebration of repetitive cycles in the Long Count versus the commemoration of one-time historical events was an introduction from Teotihuacán. Since Teotihuacán shows no evidence of using or even being aware of the Long Count calendars and since katun celebrations are dependent on having the Long Count, we find it implausible that something so fundamentally and exclusively Maya would have been introduced from Central México and a cultural area that shows no evidence of having ever used the Long Count or the katun as a basis of calculation or celebration.

39. Fahsen (1988b) also identifies Stela 28 as Great-Jaguar-Paw based on the appearance of a prominent jaguar head and paw in the lower left corner of the monument. His identification seems to be a good one, but the style of Stela 28 is a bit problematic, since it would have to mark either 8.16.0.0.0 or 8.17.0.0.0.

40. Stela 39 was found interred in Structure 5D-86–6 in the Lost World Complex (Laporte and Vega de Zea 1988), a building that sits in the center of a group built on the same plan as the contemporary Group E at Uaxactún. The huge four-staired pyramid, with its talud-tablero terraces, faces on the east a set of three buildings arranged in the same pattern as Group E at Uaxactún. Group E is known to mark the two solstice points at its outer edges and the equinox in its center. The Lost World complex is much larger in scale and has been identified by Laporte as the work of Great-Jaguar-Paw, whom he believes to be buried in the same building as the stela. The rituals ending the seventeenth katun very probably occurred in the Lost World complex, perhaps atop the great pyramid at its center.

41. The date in the surviving text corresponds to a katun ending which most investigators have interpreted as seventeen, giving a reading of 8.17.0.0.0. The name at the top of the surviving text is Jaguar-Paw, which is exactly the name occurring with this date on Stela 31. However, while looking at a cast of this monument at the Museo Nacional de Arqueología y Ethnología of Guatemala, Federico Fahsen (personal communication, 1986) suggested that the number is nineteen rather than seventeen. I resisted his suggestion at first, but it has merit. The Jaguar-Paw name is followed by a "child of mother" expression and the name of a female. Furthermore, the very first glyph could well be the *yunen* "child of parent" glyph identified by David Stuart (1985b:7) on Tikal Stela 31. Jaguar-Paw's name may, therefore, occur in a parentage statement for the king who ruled Tikal at 8.19.0.0.0, presumably Curl-Snout.

42. This date and the events that occurred on it have been the subject of speculation by Proskouriakoff as quoted by Coggins and by Mathews. Clemency Coggins, following suggestions by Proskouriakoff, has offered several variants of the same essential scenario. Coggins proposed that this date marks the arrival of foreigners in the region, which corresponded either to the death of Great-Jaguar-Paw I or to his loss of power to those foreigners. In the first scenario (Coggins 1976:142; 1979b), she proposed that Curl-Snout, the next ruler to accede at Tikal, was a foreigner from Kaminaljuyu. In the second (Coggins 1979a:42), she suggested that Curl-Snout came from El Mirador via Uaxactún

bringing Teotihuacanos with him. These Teotihuacanos then withdrew to Kaminaljuyu around A.D. 450. In yet another interpretation, Coggins (n.d.), following new information from Mathews, proposed that Curl-Snout kidnapped Smoking-Frog, whom she identifies as the daughter of Great-Jaguar-Paw at Tikal, and took her to Uaxactún on the 8.17.1.2.17 date, where he married her. Curl-Snout then took over Tikal after Great-Jaguar-Paw, his new father-in-law, died.

Peter Mathews (1985a:33–46) examined the Tikal-Uaxactún relationship in the larger framework of the Early Classic period. He pointed out that the two sites account for twenty of the thirty-five Cycle 8 monuments and twenty-two of the fifty-two known Cycle 8 dates. The date shared between them is the earliest shared date (not a period ending) now known, and in subsequent history such shared dates "record major battles," with a few recording important dynastic dates, such as births or accessions. In the records of the shared date at both sites, Mathews identified a person named "Smoking-Frog of Tikal" as the major actor along with Great-Jaguar-Paw, who let blood on this occasion.

Mathews pointed out a pattern of data that is fundamental to interpreting this event. Since Smoking-Frog appears with the Tikal Emblem Glyph at both sites, he was an ahau of Tikal who became the dominant lord at Uaxactún. The conquest of Uaxactún was apparently directed by Smoking-Frog, but Great-Jaguar-Paw, who must have been an old man at the time, also let blood. Smoking-Frog appears as the protagonist of Uaxactún monuments at 8.18.0.0.0, while the ruler Curl-Snout, who succeeded Great-Jaguar-Paw at Tikal about a year after the conquest, acts at Tikal on the same dates. At Tikal, however, Smoking-Frog's name appears on all of the Curl-Snout monuments and Curl-Snout acceded "in the land of Smoking-Frog," suggesting that the new ruler of Tikal held his throne under the authority of Smoking-Frog.

Mathews offered the following explanation for this pattern:

". . .if I am correct then the nature of the Tikal-Uaxactún ties at this time originates from the placement of Smoking-Frog or of one of his close relatives in power at Uaxactún. This could have been achieved through marriage or by conquest. The nature of the 8.17.1.4.12 event—bloodletting—could be used to support either possibility. Bloodletting was an important feature of both warfare (sacrifice of the captives) and of royal marriages (autosacrifice by the wedding couple). If the event was war, then presumably Tikal imposed a member of its own royal family as ruler of Uaxactún. If the event was marriage, then Tikal apparently married into Uaxactún's ruling dynasty. Either way, I suspect that Tikal played the dominant role in the relationship between the two sites."

We accept Mathews's scenario as the most likely, and we favor his suggestion of conquest as the type of interaction, although a royal marriage may also have resulted from the conquest. The iconography associated with representations of the events are consistently associated with war and bloodletting in Maya history.

43. This censer is composed of a zoomorphic head with a tri-lobe device over its eye. The same head appears on Stela 39 with the main sign of the Tikal Emblem Glyph and a sky sign on top of it. This combination also occurs at Copán, where the Tikal Emblem Glyph main sign is replaced by the bat of Copán in a context where the tri-lobed head can be identified as the head variant of the sign known as the "impinged bone." Combined with the sky sign, the "impinged bone" and its tri-lobed head variant identify place names or toponyms (Stuart and Houston n.d.). In these cases, the "sky–impinged bone" identify the main sign of the Emblem Glyphs as a geographic location corresponding to the polity as a place. On Stela 39, the place where the event took place is identified as Tikal. On Stela 5, it is Uaxactún, which used the split-sky sign that also identified Yaxchilán, although there is no reason to suppose that the two kingdoms were related.

44. The most elaborate example of this complex in its Maya form is on the monument of a Late Classic conqueror. Dos Pilas Stela 2 (Fig. 4:17b), depicts Ruler 3 (Houston and Mathews 1985:17) hulking over his captive, Yich'ak-Balam (Stuart 1987b:27–28), the king of Seibal. Ruler 3 wears the same balloon headdress as Smoking-Frog, but the costume is now in its complete form with a full-bodied jaguar suit, the trapezoidal sign called the Mexican Year Sign, an owl, the goggle-eyed Tlaloc image, and throwing spears and rectangular flexible shields. Piedras Negras Stela 8 (Fig. 4:17a) depicts Ruler 3 of that kingdom in the same costume as he stands on a pyramidal platform with two captives kneeling at this feet.

45. The date of the Dos Pilas event (which was also recorded on Aguateca Stela 2) and a set of related verbs called "Shell-star" events at other sites were first associated with the periodicities of Venus by David Kelley (1977b). Michael Closs (1979) and Floyd Lounsbury (1982) showed this category of event to be associated with the first appearance

of Venus as Eveningstar and the two elongation points. Lounsbury went on to add Jupiter and Saturn stationary points to the astronomical phenomenon included in this complex.

Berthold Riese (in Baudez and Mathews 1979:39) first suggested that the star-shell events were war related, a hypothesis that Mary Miller (1986b:48–51, 95–130) has brilliantly supported with her analysis of the inscriptions and imagery in Room 2 of the Bonampak murals. These paintings depict one of the most amazing battle scenes known from the history of art, all under a register that shows stars being thrown into the scene from the heavens. The day is an inferior conjunction of Venus with a heliacal rising of Morningstar probable on the next day (M. Miller 1986b:51). The day of the event, August 2, 792, was also a zenith passage and the constellations that appear in the east just before the dawn of that day, Cancer and Gemini, are also represented on the register.

The Uaxactún costume with its spearthrower, balloon headdress, and bird is regularly associated with these shell-star events. The costume also appears in scenes of self-inflicted bloodletting (Schele 1984a), such as those shown on Lintels 24 and 25 of Yaxchilán, where a drum-turban decorated with tassels occurs with the complex. Other icons in the complex include the trapezoidal design known as the Mexican Year Sign and the goggle-eyed image known as Tlaloc to the later Aztecs. Along with the balloon headdress, spearthrowers, owls, flexible shield, a jaguarian image made of mosaic pattern, and a full-body jaguar suit, this set of imagery forms a special ritual complex that meant war and sacrifice to the Maya (see Schele and M. Miller [1986:175–240]).

This complex of imagery also appears at Teotihuacán, Monte Alban, Kaminaljuyu, Cacaxtla, Xochicalco, and numerous other sites throughout Mesoamerica between A.D. 450 and 900. First discovered at Kaminaljuyu (Kidder, Jennings, and Shook 1946), this merging of traditional Maya imagery with Teotihuacán-style imagery has been taken to signal the presence of Teotihuacanos at the Maya sites, especially at Tikal (Coggins 1976, 1979a, 1979b). Teotihuacán certainly had the same complex of iconography and there it was associated with war (Pasztory 1974) and with sacrifice (Oakland 1982 and Parsons 1985). Teotihuacán has been seen by many of these researchers as the innovator of this ritual complex and the donor and dominant partner in all instances where this complex of iconography appears in non-Teotihuacán contexts. We argue that the relationship between the Maya and Teotihuacán during the Classic period is far more complex that these explanations suppose. See René Millon (1988) for his evaluation of the interaction from the viewpoint of Teotihuacán.

46. The same iconography appears in later inscriptions with an glyph juxtaposing the sign for Venus with "earth" or the main signs of Emblem Glyphs. This type of war we shall call "star-shell" war or simply "star war."

47. The coincidence of this iconographic complex with Venus and Jupiter/Saturn stations of importance to the Maya (the heliacal risings of morning and evening stars, the eastern and western elongation points of Venus, and the stationary points of Jupiter and Saturn) is overwhelming. This particular kind of war costume and related iconography occurs at the following sites associated with the following astronomical and historical events:

(1) 8.17.1.4.12—1/16/378: Uaxactún St. 5, conquest by Tikal on a day with no detected astronomical associations

(2) 9.4.3.0.7—10/19/517: Piedras Negras Lintel 12, display of captive with visiting lords 7 days before maximum elongation (-.7) of Morningstar

(3) 9.4.5.6.16—2/5/520: Calakmul (Site 2) altar (Dallas), eroded event, first appearance of Eveningstar (26 days after superior conjunction)

(4) 9.8.0.0.0—8/24/593: Lacanjá St. 1, period ending rite on the first appearance of the Eveningstar (33 days after superior conjunction)

(5) 9.8.13.10.0—1/4/607: Piedras Negras, Lintel 4, unknown event 17 days before maximum elongation (-1.7) of Eveningstar

(6) 9.8.14.17.16—6/3/608 and 9.9.12.0.0—3/10/625: Lamanai St. 9, days of no astronomical associations

(7) 9.9.15.0.0—2/23/628: Piedras Negras St. 26, period-ending rites 5 days after maximum elongation (-.14) of Morningstar

(8) 9.10.6.2.1—2/6/639: Piedras Negras Lintel 4, death of Ruler 1, retrograde before inferior conjunction of Venus

(9) 9.11.0.0.0—10/14/652: Palenque, Temple of Inscriptions middle panel, a mosaic helmet with Palenque Triad on first appearance of Eveningstar (31 days after superior conjunction)

(10) 9.11.0.0.0—10/14/652: Piedras Negras St. 34, period-ending rites on the first appearance of Eveningstar (31 days after superior conjunction)

(11) 9.11.6.1.8—10/11/658: Piedras Negras Lintel 4, war event of Ruler 2; Jupiter is 1.44 before its 2nd stationary point (345.41)

(12) 9.11.6.2.1—10/24/658: Piedras Negras Lintel 2, war event with heir and youths from Bonampak and Yaxchilán; Jupiter is .45 before its 2nd stationary point (344.46)

(13) 9.11.9.8.6—2/10/662: Piedras Negras St. 35, eroded (6 days before shell-star event); Jupiter is .40 before its 2nd stationary point (89.68)

(14) 9.11.15.0.0—7/28/667: Chicago Ballcourt Panel, ballgame sacrifice by Zac-Balam; Jupiter is .06 before its 2nd stationary point

(15) 9.12.0.0.0—7/1/672: Palenque, Temple of Inscriptions middle panel, mosaic helmet verb with Palenque Triad 5 days after maximum elongation (-.73) of Eveningstar

(16) 9.12.7.16.17—4/27/680: Calakmul (Site 2) altar (Dallas), eroded action of Lady of Site Q, 12 days after maximum elongation (-.776) of Morningstar

(17) 9.12.9.8.1—10/23/681: Yaxchilán Lintel 25, accession of Shield-Jaguar and fish-in-hand bloodletting by Lady Xoc; Jupiter is .17 after 2nd stationary point (318.27)

(18) 9.12.10.0.0—5/10/682: Copán St. 6, period-ending rites on the retrograde position after inferior conjunction of Venus

(19) 9.12.11.13.0—1/20/684: Palenque, Group of the Cross, end of Chan-Bahlum's accession rite 11 days before the maximum elongation of Morningstar (-.53)

(20) 9.12.14.10.11—11/16/686: Piedras Negras St. 8, *macah* of Lady Ahpo-Katun, 4 days before maximum elongation (-.20) of Eveningstar

(21) 9.12.14.10.14—11/19/686: Piedras Negras St. 8 and 7, death of Ruler 2, 1 day before maximum elongation (-.10) of Eveningstar

(22) 9.12.14.10.17—11/22/686: Piedras Negras St. 8, *nawah* of Lady Ahpo Katun, 2 days after maximum elongation (-.18) of Eveningstar

(23) 9.12.14.11.1—11/26/686: Piedras Negras St. 8, preaccession rite of Ruler 3, 6 days after maximum elongation (-.62) of Eveningstar

(24) 9.12.18.5.16—7/23/690: Palenque, Group of the Cross, dedication rites for the Group of the Cross, complex conjunction with Jupiter .33 after its 2nd stationary point (221.43), Saturn at its 2nd stationary (225.50), Mars at 219.20, and the moon at 232.91

(25) 9.12.19.14.12—1/10/692: Palenque, Group of the Cross, dedication of the sanctuary buildings, 23 days before maximum elongation (-1.67) of Morningstar and 8th-tropical year anniversary of Chan-Bahlum's accession

(26) 9.13.3.8.11—8/21/695: Tikal, Structure 5D-57, *nawah* by Ruler A; Jupiter is .42 before the 1st stationary point (45.64); Saturn is at 2nd station (282.4)

(27) 9.13.3.9.18—9/17/695: Tikal, Temple 1, Lintel 3, bloodletting and 13th katun anniversary of the last date on Stela 31; Jupiter is .36 after the 1st stationary point (45.70); Saturn is at its 2nd station

(28) 9.13.17.15.12—10/28/709: Yaxchilán Lintel 24, bloodletting of Lady Xoc and Shield-Jaguar; Jupiter is .58 after the 1st stationary point (117.20); Saturn at 2nd stationary point (114.92)

(29) 9.14.0.0.0—12/5/711: Naranjo St. 1, action by Smoking-Squirrel on the first appearance of Eveningstar (25 days after superior conjunction)

(30) 9.14.0.0.0—12/5/711: Piedras Negras St. 7, period-ending rites on the first appearance of Eveningstar (25 days after superior conjunction)

(31) 9.14.0.0.0—12/5/711: Tikal St. 16, period-ending rites on the first appearance of Eveningstar (25 days after superior conjunction)

(32) 9.14.9.7.2—3/9/721: Piedras Negras St. 7, 17th tun anniversary of Ruler 3's accession; Jupiter is .81 after the 2nd stationary point (81.05); Saturn at 1st (249.77)

(33) 9.15.0.0.0—8/22/731: Calakmul (Site 2) altar (Dallas), period-ending 5 days before maximum elongation (-.125) of Eveningstar

(34) 9.15.4.6.4—12/3/735: Aguateca 2 and Dos Pilas 16, star over Seibal war on the first appearance of Eveningstar (31 days after superior conjunction)

(35) 9.15.5.3.13—10/7/736: Piedras Negras St. 9, 7th tun anniversary of Ruler 4's accession, 21 days before maximum elongation (-2.66) of Eveningstar

(36) 9.16.4.1.1—5/9/755: Yaxchilán Lintels 8 and 41, capture of Jeweled-Skull by Bird-Jaguar on a day with no detected astronomical associations

(37) 9.17.0.0.0—1/24/771: Tikal St. 22, scattering rite, visible eclipse 15 days after superior conjunction of Venus

(38) 9.17.5.8.9—6/15/776: Bonampak St. 2, accession of Muan-Chaan 14 days before maximum elongation (-.74) of Eveningstar

(39) 9.17.15.3.13—1/18/786: Bonampak St. 3, capture ??? by Muan Chaan 13 days before maximum elongation (-.55) of Eveningstar

(40) 9.18.0.0.0—10/11/790: Cancuen 1, period-ending rites 14 days before maximum. elongation (-.43) of Eveningstar

(41) 9.18.1.15.15—8/16/792): Bonampak Room 2, battle to take captives on the zenith passage of sun and the inferior conjunction of Venus

(42) 10.1.0.0.0—11/30/849: Ixlú St. 2, scattering rite, 16 days after maximum elongation (-.95) of Eveningstar

To test that these astronomical associations are not the product of the natural periodicity of planetary motions and thus coincidental, we calculated the dates and planetary data for every hotun (five-tun period) in Classic history. The pattern holds. The Tlaloc-war iconography appears when a period-ending date coincided with a important Venus, Jupiter, or Saturn station, and it does not appear on dates without these associations.

If the Tlaloc complex was borrowed from Teotihuacán, an interpretation that seems likely, it may have come with the astronomical associations already in place. However, we will not be able to test that possibility since no Teotihuacán art or architectural objects have dates recorded on them. The Teotihuacanos apparently did not consider the calendar or the days on which the events of myth and history occurred to be important public information. Thus, the astronomical associations with this ritual complex may well have come into being after the Maya borrowed it and made it their own.

48. We do not understand the full four-glyph phrase yet, but the first glyph is a hand with a jewel suspended from the extended first finger. This same sign is used as the principal verb for the completion of katuns and other period endings, especially when recording the katuns with a reign. Thrice this verb is written with its phonetic spelling appended to it: once on Tortuguero Monument 6, a second time on Naranjo Altar 1, and finally on Copán Stela A (Fig. 4:18). These spellings have a shell marked by three dots superfixed to a sign identified in Landa as *ma* or surrounded by a dotted circle, generally accepted as the syllable *mo*. The shell sign is the main glyph in the verb identified in the Dresden and Madrid codices and in the inscriptions of Chichén Itzá as the "fire drill" glyph. For many years, we presumed this glyph to read *hax*, the back and forth motion of the hands that drives the drill. Recently, however, Nikolai Grube (personal communication, 1987) reinterpreted this glyph to read *hoch'*, also a term for "to drill or perforate" in Yucatec. The shell in his spelling has the value *ho*, giving the value *ho-m(a)* and *ho-m(o)* for the "completion" hand discussed above. In Chol and Yucatec, *hom* is "to end or finish (*acabarse*)" (see Aulie and Aulie 1978:66 and Barrera Vasquez 1980:231). Homophones in Yucatec mean "a boundary between property" and most important, "to knock down or demolish buildings or hills (*desplomar lo abovedado, derribar edificios, cerros*)." The latter meaning especially seems appropriate to the context of conquest.

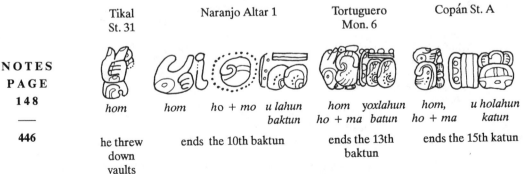

Tikal St. 31	Naranjo Altar 1			Tortuguero Mon. 6		Copán St. A	
hom	*hom*	*ho + mo*	*u lahun baktun*	*hom* *ho + ma*	*yoxlahun batun*	*hom,* *ho + ma*	*u holahun katun*
he threw down vaults	ends the 10th baktun			ends the 13th baktun		ends the 15th katun	

David Stuart (personal communication, 1988) takes the *hom* discussed above to spell the future suffix on a root ending in *-h*. Stephen Houston, following Stuart, has suggested *lah,* a word meaning "to end or finish" in Yucatec. This reading is the other possibility, although we find it less likely because in other contexts, such as the west panel of the Temple of Inscriptions, the *ma* phonetic complement is retained when other tense/aspects are distinguished by different suffixes. However, if this *lah* suggestion proves to be the correct reading, it still provides an appropriate meaning to the event—that the battle "finished" or "ended" the defeat of Uaxactún.

Regardless of which reading proves to be the correct one in the long run, the association of the "completion" hand with war events seems to be clear. On Lintel 3 of Tikal Temple 4, for example, the same verb appears with an event that took place one day after a "star-war" event against Yaxhá (see glyph C7a on the lintel).

49. Mathews (1985a:44) observed that the first of the glyphs recording this bloodletting action shows the lower half of a body sitting on its heels in the position assumed by a man when drawing blood from his penis (Joralemon 1974). Mathews suggested the glyph is a direct reference to male bloodletting. Federico Fahsen (1987) has documented other occurrences of the same verb at Tikal with the same meaning. The second verb shows a hand with its thumb extended as it grips a lancet of some sort. The same sign appears in the Early Classic version of the west glyph, which is shown on Yaxchilán Lintel 53 as a monster head biting down on the glyph for the sun. In the two examples of this verb on Stela 31, the hand with lancet has a *ba* or a *bi* sign attached to it, producing in the Maya way of spelling a term which should end in *-ab* or *-ib*. In Yucatec, the word for west in *chikin,* "bitten or eaten sun"; the word for "to bite" is *chi';* and the word for "bitten" and "to prick or puncture" is *chi'bal* (Barrera Vasquez 1980:92). The verb is apparently *chi'bah,* "he was punctured."

50. Prescott Follett (1932) compiled a useful summary of the weapons and armor depicted in Maya art as well as Colonial descriptions of warfare. Mary Miller's (1986b) analysis of the Bonampak murals gives evidence of a battle in progress while Schele (1984a), Dillon (1982), and Taube (1988b) discuss the aftermath of battle.

51. Marisela Ayala Falcón has called our attention to what is perhaps the most astounding and poignant episode in our entire story. Stela 5, the tree-stone depicting the conqueror Smoking-Frog, was set directly in front of Temple B-VIII (Fig. 4:5). Excavated by the Carnegie Institution in the thirties, this building was uniquely constructed as a mausoleum. Ledyard Smith (1950:101) describes a tomb built like a chultun directly under the floor of the upper temple and extending down to the bedrock below. He cites the type of loose fill and the construction technique used in the substructure as evidence that the tomb "chamber was constructed at the same time as the substructure" (Smith 1950:52).

Stela 5, the conquest monument, was located in the center of the temple stairs. The stela "lies only a few centimeters from the center of the lowest step of the stairway. The floor was laid at the time of the stairway and turns up to the stela, which was not put through it" (Smith 1950:52). On the other hand, Stela 4, Smoking-Frog's 8.18.0.0.0 monument, was erected by cutting through this same floor. The stairway and floor then were completed when Stela 5 was set in its place, thus identifying the temple as a victory monument constructed to celebrate the same events as Stela 5.

Of the tomb, Ledyard Smith (1950:52) said this: "It is of interest that it [Temple VIII] was probably built as a burial place; and that the tomb, which contained five skeletons, is one of the few at the site that held more than a single body; and that it is the only example of a group burial found at Uaxactún." The five people buried in it comprise the most extraordinary detail of all. Smith (1950:101) reported the skeletons included an adult female who was pregnant when she died, a second adult female, a child, and an infant. That the only group grave at Uaxactún should happen to be located in a tomb constructed inside the temple celebrating Tikal's victory is no accident. The identity of the dead as two women, an unborn child, an infant, and an older child is no coincidence either. These people were surely the wives and children of the defeated king. They were killed and placed inside the victory monument to end forever the line of kings who had ruled Uaxactún.

The defeated king himself was likely taken to Tikal to meet his end. His family stayed at Uaxactún watching the victors construct the new temple at the end of the causeway that connected the huge temple complexes of the city (Group A and B according to archaeological nomenclature). They must have known the tomb was being constructed in the substructure and who would occupy it.

The scene of their deaths can be reconstructed also. A circular shaft dropped to a ledge cut midway down and then fell another couple of meters to the bedrock floor below, dropping five meters in all. The bottom of the shaft widened on its east-west axis to form the burial chamber. The pregnant woman died and fell on her side with her knees drawn up around her unborn child. Her body lay in the southwest corner. The other woman lay along the north wall with the child lying next to her waist in the center of the tomb. The infant was thrown into the southeast corner. Plates, bowls, and jugs, probably containing food for their journey, were placed around them and then the chamber was sealed with what Smith (1950:101) called an "elaborate stucco adorno painted red. [The] adorno [was] set into the shaft and covered with the floor of the temple."

52. Despite the crucial role of weaponry in any interpretation of combat tactics, the investigation of Maya chipped-stone weapon tips remains in the preliminary stages. The hypothesis presented here, that the Teotihuacanos introduced the spearthrower as a weapon in the Maya lowlands, is not original to us. For example, Irvin Rovner (1976:46), from the vantage of Becán, and Hattula Moholy-Nagy (1976:96), from the vantage of Tikal, both note the linkage between the stemmed projectile form and imported Mexican obsidian in the time of the known Early Classic contacts. Gordon Willey (1972:161–177; 1978:102–105) provides some overview discussion of the development of lowland Maya bifacially chipped point-shaped artifacts. The relatively smaller stemmed varieties of point are characteristic of the Late Classic period. Although the function of such points is a matter for empirical investigation through microscopic inspection of edge damage, these points are in the appropriate range for projectile weapons, such as the spear flung using a throwing-stick. The relatively larger laurel-leaf-shaped points, suitable for the thrusting spears and explicitly depicted by the Classic Maya in their war art, definitely occur by Early Classic times at such sites as Uaxactún and Altar de Sacrificios and persist throughout the Late Classic. During the Late Preclassic period, the smaller stemmed varieties of bifacial point are absent from such communities as Cerros (Mitchum 1986); the characteristic pointed artifact is the large, stemmed, plano-convex macroblade "tanged dagger." This artifact is suitable for a shock weapon such as the thrusting spear, but not for a projectile weapon; it is broadly distributed in Late Preclassic times throughout the Maya region (Sheets 1976). Nevertheless, there is some preliminary evidence from even earlier contexts tentatively identified as Archaic hunter-gatherer groups in Belize (MacNeish 1981) for the presence of projectile weapons among the original inhabitants of the lowlands. We surmise that while the Maya probably always knew about the throwing-stick and its spear, it did not figure prominently in their politics until it was declared a weapon of war by Great-Jaguar-Paw. In all, the stone-artifact evidence will provide a useful arena for the further exploration of the hypothesized change in battle tactics after A.D. 400.

53. Mathews (1985a:44–45) proposed much the same interpretation, but there are problems with the calendrics of this passage, which may lead to a different interpretation. The date at the beginning of this passage is clearly 10 Caban 10 Yaxkin with G4 as the Lord of the Night. This particular combination occurred only on 8.6.3.16.17, a date much too early for the chronology of this text and its actors. Christopher Jones, Tatiana Proskouriakoff, and others (see C. Jones and Satterthwaite 1982:70) have pointed out that the accession date on Stela 4 is 5 Caban 10 Yaxkin with the same G4, and thus the date on Stela 31 has been accepted as an error. The problems with this interpretation are twofold:

(1) 8 Men is written just above this Calendar Round on Stela 31 and 8 Men is exactly two days before 10 Caban, reinforcing the likelihood of a 10 Caban reading.

(2) The clause preceding this date records the dedication of a house named *Wi-te-na*. The reconstruction of the date of this dedication event is problematic because part of the passage was destroyed in the ritual burning that accompanied deposit of Stela 31 in Temple 33. However, if the date recorded immediately before this burned area belongs to the house dedication, it took place 17 tuns, 12 uinals, and 10 kins (or 17.10.12, since the Distance Number could be read either way) after the conquest of Uaxactún. This chronology gives a date of 8.17.18.17.2 11 Ik 15 Zip (June 26, 395) or 8.17.18.15.4 12 Kan 17 Pop (May 19, 395). The relevance of this dedication date is that the 10 (or 5) Caban 10 Yaxkin event, which has been taken to be Curl-Snout's accession, took place both in "the land of Smoking-Frog" and in the *Wi-te-na*. Unless the house dedicated seventeen years after the conquest of Uaxactún carried the same name as an earlier house, the Stela 31 event must have taken place after the house was dedicated.

In this second interpretation, the day of the event would be 8.19.7.9.17 10 Caban 10 Yaxkin (September 2, 423), but the Lord of the Night would be in error, for this day requires G8. Fortunately, the historical argument we propose in this chapter does not depend on the precise date of this event, for the date is not the critical information. Regardless of the timing of the action, the protagonist clearly is Curl-Snout, but he acts "in the land of Smoking-Frog." The ahau of higher rank is Smoking-Frog.

54. The deep interaction of Tikal and Uaxactún during this period is further supported by the Early Classic murals in Uaxactún Temple XIII. The murals show two high-rank males confronting each other across a three-column-wide text. Next to them sits a palace building with three women sitting inside, and beyond the house, two registers with several scenes of ongoing rituals. The style of dress, the ceramics associated with the building, and the style of the glyphs (Marisela Ayala, personal communication, 1989) date the mural to approximately the time of Uolantún Stela 1 (8.18.0.0.0) and Tikal Stela 31 (9.0.10.0.0). The main text of the mural has the name of a person called Mah Kina Mo' (Lord Macaw) and perhaps the name of Stormy-Sky of Tikal. Most interesting, Fahsen (1988a) reports an inscription found on a headless statue in Temple 3D-43, a structure located at the juncture of the Maler and Maudslay causeways. The inscription dates to the time around 8.18.10.8.12 (November 5, 406) and it includes a character named K'u-Mo'. We have no way now of knowing if these two references to someone named Macaw refer to the same person, but the time and place are right.

55. David Stuart (in a letter dated February 10, 1988) suggested a reading of *yitan* (or *yitah*) for the T565 relationship glyph first identified by Kelley (1962) at Quiriguá. In Chorti, this term means "the sibling of." *Ihtan* is the root, while *y* is the possessive pronoun used with vowel-initial words. We (Schele n.d.e) have tested this reading at Tikal, Caracol, Chichén Itzá, and other Maya sites and found it to be productive. It is used, for example, to represent the relationship between two kings of Caracol (Rulers IV and V) who were born less than twelve years apart.

56. At Palenque and Yaxchilán, a horned owl and a shield substitute for each other in the names of the ruler Pacal and G3 of the Lords of the Night. The owl in this context appears with a spearthrowing dart penetrating its body or its head. Exactly this combination occurs in the headdress on Stela 31, which depicts the dart-pierced bird with the shield over its wing. In the title, the spearthrower dart is replaced by the spearthrower itself, so that "spearthrower-owl" and "spearthrower-shield" and combinations of the "spearthrower dart" with the bird and the shield are all variations of the same name.

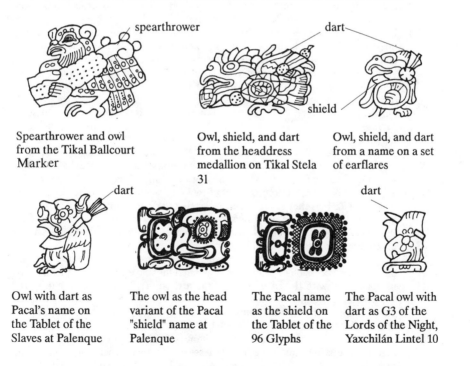

Spearthrower and owl from the Tikal Ballcourt Marker

Owl, shield, and dart from the headdress medallion on Tikal Stela 31

Owl, shield, and dart from a name on a set of earflares

Owl with dart as Pacal's name on the Tablet of the Slaves at Palenque

The owl as the head variant of the Pacal "shield" name at Palenque

The Pacal name as the shield on the Tablet of the 96 Glyphs

The Pacal owl with dart as G3 of the Lords of the Night, Yaxchilán Lintel 10

Variants of the Shield, Owl, and Spearthrower

Virginia Fields (personal communication, 1989) pointed out to me the importance of Stela 32 (Jones and Satterthwaite 1982: Fig. 55a) to the spearthrower-owl identification. This fragment was found in Problematic Deposit 22, a dedication cache intruded into the stair of Structure 5D-26–1st in the North Acropolis. The image depicts a front-view person dressed in regalia identical to the shield carried by Curl-Snout on the sides of Stela 31. However, hanging over the chest of the figure is a crested bird very similar if not identical to the bird medallion on Stormy-Sky's headdress. If Fields's identification of this bird as the owl in the spearthrower title is correct, then the title is directly associated with the war costume worn by Curl-Snout, just as we propose.

Peter Mathews (personal communication, December 1989) presented us with the final piece of the puzzle by pointing out an entry in the Cordemex dictionary of Yucatec (Barrera Vasquez 1980:342) and its relationship to the phonetic value of the cauac sign as *cu*. The entry has *ku* (*cu* in our orthography) as "the omen owl, owl, bird of prophesy in the books of Chilam Balam." This *cu* word for "owl" also occurs in Chol and in Tzeltal where it is registered as *cuh*. Since the objects at the corners of the shield are thought to have the phonetic value *hi* or *he* in glyphic contexts, the entire configuration may be the full spelling *cu-h(e)*. Mathews's observations thus identify the cauac-marked shield as a direct phonetic spelling of the owl and, just as important, with an owl specifically associated with prophecy and fortune-telling. This particular association apparently had a very ancient history that derived from the owl's prominent role in this war iconography.

57. This final event on Stela 31 took place on June 11, 439, in the Julian calendar when Venus was Morningstar and 44.93+ from the sun. The maximum elongation occurred fifteen days later on June 27 with Venus at 45.62+ from the sun, or .69+ beyond the June 11 position. However, June 11 can be taken as an arrival position for eastern elongation, the point at which Venus is farthest from the ecliptic of the sun as we see them from earth, and on that day Venus was magnitude -4.4, about as bright as it gets. This date then belongs to the same category of astronomical hierophany as the war/Tlaloc events discussed above (See Note 47).

58. The text on Stela 31 concerning Curl-Snout has proven to be extremely resistant to decipherment. The events and actors as we understand now are as follows:

(1) On 8.17.18.17.2 (June 26, 395) a temple named *Wi-te-na* was dedicated by Curl-Snout.

(2) On 8.17.2.16.17 (September 13, 379) or 8.19.7.9.17 (September 2, 423), Curl-Snout engaged in a dynastic event that involved displaying a scepter "in the land of" Smoking-Frog (see Note 53 for a discussion of this problematic date).

(3) On 8.18.0.0.0 (July 8, 396), Curl-Snout ended Katun 18 in his own land as a one-katun ahau, a title that indicates a person was under twenty years old or else still in his first katun of reign when the event happened. If he was under twenty years old more than seventeen years after his accession, he was indeed young when he acceded, perhaps explaining why Smoking-Frog appears to be the dominant ahau in the kingdom.

(4) On 8.19.5.2.5 (April 13, 421) an unknown event was done by an unknown person.

(5) On 8.18.15.11.0 (November 27, 411) another event occurred, but the record of it is lost in the damaged area of the text. We do not know who the actor was, but the event occurs on one of the most extraordinary astronomical hierophanies we have yet discovered in Maya inscriptions. Since July of 411, Jupiter and Saturn had been within four degrees of each other, hovering around an azimuth reading of 72+ as they crisscrossed each other in a triple conjunction that would finally end in March of the following year. This day occurred shortly after the second of these conjunctions just when Venus had swung out 47.22+ to its maximum elongation as Eveningstar.

Federico Fahsen (1988b) has posited that the lost event associated with this date was the accession of Stormy-Sky. We find his suggestion interesting because its fits so well with the chronology of the text on Stela 1 and the date in Burial 48, which is generally accepted as Stormy-Sky's tomb. Since Stela 1 records the "completion of the second katun" of Stormy-Sky's reign, he must have reigned at least forty years. Moreover, if 9.1.1.10.10 (March 20, 457), the date painted on the walls of Burial 48, is taken as Stormy-Sky's death (Coggins 1976:186), then the accession must have been at least two katuns earlier—or 8.19.1.10.10, at the latest. 8.19.10.0.0, the date most of us have taken as his accession date, not only falls after that limit, but its 2-katun anniversary fell on 9.1.10.0.0, nine years after the death date. In contrast, Fahsen's earlier date has its 2-katun anniversary on 9.0.15.11.0, six years before the tomb date and just after the latest date on Stela 31, 9.0.14.15.15 (C. Jones and Satterthwaite 1982:73). This chronology is much more satisfactory.

We also find support for Fahsen's suggestion in the fragmentary glyph that follows the 8.18.15.11.0 date on Stela 31. It resembles the T168:518 accession glyph that is used at Naranjo and Palenque. If this date is the accession of Stormy-Sky, then the date under #2 above is likely to correspond to the earlier placement.

(6) On 8.19.10.0.0 (February 1, 426), Stormy-Sky, the son of Curl-Snout, became king or else completed the half-period of the nineteenth katun.

59. There may have been earlier records of the event, but they have not survived into modern times or archaeologists have not yet found them.

60. The period of thirteen katuns was very important in Maya thought. The thirteen numbers of the tzolkin (260-day calendar) divided into the 7,200 days of a katun gives a remainder of +11 or -2. Thus, each time the Long Count advances one katun it reaches the same day name combined with a number two less than the starting point, as in the consecutive katun endings 6 Ahau, 4 Ahau, 2 Ahau, 13 Ahau, 11 Ahau, 9 Ahau, and so forth. It takes thirteen katuns to cycle back to the original combination. The 12 Etz'nab 11 Zip (9.0.3.9.18) of the Stela 31 passage cycled back on the katun wheel thirteen katuns later on 9.13.3.9.18 12 Etz'nab 11 Zac. On the occasion of that anniversary, the Late Classic descendant of Stormy-Sky conducted his own bloodletting and war in an episode we will encounter in the next chapter.

61. This Ballcourt Marker was found inside an altar set inside a court on the north end of Group 6C-XVI-Sub (Fialko 1988 and Laporte 1988). The altar platform was built with a single Teotihuacán-style talud-tablero terrace, a short stairway leading to its summit on which the marker was once mounted in an upright position (Fig. 4:23). We believe that this group was a nonroyal compound, probably for a favored noble lineage subordinate to the high king.

62. A ballcourt marker with depictions very similar to these murals was found on a ranch in La Ventilla near Teotihuacán in 1963 and is now in the Museo Nacional de Antropología e Historia of México. This Teotihuacán example is made in four pieces joined by tenons and, at 2.13 meters, is twice the size of the meter-high Tikal example (Bernal 1969:#8). The Denver Art Museum owns a third example, but we know nothing of its provenience.

63. This is a unique piece of Mesoamerican history. First, the lowland Maya of the Preclassic period kingship already celebrated royal events in conjunction with the ballgame played with rubber balls, as we have seen at the center of Cerros where ballcourts are linked to the image of the severed head of the Jaguar Sun. The ballgame is the fundamental metaphor of life out of death: The sacrifice of the Ancestors and their apotheosis occurs in the context of ballgames with the lords of Xibalba. The form of sacrifice associated with the ballgame is specifically decapitation; we have seen that the kings of Tikal and Uaxactún focused upon the severed head resulting from such acts. Further, we know that the severed head of the sun and the ballgame are both central to Maya concepts of warfare.

All well and good: But the lowland Maya did not play the ballgame with markers like the one found at Tikal. Their courts could have carved stones laid into the playing surfaces and sometimes rings or tenoned sculptures mounted in the side walls. The Tikal Ballcourt Marker is a Teotihuacán-style artifact that was used in an entirely different game played with a smaller ball, with sticks, and without courts. Eric Taladoire (1981) has summarized the evidence for this distinctive Early Classic ballgame in his comprehensive review of the Mesoamerican ballgame. At Teotihuacán, this kind of ballcourt marker and game are depicted in the Mural of Tlalocán, and an actual stone marker was discovered in the La Ventilla Complex at this city. Outside of Teotihuacán, examples of this kind of marker are found in the western region of Mesoamerica; one example is reported from Kaminaljuyu, which clearly had significant ties to Tikal and other lowland Maya capitals during this period (Brown 1977). The Tikal example seems to be of local manufacture, since the long inscription on its shaft is clearly Mayan and refers to local events, but its form deliberately emulates the style of the Teotihuacán game.

64. The date of this accession is somewhat problematical. The best solution gives 8.16.17.9.0 11 Ahau 3 Uayeb (May 5, 374) for the date of accession, with the alternative being 8.18.5.1.0 11 Ahau 13 Pop (May 10, 411) (Fialko 1988).

65. Pendergast (1971) found green obsidian in a Late Preclassic cache at Altun Ha, while Hammond reports green obsidian in Late Preclassic contexts at Nohmul (Hammond

n.d.). Later materials in Teotihuacán style are known from a cache at Becán (Ball 1974b, 1979, 1983), and Burials 10 and 48 at Tikal (W. R. Coe 1965a). Conversely, Maya-style artifacts have been excavated at Teotihuacán (Linne 1934, 1942 and Ball 1983). The appearance of these objects imported from the opposite region or manufactured in the style of the other culture signals the opening of an extensive interchange network that moved material goods as well as ideas and symbols throughout Mesoamerica.

66. The Tlaloc complex of imagery is particularly associated with the "star-shell" type of war we have been discussing as battle timed by Venus and Jupiter hierophanies (Schele 1979, n.d.; Lounsbury 1982; M. Miller 1986b; Closs 1979). Many of the territorial conquests in which rulers of known sites were captured are associated with this complex: Caracol's defeat of Tikal and Naranjo; Toniná's defeat of Palenque; Dos Pilas's defeat of Seibal; Piedras Negras's defeat of Pomona; Tikal's defeat of Yaxha; and more.

Most captives in Maya art are shown as individuals, some named by glyphs incised on their bodies, most unnamed and anonymous. Their captors stand on captives' bodies or display them publicly as offerings whose presentation will gain them merit with the gods. Named prisoners are a minority and those named with their kingdoms identified are rarer still. In most contexts, then, the Maya gleaned prestige from the identities of their captives as individuals as much or more than as representatives of their kingdoms. This remains true of the kingly captives, with the exception that their status as ahauob of their home kingdoms is repeatedly emphasized. If there was war that resulted in territorial conquest as well as political dominance, then these star-shell events are the likely candidates. The first and perhaps the most impressive example of this kind of war was Tikal's conquest of Uaxactún. See Note 47 for a discussion of the astronomical association of this war and sacrifice complex.

67. Coggins (1976; 1979a:259–268) has presented detailed arguments for these identifications, although the case for identifying Burial 10 as the burial place of Curl-Snout is the weaker of the two cases. We find her evidence well argued and accept her identifications.

68. Coggins (1976:177–179) remarks that this deposit was found in a dump west of the North Acropolis. She lists seven skeletons, a basalt mano and metate, olivo shells, green obsidian, a mosaic plaque, a couch shell, and thirty-eight vessels, many of them in the style of Teotihuacán. Among these vessels is one depicting the group of Teotihuacanos apparently leaving a Teotihuacán-style pyramid to arrive at a Maya temple, which Coggins speculated was in fact a record of the arrival of Teotihuacanos in the Maya lowlands.

69. It is just about this time that the cylindrical tripod spread throughout Mesoamerica and became one of the principal pottery forms of the Early Classic period through the entire cultural sphere. The shape, which provides particularly useful surfaces for displaying imagery, was adopted by all of the major cultural traditions of the time. In general the Maya style is taller in the vertical axis than the squatter style of Teotihuacán.

70. The other possibility is that the cities are Tikal, Kaminaljuyu, and Teotihuacán (Coggins 1979a:263). Kaminaljuyu is a likely candidate for the middle temple depicted on the vase which shares features of both Teotihuacán and Maya architecture. However, if Coggins's dates of A.D. 386 to 426 for this deposit are correct, the deposit is some seventy-five to a hundred years earlier than the Teotihuacán-style architecture and tombs at Kaminaljuyu. Furthermore, recent excavations in the Lost World group at Tikal by Juan Pedro Laporte (1988) have demonstrated the presence of talud-tablero architecture at Tikal by the third century A.D. A place ruled by Maya which has both styles of architecture is very probably Tikal. The two types of talud-tablero temples represented in the scene are distinguished by their roofcombs and the U-shapes marking the Maya version.

71. Marcus (1980) has also commented on these tasseled headdresses, also associating them with Teotihuacán emissaries to Monte Alban.

72. Charles Cheek (1977) proposed a model of conquest to explain the appearance of Teotihuacano architectural and ceramic styles at Kaminaljuyu, placing the time of Teotihuacán conquest in the sixth century. Kenneth Brown (1977 and personal communication, 1986) sees Kaminaljuyu as a port of trade serving as a neutral, secure ground for both lowland Maya and highland Teotihuacanos to trade upon.

At Kaminaljuyu, both lowland Maya and Teotihuacanos seem to have been present during the Middle Classic period (A.D. 400–600). Lowland Maya ceramics and jade artifacts are known at Teotihuacán, especially in the Merchants' Barrio with its curious arrangement of round buildings (Rattray 1986). Teotihuacanos also seem to have been physically present at Tikal. Moholy-Nagy (personal communication, 1986) believes there were a limited number of people of Teotihuacán ethnic origin at Tikal. This identification is based on a burial pattern consisting of cremation and the use of a pit to deposit the human remains and funerary offerings. Two of these pit burials are known: Problematic Deposit 50 found in a dump west of the North Acropolis and Problematic Deposit 22 found in the center of the North Acropolis in front of Structure 5D-26.

Coggins (1979b:42), following Proskouriakoff, suggested that the appearance of the Teotihuacán imagery at Uaxactún and Tikal signaled the arrival of a foreign people. She has suggested that Curl-Snout was in fact a Kaminaljuyu foreigner who usurped the throne of Tikal on the demise of the old dynasty. Archaeological evidence, however, documents Maya interest in green obsidian for use in cached offerings as early as the Late Preclassic period. New excavations at Tikal place the talud-tablero style of architecture at Tikal earlier than the date of the Uaxactún conquest. The lowland Maya and Teotihuacán had long been known to each other and had long traded for exotic goods originating in each others' domains. The appearance of Tikal kings in this Teotihuacán costume represents either an intensification of this contact or the adoption of a Teotihuacán ritual complex by the Maya for their own use. It does not signal the conquest of the central Petén or its dominance by foreigners.

73. Pasztory (1974) divided Tlaloc imagery into two categories, Tlaloc A, which is associated with water and agricultural fertility, and Tlaloc B, which is associated with war and sacrifice. She pointed out that the goggle-eyed imagery of Stela 31 and the Burial 10 vessels is not a Tlaloc image, but rather humans who wear goggle eyes, which she proceeded to associate with war iconography at Teotihuacán (Pasztory 1974:13–14). This war and sacrifice complex appears as the central theme of the Atetelco murals at Teotihuacán. The iconography of that complex is consistent with Teotihuacán imagery as it appears at foreign sites and may well represent a ritual or religious complex that Teotihuacán traders or political emissaries took with them as they spread outward from Teotihuacán in the fifth and sixth centuries.

Karl Taube (n.d.) has recently identified a war complex he associates with the Temple of Quetzalcoatl. The symbolism of this imagery includes the Mosaic Monster headdress, which he identifies as a War Serpent. He cites recent excavations at the Temple of Quetzalcoatl (Sugiyama 1989; Cabrera, Sugiyama, and Cowgill 1988) in which were found mass burials of warriors who were perhaps sacrificed in dedication rituals sometime during the mid-second century A.D. One of these burials contained eighteen mature males of warrior age. They were buried with obsidian points, mirrors that warriors wore on the back of their belts, war trophies in the form of human maxillas and mandibles, and shell imitations of maxillas and teeth. Other artifacts included 4,358 pieces of worked shell, many of which were drilled at one or both ends. Following suggestions by Berlo (1976), Taube suggested these pieced shells were from the Mosaic Monster (his War Serpent) headdress. These recent excavations and work on the war complex of Teotihuacán are enriching our understanding of war in Mesoamerican tradition, especially in the Tlaloc-complex we have seen at Uaxactún and Tikal.

74. Taube (n.d.) follows Rene Millon in suggesting that all of Mesoamerica saw Teotihuacán as the place where the sun and moon were created. We are not yet convinced that the Maya accepted that view, but the imagery at Teotihuacán, especially in the murals of Tetitla called the Tlalocán (Pasztory 1976), represented the city as the earthly replication of the sacred source of creation and genesis. We contend that the Teotihuacanos thought of themselves as citizens of the central sacred spot in the human plane of existence. The Maya on the other hand understood that all temples performed this function and that all kings were the embodiment of the world axis. We do not see Maya kings, their nobles, or the common folk standing in awe of Teotihuacán, no matter its internal definition of itself.

75. See the July 1982 issue of the *National Geographic Magazine* for Hammond's descriptions of this sacrificial burial.

76. However, there may be hints that this complex was associated with Venus. Pasztory (1976:245–247) associates the Atetelco warrior iconography with the sun ritual and follows Sejourne in associating the goggle-eyed warriors with half-darkened faces with the later Venus deity Tlahuizcalpantecuhtli. However, the Venus association may also be a Postclassic loan to the people of the Valley of México from the lowland Maya. The sacrificial ritual depicted at Cacaxtla in the eighth century seems to be closer to the Late Classic Maya version of the complex than to Atetelco.

77. Coggins (1979b:41–42) suggests a variant of exactly this scenario.

1. The kings changed to a costume consisting of a double-stranded necklace with a pectoral; a thick belt mounting a head-celt assemblage on the front and a backrack on the rear; a hipcloth overlaid by a pointed loincloth; and elaborate cuffs on the ankles and wrists. The headdresses vary with the particular stela and on Stelae 3 and 9 Kan-Boar wears a cape over his shoulders.

2. These staff monuments include Stelae 13, 9, 3, 7, 15, 27, 8, and 6.

3. Coggins (1976:184–208) identified Burial 48 as Stormy-Sky's grave. Chris Jones (n.d.) dates the construction of 5D-33–2nd to a time following the sealing of Burial 48. The temporal gap between the sealing of the tomb and the temple construction is unknown, but he assigns the temple construction to the period of the staff portraits. He also dates the spectacular Structure 5D-22–2nd, the huge temple on the northern edge of the Acropolis, to this same period. Arthur Miller (1986:40–50) describes the imagery of this temple in detail, although he assigns the dates of the tombs and construction phases differently from either Coggins or Jones. Miller points out that once the temple was built, the imagery was unchanged until the seventh century when it was encased by the thirty-meter-high Structure 5D-33–1st. No matter which of these chronologies proves to be correct, it is clear that the iconography depicted on these buildings was commissioned during the period of the staff kings, and that these buildings remained the principal backdrop for royal ritual in the Great Plaza until the seventh century.

4. The clearest data for ordering the monuments comes from dates and a series of "numbered successor" titles that record the numerical position of a particular king following the founder of his dynasty (Mathews 1975; Riese 1984; Schele 1986b; Grube 1988). Recorded both on monuments and on a looted pot (Robiscek and Hales 1981:234), these "numbered successor" titles allow us to reconstruct the order in which the kings reigned, and to know which kings are still missing from the record. Epigraphers still debate which monuments should be associated with which ruler. The three main theories that describe these events have been put forward by Clemency Coggins (1976), Chris Jones (C. Jones and Satterthwaite 1982), and Peter Mathews (1985a). None of these reconstructions is likely to be completely accurate: the eroded conditions and incomplete nature of the inscriptional record make study of this period in Tikal's history difficult. We present our own theory in the main text.

5. See Chapter 4, Figures 4:6 through 4:9.

6. A. Miller (1986:43–44) identifies the lower masks as "the sun still in the Underworld." The center masks he associates with the Old God effigy from Burial 10, which has the same trefoil eyelashes as the Cauac Witz Monster; and the upper masks, he sees as Venus. Although our identifications differ, the interpretative concepts are the same: These masks represent manifestations of the Hero Twins and other cosmic imagery as the sacred definition of the temple in Tikal's ritual life.

7. If we calculate the span of time between the death of the eleventh successor, Stormy-Sky, and the accession of the twenty-first successor, we end up with seventy-two years. Dividing this number by the number of kings who ruled during this period gives us an average reign of about eight years.

8. C. Jones (n.d.) says that the stairs of the twin pyramids were rebuilt at least once, suggesting that the complex was used for more than one katun celebration. He also notes the existence of two twin-pyramid complexes during this period.

9. The twin-pyramid complexes consist of two pyramids with stairways mounting the four sides of each. These platforms, which never had temples at their summits, sit on the east and west sides of a raised plaza. A row of uncarved stelae paired with plain altars are always erected in front of the west facade of the east pyramid. On the north side of the plaza, a carved stela recording the period-ending rite stands with its altar inside a roofless, walled enclosure entered through a vaulted door. On the south side of each complex is a small building which always has nine doors (see C. Jones [1969] for a detailed description of these complexes at Tikal). Dating the beginning of the twin-pyramid complex to the late fifth or early sixth century is important, for the endings of katuns and their quarter points provide one of the great regular patterns of time on which the Classic Maya system of festival and fair revolved. These complexes are unique to Tikal and they play a role of central importance in the ritual life of Tikal in the second half of the Classic period.

10. Caracol was first discovered in 1937 by Rosa Mai, a logger. He reported it to A. H. Anderson, the archaeological commissioner of Belize, who visited the site that year. Linton Satterthwaite of the University Museum conducted several field seasons between

1950 and 1958 that resulted in excavations and removal of many of its monuments to safe locations (see A. Chase and D. Chase 1987a:3–7 for a history of investigations). Arlen and Diane Chase resumed archaeological investigations in 1985, resulting in the discovery of important new inscriptions and archaeological data of major importance. Chase and Chase confirm earlier reports (Healy et al. 1980) of a very densely packed settlement. The city is situated five hundred meters high on the Vaca Plateau near the Maya Mountains of Southern Belize (A. Chase and D. Chase 1987a:1–2).

11. Proskouriakoff's work, *A Study of Classic Maya Sculpture,* was published in 1950. In this study she carefully compared the manner in which a fixed set of objects were depicted on monuments with inscribed dates in the Maya calendar. By showing how these depictions changed over time, she was able to produce a series of dated examples against which an undated monument could be compared and given a general style date. Her work still stands today as the principal means by which we formally assign stylistic dates to Maya sculptures.

12. See Proskouriakoff (1950:111–112) for her description of the hiatus.

13. Willey's (1974) brief and brilliant discussion of the hiatus as a "rehearsal" for the ninth-century collapse of southern Classic Maya civilization reviews many of the political and economic problems confronting the Maya in the wake of the collapse of extensive trade with Teotihuacán and the proliferation of competing polities in the lowlands (see also Rathje 1971). Although a "pre-historical" view, Willey prophetically pinpointed those very areas of social stress that emerged as significant in our translations of the Maya's own histories of their times. What the Maya themselves are silent on is the linkage between political and economic power. We are confident that there are more allusions to wealth and prosperity of an economic sort in the texts than we can presently identify, but the essential challenge of extending Maya history into the economic domain rests squarely in the fieldwork of archaeologists. One key will be to pursue the strategic imperishable commodities, such as obsidian, jade, and shell, from their stated functions and values in the texts into the contexts of the actual objects excavated from the earth (Freidel 1986a). Meanwhile, the hiatus remains an issue of regional dimensions in Maya research.

14. In 1960, Tatiana Proskouriakoff published a study of the distribution of monuments at the site of Piedras Negras and other sites. This study identified for the first time historical events and people in the Classic Maya inscriptions. During the next several years, she published a series of papers that changed the world of Maya studies forever by providing the keys to reconstituting their history through study of the inscriptions. These included identification of women in Maya inscriptions and art (1961b), a description of her discovery of the historical method (1961a), and finally her description of historical data in the inscriptions of Yaxchilán (1963–1964). These articles more than any others are at the heart of the decipherment and the reclamation of Maya history from the darkness of a muted past.

15. Chris Jones (n.d.) notes that almost all pre-9.7.0.0.0 monuments were deliberately effaced, while monuments after that time appear to have been damaged only accidentally. Early monuments were abraded, broken, and moved. Scars from the pecked lines that facilitated their mutilation are still in evidence. Other carvings (the back of Stela 10 and Altar 13) were rubbed smooth. Jones comments, "I would guess that this energetic onslaught was the result of a successful raid on Tikal, probably at the end of the reign of Double-Bird, the man on Stela 17."

16. A. Chase and D. Chase (1987a:33) report that Altar 21 was found in a central trench dug along the east-west axis of the ballcourt in Group A. The use of the term altar for this monument is something of a misnomer. Beginning in the Late Preclassic Period, Maya placed commemorative stones both in the center and at the ends of the plastered playing surfaces of ballcourts (Scarborough et al. 1982). These markers presumably pertained to the rules of the game and also to the rituals that kings carried out in the ballcourts. Generally, the monuments of ballcourts, including reliefs along the sides of some courts, allude to war and sacrifice. This linkage strongly suggests that the ballgame bore a metaphorical relationship to war (see Schele and M. Miller 1986: Chapter 6). Located in the center of the playing field, the altar in question is a round monument with 1 Ahau, the day upon which the katun of its dedication ended (9.10.0.0.0), and the events in the lives of the Caracol kings, Lord Water and Lord Kan II (Rulers III and V, in the dynastic list). Stephen Houston (in A. Chase n.d.), the project epigrapher, immediately recognized the implications of that remarkable inscription. A. Chase and D. Chase (1987a:60–62) proposed that the hiatus at Tikal was the direct result of its conquest by Caracol, an argument that we accept.

17. We follow the chronological analysis of Altar 21 first presented by Houston (in A. Chase n.d.; A. Chase and D. Chase 1987a:99–100). This day, 9.6.2.1.11 6 Chuen 19 Pop, corresponded to an ax event, a type of action that is associated with "shell-star" war events at Dos Pilas. Most significantly, this same glyph records what happened to 18-Rabbit, a king of Copán captured by Cauac-Sky, his contemporary at Quiriguá. Although the "ax" verb is used in astronomical contexts in the codices, it is clearly associated with war and decapitation ritual in the Classic inscriptions and on pottery (see, for example, the Altar de Sacrificios vase, *National Geographic,* December 1975, p.774).

18. Houston (in A. Chase n.d.) noted that the date of this war event, 9.6.8.4.2 7 Ik 0 Zip, corresponds to the stationary point of Venus that forewarns of inferior conjunction. The verb, a star (or Venus) sign, here followed by the main sign of the Tikal Emblem Glyph, occurs throughout the inscriptions of war events timed by Venus apparitions or Jupiter and Saturn stations. The location is indicated by the main signs of the appropriate Emblem Glyph or simply as the "earth." Here the star war took place at Tikal.

19. Clemency Coggins (1976:258) notes that this period "is characterized by the poverty of its burials." During this time there is only one burial "rich enough to have had painted ceramics." Burials in residential areas were equally poor. In an insightful and anticipatory interpretation of stylistic similarities, Coggins (1976:385–386) posited influence from Caracol into the Tikal region exactly during this period and culminating with the first stela known to have been erected after the hiatus, Stela 30 and its altar, depicting the ahau name of its katun in the style of Caracol. A. Chase and D. Chase (1987a:60–61) attribute many characteristics, especially in Burials 23 and 24, to Caracol funerary practices.

Chase and Chase (1989) report a 325 percent increase in population at Caracol following the Tikal war. There was a corresponding increase in large, single-phase construction projects both of temples and extensive terracing systems. Tomb space became so sought after that chambers were built into substructures and reused for several people before being finally sealed. Whereas Tikal saw an impoverishment of burial furniture, Caracol experienced a remarkable enrichment. D. Chase and A. Chase (1989) have suggested that much of the labor for these construction projects and the wealth of Caracol during this period was transferred from the prostrate kingdom of Tikal.

20. Houston (in A. Chase and D. Chase 1987a:91) suggested that Caracol Rulers IV and V (Lord Kan II) were brothers since they were born only twelve years apart (Ruler IV on 9.7.2.0.3 or November 30, 575, and Ruler V on 9.7.14.10.8 or April 20, 588). A reading suggested by David Stuart (1987b:27, 1988a, and n.d.) supports Houston's proposed relationship. On Stela 6, the last clause closes with the information that the half-period ending 9.8.10.0.0 was witnessed by Ruler V who was the *yitan itz'in,* "the sibling younger brother of" Ruler IV. We should also observe that the parentage of Rulers IV and V is not clearly stated in the inscriptions. The most likely reconstruction is that the throne descended from father to firstborn son, but there is some evidence of a break in the descent line with these two brothers.

21. The Emblem Glyph of this kingdom has a snake head as its main sign. It was identified with Calakmul, a site north of the Guatemala-México border, first by Joyce Marcus (1973 and 1976) and later by Jeffrey Miller (1974). Miller identified looted stelae in the Cleveland Museum of Art and the Kimbell Art Museum as coming from the "Snake site," as Calakmul is sometimes known. Although the Calakmul identification was widely accepted at first, several epigraphers began questioning it because of the unusually wide distribution of this Emblem Glyph and the damaged condition of Calakmul's monuments. Peter Mathews (1979) assembled all the then-known inscriptions, many of them looted, marked with the Snake site or its dynasty and gave the site the noncommittal designation "Site Q."

Several years ago, however, Ian Graham discovered the sawed-off remains of the looted monuments currently housed at Cleveland and Fort Worth, in a site called El Perú, located to the west of Tikal in the northwest Petén. Finding the remnants of these shattered stelae at El Perú convinced most epigraphers that the Snake site was finally to be identified as El Perú.

Recently, however, Stuart and Houston (n.d.) have once again questioned the Snake site identification based on the following grounds:

(1) Stelae from El Perú have another Emblem Glyph distinct from the Snake Emblem Glyph. This second Emblem Glyph does not appear paired with the Snake Emblem Glyph in the manner of other double Emblem Glyphs, such as

those found at Yaxchilán, Palenque, and Bonampak. This distribution suggests that the Snake Emblem Glyph appearing on El Perú Stela 30 is a reference to a foreign power.

(2) A key Snake site king named Jaguar-Paw appears in the inscriptions of several sites. His birth was recorded on Calakmul Stela 9 and also on Site Q Glyphic Panel 6. His accession was inscribed on El Perú Stela 30 and on Dos Pilas Stela 13. Finally, his capture by Tikal's Ah-Cacaw was declared in conjunction with a war event in Temple I of that city. The Tikal and Dos Pilas references are clearly to foreigners. The El Perú reference may be taken either as foreign or local, while the Site Q and Calakmul references are more likely to be local.

(3) Finally, Stuart and Houston have identified a place name consisting of a water-lily plant (*nab*) over a *chi* hand merged with a *tun* sign, resulting in the phrase *nab tunich.* This place name appears with names incorporating the Snake Emblem Glyph at Naranjo, where it is in a foreign context. The Dos Pilas inscriptions say that Jaguar-Paw's accession occurred at *nab tunich,* and most important, the ruler on Calakmul Stela 51 has *nab tunich* in his name. They feel the place is most likely to be some part of Calakmul and prefer the identification of the Snake Emblem Glyph as Calakmul.

We became convinced of the Calakmul identification when Schele noticed that a fragment in the Tamayo Collection from the side of the Fort Worth stela, recorded a "God K-in-hand" action with two persons named in association. The first of these is the protagonist of that stela, Mah Kina Balam, but his name is followed by *ichnal* and the name of the current ruler of Site Q. David Stuart (personal communication, 1988) has shown that the *ichnal* glyph means "in the company of." Given this reading, the fragmentary text records that the El Perú lord enacted the ritual "in the company of" the ruler of Calakmul, giving us strong evidence that Jaguar-Paw of Site Q was a visitor at El Perú for the ritual. Based on this interpretation, we follow Marcus, J. Miller, Stuart, and Houston in accepting Calakmul as the Site Q kingdom. However, we also acknowledge that the evidence is still not indisputable and that Site 2 may be a yet undiscovered city.

22. This same glyph names the fourth successor of the Copán dynasty who reigned about eighty years earlier (Grube and Schele 1988).

23. We have, of course, no direct evidence that Yaxchilán ever participated in the oncoming wars. However, a representative of the Calakmul king attended an important ritual conducted by the tenth king of Yaxchilán. This visit suggests they were at least on friendly terms, if not outright allies. If Cu-ix installed Ruler I on the throne of Naranjo, as Stela 25 implies, then the Naranjo ruler was very likely part of the proposed alliance against Tikal. By the middle of Katun 5, Tikal may have been surrounded by an alliance of hostile states.

24. This is the stationary point that ends the retrograde movement of Venus as it flashes across the face of the sun at inferior conjunction. The Morningstar would then resume motion in its normal direction, heading toward its maximum distance from the sun.

25. Captives, especially those of high rank, were sacrificed in a mock ball game played upon hieroglyphic stairs (Schele and M. Miller 1986:214–263 and M. Miller and Houston 1987).

26. Mathews (1977) identifies 9.5.12.0.4 as the birth date of Naranjo Ruler I based on an anniversary expression on Stela 3 and a "five-katun-ahau" title included with Ruler I's name on Stela 27. Based on this last citation, Mathews proposed that Ruler I lived into his fifth katun and ruled until at least 9.10.12.0.4, long after the conquest date. Closs (1985:71), on the other hand, takes the anniversary sequence on Stela 25 as the celebration of the accession of this ruler. Closs's interpretation has the virtue of placing the birth of this ruler earlier than 9.5.12.0.4 and placing his transition to status as a "five-katun ahau" on a correspondingly earlier date. Since we have neither a clear birth nor accession verb with any of these dates, the final interpretation will have to wait for additional information to appear. The text of Stela 25, however, clearly declares that the event which took place on that date, be it birth or accession, took place "in the land of Cu-Ix of Calakmul."

27. Heinrich Berlin (1973), citing a personal communication from Linton Satterthwaite, first commented on this 9.9.18.16.3 7 Akbal 16 Muan date that is shared between Caracol and Naranjo, although he offered no interpretation of its significance. David Kelley (1977b) suggested that it should have corresponded with the heliacal rising of Venus as Morningstar, tempering his suggestion with the caution that his data was too varied to commit to a particular answer. The most important component of his paper was

the identification of the "shell-star" complex associated with this particular category of date. Following up on Kelley's work, Michael Closs (1979) identified the "shell-star" category as Venus dates and posited that this Caracol-Naranjo date corresponded to the first appearance of Venus as Eveningstar, an association confirmed by Floyd Lounsbury and extended to include the Bonampak war scene. See Chapter 4, notes 45 and 47, for a detailed discussion of the war and astronomical associations connected with this set of dates.

28. David Stuart (1987b:29) first read this collocation as *k'u.xa.ah,* pointing out that it also occurs on a captive panel at Toniná. He notes that *k'ux* is "eat/bite/pain" in proto-Cholan. Stuart himself suggests that the event may be captive torture, a practice well documented in narrative scenes of the Classic period, but he also notes that Victoria Bricker suggested to him that it might also be cannibalism, a practice documented archaeologically in many parts of Mesoamerica, including the Maya lowlands. Freidel participated in the excavation of a deposit of butchered human bones found in a small platform at the Late Postclassic lowland Maya community of San Gervasio on Cozumel Island in 1973. The feet and hands had been sawed away from the meat-bearing limb bones. No matter the action recorded here, it boded no good for the captive.

29. Mathews (1985a:44) dates Stela 6 at 9.6.0.0.0 and identifies it as the last monument in a 200-year hiatus in monument dedication at Uaxactún.

30. Berlin (1958) first noted the mutual use of the same Emblem Glyph at both Tikal and the Petexbatún sites, although he posited that the Tikal Emblem Glyph was subtly differentiated from the Petexbatún version. Marcus (1976:63–65) suggested that the Hieroglyphic Stairs at Dos Pilas actually recorded the history of Tikal lords who conquered Dos Pilas and reigned there in the name of the regional capital. Coggins (1976:445–446) sees an offshoot of the Tikal royal family moving to Dos Pilas after the death of Stormy-Sky, and sending one of its sons back to Tikal to reestablish the old family and reign as Ruler A.

Houston and Mathews (1985:9) and Mathews and Willey (n.d.) also think it likely that Dos Pilas was established from Tikal, perhaps by a minor son or a segment of the royal family that moved out of Tikal during the hiatus. With the new information available to us, we know that this hiatus occurred because of Tikal's defeat by Caracol. They believe the Dos Pilas dynasty intruded itself into the area, using a strategy of intermarriage and war to consolidate its position. They, however, also see the Dos Pilas dynasty as independent of Tikal, a position we accept. We, furthermore, see a tension and competition between Tikal and Dos Pilas that unfolds as Tikal struggled to reestablish the prestige of its rulers.

31. According to Houston and Mathews (1985:11–12), this second son, named Shield-Jaguar, is recorded on the West Hieroglyphic Stairs at Dos Pilas.

32. The El Chorro and El Pato lords name a woman with the Dos Pilas Emblem Glyph as their mother. Mathews and Willey (n.d.) and Houston and Mathews (1985:14) note that the time involved makes their identification as sisters of the king—or at minimum, members of the royal family of Dos Pilas—a likely interpretation.

33. Unfortunately, since the first half of the stair (Hieroglyphic Stair 2, East 3) is destroyed, we have neither the exact date nor the action recorded in this passage. Since other dates on this stair occur between 9.11.9.15.9 and 9.12.10.12.4, we surmise that this action fell within the same period.

34. Stuart and Houston (n.d.) have identified the combination of a waterlily-imix glyph (*nab*) with a shell-winged dragon as the name of Lake Petexbatún. The action is called a "shell-dragon" *ti kan toc,* and may have occurred at that lake. The inscription names Jaguar-Paw as *ihtah itz'in,* the younger brother, of another Calakmul noble, who may also be named at Dos Pilas (HS2, E4).

35. Jeffrey Miller (1974) first identified the accession date of Jaguar-Paw on a looted monument in the Cleveland Art Museum. He suggested the stela was from Calakmul and was once paired with another looted monument in the Kimbell Art Museum. His pairing of the stelae was correct, but Ian Graham found the remnants of both stelae at the site of El Perú. The Cleveland stela depicts a female who records her celebration of the katun ending 9.13.0.0.0. The accession of Jaguar-Paw is the dynastic event to which this katun celebration is linked.

36. David Stuart (1987b:25–27) has read this representation of an eye as the verb *il,* "to see," supporting his reading with the phonetic spellings that can accompany or replace it.

37. Recall that Stuart and Houston (see Note 21) associate this toponym with Calakmul.

38. Houston and Mathews (1985:14–15) first published this scene and recognized its implications.

39. The second glyph in the text next to the seated figure is *ch'ok,* a glyph that Grube, Houston, and Stuart (personal communication, 1988) and Ringle (1988:14) associate with young persons who have not yet taken the throne. Our own study of this title confirms that it appears only in the names of people who are not yet kings, but their ages can range from five to forty-eight years. The title apparently refers to members of a lineage who are not in its highest rank.

40. Proskouriakoff (1961b:94) first identified this woman in the imagery and texts of Naranjo, pointing out that each of her stelae is paired with another representing a male. She remarked on the presence of the Tikal Emblem Glyph in her name, and observed that the male was born several years after the most important date of the woman. She commented, "She is doubtless older than the man, and one may infer that the relationship could be that of a mother and son." Berlin (1968:18–20) accepted Proskouriakoff's analysis, further suggesting that Tikal entered into a dynastic marriage at Naranjo, and that this woman's male offspring in turn married another woman from Tikal. Molloy and Rathje (1974) and Marcus (1976) both follow the suggestions of their predecessors, but Peter Mathews (1979) noted that the name of the father of this foreign woman in her parentage statement on Naranjo Stela 24 matches Flint-Sky-God K of Dos Pilas. Houston and Mathews (1985:11) posited two royal marriages for that king—one to a woman of Itzán, which produced the next king of Dos Pilas, and the other to a woman who produced a daughter he sent to Naranjo to marry a noble there. From this marriage came a grandson who was the next king of Naranjo. We accept Mathews's identification and suggest that the royal woman married a male noble of Naranjo, for the next king, if he was her son, carried the Naranjo Emblem Glyph, rather than that of Dos Pilas.

Berlin (1968:18) observed that the date of Lady Wac-Chanil-Ahau's arrival also occurs on Cobá Stela 1. On that monument, the date occurs in the last clause on the front in the form of a Long Count, the second notation of this kind in the text. Although the Long Count form of the date suggests that it was especially important in the inscriptional history recorded on this monument, the verb is too eroded to decipher. It appears to have involved a katun, perhaps as an anniversary, but the actor is clearly not any of the principals in the Naranjo-Dos Pilas affair to the south. The scene shows the Cobá ruler dressed as the Holmul dancer standing on top of two bound captives who are flanked by two more captives. Although we suspect the Cobá inscription records an event important to local history, the fact that the date is shared between Cobá and Naranjo may point to some important connection between the two zones.

41. Interestingly, a variant of this name occurs in a reference to a foreign wife at Yaxchilán on Lintels 5 and 41 and in a reference to the wife of the ruler Yoc-Zac-Balam of Calakmul. We can come up with a number of explanations as to why the *Wac-Chanil-Ahau* appellative had this wide distribution: It could have been a special title of royal wives, or perhaps queen mothers; it may have designated foreign women in some way; or it might have been a name popular in the Usumacinta and Petexbatún regions.

42. In the text at Tikal that records this war event, the extended finger has a bauble dangling from its tip. In this version and a related one on Caracol Stela 3, the jewel does not appear with the hand. However, this hand, both with and without the bauble, occurs in Glyph D of the Lunar Series. We had taken this common occurrence in Glyph D as evidence that both forms are equivalent, but Nikolai Grube and Barbara MacLeod (personal communication, 1990) have independently shown that the hand without the bauble and its substitutes in Glyph D read *hul,* "to arrive." They have convinced us that the two forms of the hand do not substitute for each other in most contexts. Glyph D counts the age of the moon from its *hul,* "arrival," a point defined as the first appearance of a visible crescent. In the context of the Naranjo event, they suggest that the verb is simply "she arrived," an event that was followed three days later by the dedication ritual for a pyramid named with the main sign of the Naranjo Emblem Glyph. Lady Wac-Chanil-Ahau's arrival thus reestablished the house of Naranjo's rulers.

Archaeologically, there is some evidence supporting the association of termination and dedication rituals with the act of reestablishment or founding. Both kinds of rituals are similar in form and content (Freidel 1986b). Termination rituals involving the smashing of artifacts of pottery, jade, and other materials, and the layering of these materials in white earth, are found not only upon the occasion of the permanent abandonment of buildings, but also at their reconstruction. At Cerros, the first place this ritual activity was identified and documented in the Maya region (Robin Robertson n.d.; Garber

Date and universal time: 710 June 28 (Gregorian); 24:22 U.T.
JDN and sidereal time: 1980560.515278; Mean G.S.T.: 18h 49.6m

Object	G long	G lat	G dist	R.A.	Dec.
Sun	95.45	0.00	1.017	6 23.8	+23 30
Moon	17.46	2.58	63.016	10.3	+9 17
Mercury	117.11	−2.45	0.671	7 54.7	+18 29
Venus	116.05	1.52	1.574	7 53.5	+22 35
Mars	115.22	1.20	2.584	7 49.7	+22 25
Jupiter	121.25	0.73	6.255	8 14.7	+20 44
Saturn	115.52	0.61	10.101	7 50.6	+21 47

As observed from 89.0 degrees west longitude, 17.0 degrees north latitude:

Object	Altitude	Azimuth	Mag.	Diam.	Phase(%)
Sun	0.6	294.6	−26.8	31 30.9	
Moon	−64.1	356.3	−9.4	29 43.8	39.6
Mercury	19.4	284.1	1.5	10.0	20.7
Venus	19.9	288.4	−3.9	10.7	93.3
Mars	19.0	288.4	1.8	3.6	98.9
Jupiter	24.4	285.5	−1.8	31.5	
Saturn	19.1	287.7	0.3	16.5	

(Outer diameter of Saturn's rings: 37.2 arc seconds)

1983), it is clear that the same unbroken ritual offerings which terminate a building can be part of the dedication ceremony of the new building (Walker n.d.). Since the *hul* event was followed three days later by the dedication of a house, we may very well be dealing with a prime example of a house dedication used to establish a broken dynasty.

43. Based on the identification of the verb as "accession" at other sites, and on the recurrent anniversary celebrations of this date, Michael Closs (1985) first established that this event was the accession of this child to the throne.

44. This pairing was first noted by Proskouriakoff (1961b:94). Stela 2, which depicts Smoking-Squirrel on his first katun anniversary, pairs with Stela 3, which represents Lady Wac-Chanil-Ahau. The inscription on Stela 3 connects her arrival to his anniversary. Stela 30, depicting Smoking-Squirrel on the same anniversary, couples with Stela 29, which also records her arrival as well as her initial temple dedication. Smoking-Squirrel's Stela 28 pairs with Lady Wac-Chanil-Ahau's Stela 31. Finally, Stelae 22 and 24 pair together in recording the accession of the young Smoking-Squirrel and its aftermath.

45. Graham (1975–1986, vol. 2–3:152) notes that Ucanal lies on high ground at the southwestern end of a spur of hills rising above a flat basin on the west bank of the Mopán River. The glyph name for the site is *Kan Witz*, "Precious Mountain."

46. Based on conversations with Peter Mathews (personal communication, 1989), Stephen Houston (1983) first identified this captive and discussed the war between Naranjo and Ucanal. He noted the passages on Stela 2 and 22, and recognized the same name on a pot. He also called attention to this name on Sacul Stela 1, where it appears with the date 9.16.8.16.1 5 Imix 9 Pop (February 12, 760). The text records a scepter ritual enacted by a Sacul lord "in the company of" (*yichnal* [Stuart, personal communication, 1988]) Shield-Jaguar of Ucanal. Houston pointed out that the time span (sixty-five years) between the Naranjo attack and this event makes it likely that this later Shield-Jaguar was a

namesake. He also remarked that Ucanal had reestablished the prestige of its own ruling lineage by that time.

47. In commenting on this passage, Berlin (1968:20) suggested that it names the wife of the young king as a woman from Tikal. He also posited that the woman named here is not Lady Wac-Chanil-Ahau, the daughter of Flint-Sky-God K. We agree with his suggestions, but we believe she was also from Dos Pilas. The glyphs that precede her name include "18 ???" and "Lord of the shell-winged-dragon place." This shell-winged dragon is especially associated with Dos Pilas as the toponym of Lake Petexbatún. The person named thus appears to be a lord of Dos Pilas. His name is followed by *yihtah,* "the sibling of," (Stuart 1988a) and a glyph Berlin proposed as "wife." Lounsbury (1984:178–179) has read it as *yatan,* "his wife." The male from Dos Pilas seems to be named as the "sibling of the wife" of the king. The wife was a woman of Dos Pilas. Smoking-Squirrel apparently married a woman in his grandfather's family to reinforce the alliance with Dos Pilas.

48. Venus as Morning Star was 6.93+ from the sun, while Jupiter hung at 107.82 and Saturn at 108.09, both frozen at their second stationary points. As we will see in the following chapters, this pairing of Saturn and Jupiter was carefully observed by the Maya and used to time particularly important dynastic events.

49. The data on the day in question, shown on page 460, was generated with "Planet Positions," a BASIC program written by Roger W. Sinnott, 1980.

50. In his map of the Naranjo region, Ian Graham (1975–1986, vol. 2, p. 5) used *Sacnab* as an alternative name for Lake Yaxhá. *Sacnab* is "clear lake," while *Yaxhá* is "blue water." Maler (1908–1910:70) reported that there are two lakes at the location connected by a natural channel. One of these lakes was called *Yaxhá* and the other *Sacnab.* Apparently the names he was given at the end of the nineteenth century come from the Precolumbian names of the lakes.

51. 9.14.0.0.0 is also recorded on Stela 23, but as a future event, which will follow the current events described in the narrative. The coincidence of the first appearance of Eveningstar on this katun ending was recorded at two other kingdoms. On Stela 16 at Tikal, Ah-Cacaw wears the skeletal god of Eveningstar (Lounsbury, personal communication, 1978) as his headdress, and on Stela C at Copán, 9.14.0.0.0 is connected by a Distance Number to a first appearance of the Eveningstar many years before the 4 Ahau 8 Cumku creation date.

52. Ian Graham (1975–1986, vol. 2, p. 3) reported finding this stone "on the centerline of the ballcourt at the northern extremity of the plaza" in 1972. He posited that it was moved there as the result of Postclassic or even post-Conquest activity, but we believe that the sequence of associated events suggests the placement was deliberate. Caracol conquered Naranjo and erected a stairs there to celebrate its victory. Forty years later, a recovered Naranjo conquered Ucanal and placed a piece of that stairs in the ballcourt of the kingdom they had just defeated. Others (Houston 1983:34 and Sosa and Reents 1980) have also made this connection between defeat, revival, and victory.

Peter Mathews (personal communication, 1976) suggested that triumphal stairs were forceably erected at the site of the loser by the victor. Houston also points out that this type of victory stairs has survived in remarkably good condition at sites like Seibal, Naranjo, and Resbalón, but that they were often reset in illegible order. He suggested that the dismantling and resetting in scrambled order may have been the loser's way of neutralizing the stair after they had revived their prestige. Apparently one could damage the monuments of a defeated enemy, as Caracol apparently did at Tikal, but the monuments of a victor were not to be defiled in the same way. You reset them out of reading order to neutralize them.

Interestingly, Ucanal's suffering did not end here. D. Chase and A. Chase (1989) report finding a panel at Caracol that depicts two Ucanal captives, bound and seated on legged, stone thrones. Dated at 9.18.10.0.0, the monument documents a Caracol that is once again erecting stelae and returning to its old pattern of aggression. A renewed Caracol apparently struck at the same border community that had felt the earlier wrath of a recovered Naranjo.

53. Chris Jones (n.d.) dates several important projects to the last part of Tikal's hiatus: a repaving of the North Acropolis; the completion of its present eight-temple plan; a rebuilding of the edge of the North and Central Acropolis which cut the Central Acropolis off from the East Plaza; and the remodeling of the East Plaza, which included placing a ballcourt in its center over the old Twin Pyramid Complex. Burials 23 and 24 were cut into the pyramidal substructure of Temple 5D-33–2nd, the huge masked building that fronted the North Acropolis. Jones suggests that Burial 23, the richer of the two, might

be the tomb of Shield-Skull, the father of Ruler A, whom he suspects was the patron of much of this construction.

54. His first name has been read by Chris Jones (1988:107) as Ah-Cacaw, although he also appears in the literature as Double-Comb and Ruler A. Although the reading of one of the glyphs as *ca* has been questioned, we will use Ah-Cacaw as the name of this ruler.

55. Chris Jones (1988:107) cited skeletal information from Haviland (1967).

56. Nomenclature for the phases of these buildings can be a bit confusing for people unused to archaeological conventions. The phases of construction are numbered from the outside to the inside so that Temple 32–1st refers to the last construction phase of Temple 32. Temple 33–2nd refers to the next phrase inward; 33–3rd to the next, and so on until the earliest phase of construction is reached.

57. Both Coggins (1976:380) and Chris Jones (n.d.) speculate that Burial 23, the richer of the two graves dug into Temple 33–2nd just before the last phase of construction began, contained Shield-Skull. This enigmatic person did not leave any sculpted monuments that survived, but he is recorded on Lintel 3 of Temple 1 as Ah-Cacaw's father. Jones also describes a significant building program which included Temple 5D-32–1st and the tomb of the twenty-second successor. Other buildings in the East Court and Central Acropolis may have been constructed during the reigns of the four intervening rulers. Unfortunately, since only the twenty-second ruler left us inscribed objects, we cannot know which of those rulers were responsible for the building programs. We interpret the absence of inscribed stelae during the reigns of the twenty-second through the twenty-fifth successors to have been the result of Caracol's victory; but why the same Tikal rulers left the shattered remains of their ancestors' stelae lying unattended in front of the North Acropolis, we don't know.

58. If our reconstruction of events is correct, the twenty-first ruler was captured by Lord Water of Caracol. The twenty-second ruler is in Burial 195 in Temple 5D-32, located to the immediate east of Temple 33. The central temple held the older tomb of Stormy-Sky, as well as two others inserted into the substructure shortly before the second phase of construction was buried under the third. If the twenty-fifth ruler was in Burial 23 and if Burial 24 held the twenty-fourth ruler, then three of the four kings who ruled between the defeat and Ah-Cacaw's accession are buried in the buildings fronting the North Acropolis.

59. Shook (1958:31) theorized that the stela was originally mounted in the rear chamber of Temple 5D-32. But since all other Tikal stela were erected in plaza space, we surmise that this one had been carried inside the temple from some other location. Chris Jones (n.d.) suggests that Stela 26 had been mounted in front of Temple 5D-32, while Stela 31 was originally placed in front of 5D-33. The notion that the offering deposit was situated at the physical threshold of the Otherworld portal of these temples is derived from examples of other back-wall locations of altars and symbolic representations of Otherworld beings in the sanctums of Maya temples, as detailed, for example, in Chapter 6.

60. Chris Jones (n.d.) reports that a fragment of Stela 26 was placed alongside Altar 19 (the altar to Stela 31) in a pit next to the substructure of Temple 33–1st. Since fragments from both monuments were put in the same cache, he presumes that both stelae were interred in their resting places in a single ceremonial sequence associated with the reestablishment of the Tikal dynastic lineage. Our reconstruction is somewhat different: We do not see any actual sundering in the old line as a result of the defeat by Caracol. There is no epigraphic evidence to suggest the insertion of any usurper Caracol kings; indeed, Caracol evidently did not even raise a victory monument here as they did at Naranjo. The victors apparently contented themselves with the desecration of Tikal royal historical monuments and the imposition of an effective ban on public history in the city. We interpret the ritual deposits of these two stelae—one recording a list of the kings from the lineage during its most aggressive and successful era, and the other recording its most glorious military victory—as a method of compensating for the desecration done to the monuments by the Caracol conquerors and as a means of establishing supernatural support for a new era of military success.

61. This description is based on images on the lower register of Room 1 at Bonampak. The event associated with that scene is the "fire" house-dedication ritual now known from many different sites. Although our scenario concerns the honorable deposit of a desecrated stela at Tikal, the "fire" ritual was very probably of the same type because the material placed in the caches is identical to that placed in dedication caches in other buildings at Tikal (see Note 42 for a discussion of the interrelationship of dedication and termination rituals).

62. Harrison (1970) has interpreted the presence of family residences as well as administrative and ritual houses in the Central Acropolis. We presume that these buildings functioned both as residences for the royal family and as council houses for the institutions of governance.

63. The offering plates we describe here are the flat-bottomed plates found in the lip-to-lip caches especially associated with building termination and dedication deposits. One set of this type of cache vessel (Crocker-Delataille 1985:231 [#354]) has *zac lac* incised on the side of the plate. This name associates these lip-to-lip plates with the great stone censers of Copán, which are called *zac lac tun* (Stuart 1986e). *Zac* has the meaning of "white," but also of something "artificial," in the sense of human-made. *Lac* is the word for plate, while *tun* specifies that the *zac lac* was made of stone. Both types of vessels were receptacles for offerings [and both have interiors shaped like buckets or deep pans]. Shook's report does not mention either type of *zac lac* in Temple 34, but his descriptions of the pits dug in the floor closely resemble the bucket shape inside the Copán censers. We suspect that the Maya thought of them as being the same thing; and although no plates were deposited in the Temple 34 cache pits, the material in these caches closely matches dedication offerings from other deposits which have them. Our presumption that a *zac lac* would have been used to transport the offerings is based on the many depictions of such plates in scenes of ritual activities from painted pottery. The *lac* plate was one of the principal containers for offerings of all sorts.

64. These descriptions are based on the wall paintings of Bonampak and Temple XIII from Uaxactún.

65. Shook (1958:32) reports that some of the marine materials came from the Pacific, while others came from the Atlantic. Presumably, the Tikal lord traded for material both from the Gulf of México and from the Belizean area of the Caribbean coast.

66. Flint and obsidian are associated with lightning strikes in most Maya languages and in much of their mythology. Most interestingly, the small obsidian blades found throughout the region are called *u kach Lac Mam* in modern Chol. This phrase translates as "the fingernails of the Lighting Bolt."

67. Volcanic hematite is a rare iron mineral. It occurs naturally only in the context of active volcanoes—of which there are several in the southern Maya Mountains. The crystal takes the form of flat flakes with mirror-quality surfaces. Although the crystal is virtually noncorruptible by oxidation, it can be ground into a bright reddish-purple powder that can be used for decorative purposes. This powder contains sparkling fragments of the crystal form. Volcanic hematite was highly prized as a mosaic mirror material—superior even to the iron pyrite which the lowland Maya also imported. Hematite is found in relative abundance in Late Preclassic contexts and in decreasing amounts thereafter, suggesting that the known sources in the highlands were limited and became exhausted during the course of the Classic period. The mother-of-pearl backing on this particular mirror is commensurate with the Late Preclassic volcanic hematite mirrors found in the cache of royal jewels at Cerros as described in Chapter 3.

68. The practice of deliberately smashing jade artifacts, particularly earflare assemblages, has been identified as an aspect of lowland Maya termination rituals by James Garber (1983). David Grove (1986) has suggested the presence of a similar practice at the Middle Preclassic highland Mexican center of Chalcatzingo and it has been found in relation to one of the earlier phases at Temple 10L-26 at Copán.

69. This type of bundle has long been known from narrative scenes on pottery, on carved monuments, and in the murals of Bonampak. The Quiche talked about sacred bundles called the *Pizom Q'aq'al,* which contained relics from their founding ancestors. The Tzotzil today still use bundles in the rituals of office in much the same way they were used in ancient ceremonies. Juan Pedro Laporte found a lip-to-lip cache in the Lost World group. When opened it was found to hold the same array of marine materials, lancets made from the thorns called *cuerno de toro* in modern México, jade, shell, and so forth. These objects were lying in a black substance which proved on analysis to be amate-fig bark paper, which had been painted blue and red. Around the entire offering, a band of fibrous cloth had been tied. Marisela Ayala (n.d.) was the first to identify this offering bundle with those represented in Maya imagery.

70. Bruce Love (1987:12) describes the smearing of blood on idols and stelae as these rituals are described in ethnohistorical sources.

71. In Room 1 at Bonampak, three high-ranked lords are shown being dressed in elaborate costumes. In the dedication scene on the lower register, these same three lords are shown dancing to the music of a band which marches into the picture from their right

side. On their left, high-ranked nobles move into the scene in an informal procession. These latter appear to be both witnesses and participants in the ceremonies. This same kind of dance very likely occurred in all or most dedication rites elsewhere, including Tikal.

72. Chris Jones (n.d.) notes that another cache containing fragments of Altar 19, which he associates with Stela 31, and a fragment of Stela 26 were placed in a pit next to Temple 33–1st. He sees this as evidence that Stela 26 and 31 were deposited at the same time.

73. W. R. Coe (1967:48) described the construction sequence for Temple 33–1st in detail. Coggins (1976:445–447) and Chris Jones (n.d.) both agree that this construction project was associated with Ah-Cacaw's reestablishment of the old lineage. Our understanding of this history descends from theirs, although we offer a slightly different interpretation of the data patterns. We see, for example, Temple 33–1st as both a new construction to declare the renewed authority and power of the dynasty, and as a method of ceremonially deactivating the North Acropolis. The Classic period Maya believed that sacred power and energy was accumulated in material objects (1) as they were used to contain the sacred power manifested in ritual and (2) as the actions of kings in the making of history focused the power of the cosmos onto them. To contain the accumulated power of an object which they wished to bury or discard, the Maya used a set of rituals to terminate the object formally. The dispositions of Stela 26 and 31 are examples of exactly these sorts of rituals; but these termination rituals also included drilling holes in pottery, knocking out the eyes of figures, destroying the faces of human imagery, removing color from sculpture, and many others. David Grove (1981) has proposed that this same behavior accounts for the mutilation of Olmec sculpture. Temple 33–1st seems to function like Temple 14 at Palenque. Built by Kan-Xul after his brother Chan-Bahlum's death, Temple 14 celebrates the dead brother's emergence from Xibalba. It also contains the power in the Group of the Cross by blocking the main ceremonial access into it (Schele 1988b). Temple 33–1st performs the same function at Tikal by obstructing the formal, processional access into the center of the North Acropolis, deactivating it as the ritual focus of the dynasty.

74. In an insightful analysis, Coggins (1976:371) noted this stylistic relationship of this altar to the Caracol tradition and, long before the discovery of Altar 21 at Caracol, she suggested there might have been interaction in that direction

75. We do not yet have a phonetic reading of this verb, but its association with war and captive taking is widespread. Its other significant occurrence is in the heir-designation ritual of Chan-Bahlum at Palenque. Heir-designation rites as they were portrayed at Bonampak also involved the taking and offering of captives.

76. This ritual display of captives after a battle is the war event shown most often in narrative scenes in Maya art (Schele 1984a). We can see an excellent example of this in Room 2 at Bonampak (M. Miller 1986:112–130). The event in the Tikal scene is spelled *nawah,* a term meaning "to dress or adorn" (Bricker 1986:158). Here, the action is the dressing of the captive in the garb of sacrifice. This action included stripping him of his regalia, replacing his battle garb with the cut-cloth kilt of sacrifice, replacing his ear ornaments with paper or flowers, and painting him in the color of sacrifice. Landa (Tozzer 1941:117–119) reported that blue was the color painted on the stripped bodies of sacrificial victims before they were tortured or killed.

Captives most often appear as sacrificial victims, rather than as warriors engaged directly in battle. Capture, and the rank of those captives taken, were central to the prestige of Maya nobles. Sacrificial victims also appear regularly in burials and in dedication rites. Brian Dillon (1982:44) found a deposit of sacrificial victims who were apparently lying in the belly-down position characteristic of captives when they met their fate. Captives, especially high-ranked ones, were often kept alive for years. They appeared repeatedly in all sorts of rituals, and their survival quite possibly created problems of succession in their lineages.

Peter Harrison (1989) has provided us additional information on Structure 5D-57 that enriches this piece of history considerably. At the Seventh Round Table of Palenque, he demonstrated how the builders of the Central Acropolis used the geometry of the triangle in conjunction with older buildings to establish the location of new buildings. Using this technique, Structure 5D-57 was positioned in relationship to what he calls "Great-Jaguar-Paw's clan house," known archaeologically as Structure 5D-46, a great two-storied palace built on the west end of the Central Acropolis during the Early Classic period. So important was this palace to subsequent kings that while they added to it, they were careful to retain the original structure as a part of the functioning Acropolis throughout the subsequent history of the city.

The identity of its original patron is established by a cache vessel deposited under the west stairs of 5D-46. The inscription on the pot records that it was made for the dedication of the "*k'ul na* (holy structure) of Great-Jaguar-Paw." Thus, Ah-Cacaw established the location of the building depicting his display of captives at the dedication of Temple 33 in relationship to the residence of the very ancestor whose victory over Uaxactún is celebrated on Stela 31. It was in Temple 33 that he deposited this tree-stone with such reverence. This is a remarkable folding of history back on itself and a wonderful example of the symmetries the Maya found so fascinating and useful in their construction of political history.

77. The phrase, as written here, includes the "fish-in-hand" verb that records bloodletting and vision rituals at other sites. This verb is followed by a standard phrase including *tu* and a glyph representing a lancet and an "akbal" compound. In the past, we have presumed this "akbal" glyph referred to a performance of the ritual at night, but Victoria Bricker (1986:73–74) has suggested an alternative explanation that seems to be correct. The glyph consists of the signs *ti, ya,* the "akbal" sign, and *li.* If the "akbal" sign reads syllabically as *ak',* the combination reads *ti yak'il,* "in his tongue."

78. This verb consists of T79 (value unknown) superfixed to *ta* (T565) plus the combination -*wan,* an inflectional suffix for verbs having to do with position in or the shape of space. This same glyph and variants of it occur at Palenque, Copán, and many other sites associated with the dedication rituals for monuments and houses. The "T" in the number above derives from Thompson's 1962 method of glyph transcription.

79. For a full discussion of this day and its events, see the later parts of Chapter 4. Proskouriakoff (Coggins 1976:448) first noted that this date is linked to the Temple 1 date.

80. Even more intriguing is an observation recently made by Karl Taube in his study of Teotihuacán mirrors and war imagery (Taube n.d.). Following earlier work by George Kubler (1976), Taube notes the appearance of a species of cactus found in the highlands of Central México. Both scholars have suggested that the platform under Ah-Cacaw refers directly to Teotihuacán, and Taube suggests it may refer directly to the Temple of Quetzalcoatl. We think this may be correct, but we suggest the reference is far more oblique. At the time of the carving of these lintels, Teotihuacán was in severe decline (Millon 1988), but it had been in full florescence at the time of the conquest of Uaxactún when this iconography became so popular. We suggest the reference is to the conquest of Uaxactún and the long-lasting association of that victory with the memory of the Teotihuacanos. See René Millon's (1988) evaluation of the Maya-Teotihuacán interaction in his discussion of the fall of Teotihuacán.

81. Schele (1985a) proposed a reading of *bal* or *balan* for the Emblem Glyph of Tikal. New evidence from the Primary Standard Sequence on pottery has lent support to that reading and provided a direct association to this jaguar head. David Stuart (1987b:2–7) has read one of the glyphs in this pottery text as *u tz'ibil,* "his writing."

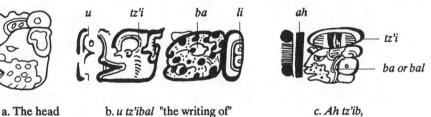

a. The head variant of the number 9

b. *u tz'ibal* "the writing of"

c. *Ah tz'ib,* "He the Scribe"

In one version of this glyph, the syllable *ba* is written with a jaguar head, and in another, *bal* appears as the head of the number 9. This last glyph standardly refers to a human head with the lower jaw covered with a jaguar pelt, and a *yax* shell sign affixed to its forehead. In many of the toponymic forms of the Tikal Emblem Glyph, the "bundle" is prefixed by *yax.* Since the main sign, as well as the head of the number 9, have phonetic values as *bal,* the name of Tikal was likely to have been *Yax Bal* or *Yax Balam.* The portrait head of the number 9, however, was also used to record the image and the name of the jaguar member of the Headband Twins, who are one of the Classic period manifestations of the Hero Twins. Tikal was apparently named as the special place of this god.

82. Lintel 3 of Temple 4 depicts the son of Ah-Cacaw seated on a throne, but the point of view is rotated 90± so that we see a front view of the king. Just as in Temple 1, the throne of the king sits atop a low stepped platform, but here the artist showed clearly the carrying bars of the Maya version of a sedan chair.

83. Chris Jones (1988:110) follows an earlier suggestion by Marcus (1976:90) that the Emblem Glyph of this noble is that of Piedras Negras, based on the identification of the prefix as a leaf. However, the main sign of the Piedras Negras Emblem Glyph consists of the syllables *yo, ki,* and *bi,* which can all appear in a variety of substitutions (Stuart 1987b:37). The snake form of the Piedras Negras Emblem Glyph is formed by simply using the head variant of *bi.* The Emblem Glyph on this bone has the "blood group" sign inverted, with the dotted part above the shell sign rather than below it. Therefore, we believe that the main sign of the Emblem Glyph of this captive noble is the snake head associated with Site Q and Calakmul.

84. Proskouriakoff (in Chris Jones 1988:109) first noted the recurrence of the death date on this bone. The other five events on MT 28 are also deaths, including that of someone named 18-Rabbit-God K on 9.14.15.4.3 and a woman on 9.14.15.6.13. The 18-Rabbit character may be named on Lintel 2 of Temple 1.

85. Chris Jones (personal communication, 1986) sees little possibility that a passage-way could have been left open to give access to the tomb. Ruler B probably oversaw the building of the substructure over the tomb of his father, although Ah-Cacaw is likely to have commissioned the lintels or at least to have overseen the information that would be put on them after his death.

86. David Stuart (personal communication, 1985) first recognized that the name phrase on Naranjo Stela 6 is the phonetic version of Smoking-Batab's name. The day sign in the Calendar Round is eroded, but the three possible readings are:

9.14.18. 4. 8 9 Lamat   11 Muan November 28, 729
9.15.11. 7.13 9 Ben   11 Muan November 25, 742
9.16. 4.10.18 9 Etz'nab   11 Muan November 22, 755

CHAPTER 6: THE CHILDREN OF FIRST MOTHER: FAMILY AND DYNASTY AT PALENQUE

1. According to one account by the family of Antonio de Solís of Tumbala in 1746, Palenque came to the attention of Europeans in the mid-eighteenth century with its "discovery" by Spaniards. During the next forty years, many visitors, both civilian and government sponsored, went to Palenque and made a series of drawings and maps of the site, which are now in archives in Seville and Madrid and at the British Museum. A set of these early drawing and commentaries by Antonio del Río and Paul Felix Cabrera appeared in *Descriptions of the Ruins of an Ancient City,* a two-volume work published by Henry Berthoud in 1822. With this publication, the ruined buildings and sculptures of Palenque came to the attention of the Western world and initiated a fascination with ancient Maya civilization that continues today. The most popular travel accounts were those written by John Stephens and Frederick Catherwood in their *Incidents of Travel in Central America, Chiapas and Yucatán,* published in 1841. These books truly brought the Maya to the attention of the Western world and were immensely popular at the time. For those interested in the history of discovery, see Graham (1971), Berlin (1970), and G. Stuart (n.d.).

2. This royal name combines the features of a snake and jaguar into one glyph block. At the Primera Mesa Redonda of Palenque, a meeting held at Palenque in December, 1973, at which most of Palenque's kings were given their modern names, we elected to use the modern Chol spelling of this name combination—*chan,* "snake," and *bahlum,* "jaguar." Later research into the phonetic complements accompanying this name has shown that it was originally pronounced more like its modern Yucatec version, *can-balam,* but we have elected to retain the original spelling of this name in order not to add confusion by creating different names for the same person.

3. The longest inscription was the Hieroglyphic Stair of Temple 26 at Copán. We have deciphered enough of that inscription to know that it recorded a detailed dynastic history of Copán, but unfortunately the stairs were found already badly eroded and out of order

for the most part. Time has not been kind to the stairs since they were uncovered in 1898 and much of what was visible then has since been worn away. This inscription is unlikely ever to be deciphered completely, making the panels of the Temple of Inscriptions at Palenque the longest intact inscription.

4. Pacal used the nine katuns leading up to and including his own lifetime as the framework for the dynastic history he inscribed. Beginning with the katun ending on 9.4.0.0.0, he recorded the last royal accession to occur before each successive katun ended. When more than one king ruled within a katun, he linked their accessions to the half-katun or the thirteen-tun point within the katun. He ended the nine katuns with 9.13.0.0.0, the twenty-year period during which he built the temple and commissioned the tablets and their history. By using this device, Pacal locked all the accessions between Chaacal I and himself to specified period endings, thus setting the whole of Palenque's history into a firm and indisputable chronological framework. This use of katun succession as the framework of history created the prototype of the katun histories that are common in the later books of Chilam Balam in Yucatán. Lounsbury (1974) first offered the chronological decipherment of the sarcophagus edge, while Berlin (1977:136) recognized the nine-katun sequence as the structural framework in which Pacal presented his history on the tablets above. For a detailed decipherment of the tablets from the Temple of Inscriptions, see Schele (1983, 1986c).

5. Inscriptions document at least three, possibly four, more generations on later tablets, bringing the total number of generations to thirteen or fourteen during the entire history of Palenque.

6. The inscriptions of Palenque never record the exact kinship relationship between Ac-Kan, Pacal I, and Lady Zac-Kuk, but we can reconstruct it based on the following information. (1) Of the two men, only Ac-Kan became the king of Palenque. The texts of the Temple of Inscriptions are complete in the record of accessions from 9.4.0.0.0 until Pacal II, and Pacal I does not appear in that record. (2) Both men died in 612, but Pacal I died on March 9 while Ac-Kan died six months later on August 11. Most important, the records of their deaths on the edge of the sarcophagus lid are reversed, with the later date recorded first, as if we are to understand these persons in the order Ac-Kan/Pacal, rather than the order of their deaths. (3) Of the two men, only Pacal I is shown as a figure on the sides of the sarcophagus, even though he was never king.

Something about their dynastic roles made it advisable to break the chronological order of the death list to put Ac-Kan before Pacal. At the same time, this something led the Maya to eliminate Ac-Kan from the portrait row and picture Pacal I instead. The most efficient explanation is that they were brothers and that the line passed through Pacal rather than Ac-Kan.

In two other examples on the sarcophagus sides, one of a pair of rulers was eliminated from the portrait gallery, and in those examples we can determine the reason. The first pair, Manik and Chaacal I were born only five and a half years apart, while the other, Chaacal II and Chan-Bahlum I, were born only a year apart. These short periods between births make a father-son relationship between these pairs impossible—they were siblings. Of the first pair of brothers, only Chaacal I appears in portraiture; and of the second pair, only Chan-Bahlum I has a place on the sarcophagus sides. Why? The answer lies in inheritance: The children of only one brother might inherit the throne. The sarcophagus sides depict the direct descent of the line from parent to child. In this interpretation, Pacal I was the sibling of Ac-Kan and he is shown because his child inherited the throne. He won his place in Pacal the Great's portrait gallery for his role as father of the next ruler, Lady Zac-Kuk, and as the grandfather of the child named for him, Pacal, who became one of the greatest American rulers in history.

7. Such tablets may well be at Palenque in the deep levels of the Palace or in some other building, for deep excavations have rarely been done at Palenque, and then often by accident. The time difference between Lady Kanal-Ikal's rule and Pacal the Great's was not long, for she was still alive when her great grandson was born. He was born on March 26, 603 and she died on November 7, 604. Her prominence in Pacal's records and the twenty-year length of her reign makes likely that Lady Kanal-Ikal commissioned inscriptions and temple constructions during her reign.

8. He was forty-three years old at the time. He was thirty-seven when his mother died and thirty-nine at his father's death.

9. The plan and design of the Temple Olvidado became the hallmarks of Palenque's architecture: double-galleried interior, thin supporting walls with multiple doors piercing

exterior walls, and trefoil vaults arching across the inner galleries. The vault system used in later buildings actually leaned the outer wall against the center wall, above the medial molding. The Palencanos never developed the true arch, but their system gave them the highest ratio of wall thickness to span width ever achieved in Maya architecture. The system also allowed them to pierce the outer walls of their buildings with more doors than any other Maya style, giving Palenque architecture the largest interior volume and best lighting known among the Maya. This innovative sequence began with the Temple Olvidado and culminated with the Group of the Cross and Houses A and D of the Palace.

10. His construction projects probably also included Houses K and L on the south ends of the eastern and western facades, and perhaps other buildings that were found in excavations of the Palace courtyards,

11. See Schele (1986a) for a full discussion of the development of Palenque's architectural style.

12. This inference of the identity of the woman named in the Temple of Inscriptions as Pacal's mother is based on the following pattern of data:

(1) The woman who appears in the equivalent chronological position in the death list on the sarcophagus is his mother, Lady Zac-Kuk.

(2) On the Oval Palace Tablet, the woman named as Pacal's mother hands him the crown that makes him king, but his father is neither named nor pictured. The parent critical to his legitimate claim to the throne is his mother rather than his father.

(3) His father, Kan-Bahlum-Mo', never appears in an accession phrase in any of the inscriptions of Palenque. Furthermore, Pacal depicts Kan-Bahlum-Mo' only on the sarcophagus where he appears as the king's father and not as a king in his own right.

(4) The goddess is born on a date deliberately contrived to have the same temporal character (see note 35) as Pacal's birth.

All of these factors emphasize that Pacal's right of inheritance descended through his mother rather than his father. Pacal's strategy for explaining the appropriateness of this pattern of descent was to establish an equation between his mother and the mother of the gods. To have named the woman who acceded shortly before his own accession with the name of the goddess is much in keeping with this strategy.

The name itself consists of the bird from the Palenque Emblem Glyph, which is a heron, with feathers in its mouth. Lounsbury (personal communication, 1977) has suggested that this is a play on the name Zac-Kuk, based on the following word plays. The word for heron in Yucatec and Chol is *zac bac*, "white bone," or some expression like "white crest." The *zac bac* reading works well as the Palenque Emblem Glyph since the main sign in the Emblem Glyph is a long bone or skull, also *bac*. Lounsbury suggests that the feathers (*kuk*) in the mouth changes *zac bac* to *zac kuk*, thus making a play on the name of Pacal's mother which was Zac-Kuk, "White (or Resplendent) Quetzal." No one has, as yet, suggested a reading for the small sign mounted atop the heron's head in the name. At the 1989 Texas Workshop on Maya Hieroglyphic Writing, Dennis Tedlock offered a different solution by linking the *zac bac* gloss with the name *Xbaquiyalo*, the first wife of Hunhunahpu and mother of Hun-Batz' and Hun-Chuen in the Popol Vuh.

13. The stairs leading up the front of the Temple of Inscriptions and those leading down to the tomb have risers about 18 inches high. Today, the inner stairs are almost always damp and slippery from condensation in the tunnellike vaults; we assume the same conditions were extant when Pacal was buried.

14. While we have no way of determining who enacted the rituals described in this scenario, the fact that these particular actions were done is clear from the archaeological record at Palenque and from records of other burial rites, especially those of Ruler 3 at Piedras Negras (Stuart 1985a). The description of the objects deposited inside the coffin and tomb are drawn from Ruz (1973) and from his description of the sacrifice of five victims (1955). The description of the scale and feel of being in the tomb comes from the days Schele spent locked inside the tomb helping Merle Greene Robertson photograph the stucco sculptures modeled on the walls.

15. The drawings which survive on the sarcophagus sides are carefully drawn and beautifully designed. However, the carving, especially in the areas at some distance from the image of the falling Pacal, are very sloppily executed. Merle Robertson and Schele take

this contrast to mean that the carving was executed at the last minute and in a rush. See Merle Robertson (1983) for a detailed photographic record of the tomb.

16. Xoc appears briefly on the Palace Tablet as the man who dedicated the north building of the Palace after Kan-Xul had been taken captive by the king of Toniná. He never became the king, but he apparently was a high-ranked official in the kingdom because he functioned as the surrogate of the captured Kan-Xul until a new king was selected from the royal clan. Given his age of thirty-three at the time of Pacal's death, we have assumed he served Pacal as well as his descendants.

17. Chaacal, in fact, did become king after Kan-Xul was taken captive and executed at Toniná. His parentage statements do not name either Chan-Bahlum or Kan-Xul as his father. He was apparently the offspring of one of the women in Pacal's lineage, perhaps a sister of Chan-Bahlum and Kan-Xul. Chac-Zutz' was a cahal, who became an important figure (maybe the war chief of the kingdom) during Chaacal's reign.

18. The offerings of the plaster heads, the plates and cups of food, the royal belt, and the slaughtered victims are located in the plans below.

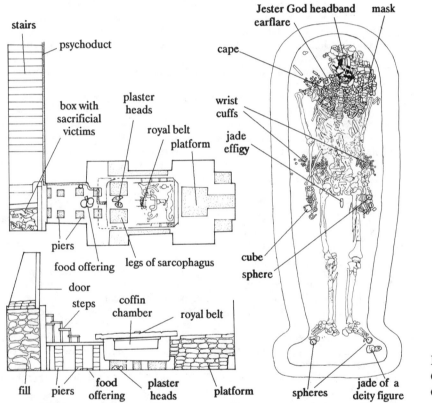

Pacal's Tomb Chamber and Coffin

19. The other possibility is that the portraits represent the great king Pacal and his wife Lady Ahpo-Hel.

20. Merle Robertson (1979) first associated the imagery on these piers with glyphic accounts of Chan-Bahlum's heir-designation. The fact that Chan-Bahlum became a living incarnation of the sun is declared by him in his own textual account of this ceremony in the Temple of the Sun in the Group of the Cross.

21. The badly damaged condition of these stucco portraits and the texts that once accompanied them preclude identifying them with security, but logically they should be the most important ancestors in Chan-Bahlum's claim to legitimacy. One possible pattern is that they all represent his father Pacal, but the headdresses, one of which is a jaguar head, suggest that they are meant to represent different individuals. The Maya often represented their names in the imagery of their headdresses. The jaguar headdress, then, may refer to Chan-Bahlum I, his great-great-great-grandfather.

22. At Bonampak, Chaan-Muan depicted the designation of his heir by showing a high-ranking noble displaying him at the edge of a pyramid. The audience on the mural consists of fourteen high-ranked individuals, but the ritual would have been held publicly, the entire community in attendance (M. Miller 1986b:59–97). At Palenque, Chan-Bahlum did not represent the audience, but we know it included everyone who stood in the plaza under the piers of the Temple of Inscriptions. In the Group of the Cross, he used a pyramid glyph to describe the action of heir-designation (Schele 1985b) as being "pyramided." The glyph actually reads *le.ma:ch'ul na* (using the transcription punctuation from Thompson's [1962] *A Catalog of Maya Hieroglyphs*) or *lem ch'ul na:* in Yucatec *lem* is glossed by Barrera Vasquez as *"meter, encajar, introducir."* To become the heir was "to introduce the child from the pyramid," exactly the scenes Chan-Bahlum displayed on the Temple of Inscriptions piers.

23. Although the first royal temple at Cerros is designed around the quincunx or five-fold principle, the later public buildings there are triadic in concept. The earliest architects created an innovative variety of building designs, but the triadic principle was the most pervasive.

24. The glyphic phrase for these small inner houses, *pib na,* consists of *pib,* the word for "underground" as in the pits used for cooking, and *na,* "edifice or building." *Pib na* is also the term for a "sweat bath" used by women after childbirth. Many cosmologies of modern Maya in Chiapas refer to a sweat bath in the heart of the mountain. This image may be intended here also.

25. The text on the Tablet of the Cross writes this second event as *yoch-te k'in-k'in,* "he became the sun."

26. All three panels have the same text on them, but the text is split in different ways in each temple. In the Temple of the Cross, it reads "ten days after he had become the stood-up one (*yoch-te acal*) and then he spoke of (*iwal chi-wa* or *che-wa*) U-Kix-Chan, Mah Kina Chan-Bahlum, the child of Pacal, Blood Lord of Palenque." In the Temple of the Foliated Cross, the first event (*yoch-te*) appears on the left panel and the second (*chi-wa*) is on the right. In the Temple of the Sun, the glyphs from the left panel survive on Maudslay's (1889–1902:Pl.86) reproduction of Waldeck's original drawing, but nevertheless some of them are readable. The first phrase reads *chumlah ti ahau le* and paraphrases "He was seated as king, Mah Kina Chan-Bahlum, Blood Lord of Palenque." The second section of the text is much more difficult, but the best probability is that it begins with a Distance Number that leads to the event ten days after the accession (9.12.11.13.0 5 Ahau 13 Kayab) and then jumps to the right tablet where the event was once written. Today only the long name phrase of the actor, Chan-Bahlum, survives on the right panel.

27. Mayanists are still debating the identification of this smaller figure. Floyd Lounsbury (in his seminar on Maya hieroglyphic writing, 1975) first proposed that he is Chan-Bahlum at his heir-designation. Since all three of the texts located near his head record this heir-designation and, in two of the three texts, a war event which took place more than a year later on 9.10.10.0.0, this interpretation has merit. In fact, it has resurfaced recently in a presentation by Basse and it has the support of David Stuart. Another alternative interpretation emerged at the 1987 Advanced Seminar on Maya Hieroglyphic Writing. Tom Jones proposed this figure represents the lineage founder, Bahlum-Kuk. Since founders also appear in accession scenes at Yaxchilán (Lintel 25) and Copán (the bench from Temple 11), this interpretation also has merit.

For the present, we still hold to the older interpretation of this shorter figure as Pacal, based on the following arguments:

(1) There is a transfer of a scepterlike object (in the Temple of the Cross a Quadripartite Scepter; in the Temple of the Foliated Cross, a Personified Perforator; and in the Temple of the Sun, a shield and eccentric-shield device). These transferred objects represent the power of the throne, and rulers at Palenque and other Maya sites wield them in scenes of rituals. If the smaller figure is Chan-Bahlum at his own heir-designation, he is already controlling these objects at age six. Lounsbury (personal communication, 1989) has suggested that this is a ritual in which the child was made acquainted with the objects he would one day wield as king. We find this interpretation less satisfying than one in which these objects are transferred from the former king, now deceased, to his son who is becoming the new king.

(2) In the heir-designation presentation on the Temple of Inscriptions piers, the size of the child (104 cm) matches closely the size of six-year-old Chol children in

the region today (M. Robertson 1979:132–133). The scale of the child presented in the Bonampak murals conforms to this size in direct proportion to the adult who holds him. The muffled figure in the Group of the Cross may be smaller than the larger figures, but he is still of a size larger than a six-year-old in proportion to the larger figure. The Temple of Inscriptions child when stretched out to full height is only 56 percent of the height of the adults who hold him, while the smaller figure in the Group of the Cross is between 73 percent and 78 percent of the height of the larger figure. According to Robertson's modern measurements, a 1.04-meter six-year-old from the Palenque region is around 60 percent of the height of a 5' 6'' (1.70m) adult.

(3) If the scene is the documentation of Chan-Bahlum's accession rites, and this interpretation is well supported by the inscriptions, then the composition format of each temple means to present this small figure as the source of power. He holds the objects of power on the inner tablet while the new king holds them on the outer panels. There is a transfer of these objects from the smaller person to the larger one as the scene moves inside to outside. The larger figure also dons the costume of kings in its most ancient and orthodox version during the transition from inside to outside: He wears minimal jewelry and a cotton hipcloth on the inside and the full costume over those minimal clothes on the outside. In addition, the larger figure takes the smaller person's place when the scene moves from the inside to the outside of the sanctuary, especially in the composition of the Temple of the Cross. The scenes in all three temples emphasize the transformation of the tall figure from heir to king in the movement from inside to outside, and within this program the smaller figure is presented as the source of Chan-Bahlum's claim to the throne—and *that* person was either Pacal, his father, or Bahlum-Kuk, the founder of his dynasty.

(4) Finally, in the heir-designation event, the six-year-old child was not the main actor, either at Palenque or at Bonampak. The child was displayed as the heir, but the father, who was the acting king, oversaw that display. At Bonampak, Chaan-Muan went to war, not the child, and at Palenque, Pacal memorialized the thirteenth-haab anniversary of this heir-designation in the Tableritos from the Subterranean building of the Palace without mentioning Chan-Bahlum at all. Chan-Bahlum, the six-year-old child, was the recipient of the action in the heir-designation rites, but the source of those actions was his father, Pacal.

The argument for identifying the smaller figure as Chan-Bahlum at his heir-designation has strengthened with the recognition that the two outer panels of the Temples of the Foliated Cross and the Sun depict Chan-Bahlum at points in his accession rituals separated by at least ten days. The fact that Chan-Bahlum appears on more than one date, involved in more than one action on the outer panels, reinforces the possibility that he is shown at two different ages and in two different actions on the inner panel. Although we believe this latter interpretation to be less probable, it is a viable possibility that must also be kept in mind.

28. The Tzotzil-speaking Maya of Zinacantan in highland Chiapas still regard the Christian crosses at the base of their sacred mountains as the doorways to the Otherworld which contains their ancestors. The shamans of this community regularly commune with the supernatural at these holy places (Vogt 1976).

29. See Schele and M. Miller (1986:76–77, 265–315) for a detailed discussion of the World Tree and its appearances in death and bloodletting iconography of the Maya.

30. The aged god on the right has never been securely identified. Kelley (1965) suggested God M, but demonstration of his identification has not materialized. The only other portrait we have of this god appears on a small incised bone, probably from the Palenque region (see Crocker-Delataille 1985: Pl. 395). The composition of these two old gods bent under the weight of the throne precisely anticipates the display of captives on Late Classic stelae from the site of Cobá (Thompson, Pollock, and Charlot 1932).

31. God L is now recognized as one of the chief gods of the Maya Underworld. Most important, he is the deity shown presiding over the gods on 4 Ahau 8 Cumku, the day of the current creation (M.D. Coe 1973:107–109). Chan-Bahlum's repeated depiction of this god asserts the ability of the king to control the effects of God L and other Xibalbans

in his community, and perhaps his ability as king to gain the willing cooperation of these gods in the affairs of the kingdom.

32. This set of gods was first noticed by Berlin (1963), who gave it the name "Palenque Triad" because it was in the Palenque inscriptions that he first saw them. Building on Berlin's identification, Kelley (1965) identified their birth dates in the Group of the Cross and suggested associations between these Maya gods and other Mesoamerican supernaturals. Lounsbury (1976, 1980, 1985) sorted out chronological problems concerning their histories and recognized the names of their parents in the Tablet of the Cross. He has also made extensive arguments concerning their identities. In Maya art, these gods appear both singly and as a triad of gods at other Maya sites. Most important, GI and GIII, the first and second-born gods, are the beings most often depicted in the very earliest public images created by the Maya during the Late Preclassic period. They are not just Palenque gods.

33. The text that records this event falls into a couplet which characterizes the action in two ways. In the first, the god *yoch-te ta chan* "entered into the sky." In the second, he dedicated a house named "*wac-ah-chan xaman waxac na GI* or "raised up sky north eight house GI." The first glyph naming the house consists of the number six prefixed to a sky glyph with two *ah* signs above it. The word for "six" is *wac*. Barrera Vasquez (1980:906) lists a homophone, *wac,* as "*cosa enhiesta*" (*enhestar* means "to erect, to set up, to hoist [up], and to raise [up]"). *Wac-ah chan* is "raised up sky." This proper name is followed by the glyph for "north" (*xaman*) and the portrait head of GI preceded by the number eight (*waxac*) and phonetic *na* ("edifice").

The most likely reference here is to the act of raising the sky from the primordial sea of creation, an act known to be part of many Mesoamerican origin myths. This house is further characterized as *yotot xaman,* "the house of the north." The same *wacah chan* phrase names the inner sanctuary of the Temple of the Cross and World Tree on its inner panel. The god's action was to establish the primary axis of the world by setting the sky in its place and establishing its order. Since this is an action twice associated with the north, we suggest it corresponded in the Maya mind to the set of the polar star and the circular movement of the constellations around that axis. In the tropics, the polar star is much lower than in the temperate zone, and the movement of the constellations through the night is even more noticeable, resembling as much as anything the shifting of patterns around the inside of a barrel. This axial pivot of the sky creates the great pattern through which the sun and the planets move and it was a pattern created by GI' 542 days or a year and a half after this era began (Schele 1987e and n.d.a).

34. Floyd Lounsbury first deciphered the chronology of this difficult passage. The text begins with a Distance Number of 8.5.0, a birth verb, and then a series of glyphs recording 4 Ahau 8 Cumku, the era date. Before Lounsbury proposed this solution, most researchers had assumed that the birth referred to the Initial Series event. In this interpretation, the Distance Number must be in error since the Initial Series date is 6.14.0 before 4 Ahau 8 Cumku, rather than the 8.5.0 written in the text. Lounsbury used known patterns of Mayan grammar to show that there are actually two different births given here, and that the name of the person born 8.5.0 before the era has been deleted from the text. The missing name, however, can be reconstructed—again by using known patterns of Mayan grammar—as the subject of the next event. The name in question is GI', the god who ordered the sky a year and a half after the era began. See Lounsbury (1980 and 1985) for a full discussion of the chronology and grammar of these passages and the identities of the gods of the Palenque Triad.

35. Lounsbury (1976) called this kind of numerology "contrived numbers." Such numbers are composed of two dates: The earlier one is usually from a time previous to the 4 Ahau 8 Cumku creation date, and the other is a historical date of significance in the present creation. The Distance Number (amount of time) that separates the two is contrived by using highly factorable numbers, so that both dates fall on the same point in time in several different cycles. The two dates manipulated by Chan-Bahlum, 12.19.13.4.0 8 Ahau 18 Zec and 9.8.9.13.0 8 Ahau 13 Pop, fall 9.8.16.9.0 or 1,359,540 days apart in the Maya Long Count. This number is 2^2 x 3^2 5 x 7 x 13 x 83 yielding the following relationships:

1,359,540 =	5,229	(26)	gives the same day number
	3,735	(364)	computing years
	1,734	(780)	Mars period and three tzolkins (3 x 260)
	1,660	(819)	same day in the 819-day quadrant

747	(1,820)	seven tzolkin/five computing-year cycle
581	(2,340)	harmonizes the Lord of the Night with the Tzolkin
415	(3,276)	places the births in the same south quadrant of the 819-day count

This puts Pacal's birth in relation to Lady Beastie's on the same day in the tzolkin (8 Ahau), the same point in the Mars cycle, and during the time when the same Lord of the Night reigned. Most important, both persons were born twenty days after time moved into the south-yellow quadrant of the 819-day count. And both quadrants began on 1 Ahau.

36. In the account of genesis given in the Popol Vuh, First Mother is a daughter of a lord of Xibalba. When the skull of First Father impregnates her by spitting in her hand, she is forced to flee to the world of humanity. As in Chan-Bahlum's story, the First Mother spans the worlds.

37. The two births are: 12.19.11.13.0 1 Ahau 8 Muan (June 16, 3122 B.C.) for GI' and 1.18.5.4.0 1 Ahau 13 Mac (November 8, 2360 B.C.) for GII. The elapsed time between them is 1.18.13.9.0 or 278,460 days. This sum factors out as 2^2 x 3^2 x 5 x 7 x 13 x 17 and gives the following patterns of cycles:

278,460 =	1,071	(260)	same day in the tzolkin
	357	(780)	same day in the Mars cycle and 3 tzolkins
	119	(2,340)	gives the same Lord of the Night
	765	(364)	computing year
	153	(1,820)	seven tzolkin/five haab cycle
	340	(819)	same day in the 819-day quadrant
	85	(3,276)	same quadrant of the four 819-day sequence (east, red, and 1 Imix)

These cycles make the two births fall on the same day in the 260-day tzolkin, on days ruled by the same Lord of the Night, and on the same day in the same quadrant of the 819-day count. The First Father, GI', was born in the last creation; his reflection in this creation is his child GII.

38. The "fish-in-hand" glyph appears on Lintels 13, 14, and 25 of Yaxchilán with scenes of the Vision Serpent, while on Lintels 39, 40, and 41, the scenes depict Bird-Jaguar and two of his wives holding Double-headed Serpent Bars. The action associated with this verb is the materialization of the Vision Serpent. Since the k'ul "holy" sign follows the "fish-in-hand" when it is inflected as a transitive root, the action is something done to the "holy" liquid of the body—in other words to "blood." This action results in the appearance of the Vision Serpent. In those examples where it is not followed by the k'ul "holy" sign, God K appears in the object slot, although we do not yet fully understand what meaning is intended. Perhaps this association of God K with "fish-in-hand" reflects the frequent appearance of this god in the mouth of the Double-headed Serpent Bar. It is the vision often brought forth by the ritual. "To manifest a vision (or a divinity)" is an appropriate paraphrase to use for the present, although the final phonetic reading of the "fish-in-hand" glyph may refer to this action metaphorically or through the vision side of the rite.

39. Constance Cortez (1986) and others have identified this bird with Vucub-Caquix of the Popol Vuh. Cortez suggests that this bird represented the idea of order in nature. When it acted with hubris, imitating the glory of the sun, the natural world was out of order. In the story of the Popol Vuh, the Hero Twins opposed Vucub-Caquix, and by defeating him, brought nature back into its proper balance and behavior once again. In this interpretation, the Celestial Bird represents an universe in which order is mediated by the king in his role as the avatar of the Hero Twins.

40. On the Tablet of the Cross, these events appear immediately behind Chan-Bahlum's legs, linked to his accession by a Distance Number.

41. Lounsbury (personal communication, 1978) was the first to recognize that Jupiter and Saturn were frozen at their stationary points less than 5+ apart in the sky. He informed Dieter Dütting of the alignment in 1980 and then Dütting and Aveni (1982) extended the hierophany to include this quadruple conjunction with Mars and the moon

also in close proximity on that day (July 20, 690, in the Julian calendar). They located the planets as follows:

Planet	Longitude	Latitude
Mars	219°.10	−2°.18
Jupiter	221°.94	+0°.83
Saturn	225°.52	+2°.04
Moon	231°.80	−1°.80

They describe the phenomena as follows: " . . . all four planets were close together (a quadruple conjunction) in the same constellation Scorpio, and they must have made quite a spectacle with bright red Antares shining but a few degrees south of the group as they straddled the high ridge that forms the southern horizon of Palenque. The night before 2 Cib 14 Mol the moon would have been just at the western end of the planetary lineup, but the night after it would have been well out of range to the east. The month before and after, Mars would have shifted appreciably away from Jupiter and Saturn. Therefore, the date of the inscription is the best one where the four were closest together." Aveni continues, "Though conjunctions of Jupiter and Saturn with given tolerance in separation are skewed to occur about five times a century, the inclusion of a third planet in the grouping reduces the frequency of occurrence to about once a century." Dütting and Aveni speculated that the Palencanos saw this conjunction as a replay of the birth of Triad gods with the moon representing their mother, Lady Beastie. This interpretation seems likely since Chan-Bahlum carefully bridged from those births to this 2 Cib 14 Mol event.

Perhaps the most remarkable new piece of information on this date was discovered independently by Stephen Houston and David Stuart (in a letter dated October 19, 1989) and Nikolai Grube (in a independent letter also dated October 19, 1989). The event on this day is written *pili u waybil* on the Tablet of the Sun and *pili u chiltin* in the other temples. Houston, Stuart, and Grube all identify *way* and its past participial *waybil* as the word meaning "nagual" or "spirit or animal counterpart." In sixteenth-century Tzotzil (a language very close to the Chol spoken at Palenque), *chi'il* is "companion, familiar thing, friend" (Laughlin 1988:189).

The verb, which is glyphically spelled *pi-lu-yi,* seems most closely related to the verb *pi'len*, which is glossed in Chol (Aulie and Aulie 1978:93) as *"acompañar* (to accompany)" and *"tener relación sexual* (to have a sexual relationship)." The second meaning is known to have been used by the Maya as a metaphor for astronomical conjunction, just the event recorded in this phrase. Grube suggested in his letter that the naguals of the Palenque Triad were in conjunction (or had come together) and that the Palencanos regarded the planets as the naguals (or spirit counterparts) of the Triad Gods. Merging his observation with Aveni's interpretation gives new and important insight into how the Palencanos thought about the events they saw in the sky: The naguals of the three Triad Gods— Jupiter, Saturn, and Mars—were reunited with the nagual of their mother—the moon.

This spectacular hierophany apparently was the trigger event for the house rites that followed over the next three days. However, this day is very near the seventy-fifth tropical year anniversary of Pacal's accession, which took place only five days after this hierophany. Considering Chan-Bahlum's preoccupation with the legitimacy of his claim to the throne, this anniversary must also have played a part in his calculations.

42. There are several possible houses that may be the Mah Kina Bahlum-Kuk Building. The Temple of the Cross is the most likely candidate because it contains the dynastic list that includes Bahlum-Kuk's name as the founder. However, the text behind Chan-Bahlum on the Temple of the Foliated Cross actually has the words *pib nah* and *yotot* following Bahlum-Kuk's name in a passage that may refer to that temple. We suspect, however, that Chan-Bahlum referred to the entire Group of the Cross as the "Mah Kina Bahlum-Kuk Building." The last and most distant possibility is the Temple of Inscriptions. Mathews (1980) identified an Initial Series date over the piers of the Temple of Inscriptions with the 819-day count appropriate to the 2 Cib 14 Mol series of events. He suggested the date intended here was the hierophany, but it was just as likely to have been 3 Caban 15

Mol, with Chan-Bahlum's dedication of his father's funerary building as the event taking place. This last solution seems the least satisfactory of the four because of Chan-Bahlum's deliberate linkage of the 3 Caban 15 Mol dedication event to the mythological dedication of GI'. To us, it is more logical to assume he would have reserved such elaborate explanations for his own buildings.

43. In the Temples of the Foliated Cross and the Sun, a Distance Number of three days stands between 3 Caban 15 Mol and this bloodletting event. However, the 3 Caban 15 Mol event is not recorded at all on the Tablet of the Cross. In that context, the Distance Number must be counted from the date of the astronomical event, 2 Cib 14 Mol. This chronology places the bloodletting on 5 Cauac 17 Mol rather than 6 Ahau 18 Mol.

44. The only surviving pier reliefs are from the Temple of the Sun. The inscription is fragmentary but the date is indisputably 9.12.19.14.12 5 Eb 5 Kayab and the verb is the same. The Initial Series date and its supplementary data were on the south pier, while the verb and actor were on the north pier. The figures on both inner piers are badly damaged, but Pier C has a flexible shield with a Tlaloc image on it. For the Maya, this Tlaloc iconography signals bloodletting and war, so that we can speculate with some certainty that the 5 Eb 5 Kayab event involved the taking and sacrifice of captives. We have lost the piers on the other two temples, but since the balustrades and sanctuary doorjambs in all three temples repeat the same basic information in the same discourse pattern, it is likely that the piers repeated the same information on all three temples.

45. Although astronomy plays an important role in the timing of the events of Chan-Bahlum's history—he ended his accession rites on a maximum elongation of Venus and dedicated the Group of the Cross during a major planetary conjunction—the dedication of the *pib na* was not timed by astronomy. Like Ah Cacaw of Tikal, he went to Tlaloc war on an important anniversary.

While the association is distant, the 5 Eb 5 Kayab dedication of the inner sanctum may also have been associated with a Venus cycle. The final event of his ten-day-long accession ritual occurred during a maximum elongation of Venus as Morningstar. The dedication of the *pib na* took place almost exactly five rounds of Venus later, but the planet was twenty days from its elongation point on that day. Chan-Bahlum may have been observing Venus as well as the tropical year in timing the dedications of the *pib na,* although it is clear that Venus was not the primary factor.

46. Only one jamb panel is preserved from each sanctuary, and of these only the panel from the Temple of the Foliated Cross is complete. Since this panel formed a joint with the outer panel, the border on the outer panel continued onto the edge of the doorjamb. Using this pattern, we can ascertain that the surviving fragments are all from the right sides of the doors. It is possible, therefore, that the left doorjambs recorded the birth of the Triad Gods, but until additional fragments are discovered, we will not know the entire pattern.

47. The clearest demonstration of the relationship of the central icon with the name of the sanctuary occurs in the Temple of the Foliated Cross. There the icon is a maize tree emerging from a monster with a kan-cross in its forehead while the name of the house is a tree sign over a kan-cross. Since this same relationship must hold for the other two temples, we can identify *wacah chan* as the name of the tree on the Tablet of the Cross. The Temple of the Sun is more difficult, but the glyph on the balustrade is a variant of the "new-sky-at-horizon" glyph that occurs as a name at Copán. Here it has *Mah Kina* preceding it, possibly as a reinforcement that the GIII shield in the icon of this temple represents the sun.

48. The term used here is the T606 glyph which has been taken as "child of mother" (Schele, Mathews, and Lounsbury n.d.). David Stuart (n.d) has recently suggested a reading of *u huntan* for this glyph, citing glosses from the Motul dictionary of Yucatec for "to take care of a thing" and "to do something with care and diligence." He suggests that the term refers to the child as the object of the mother's care and nurturing. It is this sense, as "the objects of caretaking," that the gods are related to the king—he cares for them like a mother.

49. In this context, as with the 2 Cib 14 Mol conjunction event, the gods are named as the "cared-ones" of Chan-Bahlum. This same relationship between these gods and Pacal occurs on katun-ending dates in the Temple of Inscriptions. The glyphic terms, T1.I.606:23, *u huntan,* identifies the king as the caretaker of the gods in the sense that a mother cares for her child. Since the Maya believed that the act of bloodletting literally gave birth to the gods (Stuart 1984a), we deduce that the king's role as caretaker and nourisher took place in the context of bloodletting.

The importance of this role as "nurturer of the gods" is illustrated in the Popol Vuh version of the genesis myth. The following passage describes the gods' motivation for trying again to create humanity after the first attempt had failed.

"The time for the planting and dawning is nearing. For this we must make a provider and nurturer. How else can we be invoked and remembered on the face of the earth? We have already made our first try at our work and design, but it turned out that they didn't keep our days, nor did they glorify us.

"So now let's try to make a giver of praise, giver of respect, provider, nurturer." (Tedlock 1986:79).

The way a community provided sustenance to a king was through tribute, and in Quiche the word *tzuqul,* "provider," means "nourish, support, raise, bud, sprout, be born, rear, and support by tribute" (Edmonson 1965:136). The way humanity sustained and nourished the gods was through bloodletting. When the king was in this role as "caretaker of the gods," he became their mother by giving them birth and sustenance. It is this metaphor that Chan-Bahlum used on the doorjambs of the sanctuaries.

50. Chaacal III evoked the accession of Lady Beastie in his own accession records to relate his own mother to the great founding deity of the Palenque dynasty. Kan-Xul, the younger brother of Chan-Bahlum, was captured late in his reign by a ruler of Toniná. This political disaster apparently threw the succession into confusion. Chaacal III, the next king to come to the throne, chose his accession date so that it would fall into a contrived relationship of numerology with the accession of Lady Beastie (Lounsbury 1976:220–221). Even more interesting is the fact that the date of Lady Beastie's accession, as written on the Tablet of the Cross, is in error. Two mistakes have been detected:

(1) The Distance Number that is written was calculated from the 819-day count date, 1 Ahau 18 Zotz', rather than the Initial Series date, 8 Ahau 18 Zec.

(2) To find the Calendar Round reached by the Distance Number, the scribe used 20 calculating years (1.0.4.0 in the Long Count). Each time one calculating year is added to a Calendar Round, the tzolkin day stays the same, the day of the month stays the same, but the month drops back one as follows:

1.12.19. 0. 2 9 Ik 0 Cumku + 1.0.4.0 equals

1.13.19. 4. 2 9 Ik 0 Kayab + 1.0.4.0 equals

1.14.19. 8. 2 9 Ik 0 Pax + 1.0.4.0 equals

1.15.19.12. 2 9 Ik 0 Muan + 1.0.4.0 equals

1.16.19.16. 2 9 Ik 0 Kankin + 1.0.4.0 equals

1.18. 0. 2. 2 9 Ik 0 Mac + 1.0.4.0 equals

1.19. 0. 6. 2 9 Ik 0 Ceh + 1.0.4.0 equals

2. 0. 0.10. 2 9 Ik 0 Zac + 1.0.4.0 equals

2. 1. 0.14. 2 9 Ik 0 Yax

The Distance Number written in the text falls between 12.19.13.3.0 1 Ahau 18 Zotz' (the 819-day count) and the ninth interval above. The Calendar Round written in the text is the eighth interval above, 9 Ik 0 Zac. The scribe stopped one interval short of the correct answer.

The Maya knew they had made a mistake because in the very next notation they counted from interval nine, rather than interval eight. They may have left the erroneous Calendar Round in the text because they believed the gods had caused the error. When Chaacal contrived the numerological relationship between his accession and Lady Beastie's, however, he used the erroneous Calendar Round rather than the correct one. Apparently, history as it was engraved in the stone, erroneous or not, became the gospel according to Chan-Bahlum.

CHAPTER 7: BIRD-JAGUAR AND THE CAHALOB

1. According to Teobert Maler's (1901–1903) descriptions, the temples of Yaxchilán were painted white with a red band below the medial molding.

2. Maudslay named the ruins *Menché Tinamit* after the Maya people he found living nearby. Maler (1901–1903:104) renamed the city using a combination of *yax*, "blue" or

"green," and the word *chilan*, which he thought meant "that which lies or is scattered around," referring to the fallen stones of the ruined buildings. Maler criticized Maudslay's use of what he believed was an ersatz term, and then he proceeded to supply his own. Unfortunately, Maler's coined name has stuck, although Maudslay's name was more likely what the Indians living along the river called the old city.

3. Tatiana Proskouriakoff (1963–1964) published two detailed studies of the life of Shield-Jaguar and Bird-Jaguar. These two studies remain today the finest example of historical studies of the Maya inscriptions.

4. In her study of the history of kingship and the physical orientation of buildings at Yaxchilán, Tate (1986b) identified a group of temples oriented toward the rising sun at summer solstice. Since many of the house dedication dates at Yaxchilán are on or near summer solstices, this orientation is not simply fortuitous.

5. This king's name consists of a sign representing male genitals surmounting a jaguar head. The name was probably Yat-Balam, "Penis of the Jaguar," but his name was published as "Progenitor-Jaguar" in the *National Geographic Magazine* (October 1985).

6. David Stuart (personal communication, 1984) first recognized the accession passage of Progenitor-Jaguar on Hieroglyphic Stair 1. This date is best reconstructed as 8.14.2.17.6 7 Cimi 14 Zotz'. The latest date known at Yaxchilán, 9.18.17.13.14 9 Ix 2 Zec (April 13, 808), occurs on Lintel 10, a monument of the last king in the dynasty, Mah Kina Ta-Skull. Yaxchilán was certainly abandoned within fifty years of this date.

7. The great Mayanist Tatiana Proskouriakoff published two seminal papers on her "historical hypothesis" demonstrating her belief that the contents of the Maya inscriptions were primarily historical. The first study (Proskouriakoff 1960) focused on the dynastic sequence of Piedras Negras to prove her thesis, but she did not give personal names to the Maya rulers she identified. However, in a paper published for a more general audience less than a year later, Proskouriakoff (1961a) described her methodology and gave names to these two great kings of Yaxchilán, as well as other personalities of Maya history.

The six years between 1958 and 1964 were an extraordinary time in Maya studies. Proskouriakoff's work followed a study by Heinrich Berlin (1959) that had anticipated her results. Berlin had already identified the names of historical people on the sarcophagus in the Temple of Inscriptions at Palenque. David Kelley (1962) contributed his own study of the history of Quiriguá less than a year later. With these seminal studies, we began to speak truly of Maya history as they themselves wrote it and meant it to be understood.

8. The history we present here is based on several sources, including Proskouriakoff's (1963–1964) papers, Carolyn Tate's (1986a) study of Yaxchilán architecture and statecraft, Mathews's (1975) work on early Yaxchilán history, and long-term conversations and debate with Peter Mathews, David Stuart, Sandy Bardslay, and many of Schele's students, especially Ruth Krochock and Constance Cortes. After this chapter was finished, we received a copy of Peter Mathews's (1988) dissertation on Yaxchilán and have added information from that source as it is relevant.

9. Shield-Jaguar's birth is not recorded on any of the surviving Yaxchilán monuments, but Proskouriakoff (1963–1964) was able to reconstruct it from other glyphic information as having occurred within five years of 9.10.15.0.0.

10. The third and the eighth successors were also named Bird-Jaguar, which was probably Xtz'unun-Balam in Mayan. The father of Shield-Jaguar was the third Bird-Jaguar, and his grandson, the great Bird-Jaguar, was the fourth. We shall call the grandfather 6-Tun-Bird-Jaguar because his name phrase invariably contains a 6-Tun glyph that is not included in his grandson's name.

11. Recorded on the Hieroglyphic Stairs of House C of the Palace at Palenque, the event (an "ax" war and a "capture") took place on 9.11.1.16.3 6 Akbal 1 Yax (August 28, 654). The Yaxchilán lord who participated in these events was Balam-Te-Chac, who is named a *yihtah* ("sibling") of Shield-Jaguar, the ahau of Yaxchilán. This brother does not appear in Yaxchilán's inscriptions, but at Palenque the context is clearly war and capture. Note that Shield-Jaguar had very likely already been designated heir to Yaxchilán's throne. Why else would Pacal demonstrate the importance of the Yaxchilán visitor by naming him the sibling of an eleven-year-old who was not yet a king?

12. The term used for the relationship, *ihtan*, is "sibling" in modern Chorti, but in the set of kinship terms used by many Maya people, "siblings" include the children of a father's brothers as well as one's own brothers and sisters. The Yaxchilán cohort may, therefore, have been the child of one of 6-Tun-Bird-Jaguar's brothers, rather than his son.

13. On Lintel 45, Ah-Ahaual is named "the ahau of (*yahau*)," the king of a domain named with a serpent segment with a phonetic *ni* attached. On Stela 19, this same location

is spelled with the phonetic complements *ma* and *na.* Since this same serpent-segment glyph appears in the *xaman,* "north," glyph with the value *ma* or *man,* we suggest the place was known as *Man.* This Emblem Glyph appears in several other contexts, including the name of Ruler B's mother at Tikal (see Stela 5). No one has yet associated this Emblem Glyph with a particular archaeological ruin; but in light of Shield-Jaguar's focus on this capture, the domain was important and prestigious in the Maya world.

14. This is a unique event in Maya history as we now understand it. Women were recorded in the historical inscriptions because of their roles either as wives or mothers of important Maya lords. Although two women ruled in their own right at Palenque, Temple 23 is the only major Maya monument known to have been dedicated by a woman for the express purposes of celebrating personal history. The rarity of this circumstance points to the extraordinary and pivotal importance of this woman in Yaxchilán's history.

15. At Yaxchilán, kings used two forums to display their political messages—the slab-shaped tree-stones erected in front of buildings and the lintel stones that spanned door openings into the interiors of temples. In the local tradition, tree-stones displayed two complementary scenes (Tate 1986a): A period-ending bloodletting rite was depicted on the temple side and a capture on the river side of the monument. The lintels, on the other hand, displayed only one scene; but since a building usually had several sculpted lintels, the various scenes and texts could be orchestrated into larger programs of information. The scribes favored two kinds of compositional strategies in these larger programs. They could place a series of different actions and actors in direct association within a single building or they could divide a ritual or text into parts, which were then distributed *across* the lintels of a building. By using these multiple scenes in various combinations, the king was able to construct compelling arguments for his political actions. He could interpret history by showing how individual actions were linked into the larger framework of history and cosmic necessity. Retrospectively constructed, these linkages between different rituals and events became the central voice of Yaxchilán's political rhetoric.

16. Proskouriakoff (1963–1964) reconstructed this date as 9.14.8.12.5, but Mathews (personal communication, 1979) has noted that this event recurs on Lintel 23 where the date clearly reads 9.14.14.13.17, a placement supported by the presence of G7 as the Lord of the Night on Lintel 26. We accept the later placement as the correct reconstruction.

17. There are three sequential narrative lines in these lintels: (1) the texts on the outer sides record three separate rituals in the dedication sequence of the temple (the side of Lintel 24 was destroyed when it was lightened for transport to England [Graham 1975–1986, vol. 3:54]); (2) the texts on the undersides picture the sequence of historical events; (3) they also picture the three stages of the bloodletting rite which took place on each of those historical occasions. Thus, the sculptors let us understand the action sequence of the bloodletting rite and simultaneously that this ritual took place at three different points in time. See Schele and M. Miller (1986) for more complete descriptions of the iconography and rites depicted on these lintels.

18. A second glyph, which looks like crossed torches, can be seen in the background next to the serpent's head. This is the glyph that occurs at Copán as a substitute for the lineage founder's name in "numbered succession" titles. The presence of this glyph in the name phrase referring to the figure emerging from the serpent's jaw identifies him as the founder Yat-Balam.

19. There is the possibility, of course, that other depictions once existed and are now destroyed. However, accession was not a favored subject for sculptural representation at Yaxchilán, although it was frequently recorded in glyphic texts. The only other picture of an accession known is Bird-Jaguar's on Lintel 1.

20. The bloodletting on Lintel 24 took place exactly twenty-eight years (28 x 365.25) plus four days after Shield-Jaguar's accession.

21. The only other women to hold such prominent places are Lady Zac-Kuk of Palenque and Lady 6-Sky of Dos Pilas who appears on the stela of Naranjo. The first woman was a ruler in her own right, while the second reestablished the lineage of Naranjo after a disastrous defeat at the hands of Caracol.

22. Mathews (1988:171) suggests that Lady Xoc, whom he calls Lady Fist-Fish, was probably buried in Structure 23 in Tomb 2. He describes nine carved bones found in the tomb and notes that six of them carry her name.

23. The inscription records the dedication of an object written as *pa.si.l(i).* In Chorti (Wisdom n.d.), *pasi* is glossed as "open, open up, break open, make an opening." The *pasil* is apparently the east doorway itself, which was perhaps opened up into the building to become the resting place of this lintel.

24. Tom Jones and Carolyn Jones discovered the important secrets hidden in this Lintel 23 text and presented them at the 1989 Maya Hieroglyphic Workshop at the University of Texas.

25. The main sign of the Calakmul Emblem Glyph (also known as Site Q) is a snake head. On Stela 10, exactly this main sign occurs with the female head and the word *ah po*. This is the form of the Emblem Glyph title used especially to designate women. The reader should also note that the identification of the snake Emblem Glyph is still questioned by several epigraphers. This particular version is the one Mathews identified with Site Q. It is also the Emblem Glyph of the kingdom allied to Caracol and Dos Pilas in the star wars history detailed in Chapter 5. It is interesting that the "batab" title in Lady Eveningstar's name uses the directional association "east." Berlin (1958) first suggested this title should be read "batab," a documented title in Yucatec sources meaning "ax-wielder." Although we now know the title refers to the god Chac rather than to the Yucatec title, epigraphers still use "batab" as the nickname of the title. Normal Yaxchilán versions of this title all have the "west" direction connected with their names. The change in directional association may reflect her status as a foreigner from the east.

26. Bird-Jaguar was thirteen years old when the sculpture was dedicated and about seventeen at the time of the house dedication rituals.

27. Other dates and events in Temple 23 texts include the dedication of the temple sculptures on August 5, 723; the dedication of Lintel 26 on February 12, 724; the twenty-fifth anniversary of Shield-Jaguar's accession on March 2, 726; and finally, the dedication of the temple itself on June 26, 726. (Note that this last date is very near a summer solstice [Tate:1986b].) The inscriptions describing these events also specify that they took place next to the river, probably in or very near the location of Temple 23. Stuart and Houston (n.d.) have identified glyphs naming specific topographic features within a polity. These topographic features can include *witz*, "mountain," and *nab*, "water, lake, or river," and they are often accompanied by a locative glyph called the "impinged bone." Lady Xoc's names on Lintels 24 and 25 end with a combination including T606 (perhaps another locative), the glyph for "body of water," *nab,* and the main sign of Yaxchilán's Emblem Glyph, a "split-sky." These glyphs should refer either to the river itself or just as likely to the flat shelf next to the river on which Temple 23 was built.

28. This marriage may have simply renewed an old alliance. The Early Classic lintels from Yaxchilán discussed in Chapter 5 record that an ambassador from the Calakmul king visited the tenth successor of Yaxchilán soon after he acceded to the throne. We suspect Yaxchilán was in alliance with Cu-Ix, the Calakmul king who installed the first ruler at Naranjo. He was surely allied to Caracol in the Tikal wars. The alliance of the Calakmul king with the Yaxchilán dynasty may have secured at least their agreement not to interfere, if not their active participation.

29. Her name consists of a skull with an infixed *ik* sign that Lounsbury (personal communication, 1980) has identified as Venus in its aspect of Eveningstar. This component of her name precedes a sky glyph and usually a series of titles.

30. The inverted-L shape, next to the ankles of the shorter figure on the left, faces that figure and most likely identifies it as Shield-Jaguar. The composition presses this figure against the frame, giving it less space as well as a smaller size. The monument was commissioned by Bird-Jaguar, who apparently used the scale difference and compositional device to subordinate his father, even though at the time of the event shown, Shield-Jaguar was the high king.

31. The figures shown in the ancestral cartouches above the sky register may be the parents of either actor, but the protagonist of Stela 11 is clearly Bird-Jaguar. His parents (Shield-Jaguar and Lady Eveningstar) are named glyphically as the ancestral figures on the other side of the monument. We suspect the ancestors on this side represent Bird-Jaguar's parents as well.

32. David Stuart (n.d.) has recently identified Great-Skull-Zero as the *ichan* of Bird-Jaguar's son. This relationship term stands for mother's brother in Chol, making him Lady Great-Skull-Zero's brother and Bird-Jaguar's brother-in-law. In fact, the relationships of Great-Skull-Zero and Lady Great-Skull-Zero to Bird-Jaguar's son and future heir (who was not yet born at the time of this bloodletting) are featured in the two actors' names. Here her name ends with the phrase "mother of the ahau." Lord Great-Skull-Zero's ends with *yichan ahau,* "the mother's brother of the ahau." In his name, the *chan* part of the *yichan* glyph is written with the head variant of the "sky" glyph.

33. Since both the woman and man hold Personified Perforators in their hands, they both apparently let blood in this rite.

34. The scenes on Lintels 15, 16, and 17 deliberately reproduce the same actions shown on Lintels 24, 25, and 26, which are: Lady Xoc materializing the dynasty founder at Shield-Jaguar's accession; Lady Xoc and Shield-Jaguar letting blood to celebrate the birth of his heir; and their preparation for a battle on the occasion of the dedication of the building. Bird-Jaguar's lintels show him and a wife letting blood to celebrate the birth of an heir; his capture of a noble shortly before his accession; and the vision quest of another of his wives, probably as part of the dedication rites of the building. He carefully echoes the compositions of the Structure 23 lintels, but substitutes ritual events important to his own political succession.

35. A detail of this stela was published in the *National Geographic Magazine,* October 1985:521.

36. Bird-Jaguar became a three-katun lord on 9.15.17.12.10, meaning that this stela could not have been carved until after that date. If it was originally erected in the temple where it was found, it had to have been carved after 9.16.3.16.19. It is a retrospective stela depicting this bloodletting event as a part of Bird-Jaguar's strategy of legitimization.

37. The other two lintels in this building date to April 2, 758, and June 29, 763. They depict Lady 6-Tun of Motul de San José and Lady Balam-Ix engaged in the "fish-in-hand" bloodletting rite on those dates. The Bird-Jaguar depiction is then a retrospective one, carved sometime after 763, to link the bloodletting rites of his wives to the earlier 9.15.10.0.1 ritual so important to his demonstration of legitimacy.

38. Besides the three lintels depicting this ritual at Yaxchilán, similar rituals occur in detailed depictions in the murals of Bonampak and in several pottery scenes.

39. This day was nine days after the summer solstice so that the sun rose within 1° of the solstice point. Venus was at 71.06° and frozen at the stationary point after its first appearance as Morningstar. The sun rose through Gemini, and Venus was poised near the Pleiades and the bright star we call Aldebaran. We do not know what the Maya called this star.

40. Temple 23, Lady Xoc's house, is named on Lintel 23 with an sun-eyed dog head. On Lintel 21, Temple 22 is named the *Chan-Ah-Tz'i,* both in its earlier version and in the later rebuilding dedicated by Bird-Jaguar. This ritual could have taken place anywhere in the city, but we are reconstructing it here because all of the representations of the 9.15.10.0.1 bloodletting are distributed around Lady Xoc's building. This spatial point was critical to Bird-Jaguar's quest for the throne.

41. Tom Jones (1985) provided convincing evidence that the Usumacinta was called Xocol Ha at the time of the conquest.

42. Given that Lady Xoc was around twenty years old when Shield-Jaguar acceded, she would have been between forty-five and fifty years old when Bird-Jaguar was born and very likely beyond her childbearing years. Any of her own children who were still alive would very likely have been adults or adolescents at that time.

43. At the time of this event, Shield-Jaguar was ninety-four years old ($+$ two years). Lady Xoc's birth date is not known, but sixty-seven years passed between Shield-Jaguar's accession (in which she had participated as an adult) and her death date on 9.15.17.15.14. Presuming she was at least eighteen when Shield-Jaguar acceded, she died around age eighty-five. At the time of this 9.15.10.0.1 bloodletting, she would have been in her late seventies. If she had given birth to Shield-Jaguar's child around the time of his accession, that child would have been in his late sixties by the time of our event; grandchildren would have been in their forties; great-grandchildren in their twenties; and great-great-grandchildren in their early childhood. Since most Maya did not live beyond their forties (although the elite appear to have had considerably longer lives and better food resources than the common folk), we suspect that the problem in Yaxchilán's succession may have been that the extremely long-lived Shield-Jaguar had outlived the sons he'd had by his principal wife and perhaps many of his grandsons from that marriage as well. If this was the situation, the rivalry here would have been between grandsons or perhaps great-grandsons of Lady Xoc and Shield-Jaguar on one side and the son of Shield-Jaguar and Lady Eveningstar on the other. Both claims would be equally legitimate and interpretable as a direct descent from a king, although the claim of a son would have been the stronger, especially if Shield-Jaguar publicly favored that offspring.

44. The costume was worn by nobles who aided the king in scattering rites at Yaxchilán, by nobles who witnessed an heir-designation at Bonampak, and by emissaries who delivered gifts to kings. This last scene is depicted on a painted pot in the burial of Ruler A at Tikal.

45. We cannot know the exact sequence of the events which took place during these rites. We have arranged the individuals sequentially as a narrative device, but it is also possible that all the principals drew blood at the same time. The other sequences—the dancers, the placement of the high king inside a building, the musicians, and so forth—are based on the lower register of Room 1 and Room 3 at Bonampak, and on Piedras Negras Lintel 3.

46. Representations of people undergoing bloodletting rarely show pain, and eyewitness accounts of the ritual specifically mention that the participants do not react in pain. (See Tozzer 1941:114, note 552.)

47. Exactly this sequence of events, including the change of headdresses, is shown on Stela 35.

48. David Stuart (personal communication, 1988) first identified a set of glyphs on Lintel 14 (E3-D4) and on Stela 10 and 13 at Copán as the name of the Vision Serpent in the manifestation shown on the Yaxchilán lintel.

49. Stela 2 of Bonampak shows the king's mother and his wife helping him in a sacrificial rite exactly as we have imagined in the Yaxchilán event.

50. We have reconstructed this scene from a stucco sculpture which was modeled on the rear of Temple 21 immediately behind Stela 35, which showed Lady Eveningstar in this very bloodletting rite. In the stucco relief, a large male sits in the center with another male and a female on his right and two females on his left. We propose these are the principals of the bloodletting ritual—Shield-Jaguar with Bird-Jaguar and Lady Great-Skull-Zero on his right and with Lady Xoc and Lady Eveningstar on his left.

51. M. Miller and Houston (1987) first recognized that these scenes occur not in ballcourts, but against hieroglyphic stairs.

52. On the day of the ballgame, October 21, A.D. 744, Venus was 46.218° from the sun and only five days away from its maximum elongation as Morningstar. As we have seen repeatedly, this kind of Venus date often provided the stimulus for ritual events, especially those involving war and sacrificial rites. See Lounsbury (1982).

53. A total of thirteen panels make up this sculpted stoop, which is located immediately in front of the three doors of Temple 33. The center panel, depicting Bird-Jaguar at play, is the widest and is designed to be the pivot of the entire program. Steps I, II, and III show three women, one of which is Lady Pacal (Shield-Jaguar's mother), holding Vision Serpents in their arms in rituals that perhaps began different ballgames. The fact that Bird-Jaguar's grandmother is depicted suggests that these three women represent different generations, but the inscriptions are too badly effaced to identify the other two.

The remaining ten steps portray males in the midst of the ballgame. The ball is frozen in flight, either to or from the hieroglyphic stairs. Again the badly eroded texts of some panels preclude identification of the actors pictured, but we can identify Shield-Jaguar on Step VI, Bird-Jaguar the Great on Step VII, his grandfather, 6-Tun-Bird-Jaguar III, on Step VIII, and the cahal Kan-Toc on Step X. Presumably these steps represent different ballgames, since different generations are shown engaged in play. We may also assume that Bird-Jaguar used this step to bring together all the people, king and cahal, kinsmen and allies, who were important to his status as high king.

54. The verb is the so-called "scattering" glyph without the drops. David Stuart (personal communication, 1989) has recently suggested a reading of *ye* for this hand. In proto-Cholan (Kaufman and Norman 1984:137), *ye'* is given as "take in the hand." *Lomil,* the glyph that follows, is the word for lances or other tall staffs. The actions may be another holding of the tall flapstaff. The first glyph of the highly eroded name phrase following the verbal phrases is "5 katun ahau," a title exclusively used at Yaxchilán in Shield-Jaguar's name phrase. We surmise, then, that the actor was the then-deceased Shield-Jaguar.

55. It is possible of course that Bird-Jaguar fabricated this information after the fact and that in reality he had no authority to conduct any ritual at the time of this period ending. This history was, after all, recorded *after* his accession and is thus a retrospective creation. We suspect, however, that the record is a true one. When he erected this stela sometime after his accession, that particular period ending would still have been fresh in everyone's mind. If he was required to recruit and retain alliances with cahal lineages in order to hold his throne, documenting a brazen lie would certainly, it seems to us, be a counterproductive strategy.

For this reason we assume that, by that time, he had gained enough support to participate in, if not lead, the ritual. Therefore, in his reconstruction of the story, he could declare that this rite took place in what had become his kingdom on the later date.

56. Stela 11 was erected in front of Structure 40, a temple built next to an important Shield-Jaguar temple. Before that temple stood five stelae, four recording Shield-Jaguar's greatest captures (Stelae 15, 18, 19, and 20) and the fifth recording the first flapstaff event. The proximity of the Stela 11 to Shield-Jaguar's monument, and the prominent place of Bird-Jaguar's accession in its texts (this information is recorded in the bottom register and on the edges of the stela), identify the flapstaff event and the captive presentations as events critical to Bird-Jaguar's campaign demonstrating his right to the throne.

57. On Lintel 16, Bird-Jaguar designates this captive as the cahal of a king who ruled a site named by an unknown Emblem Glyph with a snakelike head as its main sign.

58. Ix Witz (Jaguar Mountain) is another unknown kingdom. David Stuart (1987b:21) first identified its Emblem Glyph.

59. GII is also known as the Manikin Scepter or by the name Kauil.

60. These bundles were critical to the ritual lives of the Maya. In ethnohistorical sources, they hold the sources of the lineage power, and are often described as having been left by the semi-divine ancestors who founded those lineages. The bundles are recorded as holding idols, jades, eccentric flints, and similar objects. Eccentric flints and eccentric obsidians were worked into irregular, nonutilitarian shapes that often included human or deity profiles. During the Classic Period, it's fairly certain they were used to store idols such as the Manikin Scepter and the Jester Gods. A bundle has been found archaeologically in the Lost World group at Tikal (Marisela Ayala, personal communication, 1986 and n.d.). Made of ficus-bark paper tied closed with a woven-fiber band, the bundle was inside a lip-to-lip cache made of an angle-sided plate with an identical plate inverted and set over it as the lid. The bundle inside held the remains of marine creatures and the thorns used in bloodletting. Other similar caches regularly contain bloodletting instruments such as thorns, stingray spines, obsidian, and flint blades. Archaeologists found human blood on one such flint blade discovered in a cache at Colha, Belize (Dan Potter, personal communication, 1987). Merle Robertson (1972) first proposed the association of these bundles with the bloodletting rite, a suggestion that has since been confirmed archaeologically. This lintel at least partially confirms her hypothesis, for the verb written in the text over the woman's head states that she will soon let blood.

61. The text records that she will let blood by naming *Chanal Hun Winik Chan*, the particular Vision Serpent she will manifest.

62. The text on this lintel is very badly eroded, but based on a detailed examination of the original stone, Tate (1986a:336) has proposed readings of 9.16.6.11.0 3 Ahau 3 Muan or 9.17.6.15.0 3 Ahau 3 Kankin. We think this structure was built by Bird-Jaguar. The lintel, therefore, should be dated to the earlier of these two possibilities.

63. Tate (1986a:307) argues that the careless sculptural style and the lack of a date resembles the very late style used by the last documented ruler of Yaxchilán. However, since the building is part of Bird-Jaguar's program to legitimize himself, we suggest that the scene depicts the first Shield-Jaguar flapstaff event that is also shown on Stela 50.

64. This woman has the Ik Emblem Glyph in her name, like the woman on Lintels 15 and 39. Here, however, two different people seem to be named: on Lintels 15 and 29 the woman has the title Lady 6-Tun preceding the Emblem Glyph, whereas on Lintels 41 and 5 the woman has Lady 6-Sky-Ahau as her name. If these are separate women, then Bird-Jaguar is associated with four women—Lady Great-Skull-Zero (the mother of his child), Lady Balam of Ix Witz, and these two ladies from Motul de San José.

65. The Lintel 42 name phrase of this cahal has the "captor of Co-Te-Ahau" title that appears consistently in this fellow's name phrase.

66. Tate (1985) has argued this woman is the same Lady Balam of Ix Witz. However, since that lady had already appeared on Lintel 43 two days earlier, we think it more likely that Bird-Jaguar wished to associate yet another of his wives with this bloodletting sequence. We suspect she is the second wife from Motul de San José.

67. On lintels carved after the date of this capture, both men, whenever they named themselves, included the names of the captives in their titles. They did this regardless of whether or not the narrative action was set before or after the capture itself.

The scene we are discussing here may not be the actual capture, for the captives are already stripped and wearing the cut cloth that signifies sacrifice. This event probably occurred after the capture when the victims are displayed and torture begins. See the fourth wall of Bonampak Room 2 for a graphic description of this phase of the ritual (M. Miller 1986b:113–130, Pl. 2).

68. The two protagonists are about the same height, but more important, the two scenes occupy an equal amount of compositional space. Bird-Jaguar is contrasted to Kan-

Toc by the more elaborate detail of his costume and by the larger size of the text referring to his actions. Kan-Toc's inscription is the smaller secondary text between the figures.

69. Lintel 54 was over the center door, while Lintel 58 was on the left and 57 on the right.

70. David Stuart (n.d.) first read the glyph for this relationship and recognized that it clarified the role Great-Skull-Zero played in Bird-Jaguar's history.

71. Notice that Chel-Te is represented on both lintels as approximately the same size as his father, in spite of the fact that he was five on 9.16.5.0.0 and fourteen on 9.16.15.0.0. His smaller scale is apparently designed to represent him as simply "child."

72. This is the temple housing the western set of duplicating lintels, which include Bird-Jaguar and his cahal Kan-Toc at the capture of Jeweled-Skull; a bird-scepter ritual with Lady 6-Sky-Ahau; a basket-staff event with Kan-Toc; and a bundle/Manikin Scepter event with another wife. Temple 1 exalts the cahal Kan-Toc, very probably to seal his alliance to Bird-Jaguar during his life and to his son after Bird-Jaguar's death.

73. The name of this person is a jaguar head holding a cauac sign in a paw raised beside its head. This position is one of the variants of the penis glyph in the founder's name. This visitor appears to be named Yat-Balam, but obviously he cannot be the founder of Yaxchilán's dynasty, who was long dead. Either he is a namesake, or the Piedras Negras lord is flattering the Yaxchilán lord by using the founder's name for him.

74. Proskouriakoff (1961a) first identified these figures as youths and suggested that this is an heir-designation rite.

CHAPTER 8: COPÁN: THE DEATH OF FIRST DAWN ON MACAW MOUNTAIN

1. The name of the last great king of that community, Yax-Pac, means "First Sun-at-Horizon" or "First Dawn." *Mo'-Witz,* or "Macaw Mountain," was a sacred place in or near the community alluded to by several Late Classic kings there. The death of Yax-Pac was indeed the death of first dawn in the valley, for the contentious rivalry between the kings and their nobility was a key factor in the demise of the kingdom.

2. Many of the ideas presented in this chapter are the result of collaboration among Dr. William Fash, Barbara Fash, Rudy Larios, David Stuart, Linda Schele, and many other people who have worked on the Copán Mosaics Project and the Copán Acropolis Project. William Fash (1983a; Fash and Schele [1986]; Fash and Stuart [n.d.]) first suggested that nonroyal lineages competing with the royal house of Copán contributed to the collapse of central power in the valley.

3. Data on the history of the Copán Valley is drawn from William Fash's (1983a) study of the process of state formation in the valley. Found in the deepest levels under Group 9N-8 (Fash 1985), the earliest deposit at Copán consisted of ceramics; obsidian; bones of deer, turtle, rabbit, and peccary; burned earth; and carbon. Fash interpreted this as a seasonal camp. Viel, the ceramist for the Proyeto Arqueología de Copán, associates this early ceramic phase, Rayo, with the Cuadros phase of the Soconusco Coast and the Tok phase at Chalchuapa (Fash 1983a:155). The pottery included brushed tecomates and flat-bottomed, flaring-walled bowls decorated with shell stamping, red slip, and hematite paint.

4. William Fash (1985 and n.d.a) describes this cemetery in detail and associates its ceramics directly with the Middle Preclassic ceramics discovered by Gordon (1898) in the caves of the Sesemil region of the valley, which Fash interprets as part of a very early burial complex. He (1983a:157–158) cites Middle Preclassic occupations in Group 9N-8, the Bosque, and in the Main Group, while cautioning that the full settlement pattern cannot be reconstructed from the present data. Of the rich burials containing jade, those referred to as Burials VIII-27 and IV-35, he comments that only Burial V at La Venta (Veracruz, México) rivals the Copán tombs in quantity and quality of jade. He takes the jade and the pottery incised with Olmec imagery to "indicate intimate familiarity with heartland Olmec ritual practices."

5. See Schele and M. Miller (1986: 70, 80, 104, 119, Pl. 17, 28–30) for a discussion of some of the jade and ceramics from this early period.

6. William Fash (1983a:176) sees this growing density in settlement on the best agricultural lands as the result of social and political motivations which gradually usurped subsistence needs. As the dynasty established itself at the Acropolis, Copanecs found it advantageous to place their residential groups as near the king as possible, and thus gave over their best agricultural lands to the burgeoning population. Fash speculated that events

taking place in the city were important enough to lure people into settling areas previously occupied by permanent agricultural settlements. In one of the zones of occupation, El Cerro de las Mesas, people deliberately chose inconvenient locations for settlement, perhaps for purposes of defense or for some as yet undetected religious or political reasons.

7. The noncalendric text on Stela 17 does not survive, but phrases in the 8.6.0.0.0 texts on Stela I (Smoking-Imix-God K) are repeated in the record of the same event on Stela 4 (18-Rabbit) (Stuart 1986b). The second event on Stela I is unfortunately destroyed, but the last glyph in the text records the main sign of the Copán Emblem Glyph with the "impinged bone" sign that identifies its function here as a location—the kingdom of Copán as a physical entity with a geographical location. This is equivalent to the locational forms of the Tikal Emblem Glyph we encountered on Tikal Stela 39 in Chapter 5. This reference appears to be to the founding of the kingdom itself (Schele 1987b).

Altar I' also has an early date (Morley 1920:192) of 7.1.13.15.0 or October 9, 321 B.C., a date remarkably close to the beginning of Copán's Late Preclassic decline. Unfortunately, the Copanecs did not record the event occurring on that date.

8. Excavations in the 1988 and 1989 seasons of the Copán Acropolis Project under the direction of Dr. William Fash have uncovered buildings and inscribed monuments contemporary to Yax-Kuk-Mo's reign.

9. Sylvanus Morley in his *Inscriptions of Copán* (1920) worked out much of the chronology of Copán's inscriptions. Later scholars, including David Kelley (1962; 1976:238–240), Joyce Marcus (1976), Gary Pahl (1976), Berthold Riese (n.d.; 1988; Riese and Baudez 1983), and David Stuart, Nikolai Grube, Linda Schele, and others in the *Copán Notes* have revised Morley's chronology and identified a series of Copanec rulers. Peter Mathews (n.d.) first noted "numbered succession" titles at Yaxchilán and Copán, which Riese (1984) subsequently demonstrated had a wide distribution in the Maya inscriptions. The identification of Yax-Kuk-Mo' as the founder began when David Stuart managed to identify his dates as belonging to the fifth century. Stuart communicated his finding to William Fash in a letter dated November 1985. Collaborative work between Stuart and Schele (1986a and Schele 1986b) led to Yax-Kuk-Mo's identification as the dynastic founder. Later Copán kings reckoned the establishment of their dynasty from the reign of Yax-Kuk-Mo' and gave themselves titles which reflected their numerical position in the line following him: for example, Smoke-Imix-God K called himself "the twelfth successor of Yax-Kuk-Mo'." However, we also note that Yax-Kuk-Mo' was not the true founder of the kingdom, nor its first ruler. Stuart (personal communication, 1985) identified the notation of an even earlier king as a "first successor" on Stela 24.

10. See Carlson (1977) for a history of the astronomical conference interpretation of Altar Q and an evaluation of the evidence. David Stuart (personal communication, 1984) first suggested that the dates on Altar Q are early, rather than contemporary with the altar itself. Joyce Marcus (1976:140–145) first suggested that the Altar Q figures are portraits of rulers, while Riese (n.d.) identified the entire composition as Copán's sixteen rulers seated in the numerical order of their succession.

11. The first event is a "God K-in-hand" event. This verb is associated with the display of scepters and is specified by a noun incorporated into the hand holding the scepter or appended to the rear of that hand. The second event is spelled *ta.li,* a verb which in Chol and Chorti (the language of the Copán region) means "to come" or "to arrive." In both phrases, the glyph that follows the verb appears in later texts as a replacement for the name of Yax-Kuk-Mo' in numbered successor titles. It appears to refer to the idea of "founder," or perhaps "lineage," in some way we do not yet understand.

12. William Fash (personal communication, 1989) has found this monument, broken into three parts and deposited in a building under Temple 10L-26, the building of the famous Hieroglyphic Stairs of Copán. The date on this monument is exactly the same as that on Stela J, 9.0.0.0.0. The front of the te-tun records the date and the king who reigned when this great period ending turned. David Stuart (in Stuart et al. 1989) found the fragmentary remnant of Yax-Kuk-Mo's name on the last glyph block in this passage, thus confirming that he was reigning. The protagonist and owner of the te-tun, however, was his son, the second ruler in the Altar Q list. We have confirmation, therefore, from a monument carved during or soon after his lifetime that Yax-Kuk-Mo' was indeed a real historical person. Furthermore, this monument was treated with special reverence, carefully cached inside the temple before it was buried in preparation for the next stage of construction. When a later descendant evoked ancestral greatness by constructing the Hieroglyphic Stairs, he chose to put it in this location very probably because he knew a temple of the founder of his line lay deep under Temple 10L-26.

13. In the interim nomenclature used by the Copán Acropolis Project, buildings are designated by bird names, substructures by colors, and floors by names of archaeologists and other persons. This early temple has been dubbed Papagayo ("Macaw") until the history and various levels of the main structure, 10L-26, are fully known and numbered.

14. Strömsvik (1952:198) published a drawing of a mask he found on a terrace under Structure 10L-26 (The Temple of the Hieroglyphic Stairs). He considered the terrace to be contemporary with the first Ballcourt. Investigations in the Copán Archaeological Project have refined the chronology dating the first phase of the Ballcourt and the earliest floors of 10L-26 to the last half of the Bajic phase (A.D. 300–400) (Cheek 1983:203). During the *Copán Mosaics Project* (1985–present), Dr. William Fash has continued Strömsvik's work and found even earlier platforms and structures, some of which are decorated with massive stucco sculptures. They have also found predynastic levels, but the relationship of those levels to Papagayo Temple and other early levels of the Acropolis are still under investigation. Since Stela 63 was set in the floor when Papagayo was constructed, that temple can be dated to between 9.0.0.0.0 and 9.0.5.0.0 (435–440). It was constructed after Ballcourt I was in place, but throughout the subsequent history of the kingdom, the temple in this location (in whatever manifestation) was always associated with one or another of the various stages of the Ballcourt.

15. In the summer of 1989, Schele talked with Rudy Larios, Richard Williamson, and William Fash about the architectural history of this early temple. Although analysis of the archaeological data has just begun, all three archaeologists agree that Stela 63 was set in the back chamber of this building when it was built. This dates the construction to the reign of Yax-Kuk-Mo's son, who was presumably the second successor. At a later time, the fourth successor, Cu-Ix, then placed his step in front of the temple to associate himself with the founder. Larios also has clear evidence that the construction of Papagayo is atop another large platform, which may date to the reign of Yax-Kuk-Mo'. Furthermore, that platform is atop yet another huge platform that must be from predynastic times. The excavations have not yet reached bedrock so that we anticipate finding even earlier structures during the next few field seasons.

16. Papagayo Temple was uncovered during the 1988 field season of the Copán Mosaics Project under the direction of Dr. William Fash. The step sits in front of Stela 63, which had been erected in the rear chamber by the second ruler when the temple was built. The step has a now-damaged inscription consisting of thirty glyphs on top of the step and a single row on the front edge. The name of the fourth successor occurs on this edge and also on Stela 34, a fragment of which was found lying on the plaza just west of Stela J (Grube and Schele 1988). The stela fragment had been recut and used (perhaps as a cache) in some as yet unidentified construction. We now know that Papagayo was open at least through the reign of the fourth successor and perhaps later.

17. The dates and names in this historical reconstruction are drawn from analyses by David Stuart (1984 letter to Fash and 1987) and in the *Copán Notes,* a series of short research reports produced during the Copán Mosaics Project. Copies are on file in the Archives of the Instituto Nacional de Antropología e Historia in Tegucigalpa and Copán, Honduras, and at the University of Texas at Austin. Notes of particular interest to the dynastic history are Notes 6, 8, 14–17 from the 1986 season, and Notes 20–22 and 25–26 from the 1987 season, and Notes 59–67 from the 1989 season.

18. The ritual demarcation of space to facilitate the entry of powerful people into the Otherworld spans Maya history from the Late Preclassic construction of the four-posted temple summits, such as Structure 5C-2nd at Cerros, to the historical treatise of the early Colonial period called the "ritual of the bacabs" (Freidel and Schele 1988; Roys 1965). Present-day Maya shamans continue this practice in their construction of "corrals" (Vogt 1976) and altars. The posts of the sacred spaces given in the prayers of the "ritual of the bacabs" are called *acantun,* "upright or set-up stones"; and *acante',* "upright or set-up trees." Stelae at Copán are specifically called te-tun or "tree-stone." Smoke-Imix-God K departed from normal practice by using stelae to demarcate the entire core area of his kingdom, while under most circumstances Maya kings used stelae as the permanent markings of the central position held by themselves within the sacred space during their entry into the Otherworld.

19. William Fash (1983a:217–232) suggested that these outlying stelae were erected to mark the establishment of a state under Smoke-Imix-God K around A.D. 652. Much of the epigraphic evidence he cites in that study has since been replaced or reinterpreted. For example, the Early Classic history of Copán is far more detailed and regular than it appeared to be in 1983. While we now question if Smoke-Imix-God K changed the system

at Copán as much as it once appeared that he had, he was still responsible for placing inscribed monuments throughout the valley. Smoke-Imix-God K also erected a stela at Santa Rita (Stela 23) and, at about this same time, the lords of Río Amarillo (Schele 1987d) inscribed altars acknowledging the rule of Copán's high king. While Smoke-Imix-God K may have inherited a polity that already qualified as a state, he extended its domain farther than it had ever been before.

20. David Stuart (1987a) first identified the name on Quiriguá Altar L as Smoke-Imix-God K. The record of the Copán king occupies the outer rim text, while another date and event are recorded in the interior. The interior date, 9.11.0.11.11, falls 231 days after the period ending. The event phrase includes the glyph *ta yuc.* This term *yuc* is the Chorti word for "join things, unite, a joining, union" (Wisdom n.d.:771). Smoke-Imix may then have united or joined that polity to his own.

This action explains why the first great ruler of Quiriguá, Cauac-Sky, recorded that he acceded *u cab,* "in the territory of" 18-Rabbit of Copán. Quiriguá was in the hegemony of Copán after 18-Rabbit's predecessor "joined" it to the kingdom. Further evidence supporting the conclusion that Smoke-Imix actually brought Quiriguá under his hegemony comes from later rulers' practice of citing themselves as "Black Copán Ahau" and of claiming descent from Yax-Kuk-Mo' as their founder (Schele 1989c).

21. Etsuo Sato (1987) interprets the appearance of polychrome in the Valley of La Venta as evidence of elites who had access to exotic pottery. He sees these elites as being both heavily influenced by Copanecs and in contact with peoples at Naco and in the Sula Valley.

22. These monuments include the bifaced Stela C (9.14.0.0.0), Stela F (9.14.10.0.0), Stela 4 (9.14.15.0.0), Stela H (9.14.19.5.0), Stela A (9.14.19.8.0 or 9.15.0.3.0), Stela B (9.15.0.0.0), and finally, Stela D (9.15.5.0.0). Stela C, the first monument in this set, dates to the same first appearance of Venus celebrated by Ah Cacaw on Stela 16 at Tikal (see Chapter 6). Stela C reflects this association with Venus by linking the period ending to a Venus date occurring before the beginning of this creation. Other analyses have placed Stela C at later dates, but the text specifies that the stela was erected (*tz'apah*) on 9.14.0.0.0.

23. In the 1987 excavations, William Fash drove a tunnel into the rear of the platform directly under the temple. Although no cache was found, the excavation uncovered a muzzle stone exactly the same size and shape as the corner Witz Monsters that decorated the 18-Rabbit temple. With present data, we have no way of determining which king commissioned the earlier phase of the building, but clearly that earlier building displayed the same iconography as the later version. See Larios and W. Fash (n.d.) for a preliminary analysis of the final phases of Temples 22 and 26.

24. Two broken fragments with inscriptions were set in the step of the final phase of this temple. One records the first katun anniversary of 18-Rabbit's accession (David Stuart personal communication, 1987) and the other is the death date of Smoke-Imix-God K (Schele 1987a). These two dates as well as the style of the God N sculpture found cached in the later building identify the time of the earlier building as the second half of the reign of 18-Rabbit.

25. William Fash (1983a:236–237) cites Viel's analysis of the source of Ulua polychrome as the Comayagua Valley, rather than the Sula Valley. Furthermore, caches found within the Early Classic phases of Structure 10L-26 (the Temple of the Hieroglyphic Stairs) include greenstone beads and earflares identical in technical workmanship and design to the greenstone artifacts excavated at the central Honduran site of El Cajón by Kenneth Hirth (1988).

26. Rebecca Storey (1987 and personal communication) documents evidence for death rates higher than birth rates in the Copán pocket during the Late Classic period. 18-Rabbit had to recruit newcomers from outside the valley to keep the population growing, and his strategy apparently succeeded, for by the end of the eighth century, population exceeded the capacity of the Copán pocket to sustain them.

27. Kelley (1962:324), following a suggestion by Proskouriakoff, pointed out the *u cab* expressions at Quiriguá, noting that *cab* means "town, place, and world." David Stuart (1987a) first interpreted this passage to indicate that Cauac-Sky's installation was under 18-Rabbit's authority and perhaps even took place at Copán. This interpretation is in keeping with his identification of the protagonist of Quiriguá Altar L as Smoke-Imix-God K of Copán.

28. Morley (1915:221) first noted that this 9.15.6.14.6 6 Cimi 4 Zec date was important to Quiriguá's history, while Kelley (1962:238) suggested that it referred to "a conquest of Quiriguá by Copán, or perhaps to the installation of a Copanec ruler at Quiriguá."

Proskouriakoff (1973:168) took the prominence of the date at Quiriguá to indicate that the Quiriguá ruler had the upper hand in the encounter. Following her mentor's suggestions, Marcus (1976:134–140) pointed out that Cauac-Sky, the ruler of Quiriguá, was the "captor of" 18-Rabbit, the king of Copán. She correctly identified the event as a battle in which Quiriguá achieved independence of Copán.

The verb associated with this date consists of an "ax" followed by the T757 auxiliary verb. This verb records "astronomical" events in the codices, and at Dos Pilas and other sites it appears with "star-shell" war events (see Schele 1982:351 for a listing). In most of the examples from the Classic inscriptions, the event appears to be "battle," but on pottery, the "ax" glyph is particularly associated both with scenes of decapitation and with the names of gods shown in the act of self-inflicted decapitation (one example occurs on the famous painted pot from Altar de Sacrificios). This association with sacrifice opens the possibility that the action recorded is execution by decapitation. Nikolai Grube (personal communication, 1989) and Jorge Orejel (n.d.) have both suggested a reading of *ch'ak,* "to decapitate," for the glyph.

29. The case of Copán is not entirely unique. Palenque suffered a similar disaster when Kan-Xul, the younger brother and successor of Chan-Bahlum, was captured by Toniná and presumably sacrificed. Palenque, like Copán, did not enter into a hiatus, but rather continued under the aegis of its old dynasty. The political reactions at both Copán and Palenque included, however, the emergence of the lesser nobility as players in the game of history. In both kingdoms, the kings struggled in vain to reassert the centrality of the dynasty.

30. Smoke-Monkey's accession appears on the base of Stela N and on Steps 40 and 39 of the Hieroglyphic Stairs as 9.15.6.16.5 6 Chicchan 3 Yaxkin (Stuart and Schele 1986b), a day on which Venus was 45.68° from the sun.

31. This date is recorded on the north panel of the east door of Temple 11 as 5 Cib 10 Pop or 9.15.15.12.16 5 Cib 9 Pop (the correct form of the Calendar Round). On this date, the Eveningstar was 7.09° beyond the sun, enough for first visibility after superior conjunction. The action recorded on this date is "it appeared, the Great Star." Previously, Schele (Schele and M. Miller 1986:123) had placed this first appearance forty-six days after the accession of the next king, Smoke-Shell, but the Long Count used for that date was in error. Smoke-Shell acceded on 9.15.17.13.10 11 Oc 13 Pop or February 18, 749, fourteen days after Smoke-Monkey's death.

32. On the base of Stela N, the name of Smoke-Shell's father follows an *yune* "child of" statement. In that phrase, he is named as a Turtle Shell Ahau (Schele and Grube 1988). The turtle-shell glyph in this title is a variant of the God N (Pauahtun) glyph that names the lord whose accession is recorded in the north-south text-bands on the base. In that clause, the "Pauahtun Ahau" is clearly named as the former king, Smoke-Monkey. The fifteenth successor, Smoke-Shell, was therefore the child of the fourteenth successor, Smoke-Monkey.

33. William Fash (personal communication, 1989) holds open the possibility that Smoke-Monkey may have started some of the work on the final stage of Temple 26. Considering that six years passed between Smoke-Shell's accession and the dedication of the building on 9.16.4.1.0 (Stuart and Schele 1986b), the project may well have been begun during Smoke-Monkey's reign.

34. The date of this dedication event is recorded on the center strips on the eastern incline of the Ballcourt. Although reconstructing the date is problematic, it appears to record the Calendar Round 10 Ben 16 Kayab (or less likely 10 Kan 17 Kayab). The 10 Ben possibility falls on 9.15.6.8.13, a day only 113 days before 18-Rabbit's death at Quiriguá. 18-Rabbit's accession is recorded in an Initial Series date in the same text, thus confirming that he commissioned the final phase of the Ballcourt (Schele, Grube, and Stuart 1989). Rudy Larios (personal communication, 1989) has confirmed that Ballcourt III is associated with Structure 10L-26–2nd, the level under the final phase. This juxtaposition of the dedication date with the capture opens the possibility that 18-Rabbit may have been taken captive in a battle to secure sacrificial victims for his new ballcourt.

The proper name of Ballcourt III is recorded on the Hieroglyphic Stairs on fragments now mounted in Step 44. These fragments include an unreadable date and the name of the Ballcourt as the *Ox Ahal Em* Ballcourt (Schele and Freidel n.d.). The proper name translates as "Thrice-Made Descent" and relates to the mythological events recorded on the Ballgame Panel from Temple 33 at Yaxchilán (Fig. 7:7).

The "thrice-made" event is recorded as a descent in this naming and as a decapitation sacrifice at Yaxchilán, but the references are the same. Both the descents and the sacrifices refer to the Popol Vuh myth. The first descent and sacrifice was of Hun-Hunahpu and Vucub-Hunahpu, the first set of Twins. The second descent into Xibalba, which resulted in the second sacrifice, was made by the Hero Twins, Hunahpu and Xbalanque. They sacrificed each other in order to trick the Lords of Death into defeat. The third descent is that of the king in his guise as the avatar of the Hero Twins. This descent can be accomplished by two means—his own ecstatic journey through bloodletting or by the decapitation of a captive who goes as his messenger. The Ballcourt was then a portal to the Underworld as was the inner sanctum of the temple. The iconography of all three sets of Ballcourt Markers reflects this idea, for each shows the confrontation of the Hero Twins with a Lord of Death (Schele and M. Miller 1986:251–252, 257) through a quadrifoil shape. This shape symbolized the mouth of the cave and the opening to the Otherworld from Olmec times onward. The playing alley was like a glass-bottomed boat with transparent windows opening on to the Underwater domain of Xibalba. There, the great confrontation of humanity with death played itself out in the myths that became the Popol Vuh. Captives played a losing game and were dispatched in the "thrice-made descent." Ironically, 18-Rabbit himself may have been dispatched by exactly this means.

35. It has about twelve hundred glyph blocks, but most of the blocks hold two or more words. There are generally thirty-five glyphs per step and a minimum of sixty-four steps. Some of the steps have figures in the center, which reduces the number of words per step, but recent excavation suggests there were more than the sixty-four reconstructed stairs. 2,200 is about the right count.

36. Marcus (1976:145) first noted the appearance of the Palenque Emblem Glyph on Copán Stela 8, a monument we now know records that Yax-Pac was the child of this woman. When she traveled to Copán, she apparently brought a royal belt inscribed with the names of family members, which her descendants at Copán inherited and passed down through *their* family. By an unknown process, this belt traveled to Comayagua, where it was bought from an Indian at the end of the nineteenth century and given to the British Museum (Schele and M. Miller 1986:82, Pl. 21).

37. William Fash (1983b) identified the household groups in the Copán with *sian otot,* the Chorti Maya patrilocal residential system documented in detail by Wisdom (1940). He posits that the ancient settlement pattern reflects a system similar to the modern one, thus identifying the numerous residential compounds as patrilineal residences.

38. William Fash (1983a:192–195) gives a count of 1,489 structures (not including invisible structures or those washed away by the Río Copán) within the 2.1 km² entered on the Ballcourt. He allows five people per structure and assumes that 84 percent of the total structures were residential, arriving at a density of 2,977 people per square kilometer. Webster (1985:24) accepts a figure of 15,000 to 20,000 for the Copán pocket and a density of 5,000/km² for the Sepulturas and Bosque zones. The rural zones were less densely settled with an overall density of 100/km². Webster (1985:50) argued for a maximum population of 20,000 for the entire Copán drainage, and he communicates that Sanders believes that the densities near the Acropolis were too high to have been supported by any feasible agricultural methods available to the Copanecs in the eighth century. The hinterlands around Copán supported the dense populations in the pocket.

39. William Fash (1983a:305–308) calculates that the pocket's capacity to support about 10,000 people was exceeded by a significant factor in the eighth century, forcing shorter fallow periods as well as massive deforestation. The loss of topsoil on the intramountain zones, he suggests, led to a depletion of the soils that was so permanent that only pine forest could survive in these highly acidic areas, even today. He further notes that deforestation affected local rainfall and exacerbated the problem further. All of this occurred simultaneously, exactly when the nucleated zone around the Acropolis was occupied by up to 15,000 people, 50 percent more than could have subsisted on the agricultural base within the pocket. It was a prescription for disaster.

40. In the most recent tunneling under the East Court, Robert Sharer and Alfonso Morales (personal communication, 1989) have found a sharp division between buildings constructed with rough stone covered by thick plaster surfaces and those built with finely finished coursing covered with thin plaster. Sharer (personal communication, 1989) tentatively dates this building to the first half of the seventh century—that is, to the end of Butz'-Chan's reign or to the first half of Smoke-Imix-God K's. About this time, the Copanecs apparently switched from plaster to stone as the medium of architectural sculpture, thus suggesting that the wood necessary for making plaster had become a rare commodity. Certainly by 18-Rabbit's reign, stone was the primary medium for architectural sculpture. Indeed, the building under his version of Temple 22 also used stone as its

sculptural medium. If this is the correct interpretation, then the valley environs may have been seriously deforested by the beginning of the Late Classic period.

41. Rebecca Storey (1987 and personal communication, 1987–1989) has documented severe stress in the Copán Valley populations, especially in the eighth century. This stress was indicated in skeletons found in elite contexts as well as those excavated from the lower strata of Copán society. She notes high death rates for people between five and sixteen, exactly the ages that should have had the lowest rate of death, and she has also found evidence of widespread anemia. In her words, the people who lived in the valley during the eighth century were sick and getting sicker, and this was true for the elite as well as commoners.

42. This is the earliest monument of Yax-Pac left to posterity. In light of its period-ending association, it may well be his first foray into public history.

43. In 1985, David Stuart made a new drawing of the stair under Temple 11 at the end of a tunnel driven by Strömsvik. He recognized that the text records the dedication of Structure 11-Sub 12, a temple that originally stood on a platform that was the same height as the floor of the West Court.

44. Mary Miller (1986:83–84; 1988; M. Miller and Houston [1987:59]) pointed out this association of ballgame scenes, hieroglyphic stairs, and sacrificial scenes, and identified the Reviewing Stands at Copán as the sides of a false ballcourt. She identified the location as underwater and the rising god on the stairway as Chac-Xib-Chac.

45. Barbara Fash (personal communication, 1989) informs us that Proskouriakoff commented on these crocodiles in the field notes she kept while working on reconstruction drawings for the Carnegie expedition under Strömsvik.

46. See Schele (1987c) for an analysis of the chronology and events recorded in this inscription. The date and event is repeated on the west panel of the north door above in Temple 11, where Smoke-Shell, Yax-Pac's predecessor, appears as the protagonist. We suggested the event corresponded to his apotheosis and emergence from the Underworld after he had defeated the Lords of Death (see Schele and M. Miller 1986:265–300).

47. He dedicated the Reviewing Stand 9.16.18.2.12 8 Eb 15 Zip (March 27, 769) and Altar Z on 9.16.18.9.19 12 Cauac 2 Zac (August 21, 769). The last glyph in the altar text is *ya.tz'i:ni,* spelling the word *yatz'in.* It occurs in the name of a person (not the king) given in a second clause. Since *yitz'in* is "younger brother," and since no *yatz'* or *yatz'in* word with an appropriate meaning occurs in either the Yucatecan or Cholan languages, we suspect this glyph may identify this second person as the "younger brother of the king."

48. 9.17.0.0.0 13 Ahau 18 Cumku (January 24, 771) has long been known as an eclipse date from its appearance in the eclipse tables of the Dresden Codex. David Kelley (1977: 406) noted that the glyph recording "dark of the moon" for 9.17.0.0.0 on Quiriguá Stela E is closely related to the glyph recording the same eclipse station on Dresden, page 51b at B1. At Tikal, this solar eclipse darkened 20 percent of the sun beginning at 12:49 P.M. and ending at 3:09 P.M. (Kudlek 1978). It is registered in the inscriptions of Quiriguá on Stela E and at Copán on the east panel of the south door of Temple 11. The first appearance of the Eveningstar is also recorded in Temple 11 (south panel, west door) on the day 9.17.0.0.16 3 Cib 9 Pop (February 9, 771). Venus was separated from the sun by 7.46+ and high enough to be observed above Copán's mountainous horizon.

49. On 9.17.0.0.0, Yax-Pac also dedicated Altar 41, recording the dedication rituals on two of the edges of the flat slab, and the Cosmic Monster and a toad on the other two edges. This altar reflects the cosmic nature of this katun ending.

50. Temple 21 has fallen into the cut made by the Copán River along the eastern edge of the Acropolis. We have no information on its patron, but fragments found on the platform behind it include Tlaloc-war iconography among other motifs.

51. Although very little evidence survives, William Fash and I have surmised the north door was in fact carved as a monster mouth based on some of the fragments lying on the stairway below the temple. Principal among these fragments are huge stones carved with parallel curving lines that appear to represent the palette of an open mouth.

52. Both Bill and Barbara Fash argued in their comments on this chapter that we have proof for only two of these Pauahtun figures. One head is located under the huge ceiba tree that stands over the northeast corner of the building, and the other lies among the fragments in the Plaza below the temple. Since no evidence of Pauahtunob has been found on the south side, the design probably had the cosmic arch of heaven only on the northern facade that faced out toward the Great Plaza. Barbara Fash also pointed out to us that Proskouriakoff mentioned in her field notes seeing and recognizing segments

of the reptilian body of the Cosmic Monster in the rubble associated with Temple 11.

53. A summary of the events as we understood them in 1985 appears in Schele and M. Miller (1986:123). In the 1987 field season, David Stuart worked extensively with these texts and supervised the reconstruction of several of the most important panels, particularly the two west panels in the north-south corridor. In November 1987, Schele reconstructed additional parts of the north panel of the west door. These reconstructions and corrections have allowed a much more accurate understanding of the chronology and events, which are as follows:

a. North door, east panel. The accession of Yax-Pac on 9.16.12.6.16 6 Caban 10 Mol (July 2, 763).

North door, west panel. The dedication of the Reviewing Stand and perhaps the apotheosis of Smoke-Shell on 9.16.18.2.12 8 Eb 15 Zip (March 27, 769). 9.14.15.0.0 (September 17, 726) continues to the south door, where the actor is recorded.

b. South door, east panel. The finish of the 9.14.15.0.0 event with 18-Rabbit as the actor. The 9.17.0.0.0 period ending and eclipse.

South door, west panel. The 9.17.2.12.16 1 Cib 19 Ceh (September 26, 773) dedication of the Temple. David Stuart recognized the nature of this event in his 1987 work.

c. East door, north panel. The first appearance of Venus as Eveningstar on 9.15.15.12.16 5 Cib 9 Pop (February 15, 747), an unknown event on 9.17.1.3.5 9 Chicchan 13 Zip (March 24, 772), and a repetition of the 9.17.2.12.16 event, but specified for the *xay*, "crossing," of the interior corridors.

East door, south panel. The 819-day count and Long Count for the dedication date, 9.17.2.12.16 (continues to west door).

d. West door, north panel. Continuation of the date from east door and the dedication event. 9.17.5.0.0 period-ending ritual and the latest date in the building.

West door, south panel. The dedication event and the 9.17.0.0.16 3 Cib 9 Pop (February 9, 771) first appearance of the Eveningstar.

54. The text and figures on this bench are described and analyzed in Schele and M. Miller (1986:123–125), but some new information of interest has surfaced since that analysis. Each of the twenty personages sits on a glyph, but in 1986 we thought the glyphs did not name any of Copán's rulers. David Stuart (personal communication, 1987) has suggested the glyph under Personage 14 refers to the seventh successor, and that the one under Personage 15 is identical to the name of the eleventh successor. However, even with several glyphs associated with the names of particular rulers, the glyphs do not appear to record a series of personal names, but rather a continuous text. Furthermore, I had erroneously taken all ten glyphs on the left side to be in mirror image, signaling that the order of the figures unfolded outward from the central text. This interpretation is wrong. The glyphs under the first four personages on the left (Personages 1–4) read in the correct order. The left text is then broken into at least two clauses. One is written in proper reading order and records the dedication of the bench. The second one we do not yet understand, but we know it is related to the dynastic history of the kingdom. This new analysis does solve one problem in the previous interpretation—there are sixteen successors in the dynasty, including Yax-Pac, but twenty figures on the bench. With the separation of four of these figures and their glyphs into a separate clause, the number of dynasts depicted now becomes the correct one, sixteen.

55. The ambitious size of the building exceeded the technological capabilities of the Copanecs and caused problems almost immediately. The east-west gallery was simply too wide for the capability of a corbeled vault, especially with the weight of a second story above it. The new walls built by the architects to support the failing vault narrowed the interior corridor to half its former width and severely constricted the readability of the inscriptions. Some of these inscriptions appear to have been covered over, especially those on the west side.

56. Ricardo Argurcia (personal communication, 1989), co-director of the Copán Acropolis Project, informed us that the building immediately under the final phase of Temple 16 faced east instead of west. He suspects that the entire West Court was not formulated architecturally until Yax-Pac built Temple 11 and 16. If his assessment is correct, then Yax-Pac deliberately created the primordial sea and the Underworld in this West Court as a part of his political strategy.

57. Williamson, Stone, and Morales (1989) have connected the iconography of Temple 16 to the Tlaloc-war imagery we have discussed throughout this book. Ricardo Argurcia's (personal communication, 1989) excavations of Temple 16 have proved beyond doubt that the last phase was built during Yax-Pac's reign. This new dating clearly

connects Temples 11 and Temple 16 as part of a unified project, very probably conceived and executed together. The iconography of the West Court with its death and Underwater imagery was intentionally created as a single statement, rather than accumulated through several reigns.

58. William Fash (1983a:310–314) first proposed that Yax-Pac used this kind of strategy in dealing with the factionalism evident in the archaeology associated with the latest phrase of Copán life. The epigraphic information upon which he based his ideas has changed drastically since his initial presentation, but our analysis of Yax-Pac's strategy grows from his initial insights.

The houses we talk about are the principal structures in large, multiple-court residential compounds. These particular structures have benches in them, as do a large number of buildings in the residential compounds, but in general they are large and more elaborately decorated than adjacent buildings. The function of these benches is debated, with some researchers asserting they were simply beds. Clearly, some functioned as sleeping platforms, but the Maya themselves called them *chumib*, "seat." From pottery scenes, we deduced that the benches served a number of purposes, including sleeping, working, the conducting of business, audiences with subordinates, and a variety of rituals. The structures with these inscribed "seats" were very probably the rooms from which the lineage heads conducted the business critical to their peoples. They were called *otot*, "house," by the Maya, but they are houses in the sense that modern people sometimes have offices in their homes. These structures were more than residential.

59. For a description of this group under its older designation CV-43, see Leventhal (1983).

60. This bench text begins with a date corresponding to the dedication of the building in which it is housed. The chronology leads to a future (at the time of the inscribing) enactment of the scattering rite by Yax-Pac on 9.17.10.0.0. The date of the dedication is difficult to decipher but 9.17.3.16.15 is one of the more likely possibilities. The event is the God N dedication event of a house by an offering which had something to do with Smoke-Shell. Since that ruler was long dead at the time of the dedication, we presume this was a offering "to" rather than "from" Smoke-Shell (Schele 1989a). The alternative explanation is that the date of the dedication fell within the reign of Smoke-Shell, but that it was not commemorated by the installation of this bench until shortly before 9.17.10.0.0. In this scenario, both kings would have been active participants.

61. Altar W' was set in this same group. Dated at 9.17.5.9.4, the text celebrated the dedication of that altar and names the lineage head as the "third successor" of a person named Skull, who was a ballplayer. Presuming this person was the founder of this particular lineage, he may have been the lord who built the structure with the monkey/God N scribe in the time of 18-Rabbit.

62. Berthold Riese (in Webster, W. Fash, and Abrams 1986:184) had originally dated this monument to 9.17.16.13.10 11 Oc 3 Yax. Grube and Schele (1987b) proposed a different reading of the day as 11 Ahau and placed the Long Count at 9.19.3.2.0. Stuart, Grube, and Schele (1989) have proposed a new reading of the haab as 3 Ch'en rather than 3 Yax. This new combination gives 9.17.10.11.0 11 Ahau 3 Ch'en, a placement that is far more in keeping with the style of the carving and with the notation that Yax-Pac was in his first katun of reign when the house dedication occurred.

63. David Stuart (personal communication, 1985) first identified the name phrase of Yahau-Chan-Ah-Bac. This man's relationship to the king can be deduced from two monuments (Schele and Grube 1987a). The parentage statements of the king, given on Stela 8, and Yahau-Chan-Ah-Bac's, given on Altar U, name the same woman of Palenque as their mother. Yax-Pac's father is never given, but we deduce he was Smoke-Shell's son, based on his position as the sixteenth successor. The younger half brother was, however, not the son of Smoke-Shell. Since Yax-Pac was under twenty at the time of his accession, and since his father reigned for less that fifteen years, we speculate that Smoke-Shell died while his wife was still young. She produced his heir in Yax-Pac, but after his death she remarried and produced another son by a different father, making Yahau-Chan-Ah-Bac a half brother. On Altar U (Fig. 8:19), her name includes her status as the mother of the king.

64. Venus was 46.35° from the sun on the anniversary and 46.21° on the bloodletting five days later.

65. There are some important differences between the Altar T figures and those on Altar Q, Altar L, and the bench from Temple 11. The latter three monuments depict human figures all wearing a particular kind of breast ornament which appears to be

associated with ruling lords at Copán and, interestingly enough, with the noble whose portrait was carved on Stela 1 from Los Higos, one of the largest sites in the La Venta Valley to the north at the edge of Copán's hegemony. The Altar T figures were a mixture of fully human representations and fantastic beasties on the sides. We do not know whether these figures are to be interpreted as a glyphic text or as beings called from Xibalba, but they are clearly not meant to be understood as ancestors. Furthermore, the four fully human figures on the front surface are not identified by names. We do not know which represents Yahau-Chan-Ah-Bac, or whether to interpret the four figures as ancestors or contemporary patriarchs. Regardless of our confusion, the imagery on the altar clearly evokes Altar Q and the Temple 11 bench, both of which were in place when Altar T was carved.

66. Stuart (1986a) first identified the proper name of Altar U. See Schele and Stuart (1986b, 1986c) for analysis of the chronology and inscription on Altar U.

67. The name is written *Yax.k'a:ma:la.ya* or *Yax K'amlay*. Nikolai Grube (personal communication, 1988) brought to our attention that the root *k'am* in Yucatec means "to serve another," as well as "obligation, offering of the first fruits, and offering." *K'amtesah* is "administrator or he who serves" (Barrera Vasquez 1980:371). Chorti (Wisdom n.d.:607) has *k'am* as "use, service, value" and *k'amp'ah* as "be of use or value, serve, be occupied with." If, as Grube suggests, *-lay* is a derivational suffix, then this man may have been known by the office he fulfilled—"First Steward (or Administrator)."

In earlier analyses, we had taken this Yax-Kamlay glyph to be a title taken by Yahau-Chan-Ah-Bac upon his seating. However, in the summer of 1989, David Stuart found this same name on Stela 29, on the new altar from Temple 22a, and on a house model located near a residential building just south of the Acropolis. He convinced us that Yax-Kamlay and Yahau-Chan-Ah-Bac were, in fact, two different individuals. The relationship of Yax-Kamlay to Yax-Pac is less clear than that between the king and Yahau-Chan-Ah-Bac. Nikolai Grube and Schele speculate that a glyph in his name on Altar U reading *i.tz'i.ta* is an unpossessed form of "younger brother." If this reading is correct, then he would have been a younger full brother of the king. At present, however, this reading is only a possibility. Confirmation of the proposed relationship must wait until incontrovertible evidence is found.

68. On the eastern side of Stela 5, the Serpent Bar holds two tiny ancestral figures in its gaping mouths. On the northern, left side of the king, the ancestor holds a stingray spine, while on the southern, right side, another holds the bowl full of the blood that has brought him forth from the Otherworld.

69. We refer here to Stela 6, which was mounted in a small, unexcavated compound about a hundred meters west of Stela 5. From a point fifty meters to the south and equidistant from each, both tree-stones can be seen.

70. Here we have Yax-Pac pausing after he has left the causeway that led west from the Acropolis to a large complex on the slope above and to the east of Stela 5. From his position, he would have seen the east face of Stela 5, and after walking fifty meters to the west, he would have seen the west face of Stela 5 and the front of its nearby companion, Stela 6. The latter monument celebrated 9.12.10.0.0, a date which corresponded to a stationary point ending the retrograde motion of Venus after its heliacal rising as Morningstar. The same monument has the first historical record of a ritual action by 18-Rabbit, who was to become king after the death of Smoke-Imix.

71. This was the glyphic name of Temple 11 recorded on the west panel of the south door (Stuart, personal communication, 1988).

72. We are supposing Yax-Pac was standing on the west causeway due south of Stelae 5 and 6. On that day, January 25, 793, the sun would have risen above the far mountainous rim of the valley (about 8° of altitude) at 112° azimuth. From the vantage point we have taken, the sun would appear in a line directly between Temple 16 and Temple 11, but Temple 11 would have dominated the scene.

73. The identification of Temple 22a is the result of brilliant work by Barbara Fash (1989 and B. Fash et al. n.d.). In working with the sculpture excavated in the fallen debris around Temple 22a, Fash associated the *pop*, "mat," signs that were built into the entablatures of all four sides of the building with the ethnohistorical term for "council houses" documented in post-Conquest sources. Known as Popol Nah, these buildings were specifically designed for meetings of community councils. Fash points out that Temple 22a is the only major public building in the Acropolis that has a large front patio attached to the building. Since it provides more floor space than the interior, she suggests that the major lords of the Copán kingdom came here to counsel with the king in meetings that

must have resembled the conciliar assemblage of lords that we have seen on Piedras Negras Lintel 3 (see Fig. 7.21).

In the summer of 1989, she found even more remarkable evidence by asking Tom and Carolyn Jones to work with the fragments of huge glyphs that had been found around Temple 22a in recent excavations. They managed to reassemble enough of these glyphs to identify them as a series of locations. Later work by Fash confirmed the likelihood that beautifully carved figures sat in niches above these locations. Given the combination of richly dressed figures with a toponymic, it seems likely that the figures simply read "ahau of that location." The Popol Nah then may have been graced not only by mat signs marking its function as a council house, but with representations of the ahauob who ruled subdivisions of the kingdoms (or principal locations within it) for the kings. It is not unlike a modern meeting of state governors who come to counsel the president.

The dating of Temple 22a is more complicated. Barbara Fash and David Stuart managed to put together a series of glyphs that also went around the building above the mat signs. They are clearly day signs reading 9 Ahau, which should in this context and without any additional calendric information refer to an important period-ending date. The only 9 Ahau that falls on a hotun (5-tun) ending within the time that is archaeologically and stylistically feasible is 9.15.15.0.0 9 Ahau 18 Xul (June 4, 746). This falls shortly before Smoke-Monkey's death, so that the Popol Nah may be the only surviving construction from his reign. The sculptural style and the figures deliberately emulate Temple 22, the magnificent temple built by 18-Rabbit, but Smoke-Monkey seems to have elevated conciliar rule to new status at Copán by placing this building in such a prominent place. Perhaps he found such a change in the long-standing practice of governance to be prudent after 18-Rabbit's ignominious end.

74. This oddly shaped altar-bench was found in the rear chamber of Temple 22a during the 1988 field season. Four important dates are featured in its chronology. These include 9.18.5.0.0 4 Ahau 13 Ceh (September 15, 795, a day recorded with Yahau-Chan-Ah-Bac here and on Altar U); 9.17.9.2.12 3 Eb 0 Pop (January 29, 780, the date Yax-Kamlay was seated); 9.17.10.0.0 (December 2, 789, an important period ending and anchor for the chronology); and 9.17.12.5.17 4 Caban 10 Zip (March 19, 783, the first katun anniversary of Yax-Pac's own accession). All three major actors, Yahau-Chan-Ah-Bac, Yax-Kamlay, and Yax-Pac are mentioned. It is interesting that the undated Stela 29 (Altar O' under Morley's designations), which is almost exactly the same size and style as this altar, also mentions Yax-Kamlay and Yax-Pac. It was found in the East Court and may originally have been paired with the Temple 22a stone (Schele et al. 1989). W. Fash (personal communication, 1989) believes the wear pattern, the position, and the shape of the stone suggest it was part of a seat, perhaps the backrest.

75. The use of large zoomorphic altars at Copán was initiated by 18-Rabbit, but these altars were usually associated with stelae. Other altars, usually all glyphic, had been known since Smoke-Imix-God K's reign, but those rarely combined inscriptions and figures. The first experiment utilizing this combined format was Yax-Pac's Altar Q, but Altars U and T represent innovative experiments in both style and size. Since Quiriguá rulers were experimenting with large boulder sculpture during the same period, Copán's abandonment of the stela format may signify synergy between both the artists and rulers of the two sites.

76. William Fash (personal communication, 1989) informs us that bone, jade, and alabaster fragments were found inside the tomb, so it had definitely been occupied. Who occupied it, we don't know. The stela commemorating Yax-Pac's death was set in the corner formed by the west wall of the substructure and the wall that formed an entry gate to the East Court. It was juxtaposed to Temple 18 in a way that would be expected if Yax-Pac was buried there twenty years after the dates inscribed on the building. The tomb was constructed so that it could be entered after the building of the temple was completed. However, without inscriptions to identify the occupant, his identity will remain a matter of speculation.

77. While it is true that kings are shown holding weapons on the Temple 26 stairs, there they are sitting on thrones in the passive mode. They are not actively going to or returning from battle.

78. Two other monuments can be dated to the twelve years between the end of Katun 18 and the king's anniversary. Altar R, which was found on the platform in front of Temple 18, commemorates Yax-Pac's accession and another event which took place on 9.18.2.8.0 7 Ahau 3 Zip (March 9, 793). The other monument, Altar F', was found behind Structure 32 (Morley 1920:373) in a residential compound just south of the Acropolis (Fig. 8:11). This square altar has binding ribbons engraved around its perimeter and a text of sixteen

glyphic blocks. It is a difficult text, which records the accession of yet another lineage head to an office which we do not yet understand (Schele 1988a). All we can say about this office is that it was not the office of ahau. The accession took place on 9.17.4.1.11 2 Chuen 4 Pop (775 February 3, 775) and its twenty-fourth tun anniversary on 9.18.8.1.11 10 Chuen 9 Mac (September 30, 798). The text records that the anniversary ritual occurred in the company of Yax-Pac, who was in his second katun of reign.

79. We have already discussed a royal visit from Bird-Jaguar to Piedras Negras, but in general, the kings preferred to send ahauob as their representatives. See Schele and Mathews (n.d.) for a discussion of these visits and other patterns of interaction between Classic period kingdoms.

80. See Baudez and Dowd (1983:491–493) for the analysis of the iconography and inscriptions in Temple 18. Just below that building, the latest date associated with Yax-Pac was on Stela 11. Riese argues that the opening date in that text, which is written as 6, 7, or 8 Ahau, must be later than 9.18.0.0.0 based on the "3-katun ahau" title in Yax-Pac's name. Since naked ahau dates are usually associated with period endings, the following Long Count positions are possible:

9.16.15.0.0 7 Ahau 18 Pop
9.17. 5.0.0 6 Ahau 13 Kayab
9.19.10.0.0 8 Ahau 8 Xul

Since Yax-Pac's numbered katun titles refer to katuns of reign, rather than to katuns of life as at most other sites (Schele 1989b), they cannot be used to estimate his age. However, they do confirm the placement of the Stela 11 date. He was a 1-katun ahau between 9.16.12.5.17 and 9.17.12.5.17; a 2-katun ahau between 9.17.12.5.17 and 9.18.12.5.17; and, a 3-katun ahau between 9.18.12.5.17 and 9.19.12.5.17. Since the first dates fall before his accession, and the second within his second katun of reign, only the third date, 9.19.10.0.0, is a possibility.

81. Stuart (1984, 1988c) has made a direct connection between the imagery of Vision Serpents and the Double-headed Serpent Bar.

82. On the sarcophagus of Palenque, the king Pacal falls into Xibalba with the same smoking image in his forehead as a sign of his transformation in death (Schele 1976:17). Several people have noted the same smoking shapes with the figures on Altar L, but in that scene, the devices penetrate the turban headdresses. On the Palenque sarcophagus and Stela 11, the celts penetrate the flesh of the head itself.

83. There is also a possibility that the text refers to a branch of the lineage deriving from 18-Rabbit-Serpent, a name also recorded on Stela 6. The glyph between this 18-Rabbit's name and Yax-Kuk-Mo' is *u loch,* a term for "fork (as of a tree)" in Yucatec and "to fold or bend" in Chorti. We are presuming, for the present, that 18-Rabbit-Serpent is the same person as 18-Rabbit-God K, for this former name appears on Stela 6, dated just eight years before 18-Rabbit-God K's accession. David Stuart (personal communication, 1987) has expressed doubts, however, that the two 18-Rabbits are the same person, and that possibility must remain open. In late 1989, another alternative occurred to us—that the 18-Rabbit-Serpent name phrase refers to the special Tlaloc-war Vision Serpent on the front of Stela 6 and presumably also on Stela 11. In this interpretation, the "fish-in-hand" verb in the Stela 6 text refers to the appearance of this particular Vision Serpent, while *u loch,* the phrase on Stela 11, also means "to hold something crosswise in the arms"—exactly the position of the Vision Serpent on both stelae.

84. Grube and Schele (1987a) identified this ruler and read his name glyph as *U-Cit-Tok',* "the patron of flint." The Calendar Round of his accession, 3 Chicchan 3 Uo, can fit into the dynastic sequence at Copán only at this Long Count position.

85. The office into which U-Cit-Tok was seated does not appear in the text, but this may be the result of a historical accident. If we assume that the original intention was to carve all four sides of the monument, as is the case with most other altars at Copán, then the inscription would probably have continued onto one of the other sides. Since the carving was never finished, the text ends abruptly in the middle of a sentence.

86. Morley (1920:289) first suggested that Altar L is in an unfinished state, a conclusion Barbara Fash (personal communication, 1987) also made when she drew the altar. She was the individual who brought this to our attention.

87. Both William Fash and Rebecca Storey (personal communication, 1986–1987) have described this incident to us.

88. This estimate comes from Rebecca Storey (personal communication, 1987), the physical anthropologist who is investigating the skeletal remains from the burials of Copán.

CHAPTER 9: KINGDOM AND EMPIRE AT CHICHÉN ITZÁ

1. The Great Collapse of the ninth century is one of the major social disasters of Precolumbian history (see Culbert 1973). E. W. Andrews IV (1965; 1973) underscored the fact that the northern lowland states of the ninth and tenth centuries were enjoying prosperity and expansion in the wake of the Great Collapse of the southern lowland kingdoms. Recent discussion and analysis of the relative destinies of northern and southern lowland Maya (Sabloff and E. W. Andrews V 1986) points to a significant overlap in timing between the fall of the southern kingdoms, the rise of the northern kingdoms, and ultimately, the rise of the conquest state of Chichén Itzá.

2. The most famous architectural style of the northern lowlands is the exquisite Puuc veneer stone masonry (Pollock 1980), regarded by many scholars as the epitome of Maya engineering and masonry skill. This style emerges in the Late Classic and persists through the Early Postclassic period (Sabloff and E. W. Andrews V 1986). The north central peninsular region also displays a style called Río Bec (Potter 1977); and between the central peninsular Río Bec sites and the concentration of Puuc-style cities in the hills to the north and west, there are communities with architecture of another, related style called Chenes (Pollock 1970). The northern tradition includes the temple-pyramid complex of the southern kingdoms, but there is also an emphasis on constructing many-roomed structures atop large solid pyramids. This change in emphasis may reflect a particular focus upon activities and events involving assemblies of leaders as opposed to the cultic focus upon rulers expressed in temple pyramids (Freidel 1986a) seen in the Late Classic southern lowlands.

3. The Maya of the time of the Conquest were still literate in their own system of writing. The most famous aboriginal treatises are the Books of Chilam Balam (Edmonson 1982, 1986), which are principally records of the katuns and their prophecies. These books are named after the last great Maya prophet: *chilam,* "interpreter [of the gods]," and *balam,* "jaguar," which was probably his family name. Roys (1967:3 and 182–187) suggested that Chilam Balam lived during the last decades of the fifteen century or perhaps during the first part of the sixteenth century and that his lasting fame came from his foretelling the appearance of strangers from the east who would establish a new religion. Roys (1967:3) says, "The prompt fulfilment of this prediction so enhanced his reputation as a seer that in later times he was considered the authority for many other prophecies which had been uttered long before his time. Inasmuch as prophecies were the most prominent feature of many of the older books of this sort, it was natural to name them after the famous sooth sayer."

The Books of Chilam Balam were recorded in the Yucatec Maya language, but written in Spanish script. The "prophecies" offered do have components that resemble the Western idea of fortune-telling, but the foretelling is based on detailed accounts of the major historical events and political struggles between competing communities and families from the late Precolumbian through the Colonial periods. Dennis Puleston (1979) argued that the fatalistic beliefs of the Maya and their acceptance of the essential cyclicality of time transformed such records of the past into rigid predictions of the future. We have tried to show in previous chapters that the Maya implementation of history as a guide to the future was subtle and politically imaginative. Bricker (n.d.) provides an elegant proof that some passages in the Books of Chilam Balam are direct transliterations of the glyphic originals. Archaeologists have been wrestling with these fragmentary historical accounts from the vantage of the record from excavation and survey for many years (Tozzer 1957; Pollock, Roys, Proskouriakoff, and Smith 1962; Ball 1974a; Robles and A. Andrews 1986; A. Andrews and Robles 1985).

4. As noted in Chapter 1, evidence from linguistic reconstructions and particular spellings in the Classic inscriptions indicate that Yucatec was spoken by the peoples occupying the northern and eastern sections of the Yucatán Peninsula. This zone included at least the modern regions of Yucatán, Quintana Roo, Belize, and the eastern third of the Petén. Northern and southern lowlands were linked in the Preclassic period by means of shared ceramic styles and by trade materials such as greenstone and chert brought through the southern lowlands or from them. In return, the northern lowland peoples may have traded sea salt (Freidel 1978; E. W. Andrews V 1981) from beds along their northern and western coasts. The northern lowland Maya participated in the early establishment of the institution of kingship, as seen in the famous bas-relief carved into the mouth of the cave of Loltún, which depicts a striding ahau wearing the Jester God diadem and the

severed jaguar head with triple plaques on his girdle (Freidel and A. Andrews n.d.). Stylistically, this image dates to the Late Preclassic period.

5. Our story of Chichén Itzá is based on less secure data than the stories we have offered about the southern kings. The northern Maya cities, with the notable exception of Dzibilchaltún on the northwestern plain, have not enjoyed the extensive and systematic investigations aimed at cultural interpretation that have been carried out at several of the southern cities we have written about. At Dzibilchaltún, E. Wyllys Andrews IV conducted long-term and systematic research (E. W. Andrews IV and E. W. Andrews V 1980). The settlement-pattern work at this site (Kurjack 1974) first alerted Maya scholars to the enormous size of some of these cities, a fact which took a long time to be accepted. Work of this quality and detail is only now in progress at sites like Cobá, Isla Cerritos, Sayil, Ek Balam, and Yaxuná.

Furthermore, in spite of the efforts of many epigraphers over more than sixty years, the hieroglyphic texts of the north are not as well understood as those of the south, partly because they have a higher percentage of phonetic signs and their calligraphy is far more difficult to read. The first date to be deciphered in the Chichén inscriptions was the Initial Series date 10.2.9.1.9 9 Muluc 7 Zac (Morley 1915). During the following two decades, the Carnegie Institution of Washington conducted the excavations that uncovered the remainder of the presently known hieroglyphic monuments of the Chichén Itzá corpus (Martin 1928; Morley 1925, 1926, 1927, 1935; Ricketson 1925; Ruppert 1935). Hermann Beyer's (1937) structural analysis laid the foundation for later epigraphic research on this body of texts, while Thompson (1937) was the first to explain the tun-ahau system of dating used at Chichén Itzá. Tatiana Proskouriakoff (1970) raised difficult questions about the presence of Maya inscriptions on "Toltec" architecture at the site.

David Kelley (1968; 1976; 1982) has been working with the texts of Chichén Itzá and Uxmal for many years, and he must be credited with the identification of several key relationship terms in the complex and partially understood network of family ties among nobles of the Chichén community. His structural analyses and interpretations have pushed far beyond the work of previous researchers. He also identified the inscriptional name, Kakupacal (Kelley 1968), an Itzá warrior mentioned in the Books of Chilam Balam, as an ancient ruler of Chichén Itzá. His important work inspired Michel Davoust (1977, 1980), who vigorously pursued the hypothesis that Chichén Itzá was ruled by a dynasty whose names are preserved in the texts.

James Fox (1984a, 1984b, n.d.) has made several major contributions to the unraveling of the Chichén Itzá texts; most notably, he correctly identified the Emblem Glyph of this capital. Jeff Kowalski (1985a, 1985b, 1989; Kowalski and Krochock, n.d.) has made substantial headway in the analysis of texts from Uxmal and other Terminal Classic communities of the north, including Chichén Itzá. Ian Graham, master of the Corpus of Hieroglyphic Writing Project at Harvard University, has generously allowed scholars to work with his drawings of northern lowland texts. David Stuart has contributed fundamentally to the interpretation of the political organization of Chichén Itzá, both in his publications (Stuart 1988a; Grube and Stuart 1987) and in his generous sharing of work in progress through personal communications. Stuart's decipherment of the sibling relationship at Chichén is the cornerstone of an epigraphic interpretation of conciliar rule there.

Finally, we draw heavily upon the work in progress of Ruth Krochock (1988) whose master's thesis on the lintels of the Temple of the Four Lintels is a tour de force of method. It is a programmatic breakthrough in the interpretation of the political rhetoric of Chichén Itzá as focused upon the simultaneous participation of contemporary leaders in dedication rituals. Our attempts to push beyond Krochock's interpretation are based upon intensive consultation with her and with Richard Johnson, Marisela Ayala, and Constance Cortez at the 1988 Advanced Seminar in Maya Hieroglyphic Writing at Austin and with Ruth, Jeff Kowalski, John Carlson, and others at the 1989 workshop. They are further based upon continued correspondence with Ruth Krochock. We appreciate her helpful advice and words of sensible caution. We also note that Virginia Miller (1989) has independently made many of the same associations between the Tlaloc-warrior of Classic period iconography and the Toltec warriors of Chichén Itzá.

6. The actual extent of Chichén Itzá has never been documented, since only the central core of the city has been mapped. The description of the city's limits we use here is an estimate attributed to Peter Schmidt by Fernando Robles and Anthony Andrews (1986). In the *Atlas of Yucatán,* Silvia Garza T. and Edward Kurjack provide an estimate of thirty square kilometers (Garza T. and Kurjack 1980).

The traditional interpretation of the history of Chichén Itzá (Tozzer 1957) holds that the city was occupied several times by different groups of people, generally moving from a Maya "old" Chichén to a Toltec Mexican "new" Chichén represented in the great northern center of the city. We support the view, as recently argued by Charles Lincoln (1986), that Chichén Itzá was a single city continuously occupied through its history. As Lincoln points out, the notion of an early Maya Chichén makes little sense, for it would leave the city without a discernible spatial center. The Maya were quite flexible in their city planning, but no Maya capital lacks an easily identified center.

Viewed as a single city, Chichén Itzá is strikingly diverse and cosmopolitan in its public and elite architecture, registering styles from both Maya country and from México. Traditionally, Chichén Itzá's Mexican cultural expression has been attributed to a conquest of the northern lowlands by Toltec Mexicans operating out of their capital in Tula Hidalgo, México (see Diehl 1981 on Tula). George Kubler (1975) argued that Tula displays only a fraction of the political program and architectural design found at Chichén Itzá, and it is more likely that Chichén was the dominant community in the acknowledged relationship with Tula. To be sure, Maya groups collaborated with Gulf Coast and Mexican peoples, probably merchant-warrior brotherhoods of a kind that later facilitated the economy of the Aztec Empire; but the Maya civilization was the fundamental source of ideas and imagery in this new government. We believe that Kubler is correct and that Chichén Itzá developed into a truly Mesoamerican capital, like Teotihuacán before it. This was perhaps the only time in Maya history that their culture stood center stage in the Mesoamerican world. Because we regard the great period of Chichén Itzá to be Mesoamerican and Maya, and not the product of a Toltec invasion, we use the traditional attribution of "Toltec" Chichén Itzá in quotations.

7. We will generally avoid as much as possible any references to the histories and chronicles, collectively termed the Chilam Balams, passed down to the time of the Europeans. No doubt there is significant historical information in these texts, but despite the brilliant efforts of Joseph Ball (1974a; 1986) and other scholars who worked before the Chichén texts had been even partially deciphered, it will take much future work to coordinate, in any useful way, the evidence of archaeology and epigraphy with that of ethnohistory. These histories are fraught with metaphorical allusions and political manipulations. Some essential assertions of the chronicles are confirmed by archaeology, principally the fact that foreigners entered the northern lowlands and, in alliance with native nobility, established new states such as Chichén Itzá. Some key figures in the historical narratives can also be found in the ancient texts, figures such as Kakupacal of Chichén Itzá (Kelley 1968). Eventually, there will be an historical framework that accounts for all of these forms of evidence.

8. The timing of the rise of the Puuc cities relative to the southern kingdoms is still a matter of controversy. Most specialists feel comfortable in dating the beginning of the Puuc florescence at about 800 A.D. or a half century earlier (Robles and A. Andrews, 1986:77). This date would establish contemporaneity of at least half a century between the kings of the Puuc and those of the south.

9. Jeff K. Kowalski (1985a; 1985b; 1987) in his study of Uxmal has carried out the most extensive investigation of the political organization of the Puuc cities as revealed in iconography and epigraphy.

10. These terms were popularized by J.E.S. Thompson (1970), who proposed that these were barbarian "Mexicanized Maya" who, through energetic trade, warfare, and diplomacy, penetrated the lowlands from their homeland in the swampy river country bordering the Maya domains on the west and established a new hegemony in the period of the Great Collapse. While the details are controversial, most scholars presently adhere to the general notion of a Putún or Chontal movement into the lowlands in Terminal Classic times (Sabloff and E. W. Andrews V 1986).

At some point in their peregrinations, the Itzá, often regarded as one group of Putún Maya, established cities along the western coast of the Yucatán peninsula, at Chanpotón— Chan Putún—and elsewhere in Campeche. Edmonson (1986), in his translations of the Chilam Balam books, would place this Itzá settlement prior to their incursions into the center of the peninsula to establish Chichén Itzá. The archaeology of this western coastal region is intriguing, but poorly known. On the one hand, there is the city of Xcalumkin (Pollock 1980) with its veneer mosaic architecture; Late Classic hieroglyphic dates on texts; and use of the ahau-cahal relationship, an innovation which originated in the Western Rivers district of the south at kingdoms such as Yaxchilán. On the other hand, there is Chunchucmil, situated to the north and very close to the rich salt beds of the western coast (Vlchek, Garza, and Kurjack 1978; Kurjack and Garza 1981). This Classic period city covers some six or more square kilometers and has densely packed house lots, temples, and pyramids. Until we have better archaeological control over this region, we will be required to treat the garbled history of its occupation with great caution.

11. Robles and A. Andrews's (1986) review of the evidence for the settlement size and organization of Cobá. See also Folan, Kintz, and Fletcher (1983) and Folan and Stuart (1977) for discussion of the settlement patterns at Cobá.

12. Stone roads, *sacbe,* were built by Maya from the Preclassic period onward. Although these roads no doubt could have served prosaic functions, such as commerce and rapid mobilization of troops, all of our descriptions from observers after the Conquest (Freidel and Sabloff 1984) show that such roads functioned principally as pathways for ceremonial processions and pilgrimages among related nobilities. Such rituals were, in all the cases we have come across, political statements of obligation and responsibility. Kurjack and E. W. Andrews V (1976) establish the archaeological case for such an interpretation of settlement hierarchy linked by intersite roads. The roadways of Cobá have been extensively reported on by Antonio Benavides C. (1981).

13. The original homeland of the Itzá is a matter of continuing dispute. They may have been speakers of a Maya language, probably Chontal, and the best guess places their original communities in the Chontalpa, a stretch of flat, swampy land to the east of the mighty Usumacinta and north of the Petén. The garbled histories of the Chilam Balam books give some reason to suspect that the Itzá established sizable communities along the western coast of the peninsula (perhaps even some of the Puuc-style communities on this coast were Itzá) before making their bid for hegemony in Yucatán by controlling the coastlands. The Maya of the Tabasco-Campeche coastlands were multilingual at the time of the Spanish Conquest. Many of them spoke Nahuatl, the language of the Aztec Empire, and they were astute, opportunistic merchants and warriors (Thompson 1970). Archaeological survey of the western and northern coasts by Anthony Andrews (1978) confirms the presence of coastal enclaves with pottery diagnostic of the Sotuta Ceramic Sphere associated with Chichén Itzá and the Itzá incursions. Certainly, the people who established Chichén Itzá as a great capital had adopted many ideas of governance from México (Wren n.d.). Hence it is likely that they had Mexican allies in their adventures on the peninsula.

14. The pottery associated with Chichén Itzá, and its "Itzá" occupation, is called Sotuta Sphere. This survey work along the coast has been carried out primarily by Anthony Andrews (1978). Much of what follows is based upon the syntheses of Andrews and Fernando Robles (A. Andrews and Robles 1985; Robles and A. Andrews 1986). The wide range of Mexican sources of obsidian traded by the Itzá is documented at Isla Cerritos (A. Andrews, Asaro, and Cervera R. n.d.).

15. This important site is undergoing long-term investigation by Anthony Andrews and Fernando Robles and their colleagues.

16. Izamal boasts one of the largest pyramids in the northern lowlands. Surface remains of monumental stucco masks which decorated the pyramid, along with the cut-stone monolithic-block facading on its terraces, indicate that its major period of construction dates to the Early Classic, long before the Terminal Classic incursions of the Itzá (Lincoln 1980). In the absence of further field investigation, we cannot say how substantial the community may have been at the time of the incursion. Clearly, however, the great pyramid on this otherwise flat plain constituted a famous geographic marker which the Itzá could refurbish as a capital with little additional labor investment.

David Stuart (personal communication, 1988) has alerted us to the fact that ethnohistorical documents (Lizana 1892: Chapter 2) describe Izamal as the capital of a lord named Hun-Pik-Tok, warrior captain of an army of "8,000 flints." He also identified the same name, Hun-Pik-Tok, in the inscription of the Casa Colorada and on the lintel from Halakal. Hence there is both ethnohistorical and epigraphic evidence to support the hypothesis that Izamal was an established capital of the Itzá at the time of the temple dedications at Chichén Itzá. These dedications occurred during Katun 2 of the tenth baktun, the likely time of Chichén Itzá's founding as the principal city of the Itzá. Hun-Pik-Tok and Kakupacal, a famous lord of Chichén Itzá mentioned several times in these dedication events throughout that city, are both mentioned on the Casa Colorada, so we can surmise they were contemporaries.

Hun-Pik-Tok reappears on a monument from Halakal, a small satellite community of Chichén Itzá to the east of that city. Most interesting is the fact that Hun-Pik-Tok and another lord named on a lintel from the Akab Tzib from Chichén Itzá *are both* named as vassal lords of Jawbone-Fan, who was a *K'ul Cocom* (Grube and Stuart 1987:8–10).

Archaeologically, Lincoln (1986) has noted the presence of Sotuta ceramics at Izamal.

It may well prove significant that both Chichén Itzá and Yaxuná, the frontier community of the Cobá state, are both roughly halfway between Izamal and Cobá. This is the zone of struggle between the Itzá and the kings of Cobá. As we have seen in the case of the great wars between Caracol, Tikal, and Naranjo, struggle between hegemonic Maya states could focus on the border communities between them—in their case Yaxha and Ucanal, which sat roughly halfway between Tikal and Caracol.

17. Calculation of the size of southern lowland kingdoms is still a tricky business (see Chapter 1). Peter Mathews (1985a and 1985b) posits that emblem-bearing polities constituted the principal states which claimed territorial domain over the smaller communities ruled by second-and third-rank nobility. On this basis, and taking into account exceptional conquest events such as Tikal's incorporation of Uaxactún, the largest southern lowland hegemonies were on the order of 2,500 square kilometers in size. Recently (April 1989), Arthur Demarest and Stephen Houston have suggested in oral reports that the kingdom of Dos Pilas may have encompassed 3,700 square kilometers. This remains to be confirmed though field investigation. Calculation of the size of the Cobá state at the time when the great causeway linking it to Yaxuná was built is based upon Robles and A. Andrews's map (1986: Fig. 3:4) and the following premises. First, Cobá controlled the coastlands directly fronting the kingdom on the east, some 25 kilometers distant from the capital. This information is based upon study of the distribution of distinctive ceramics of the Cobá Western Cepech Sphere relative to the distribution of Chichén-related Sotuta Sphere ceramics along that coast. Chichén Itzá evidently skirted the coast in front of Cobá when it established communities on the Island of Cozumel (see Freidel and Sabloff 1984; A. Andrews and Robles 1985).

Second, this estimate of kingdom size is calculated by allowing for a corridor of 25 kilometers surrounding the great causeway along its entire route. This figure provides us with a minimal support population for labor, sustenance, and defense during the construction. The timing of the construction of the causeway is equally tricky relative to the war between Chichén Itzá and Cobá. Robles (1980) places its construction at the beginning of the Terminal Classic period, about A.D. 800. We believe that the war between Cobá and Chichén Itzá was under way in earnest by the middle of the ninth century, for the spate of dedications defining Chichén Itzá's first major temples occurs between A.D. 860 and 880. Present evidence does not allow final resolution of the two possibilities: Either Cobá built the causeway in response to the incursion of the Itzá, as we have postulated in this chapter, or, alternatively, they built the causeway to declare a hegemonic kingdom prior to the Itzá threat. The latter possibility opens the intriguing prospect that the Itzá were posing as "liberators" of the central north, appealing to peoples already subjugated by Cobá. This was a tactic used frequently by conquerors in the ancient world. Sargon of Akkad "liberated" Sumer from rival indigenous hegemonic states in Mesopotamia.

18. The regalia of some lords of the Yaxuná polity shows a striking resemblance to that of lords in tribute procession at Chichén Itzá.

19. Research at Dzibilchaltún (E. W. Andrews IV and E. W. Andrews V 1980) documents a dramatic decline and eventual cessation of public construction with the arrival of Sotuta Sphere ceramics in the city. E. W. Andrews and E. W. Andrews (1980:274) place that arrival at about A.D. 1000, but since these diagnostic ceramics occur in above-floor deposits of earlier buildings, they warn that the A.D. 1000 date may be too late for the change. Our own scenario would place the collapse of Dzibilchaltún about 100 years earlier.

20. Recent excavations by the Centro Regional de Yucatán (of the Instituto Nacional Autónoma de México) show the presence of Sotuta Sphere ceramics in the main plaza areas of Uxmal (Tomas Gallareta N., personal communication, 1987).

21. The interpretation of events at Yaxuná and, through the Yaxuná record, of Chichén Itzá's wars with the Puuc cities and Cobá, is based upon ongoing research by Southern Methodist University, sponsored by the National Endowment for the Humanities, the National Geographic Society, and private donors (Freidel 1987).

22. The Advanced Seminar on the Maya Postclassic at the School of American Research, Santa Fe (Sabloff and E. W. Andrews V 1986), concentrated attention on this problem. See especially the contribution by Charles Lincoln (1986).

23. Tatiana Proskouriakoff (1970) firmly pointed out the fact that "Toltec" art was found in direct association with Maya hieroglyphic texts and questioned the then popular interpretation that the people who dominated Chichén Itzá at the time of the creation of this art were illiterate foreigners. There is no reason to suppose that any rulers of the Maya

before the European Conquest were illiterate, for all of the Maya kings used the calendrics predicated upon literacy as a political tool (Edmonson 1986). Further, the gold disks dredged from the sacred cenote, clearly pertaining to the late or "Toltec" period as identified by the iconography, have glyphic inscriptions (S. K. Lothrop 1952). A gold-handled bone bloodletter from the cenote (Coggins and Shane 1984) also carries a glyphic inscription. The fact that these objects are made from gold (a medium ignored by or unknown to Classic period kings) identifies them as late. Finally, Linea Wren (n.d.) and Ruth Krochock (1988) have reported the discovery of a portable hemispherical sacrificial stone from Chichén Itzá that carries a glyphic inscription. This stone also depicts a duplicate of the decapitation scenes that decorate the playing-wall panels of the Great Ballcourt, a clearly late Chichén building.

But the matter of the literacy of the audience of late Chichén Itzá, the city that built the final temples and courts of the great platform, is far from secure. As Charlot pointed out (Morris, Charlot, and Morris 1931), processional figures in the great assemblies of the northern center often have glyphlike emblems floating above their heads. For the most part, these are not identifiable as Maya glyphs. Some look like Mexican glyphs and others are indecipherable. Were these portrayed peoples truly illiterate, or were they simply complying with the current customs of Mesoamerican elite public display, in which literacy played no part? We can pose the question, but we cannot answer it yet.

24. Ruth Krochock (n.d.) must be credited with the fundamental identification of the simultaneity of participants in dedication rituals at Chichén, with particular reference to the lintels in the Temple of the Four Lintels. The family relationships posited in the following discussion are predicated principally upon the syllabic identification of *yitah,* the "sibling" relationship glyph linking protagonists into single generations (Stuart 1988a: Fig. 54g–i; personal communication, 1988), and upon "child of mother" and "mother of" relationships discussed by Krochock (1988).

25. The technical name for this building is Structure 3C1 in the nomenclature of the Carnegie Institution of Washington (Ruppert 1952:34).

26. This rather stunning insight was first presented in a graduate seminar on "Caching Rituals and Their Material Remains" held at the University of Texas at Austin, spring semester, 1989. Using the caches of the city as her clues and examining the archaeology of the High Priest's Grave, Annabeth Headrick proposed that this temple and the seven-lobed cave under it are early in Chichén's history and functioned as the prototype of later buildings to the north, such as the Castillo and the captive procession in front of the Temple of the Warriors.

The inscription on one of the inner columns (Lincoln 1986:Fig. 5:1) of the temple accompanies the image of a captive rendered in the style of the Temple of the Warriors columns. The Long Count for the 2 Ahau 18 Mol Calendar Round has been interpreted as 10.8.10.11.0 because that date falls within a katun ending on 2 Ahau, the last glyph in the text. However, the 2 Ahau does not occur within the expected formula phrase for Yucatec-style dates. We think it may simply refer to the opening Calendar Round date and not to the katun within which that date fell. In this alternative interpretation, the date of the column could as easily be 10.0.12.8.0 (July 3, 842) or 10.3.5.3.0 (June 7, 894). Furthermore, the earliest placement, 10.0.12.8.0 2 Ahau 18 Mol, has the virtue of making the date of the High Priest's Grave the earliest known date at Chichén Itzá. Headrick associated the cave under this temple with Chicomoztoc, the origin cave of seven lobes famous from Aztec myth. The presence of this cave points to the High Priest's Grave as an "origin" building in the cosmic landscape of Chichén Itzá, exactly as the cave under the Pyramid of the Sun at Teotihuacán marks it as an "origin" temple (Heyden 1981).

27. This new fire, called *suhuy kak,* "virgin fire," was described by Landa in his *Relación de Yucatán* (Tozzer 1941:153 155, 158) in association with a number of different ritual occasions, including the New Year ceremonies and the Festival of Kukulcan at Maní.

28. Ruth Krochock (1988) makes a persuasive case for the association of such sacrifice with the images on the Four Lintels. In the Chilam Balam books (Edmonson 1986), a great serpent deity at Chichén Itzá, named *hapay can,* "sucking snake," is said to have demanded many nobles from other communities as sacrificial victims.

29. James Fox (n.d.) recently identified this date as an important Jupiter date. In fact it is also a Saturn date, for Jupiter (253.81+) and Saturn (259.97+) had just begun to move after they had hung frozen against the star fields at their second stationary points for about forty days. This is the same hierophany recorded at Palenque on the 2 Cib 14 Mol house dedication and on Lady Xoc's bloodletting (Lintel 24) at Yaxchilán. David

Stuart (personal communication, 1989) noticed that the glyph appearing with the 2 Cib 14 Mol event (*pil* or *pul*) also recurs in the Casa Colorada text. Unfortunately, there it is recorded with the 7 Akbal event, which has no obvious astronomical associations.

30. Karl Ruppert (1952) has described the architecture at Chichén Itzá and provides a map showing the survey squares that are the basis for this nomenclature.

31. The Maya used stone axes in battle, but there are also abundant images documenting that the ax was also specifically a sacrificial instrument (Schele and M. Miller 1986).

32. These knives are especially evident in the sacrificial scenes of the gold battle disks (S. K. Lothrop 1952).

33. The final three glyphs in the names of the three persons to the left of the drawing are *uinic* titles. These titles declare that these men are *uinic,* that is to say, "men (in the sense of humans)" of a particular rank or location. Unfortunately, we do not yet know how to read that rank.

34. Patio Quad structures, also called Gallery Patio Structures, have several diagnostic features which can occur in varying combinations: (1) sunken central patios; (2) masonry shrines built against the back wall; (3) colonnaded front rooms; and (4) colonnades bordering the central patio. Generally, the plan of the building is square and the walls are of masonry. Based upon settlement location and associated excavated debris at Chichén Itzá, Freidel (1981b) proposed that these buildings are elite residences. These buildings occur rarely in the Maya area outside of Chichén Itzá. Examples are known at Nohmul in Belize (D. Chase and A. Chase 1982) and on Cozumel Island (Freidel and Sabloff 1984: Fig. 26a), but they also occur in the contemporary highland communities of México (e.g., in the Coxcatlan area, Sisson 1973).

35. Tatiana Proskouriakoff (1970) pointed out some time ago that the association of glyphic texts with typical "Toltec" images in the case of this building suggests that the patrons of the latest artistic and architectural programs of the city were not illiterate foreigners.

36. David Stuart (personal communication, 1987) pointed out to us a reference in Landa to a set of brothers who ruled at Chichén Itzá. They purportedly came from the west and built many beautiful temples in the city (Tozzer 1941:19, 177).

37. Ralph Roys (in Pollock et al. 1962) extensively discusses the political organization of the Mayapán Confederacy, which was ruled by this principle. Edmonson (1986) translates *multepal* as "crowd rule." Barrera Vasquez (1980:539–540, 785) glosses *multepal* as "united government (or confederation) that was prevalent during the dominion of Mayapán until the middle of the fifteenth century when a great revolution resulted in the destruction of that city." *Mul* is listed as "in combination, to do something communally or between many. . ." and "in a group." *Tepal* is "to reign and to govern."

38. Mayapán, although a relatively unspectacular ruin by Maya standards (J. Eric Thompson called it "a flash in the Maya pan"), has exceptionally well-preserved remains of buildings made with stone foundations and wooden superstructures. The Carnegie Institution of Washington (Pollock et al. 1962) carried out long-term work at the site, so we have a lot of information on its organization. Essentially, both Chichén Itzá and Mayapán show a central focus upon a four-sided pyramid associated with colonnaded halls. Although the halls at Mayapán are organized in a circle around the pyramid, while the halls at Chichén Itzá are to one side of its great northern central platform, neither of these arrangements is comparable to the vaulted masonry buildings found in Puuc cities and in the southern cities described in previous chapters. Contact-period colonnaded halls (Freidel and Sabloff 1984) functioned as assembly halls for men in public service, as schools for boys being trained in the arts of war and in the essentials of the sacred life, as dormitories for men fasting in preparation for festivals, and as quarters for militia. These halls were not the public residences of important people. Noble residences (Smith in Pollock et al. 1962) were to be found throughout the city of Mayapán. We have seen that the buildings which were equivalent to the colonnaded halls found in southern kingdoms, such as the Palace of Pacal at Palenque, were the public lineage houses of dynasties. Multepal, then, has its material expressions in the organization of the communities in which this form of government prevailed.

39. Ralph Roys (1962:78) gives the fall of Mayapán as occurring in a Katun 8 Ahau, ca. A.D. 1451.

40. The *cocom* reading was first identified in the texts of Chichén Itzá by Grube and Stuart (1987:10).

41. James Fox (1984b) identified this combination of signs as the Chichén Itzá Emblem Glyph.

42. Our interpretation of the architectural and artistic program of the Temple of the Warriors complex draws heavily upon the skill and brilliance of Jean Charlot, an artist and iconographer. Charlot, along with Ann Axtel Morris and Earl Morris (Morris et al. 1931), published articles on the bold and comprehensive architectural excavations and restorations carried out in these buildings by the Carnegie Institution of Washington earlier in this century. Charlot proposed the hypothesis that the reliefs are attempts at public portraiture. He based this evaluation upon the fact that the artists depicted individualistic detail both in the warriors' regalia and in their faces, where preserved. Charlot also noted the intriguing presence of glyphlike elements floating above a number of the individuals. These symbols are not recognizable as true Maya glyphs, but they do seem to distinguish these people one from another. It is perplexing that the artisans did not use known glyphs to convey such information, for the elite of Chichén Itzá were certainly aware of glyphic writing throughout the history of the city. Such late and diagnostic media as the gold battle disks and other gold artifacts from the cenote (S. K. Lothrop 1952) carry glyphic inscriptions.

43. Actual specimens of the throwing spears and the parry sticks were cast into the cenote at Chichén Itzá and were retrieved by modern scholars. They are housed in the museum in Mérida.

44. The Itzá Maya especially favored the goddess Ix-Chel, Lady Rainbow, consort of the high god Itzamna and the patroness of weaving, childbirth, sorcery, and medicine. The island of Cozumel was sacred to Ix-Chel at the time of the Conquest and was also a strategic sanctuary of an oracle of the goddess. Cozumel Island was controlled by the Itzá during the height of their power and the oracle may have originated during that time. The depictions of old women at Chichén include some with skull heads who are dancing with old Pauahtunob. These may well represent the goddess. The woman in this procession, however, is no doubt a real person just like the other portraits. Either she is a representative of the goddess, or possibly she is the matriarch of the principal sodality. Recall that the genealogies of Chichén Itzá describe the descent of the principal group of brothers from their mother and grandmother. In that case, the procession would have occurred in the time of the great captains who dedicated the lintels throughout the city.

45. Tozzer (1941:121) describes the binding of limbs with cotton-cloth armor in preparation for war.

46. This is the High Priest's Grave. The seven-lobed cave was reached by an artificial shaft, sealed by seven graves filled with bones and a wealth of sacred objects, such as rock crystals, jade, shell, clay vessels, and more (see Thompson 1938; Marquina 1964:895–896).

47. Landa in Tozzer (1941:93–94) describes this form of mock battle in the following way: "One is a game of reeds, and so they call it *Colomche,* which has that meaning. For playing it, a large circle of dancers is formed with their music, which gives them the rhythm, and two of them leap to the center of the wheel in time to it, one with a bundle of reeds [the shafts of throwing spears and arrows are so termed in this text], and he dances with these perfectly upright; while the other dances crouching down but both keeping within the limits of the circle. And he who has the sticks flings them with all his force at the second, who by the help of a little stick catches them with a great deal of skill."

48. This scenario is highly speculative, but it is also commensurate with the fact that the bound prisoners in processions at Chichén Itzá are usually displayed in full regalia and not stripped for sacrifice as in southern Classic depictions. One way to account for this iconography is to propose that there were ritual events that combined mock battle and formal sacrifice. The Maya at the time of the Spanish Conquest practiced arrow sacrifice which indeed did combine elements of battle and sacrifice (Tozzer 1941:118), but here the victim was stripped naked in Classic Maya fashion before being tied to a post.

The closest example of what we envision here is found at the Late Classic site of Cacaxtla in highland México (Foncerrada de Molina 1978; Kubler 1980). Here beautifully preserved polychrome-painted murals depict a sacrificial slaughter of battle captives. Some of the victims in this scenes are stripped, but others, including the leader of the losing side, wear full regalia and still carry shields. They are shown with gaping wounds in their flesh from knife and dart wounds and one is depicted dismembered at the waist. There is a sense of a dramatic public slaughter of captives taken in battle.

Although the Cacaxtla murals are a long way from the Maya lowlands, their iconography and style show clear connections to the Maya and they are roughly contemporary to or slightly earlier than Chichén Itzá. Badly ruined murals from the Puuc site of Mulchic (Barrera Rubio 1980:Fig. 3) include not only battle scenes, but also sacrificial scenes in which knife-wielding lords bend over a victim who is wearing an elaborate headdress. The body of the victim is eroded, but this headdress suggests that he was in full regalia at the time of sacrifice. This example is close enough in space and time to the Chichén Itzá context to offer encouragement that future discoveries of mural scenes in the northern lowlands will either confirm or disconfirm the existence of mock-battle sacrifice in the region. Meanwhile, we hold that the transformation of highborn captives from sacrificial victims to members of the confederacy is the most promising political hypothesis for the success of Chichén Itzá.

49. Arthur Miller (1977) coined these terms for the two major images in the murals of the Upper Temple of the Jaguars, one of the three buildings attached to the Great Ballcourt complex containing political imagery.

50. We are accepting that the Sun Disk at Chichén Itzá is equivalent to the "ancestor cartouche" of Classic period iconography to the south. The conjunction of images that leads us to this conclusion is found especially in the upper registers of stela imagery in the Late Classic period. At Yaxchilán, figures identified glyphically and by image as the mother and father of the protagonist sit in cartouches (Proskouriakoff 1961a:18, 1963–1964:163; Schele 1979:68; Stuart 1988:218–219) often shown with snaggle-toothed dragons in the four corners (see Fig. 10:2). In contrast to the Yaxchilán pattern, Caracol monuments show Vision Serpents emerging from bowls and sky bands in the upper register. Some of the people emerging from the open maw of these serpents are identified glyphically as the parents of the protagonists (Stone, Reents, and Coffman 1985:267–268). In Terminal Classic renditions, the serpent and the cartouche are replaced by dotted scrolls David Stuart (1984) identified as the blood from which the vision materializes. At Jimbal and Ucanal, the characters floating in these blood scrolls are the Paddler Gods and warriors carrying the regalia of Tlaloc war. At Chichén Itzá, the same spearthrower-wielding warriors emerge from Vision Serpents on the gold disks from the Cenote and from sun disks in the upper register of the Temple of the Warriors columns. To us, this consistent association of Vision Serpents, the Ancestor Cartouches, Blood/Vision Scrolls, and Warriors with spearthrower and darts form a cluster of ancestor-vision imagery, which includes Captain Sun Disk of the Chichén Itzá representations.

Several other scholars have also dealt with this imagery, but none have proposed the argument we present here. In a discussion of Yaxchilán Stela 1, David Stuart (1988:181) noted the correspondence between the ancestor cartouches of the Classic period and the Central Mexican sun disk. However, Stuart did not associate those ancestral images with the sun disk and Tlaloc-warrior presentations at Chichén Itzá. Charles Lincoln (n.d.) noted the correspondence between the Sun Disk at Chichén Itzá and the cartouches at Yaxchilán, but he argued that the disks at Yaxchilán are specifically dualistic and pertain to the sun and moon. Actually, Spindin (1913:91–92) got closest by associating the sun imagery of the Classic period ancestor cartouches with these sun disk icons from Chichén Itzá and suggested a Maya origin for both.

51. See Kelley (1982, 1983:205, and 1984) and Lincoln (1986:158) for arguments concerning these characters.

52. Ruth Krochock (1988) makes the persuasive case that the feathered serpent is, in fact, the Blood Vision Serpent of traditional Maya royal ritual. She suggests that the bird image connected with it might be related to the Principal Bird Deity, who is, in turn, linked with the World Tree. At the same time, there are strong associations between the eagle and heart sacrifice in Mexican religion.

53. Mary Miller and Stephen Houston (1987) have documented the fact that ballgame sacrifice took place on grand stairways outside of ballcourts.

54. This link between the ballgame and war was discussed in the context of Preclassic ballcourts at Cerros in Chapter 3. The people of Chichén Itzá and their enemies all used the ballgame as a metaphor for the wars they were fighting. At Chichén Itzá, a small ballcourt directly west of the Mercado Patio Quad hall has a bas-relief procession of warriors pushing captives before them (Ruppert 1952). This composition is nearly identical to a relief procession at the site of X'telhu, one of the satellites of Yaxuná, which shows the warriors wearing the skin apron and tight leather belt of the ballgame in one of its forms. At Yaxuná, the Ballcourt Complex is the only original construction dating to the Terminal Classic period when the war was waged. The severed head of the victim of sacrifice in the ballcourt or in ballgame ritual was closely associated by all of the contenders with the image of a skull from which waterlilies emerge. This skull with emerging waterlilies was a symbol of fertility and renewal (Freidel 1987). This head is at the center of the baseline in the battle scene illustrated here.

55. The skull-rack platform at Chichén Itzá has the standard form of such structures, but its walls are carved with the images of skulls set in rows. Tozzer (1957:218–219) associated this gruesome imagery with the practice of taking heads as trophies of war and relics of the dead, both of famous lords who died naturally and captives who died in sacrifice. The trophies from sacrificial rituals and battle were preserved on great wooden racks called *tzompantli* by the Aztec (Tozzer 1957:130–131) that were contructed in the most important sacred spaces at Tenochtitlan, the capital of the Aztecs, and at Chichén Itzá, the capital of the Itzá Maya.

56. These relationships, evidently linking three male individuals, are found on a monument from Uxmal described by Jeff Kowalski (1985b). He identified the glyph as a relationship, although Stuart's *itah* decipherment was not then known.

CHAPTER 10: THE END OF A LITERATE WORLD AND ITS LEGACY TO THE FUTURE

1. Tozzer (1941:28) quotes from Gaspar Antonio Chi, Landa's Yucatec informant: "They had written records of important things which had occurred in the past . . . the prognostications of their prophets and the lives of their lords; and for the common people, of certain songs in meter . . . according to the history they contained."

2. The Maya of the Postclassic period did enjoy commercial prosperity and brisk trade with peoples beyond their borders. Their homes were well built and their technology was generally on a par with that of their ancestors, although, unlike the Classic period peoples, they used metal. The lords of the Late Postclassic Maya, however, simply did not have the command of the social energy of their people that the lords of the Classic period could bring to bear on public works, especially central monumental architecture. It is not that these people were less devout than their ancestors: They built many shrines and temples, but these were as frequently dedicated to gods as to ancestors and as frequently found in homes as in centers. Some Mayanists regard this change not as a dissipation of energy so much as a reorientation to other goals, particularly the material well-being of the rising mercantile cadres, the *p'olomob*. Be that as it may, the Postclassic Maya who greeted the Spaniards were at best between eras of greatness.

3. The first systematic study of the collapse was conducted as a School of American Research seminar (Culbert 1973). Several recent books have concentrated on the problem of the collapse from the viewpoint of Teotihuacán's collapse in the eighth century (Diehl and Berlo 1989); from the viewpoint of Postclassic archaeology in northern Yucatán and the Petén (Sabloff and Andrews V 1986a); and as a worldwide phenomenon (Yoffee and Cowgill 1988).

4. The only such system to be excavated in the immediate vicinity of a center which rose and then collapsed, Cerros in Belize (Scarborough 1983), shows that the canals silted in beyond use within a century of the political abandonment.

5. This inscription includes the earliest known usage of a calendric name in a Classic Maya name phrase. This tradition of naming a child for the day in the tzolkin on which he was born was prominent among peoples of western Mesoamerica, such as the Zapotec, the Mixtec, the Cacaxtlanos, the Huastecs of El Tajín, and presumably, the Teotihuacanos, but the Classic Maya used an entirely different system. Since the clay in the pot came from the plain in front of Palenque, we suggest that the man whose accession is recorded in the text or perhaps the person who gave the vase to the Palencano lord in whose grave it was found was one of the Putún Maya.

6. Robert Rands (personal communication, 1975) discovered that the clay has chemical traces produced by the grasses out on the plain. It was manufactured in the region where the Putún Maya are thought to have lived.

7. Lauro José Zavala (1949) reported finding this skeleton in the rubble of the west end of south gallery of the House AD in the Palace. He speculated that the man was accidentally caught in the collapse of the vault and never dug out.

8. The portrayal of the captive lords of Pomoná in their anguish is intensely personal and intimate, among the finest portraits ever achieved by Maya artists. The artists's concentration on the victims leads Mary Miller to believe that they were vassals from the defeated town who were forced to carve this monument in tribute to their conquerors. If this was the case, then Pomoná at least survived as a place of skilled artisans until the opening of the ninth century A.D.

9. We met this Calakmul king in Chapter 4. He installed the first ruler of Naranjo

on his throne and he apparently sent a visitor to participate in rituals conducted by the contemporary king at Yaxchilán, who may have been an ally.

10. Demarest, Houston, and Johnson (1989) report that this log palisade was built around the central plaza of Dos Pilas during the last years of its occupation. They also report that Punta de Chamino, a site built on the end of a peninsula jutting into Lake Petexbatún, has massive fortifications across the neck of the peninsula. Warfare was endemic and highly destructive during the last years of the Petexbatún confederacy.

11. Jeff Kowalski (1989) has traced the Itzá style up the Usumacinta to Seibal and this set of late sites in the highlands of Chiapas.

12. The Classic diaspora into the adjacent highlands is subject to continued interest and interpretation. See John Fox (1980, 1989) and David Freidel (1985a) for some consideration of the issues.

13. The notable community here is Lamanai (Pendergast 1986), an ancient center and community which not only survived the collapse but continued to flourish up to the Spanish Conquest. Although clearly participants in the Maya elite world of the Classic period, Lamanai rulers raised few stelae during their history. But there is no certain correlation of historical kingship and the success or failure of government in Belize: Altun Ha, another center of great antiquity and wealth, never raised stelae and yet it succumbed in the time of the collapse. The Belizean situation underscores the fact that historical kingship was a major strategy of Maya governance, but not the only one. Maya centers rose and fell throughout the lowlands without raising stelae or declaring other public inscriptions. Yet at the same time, the correlation between the collapse of lowland society and the failure of historical kingship demonstrates the centrality of this institution, despite the examples of survival beyond the silencing of the historical record. Nevertheless, there are many and complex relationships between historical kings and their nonhistorical counterparts to be worked out in the future (see Freidel 1983).

14. Sabloff and Willey (1969) first suggested that Seibal's late florescence resulted from the intrusion and takeover by non-Petén foreigners. Rands (1973) suggested that the ceramics associated with that intruding group are related to the Fine Paste wares from the Palenque-Tabasco region. These foreigners appear to have been Thompson's Putún Maya (see note 18) who gave rise both to the Itzá of Yucatán and the invaders who took Fine Orange ceramics with them as they went up the Usumacinta River.

15. The four-sided pyramid is a very old architectural design among the Maya, going back into the Preclassic period at such sites as Tikal and Uaxactún. Although it occurs periodically throughout the Classic period, it seems to have enjoyed resurgence to a position of special prominence in the Terminal Classic period. See Fox (1989) for a discussion of the quadripartite principle in the consolidation of segmentary lineages into new states in the Postclassic period.

16. David Stuart (1987:25–26) first read the verb in this passage as *yilah,* "he saw it," and realized that the Seibal passage record a visit by foreign lords to participate in the period-ending rites conducted by Ah-Bolon-Tun.

17. See Jeff Kowalski's (1989) very useful comparison of the Seibal iconography to that of Chichén Itzá. In particular, Kowalski identifies an element called the "knife-wing" in the headdress of one of Ah-Bolon-Tun's stelae. This element is important in the serpent-bird of prophecy iconography of lintels at Chichén Itzá (Krochock 1988). This complex, in turn, ties into the Vision Serpent–ancestor iconography of Captain Sun Disk, described in this chapter.

18. Sabloff and Willey (1967) proposed that the southern lowlands might have experienced invasion by barbarians moving up the Western Rivers district at the time of the Collapse. One impressive pattern was the introduction of fine-paste wares from the Tabasco region in conjunction with the barbarian Maya stelae at Seibal. Thompson (1970:3–47) called these invaders Putún and proposed they were Chontal-speaking Maya who had lived in Tabasco for most of the Classic period. He suggested that they expanded upriver in the chaos at the end of the Classic period. Kowalski (1989) and Ball and Taschek (1989) accept Thompson's scenario and have added new support to the hypothesis.

19. Don Rice (1986:332) argued from ceramic, stylistic, and architectural evidence that the late occupants of Ixlú were intruders. Because the shape of the benches built inside the buildings at Ixlú resembles those of late Seibal, he (1986:336) suggested they migrated to Lake Petén-Itzá from Seibal.

20. Peter Mathews (1976) long ago showed the affinity of this Ixlú altar to a text on Stela 8 at Dos Pilas. This parallelism suggests that the Ixlú lords might have been refugees from the collapse of the Petexbatún state.

21. A column from Bonampak now in the St. Louis Art Museum names its Bonampak protagonist as the *yahau,* "subordinate lord," of the king of Toniná.

22. Mary Pohl (1983) has reviewed the archaeological evidence for the ceremonial caching of owls, noting that pygmy owls were favored by the Maya. The iconography of owls is not so specific as to require identification of the carved images as pygmy owls, but these are what the Maya deposited. Pygmy owls, according to Pohl, frequent the mouths of caves and hence inspire denotation as messengers from the Otherworld. These pygmy owls may refer to the bird of omen called *cuh* in Yucatec, Chol, and Tzeltal and the owl of the spearthrower-shield-owl title we first encountered with Jaguar-Paw, the conqueror of Uaxactún.

23. The Feathered Serpent could also be represented as a raptorial bird that tore out the hearts of sacrificial victims. The taloned-Kukulcan images that decorated the Temple of the Warriors display an ancestral head peering out from between its open beak, in an analog to Classic-period depictions of ancestors peering out of the mouth of the Vision Serpent.

24. See the discussions by Tatiana Proskouriakoff and Samuel K. Lothrop of these disks and their correspondences to southern lowland imagery and texts (Lothrop 1952).

25. Scholars have long recognized the significant impact of Maya influence on sites like Xochicalco and Cacaxtla. Now that we have recognized the place of Tlaloc warfare in Classic Maya imagery, we see that Chichén Itzá's representation of war is clearly not inspired by the Toltec, but by the Maya past. Tlaloc warfare as it is represented at Cacaxtla seems also to be inspired by the Maya model rather than that of Teotihuacán. Furthermore, as George Kubler suggested, Tula, Hidalgo, the capital of the Toltec, may well have emulated the Temple of the Warriors at Chichén Itzá rather the reverse. Mary Miller (1985) has shown that the famous Chac Mool figure of Postclassic Mesoamerica derives from Maya imagery of captives and sacrificial victims.

26. The word *can* also means "four" and "sky," so that the name also might have meant "four-star" or "sky-star." Avendaño (Stuart and Jones n.d.) said that the name meant "the star twenty serpent."

27. The accounts of the Conquest of the Itzá of Lake Petén-Itzá were published by Philip A. Means (1917). Dennis Puleston (1979) was the first to connect the prophesies of the Books of the Chilam Balam with Can-Ek's reaction and the newly recovered histories of the Classic period.

28. The trip we describe here is a new entrada recorded in a manuscript George Stuart discovered in 1989. He provided us with a copy of the transcription, translations, and the commentary written by Grant Jones (Stuart and Jones n.d.) and has very graciously allowed us to use the events of the entrada and the description of Can-Ek contained in this document.

29. The size difference between the elite and commoners is one that is documented from Preclassic times onward. Can-Ek's light complexion may have resulted from a life-style that kept him out of the fierce tropical sun far more than his subordinates.

30. The cloth of costumes in the Bonampak murals also have glyphs drawn on them, and the ahaus in the first room wear ankle-long white capes amazingly like Avendaño's description.

31. Avendaño (Means 1917:128) says, "We had to observe and wonder on some rocks or buildings on some high places—so high that they were almost lost to sight. And when we caught sight of them clearly, the sun shining on them in full, we took pleasure in seeing them; and we wondered at their height, since without any exaggeration it seemed impossible that work could have been done by hand, unless it was with the aid of the devil, whom they say they adore there in the form of a noted idol."

32. This and all other direct quotations come from Avendaño's own description of this entrada as they were translated by Means (1917).

33. Avendaño's description (Means 1917:137) is full of the irritation the Spanish felt at the uninvited and intimate attention.

34. This episode (Means 1917:140) recalls the threats presented by the Chacans in Avendaño's first visit.

35. This episode is recorded in Means (1917:140).

36. This 12.3.19.11.14 1 Ix 17 Kankin date is March 13, 1697, in the Gregorian calendar. In the Julian calendar, this day fell on 12.3.19.11.4 4 Kan 7 Kankin.

37. Dennis Puleston (1979) first connected this particular prophecy to Can-Ek's surrender and tried to show that the katun prophecies of the Books of the Chilam Balam were derived at least partially from Classic and Postclassic history. He suggested that

Can-Ek's fatalism was characteristic of Prehispanic Maya historical thought also. The imminent arrival of Katun 8 Ahau was just as likely to have been the stimulus. 8 Ahau is repeatedly associated with the collapse of kingdoms and the change of governments.

38. See Tozzer (1941, 77–78) for discussion of the suppression of Maya native literature.

39. Martín was the director of the Proyecto Lingüistico "Francisco Marroquín," an organization started in the 1960s to train native speakers in linguistics so that they could record and study their own languages.

40. Nicholas Hopkins and Kathryn Josserand also helped give the workshop. Nora England of the University of Iowa translated the English version of the workbook into Spanish with the help of Lola Spillari de López. Steve Eliot of CIRMA printed and reproduced the Spanish-version workbook and CIRMA provided support and a room for workshop sessions.

41. In 1989, Linda Schele returned to Antigua to give a second workshop. An extra day added to the workshop gave time to finish the full analysis of the Tablet of the 96 Glyphs. The final session heard a translation of that inscription read in all the languages of participants—English, Spanish, Classical Maya, Chorti, Pocoman, Cakchiquel, Quiche, Achi, Ixil, Mam, Jalcaltec, and Kanhobal.

42. The correlation we have used throughout this book set 594,285 days between the zero date in the Maya calendar and the zero date in the Julian calendar, January 1, –4712. Although we believe this is the correct correlation, it is two days out of agreement with the calendars that are still maintained by the Maya of the Guatemala highlands. The correlation that brings the ancient and modern calendars into agreement sets 584,283 days between the two zero dates. In this second correlation, July 23, 1987, falls on 12.18.14.3.17 3 Caban 5 Xul.

GLOSSARY OF GODS AND ICONS

1. See Cortez (1986) for a full discussion of the Principal Bird Deity in Late Preclassic and Early Classic contexts.

2. In this scene, Chac-Xib-Chac rises from the waters of the Underworld in a visual representation of the first appearance of the Eveningstar (Schele and M. Miller 1986: Pl. 122). GI of the Palenque Triad, who shares many features with Chac-Xib-Chac, is also associated with Venus, principally through his birth date, 9 Ik, a day associated with Venus throughout Mesoamerican mythology. Hun-Ahau of the Headband Twins is yet another aspect of Venus for he shows up in the Dresden Codex as a manifestation of Morningstar. All three of these gods are thus associated with one or another apparition of Venus and may represent different aspects of the same divine being.

3. Thompson (1934 and 1970b) thoroughly discussed these directional sets of gods and their associations. M.D. Coe (1965) associated this directional organization of gods with the functions and layouts of Yucatecan villages. He (Coe 1973:14–15) also demonstrated that the gods identified by Thompson as bacabs are the Pauahtuns of the codices and ethnohistorical sources.

4. This palace scene with the Young Goddesses of Two and the rabbit scribe is painted on a pot now in the Princeton University Museum (Schele and M. Miller 1986:115a). The creation on 4 Ahau 8 Cumku is depicted on the Pot of the Seven Gods (M.D. Coe 1973:106–109).

5. See Taube (1985) for a full discussion of the Maize God and his place in Classic Maya iconography.

6. Examples of the Paddlers in the inscriptions of Copán represent the Old Stingray God with *kin* signs on his cheeks and the Old Jaguar God with *akbal* signs (Schele 1987f).

7. The alphabetic designations of god images derive from a distributional study of gods and their name glyphs in the Dresden Codex. Not wishing to presume the meaning of the names, Schellhas (1904) used the alphabet as a neutral designation system.

8. See David Stuart (1987b:15–16).

9. David Stuart (1988c and 1984) outlined much of the evidence linking the Serpent Bar to the symbolism of the vision rites.

10. David Stuart (1988c) first outlined how this merging of images and functions is distributed in Maya images.

REFERENCES

1971 *The Compact Edition of the Oxford English Dictionary.* Vol. I. Oxford University.

ABERLE, DAVID F.
1987 Distinguished Lecture: What Kind of Science Is Anthropology? *American Anthropologist* 89(3):551–566.

ADAMS, RICHARD E. W., WALTER E. BROWN, AND T. PATRICK CULBERT
1981 Radar Mapping, Archaeology, and Ancient Maya Land Use. *Science* 213:1457–1463.

ANDREWS, ANTHONY P.
1978 Puertos costeros del Postclásico Temprano en el norte de Yucatán. *Estudios de Cultura Maya* 11:75–93. México: Universidad Nacional Autónoma de México.

ANDREWS, ANTHONY P., FRANK ASARO, AND PURA CERVERA RIVERO
n.d. The Obsidian Trade at Isla Cerritos, Yucatán, México. *Journal of Field Archaeology* (in press).

ANDREWS, ANTHONY P., TOMÁS GALLARETA N., FERNANDO ROBLES C., RAFAEL COBOS P.
1984 *Isla Cerritos Archaeological Project: A Report of the 1984 Field Season,* Report submitted to the Committee for Research and Exploration, National Geographic Society, Washington, D.C.

ANDREWS, ANTHONY P., AND FERNANDO ROBLES C.
1985 Chichén Itzá and Cobá: An Itzá-Maya Standoff in Early Postclassic Yucatán. In *The Lowland Maya Postclassic,* edited by Arlen F. Chase and Prudence M. Rice, 62–72. Austin: University of Texas Press.

ANDREWS, E. WYLLYS, IV
1965 Archaeology and Prehistory in the Northern Maya Lowlands: An Introduction. In *Handbook of Middle American Indians,* Vol. 2, edited by Robert Wauchope and Gordon R. Willey, 288–330. Austin: University of Texas Press.
1973 The Development of Maya Civilization After Abandonment of the Southern Cities. In *The Classic Maya Collapse,* edited by T. Patrick Culbert, 243–265. A School of American Research Book. Albuquerque: University of New Mexico Press.

ANDREWS, E. WYLLYS, IV, AND E. WYLLYS ANDREWS V
1980 Excavations at Dzibilchaltún, Yucatán, México. *Middle American Research Institute* Pub. 48. New Orleans: Tulane University.

ANDREWS, E. WYLLYS, V
1981 Dzibilchaltún. In *Supplement to the Handbook of Middle American Indians* 1, edited by Victoria Bricker and Jeremy A. Sabloff with the assistance of Patricia Andrews, 313–344. Austin: University of Texas Press.

ANDREWS, E. WYLLYS, V, AND JEREMY A. SABLOFF
1986 Classic to Postclassic: A Summary Discussion. In *Late Lowland Maya Civilization,* edited by Jeremy A. Sabloff and E. Wyllys Andrews V, 433–456. A School of American Research Book. Albuquerque: University of New Mexico Press.

ANDREWS, E.WYLLYS, V, AND JEREMY A. SABLOFF, EDITORS
1986a *Late Lowland Maya Civilization.* A School of American Research Book. Albuquerque: University of New Mexico Press.

ASHMORE, WENDY
1981 *Lowland Maya Settlement Patterns,* edited by W. Ashmore. A School of American Research Book. Albuquerque: University of New Mexico Press.

AULIE, H. WILBUR, AND EVELYN W. DE AULIE
1978 Diccionario Ch'ol-Español: Español-Ch'ol. *Serie de Vocabulario y Diccionarios Indigenas "Mariano Silva y Aceves" 21.* México: Instituto Lingüístico de Verano.

AYALA FALCÓN, MARISELA
n.d. El bulto ritual de Mundo Perdido, Tikal, y los bultos mayas. A MS in the possession of the authors.

BALL, JOSEPH
1974a A Coordinate Approach to Northern Maya Prehistory: A.D. 700–1000. *American Antiquity* 39 (1):85–93.
1974b A Teotihuacán-style Cache from the Maya Lowlands. *Archaeology* 27:2–9.
1979 Southeastern Campeche and the Mexican Plateau: Early Classic Contact Situation. *Actes du XXII Congrès International de Américanistes* 8:271–280. Paris.
1983 Teotihuacán, the Maya, and Ceramic Interchange: A Contextual Perspective. In *Highland-Lowland Interaction in Mesoamerica: Interdisciplinary Approaches,* edited by Arthur G. Miller, 125–146. Washington, D.C.: Dumbarton Oaks Research Library and Collection.
1986 Campeche, the Itzá, and the Postclassic: A Study in Ethnohistorical Archaeology. In *Late Lowland Maya Civilization, Classic to Postclassic,* edited by Jeremy A. Sabloff and E. Wyllys Andrews V, 379–408. A School of American Research Book. Albuquerque: University of New Mexico Press.
1989 Ceramics of the Lowlands. A paper presented at the Dumbarton Oaks Conference, "At the Eve of the Collapse: Ancient Maya Societies in the Eighth Century A.D.," held on October 7–8, 1989.

BALL, JOSEPH, AND JENNIFER TASCHEK
1989 Teotihuacán's Fall and the Rise of the Itzá: Realignments and Role Changes in the Terminal Classic Maya Lowlands. In *Mesoamerica After the Decline of Teotihuacán: A.D. 700–900,* edited by Richard Diehl and Janet Berlo, 187–200. Washington, D.C.: Dumbarton Oaks Research Library and Collection.

BARRERA RUBIO, ALFREDO
1980 Mural Paintings of the Puuc Region in Yucatán. In *Third Palenque Round Table, 1978,* edited by Merle Greene Robertson, 173–182. Austin: University of Texas Press.

BARRERA VASQUEZ, ALFREDO
1980 *Diccionario Maya Cordemex, Maya-Español, Español-Maya.* Mérida: Ediciones Cordemex.

BAUDEZ, CLAUDE F., AND ANNE S. DOWD
1983 La decoración de Templo 18. In *Introducción a la arqueología de Copán, Honduras,* Tomo II, 447–500. Tegucigalpa: Instituto Hondureño de Antropología e Historia.

BAUDEZ, CLAUDE F., AND PETER MATHEWS
1979 Capture and Sacrifice at Palenque. *Tercera Mesa Redonda de Palenque,* edited by Merle Greene Robertson and Donnan Call Jeffers, 31–40. Palenque: Pre-Columbian Art Research, and Monterey: Herald Printers.

BENAVIDES C., ANTONIO
1981 *Los Caminos de Cobá y sus implicaciones sociales.* México: Instituto Nacional de Antropología e Historia.

BERLIN, HEINRICH
1958 El glifo "emblema" en las inscripciones mayas. *Journal de la Société des Américanistes,* n.s. 47:111–119. Paris.

REFERENCES

510

1959 Glifos nominales en el sarcófago de Palenque. *Humanidades* 2(10):1–8. Guatemala: Universidad de San Carlos de Guatemala.

1963 The Palenque Triad. *Journal de la Société des Américanistes,* n.s. 52:91–99. Paris.

1968 Estudios Epigraphicos II. *Antropología e Historia de Guatemala, vol. xx, no. 1,* 13–24. Guatemala: Instituto de Antropología e Historia de Guatemala.

1970 Miscelánea palencano. *Journal de la Société des Américanistes,* LIX:107–135.

1973 Contribution to the Understanding of the Inscriptions of Naranjo. *Bulletin de la Société Suisse des Américanistes* 37:7–14. Translated by Christopher Jones.

1977 *Signos y significados en las inscripciones mayas.* Guatemala: Instituto Nacional del Patrimonia Cultural de Guatemala.

BERLO, JANET

1976 The Teotihuacán Trapeze and Ray Sign: A Study of the Diffusion of Symbols. M.A. thesis, Department of the History of Art, Yale University.

BERNAL, IGNACIO

1969 *100 Masterpieces of the Mexican National Museum of Anthropology.* New York: Harry N. Abrams, Inc.

BEYER, HERMANN

1937 Studies of the Inscriptions of Chichén Itzá. In *Contributions to American Archaeology No. 21. Carnegie Institution of Washington Pub. 483.* Washington, D.C.

BRICKER, VICTORIA

1986 A Grammar of Mayan Hieroglyphs. *Middle American Research Institute Pub. 56.* New Orleans: Middle American Research Institute, Tulane University.

n.d. The Last Gasp of Maya Hieroglyphic Writing in the Books of Chilam Balam of Chumayel and Chan Kan. In *Word and Image in Maya Culture,* edited by William Hanks and Don Rice. Salt Lake City: University of Utah Press (in press).

BROWN, KENNETH L.

1977 The Valley of Guatemala: A Highland Port of Trade. In *Teotihuacán and Kaminaljuyu: A Study in Prehistoric Culture Contact,* edited by William T. Sanders and Joseph W. Michels, 1–204. *The Pennsylvania State University Press Monograph Series on Kaminaljuyu.* University Park: Pennsylvania State University Press.

CABRERA CASTRO, RUBÉN, SABURO SUGIYAMA, AND GEORGE COWGILL

1988 Summer 1988 Discoveries at the Feathered Serpent Pyramid. A paper presented at the 1988 Dumbarton Oaks Conference on "Art, Polity, and the City of Teotihuacán."

CARLSON, JOHN

1977 Copán Altar Q: the Maya Astronomical Conference of A.D. 763? In *Native American Astronomy,* edited by Anthony Aveni, 100–109. Austin: University of Texas Press.

CARR, H. S.

1986a Faunal Utilization in a Late Preclassic Maya Community at Cerros, Belize. Ph.D. dissertation, Department of Anthropology, Tulane University.

1986b Preliminary Results of Analysis of Fauna. In *Archaeology at Cerros, Belize, Central America, Vol. 1, An Interim Report,* edited by R. A. Robertson and D. A. Freidel, 127–146. Dallas: Southern Methodist University Press.

CHASE, ARLEN F.

n.d. Cycles of Time: Caracol and the Maya Realm. In *Sixth Palenque Round Table, 1986, Vol. VII,* edited by Merle Robertson. Norman: University of Oklahoma Press (in press).

CHASE, ARLEN F., AND DIANE Z. CHASE

1987a Investigations at the Classic Maya City of Caracol, Belize: 1985–1987. *Pre-Columbian Art Research Institute, Monograph 3.* San Francisco: Pre-Columbian Art Research Institute.

1987b *Glimmers of a Forgotten Realm: Maya Archaeology at Caracol, Belize.* Orlando: University of Central Florida.

CHASE, DIANE Z., AND ARLEN F. CHASE

1982 Yucatec Influence in Terminal Classic Northern Belize. *American Antiquity* 47:- 596–614.

1986 *Offerings to the Gods: Maya Archaeology at Santa Rita, Corozal.* Orlando: University of Central Florida.

1989 Caracol Update: Recent Work at Caracol, Belize. A paper presented at the Seventh Round Table of Palenque, held in Palenque, Chiapas, México, in June 1989.

CHEEK, CHARLES

1977 Excavations at the Palangana and the Acropolis, Kaminaljuyu. *Teotihuacán and Kaminaljuyu: A Study in Prehistoric Culture Contact,* edited by William T. Sanders and Joseph W. Michels. The Pennsylvania State University Press Monograph Series on Kaminaljuyu. University Park: Pennsylvania State University Press.

1983 Excavaciones el la Plaza Principal. *Introducción a la Arqueología de Copán, Honduras. Tomo II,* 191–290. Tegucigalpa: Instituto Hondureño de Antropología e Historia.

CLIFF, MAYNARD B.

1986 Excavations in the Late Preclassic Nucleated Village. In *Archaeology at Cerros, Belize, Central America, Vol. 1, An Interim Report,* edited by R. A. Robertson and D. A. Freidel, 45–63. Dallas: Southern Methodist University Press.

CLOSS, MICHAEL

1979 Venus in the Maya World: Glyphs, Gods and Associated Phenomena. In *Tercera Mesa Redonda de Palenque, Vol. IV,* edited by Merle Greene Robertson and Donnan Call Jeffers, 147–172. Palenque: Pre-Columbian Art Research Center.

1985 The Dynastic History of Naranjo: The Middle Period. In *The Palenque Round Table Series, Vol. VII,* gen. editor, Merle Greene Robertson; vol. editor, Virginia M. Fields, 65–78. San Francisco: The Pre-Columbian Art Research Institute.

COE, MICHAEL D.

1960 Archaeological Linkages with North and South America at La Victoria, Guatemala. *American Anthropologist* 62:363–393.

1965 A Model of Ancient Community Structure in the Maya Lowlands. *Southwestern Journal of Anthropology* 21:97–114.

1973 *The Maya Scribe and His World.* New York: The Grolier Club.

1978 *Lords of the Underworld: Masterpieces of Classic Maya Ceramics.* Princeton: The Art Museum, Princeton University.

1982 *Old Gods and Young Heroes: The Pearlman Collection of Maya Ceramics.* Jerusalem: The Israel Museum.

COE, WILLIAM R.

1959 Piedras Negras Archaeology: Artifacts, Caches, and Burials. *University Museum Monograph 18.* Philadelphia: University of Pennsylvania.

1965a Tikal, Guatemala, and Emergent Maya Civilization. *Science.* 147:1401–1419.

1965b Tikal: Ten Years of Study of a Maya Ruin in the Lowlands of Guatemala. *Expedition* 8:5–56.

1967 *Tikal: A Handbook of Ancient Maya Ruins.* Philadelphia: University Museum, University of Pennsylvania.

COGGINS, CLEMENCY

1976 *Painting and Drawing Styles at Tikal: An Historical and Iconographic Reconstruction.* Ann Arbor: University Microfilms.

1979a A New Order and the Role of the Calendar: Some Characteristics of the Middle Classic Period at Tikal. In *Maya Archaeology and Ethnohistory,* edited by Norman Hammond and Gordon R. Willey, 38–50. Austin: University of Texas Press.

1979b Teotihuacán at Tikal in the Early Classic Period. *Actes de XLII Congrès International des Américanistes* 8:251–269. Paris.

1983 An Instrument of Expansion: Monte Alban, Teotihuacán, and Tikal. In *Highland-Lowland Interaction in Mesoamerica: Interdisciplinary Approaches,* edited by Arthur G. Miller, 49–68. Washington, D.C.: Dumbarton Oaks Research Library and Collection.

n.d. There's No Place Like *Hom.* A paper presented at "Elite Interaction Among the Classic Maya," a seminar held at the School of American Research, Santa Fe, October 1986.

COGGINS, CLEMENCY C., AND ORRIN C. SHANE III

1984 *Cenote of Sacrifice: Maya Treasures from the Sacred Well at Chichén Itzá.* Austin: University of Texas Press.

CORTEZ, CONSTANCE

1986 The Principal Bird Deity in Late Preclassic and Early Classic Maya Art. M.A. thesis, University of Texas at Austin.

COWGILL, GEORGE L.

1979 Teotihuacán, Internal Militaristic Competition, and the Fall of the Classic Maya. In *Maya Archaeology and Ethnohistory,* edited by Norman Hammond and Gordon

R. Willey, 51–62. Austin: University of Texas Press.

CRANE, C. J.

1986 Late Preclassic Maya Agriculture, Wild Plant Utilization, and Land-Use Practices. In *Archaeology at Cerros, Belize, Central America, Vol. 1, An Interim Report,* edited by R. A. Robertson and D. A. Freidel, 147–166. Dallas: Southern Methodist University Press.

CROCKER-DELATAILLE, LIN

1985 The Maya. In *Rediscovered Masterpieces of Precolumbian Art.* Boulogne, France: Editions Arts 135.

CULBERT, T. PATRICK

1973 *The Classic Maya Collapse,* edited by T. Patrick Culbert. A School of American Research Book. Albuquerque: University of New Mexico Press.

1977 Early Maya Development at Tikal, Guatemala. In *The Origins of Maya Civilization,* edited by Richard E. W. Adams, 27–43. A School of American Research Book. Albuquerque: The University of New Mexico Press.

1988 The Collapse of Classic Maya Civilization. In *The Collapse of Ancient States and Civilizations,* edited by Norman Yoffee and George L. Cowgill, 69–101. Tucson: The University of Arizona Press.

DAVOUST, M.

1977 *Les chefs mayas de Chichén Itzá.* A manuscript circulated by the author. Angiers, France.

1980 Les premiers chefs mayas de Chichén Itzá. *Mexicon* II(2), May.

DEMAREST, ARTHUR A.

1986 The Archaeology of Santa Leticia and the Rise of Maya Civilization. *Middle American Research Institute* Pub. 52. New Orleans: Tulane University.

DIEHL, RICHARD A.

1981 Tula. In *Supplement to the Handbook of Middle American Indians,* gen. editor, Victoria R. Bricker; vol. editor, Jeremy A. Sabloff, with the assistance of Patricia A. Andrews, 277–295. Austin: University of Texas Press.

DIEHL, RICHARD A., AND JANET C. BERLO, EDITORS

1989 *Mesoamerica After the Decline of Teotihuacán: A.D. 700–900.* Washington, D.C.: Dumbarton Oaks Research Library and Collection.

DILLON, BRIAN

1982 Bound Prisoners in Maya Art. *Journal of New World Archaeology* 5(1):24–45. Los Angeles: Institute of Archaeology, University of California at Los Angeles.

DRANE, JOHN W.

1983 *The Old Testament Story: An Illustrated Documentary.* San Francisco: Harper & Row, Publishers.

DÜTTING, DIETER, AND ANTHONY F. AVENI

1982 The 2 Cib 14 Mol Event in the Palenque Inscriptions. *Zeitschrift für Ethnologie* 107. Branschweig.

EDMONSON, MUNRO

1965 Quiche-English Dictionary. *Middle American Research Institute, Tulane University,* Pub. 30. New Orleans.

1971 The Book of Counsel: The Popol Vuh of the Quiche Maya of Guatemala. *Middle American Research Institute, Tulane University,* Pub. 35. New Orleans.

1982 *The Ancient Future of the Itzá: The Book of Chilam Balam of Tizimin.* Austin: University of Texas Press.

1986 *Heaven Born Mérida and Its Destiny: The Book of Chilam Balam of Chumayel.* Austin: University of Texas Press.

ELIADE, MIRCEA

1970 *Shamanism: Archaic Techniques of Ecstasy.* Translated from the French by Willard R. Trask. Bollingen Series LXXVI. Princeton: Princeton University Press.

FAHSEN, FEDERICO

1987 A Glyph for Self-Sacrifice in Several Maya Inscriptions. *Research Reports on Ancient Maya Writing 11.* Washington, D.C.: Center for Maya Research.

1988a A New Early Classic Text from Tikal. *Research Reports on Ancient Maya Writing 17.* Washington, D.C.: Center for Maya Research.

1988b Los personajes de Tikal en el Clásico Temprano: la evidencia epigráfica. In *Primer Simposio Mundial Sobre Epigrafía Maya,* 47–60. Guatemala City: Asociación Tikal.

FARRIS, NANCY M.
1984 *Maya Society Under Colonial Rule: The Collective Enterprise of Survival.* Princeton: Princeton University Press.
FASH, BARBARA
n.d. Temple 20 and the House of Bats. A paper presented at the Seventh Round Table of Palenque, in Palenque, Chiapas, México, June 1989.
FASH, BARBARA, WILLIAM FASH, SHEREE LANE, RUDY LARIOS, LINDA SCHELE, AND DAVID STUART
n.d. Classic Maya Community Houses and Political Evolution: Investigations of Copán Structure 22A. A paper submitted to the *Journal of Field Archaeology.* September 1989.
FASH, WILLIAM
1983a Classic Maya State Formation: A Case Study and Its Implications. Ph.D. dissertation, Department of Anthropology, Harvard University.
1983b Deducing Social Organization from Classic Maya Settlement Patterns: A Case Study from the Copán Valley. In *Civilization in the Ancient Americas: Essays in Honor of Gordon R. Willey,* edited by Richard M. Leventhal and Alan L. Kolata, 261–288. Albuquerque: University of New Mexico Press, and Cambridge: Peabody Museum of Archaeology and Ethnology, Harvard University.
1983c Reconocimiento y excavaciones en el valle. *Introducción a la arqueología de Copán, Honduras,* 229–470. Tegucigalpa: Instituto Hondureño de Antropología e Historia.
1985 La secuencia de ocupación del Grupo 9N-8, Las Sepulturas, Copán, y sus implicaciones teóricas. *Yaxkin* VIII:135–149. Honduras: Instituto Hondureño de Antropología e Historia.
1986 La fachada de la Estructura 9N-82: composición, forma e iconografía. In *Excavaciones en el area urbana de Copán,* 157–319. Tegucigalpa: Secretaria de Cultura y Turismo, Instituto Hondureño de Antropología e Historia.
1989 The Sculpture Facade of Structure 9N-82: Content, Form, and Meaning. In *The House of the Bacabs,* edited by David Webster. Washington, D.C.: Dumbarton Oaks Research Library and Collection.
n.d. A Middle Formative Cemetery from Copán, Honduras. A paper delivered at the annual meeting of the American Anthropological Association, 1982. Copy in possession of the authors.
FASH, WILLIAM, AND LINDA SCHELE
1986 The Inscriptions of Copán and the Dissolution of Centralized Rule. A paper given at the symposium on "The Maya Collapse: The Copán Case" at the Fifty-first Meeting of the Society of American Archaeology, New Orleans.
FASH, WILLIAM, AND DAVID STUART
n.d. Interaction and Historical Process in Copán. In *Classic Maya Political History: Archaeological and Hieroglyphic Evidence,* edited by T. P. Culbert. A School of American Research Book. Cambridge: Cambridge University Press (in press).
FIALKO, VILMA
1988 El Marcador de Juego de Pelota de Tikal: nuevas referencias epigráficas para el Clásico Temprano. In *Primer Simposio Mundial Sobre Epigrafía Maya,* 61–80. Guatemala City: Asociatión Tikal.
FIELDS, VIRGINIA
n.d. Political Symbolism Among the Olmecs. An unpublished paper on file, Department of Art History, University of Texas, Austin, dated 1982.
FOLAN, WILLIAM J., ELLEN R. KINTZ, AND LORAINE A. FLETCHER
1983 *Cobá: A Classic Maya Metropolis.* New York: Academic Press.
FOLAN, WILLIAM J., AND GEORGE E. STUART
1977 El Proyecto Cartográfico Arqueológico de Cobá, Quintana Roo: Informes Interinos Numeros 1,2, y 3, *Boletín de la Escuela de Ciencias Antropológicas de la Universidad de Yucatán* 4(22–23):15–71.
FOLLETT, PRESCOTT H. F.
1932 War and Weapons of the Maya. In *Middle American Papers. Middle American Research Series 4,* edited by Maurice Ries, 373–410. New Orleans: Tulane University.
FONCERRADA DE MOLINA, MARTA
1978 La pintura mural de Cacaxtla. *Anales del Instituto de Investigaciones Estéticas* 46. México: Universidad Nacional Autónoma de México.

FOX, JAMES

1984a Polyvalance in Maya Hieroglyphic Writing. In *Phoneticism in Mayan Hieroglyphic Writing*, edited by John Justeson and Lyle Campbell, 17–76. Albany: Institute for Mesoamerican Studies, State University of New York.

1984b The Hieroglyphic Band in the Casa Colorada. A paper presented at the American Anthropological Association, November 17, 1984, Denver, Colorado.

n.d. Some Readings Involving Dates at Chichén Itzá. A paper presented at "The Language of the Maya Hieroglyphs," a conference held at the University of California at Santa Barbara, February 1989.

FOX, JOHN W.

1980 Lowland to Highland Mexicanization Processes in Southern Mesoamerica. *American Antiquity* 45(1):43–54.

1987 *Maya Postclassic State Formation: Segmentary Lineage Migration in Advancing Frontiers.* Cambridge: Cambridge University Press.

1989 On the Rise and Fall of *Tuláns* and Maya Segmentary States. *American Anthropologist* 91(3):656–681.

FREIDEL, DAVID A.

1978 Maritime Adaptation and the Rise of Maya Civilization: The View from Cerros, Belize. In *Prehistoric Coastal Adaptations,* edited by B. Stark and B. Voorhies, 239–265. New York: Academic Press.

1979 Cultural Areas and Interaction Spheres: Contrasting Approaches to the Emergence of Civilization in the Maya Lowlands. *American Antiquity* 44:6–54.

1981a Civilization as a State of Mind: The Cultural Evolution of the Lowland Maya. In *The Transition to Statehood in the New World,* edited by Grant D. Jones and Robert Kautz, 188–227. Cambridge: Cambridge University Press.

1981b Continuity and Disjunction: Late Postclassic Settlement Patterns in Northern Yucatán. In *Lowland Maya Settlement Patterns,* edited by Wendy Ashmore, 311–332. A School of American Research Book. Albuquerque: University of New Mexico Press.

1981c The Political Economics of Residential Dispersion Among the Lowland Maya. In *Lowland Maya Settlement Patterns,* edited by Wendy Ashmore, 371–382. A School of American Research Book. Albuquerque: University of New Mexico Press.

1983 Political Systems in Lowland Yucatán: Dynamics and Structure in Maya Settlement. In *Prehistoric Settlement Patterns: Essays in Honor of Gordon R. Willey*, edited by Evon Z. Vogt and Richard M. Leventhal, 375–386. Albuquerque: University of New Mexico Press, and Cambridge: Peabody Museum of Archaeology and Ethnology, Harvard University.

1985 Polychrome Facades of the Lowland Maya Preclassic. In *Painted Architecture and Polychrome Monumental Sculpture in Mesoamerica,* edited by E. Boone, 5–30. Washington, D.C.: Dumbarton Oaks Research Library and Collection.

1985s New Light on the Dark Age: A Summary of Major Themes. In *The Lowland Maya Postclassic*, edited by Arlen F. Chase and Prudence M. Rice, 285–309. Austin: University of Texas Press.

1986a Terminal Classic Lowland Maya: Successes, Failures, and Aftermaths. In *Late Lowland Maya Civilization: Classic to Postclassic,* edited by Jeremy A. Sabloff and E. Wyllys Andrews V, 409–430. A School of American Research Book. Albuquerque: University of New Mexico Press.

1986b Introduction. In *Archaeology at Cerros, Belize, Central America, Vol. 1: An Interim Report,* edited by Robin A. Robertson and David A. Freidel, xiii–xxii. Dallas: Southern Methodist University Press.

1986c The Monumental Architecture. In *Archaeology at Cerros, Belize, Central America, Vol. 1: An Interim Report,* edited by Robin A. Robertson and David A. Freidel, 1–22. Dallas: Southern Methodist University Press.

1987 *Yaxuna Archaeological Survey: A Report of the 1986 Field Season.* Dallas: Department of Anthropology, Southern Methodist University.

n.d. *The Monumental Architecture: Archaeology at Cerros, Belize, Central America, Vol. 5.* Dallas: Southern Methodist University Press (in preparation).

FREIDEL, DAVID A., AND ANTHONY P. ANDREWS

n.d. The Loltun Bas-relief and the Origins of Maya Kingship. *Research Reports on Ancient Maya Writing.* Washington, D.C.: Center for Maya Research (in press).

FREIDEL, DAVID A., MARIA MASUCCI, SUSAN JAEGER, ROBIN A. ROBERTSON
n.d. The Bearer, the Burden, and the Burnt: The Stacking Principle in the Iconography of the Late Preclassic Maya Lowlands. In *Sixth Palenque Round Table, Vol. VII,* edited by Merle Greene Robertson. Norman: the University of Oklahoma Press (in press).

FREIDEL DAVID A., AND JEREMY A. SABLOFF
1984 *Cozumel: Late Maya Settlement Patterns.* New York: Academic Press.

FREIDEL, DAVID A., AND VERNON L. SCARBOROUGH
1982 Subsistence, Trade and Development of the Coastal Maya. In *Maya Agriculture: Essays in Honor of Dennis E. Puleston,* edited by K. V. Flannery, 131–155. New York: Academic Press.

FREIDEL, DAVID A., AND LINDA SCHELE
1988a Kingship in the Late Preclassic Lowlands: The Instruments and Places of Ritual Power. *American Anthropologist* 90(3):547–567.

1988b Symbol and Power: A History of the Lowland Maya Cosmogram. In *Maya Iconography,* edited by Elizabeth Benson and Gillett Griffin, 44–93. Princeton: Princeton University Press.

n.d. Dead Kings and Living Mountains: Dedication and Termination Rituals of the Lowland Maya. In *Word and Image in Maya Culture,* edited by William Hanks and Don Rice. Salt Lake City: University of Utah Press (in press).

FURST, PETER T.
1976 Fertility, Vision Quest and Auto-Sacrifice: Some Thoughts on Ritual Blood-letting Among the Maya. In *The Art, Iconography, and Dynastic History of Palenque, Part III: Proceedings of the Segunda Mesa Redonda de Palenque,* edited by Merle Greene Robertson, 211–224. Pebble Beach, Calif.: Robert Louis Stevenson School.

GARBER, JAMES F.
1983 Patterns of Jade Consumption and Disposal at Cerros, Northern Belize. *American Antiquity* 48(4):800–807.

1986 The Artifacts. In *Archaeology at Cerros, Belize, Central America, Vol. 1: An Interim Report,* edited by R. A. Robertson and D. A. Freidel, 117–126. Dallas: Southern Methodist University Press.

GARZA TARAZONA DE GONZALEZ, SILVIA, AND EDWARD B. KURJACK
1980 *Atlas arqueológico del estado de Yucatán,* Tomo 1. Mérida: Instituto Nacional de Antropología e Historia.

GIBSON, ERIC C., LESLIE C. SHAW, AND DANIEL R. FINAMORE
1986 Early Evidence of Maya Hieroglyphic Writing at Kichpanha, Belize. *Working Papers in Archaeology,* No. 2. San Antonio: Center for Archaeological Research, The University of Texas at San Antonio.

GORDON, GEORGE BYRON
1898 Caverns of Copán. *Memoirs of the Peabody Museum of Archaeology and Ethnology, Harvard University,* Vol. I (5). Cambridge.

GRAHAM, IAN
1971 *The Art of Maya Hieroglyphic Writing.* Cambridge: President and Fellows of Harvard College, and New York: Center for Inter-American Relations, Inc.

1975–1986 *Corpus of Maya Hieroglyphic Inscriptions.* Cambridge: Peabody Museum of Archaeology and Ethnology, Harvard University.

GROVE, DAVID
1981 Olmec Monuments: Mutilation as a Clue to Meaning. In *The Olmec and Their Neighbors: Essays in Memory of Matthew W. Stirling.* Washington, D.C.: Dumbarton Oaks Research Library and Collections.

1986 *Ancient Chalcatzingo.* Austin: University of Texas Press.

GRUBE, NIKOLAI
1988 Städtegründer und "Erste Herrscher" in Hieroglyphentexten der Klassischen Mayakultur. *Archiv für Völkerkunde,* 69–90. Wien: Museum für Völkerkunde.

GRUBE, NIKOLAI, AND LINDA SCHELE
1987a U-Cit-Tok', the Last King of Copán. *Copán Note 21.* Copán, Honduras: Copán Mosaics Project and the Instituto Hondureño de Antropología e Historia.

1987b The Date on the Bench from Structure 9N-82, Sepulturas, Copán, Honduras. *Copán Note 23.* Copán, Honduras: Copán Mosaics Project and the Instituto Hondureño de Antropología e Historia.

1988 Cu-Ix, the Fourth Ruler of Copán and His Monuments. *Copán Note 40.* Copán,

Honduras: Copán Mosaics Project and the Instituto Hondureño de Antropología e Historia.

GRUBE, NIKOLAI, AND DAVID STUART
1987 Observations on T110 at the Syllable *ko*. *Research Reports on Ancient Maya Writing* No. 8. Washington, D.C.: Center for Maya Research.

HAMILTON, RACHEL
n.d. The Archaeological Mollusca of Cerros, Belize. Manuscript to be included in the final reports of the Cerros Project, dated 1988.

HAMMOND, NORMAN
1982 Unearthing the Oldest Maya. *National Geographic Magazine* 162:126–140.
n.d. Excavation and Survey at Nohmul, Belize, 1986. A paper presented at the Fifty-first Annual Meeting of the Society for American Archaeology, New Orleans, April 1986.

HAMMOND, N., D. PRING, R. WILK, S. DONAGHEY, F. P. SAUL, E. S. WING, A. G. MILLER, AND L. H. FELDMAN
1979 The Earliest Lowland Maya? Definition of the Swazy Phase. *American Antiquity* 44:92–110.

HANSEN, RICHARD
1984 Excavations on Structure 34 and the Tigre Area, El Mirador, Petén, Guatemala: A New Look at the Preclassic Lowland Maya. A master's thesis, Department of Anthropology, Brigham Young University.
1989 Las investigaciones del sitio Nakbe, Petén, Guatemala: Temporada 1989. A paper delivered at the Tercer Simposio del Arqueología Guatemalteca, Guatemala City, July 1989.

HARRISON, PETER
1970 The Central Acropolis, Tikal, Guatemala: A Preliminary Study of the Functions of Its Structural Components During the Late Classic Period. A Ph.D dissertation, Department of Anthropology, University of Pennsylvania.
1989 Architecture and Geometry in the Central Acropolis at Tikal. A paper presented at the Seventh Round Table of Palenque, held in Palenque, Chiapas, México, in June 1989.

HAVILAND, WILLIAM A.
1967 Stature at Tikal, Guatemala: Implications for Ancient Maya Demography and Social Organization. *American Antiquity* 32:316–325.
1968 Ancient Lowland Maya Social Organization. In *Archaeological Studies in Middle America. Middle American Research Institute, Tulane University* Pub. 26, 93–117. New Orleans.
1977 Dynastic Genealogies from Tikal, Guatemala: Implications for Descent and Political Organization. *American Antiquity* 42:61–67.

HEALY, P. F., J. D. H. LAMBERT, J. T. ARNASON, AND R. J. HEBDA
1983 Caracol, Belize: Evidence of Ancient Maya Agricultural Terraces. *Journal of Field Archaeology* 10:773–796.

HEYDEN, DORIS
1981 Caves, Gods, and Myths: World-View and Planning in Teotihuacán. In *Mesoamerican Sites and World-Views,* edited by Elizabeth Benson, 1–37. Washington, D.C.: Dumbarton Oaks Research Library and Collections.

HIRTH, KENNETH
1988 Beyond the Maya Frontier: Cultural Interaction and Syncretism Along the Central Honduran Corridor. In *The Southeast Classic Maya Zone,* edited by Elizabeth Boone and Gordon Willey, 297–334. Washington, D.C.: Dumbarton Oaks Research Library and Collection.

HOPKINS, NICHOLAS
n.d. Classic-Area Maya Kinship Systems: The Evidence for Patrilineality. A paper presented at the Taller Maya VI, San Cristóbal, July 1982.

HOPKINS, NICHOLAS, J. KATHRYN JOSSERAND, AND AUSENSIO CRUZ GUZMÁN
1985 Notes on the Chol Dugout Canoe. *Fourth Palenque Round Table, 1980, Vol. VI,* edited by Elizabeth Benson, 325–329. San Francisco: Pre-Columbian Art Research Institute.

HOUSTON, STEPHEN
1983 Warfare Between Naranjo and Ucanal. *Contribution to Maya Hieroglyphic Decipherment I,* 31–39. New Haven: HRAflex Books, Human Relations Area Files, Inc.

1984 An Example of Homophony in Maya Script. *American Antiquity* 49:790–805.

HOUSTON, STEPHEN, AND PETER MATHEWS

1985 The Dynastic Sequence of Dos Pilas. *Pre-Columbian Art Research Institute, Monograph 1.* San Francisco: Pre-Columbian Art Research Institute.

HOUSTON, STEPHEN, AND DAVID STUART

1989 The *Way* Glyph: Evidence for "Co-essences" Among the Classic Maya. *Research Reports on Ancient Maya Writing* 30. Washington, D.C.: Center for Maya Research.

JOESINK-MANDEVILLE, LEROY R. V., AND SYLVIA MELUZIN

1976 Olmec-Maya Relationships: Olmec Influence in Yucatán. In *Origins of Religious Art and Iconography in Preclassic Mesoamerica,* edited by H. B. Nicholson, 89–105. Los Angeles: UCLA Latin American Center Publications and Ethnic Arts Council of Los Angeles.

JONES, CHRISTOPHER

1969 The Twin Pyramid Group Pattern: A Classic Maya Architectural Assemblage at Tikal, Guatemala. Ph.D dissertation, University of Pennsylvania. Ann Arbor: University Microfilms.

1988 The Life and Times of Ah Cacaw, Ruler of Tikal. In *Primer Simposio Mundial Sobre Epigraphía Maya,* 107–120. Guatemala: Asociación Tikal.

n.d. Patterns of Growth at Tikal. In *Classic Maya Political History: Archaeological and Hieroglyphic Evidence*, edited by T. P. Culbert. A School of American Research Book. Cambridge: Cambridge University Press (in press).

JONES, CHRISTOPHER, AND LINTON SATTERTHWAITE

1982 The Monuments and Inscriptions of Tikal: The Carved Monuments. *Tikal Report No. 33: Part A. University Museum Monograph 44.* Philadelphia: The University Museum, University of Pennsylvania.

JONES, TOM

1985 The Xoc, the Sharke, and the Sea Dogs: An Historical Encounter. In *Fifth Palenque Round Table, 1983, Vol. VII,* gen. editor, Merle Greene Robertson; vol. editor, Virginia M. Fields, 211–222. San Francisco: The Pre-Columbian Art Research Institute.

JORALEMON, DAVID

1974 Ritual Blood-Sacrifice Among the Ancient Maya: Part I. *Primera Mesa Redonda de Palenque, Part II,* edited by Merle Greene Robertson, 59–76. Pebble Beach, Calif.: Robert Louis Stevenson School.

JUSTESON, JOHN, AND PETER MATHEWS

1983 The Seating of the *Tun:* Further Evidence Concerning a Late Preclassic Lowland Maya Stela Cult. *American Antiquity* 48:586–593.

KAUFMAN, TERRENCE S., AND WILLIAM M. NORMAN

1984 An Outline of Proto-Cholan Phonology, Morphology, and Vocabulary. In *Phoneticism in Mayan Hieroglyphic Writing,* edited by Lyle Campbell and John S. Justeson, 77–167. Albany: Center for Mesoamerican Studies, State University of New York at Albany.

KELLEY, DAVID

1962 Glyphic Evidence for a Dynastic Sequence at Quiriguá, Guatemala. *American Antiquity* 27:323–335.

1965 The Birth of the Gods at Palenque. In *Estudios de Cultura Maya* 5, 93–134. México: Universidad Nacional Autónoma de México.

1968 Kakupacal and the Itzás. *Estudios de Cultura Maya* 7:255–268. México: Universidad Nacional Autónoma de México.

1975 Planetary Data on Caracol Stela 3. In *Archaeoastronomy in Pre-Columbian America,* edited by Anthony Aveni, 257–262. Austin: University of Texas Press.

1976 *Deciphering the Maya Script.* Austin: University of Texas Press.

1977a A Possible Maya Eclipse Record. In *Social Processes in Maya Prehistory: Studies in Honour of Sir Eric Thompson.* New York: Academic Press.

1977b Maya Astronomical Tables and Inscriptions. In *Native American Astronomy,* edited by Anthony Aveni, 57–74. Austin: University of Texas Press.

1982 Notes on Puuc Inscriptions and History. In *The Puuc: New Perspectives: Papers Presented at the Puuc Symposium, Central College, May 1977, Supplement,* edited by Lawrence Mills. Pella, Iowa: Central College.

1983 The Maya Calendar Correlation Problem. In *Civilization in the Ancient Americas:*

Essays in the Honor of Gordon R. Willey, edited by Richard Leventhal and Alan Kolata, 157–208. Albuquerque: University of New Mexico Press.

1984 The Toltec Empire in Yucatán. *Quarterly Review of Archaeology* 5:12–13.

KIDDER, ALFRED, JESSE D. JENNINGS, AND EDWIN M. SHOOK

1946 Excavations at Kaminaljuyu, Guatemala. *Carnegie Institution of Washington, Pub. 561.* Washington, D.C.: Carnegie Institution of Washington.

KIRCHHOFF, PAUL

1943 Mesoamerica. *Acta Americana* 1, no. 1, 92–107.

KNOROZOV, YURI

1952 Ancient Writing of Central America. An unauthorized translation from *Sovietskaya Etnografiya* 3:100–118.

KOWALSKI, JEFF K.

1985a Lords of the Northern Maya: Dynastic History in the Inscriptions. *Expedition* 27(3):50–60.

1985b An Historical Interpretation of the Inscriptions of Uxmal. In *Fourth Palenque Round Table, 1980, Vol. VI,* edited by Merle Greene Robertson and Elizabeth P. Benson, 235–248. San Francisco: Pre-Columbian Art Research Institute.

1987 *The House of the Governor: A Maya Palace at Uxmal, Yucatán, México.* Norman: University of Oklahoma Press.

1989 Who Am I Among the Itzá?: Links between Northern Yucatán and the Western Maya Lowlands and Highlands. In *Mesoamerica After the Decline of Teotihuacán: A.D. 700–900,* edited by Richard Diehl and Janet Berlo, 173–186. Washington, D.C.: Dumbarton Oaks Research Library and Collection.

KOWALSKI, JEFF K., AND RUTH KROCHOCK

n.d. Puuc Hieroglyphs and History: A Review of Current Data. Paper presented at the American Anthropological Meetings, Chicago, November 1987.

KROCHOCK, RUTH

1988 The Hieroglyphic Inscriptions and Iconography of Temple of the Four Lintels and Related Monuments, Chichén Itzá, Yucatán, México. M.A. thesis, University of Texas at Austin.

n.d. Dedication Ceremonies at Chichén Itzá: The Glyphic Evidence. *The Sixth Round Table of Palenque.* Norman: University of Oklahoma Press (in press).

KUBLER, GEORGE

1969 Studies in Classic Maya Iconography. *Memoirs of the Connecticut Academy of Arts and Sciences XVIII.* Hamden: Archon Books.

1975 *The Art and Architecture of Ancient America: The Mexican, Maya and Andean Peoples,* 2nd ed. Harmondsworth, England: Penguin Books.

1976 The Double-Portrait Lintels at Tikal. *Actas del XXIII Congreso Internacional de Historia del Arte España Entre el Mediterráneo y el Atlántico.* Granada.

1980 Electicism at Cacaxtla. In *Third Palenque Round Table, 1978, Part 2,* edited by Merle Greene Robertson, 163–172. Austin: University of Texas Press.

KUDLEK, MANFRED

1978 Solar Eclipses Visible at Tikal, -1014 to +2038. A copy of tables run in Hamburg on December 14, 1978. Copy in possession of author.

KURJACK, EDWARD B.

1974 Prehistoric Lowland Maya Community and Social Organization: A Case Study at Dzibilchaltún, Yucatán, México. *Middle American Research Institute, Tulane University* Pub. 38. New Orleans.

KURJACK, EDWARD B., AND E. WYLLYS ANDREWS V

1976 Early Boundary Maintenance in Northwest Yucatán, México. *American Antiquity* 41:318–325.

KURJACK, EDWARD B., AND SILVIA GARZA T.

1981 Pre-Columbian Community Form and Distribution in the Northern Maya Area. In *Lowland Maya Settlement Patterns,* edited by W. Ashmore, 287–309. A School of American Research Book. Albuquerque: University of New Mexico Press.

LAPORTE MOLINA, JUAN PEDRO

1988 Alternativas del Clásico Temprano en la relación Tikal-Teotihuacán: Grupo 6C-XVI, Tikal, Petén, Guatemala. A Dissertation for a Doctoral en Antropología, Universidad Nacional Autónoma de México.

LAPORTE MOLINA, JUAN PEDRO, AND LILLIAN VEGA DE ZEA

1988 Aspectos dinásticos para el Clásico Temprano de Mundo Perdido, Tikal. In *Primer*

Simposio Mundial Sobre Epigrafía Maya, 127–141. Guatemala: Asociación Tikal.

LARIOS, RUDY, AND WILLIAM FASH

1985 Excavación y restauración de un palacio de la nobleza maya de Copán. *Yaxkin* VIII, 11–134. Honduras: Instituto Hondereño de Antropología e Historia.

n.d. Architectural History and Political Symbolism of Temple 22, Copán. A paper presented at the Seventh Round Table of Palenque, in Palenque, Chiapas, México, June 1989.

LEVENTHAL, RICHARD

1983 Household Groups and Classic Maya Religion. In *Prehistoric Settlement Patterns:. Essays in Honor of Gordon R. Willey,* edited by Evon Z. Vogt and Richard M. Leventhal, 55–76. Albuquerque: University of New Mexico Press, and Cambridge: Peabody Museum of Archaeology and Ethnology, Harvard University.

LEYENAAR, TED J. J.

1978 *Ulama: The Perpetuation in México of the Pre-Spanish Ball Game Ullamaliztli.* Leiden, The Netherlands: Rijkmuseum voor Volkenkunde.

LINCOLN, CHARLES

1980 A Preliminary Assessment of Izamal, Yucatán, México. B.A. thesis, Tulane University.

1986 The Chronology of Chichén Itzá: A Review of the Literature. In *Late Lowland Maya Civilization: Classic to Postclassic,* edited by Jeremy A. Sabloff and E. Wyllys Andrews V, 141–196. A School of American Research Book. Albuquerque: University of New Mexico Press.

n.d. Dual Kingship at Chichén Itzá. A paper presented at "Chichén Itzá: Recent Advances in Archaeology, Epigraphy, and Art History," a symposium held at the 53rd annual meeting of the Society of American Archaeology, in Phoenix, Arisona, April 1988.

LINNE, S.

1934 Archaeological Researches at Teotihuacán, México. *The Ethnological Museum of Sweden, New Series* No. 1. Stockholm.

1942 Mexican Highland Cultures. *Ethnological Museum of Sweden, New Series* No. 7. Stockholm.

LIZANA, FR. BERNARDO DE

1892 *Historia Conquista Espiritual de Yucatán.* El Museo Nacional de México. México: Imprenta del Museo Nacional.

LOTHROP, SAMUEL K.

1952 Metals from the Cenote of Sacrifice, Chichén Itzá, Yucatán. *Memoirs of the Peabody Museum of Archaeology and Ethnology, Vol. X, No. 2.* Cambridge: Peabody Museum of Archaeology and Ethnology, Harvard University.

LOUNSBURY, FLOYD G.

1974 The Inscription of the Sarcophagus Lid at Palenque. *Primera Mesa Redonda de Palenque, Part II,* edited by Merle Greene Robertson, 5–20. Pebble Beach, Calif.: Robert Louis Stevenson School.

1976 A Rationale for the Initial Date of the Temple of the Cross at Palenque. In *The Art, Iconography, and Dynastic History of Palenque, Part III: Proceedings of the Segunda Mesa Redonda de Palenque,* edited by Merle Greene Robertson, 211–224. Pebble Beach, Calif.: Robert Louis Stevenson School.

1978 Maya Numeration, Computation, and Calendrical Astronomy. In *Dictionary of Scientific Biography,* edited by Charles Coulson Gillispie, XV:759–818. New York: Charles Scribner's Sons.

1980 Some Problems in the Interpretation of the Mythological Portion of the Hieroglyphic Text of the Temple of the Cross at Palenque. In *Third Palenque Round Table, 1978, Part 2,* edited by Merle Greene Robertson, 99–115. Palenque Round Table Series Vol. 5. Austin: University of Texas Press.

1982 Astronomical Knowledge and Its Uses at Bonampak, México. In *Archaeoastronomy in the New World,* edited by A. F. Aveni, 143–169. Cambridge: Cambridge University Press.

1984 Glyphic Substitutions: Homophonic and Synonymic. In *Phoneticism in Mayan Hieroglyphic Writing,* edited by John S. Justeson and Lyle Campbell, 167–184. Albany: Institute for Mesoamerican Studies, State University of New York.

1985 The Identities of the Mythological Figures in the "Cross Group" of Inscriptions at Palenque. In *Fourth Round Table of Palenque, 1980, Vol. 6,* gen. editor, Merle

Greene Robertson; vol. editor, Elizabeth Benson, 45–58. San Francisco: Pre-Columbian Art Research Institute.

LOUNSBURY, FLOYD G., AND MICHAEL D. COE
1968 Linguistic and Ethnographic Data Pertinent to the "Cage" Glyph of Dresden 36c. *Estudios de Cultura Maya* 7:269–284. México: Universidad Nacional Autónoma de México.

LOVE, BRUCE
1987 Glyph T93 and Maya "Hand-scattering" Events. *Research Reports on Ancient Maya Writing* 5. Washington, D.C.: Center for Maya Research.

LOWE, GARETH W.
1977 The Mixe-Zoque as Competing Neighbors of the Early Lowland Maya. In *The Origins of Maya Civilization,* edited by R. E. W. Adams, 197–248. A School of American Research Book. Albuquerque: University of New Mexico Press.

MACLEOD, BARBARA, AND DENNIS PULESTON
1979 Pathways into Darkness: The Search for the Road to Xibalba. *Tercera Mesa Redonda de Palenque, Vol. IV,* edited by Merle Green Robertson, 71–79. Palenque: Pre-Columbian Art Research, and Monterey: Herald Printers.

MACNEISH, RICHARD S.
1981 *Second Annual Report of the Belize Archaic Archaeological Reconnaissance.* Andover, Mass.: Robert S. Peabody Foundation for Archaeology, Phillips Academy.
1982 *Third Annual Report of the Belize Archaic Archaeological Reconnaissance.* Andover, Mass.: Robert S. Peabody Foundation for Archaeology, Phillips Academy.

MALER, TEOBERT
1901–1903 Researches in the Central Portion of the Usumasintla Valley. *Memoirs of the Peabody Museum of American Archaeology and Ethnology, Harvard University* II. Cambridge.
1908–1910 Explorations of the Upper Usumasintla and Adjacent Region. *Memoirs of the Peabody Museum of American Archaeology and Ethnology, Harvard University* IV. Cambridge.

MARCUS, JOYCE
1973 Territorial Organization of the Lowland Maya. *Science* 180:911–916.
1976 *Emblem and State in the Classic Maya Lowlands: An Epigraphic Approach to Territorial Organization.* Washington, D.C.: Dumbarton Oaks Research Library and Collection.
1980 Zapotec Writing. *Scientific American* 242:50–64.

MARQUINA, IGNACIO
1964 *Arquitectura prehispánica.* México: Instituto Nacional Autónoma de México.

MARTIN, PAUL S.
1928 Report on the Temple of the Two Lintels. In *Carnegie Institution of Washington Year Book 27,* 302–305. Washington, D.C.

MATHENY, RAY T.
1986 Early States in the Maya Lowlands During the Late Preclassic Period: Edzna and El Mirador. In *City-States of the Maya: Art and Architecture,* edited by Elizabeth P. Benson, 1–44. Denver: Rocky Mountain Institute for Precolumbian Studies.
1987 El Mirador: An Early Maya Metropolis Uncovered. *National Geographic Magazine,* September 1987, 317–339.

MATHEWS, PETER
1975 The Lintels of Structure 12, Yaxchilán, Chiapas. A paper presented at the Annual Conference of the Northeastern Anthropological Association, Wesleyan University, October 1975.
1976 The Inscription on the Back of Stela 8, Dos Pilas, Guatemala. A paper prepared for a seminar at Yale University. Copy provided by author.
1977 Naranjo: The Altar of Stela 38. An unpublished manuscript dated August 3, 1977, in the possession of the authors.
1979 Notes on the Inscriptions of "Site Q." Unpublished manuscript in the possession of the authors.
1980 The Stucco Text Above the Piers of the Temple of the Inscriptions at Palenque. *Maya Glyph Notes, No. 10.* A manuscript circulated by the author.
1985a Maya Early Classic Monuments and Inscriptions. In *A Consideration of the Early Classic Period in the Maya Lowlands,* edited by Gordon R. Willey and Peter Mathews, 5–54. Albany: Institute for Mesoamerican Studies, State University of New York at Albany.

1985b Emblem Glyphs in Classic Maya Inscriptions. A paper presented at the Annual Meeting of the Society of American Archaeology, Denver, 1985.

1986 Late Classic Maya Site Interaction. A paper presented at "Maya Art and Civilization: The New Dynamics," a symposium sponsored by the Kimbell Art Museum, Fort Worth, May 1986.

1988 The Sculptures of Yaxchilán. A Ph.D dissertation, Department of Anthropology, Yale University.

MATHEWS, PETER, AND JOHN S. JUSTESON
1984 Patterns of Sign Substitution in Mayan Hieroglyphic Writing: "The Affix Cluster." In *Phoneticism in Mayan Hieroglyphic Writing,* edited by John S. Justeson and Lyle Campbell, 212–213. Albany: Institute for Mesoamerican Studies, State University of New York at Albany.

MATHEWS, PETER, AND GORDON WILLEY
n.d. Prehistoric Polities in the Pasión Region: Hieroglyphic Texts and Their Archaeological Settings. In *Classic Maya Political History: Archaeological and Hieroglyphic Evidence,* edited by T. P. Culbert. A School of American Research Book. Cambridge: Cambridge University Press (in press).

MAUDSLAY, ALFRED P.
1889–1902 *Archaeology: Biologia Centrali-Americana.* Vol. 1. London: Dulau and Co. Reprint edition, 1974, Milparton Publishing Corp.

MEANS, PHILIP AINSWORTH
1917 History of the Spanish Conquest of Yucatán and of the Itzás. *Papers of Peabody Museum of American Archaeology and Ethnology, Harvard University,* Vol. 7. Cambridge, Mass.

MILLER, ARTHUR G.
1977 Captains of the Itzá: Unpublished Mural Evidence from Chichén Itzá. In *Social Process in Maya Prehistory: Studies in Honour of Sir Eric Thompson,* edited by Norman Hammond, 197–225. London: Academic Press.

1986 *Maya Rulers of Time: A Study of Architectural Sculpture at Tikal, Guatemala. Los Soberanos Mayas del Tiempo: Un Estudio de la Escultura Arquitectónica de Tikal, Guatemala.* Philadelphia: the University Museum.

MILLER, JEFFREY
1974 Notes on a Stelae Pair Probably from Calakmul, Campeche, México. In *Primera Mesa Redonda de Palenque, Part I,* edited by Merle Greene Robertson, 149–162. Pebble Beach, Calif.: Robert Louis Stevenson School.

MILLER, MARY E.
1985 A Re-examination of Mesoamerican Chacmool. *The Art Bulletin* LXVII:7–17.

1986a Copán: Conference with a Perished City. In *City-States of the Maya: Art and Architecture,* edited by E. Benson, 72–109. Denver: Rocky Mountain Institute for Pre-Columbian Studies.

1986b *The Murals of Bonampak.* Princeton: Princeton University Press.

1988 The Meaning and Function of the Main Acropolis, Copán. In *The Southeast Classic Maya Zone,* edited by Elizabeth Boone and Gordon Willey, 149–195. Washington, D.C.: Dumbarton Oaks Research Library and Collection.

MILLER, MARY E., AND STEPHEN D. HOUSTON
1987 The Classic Maya Ballgame and Its Architectural Setting: A Study in Relations Between Text and Image. *RES* 14, 47–66.

MILLER, VIRGINIA
1989 Star Warriors at Chichén Itzá. In *Word and Image in Maya Culture: Explorations in Language, Writing, and Representation,* edited by William F. Hanks and Don S. Rice, 287–305. Salt Lake City: University of Utah Press.

MILLON, RENÉ
1981 Teotihuacán: City, State, and Civilization. In *Handbook of Middle American Indians, Supplement 1,* edited by Jeremy A. Sabloff with the assistance of P. A. Andrews, 198–243. Austin: University of Texas Press.

1988 The Last Years of Teotihuacán Dominance. In *The Collapse of Ancient States and Civilizations,* edited by Norman Yoffee and George L. Cowgill, 102–175. Tucson: The University of Arizona Press.

MITCHUM, B.
1986 Chipped Stone Artifacts. In *Archaeology at Cerros, Belize, Central America, Vol. 1, An Interim Report,* edited by R. A. Robertson and D. A. Freidel, 105–115. Dallas: Southern Methodist University Press.

MOHOLY-NAGY, HATTULA

1976 Spatial Distribution of Flint and Obsidian Artifacts at Tikal, Guatemala. In *Maya Lithic Studies: Papers from the 1976 Belize Field Symposium,* edited by Thomas R. Hester and Norman Hammond, 91–108. Special Report No. 4. San Antonio: Center for Archaeological Research, The University of Texas at San Antonio.

MOLLOY, JOHN P., AND W. L. RATHJE

1974 Sexploitation Among the Late Classic Maya. In *Mesoamerican Archaeology: New Approaches,* edited by Norman Hammond, 430–444. Austin: University of Texas Press.

MORLEY, SYLVANUS GRISWOLD

1915 *An Introduction to the Study of Maya Hieroglyphics.* New York: Dover Publications. 1975 reprint.

1920 The Inscriptions at Copán. *The Carnegie Institution of Washington Pub. 219.* Washington, D.C.

1926 The Chichén Itzá Project. *Carnegie Institution of Washington Year Book 26,* 259–273. Washington, D.C.

1927 Archaeology. *Carnegie Institution of Washington Year Book 26,* 231–240. Washington, D.C.

1935 Inscriptions at the Caracol. In *The Caracol of Chichén Itzá, Yucatán, México. Carnegie Institution of Washington Pub. 454,* edited by Karl Ruppert. Washington, D.C.

MORRIS, EARL H., JEAN CHARLOT, AND ANN AXTELL MORRIS

1931 The Temple of the Warriors at Chichén Itzá, Yucatán, Vols. 1 and 2. *Carnegie Institution of Washington Pub. 406.* Washington, D.C.

NAKAMURA, SEIICHI

1987 Proyecto Arqueológico La Entrada, Temporada 1986–1987: resultados preliminares e interacción interregional. A paper presented at IV Seminario de Arqueología Hondureña, held in La Ceiba, Altántida, Honduras, June 22–26.

OAKLAND, AMY

1982 Teotihuacán: The Blood Complex at Atetelco. A paper prepared for a seminar on the transition from Preclassic to Classic times, held at the University of Texas, 1982. Copy in possession of author.

OREJEL, JORGE

n.d. An Analysis of the Inscriptions of the Petex Batun Region. A paper prepared for the graduate seminar on Maya Hieroglyphic Writing, University of Texas, 1988.

PAHL, GARY

1976 Maya Hieroglyphic Inscriptions of Copán: A Catalogue and Historical Commentary. Ph.D dissertation, University of California. Ann Arbor: University Microfilms.

PARSONS, MARK

1985 Three Thematic Complexes in the Art of Teotihuacán. A paper prepared at the University of Texas. Copy in possession of author.

PASZTORY, ESTHER

1974 The Iconography of the Teotihuacán Tlaloc. *Studies in Pre-Columbian Art and Archaeology* 15. Washington, D.C.: Dumbarton Oaks Research Library and Collection.

1976 *The Murals of Tepantitla, Teotihuacán.* New York: Garland Publishing.

PENDERGAST, DAVID M.

1971 Evidence of Early Teotihuacán-Lowland Maya Contact at Altun Ha. *American Antiquity* 35:455–460.

1981 Lamanai, Belize: Summary of Excavation Results 1987–1980. *Journal of Field Archaeology* 8(1):29–53.

1986 Stability Through Change: Lamanai, Belize, from the Ninth to the Seventeenth Century. In *Late Lowland Maya Civilization, Classic to Postclassic.* Edited by Jeremy A. Sabloff and E. Wyllys Andrews V, 223–249. A School of American Research Book. Albuquerque: University of New Mexico Press.

POHL, MARY

1983 Maya Ritual Faunas: Vertebrate Remains from Burials, Caches, Caves and Cenotes in the Maya Lowlands. In *Civilization in the Ancient Americas: Essays in Honor of Gordon R. Willey,* edited by Richard M. Leventhal and Alan L. Kolata, 55–103. Albuquerque: University of New Mexico Press, and Cambridge: Peabody Museum of Archaeology and Ethnology, Harvard University.

POLLOCK, H.E.D.

1970 Architectural Notes on Some Chenes Ruins. In *Monographs and Papers in Maya Archaeology, Papers of the Peabody Museum of Archaeology and Ethnology, Vol. 61,* edited by William R. Ballard, Jr., 1–87. Cambridge: Peabody Museum, Harvard University.

1980 The Puuc: An Architectural Survey of the Hill Country of Yucatán and Northern Campeche, México. *Memoirs of the Peabody Museum of Archaeology and Ethnology, Harvard University, Vol. 19.* Cambridge.

POLLOCK, H.E.D., RALPH L. ROYS, TATIANA PROSKOURIAKOFF, AND A. LEDYARD SMITH

1962 Mayapán, Yucatán, México. *Carnegie Institution of Washington Pub. 619.* Washington, D.C.

POTTER, DAVID F.

1977 Maya Architecture of the Central Yucatán Peninsula. *Middle American Research Institute, Tulane University* Pub. 44. New Orleans.

PROSKOURIAKOFF, TATIANA

1950 A Study of Classic Maya Sculpture. *Carnegie Institution of Washington Pub. 593.* Washington, D.C.

1960 Historical Implications of a Pattern of Dates at Piedras Negras, Guatemala. *American Antiquity* 25:454–475.

1961a Lords of the Maya Realm. *Expedition* 4(1):14–21.

1961b Portraits of Women in Maya Art. *Essays in Pre-Columbian Art and Archaeology,* edited by Samuel K. Lothrop and others, 81–99. Cambridge: Harvard University Press.

1963–1964 Historical Data in the Inscriptions of Yaxchilán, Parts I and II. *Estudios de Cultura Maya* 3:149–167 and 4:177–201. México: Universidad Nacional Autónoma de México.

1970 On Two Inscriptions at Chichén Itzá. In *Monographs and Papers in Maya Archaeology, Papers of the Peabody Museum of Archaeology and Ethnology, Harvard University, Vol. 67,* edited by William R. Ballard, Jr., 459–467. Cambridge.

1973 The Hand-Grasping-Fish and Associated Glyphs on Classic Maya Monuments. In *Mesoamerican Writing Systems,* edited by Elizabeth P. Benson, 165–178. Washington, D.C.: Dumbarton Oaks Research Library and Collection.

PULESTON, DENNIS

1976 The People of the Cayman/Crocodile: Riparian Agriculture and the Origins of Aquatic Motifs in Ancient Maya Iconography. In *Aspects of Ancient Maya Civilization,* edited by François-Auguste de Montequin, 1–26. Saint Paul: Hamline University.

1977 The Art and Archaeology of Hydraulic Agriculture in the Maya Lowlands. In *Social Process in Maya Prehistory: Studies in Honour of Sir Eric Thompson,* edited by Norman Hammond, 449–469. London: Academic Press.

1979 An Epistemological Pathology and the Collapse, or Why the Maya Kept the Short Count. In *Maya Archaeology and Ethnohistory,* edited by Norman Hammond and Gordon R. Willey, 63–71. Austin: University of Texas Press.

RATHJE, WILLIAM L.

1971 The Origin and Development of Lowland Classic Maya Civilization. *American Antiquity* 36(3):275–85.

RATTRAY, EVELYN

1986 A Gulf Coast-Maya Enclave at Teotihuacán. A paper presented at the Fifty-first Annual Meeting of the Society for American Archaeology, New Orleans, April 1986.

RECINOS, ADRIAN

1950 *Popol Vuh, the Sacred Book of the Ancient Quiche Maya.* Translated by Delia Goetz and S. G. Morley. Norman: University of Oklahoma Press.

RICE, DON S.

1986 The Petén Postclassic: A Settlement Perspective. In *Late Lowland Maya Civilization, Classic to Postclassic,* edited by Jeremy A. Sabloff and E. Wyllys Andrews V, 301–344. A School of American Research Book. Albuquerque: University of New Mexico Press.

RICKETSON, OLIVER G., JR.

1925 Report on the Temple of the Four Lintels. *Carnegie Institution of Washington Year Book 24,* 267–69. Washington, D.C.

RICKETSON, OLIVER G., AND EDITH B. RICKETSON
1937 Uaxactún, Guatemala: Group E 1926–1931. *Carnegie Institution of Washington Pub. 477.* Washington, D.C.

RIESE, BERTHOLD
1984 Hel hieroglyphs. In *Phoneticism in Mayan Hieroglyphic Writing,* edited by John S. Justeson and Lyle Campbell, 263–286. Albany: Institute for Mesoamerican Studies, State University of New York at Albany.
1988 Epigraphy of the Southeast Zone in Relation to Other Parts of Mesoamerica. In *The Southeast Classic Maya Zone,* edited by Elizabeth Boone and Gordon Willey, 67–94. Washington, D.C.: Dumbarton Oaks Research Library and Collection.
n.d. Notes on the Copán Inscriptions. On file in the archives of the Proyeto Arqueología de Copán, Copán, Honduras.

RIESE, BERTHOLD, AND CLAUDE F. BAUDEZ
1983 Esculturas del las Estructuras 10L-2 y 4. In *Introducción a la Arqueología de Copán, Honduras,* Tomo II, 143–190. Tegucigalpa: Instituto Hondureño de Antropología e Historia.

ROBERTSON, MERLE GREENE
1972 The Ritual Bundles of Yaxchilán. A paper presented at the symposium on "The Art of Latin America," Tulane University, New Orleans. Copy in possession of author.
1979 An Iconographic Approach to the Identity of the Figures on the Piers of the Temple of Inscriptions, Palenque. *Tercera Mesa Redonda de Palenque, Vol. IV,* edited by Merle Greene Robertson and Donnan Call Jeffers, 129–138. Palenque: Pre-Columbian Art Research, and Monterey: Herald Printers.
1983 The Temple of the Inscriptions. *The Sculpture of Palenque, Vol. I.* Princeton: Princeton University Press.

ROBERTSON, ROBIN
1983 Functional Analysis and Social Process in Ceramics: The Pottery from Cerros, Belize. In *Civilization in the Ancient Americas: Essays in Honor of Gordon R. Willey,* edited by Richard M. Leventhal and Alan L. Kolata, 105–142. Albuquerque: University of New Mexico Press.
n.d. *Archaeology at Cerros, Belize, Central America, The Ceramics.* Dallas: Southern Methodist University Press (forthcoming).

ROBERTSON, ROBIN A., AND DAVID A. FREIDEL, EDITORS
1986 *Archaeology at Cerros, Belize, Central America, Vol. 1, An Interim Report.* Dallas: Southern Methodist University Press.

ROBISCEK, FRANCIS, AND DONALD HALES
1981 *The Maya Book of the Dead. The Ceramic Codex.* Charlottesville: The University of Virginia Museum. Distributed by the University of Oklahoma Press.

ROBLES C., FERNANDO
1980 La secuencia cerámica de la región de Cobá, Quintana Roo. M.A. thesis, Escuela Nacional de Antropología e Historia and Instituto Nacional de Antropología e Historia, México, D.F.

ROBLES C., FERNANDO, AND ANTHONY P. ANDREWS
1986 A Review and Synthesis of Recent Postclassic Archaeology in Northern Yucatán. In *Late Lowland Maya Civilization,* edited by Jeremy A. Sabloff and E. Wyllys Andrews V, 53–98. A School of American Research Book. Albuquerque: University of New Mexico Press.

ROVNER, IRWIN
1976 Pre-Columbian Maya Development of Utilitarian Lithic Industries: The Broad Perspective from Yucatán. In *Maya Lithic Studies: Papers from the 1976 Belize Field Symposium,* edited by Thomas R. Hester and Norman Hammond, 41–53. Special Report No. 4. San Antonio: Center for Archaeological Research, the University of Texas at San Antonio.

ROYS, RALPH L.
1943 The Indian Background of Colonial Yucatán. *Carnegie Institution of Washington Pub. 548.* Washington, D.C.
1957 The Political Geography of the Yucatán Maya. *Carnegie Institution of Washington Pub. 613.* Washington, D.C.
1962 Literary Sources for the History of Mayapán. In *Mayapán, Yucatán, México. Carnegie Institution of Washington Pub. 619.* Washington, D.C.
1965 *Ritual of the Bacabs.* Norman: University of Oklahoma Press.

1967 *The Book of the Chilam Balam of Chumayel.* Norman: University of Oklahoma Press.

RUPPERT, KARL

1935 The Caracol of Chichén Itzá, Yucatán, México. *Carnegie Institution of Washington Pub. 454.* Washington, D.C.

1952 Chichén Itzá, Architectural Notes and Plans. *Carnegie Institution of Washington, Pub. 595.* Washington, D.C.

RUZ LHUILLIER, ALBERTO

1955 Exploraciones en Palenque 1952. In *Anales del Instituto Nacional de Antropología e Historia* VI:82–110. México: Secretaria de Pública.

1973 El Templo de las Inscripciones. *Instituto Nacional de Antropología e Historia, Colección Científica, Arqueología 7.* México.

SABLOFF, JEREMY A., AND E. WYLLYS ANDREWS V

1986 *Late Lowland Maya Civilization, Classic to Postclassic,* edited by Jeremy A. Sabloff and E. Wyllys Andrews V. A School of American Research Book. Albuquerque: University of New Mexico Press.

SABLOFF, JEREMY A., AND GORDON R. WILLEY

1967 The Collapse of Maya Civilization in the Southern Lowlands: A Consideration of History and Process. *Southwestern Journal of Anthropology* 23(4):311–336.

SANDERS, WILLIAM T., AND JOSEPH W. MICHELS, EDS.

1977 *Teotihuacán and Kaminaljuyu: A Study in Prehistoric Culture Contact. The Pennsylvania State University Press Monograph Series on Kaminaljuyu.* University Park: Pennsylvania State University Press.

SANTLEY, ROBERT S.

1983 Obsidian Trade and Teotihuacán Influence in Mesoamerica. In *Highland-Lowland Interaction in Mesoamerica: Interdisciplinary Approaches,* edited by Arthur G. Miller, 69–124. Washington, D.C.: Dumbarton Oaks Research Library and Collection.

SATO, ETSUO

1987 Resultados preliminares del analísis de la cerámica en el Valle de La Venta, La Entrada. A paper presented at the IV Seminario de Arqueología Hondureño, held in La Ceiba, Honduras, June 1987.

SCARBOROUGH, VERNON L.

1983 A Late Preclassic Water System. *American Antiquity* 48:720–744.

1986 Drainage Canal and Raised Field Excavations. In *Archaeology at Cerros, Belize, Central America, Vol. 1, An Interim Report,* edited by R. A. Robertson and D. A. Freidel, 75–87. Dallas: Southern Methodist University Press.

SCARBOROUGH, V. L., B. MITCHUM, H. S. CARR, AND D. A. FREIDEL

1982 Two Late Preclassic Ballcourts at the Lowland Maya Center of Cerros, Northern Belize. *Journal of Field Archaeology* 9:21–34.

SCHELE, LINDA

1976 Accession Iconography of Chan-Bahlum in the Group of the Cross at Palenque. *The Art, Iconography, and Dynastic History of Palenque, Part III. Proceedings of the Segunda Mesa Redonda de Palenque,* edited by Merle Greene Robertson, 9–34. Pebble Beach, Calif.: Robert Louis Stevenson School.

1979 Genealogical Documentation in the Tri-Figure Panels at Palenque. *Tercera Mesa Redonda de Palenque, Vol. IV,* edited by Merle Greene Robertson, 41–70. Palenque: Pre-Columbian Art Research, and Monterey: Herald Printers.

1981 *Notebook for the Maya Hieroglyphic Writing Workshop at Texas.* Austin: Institute of Latin American Studies, University of Texas.

1982 *Maya Glyphs: The Verbs.* Austin: University of Texas Press.

1983a Human Sacrifice Among the Classic Maya. In *Ritual Human Sacrifice in Mesoamerica,* edited by E. P. Benson, 7–48. Washington, D.C.: Dumbarton Oaks Research Library and Collection.

1983b *Notebook for the Maya Hieroglyphic Writing Workshop at Texas.* Austin: Institute of Latin American Studies, University of Texas.

1984a Human Sacrifice Among the Classic Maya. In *Ritual Human Sacrifice in Mesoamerica,* edited by Elizabeth Boone, 7–49. Washington, D.C.: Dumbarton Oaks Research Library and Collection.

1984b *Notebook for the Maya Hieroglyphic Writing Workshop at Texas.* Austin: Institute of Latin American Studies, University of Texas.

1985a Balan-Ahau: A Possible Reading of the Tikal Emblem Glyph and a Title at Palenque. *Fourth Round Table of Palenque, 1980, Vol. 6,* gen. editor, Merle Greene Robertson; vol. editor, Elizabeth Benson, 59–65. San Francisco: Pre-Columbian Art Research Institute.

1985b Some Suggested Readings of the Event and Office of Heir-Designate at Palenque. *Phoneticism in Mayan Hieroglyphic Writing,* 287–307. Albany: Institute of Mesoamerican Studies, State University of New York at Albany.

1985c The Hauberg Stela: Bloodletting and the Mythos of Classic Maya Rulership. In *Fifth Palenque Round Table 1983, Vol. VII,* gen. editor, Merle Greene Robertson; vol. editor, Virginia M. Fields, 135–151. San Francisco: The Pre-Columbian Art Research Institute.

1986a Architectural Development and Political History at Palenque. In *City-States of the Maya: Art and Architecture,* edited by Elizabeth P. Benson, 110–138. Denver: Rocky Mountain Institute for Pre-Columbian Studies.

1986b The Founders of Lineages at Copán and Other Maya Sites. *Copán Note 8.* Copán, Honduras: Copán Mosaics Project and the Instituto Hondureño de Antropología e Historia.

1986c *Notebook for the Maya Hieroglyphic Writing Workshop at Texas.* Austin: Institute of Latin American Studies, University of Texas.

1986d Yax-K'uk'-Mo' at Copán: Lineage Founders and Dynasty at Ancient Maya Cities. *Copán Note 8.* Copán, Honduras: Copán Mosaics Project and the Instituto Hondureño de Antropología e Historia.

1987a A Possible Death Date for Smoke-Imix-God K. *Copán Note 26.* Copán, Honduras: Copán Mosaics Project and the Instituto Hondureño de Antropología e Historia.

1987b Stela I and the Founding of the City of Copán. *Copán Note 30.* Copán, Honduras: Copán Mosaics Project and the Instituto Hondureño de Antropología e Historia.

1987c The Reviewing Stand of Temple 11. *Copán Note 32.* Copán, Honduras: Copán Mosaics Project and the Instituto Hondureño de Antropología e Historia.

1987d Notes on the Río Amarillo Altars. *Copán Note 37.* Copán, Honduras: Copán Mosaics Project and the Instituto Hondureño de Antropología e Historia.

1987e *Notebook for the Maya Hieroglyphic Writing Workshop at Texas.* Austin: Institute of Latin American Studies, University of Texas.

1987f New Data on the Paddlers from Copán Stela 7. *Copán Note 29.* Copán, Honduras: Copán Mosaics Project and the Instituto Hondureño de Antropología e Historia.

1988a Altar F' and the Structure 32. *Copán Note 46.* Copán, Honduras: Copán Mosaics Project and the Instituto Hondureño de Antropología e Historia.

1988b The Xibalba Shuffle: A Dance After Death. In *Maya Iconography,* edited by Elizabeth Benson and Gillett Griffin, 294–317. Princeton: Princeton University Press.

1989a A House Dedication on the Harvard Bench at Copán. *Copán Note 51.* Copán, Honduras: Copán Mosaics Project and the Instituto Hondureño de Antropología e Historia.

1989b The Numbered-Katun Titles of Yax-Pac. *Copán Note 65.* Copán, Honduras: Copán Mosaics Project and the Instituto Hondureño de Antropología e Historia.

1989c Some Further Thoughts on the Copán-Quiriguá Connection. *Copán Note 67.* Copán, Honduras: Copán Mosaics Project and the Instituto Hondureño de Antropología e Historia.

n.d.a House Names and Dedication Rituals at Palenque. In *Visions and Revisions.* Albuquerque: University of New Mexico Press (in press).

n.d.b The Demotion of Chac-Zutz': Lineage Compounds and Subsidiary Lords at Palenque. In the *Sixth Round Table of Palenque,* gen. ed., Merle Green Robertson. Norman: University of Oklahoma Press (in press).

n.d.c The Tlaloc Heresy: Cultural Interaction and Social History. A paper given at "Maya Art and Civilization: The New Dynamics," a symposium sponsored by the Kimbell Art Museum, Fort Worth, May 1986.

n.d.d Blood-letting: A Metaphor for "Child" in the Classic Maya Writing System. A manuscript prepared in 1980 for an anthology in honor of Floyd G. Lounsbury.

n.d.e Brotherhood in Ancient Maya Kingship. A paper presented at the SUNY, Albany, conference on "New Interpretation of Maya Writing and Iconography," held October 21–22, 1989.

SCHELE, LINDA, AND DAVID FREIDEL

n.d. The Courts of Creation: Ballcourts, Ballgames, and Portals to the Maya Otherworld. In *The Mesoamerican Ballgame,* edited by David Wilcox and Vernon
Scarborough. Tucson: University of Arizona Press (in press).

SCHELE, LINDA, AND NIKOLAI GRUBE

1987a The Brother of Yax-Pac. *Copán Note 20.* Copán, Honduras: Copán Mosaics
Project and the Instituto Hondureño de Antropología e Historia.

1988 The Father of Smoke-Shell. *Copán Note 39.* Copán, Honduras: Copán Mosaics
Project and the Instituto Hondureño de Antropología e Historia.

SCHELE, LINDA, NIKOLAI GRUBE, AND DAVID STUART

1989 The Date of Dedication of Ballcourt III at Copán. *Copán Note 59.* Copán, Honduras: Copán Mosaics Project and the Instituto Hondureño de Antropología e
Historia.

SCHELE, LINDA, AND PETER MATHEWS

n.d. Royal Visits Along the Usumacinta. In *Classic Maya Political History: Archaeological and Hieroglyphic Evidence,* edited by T. P. Culbert. A School of American
Research Book. Cambridge: Cambridge University Press (in press).

SCHELE, LINDA, PETER MATHEWS, AND FLOYD LOUNSBURY

n.d. Parentage Expressions from Classic Maya Inscriptions. Manuscript dated 1983.

SCHELE, LINDA, AND JEFFREY H. MILLER

1983 The Mirror, the Rabbit, and the Bundle: Accession Expressions from the Classic
Maya Inscriptions. *Studies in Pre-Columbian Art & Archaeology* no. 25. Washington, D.C.: Dumbarton Oaks Research Library and Collection.

SCHELE, LINDA, AND MARY ELLEN MILLER

1986 *The Blood of Kings: Dynasty and Ritual in Maya Art.* New York: George Braziller,
Inc., in association with the Kimbell Art Museum, Fort Worth.

SCHELE, LINDA, AND DAVID STUART

1986a Te-tun as the Glyph for "Stela." *Copán Note 1.* Copán, Honduras: Copán Mosaics
Project and the Instituto Hondureño de Antropología e Historia.

1986b The Chronology of Altar U. *Copán Note 3.* Copán, Honduras: Copán Mosaics
Project and the Instituto Hondureño de Antropología e Historia.

1986c Paraphrase of the Text of Altar U. *Copán Note 5.* Copán, Honduras: Copán
Mosaics Project and the Instituto Hondureño de Antropología e Historia.

SCHELE, LINDA, DAVID STUART, NIKOLAI GRUBE, AND FLOYD LOUNSBURY

1989 A New Inscription from Temple 22a at Copán. *Copán Note 57.* Copán, Honduras:
Copán Mosaics Project and the Instituto Hondureño de Antropología e Historia.

SCHELLHAS, PAUL

1904 Representation of Deities of the Maya Manuscripts. *Papers of the Peabody
Museum of American Archaeology and Ethnology, Harvard University* 4(1). Cambridge.

SELER, EDUARD

1911 Die Stuckfassade von Acanceh in Yucatán. In *Sitzungsberichte der Königlich
Preussischen Akademie der Wissenschaften* 47:1011–1025.

SERVICE, ELMAN R.

1975 *Origins of the State and Civilization: The Process of Cultural Evolution.* New York:
W. W. Norton and Company.

SHARER, ROBERT J.

1988 Early Maya Kingship and Polities. A paper presented a the IV Texas Symposium,
"Early Maya Hieroglyphic Writing and Symbols of Rulership: The Archaeological
and Epigraphic Evidence for Maya Kingship and Polities," March 10, 1988. Austin: the University of Texas.

SHEETS, PAYSON D.

1976 The Terminal Preclassic Lithic Industry of the Southeast Maya Highlands: A
Component of the Proto-Classic Site-Unit Intrusions in the Lowlands? In *Maya
Lithic Studies: Papers from the 1976 Belize Field Symposium,* edited by Thomas R.
Hester and Norman Hammond, 55–69. Special Report No. 4. San Antonio: Center
for Archaeological Research, the University of Texas at San Antonio.

SHOOK, EDWIN M.

1958 The Temple of the Red Stela. *Expedition* 1(1):26–33.

SISSON, EDWARD B.

1973 First Annual Report of the Coxcatlan Project. *Tehuacán Project Report No 3.*
Andover, Mass.: R. S. Peabody Foundation for Archaeology, Phillips Academy.

SMITH, A. LEDYARD
1950 Uaxactún, Guatemala: Excavations of 1931–1937. *Carnegie Institution of Washington Pub. 588.* Washington, D.C.
SOSA, JOHN, AND DORIE REENTS
1980 Glyphic Evidence for Classic Maya Militarism. *Belizean Studies* 8(3):2–11.
SPINDEN, HERBERT J.
1913 A Study of Maya Art, Its Subject Matter and Historical Development. *Memoirs of the Peabody Museum of American Archaeology and Ethnology, Harvard University, VI.* Cambridge.
SPUHLER, JAMES N.
1985 Anthropology, Evolution, and "Scientific Creationism." *Annual Review of Anthropology* 14:103–133.
STEPHENS, JOHN L., AND FREDERICK CATHERWOOD
1841 *Incidents of Travels in Central American, Chiapas, and Yucatán.* Harper and Brothers, New York. Reprint: New York: Dover Publications, 1969.
STONE, ANDREA, DORIE REENTS, AND ROBERT COFFMAN
1985 Genealogical Documentation of the Middle Classic Dynasty of Caracol, El Cayo, Belize. In *Fourth Palenque Round Table, 1980, Vol. VI,* edited by Elizabeth Benson, 267–276. San Francisco: Pre-Columbian Art Research Institute.
STOREY, REBECCA
1987 Mortalidad durante el Clásico Tardio en Copán y El Cajón. A paper presented at the IV Seminario de Arqueología Hondureño, held in La Ceiba, Honduras, June 1987.
STRÖMSVIK, GUSTAV
1952 The Ball Courts at Copán. *Contributions to American Anthropology and History* 55:185–222. Washington, D.C.: Carnegie Institution of Washington.
STUART, DAVID
1984a Blood Symbolism in Maya Iconography. *RES* 7/8, 6–20.
1984b Epigraphic Evidence of Political Organization in the Usumacinta Drainage. Unpublished manuscript in possession of the authors.
1985a The Inscription on Four Shell Plaques from Piedras Negras, Guatemala. In *The Fourth Palenque Round Table, 1980, Vol. 6,* gen. editor, Merle Greene Robertson; vol. editor, Elizabeth Benson, 175–184. San Francisco: Pre-Columbian Art Research Institute.
1985b A New Child-Father Relationship Glyph. *Research Reports on Ancient Maya Writing, 1 & 2,* 7–8. Washington, D.C.: Center for Maya Research.
1986a The Hieroglyphic Name of Altar U. *Copán Note 4.* Copán, Honduras: Copán Mosaics Project and the Instituto Hondureño de Antropología e Historia.
1986b The Chronology of Stela 4 at Copán. *Copán Note 12.* Copán, Honduras: Copán Mosaics Project and the Instituto Hondureño de Antropología e Historia.
1986c The Classic Maya Social Structure: Titles, Rank, and Professions as Seen from the Inscriptions. A paper presented at "Maya Art and Civilization: The New Dynamics," a symposium sponsored by the Kimbell Art Museum, Fort Worth, May 1986.
1986d The "Lu-bat" Glyph and its Bearing on the Primary Standard Sequence. A paper presented at the "Primer Simposio Mundial Sobre Epigrafía Maya," a conference held in Guatemala City in August 1986.
1986e A Glyph for "Stone Incensario." *Copán Note 1.* Copán, Honduras: Copán Mosaics Project and the Instituto Hondureño de Antropología e Historia.
1987a Nuevas interpretaciones de la historia dinástica de Copán. A paper presented at the IV Seminario de Arqueología Hondureño, held in La Ceiba, Honduras, June 1987.
1987b Ten Phonetic Syllables. *Research Reports on Ancient Maya Writing 14.* Washington, D.C.: Center for Maya Research.
1988a Letter dated February 10, 1988, circulated to epigraphers on the *ihtah* and *itz'in* readings.
1988b Letter to author dated March 8, 1988, on the *iknal/ichnal* reading.
1988c Blood Symbolism in Maya Iconography. In *Maya Iconography,* edited by Elizabeth Benson and Gillett Griffin, 175–221. Princeton: Princeton University Press.
n.d. Kinship Terms in Mayan Inscriptions. A paper prepared for "The Language of Maya Hieroglyphs," a conference held at the University of California at Santa Barbara, February 1989.

STUART, DAVID, NIKOLAI GRUBE, AND LINDA SCHELE
1989 A New Alternative for the Date of the Sepulturas Bench. *Copán Note 61.* Copán, Honduras: Copán Mosaics Project and the Instituto Hondureño de Antropología e Historia.

STUART, DAVID, NIKOLAI GRUBE, LINDA SCHELE, AND FLOYD LOUNSBURY
1989 Stela 63: A New Monument from Copán. *Copán Note 56.* Copán, Honduras: Copán Mosaics Project and the Instituto Hondureño de Antropología e Historia.

STUART, DAVID, AND STEPHEN HOUSTON
n.d. Classic Maya Place Names. *Research Reports on Ancient Maya Writing.* Washington, D.C.: Center for Maya Research.

STUART, DAVID, AND LINDA SCHELE
1986a Yax-K'uk'-Mo', the Founder of the Lineage of Copán. *Copán Note 6.* Copán, Honduras: Copán Mosaics Project and the Instituto Hondureño de Antropología e Historia.

1986b Interim Report on the Hieroglyphic Stair of Structure 26. *Copán Note 17.* Copán, Honduras: Copán Mosaics Project and the Instituto Hondureño de Antropología e Historia.

STUART, GEORGE
n.d. Search and Research: An Historical and Bibliographic Survey. In *Ancient Maya Writing.* Austin: University of Texas Press (in preparation).

STUART, GEORGE, AND GRANT JONES
n.d. Can Ek and the Itzas: New Discovered Documentary Evidence. Washington, D.C.: Center for Maya Research (in preparation).

SUGIYAMA, SABURO
1989 Burials Dedicated to the Old Temple of Quetzalcoatl at Teotihuacán, México. *American Antiquity* 54(1):85–106.

TALADOIRE, ERIC
1981 Les terrains de jeu de balle (mesoamérique et sud-oest des Etats-Unis). *Etudes Mesoaméricaines Série II:4,* Mission Archaeologique et Ethnologique Française au Mexique.

TAMBIAH, STANLEY J.
1977 The Galactic Polity: The Structure of Traditional Kingdoms in Southeast Asia. *Annals of New York Academy of Sciences* 293:69–97.

TATE, CAROLYN
1985 Las mujeres de la nobleza de Yaxchilán. A paper presented at the "Primer Simposio Internacional de Mayistes," a conference held in México, D.F.

1986a The Language of Symbols in the Ritual Environment at Yaxchilán, Chiapas. A Ph.D dissertation, University of Texas at Austin.

1986b Summer Solstice Ceremonies Performed by Bird Jaguar III of Yaxchilán, Chiapas, México. *Estudios de Cultura Maya* XVI:85–112. México: Universidad Nacional Autónoma de México.

TAUBE, KARL
1985 The Classic Maya Maize God: A Reappraisal. In *Fifth Palenque Round Table, 1983, Vol. VII,* gen. editor, Merle Greene Robertson; vol. editor, Virginia M. Fields, 171–181. San Francisco: The Pre-Columbian Art Research Institute.

1988a A Prehispanic Maya Katun Wheel. *Journal of Anthropomorphic Research* 44:-183–203.

1988b A Study of Classic Maya Scaffold Sacrifice. In *Maya Iconography,* edited by Elizabeth Benson and Gillett Griffin, 331–351. Princeton: Princeton University Press.

n.d. The Temple of Quetzalcoatl and the Cult of Sacred War at Teotihuacán. Unpublished manuscript provided by the author.

TEDLOCK, DENNIS
1985 *Popol Vuh: The Definitive Edition of the Mayan Book of the Dawn of Life and the Glories of God and Kings.* New York: Simon and Schuster.

THOMPSON, J. ERIC S.
1934 Sky Bearers, Colors and Directions in Maya and Mexican religion. *Carnegie Institution of Washington Pub. 436, Contribution 10.* Washington, D.C.

1937 A New System for Deciphering Yucatecan Dates with Special Reference to Chichén Itzá. *Carnegie Institution of Washington Pub. 483, Contribution 22.* Washington, D.C.

1938 *The High Priest's Grave.* Chicago: Field Museum of Chicago.

1944 The Fish as a Maya Symbol for Counting. *Theoretical Approaches to Problems No.2.* Cambridge, Mass.: Carnegie Institution of Washington, Division of Historical Research.

1950 Maya Hieroglyphic Writing: An Introduction. *Carnegie Institution of Washington Pub. 589.* Washington, D.C.

1961 A Blood-Drawing Ceremony Painted on a Maya Vase. *Estudios de Cultura Maya* I:13–20. México: Universidad Nacional Autónoma de México.

1962 *A Catalog of Maya Hieroglyphics.* Norman: University of Oklahoma Press.

1970a *Maya History and Religion.* Norman: University of Oklahoma Press.

1970b The Bacabs: Their Portraits and Glyphs. In *Monographs and Papers in Maya Archaeology, Papers of the Peabody Museum of Archaeology and Ethnology, Vol. 61* edited by William R. Bullard, Jr. Cambridge: Peabody Museum, Harvard University.

1971 *Maya Hieroglyhic Writing: An Introduction.* Norman: University of Oklahoma Press.

1977 The Hieroglyphic Texts of Las Monjas and Their Bearing on Building Activities. In *Las Monjas* by John Bolles. Norman: University of Oklahoma Press.

THOMPSON, J. E. S., H. E. D. POLLOCK, AND J. CHARLOT
1932 A Preliminary Study of the Ruins of Cobá, Quintana Roo. *Carnegie Institution of Washington Pub. 424.* Washington, D.C.

TOZZER, ALFRED M.
1941 Landa's Relación de las Cosas de Yucatán: A Translation. *Papers of the Peabody Museum of American Archaeology and Ethnology, Harvard University,* Vol. XVIII. Reprinted with permission of the original publishers by Kraus Reprint Corporation, New York, 1966.

1957 Chichén Itzá and Its Cenote of Sacrifice: A Comparative Study of Contemporaneous Maya and Toltec. *Memoirs of the Peabody Museum of Archaeology and Ethnology, Harvard University,* XI and XII. Cambridge.

TURNER, B. L., II
1983 Comparison of Agrotechnologies in the Basin of México and Central Maya Lowlands: Formative to the Classic Maya Collapse. In *Highland-Lowland Interaction in Mesoamerica: Interdisciplinary Approaches,* edited by Arthur G.Miller, 13–47. Washington, D.C.: Dumbarton Oaks Research Library and Collection.

TURNER, B. L., II, AND PETER D. HARRISON
1981 Prehistoric Raised Field Agriculture in the Maya Lowlands: Pulltrouser Swamp, Northern Belize. *Science* 213:399–405.

VALDÉS, JUAN ANTONIO
1987 Uaxactún: recientes investigaciones. *Mexicon* 8(6):125–128.

1988 Los mascarones Preclássicos de Uaxactún: el caso del Grupo H. In *Primer Simposio Mundial Sobre Epigraphía Maya,* 165–181. Guatemala City: Asociación Tikal.

VLCHEK, DAVID T., SILVIA GARZA DE GONZALEZ, AND EDWARD B. KURJACK
1978 Contemporary Farming and Ancient Maya Settlements: Some Disconcerting Evidence. In *Pre-Hispanic Maya Agriculture,* edited by Peter D. Harrison and B. L. Turner II, 211–223. Albuquerque: University of New Mexico Press.

VOGT, EVON Z.
1964 The Genetic Model and Maya Cultural Development. In *Desarollo Cultural de los Mayas,* edited by E. Z. Vogt and A. Ruz, 9–48. México: Universidad Nacional Autónoma de México.

1976 *Tortillas for the Gods: A Symbolic Analysis of Zinacanteco Rituals.* Cambridge: Harvard University Press.

n.d. Indian Crosses and Scepters: The Results of Circumscribed Spanish-Indian Interactions in Mesoamerica. A paper presented at "Word and Deed: Interethnic Images and Responses in the New World," a conference held in Trujillo, Spain, December 12–16, 1988.

WALKER, DEBRA S.
n.d. A Context for Maya Ritual at Cerros, Belize. A paper presented at the Advanced Seminar on Maya Hieroglyphic Writing, Austin, Texas, March 21, 1986.

WAUCHOPE, ROBERT
1938 Modern Maya Houses: A Study of Their Significance. *Carnegie Institution of Washington Pub. 502.* Washington, D.C.

WEBSTER, DAVID

1976 Defensive Earthworks at Becan, Campeche, México: Implications for Maya Warfare. *Middle American Research Institute, Tulane University Pub. 41.* New Orleans.

1977 Warfare and the Evolution of Maya Civilization. In *The Origins of Maya Civilization,* edited by R. E. W. Adams, 335–371. A School of American Research Book. Albuquerque: University of New Mexico Press.

1979 Cuca, Chacchob, Dzonot Ake: Three Walled Northern Maya Centers. *Occasional Papers in Anthropology Number 11,* Department of Anthropology. University Park: The Pennsylvania State University.

1985 Recent Settlement Survey in the Copán Valley, Copán, Honduras. *Journal of New World Archaeology* V(4):39–63.

WEBSTER, DAVID L., WILLIAM L. FASH, AND ELLIOT M. ABRAMS

1986 Excavaciones en el Conjunto 9N8: Patio A (Operación VIII). In *Excavaciónes en el area urbana de Copán,* 157–319. Tegucigalpa: Secretaria de Cultura y Turismo, Instituto Hondureño de Antropología e Historia.

WILLEY, GORDON R.

1972 The Artifacts of Altar de Sacrificios. *Papers of the Peabody Museum of Archaeology and Ethnology, Harvard University Vol. 64(1).* Cambridge.

1974 The Classic Maya Hiatus: A Rehearsal for the Collapse? In *Mesoamerican Archaeology: New Approaches,* edited by Norman Hammond, 417–430. London: Duckworth.

1978 Excavations at Seibal, Department of Petén, Guatemala, Number 1, Artifacts. *Memoirs of the Peabody Museum of Archaeology and Ethnology, Harvard University Vol. 14.* Cambridge.

WILLEY, GORDON, AND RICHARD LEVENTHAL

1979 Prehistoric Settlement at Copán. In *Maya Archaeology and Ethnohistory,* edited by Norman Hammond and Gordon R. Willey, 75–102. Austin: University of Texas Press.

WILLIAMSON, RICHARD, DONNA STONE, AND ALFONSO MORALES

1989 Sacrifice and War Iconography in the Main Group, Copán, Honduras. A paper presented at the Seventh Round Table of Palenque, in Palenque, Chiapas, México, June 1989.

WISDOM, CHARLES

1940 *The Chorti Indians of Guatemala.* Chicago: University of Chicago Press.

n.d. Materials on the Chorti Languages. Collection of Manuscripts of the Middle American Cultural Anthropology, Fifth Series, No. 20. Microfilm, University of Chicago.

WREN, LINEA

n.d. Elite Interaction During the Terminal Classic Period of the Northern Maya Lowlands: Evidence from the Reliefs of the North Temple of the Great Ballcourt at Chichén Itzá. In *Classic Maya Political History: Archaeological and Hieroglyphic Evidence,* edited by T. P. Culbert. A School of American Research Book. Cambridge: Cambridge University Press (in press).

YOFFEE, NORMAN, AND GEORGE L. COWGILL, EDITORS

1988 *The Collapse of Ancient States and Civilizations.* Tucson: The University of Arizona Press.

ZAVALA, LAURO JOSÉ

1951 Informe personal de exploraciones arqueológicas: segunda temporada 1950. An unpublished report provided by Alberto Ruz Lhull

REFERENCES

———

INDEX